DATE DUE

Oct 4 '68			
Oct 29 68			
~~Nov 19 70~~			
~~Nov 18 74~~			
GAYLORD			PRINTED IN U.S.A.

The Testaments of the
Grand Princes of Moscow

The Cap of Monomakh

The Testaments of the
Grand Princes of Moscow

TRANSLATED AND EDITED
WITH COMMENTARY BY

Robert Craig Howes

OAKLAND UNIVERSITY

CORNELL UNIVERSITY PRESS

Ithaca, New York

This work has been brought to publication with the
assistance of a grant from the Ford Foundation.

Library of Congress Catalog Card Number: 67–12485

PRINTED IN THE UNITED STATES OF AMERICA
BY KINGSPORT PRESS, INC.

To my mother and father

Acknowledgments

LONG recognized as important sources for the study of Russian history, the testaments of the Grand Princes of Moscow have never been readily available to the Western student. I undertook the translation of these documents at Cornell University in 1959, at the suggestion of Professor Marc Szeftel. During much of my work on the documents, Professor Szeftel aided me immeasurably by assisting in the translation and elucidation of a number of the more difficult passages and by offering many helpful suggestions. His high standards of scholarship and profound understanding of Russian history encouraged me to pursue my work on the testaments. If there is value in this book, much credit should go to Marc Szeftel; obviously, he is not responsible for any errors or shortcomings. For these I am solely responsible.

I should also like to record my appreciation of the assistance and encouragement given me by several members of the Department of History of Cornell University and by a number of my colleagues at Oakland University. Moreover, my students at Oakland, Robert Devlin, Rita Murphy, and Nancy Zajack, worked long and well in maintaining files and in proofreading the manuscript.

Several faculty research grants from Oakland University aided me in carrying out my work.

I am especially grateful to Marian Wilson who typed, retyped, and proofread the entire manuscript. Mrs. Wilson's broad knowledge, high standards of accuracy, and unbounded enthusiasm for scholarship contributed much to the successful completion of this book.

R. C. H.

Rochester, Michigan
July 1966

Contents

Contents

Part Three: Translations of the Testaments

Illustrations

Abbreviations

THE two source abbreviations used throughout this book are:

DDG *Dukhovnyye i dogovornyye gramoty velikikh i udel'-
nykh knyazey XIV–XVI vv.* (Testaments and Treaties
of the Grand and Patrimonial Princes of the XIV–XVI
Centuries). Ed. L. V. Cherepnin and S. V. Bakhrushin.
Moscow-Leningrad, 1950.

PSRL *Polnoye sobraniye russkikh letopisey* (Complete Collection of Russian Chronicles). 30 vols. to date. See Bibli-
ography.

Introduction

THE testaments of the Grand Princes of Moscow are among the most important primary sources for the study of Russian history from the fourteenth through the sixteenth centuries. Thirteen testaments are extant, either in the original or in copies: the testament of Grand Prince Ivan I Danilovich Kalita (*c.* 1339), the testament of Grand Prince Semen Ivanovich the Proud (1353), the testament of Grand Prince Ivan II Ivanovich the Fair (1358), a fragment of the first testament of Grand Prince Dmitriy Ivanovich Donskoy (*c.* 1375), the second testament of Grand Prince Dmitriy Ivanovich Donskoy (1389), three testaments of Grand Prince Vasiliy I Dmitriyevich (*c.* 1406 or 1407, *c.* 1417, and 1423), the testament and codicil to the testament of Grand Prince Vasiliy II Vasil'yevich the Blind (1461–1462), the testament of Grand Prince Ivan III Vasil'yevich the Great (1503–1504), the testamentary writ of Grand Prince Vasiliy III Ivanovich (1523), and the testament of Grand Prince and Tsar Ivan IV Vasil'yevich the Terrible (1572). It was the accepted custom for the ruler of Muscovy to leave a testament to his princess and his children, and we have at least one testament for each of the "legitimate" grand princes except Vasiliy III. Although Vasiliy's testament has been lost, he is represented in this collection by a brief testamentary writ that is essentially a codicil to his earlier testament.

From 1339 to 1572 (the probable dates of Ivan Kalita's and Ivan the Terrible's testaments) a number of extremely important developments occurred in Russia. During this period the House of Moscow consolidated its power, to become the dominant force in reunifying the Russian lands and in beginning the expansion that culminated in the formation of the Russian Empire early in the eighteenth century. The period witnessed the gradual weakening and final eclipse of Tartar domination over northeastern Russia, as well as the retreat of the Grand Principality of Lithuania before the advance of Muscovy in the west and southwest. The city states of Novgorod and Pskov—the "northern Russian democracies"—declined and were finally absorbed by Moscow during the same period that saw the growth of the "service state" and the *pomest'ye* system. Yet when the testament of Ivan the Terrible was written, the entire structure of the Muscovite state, so laboriously constructed over three centuries, was threatened with complete dissolution.

This period of the testaments was replete with events of extreme importance, yet few materials remain for the historian. Among these, the testaments of the grand princes are primary sources of paramount significance—sources essential to an understanding of medieval Russia.

It should be recognized at the outset that these documents do not offer a narrative of events in Russian history. Their purpose was limited, and they were written for contemporaries whose understanding of terms, recognition of place names, and appreciation of allusions was assumed by the writer. Much of the valuable information they contain would be meaningless to us without reference to such contemporary narrative sources as the Chronicles.

What information do the testaments contain, and what problems do they raise? The testaments of the grand princes present, first of all, a catalogue of the territorial acquisitions of Moscow, ranging from such inconsequential places as Ivan Kalita's village Vsedobrich', "which I purchased," to Ivan the Great's "patrimony, the Grand Principality of Novgorod," with which he blessed his son, Vasiliy III. Unfortunately, it is exceptional for a prince even to suggest the method by which this or that major territory came into his possession. He assumed, of course, that the persons for whom the testament was intended knew how the territory had been acquired. Nevertheless, the student is faced with the recurring question: How did the prince come into possession of such and such a holding that he now so laconically bequeaths to one of his sons? Sometimes this question can be answered by reference to the Chronicles; at other times it cannot.

The testaments of the Grand Princes of Moscow are, however, more than mere catalogues of the territorial acquisitions of the House of Ivan Kalita. They are sources of information on the nature of territorial-administrative divisions in medieval Russia and on the nature of princely administration in the fourteenth through the sixteenth centuries. The light shed on the system, which existed during this period, of holding Moscow by thirds is particularly valuable. Considerable information on the prince's household—his officers, his slaves, his tenants, and others—can be gleaned from the testaments, as can information on the tax system of Old Russia. The testaments contain some, though sparse, information on the social classes of the times, and the lists of material objects bequeathed by the grand princes to members of their families give us some idea of the level of material culture of the period. The testaments also offer an idea of the changing concept of the state and the changing role of the grand prince between the time of Ivan Kalita and Ivan the Terrible.

Unfortunately, except for the testament of Ivan the Terrible, these documents offer little information about the personalities of the princes themselves, for, generally speaking, they were written in the same stereotyped style and repeated the same basic formulas. In this connection it is difficult not to agree with V. O. Klyuchevskiy, who wrote that "the grand princes of Moscow appear . . . as rather pallid figures, following one another on the throne of the grand prince under the name of Ivan, Semen, another Ivan, Dmitriy, Vasiliy, and another Vasiliy. Looking carefully at them it is easy to discern that they are not original personalities who pass before us, but a monotonous repetition of one and the same family type. All the Moscow princes before Ivan III are as alike as two drops of water, so that the observer sometimes has difficulty in determining which one is Ivan and which one is Vasiliy." [1]

[1] *Sochineniya* (Moscow, 1956–1959), II, 49.

PART ONE

Survey of the Testaments

CHAPTER 1

The Growth of Moscow to 1325

ALTHOUGH there are remains of neolithic settlements in the Moscow area and there is little doubt that some type of settlement existed on the present site of the city as early as the tenth—perhaps eleventh—century, the origin of Moscow is still obscure. There are a number of legends which tell of its founding.[1] According to one legend, Prince Oleg the Wise, while traveling from Novgorod to Kiev in the year 882, chanced to encamp at the confluence of the Neglinnaya and Moskva rivers, where he ordered that a fortified settlement, or burg (*gorodok*), be established. This *gorodok* and the "fine villages" surrounding it, the legend continues, later came into the possession of a certain Stepan Ivanovich Kuchka, a boyar of the old city of Suzdal'. Another legend relates that Prince Yuriy Dolgorukiy (Prince of Suzdal' from 1120 to 1155 and of Kiev from 1155 to 1157), while on his way from Kiev to Suzdal', sojourned at the patrimonial estate of the boyar Stepan Ivanovich Kuchka. Perhaps Kuchka did not show proper respect for the prince; in any case, Yuriy ordered his host to be killed and his body thrown into a pond. Then the prince, apparently taking a liking to his victim's estate, commanded that a *gorodok* be built on the rise of ground where the Kremlin now stands. Moreover, he gave orders that a second *gorodok* be constructed to the northeast of the

[1] See A. V. Ekzemplyarskiy, *Velikiye i udel'nyye knyaz'ya severnoy Rusi v" tatarskiy period", s" 1238 po 1505 g.* (St. Petersburg, 1889), II, 270; S. V. Bakhrushin, A. A. Novosel'skiy, A. A. Zimin, and N. V. Ustyugov, *Istoriya Moskvy* (Moscow, 1952), Vol. I; M. N. Tikhomirov, *Drevnyaya Moskva* (Moscow, 1947); M. N. Tikhomirov, *Srednevekovaya Moskva v XIV–XV vekakh* (Moscow, 1957); and M. N. Tikhomirov, "Osnovaniye Moskvy i Yuriy Dolgorukiy," *Izvestiya Akademii Nauk SSSR: Seriya istorii i filosofii*, V, No. 2 (1948), 143–148.

first; this second *gorodok*, so the legend goes, he named Kitay, in honor of his son, Andrey, whose Polovetsian name was Kitay.[2]

Moscow is first mentioned in the Chronicles in the entry for 1147. Prince Yuriy Dolgorukiy, returning to Suzdal' after having plundered certain of the Novgorod volosts and having seized Novyy Torg and "all the [land along the] Msta," summoned his powerful ally, Prince Svyatoslav Ol'govich of Chernigov, saying, "Come to me, brother, to Moscow." Prince Svyatoslav and his

[2] If the mother was not Russian, the child was sometimes given a name from the mother's language. Prince Andrey's mother was a Polovetsian, the daughter of Khan Aepa, and Andrey was named Kitay (*PSRL*, I, 120; *Russkiy biograficheskiy slovar'*, 25 vols. to date [St. Petersburg, 1896–1918], Vol. Al–Bes; *Povest' vremennykh let*, ed. V. P. Adrianova-Peretts [Moscow-Leningrad, 1950], II, 432). P. V. Sytin believes that the origin of the name *Kitay-gorod* is in the Mongol word *kitay*, 'middle' (Cathay, the Middle Kingdom?). If Sytin's explanation is correct, then Kitay-gorod was simply the "middle fortress" or "middle city" and any attempt to associate the name with Andrey Bogolyubskiy appears a bit farfetched. During the twelfth and thirteenth centuries Kitay-gorod was indeed in the center of Moscow. In fact it was almost entirely within the present limits of the Kremlin. By the end of the fourteenth century it had, however, been almost entirely forced out of this area. Following the rebuilding of the Kremlin by Ivan III between 1485 and 1495, Kitay-gorod was completely excluded from the Kremlin and occupied its present site. Kitay-gorod, or the Great Posad (*posad*, 'settlement outside the *gorod* proper,' 'suburb'), as it was known after about 1500, is that part of Moscow lying just northeast of the Kremlin (P. V. Sytin, *Iz istorii moskovskikh ulits* [3rd ed.; Moscow, 1958], pp. 67–108 and Schematic Plan of Moscow facing p. 824).

Tatishchev recounts the legend of the death of Kuchka and the founding of the *grad* Moscow in some detail. According to this legend the wife of Kuchka, *tysyatskiy* of Suzdal', was one of Prince Yuriy's numerous lovers. Kuchka, finding the situation unbearable, took his wife to his village on the Moskva River and confined her there. Yuriy, who was on the way to Torzhok at the time, left his men, hurried to Kuchka's village "in great anger," killed Kuchka "without having made inquiries," and gave Kuchka's daughter in marriage to his son Andrey. While waiting for the wedding to take place, Yuriy ordered that a *grad* be built on the site and sent for Prince Svyatoslav and his son, Prince Oleg (see V. N. Tatishchev, *Istoriya Rossiyskaya* [*v semi tomakh*] [Moscow-Leningrad, 1962–1966], II, 170–171).

4

son, Prince Oleg, came to Moscow at the bidding of Yuriy, and on the following day a mighty feast (*obed silen*) took place.[3] It is apparent that in 1147 Moscow belonged to Prince Yuriy and hence to Suzdal'.

The next reference to Moscow appears in the *Tver' Chronicle* under the year 1156: "That same year Prince Yuriy Volodimerich founded the city [*grad*] of Moscow, also at the mouth of the Neglinnaya, above the Yauza." Although the text of this report in the *Tver' Chronicle* is somewhat ambiguous, it appears that the translation given above is correct and that the *gorod* (the Kremlin) built in 1156 stood on the same spot on which there had been an earlier fortified settlement.[4]

There are only three references to Moscow in the Chronicles between 1156 and the coming of the Tartars in 1237. In the year 1176, we are told, Mikhalko and Vsevolod Yur'yevichi (brothers of the murdered Andrey Bogolyubskiy) were on their way from Chernigov to Vladimir, when one of the princes fell ill and "they went with him as far as Kuchkovo, that is to say, to Moscow."[5]

Moscow is mentioned in the Chronicles under the years 1176–1177 in connection with the struggle between Rostov and Vladimir for supremacy in northeastern Russia. As one of the minor cities of the Volga-Oka mesopotamia, Moscow was bound to be affected by the outcome of this struggle. When Grand Prince Mikhail (Mikhalko) Yur'yevich of Rostov and Vladimir

[3] *PSRL*, VIII, 38.

[4] "Togo zhe leta knyaz' velikiy Yuriy Volodimerich zalozhi grad" Mosk'vu, na ustnizhe Neglinny, vyshe reky Auzy" (*PSRL*, XV, 225). As Tikhomirov points out, the phrase *na ustnizhe Neglinny* does not "sound right." It suggests that the *grad* was built below the mouth of the Neglinnaya, but the phrase is awkward and there is little doubt that the scribe erred. Tikhomirov cites the corresponding passage in an unpublished copy of the *Tver' Chronicle*, which reads: "Knyaz' velikiy Yuriy Volodimerich zalozhi Moskvu na ustii zhe Neglinny, vyshe reki Yauzy." This is doubtless the reading to be accepted (see *Srednevekovaya Moskva*, pp. 6–7).

[5] *PSRL*, II, 600. Kuchkovo was the village of the aforementioned boyar Stepan Ivanovich Kuchka.

died in June 1177, his nephew Mstislav was summoned to be prince in Rostov and Suzdal'. The men of Vladimir, on the other hand, called Vsevolod, Mikhail's brother, to be their prince. "And he [Vsevolod] straightway came to them. And they came out to him before the Golden Gates [of the city of Vladimir], and they affirmed themselves to him and to his children by kissing the holy and life-giving cross of the Lord; and he came into the city of Vladimer' and sat on the throne."

Mstislav and the men of Rostov were not willing to accept Vsevolod as Grand Prince of Vladimir, and they decided to go to war over the issue. The men of Rostov moved against Vladimir, but Vsevolod did not wish to fight and, having had a vision of the Cathedral of the Holy Mother of God and the whole city of Vladimir "standing in the air," he suggested to Mstislav that the latter rule in Rostov, that Vsevolod rule in Vladimir, and that they both rule in Suzdal'. The proposition appealed to Mstislav but not to the men of Rostov, who insisted that "although you wish to do thus we do not wish it; for the city of Vladimer' is not your princedom but our minor city, and our peasants live in it and our slaves, masons and workers in wood, and ploughmen."

A battle took place near Yur'yev and "the Lord God and the Most Pure Mother of God aided Prince Vsevolod Yur'yevich and he was victorious over Prince Mstislav Rostislavich." Mstislav fled to Novgorod and, when that city would not accept him ("You went in search of another princedom and, having quit us, left with us only your son"), he proceeded to Ryazan', where his brother-in-law, Gleb Rostislavich, reigned. Here he "began to pray and weep" that Gleb move against Vladimir. Gleb hesitated, but at last "set out in war to Moscow and burned all of Moscow, the city [i.e., the Kremlin], the [Moscow] volosts and villages, and captured all." Vsevolod moved against Gleb, but returned to Vladimir, saying, "May God's will be done and may the Lord God and His Most Pure Mother take vengeance upon him." In the meantime Gleb had returned to Ryazan'. The war was resumed that winter (1177–1178) and Gleb and Mstislav were both captured. Gleb died in prison in Vladimir; Mstislav was blinded (perhaps) and set free. This was the end of the struggle between Rostov and Vladimir. The victory went to Vladimir and its prince, Vsevolod Yur'yevich Big Nest.[6]

In the year 1212, the Chronicle reports that Vladimir, a younger son of Vsevolod Big Nest, was prince in Moscow. Vladimir, however, was transferred the following year to Pereyaslavl' Yuzhnyy.[7]

Though the Chronicles do not give the exact date, Moscow was burned by the Tartars late in 1237 or early in 1238. The "accursed sons of Hagar" seized the grand prince's son, Vladimir, who was in Moscow, probably serving as his father's lieutenant in defending the city against the invading army of Khan Batu.[8]

The next mention of a prince of Moscow appears under the year 1248, when Mikhail the Brave (*Khorobit*) is called Prince of Moscow. Mikhail, usually considered the first prince to hold Moscow as his patrimonial principality (*udel*), appears to have ruled in Moscow until 1248, the year in which he drove his uncle, Svyatoslav Vsevolodovich, from Vladimir and occupied the throne of the Grand Principality. That same year Mikhail was killed in a battle with the Lithuanians on the Protva River, and, as he left no children, Moscow must have escheated to the Grand Principality upon his death.[9]

Moscow appears again in an entry for 1283. In that year "the men of Novgorod and the Grand Prince of Tver', Svyatoslav, with the men of Tver', and Grand Prince [*sic*] Daniil of Mos-

[6] This account and all quotations are from *PSRL*, X, 1–6. Note that this source identifies Prince Mstislav Rostislavich as the "grandson of Mstislav, the great-grandson of Vladimir Monomakh," whereas he must have been the grandson of Yuriy, the great-grandson of Vladimir Monomakh.

[7] *PSRL*, VII, 118–119, and S. M. Solov'yev, *Istoriya Rossii s drevneyshikh vremen* (Moscow, 1959–1966), I, 627–628.

[8] The burning of Moscow and the seizing of Prince Vladimir took place between December 21, 1237 (when Ryazan' fell to Batu), and February 3, 1238 (when the Tartars approached the city walls of Vladimir). The Chronicles do not give the exact date (*PSRL*, VII, 139–140, XV, 368, and XXV, 127; see also Ekzemplyarskiy, II, 272–273).

[9] *PSRL*, XV, 395, VII, 156, and XV, 395; Solov'yev, II, 155; and Ekzemplyarskiy, II, 273.

cow, with the men of Moscow, marched to Pereyaslavl' against Grand Prince Dmitriy Aleksandrovich." [10] It is probable that Daniil, the son of Aleksandr Nevskiy, had received Moscow as his *udel* in 1276 from his older brother Dmitriy, when the latter became Grand Prince of Vladimir. [11]

The remarkable growth of the *udel* of Moscow began with the reign of Daniil Aleksandrovich (1276?–1303). In 1300, for a cause unknown, Prince Daniil undertook a campaign against Prince Konstantin of Ryazan'. The men of Moscow and the men of Ryazan' met in battle near the city of Pereyaslavl' Ryazanskiy—a battle in which the Muscovites were victorious. As a result of this campaign, Moscow acquired a section of territory north of the Oka River previously held by Ryazan'. (Konstantin of Ryazan' was apparently supported by Tartar troops, and it is significant that the prince of Moscow was prepared even at this early date to undertake a campaign against such a force.) The Ryazan' lands, which included the towns of Kolomna and Serpukhov, marked the beginning of a remarkable series of acquisitions which was to culminate in Moscow's becoming the center of all the Russian lands. [12]

A second important step in the territorial growth of the Moscow *udel* occurred in 1302, when Daniil's nephew, Prince Ivan of Pereyaslavl' Zalesskiy, died. In the words of the Chronicle: "In the year 6810 [1302]. Prince Ivan Dmitriyevich died in Pereyaslavl' on May 15; he had no offspring and he gave his patrimony, Pereyaslavl', to Prince Daniil Aleksandrovich of Moscow, for he loved him more than all the others." [13] It is not known why Ivan bequeathed his patrimony to his uncle. Ivan had quarreled with Prince Mikhail Yaroslavich of Tver' at a meeting of princes held the previous year in Dmitrov, and possibly this quarrel had some bearing on his action. Furthermore,

[10] *PSRL*, V, 200.

[11] *PSRL*, VII, 173, and Ekzemplyarskiy, II, 273.

[12] "That same autumn [6809] Prince Daniil of Moscow made war against Ryazan', and they fought near Pereyaslavl' city, and Prince Daniil was victorious, and he killed many Tartars, and, having seized Prince Konstantin, he led him to Moscow" (*PSRL*, VII, 183).

[13] *PSRL*, VII, 183.

Grand Prince Andrey Aleksandrovich had coveted Pereyaslavl' and Daniil of Moscow had supported Ivan's defence of his patrimony. The gift of Pereyaslavl' to the Prince of Moscow demonstrates that at this time the northern Russian princes viewed their patrimony, their volost, as personal property; theoretically Prince Ivan's *udel* should have escheated to the Grand Principality of Vladimir at his death. In any case, the addition of Pereyaslavl' Zalesskiy to their patrimony was a significant gain for the Grand Princes of Moscow.[14]

Prince Daniil died on March 4, 1303, and his *udel*, now consisting of the Moscow volost, of Kolomna, Serpukhov, and other lands along the left bank of the Oka, and of Pereyaslavl' Zalesskiy, passed to his oldest son, Yuriy Danilovich. At the time, Yuriy was in Pereyaslavl' serving as his father's lieutenant. The Chronicle observes that "that same spring Prince Yuriy Danilovich of Moscow, the grandson of Aleksandr [Nevskiy], the great-grandson of Yaroslav, the great-great-grandson of Vsevolod, with his brothers marched in war to Mozhaysk and seized it, and he seized Prince Svyatoslav [Glebovich] and led him to Moscow."[15] This laconic report gives no hint of the reason for Moscow's aggression against Mozhaysk; whatever the reason, the time was well chosen, for Grand Prince Andrey Aleksandrovich of Vladimir was absent at the Horde. The acquisition of Mozhaysk was the third important step in Moscow's early growth.

Shortly after Grand Prince Andrey's son Boris Andreyevich died in Kostroma in 1304, Yuriy of Moscow attempted to seize that city. But Yuriy's brother Boris Danilovich, his emissary to Kostroma, was unable to maintain his position there; the local boyars seized him and took him to Tver'.[16] Andrey Aleksandrovich's death in 1304 marked the beginning of a struggle between Yuriy of Moscow and Mikhail Yaroslavich of Tver' for the Grand Principality of Vladimir. Initially Mikhail was victorious, assuming the throne in 1305. But Yuriy obtained the patent to the Grand Principality from Khan Uzbek in 1317, and

---

[14] See Ekzemplyarskiy, II, 274, and Solov'yev, II, 197.
[15] *PSRL*, X, 174.   [16] *PSRL*, VII, 184.

the conflict between Moscow and Tver' continued. Prince Mikhail was murdered by the Tartars in 1318;[17] in 1325 Prince Yuriy was killed in the Horde by Dmitriy, the son of Mikhail of Tver'. Yuriy's youngest brother, Ivan Danilovich Kalita,[18] succeeded him as Prince of Moscow, though not as Grand Prince of Vladimir.

In such fashion was the territorial expansion of Moscow begun during the reign of Daniil and continued during the reign of Yuriy. By 1325 the Principality of Moscow consisted not only of the original territory surrounding the city (the Moscow volost) but of Pereyaslavl', Kolomna, Serpukhov, the territory between the former southern boundary of Moscow and the Oka River, and Mozhaysk. The Grand Principality of Vladimir was not yet firmly in the possession of the House of Moscow, for in 1326 the khan granted the patent to the Grand Principality to Aleksandr Mikhaylovich of Tver', the younger son of the murdered Prince Mikhail (who was later canonized). Permanent possession of that prize remained for Ivan Kalita to acquire in 1328, when he received the patent from Khan Uzbek.[19]

[17] *PSRL*, VIII, 184, and XXV, 161.

[18] *PSRL*, VII, 199. For an account of the life of Yuriy, see Ekzemplyarskiy, I, 59–69.

[19] *PSRL*, XXV, 168. It should be noted that Pereyaslavl' was later not considered part of Moscow, but part of the Grand Principality of Vladimir. Kolomna, Serpukhov, and land north of the Oka were in fact acquired by Moscow in 1300. This acquisition was "legalized" in 1306 when Yuriy ordered the execution of Prince Konstantin of Ryazan', who was a prisoner in Moscow (see *PSRL*, VII, 184).

CHAPTER 2

The Growth of Moscow
under the Grand Princes

THE contributions made by each of the Grand Princes of Moscow to the territorial growth of Muscovy can be determined in part by evidence in the testaments. Although the conclusions in this chapter are based primarily on that evidence, I have taken into account acquisitions not mentioned in the testaments that are identified or suggested in other sources. In this chapter I enumerate the disposition of major holdings by each prince and attempt to determine those holdings that each prince acquired. I discuss in some detail the acquisition of Rostov and Mozhaysk as examples of acquisitions of two different types. Brief information on most of the other major acquisitions can be found in the notes to the texts of the testaments. For a complete list of the dispositions of territories by the various testaments, see the Appendix.

IVAN I DANILOVICH KALITA (1304–1341)

Ivan Kalita became Grand Prince of Moscow in 1325 and Grand Prince of Moscow and Vladimir in 1328. He inherited as his patrimony the original Moscow Principality (the city of Moscow and Moscow District), Kolomna, Serpukhov, the area north of the Oka River, and Pereyaslavl'.[1]

The two variants of Kalita's testament were probably written in 1339. In them he left the overwhelming majority of his holdings to his three sons, Semen, Ivan, and Andrey. Each son re-

---

[1] The original documents frequently refer to districts (or lands, or principalities) merely by the name of the principal city thereof, and I have often followed this custom. It should be understood that the reference here, for example, is to Kolomna District.

ceived a third of the city of Moscow, or, more specifically, the customs of the city (except for the *osmnicheye*, a special surtax on trade) were to be shared equally by the three princes. Yet the wording of his testament also suggests that each son was to hold a definite area of the city: "But my sons shall share the *tamga* and the other city revenues; in the same manner they shall also share the *myto*, that which is in the district of each shall be his." Moreover, the three princes were to share the quitrent in honey of Vasiliy's Department. This division was the beginning of the famous holding of Moscow by thirds.

In addition to his third of Moscow, Semen received Mozhaysk, Kolomna, and a number of lesser holdings (volosts, villages, and other settlements). In all, twenty-seven cities,[2] volosts, and settlements were left to Semen. It should be noted that, beginning with this testament, Kolomna—an outpost near the border with Ryazan'—was always kept in the senior line of the House of Moscow.

Ivan, Kalita's second son, in addition to his third of Moscow, received Zvenigorod, Ruza, and a number of scattered villages, for a total of twenty-three. Andrey, the third son of the grand prince, received Serpukhov, the volost Lopasnya (taken from Ryazan' in 1301), and the *burgs* Shchitov and Peremyshl', for a total of twenty-one, in addition to his third of Moscow.

Lesser holdings were bequeathed to Ul'yana, the wife of the grand prince, and to the "younger children," who are unidentified. These holdings consisted of nine volosts, seventeen villages, two *svobodkas* (free settlements), and one settlement or locality of unknown type (Ramen'ye), for a total of twenty-nine. The Moscow *osmnicheye*, a special surtax on trade, was also to be Ul'yana's.

Boris Vorkov, a landowner obscure yet famous because mentioned in this testament, was confirmed in his right to hold the village Bogorodicheskoye (the village "of the Mother of God") in Rostov, which Ivan had purchased, "if he serves one of my sons." The monastery of St. Aleksandr on the Kostroma River, which Kalita had purchased and given to his wife, was granted

---

[2] Here and throughout this study the word "city" is merely a translation of *gorod* (or *grad*). See Chapter 3.

three villages "for the memory of my soul (*sobe v pomi-nan'ye*)."

Solely on the basis of the information in his testament, it appears that the territorial acquisitions of Ivan Kalita were insignificant, especially when compared to those of his father and older brother. The major place names mentioned in the testament were within the territory that he had inherited. His testament does, however, list thirteen villages and two small villages, and one monastery, that were clearly his acquisitions, for the method in which he acquired them is indicated. Of the fifteen villages, eight were purchased by the grand prince himself, four (the villages on the Mas River) were obtained either by purchase or by exchange from the metropolitan, one was purchased by Ivan's grandmother and had come into his possession, one had been in the possession of an unidentified princess, and one was acquired in exchange for another village. Kalita purchased the Monastery of Saint Aleksandr on the Kostroma River. He also purchased ". . . tsya on the Mas" River from a certain Afiney; the original of the second variant of the document is torn at this place, and the passage does not appear at all in the original of the first variant.

The fact that the great majority of these acquisitions were not located within the boundaries of Kalita's patrimony is significant. Of the fifteen villages that were clearly his acquisitions, one was in the Novgorod Land, four were on the Mas (probably also in Novgorod, for the river was likely the Msta), one was in Vladimir, two were in Yur'yev, one was in Rostov, one was in Dmitrov, two were in Kostroma, and only three were in Moscow District, on the Kerzhach River. Further, the Monastery of Saint Aleksandr was in Kostroma and the unidentifiable purchase on the Mas was probably in Novgorod.

It is probable that some of the other settlements mentioned in the testament were also Kalita's acquisitions, although they are not specifically so identified. For example, the village Ryukhovskoye, in Volok Lamskiy District, may have been an acquisition of the grand prince, for he apparently held this district for a time.[3] It also appears that Ivan Kalita acquired the

[3] See below, Text 9, n. 42.

volost Kist'ma and the villages Ontonovskiye, in Bezhetskiy Verkh District, for these were identified in the second testament of Grand Prince Vasiliy I as "the acquisition of my great-grandfather."

The settlements acquired by Ivan Kalita were probably the "prince's own," his personal property. At least some of them were located in principalities whose rulers were still nominally independent, although subject to the senior prince of northeastern Russia—the Grand Prince of Vladimir—and, ultimately, to the Golden Horde of the Tartars, of which northeastern Russia was merely an *ulus*, or province.

In the second testament of Ivan's grandson, Dmitriy Donskoy, the vast areas of Galich, Beloozero, and Uglich are referred to as the purchase of Dmitriy's grandfather. No mention is made of these "purchases" in Kalita's testament. It is possible, of course, that Ivan acquired these territories after he wrote his testament, that is, sometime between 1339 and 1341. Yet if this were the case, why are these areas not mentioned in the testaments of Kalita's sons, Semen and Ivan Ivanovich? N. M. Karamzin believed that these areas were acquired shortly before the death of Kalita and that they were considered part of the Grand Principality of Vladimir and not part of the Principality of Moscow. As S. M. Solov'yev points out, however, it is unlikely that the prince of Moscow added three such important cities to the Grand Principality of Vladimir when he did not know whether his son would receive the patent to the Grand Principality. Solov'yev believed that Ivan did acquire these areas, but that their original princes remained as proprietary princes, subordinate to the prince of Moscow. Cherepnin believes that a third variant of Kalita's testament existed, listing Galich, Beloozero, and Uglich as purchases of the prince of Moscow, but that this variant did not receive the khan's approval.[4]

No mention is made in Kalita's testament of the Grand Princi-

[4] N. M. Karamzin, *Istoriya gosudarstva rossiyskago* (St. Petersburg, 1842), IV, 151–152; S. M. Solov'yev, *Istoriya Rossii s drevneyshikh vremen* (Moscow, 1959–1966), II, 342, n. 417; and L. V. Cherepnin, *Russkiye feodal'nyye arkhivy, XIV–XV vv.* (Moscow-Leningrad, 1948–1951), I, 17–19.

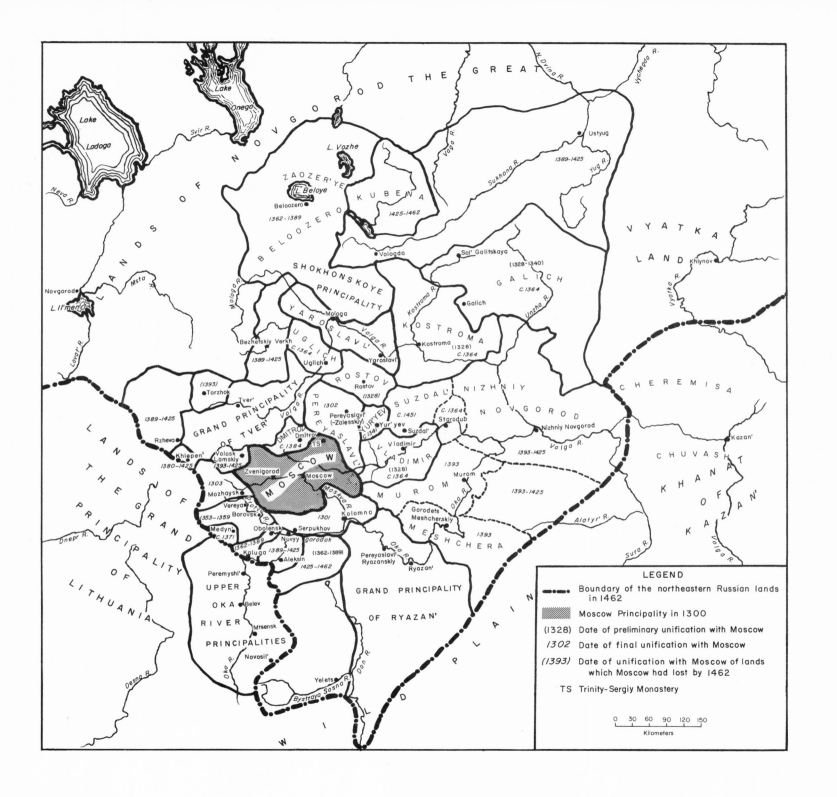

LEGEND

·–·–·–· Boundary of the northeastern Russian lands in 1462

▨ Moscow Principality in 1300

(1328) Date of preliminary unification with Moscow

1302 Date of final unification with Moscow

(1393) Date of unification with Moscow of lands which Moscow had lost by 1462

TS Trinity-Sergiy Monastery

0 30 60 90 120 150
Kilometers

Map of northeastern Russia in the fourteenth and fifteenth centuries. (Based on the map entitled "Growth of the Moscow Principality and the Unification of the Russian Lands from the End of the XIII Century to 1462" in B. D. Grekov, L. V. Cherepnin, and V. T. Pashuto, *Ocherki istorii SSSR: Period feodalizma IX–XV v.v., Chast' vtoraya, Ob"yedineniye russkikh zemel' vokrug Moskvy i obrazovaniye russkogo tsentralizovannogo gosudarstva* [Moscow, 1953].)

pality of Vladimir, to which Ivan received the khan's patent in
1328. Neither is Pereyaslavl' (listed above as part of Ivan's
patrimony) mentioned, an omission which supports the assumption that Pereyaslavl' was in fact considered part of the Grand
Principality of Vladimir, even though it had been bequeathed to
Ivan's father, Daniil, in 1302. Ivan Kalita, who held the office of
Grand Prince of Vladimir at the pleasure of the Golden Horde,
did not bequeath the Grand Principality to his eldest son, nor did
his two successors, for it was not yet their "patrimony." [5]

[5] The Grand Principality of Vladimir—whose prince held a seniority,
dating from the days of Andrey Bogolyubskiy, which was even at the
time of Kalita more traditional than real—lay along both sides of the
Klyazma River, east of the Principality of Moscow.

Dmitriy Konstantinovich the Elder, Prince of Suzdal', was Grand
Prince of Vladimir from 1360 to 1364 (*PSRL*, VIII, 11–13). Prince Yuriy
Dmitriyevich (the second son of Ivan Kalita's grandson, Dmitriy Don-
skoy) "sat on the Grand Princedom [of Vladimir]" in the spring of 1434,
having driven his nephew, Prince Vasiliy Vasil'yevich (the oldest son of
Kalita's great-grandson, Vasiliy Dmitriyevich), from Moscow. Follow-
ing the sudden death of Yuriy Dmitriyevich in June, 1434, his son,
Vasiliy the Cross-Eyed, claimed to be Grand Prince of Moscow [and
Vladimir?] for about a month, after which he was driven from Moscow
by his cousin, Vasiliy Vasil'yevich, who once more became grand prince
(*PSRL*, VIII, 98–99).

As early as the beginning of the reign of Vasiliy II, the struggle among
the princes was for Moscow and not for Vladimir. For instance, references in the Chronicles under the year 1434 are to the "Grand Principality of Moscow" or to the "Grand Princedom in Moscow" (see *PSRL*, V,
266, and VIII, 98).

Nothing is said in Ivan's testament of those actions of his which were
so important in strengthening the power and prestige of Moscow. He
actively interfered in the affairs of other principalities and of Novgorod
and Pskov, almost from the very beginning of his reign. For instance, in
1327, with a powerful Tartar force, he plundered Tver', Kashin, and
Novyy Torg (*PSRL*, VII, 200). He sent his lieutenants into Rostov. In
1329 he occupied the throne of Novgorod and in 1332 he seized the
Novgorod minor cities of Torzhok and Bezhetskiy Verkh, because the
men of Novgorod had refused to pay a ransom: "In the year 6840
[1332] . . . Grand Prince Ivan returned from the Horde and raised his
anger against Nov"grad, demanding of them silver from beyond the
Kama, and for this [that they refused to pay it] took Torzhok and
Bezhich'kiy Verkh, in violation of his oath" (see *Novgorodskaya per-*

SEMEN IVANOVICH THE PROUD (1317–1353)

Semen the Proud was Grand Prince of Vladimir and Moscow from 1341 to 1353. By his testament, written in 1352 just after his two small sons had died of the plague, he left all of his holdings to his third wife, Princess Mariya, daughter of Prince Aleksandr Mikhaylovich of Tver'. These holdings included Semen's third of Moscow, Kolomna, Mozhaysk, and a number of volosts and villages (twenty volosts and villages and the villages "near Moscow in the city district").

By the terms of this testament one village (Deigunin'skoye, Moscow District), left to Princess Ul'yana and the "younger children" by the testament of Ivan Kalita, was given to Princess Mariya. This is an early indication of a custom destined to be of no small importance in the consolidation of lands by the oldest son of the main line of the House of Moscow: lands left to the widow of the grand prince passed to the succeeding grand prince or to his wife. This custom is illustrated in later testaments by the provision, which becomes almost a formula, that such and such a property should be held by such and such a princess "during her lifetime" and that "after her death" it should pass to one of the male heirs of the testator.

Semen's testament indicates that his territorial acquisitions were meager, despite the fact that "all the Russian princes were given under his hand." The village Deigunin'skoye has been mentioned above. Apparently Semen also acquired two volosts (Zayachkov and Zabereg) and three villages. Zayachkov he received from his aunt, Princess Anna; he purchased Zabereg and the three villages. Six other villages are mentioned for the first time in Semen's testament, but with no hint as to how they were acquired. The location of these acquisitions (and uncertain acquisitions) indicates that Semen, like his father, did not hesitate to acquire holdings outside his patrimony. Although the location of the volosts Zayachkov and Zabereg is not known, the three

vaya letopis' starshego i mladshego izvodov, ed. A. N. Nasonov and M. N. Tikhomirov [Moscow-Leningrad, 1950], p. 342 and, for the citation, p. 344).

16

villages that Semen purchased were in Pereyaslavl', Vladimir, and Dmitrov districts, respectively. Among the villages that may have been acquired by Semen, three were probably in Moscow, one in Pereyaslavl', one in Kostroma, and one in Sulishin *pogost*, whose location is not known.

It should be noted that Kashira, a city on the Oka River about sixty kilometers southwest of Kolomna, is mentioned in the testament of Ivan II as belonging to Princess Mariya Aleksandrovna. Hence it too may have been Semen's acquisition.

No mention is made in this testament of the Grand Principality of Vladimir, although Semen was Grand Prince of Vladimir throughout his reign in Moscow.

IVAN II IVANOVICH THE FAIR (1326–1359)

After the death of Semen the Proud in 1353, his brother Ivan became Grand Prince of Moscow. A year later he received the patent to the Grand Principality of Vladimir as well. His testament was probably written in 1358; the principal legatees were his sons, Dmitriy and Ivan, and his nephew, Vladimir Andreyevich. Ivan bequeathed two thirds of Moscow—his share and the share Semen had bequeathed to Princess Mariya—to his two sons. At the same time he confirmed the right of his nephew, Vladimir Andreyevich, to the third of Moscow that he had inherited from his father. In addition, Dmitriy received Mozhaysk and Kolomna, Ivan received Zvenigorod and Ruza, and Vladimir Andreyevich was to "manage the district of his father" (Serpukhov) and to receive the burg Novyy (at the mouth of the Protva) in place of Lopasnya, which had been lost to Ryazan'. Provisions were also made for the lifetime holdings of Princess Aleksandra, Princess Mariya (the widow of Semen), and Princess Ul'yana (the widow of Ivan Kalita).[6] Bequests were made to two monasteries (Saint Aleksandr in Kolomna and the Holy Mother of God in Krutitsy) and to two churches (the Holy Mother of God in Moscow and Saint Mikhail in Moscow). Of obvious importance is the fact that the former hold-

[6] Apparent inconsistencies in the lands bequeathed to Mariya, Aleksandra, and Ul'yana exist (see below, Text 3, nn. 27 and 38).

ings of Semen (including Mozhaysk and Kolomna), although bequeathed to Princess Mariya by Semen's testament, were disposed of by the testament of Ivan II.

The burg Novyy is mentioned for the first time in the testament of Ivan II. Lopasnya had been lost to Ryazan' in 1353, but Ivan had "taken away" other lands, including the burg Novyy, from Ryazan'.[7] The city of Kashira also appears for the first time in Ivan's testament, where it is identified as belonging to Princess Mariya, the widow of Semen. According to this testament, Mariya was to hold Kashira during her lifetime, but upon her death it was to pass to Prince Dmitriy. Kashira is not mentioned in Semen's testament.

A number of Kolomna villages and volosts are first mentioned in the testament of Ivan II, but they can hardly be considered "new acquisitions," for all of Kolomna and its volosts had been part of the patrimony of Semen. Actually, on the basis of his testament, Ivan's acquisitions were negligible. He did assert control over major holdings bequeathed to his sister-in-law, Princess Mariya; these holdings are listed in the Appendix, although in a strict sense they can hardly be considered acquisitions of Moscow. The burg Novyy and "the Ryazan' localities on this side of the Oka that I [Ivan II] have acquired" were new, but they were gained after the loss of Lopasnya to Ryazan'. Incidentally, Ivan II seems to have feared that other lands north of the Oka might be lost to Ryazan' through interference by the Horde.[8]

The Grand Principality of Vladimir is not mentioned, although Ivan II was its grand prince at the time of his death.

DMITRIY IVANOVICH DONSKOY
(1350 [or 1351]–1389)

Dmitriy Donskoy ruled as Grand Prince of Moscow from 1359 and as Grand Prince of Vladimir and Moscow from 1364. He wrote two testaments: the first, of which the latter part only is extant, is tentatively dated 1375; the second was written in 1389.

[7] *PSRL*, X, 227.
[8] Concerning Ivan II's fear that the Tartars might assist Ryazan' in reacquiring the lands taken away by Moscow, see Commentary to Text 3.

The extant portion of the first testament bequeathed Ruza and several volosts and villages to Dmitriy's oldest son, Vasiliy Dmitriyevich; it provided that any villages or novalia (*pochinki*) purchased by the grand prince or by his father, or any villages that had belonged to his younger brother Ivan, who had died in 1364, should pass to his son Vasiliy, to his wife Yevdokiya, and to his younger children. This testament also confirmed his father's gift of the village Pavlovskoye to the Monastery of Saint Aleksandr.

The chief legatees of Dmitriy's second testament were his five sons (Vasiliy, Yuriy, Andrey, Petr, and Ivan); his cousin, Vladimir Andreyevich; his wife, Princess Yevdokiya; and his yet unborn son Konstantin.

Dmitriy willed his shares of Moscow (two thirds, for he had acquired his brother Ivan's share when the latter died in 1364) to his four oldest sons, Vasiliy, Yuriy, Andrey, and Petr. He also confirmed the right of his cousin, Vladimir Andreyevich, to hold the third of Moscow that Vladimir had inherited from his father. To his oldest son, Vasiliy, Dmitriy also bequeathed Kolomna, a number of villages in Moscow and Yur'yev districts, and one village in Rostov District. He also "blessed" his son with his "patrimony, the Grand Princedom [of Vladimir]." This is the first instance in which the Grand Principality was willed to a son by one of the princes of Moscow. Dmitriy's second son, Yuriy, received Zvenigorod and Ruza (both of which had been the patrimony of the deceased Ivan Ivanovich), a number of villages (including the famous Bogorodicheskoye in Rostov that had been held by Boris Vorkov), and Galich, "my grandfather's purchase." To Andrey, his third son, the grand prince left Mozhaysk with its volosts and "outlying volosts"; Vereya (called in the testament an "outlying volost" of Mozhaysk); Kaluga; the city of Medyn', which, with the volost Tov (location unknown), "my boyar, Fedor Andreyevich, in our common struggle, took away from the men of Smolensk"; Beloozero, "yet [another] purchase of my grandfather"; and several villages in Moscow and one in Yur'yev. Dmitriy Donskoy's second testament provided that his fourth son, Petr, was to receive Dmitrov; "yet [another] purchase of my grandfather, Ugleche

Plain" (Uglich); a number of volosts in Moscow District; one village and one *pogost* in Moscow District; one village in Yur'yev; and the volosts Toshna (Uglich District) and Syama (Dmitrov District). Syama may have been purchased by Ivan Kalita; the wording of the testament is not clear. To his fifth son, Ivan, Dmitriy Donskoy bequeathed two volosts, one village, and the *novale* Sokhon'skiy, "which has been given up by Prince Vladimir [Andreyevich]." An interesting passage in the testament relates to Ivan: Ivan was to be "free" in his patrimony, that is, he could give it "to whichsoever brother is kind to him." [9]

Princess Yevdokiya Dmitriyevna, wife of the grand prince, was granted a number of volosts, villages, and other settlements in the Grand Principality and in the patrimonial principalities (*udely*) of her sons Vasiliy, Yuriy, Andrey, and Petr. The testament provided that at Yevdokiya's death these holdings were to revert to the prince in whose patrimony they were located. Yevdokiya also received a number of scattered villages and other settlements that had been purchased or acquired in an unspecified manner by the grand prince or by Yevdokiya herself. Other holdings were identified as coming from Princess Fedosiya, Dmitriy's aunt. Two hamlets which Prince Vladimir "took away from Lytkin'skoye, the village of my princess, [and added] to Berendeyeva *sloboda*" were confirmed as hers. Moreover, she was free in these holdings; she could dispose of them as she saw fit.

Grand Prince Dmitriy also provided for his unborn child: "And if God gives me a son, my princess shall also give a share to him, taking portions from each of his older brothers."

According to the second testament, if any of the grand prince's sons should die, Princess Yevdokiya was to divide his patrimonial principality among the remaining sons. Similarly, if a son were to lose part of his patrimonial principality, the testament stipulated that Yevdokiya was to compensate him by allotments taken from the holdings of the other sons. If Vasiliy, the

[9] Ivan was the fifth and probably youngest son of Dmitriy at the time of the writing of the testament in 1389. His inheritance was negligible when compared with that of his older brothers or with the prospective inheritance of his as yet unborn brother, Konstantin (see Text 5, n. 23).

oldest son, were to die, his patrimonial principality (presumably including the Grand Principality of Vladimir) was to pass to the "son who follows him," that is, to his oldest surviving brother. The latter's patrimony would then be divided among the remaining sons by Princess Yevdokiya.

A fairly large number of comparatively minor place names appear for the first time in this testament (see the Appendix). Some of the villages were purchased by Dmitriy or Yevdokiya, while a number of holdings (volosts, villages, and *novalia*) are listed as their acquisitions (*primysly*).

On the basis of his two testaments it would appear that the principal territorial acquisitions of Dmitriy Donskoy were the holdings, including Zvenigorod and Ruza, of his younger brother, Ivan; Dmitrov (method of acquisition unknown); Kaluga; and Medyn'. The vast lands of Galich, Beloozero, and Uglich, which are mentioned for the first time in the second testament, are identified as "purchases of my grandfather" and cannot be considered acquisitions of Grand Prince Dmitriy's, although it is possible that under his rule Moscow's control over these areas became more firmly established. Possibly, possession of these lands by the princes of Moscow was tentative prior to the writing of Dmitriy's second testament and undisputed control was not acquired until some time during his reign.

VASILIY I DMITRIYEVICH (1371–1425)

Vasiliy I was Grand Prince of Vladimir and Moscow from 1389 to 1425. He left three testaments: the first was written in 1406 or 1407, the second probably in 1417, and the third probably in 1423.

The First Testament of Vasiliy I

The principal legatees of Vasiliy's first testament were his son, Ivan Vasil'yevich (an older son, Yuriy, had died in 1400); his youngest brother, Konstantin Dmitriyevich; and his wife, Sofiya Vitovtovna.

To Ivan, Vasiliy bequeathed his third of Moscow and Kolomna with its volosts. In this first testament Vasiliy did not bequeath the Grand Principality of Vladimir to his son, although he did not ignore the question, writing, "And if God grants that my son, Prince Ivan, should hold the Grand Princedom, then my princess [shall receive], from Pereyaslavl', Kinela." He also entertained the possibility that Ivan would hold Nizhniy Novgorod and Murom, for he wrote that "if God should grant that my son hold Nov"gorod Nizhnii and Murom", then my princess [shall receive] from Nov"gorod one half of the customs."

To his youngest brother, Konstantin, Vasiliy left the volost Toshnya (Uglich District) and the city of Ustyuzhna. This bequest was apparently in fulfillment of the provision of Dmitriy Donskoy's second testament that provided allotments for Dmitriy's unborn son.

To Sofiya, daughter of Vitovt of Lithuania, Vasiliy bequeathed a large number of scattered volosts, villages, and other settlements. The testament stipulated that, if Ivan Vasil'yevich were to marry, these holdings were to pass to his wife. As her widow's portion, Sofiya was granted two villages in Yur'yev District. Certain properties of Princess Yevdokiya, mother of the grand prince, were also to come to Sofiya at Yevdokiya's death. These properties were the volost Pesochna and the village Malino, both of Kolomna District.

A number of Vasiliy's purchases and acquisitions are listed in the first testament; for example, Ukhtyushka, a volost of Vologda District that was willed to Princess Sofiya, and "Fedor Sviblo's villages in Ustyug," which were also willed to Sofiya. Also mentioned were several villages in Yur'yev District which the grand prince had obtained by exchange from his mother, Princess Yevdokiya.

The Second Testament of Vasiliy I

Ivan Vasil'yevich died in 1417, and Vasiliy's second testament was probably written soon afterward. The principal legatees of the second testament were Vasiliy's wife, Princess Sofiya, and his oldest surviving son, Vasiliy Vasil'yevich.

To his son, Vasiliy Vasil'yevich, the grand prince bequeathed his third of Moscow, Kolomna with its volosts, Murom ("my acquisition"), and the Grand Principality of Vladimir. He tentatively granted his son Nizhniy Novgorod, for he wrote: "And if God gives me Nov"gorod" Nizhnii, then I also bless my son, Prince Vasiliy, with Nov"gorod" Nizhnii, with all."

The second testament, unlike the first, did not leave any territories to Konstantin, the grand prince's younger brother. Like the first, it left numerous scattered volosts, villages, and other settlements, and a third of the Moscow *tamga*, to the grand prince's wife, Sofiya Vitovtovna. It also stipulated that if God granted Nizhniy Novgorod to the grand prince, then Sofiya was to receive half of all its customs.

A number of smaller settlements were listed for the first time in this testament, many identified as either purchases or acquisitions of the grand prince or of Princess Sofiya.

The Third Testament of Vasiliy I

The third testament of the grand prince is quite similar to the second, with one important difference. As in the first testament, though not in the second, Vasiliy bequeathed the Grand Principality of Vladimir to his son with the proviso, "and if God gives to my son the Grand Princedom." It would seem that in 1423 Vasiliy was not as sure as he had been about six years earlier that his son would be in a position to hold the Grand Principality of Vladimir. By the time he wrote the third testament, however, Vasiliy must have gained firm control of Nizhniy Novgorod, for he granted this principality (and Murom) outright to his son.

No provision was made for Konstantin Dmitriyevich in the third testament. Vasiliy stipulated that Princess Sofiya's holdings were to be hers until she died; thereafter, except for the volost Gzhelya (Kolomna District) and the village Semchin'skoye, her holdings were to pass to Vasiliy Vasil'yevich.

On the basis of evidence in his three testaments it would appear that the principal acquisitions of Vasiliy I were Nizhniy Novgorod; Murom; and a number of volosts, villages, and other holdings that were identified as purchases or acquisitions of the grand prince or princess, such as the volost Ukhtyushka in Vologda and Fedor Sviblo's villages in Ustyug. Rzheva (modern Rzhev), an outlying city and volost of the Grand Principality of

Tver', was also acquired during Vasiliy's reign. There is also evidence that he held Volok Lamskiy, at least for a time, and Vyatka.[10]

VASILIY II VASIL'YEVICH (1415–1462)

Vasiliy II was Grand Prince of Moscow from 1425 and Grand Prince of Vladimir and Moscow from 1432 until his death in 1462. The principal legatees of his will, written in 1461 or 1462, were his sons, Ivan, Yuriy, Andrey the Elder, Boris, and Andrey the Younger, and his wife, Mariya Yaroslavna.

To his oldest son, Ivan, Vasiliy II bequeathed the Grand Principality of Vladimir, the Moscow third willed to Vasiliy by his father, Kolomna, Vladimir city (as distinct from the Grand Principality of Vladimir), Pereyaslavl', Kostroma, Galich, Ustyug, Vyatka, Suzdal', Nizhniy Novgorod, Murom, Yur'yev, Borovsk, Kaluga, Aleksin, and a number of smaller and less important areas and settlements. To his second son, Yuriy, Vasiliy bequeathed one half of Prince Vladimir's third of Moscow, the "year" of Konstantin Dmitriyevich in Moscow,[11] Dmitrov, the volosts beyond the Moskva River, Mozhaysk, Medyn', Serpukhov, Khotun', and a number of scattered volosts, villages, and other settlements, including those given to Yuriy by his grandmother, Sofiya Vitovtovna. Andrey the Elder, Vasiliy's third son, was given one half of the third of Prince Vladimir in Moscow, Uglich, Bezhetskiy Verkh, Zvenigorod, and scattered volosts and villages, including some of the former holdings of Prince Yuriy Dmitriyevich. The fourth son, Boris, was to receive the "year" of Prince Ivan of Mozhaysk in Moscow, Rzheva, Volok Lamskiy, Ruza, and scattered volosts and vil-

---

[10] Concerning Rzheva and Volok Lamskiy ("Lama River Portage"), see below, Text 9, nn. 41 and 42. Vyatka figured in an agreement between Vasiliy II and Yuriy Dmitriyevich of Galich, in 1428: "Also concerning that which my father, Grand Prince Vasiliy Dmitriyevich, granted to you, Vyatka . . ." (for text of this agreement, see *DDG*, pp. 63–67).

[11] Concerning the thirds of, and "years" in, Moscow, see below, Chapter 5.

lages, including those given him by his maternal grandmother, Mariya Goltyayeva. Vasiliy's fifth son, Andrey the Younger, was granted the "year" of Prince Petr Dmitriyevich in Moscow, Vologda, Kubena and Zaozer'ye, and scattered volosts and villages.

The testament confirmed the right of three of the grand prince's sons—Yuriy, Andrey the Elder, and Boris—to those holdings bequeathed them by the testament of their grandmother, Princess Sofiya.

By the provisions of this testament, Mariya Yaroslavna, Vasiliy's wife, was to receive the Sreten'ye half of Rostov, with the proviso that the Rostov princes would continue to "manage" in the same manner as under Vasiliy II. At Princess Mariya's death, the Sreten'ye half of Rostov was to pass to Prince Yuriy. Mariya was also granted scattered volosts and villages from the patrimonial principalities of her sons; she was to hold these lands during her lifetime and at her death they were to go, with the exception of those lands or settlements she had purchased, to the son in whose patrimonial principality they were located. Princess Mariya also received one half of the Moscow and Nizhniy Novgorod customs as lifetime holdings.

The first bequeathal in this testament is that of the Grand Principality itself, indicating that, in contrast with his father, Vasiliy II had no doubts that his son would be able to hold the Grand Principality. And it is interesting to note that lands formerly considered to be part of the Grand Principality of Vladimir—Vladimir, Pereyaslavl', Kostroma, and Yur'yev—are treated as separate entities in this testament. Also of interest is the location of the lands left to the younger sons of the grand prince. These lands, without exception, were in the north, west, or south; the vast areas of Ustyug, Vyatka, Suzdal', Nizhniy Novgorod, and Murom—all in the east or northeast—were willed in their entirety to the oldest son, Ivan Vasil'yevich.

Grand Prince Vasiliy II wrote a codicil to his testament in either 1461 or 1462. This document is concerned primarily with the allotment of additional lifetime holdings to Princess Mariya Yaroslavna. It also provides for the bequest of a court (*dvor*) to each of the three oldest sons, Ivan, Yuriy, and Andrey. The grand prince also confirmed the right of Fedor Basenok, a boyar and voivode who supported Vasiliy throughout his reign, to hold two villages in Kolomna which had been granted him by the grand prince's mother, Sofiya. Upon the death of Basenok these villages were to pass to Princess Mariya.

Beginning with the testament of Vasiliy II, it is useful to distinguish between two main types of territorial acquisition. The first type consists of territories acquired for the first time by a Grand Prince of Moscow; the second type is made up of lands which had once been in the possession of one of the grand princes, had been lost, and then were recovered. Many of the latter type had been lost to the main line of the House of Moscow as a result of their having been bequeathed to one of the younger sons of the grand prince; others were temporarily lost by being granted to a member of one or another of the collateral lines of the House or to someone who had performed a service to the Prince of Moscow.

The following acquisitions of Vasiliy II belong to the second type, i.e., they were holdings which had once belonged to Moscow, had been lost, and now were acquired by Vasiliy: Galich (after the defeat of Prince Dmitriy Shemyaka in a battle near Galich city in 1450), Vyatka, Serpukhov and Borovsk (in 1456, from Prince Vasiliy Yaroslavich of Serpukhov and Borovsk), Kaluga and Aleksin (in 1454, from Prince Ivan Andreyevich, concerning whom see below), Dmitrov (by an agreement concluded between Vasiliy II and Prince Vasiliy Yaroslavich sometime between 1450 and 1454); Mozhaysk and Medyn' (from Prince Ivan Andreyevich in 1454), Zvenigorod (from Prince Vasiliy Yaroslavich in 1456), Ruza (from either Prince Dmitriy Shemyaka or Prince Vasiliy Yaroslavich), Uglich (probably from Prince Dmitriy Shemyaka in 1447), and Rzheva (from Prince Dmitriy Shemyaka by treaty in 1447).

On the basis of his testament it would appear that the following major territories acquired by Vasiliy II belonged to the first type of acquisition: Ustyug, Suzdal', Khotun', Bezhetskiy Verkh, Vologda, Kubena, Zaozer'ye, and the Sreten'ye half of Rostov. The acquisition of Rostov is of considerable interest and should be discussed in some detail. (For information on the other acquisitions listed, see the notes to Text 9.)

Rostov

Located on Lake Nero about 200 kilometers north and slightly east of Moscow, Rostov is one of the oldest of Russian cities.[12] During the early part of the twelfth century it was the most powerful city in the northeast. During the reign of Prince Yuriy Dolgorukiy (1120–1157), however, Rostov began to lose its power and prestige: Yuriy and his headstrong son, Andrey Bogolyubskiy (1157–1175), were in conflict with the Rostov city assembly (*veche*) and with some of the old boyar families of the Rostov-Suzdal' Land. This assumption is supported by the fact that the leaders of the successful plot to murder Prince Andrey were members of one of these old families, the Kuchkas.[13] Prince Yuriy himself resided in Suzdal', rather than in Rostov, for most of his reign. When he became Grand Prince of Kiev in 1155 he was followed as Prince of Rostov-Suzdal' by his son, Andrey. With Andrey's acquisition of seniority among the princes of northeastern and Kiev Russia, the capital of Rostov-Suzdal' was once more moved, this time to Vladimir-on-the-Klyazma. Andrey chose not to move to Kiev. Now Vladimir was not only the capital of the Rostov-Suzdal'-Vladimir Land but also the residence of the senior princes of all Rus'.

During Prince Andrey's reign, Rostov attempted to reassert its supremacy over its two former minor cities (*prigorody*), Suzdal' and Vladimir. The plot to murder Prince Andrey, mentioned above, was part of this attempt. In the struggle for the Grand Princedom which followed Andrey's death, Rostov once more clashed with Vladimir, but this struggle ended in the latter's favor. Rostov had lost its former position of political domi-

[12] "And [following the death of his brothers Sineus and Truvor], Ryurik took power and distributed cities to his men; to one he gave Polotesk" [Polotsk], to another, Rostov, and to [yet] another, Beloozero" (*Povest' vremennykh let*, ed. V. P. Adrianova-Peretts, text prepared by D. S. Likhachev, trans. D. S. Likhachev and B. A. Romanov [Moscow-Leningrad, 1950], I, 18).

[13] Concerning Stepan Ivanovich Kuchka, see above, Chapter 1, n. 2.

nance and henceforth was to be a principality subordinate to the Grand Principality of Vladimir.[14]

Toward the end of the reign of Vsevolod Big Nest (*Bol'shoye Gnezdo*)—Grand Prince of Vladimir and the brother of Andrey Bogolyubskiy—it appeared for a time that Rostov might regain its position of dominance in northeastern Russia. In 1207 Big Nest had granted Rostov and "5 other cities" to his son, Konstantin Vsevolodovich,[15] but later, sensing his approaching death (1212), the grand prince decided to grant the throne of Vladimir (the "grand princely throne") to his oldest son, Konstantin, and name his second son, Yuriy, Prince of Rostov. Konstantin, however, did not wish to give up Rostov, and he sent his father the following message:

Father, if you desire to make me the senior [prince], then give me the old capital city of Rostov and, in addition, Vladimir; or, if you prefer so to do, give me Vladimir and, in addition to it, Rostov.[16]

These words angered Vsevolod, and on the advice of Bishop Ioann of Vladimir, he presented the Grand Princedom to his younger son, Yuriy. Konstantin was not content with this decision, however, and complained: "Now is it possible for the junior [prince] to sit on the throne of our father, and not possible for me, the senior, [to do so]?"[17] In the ensuing struggle it appeared for a time that Yuriy would prevail over his older brother. But with the intervention of Mstislav the Daring (*Udaloy*) on the side of Novgorod in a struggle that developed between that city and Yaroslav of Pereyaslavl' (the younger brother of Konstantin and Yuriy), Konstantin found himself allied with the winning side and received Vladimir and the Grand Princedom. Prince Yuriy was relegated to the compara-

[14] See A. Ye. Presnyakov, *Obrazovaniye velikorusskago gosudarstva* (Petrograd, 1918), pp. 26–39, and A. V. Ekzemplyarskiy, *Velikiye i udel'nyye knyaz'ya severnoy Rusi v" tatarskiy period", s" 1238 po 1505 g.* (St. Petersburg, 1889), II, 13–16, and above, Chapter 1.

[15] *PSRL*, VII, 115. The identity of these five cities has not been definitely established. They were probably Yaroslavl', Suzdal', Uglich, Beloozero, and, perhaps, Ustyug (see Ekzemplyarskiy, II, 15, n. 63, and 66, n. 215).

[16] Solov'yev, I, 604. Cf. *PSRL*, X, 63   [17] Solov'yev, I, 606.

tively minor city of Radilov on the Volga. The year was 1216.[18]

Konstantin remained in Vladimir, made peace with his brother Yuriy, gave him Suzdal', and promised him Vladimir. With the unification of Vladimir and Rostov in the person of Grand Prince Konstantin, Rostov's prospects were once more brighter. Yet the hopes of Rostov—that it might once more regain its position of predominance in the northeast—were dashed with the untimely death of Prince Konstantin in 1218 and the passing of the Grand Princedom to Prince Yuriy.[19]

Shortly before his death, Grand Prince Konstantin had divided his patrimony, which included Rostov, among his three sons. To his oldest son, Vasil'ko, he gave Rostov; to his second son, Vsevolod, he gave Yaroslavl';[20] and to his youngest son, Vladimir, he granted Uglich.[21] Yaroslavl' was never again a part of the patrimony of the Prince of Rostov, and the formerly mighty principality was also diminished by the temporary alienation of Uglich.

It is from Vasil'ko Konstantinovich that the House of Rostov proper takes its start. Vasil'ko, who was born in 1209, ruled as Prince of Rostov from 1218 until his death at the hands of the Tartars in 1238.[22]

[18] See Solov'yev, I, 606–617, for a detailed account of this struggle.

[19] *PSRL*, VII, 126. Ironically, the "gatherers-in of the Russian lands," the House of Moscow, were descended neither from Prince Konstantin nor from Prince Yuriy (who was killed in the Tartar holocaust of 1238), but from the fourth son of Big Nest, Prince Yaroslav Vsevolodovich of Pereyaslavl', the tormentor of Novgorod and the victim of the wrath of Mstislav the Daring. Incidentally, Yaroslav's second wife—the mother of Aleksandr Nevskiy—was the daughter of Mstislav.

[20] *PSRL*, VIII, 125.   [21] Ekzemplyarskiy, II, 125.

[22] The Chronicle speaks in glowing terms of this prince, who led the men of Rostov against the Tartars in the famous Battle on the Sit' River (March 4, 1238): "For Vasil'ko Konstantinovich was exceeding brave, and fair of face, and bright of eye, and large in body, and exceeding generous and strong . . . and charitable to all, and generous, and gifted, and kind to his boyars and servants . . . and in no way did he bear a grudge . . . and no one who served another prince following his death could forget his love and affection" (*PSRL*, X, 111).

Vasil'ko was captured by the Tartars during the Battle on the Sit'. They attempted to induce him to join cause with them against the

In the history of Rostov between the Tartar invasion of northeastern Russia (1237–1238) and the reign of Ivan Kalita of Moscow, only a few events need be mentioned. Of the two sons of Vasil'ko, Boris and Gleb, the former ruled in Rostov and the latter, until the death of his brother in 1277, ruled in Beloozero. When Boris died, Gleb "sat on the Rostov throne," giving his patrimony, Beloozero, to his son, Prince Mikhail Glebovich. Prince Gleb died the following year (1278) [23] and was succeeded as Prince of Rostov by his nephews, Dmitriy and Konstantin, the sons of Boris Vasil'kovich. In 1279 Prince Dmitriy seized "the volosts of Prince Mikhail Glebovich [Beloozero?] in sin and great injustice," [24] and in 1285 Prince Roman Vladimirovich of Uglich died and his patrimony was reunited to Rostov. Following this enlargement of Rostov a redivision of the lands of that principality took place, with Dmitriy probably receiving Uglich, Konstantin receiving Rostov and Ustyug, and Mikhail once more receiving Beloozero. [25] Under the year 1289 the Chronicle reports that Prince Dmitriy once more occupied the throne of Rostov.

Dmitriy died in 1294, however, and was succeeded by his brother, Konstantin. Konstantin's son, Aleksandr, became Prince of Uglich. [26] In the year 1297 Prince Yuriy Danilovich of Moscow was married "in Rostov." The wording of the Chronicle is such that it may be assumed that Yuriy's bride was Konstantin's daughter, although this has not been definitely established. [27]

Prince Konstantin Borisovich died in 1307, "in the Horde." [28]

Russians and, when he refused, they killed him (see *PSRL*, X, 110–111 [where these events are erroneously listed under the year 1237], and *PSRL*, XXV, 128–129).

[23] *PSRL*, V, 199.   [24] *PSRL*, VII, 174.

[25] There is some inconsistency in the chronicles concerning this redivision of Rostov (see Ekzemplyarskiy, II, 26, n. 106). Henceforth Beloozero was to be an independent principality until its acquisition by Moscow.

[26] *PSRL*, VII, 179 and 181.

[27] "In the year 6805 [1297]. Prince Yuriy Danilovich was married in Rostov. That same year the men of Novgorod founded . . ." (*PSRL*, VII, 181). See also Ekzemplyarskiy, II, 34.

[28] *PSRL*, VII, 185.

He had at least two sons, the second of whom, Aleksandr, had become Prince of Uglich upon the death of Konstantin's older brother, Dmitriy, in 1294. Very little is known about Konstantin's older son, Vasiliy. According to Ekzemplyarskiy there are in the Chronicles only two references to Vasiliy. The first, under the year 1291, reports his birth; the second, under the year 1316, reads:

That same year [6824/1316] there came from the Horde Prince Vasiliy Konstantinovich and with him the Tartar emissaries Sabanchey and Kazanchiy, and they inflicted much injury upon Rostov.[29]

If Vasiliy was Prince of Rostov at this time, why did he act in this manner? Ekzemplyarskiy theorizes that this action of Vasiliy's may have been directly related to the struggle between Yuriy of Moscow (Vasiliy's brother-in-law) and Mikhail of Tver' for the Grand Principality of Vladimir. In the following year (1317) Yuriy of Moscow returned from the Golden Horde with Tartar troops. He was met by Prince Mikhail and the latter's allies—the princes of Suzdal'—but war was averted; Prince Mikhail gave up the throne of Vladimir to Prince Yuriy.[30] The Prince of Rostov probably could not remain neutral in this struggle; if the princes of Suzdal' were Prince Mikhail's allies, then, in the view of Ekzemplyarskiy, it is reasonable to believe that Vasiliy Konstantinovich of Rostov was allied with his brother-in-law, Yuriy of Moscow. If so, the emissaries who came to Rostov with Vasiliy in 1316 may have been members of an advance party of those Tartars who were to come from the Horde with Yuriy of Moscow in 1317. But why was it that "they inflicted much injury upon Rostov"? The question remains unanswered.[31]

The date of Prince Vasiliy's death is not known; it is known, however, that he had two sons, Fedor and Konstantin.[32]

In 1318 Rostov was invaded and sacked by the Tartars. As the chronicler wrote:

[29] *PSRL*, V, 206.
[30] That same winter, however, Yuriy and the Tartars were defeated by Mikhail near Tver' (*PSRL*, VII, 187–188, and XXV, 161).
[31] See Ekzemplyarskiy, II, 34–36.   [32] Ekzemplyarskiy, II, 36.

In the year 6826 there came to Rus' a savage emissary named Kochka and, near Kostroma, he killed 100 and 20 men, and then he went and plundered the city of Rostov, and he despoiled the Church of the Holy Mother of God, and he burned monasteries and villages, and he took the people prisoner.[33]

The Prince of Rostov in 1318 may have been Yuriy, the only son of Prince Aleksandr Konstantinovich of Uglich, for under the year 1320 the chronicler reports that "Prince Yuriy Aleksandrovich of Rostov died." [34] Prince Yuriy left no children and he was followed by his cousins, Fedor and Konstantin, the sons of his uncle, Prince Vasiliy Konstantinovich.[35]

By 1320 the once mighty Principality of Rostov had been reduced to a fraction of its former size. As late as 1285 this principality had included, in addition to Rostov proper, the areas (*volosti*) of Uglich, Beloozero, and Ustyug. In 1320 Uglich may still nominally have been part of the Principality of Rostov, for no mention is made in the Chronicles of a Prince of Uglich between the death of Aleksandr Konstantinovich (1302) and the reign of Dmitriy Donskoy (1360–1389).[36] Beloozero, as was pointed out above, was probably returned to Prince Mikhail Glebovich, the cousin of princes Dmitriy Borisovich and Konstantin Borisovich of Rostov, in 1286. Thereafter, the Principality of Beloozero remained in the hands of the descendants of Prince Mikhail until it was incorporated into Muscovy.[37] Ustyug, on the other hand, may still have been part of the Principality of Rostov in 1320; it at least still maintained some of its traditional connections with the House of Rostov.[38] Thus, in 1320 the Principality of Rostov consisted only of Rostov District proper, with Uglich and Ustyug still probably having some tenuous connections with their former master.

As stated above, Prince Yuriy Aleksandrovich of Rostov died

---

[33] *PSRL*, VII, 188.   [34] *PSRL*, VII, 198.

[35] Ekzemplyarskiy, II, 37.   [36] Ekzemplyarskiy, II, 132.

[37] Concerning the possible purchase of Beloozero and Uglich by Ivan Kalita, see above, p. 14.

[38] See *Ustyuzhskiy letopisnyy svod (Arkhangelogorodskiy letopisets)*, text prepared by K. N. Serbina (Moscow-Leningrad, 1950), p. 53 (under the year 1364) and p. 66 (under the year 1397).

in 1320 and Rostov passed to his two cousins, Fedor and Konstantin. It was under these two princes that Rostov was divided and "Prince Fedor received the Sreten'ye Region [*storona*] and Konstantin the Borisoglebsk Region." This division probably occurred in 1328.[39]

In the meantime, Prince Ivan Kalita of Moscow was asserting his authority over Rostov. In the "Tale of Saint Sergiy," the chronicler, writing of the reign of Kalita, bemoaned the fate of the once mighty Rostov:

And there began much rapine, that is Ivan obtained the Grand Princedom of Moscow, and Rostov was together with Moscow. Alas, alas then for the city of Rostov, and even worse for its princes, because their power, and wealth, and honor, and glory were taken away from them; and they appertained (*potyagnusha*) to Moscow, and there came out an order from Grand Prince Ivan Danilovich and from Moscow to Rostov there was sent a certain voivode—one of the magnates—by the name of Vasiliy, with the epithet Kochev, and with him Minyay. Scarcely had he entered into the city of Rostov but they lay great force on the city and on those living in it, and not a little of the wealth of the people of Rostov was forcibly taken away from them by the Muscovite.[40]

[39] Karamzin, IV, 117, n. 303, which cites "the genealogical books" as its source.

I have been unable to find mention of this division of Rostov in the Chronicles. Neither have I determined just what parts of Rostov were included in the Sreten'ye Region and the Borisoglebsk Region. It is quite possible that these were the names of churches or monasteries in or near Rostov city. The word *sreten'ye* means "Presentation (of the Infant Jesus in the Temple)." The term *Borisoglebsk* (the combined adjectival form of the proper names Boris and Gleb) may be a reference to the two Russian princes so named who were martyred in the eleventh century. Boris was a prince of Rostov. On the other hand it may refer to the two sons of Prince Vasil'ko of Rostov, Boris and Gleb. For the date of this division, see Ekzemplyarskiy, II, 40.

[40] Karamzin, IV, 117, n. 303, which quotes from the *Nikon Chronicle*. The "Tale of Saint Sergiy" is found under the year 1392 (*PSRL*, XI, 128).

Solov'yev believed that Kochev's mistreatment of Rostov took place when Vasiliy Konstantinovich was Prince in Rostov (II, 234). Although the date of Prince Vasiliy's death is not known, it is probable that he died sometime before 1320, the year under which the Chronicle reports that Yuriy of Rostov died (*PSRL*, VII, 198). It is difficult to disagree with

The Sreten'ye Region was the first portion of the Principality of Rostov to be acquired by Moscow. As pointed out above, in about 1328 this region became the peculiar domain of Prince Fedor Vasil'yevich of Rostov, who ruled from 1320 to 1330 or 1331.[41] He was followed by his son, Andrey Fedorovich, who ruled until his death in 1409.[42] During the long reign of Prince Andrey Fedorovich, the princes of Moscow continued to increase their influence over Rostov, as is shown by the following.

In 1360 Prince Konstantin Vasil'yevich—Prince Andrey's uncle, who had received the Borisoglebsk Region of Rostov in about 1328—took advantage of the disturbed conditions resulting from the struggle between princes Dmitriy Ivanovich of Moscow and Dmitriy Konstantinovich of Suzdal' for the Grand Princedom of Vladimir by going to the Horde and obtaining the khan's patent to *all* of the Principality of Rostov.[43] For a time Prince Andrey apparently did nothing to counteract this threat to his position, but in 1362 the Chronicle reports that "there came about enmity" between princes Andrey Fedorovich and

---

Ekzemplyarskiy's supposition that Prince Vasiliy Konstantinovich died about 1316, the last year in which he is mentioned in the Chronicles (*Velikiye i udel'nyye knyaz'ya*, II, 36). If Prince Vasiliy did die in 1316 then he could not have been Prince of Rostov when the events related in the "Tale of Saint Sergiy" took place, i.e., following the date that "Ivan obtained the Grand Princedom of Moscow."

It is, of course, possible that the chronicler was mistaken and that Kochev's mistreatment of Rostov took place before Ivan obtained the Grand Princedom of Moscow. As a matter of fact, it is possible that the incident described in the "Tale of Saint Sergiy" is to be related to the sacking of Rostov in 1318, for in that year "there came to Rus' a savage emissary named Kochka [cf. Kochev] and . . . he went and plundered the city of Rostov" (see above, p. 32). Moreover, it is conceivable that the chronicler, writing years later, associated Kochev (Kochka?) with the Grand Prince of Moscow (Yuriy, not Ivan), for it was in only the preceding year (1317) that "there came from the Horde Grand Prince Yuriy Danilovich . . . and he brought with him Tartars . . ." (*PSRL*, XXV, 161).

[41] *PSRL*, VII, 202, and XXV, 170, report that Prince Fedor Vasil'yevich died in 1330. *PSRL*, X, 204, reports that he died on March 28, 1331.

[42] Ekzemplyarskiy, II, 42.   [43] *PSRL*, X, 232.

Konstantin Vasil'yevich.[44] In 1363 Prince Andrey, who was in Pereyaslavl' at the time, marched against Rostov with a large army, apparently hoping to regain his patrimony, the Sreten'ye half of Rostov, by force of arms. With him were troops under the command of Prince Ivan of Rzhev.[45] The princes of Rzhev were in the service of the Grand Prince of Moscow at this time and in all probability Prince Ivan was aiding Andrey of Rostov with the approval of Grand Prince Dmitriy Ivanovich. It is even possible that Muscovite troops accompanied Andrey and Ivan in the campaign against Rostov and Prince Konstantin.[46] Prince Andrey became prince again in Rostov.[47] In reporting the events relating to the acquisition of the Grand Principality of Vladimir by Dmitriy of Moscow in the year 1363, the *Trinity Chronicle* reads as follows:

In the year 6871 [1363] Grand Prince Dmitriy Ivanovich arrived in Vladimir with his brothers and with all the Russian princes, and with all the boyars, and there came to him from the Horde an emissary from Tsar Abdullah, with patents; now Grand Prince Dmitriy Ivanovich released the emissary and himself proceeded to Pereyaslavl'. That same year Prince Dmitriy Konstantinovich arrived in the city of Vladimir and again, for the second time, sat on the Grand Princedom. . . . And they brought to Prince Dmitriy Ivanovich from Tsar Mamay the patent to the Grand Princedom and he sat on the Princedom. Hearing this, Grand Prince Dmitriy Ivanovich drove him [Dmitriy Konstantinovich] again from his patrimony, the Grand Princedom of Vladimir, to his city of Suzdal'. Not only this, but he went thither, to Suzdal', in war, and, having stood several days near Suzdal', they made peace among themselves. Also over the Prince of Rostov.[48]

Of particular interest is the last sentence, or phrase: "Also over the Prince of Rostov"; it would indicate that this peace was not as much an agreement arrived at with the concurrence of both sides as it was a cessation of hostilities with the Prince of Moscow dictating the terms to his vanquished competitor, Dmitriy

[44] *PSRL*, XV, 428.   [45] *PSRL*, V, 229.

[46] Ekzemplyarskiy, II, 40–41.   [47] *Ustyuzhskiy letopisnyy svod*, p. 53.

[48] *Troitskaya letopis'*, reconstructed text by M. D. Priselkov (Moscow-Leningrad, 1950), pp. 378–379.

Konstantinovich, and the latter's ally, Konstantin Vasil'yevich of Rostov. This fact, in addition to the assistance given to Prince Andrey of Rostov by Prince Ivan of Rzhev, leaves little doubt that Andrey was an ally, if not a servant, of the Grand Prince of Moscow.[49]

Prince Andrey remained loyal to the Grand Prince of Moscow, who had aided him in recovering his "patrimony" from his uncle. Thus, in 1371, when Prince Mikhail Aleksandrovich of Tver' returned from the Horde with the khan's patent to the Grand Principality of Vladimir, Andrey accompanied Grand Prince Dmitriy Ivanovich when the latter set out for the Horde on June 15.[50] In 1375 Prince Andrey Fedorovich participated in Grand Prince Dmitriy's campaign against Tver'.[51] Andrey also took part in the Battle of Kulikovo Plain in 1380.[52]

During the reign of Prince Andrey the princes of Moscow acquired a number of holdings in the Principality of Rostov. Thus, Ivan Kalita, in his testament, mentioned the village Bogorodicheskoye, in Rostov, which he had purchased. Grand Prince Dmitriy Donskoy willed the village Vasil'yevskoye, Rostov District, to his son, Vasiliy. In his first testament, Grand Prince Vasiliy Dmitriyevich bequeathed his acquisitions in Rostov (not identified) to his princess, Sofiya Vitovtovna.

The identity of the descendant of Prince Andrey who sold his patrimony—the Sreten'ye half of Rostov—to Moscow has not been definitely established. It seems probable that it was Prince Ivan (dates unknown), the oldest son of Prince Andrey, and that he sold his patrimony to Grand Prince Vasiliy I of Moscow.[53] Yet if this were the case, then why was this purchase not

[49] Ekzemplyarskiy, II, 40–41. A further indication that Prince Konstantin was defeated by the joint forces of Andrey of Rostov and Dmitriy of Moscow is the fact that in the following year, 1364, Prince Konstantin fled to Ustyug (*Ustyuzhskiy letopisnyy svod*, p. 53).

[50] *PSRL*, VIII, 18. Grand Prince Dmitriy Ivanovich returned from the Horde in the autumn of the same year, having recovered the patent to the Grand Princedom (*PSRL*, VIII, 18).

[51] *PSRL*, VIII, 22–23.   [52] Karamzin, V, 39.

[53] Ekzemplyarskiy, II, 42, which cites Dolgorukov's "Russian Genealogical Book."

reflected in the testaments of Vasiliy I? The first reliable reference to the acquisition of Rostov by Moscow is found in the testament of Vasiliy II:

And to my princess I give Rostov with all that appertained to it, and with its villages [and it shall be hers] during her lifetime. And the Rostov princes who managed [*vedali*] [Rostov] under me, the grand prince, now [they] shall hold [it] in the same manner under my princess, and my princess shall not interfere with them in this. And when God takes my princess, then my princess shall give Rostov to my son Yuriy, and he shall hold [it] in the same way in which his mother held it, so that the [Rostov] princes may manage that which is theirs and may hold it in the same manner [as that in which they held it under me].

Dolgorukov's "Russian Genealogical Book," cited by Ekzemplyarskiy, reports that Prince Ivan sold his share of Rostov to Grand Prince Vasiliy Dmitriyevich. The accuracy of this report is suspect because of the fact that the acquisition of Rostov was not reflected in any of the testaments of Vasiliy I. It is possible, as Ekzemplyarskiy suggests,[54] that Prince Ivan did sell the Sreten'ye half of Rostov to Vasiliy I and that this fact was not disclosed in the latter's testaments because of some agreement between the two princes which prevented the Grand Prince of Moscow from exercising complete and unlimited control over his purchase. It is also possible, however, that Dolgorukov's "Russian Genealogical Book" is in error and that Prince Ivan actually sold his half of Rostov to Vasiliy II of Moscow. The testament of the latter clearly indicates that the Sreten'ye half of Rostov was part of the Grand Principality of Moscow in 1462.

Mozhaysk

Included among the acquisitions of Vasiliy II is Mozhaysk, an example of the second type of acquisition (i.e., it had once been in the possession of the main line of the House of Moscow, then

---

[54] II, 43, n. 150.

lost, then reacquired). The manner in which it finally became a part of the Grand Principality of Moscow differs somewhat from the way in which Rostov was incorporated.

Mozhaysk stands on the upper reaches of the Moskva River and it is, therefore, quite understandable why this principality, which had been in the hands of the princes of Smolensk, was one of the first acquisitions of the expanding principality of Moscow.[55] It appeared for a time that Mozhaysk—together with Kolomna, on the lower reaches of the Moskva River, which had been annexed in 1300—was to be an integral part of the grand-princely patrimonial principality (*veliko-knyazheskiy udel*) of Moscow, for, having passed to Prince Ivan Kalita on the death of Grand Prince Yuriy Danilovich in 1325, Mozhaysk, with all its volosts, was bequeathed to the former's oldest son, Prince Semen Ivanovich, who bequeathed all his holdings—including Mozhaysk, with its volosts—to his third wife, Princess Mariya.

Ivan II, who succeeded his brother as grand prince when the latter died in 1353, appears to have had control over the former holdings of Grand Prince Semen despite the fact that they had been willed to Semen's wife.[56] In his testament, tentatively dated 1358, Ivan II bequeathed Mozhaysk, with all its volosts, to his oldest son, Dmitriy. Mozhaysk was still part of the grand-princely patrimonial principality.

Mozhaysk was temporarily removed from the control of the Grand Prince of Moscow by the second testament of Grand Prince Dmitriy Ivanovich, written in 1389, the year of Dmitriy's death. In this testament Mozhaysk "with all its volosts . . . and with its villages, and with all its customs, and with its outlying volosts" was bequeathed to the third son of the grand prince, Andrey Dmitriyevich, subsequently known as the Prince of Mozhaysk.

Prince Andrey died in 1432.[57] Although no testament of this prince has been preserved it is quite certain that he wrote one, leaving his patrimonial principality to his two sons, Ivan and

[55] See above, Chapter 1.
[56] Grand Princess Mariya Aleksandrovna lived until 1399 (*PSRL*, XXV, 228).
[57] *PSRL*, VIII, 96.

Mikhail. The older son, Ivan, received Mozhaysk; Mikhail received Vereya, Beloozero, and other holdings.[58]

The date of the birth of Prince Ivan Andreyevich, the second patrimonial prince of Mozhaysk, is not known. He played an important role in the struggle between Vasiliy II on the one hand and Prince Yuriy Dmitriyevich and his sons on the other, for possession of the Grand Principality of Moscow. For a time in 1434 Prince Ivan Andreyevich was allied with Grand Prince Vasiliy II against their uncle, Prince Yuriy Dmitriyevich, participating with Vasiliy in the battle near Rostov in the spring of 1434 in which Yuriy was victorious. Prince Ivan, who had fled to Tver', did not remain loyal to Vasiliy II but, deserting the latter's cause, went over to Prince Yuriy and participated with the latter in the capture of Moscow (1434). Two years later, however, we find Ivan allied once more with Vasiliy II against Vasiliy the Cross-Eyed, the son of the deceased Prince Yuriy Dmitriyevich.[59]

Prince Ivan Andreyevich and his brother both participated, as the allies of Grand Prince Vasiliy II, in the battle on the Kamenka River near Suzdal' in July 1445, in which the Russians were defeated by the Tartars.[60] But Prince Ivan Andreyevich once more betrayed Grand Prince Vasiliy. It was Prince Ivan who—together with Nikita Konstantinovich Dobrynskiy, a boyar of Prince Yuriy's son, Dmitriy Shemyaka—seized Grand Prince Vasiliy Vasil'yevich in the Trinity-Sergiy Monastery shortly after his return from Tartar captivity. They carried the grand prince to Moscow where he was blinded by Shemyaka in February, 1446.[61]

[58] Sources of this information are the "Agreement of Grand Prince Vasiliy Vasil'yevich with Prince Ivan Andreyevich of Mozhaysk," dated 1447 (*DDG*, pp. 146–148), and the "Agreement of Grand Prince Vasiliy Vasil'yevich with Prince Mikhail Andreyevich of Vereya and Beloozero," dated June 19, 1447 (*DDG*, pp. 126–128).

[59] *PSRL*, VIII, 98–99.

[60] Grand Prince Vasiliy II and Prince Mikhail were both captured by the Tartars during this battle. "And Prince Ivan Andreyevich was greatly wounded and was knocked from his horse but another horse was given to him and he fled" (*PSRL*, VIII, 112).

[61] *PSRL*, VIII, 115–116.

In the following year, after Vasiliy II had regained the Grand Princedom, Shemyaka and Ivan Andreyevich concluded an armistice with the grand prince.[62] Still Prince Ivan Andreyevich did not remain loyal to Grand Prince Vasiliy II. In a sworn writ (*krestotseloval'naya zapis'*) to King Casimir of Poland, dated February 5, 1448, Ivan's father-in-law, Prince Fedor Vorotynskiy, speaking for his son-in-law, promised King Casimir the cities of Rzhev and Medyn' if the Polish king undertook to aid the Prince of Mozhaysk in acquiring the Moscow Princedom.[63] In 1449 Prince Ivan Andreyevich, once more allied with Dmitriy Shemyaka, participated with the latter in a campaign against Kostroma. Grand Prince Vasiliy II, accompanied by Metropolitan Iona, went forth to meet them, but stopped at the village Rudino, near Yaroslavl'. Princes Dmitriy and Ivan moved against the grand prince but, before fighting broke out, Prince Ivan deserted his ally and once more swore allegiance to Vasiliy II. It was at this time that the grand prince granted Bezhetskiy Verkh to his cousin, Ivan.[64]

Prince Dmitriy Shemyaka died in 1454. In the following year Grand Prince Vasiliy II seized Mozhaysk. The Chronicle reports that the grand prince, having seized the city of Mozhaysk and, "having mercy on all those in that city, favored them and, placing his lieutenants [in the city], returned to Moscow." Prince Ivan Andreyevich fled to Lithuania.[65] Mozhaysk was

[62] See the "Armistice Agreement of Princes Ivan Andreyevich of Mozhaysk and Mikhail Andreyevich of Vereya and Beloozero with Grand Prince Vasiliy Vasil'yevich" (*DDG*, pp. 140–142).

[63] For the text of this sworn writ, see *DDG*, pp. 149–150.

[64] *PSRL*, V, 269.

[65] *PSRL*, VIII, 144. In Lithuania Prince Ivan Andreyevich was granted Chernigov, Starodub (Seversk), Gomel', and Lyubech (Ekzemplyarskiy, II, 327). The Chronicle (*PSRL*, VIII, 144) reports that Vasiliy II moved against Ivan because of the latter's incorrigibility (*neispravleniye*). Vasiliy certainly had ample reason to distrust the Prince of Mozhaysk. In addition to the actions of Prince Ivan that have been related above it is probable that Vasiliy had another cause for distrusting the former. In a letter to Misail, Bishop of Smolensk, written after the flight of Ivan to Lithuania, Metropolitan Iona referred to that prince's refusal to send assistance against the forces of Khan Sedi Akhmet of the Blue (Nogay) Horde who invaded Muscovy in 1449 and in 1451 (see Ekzemplyarskiy, II, 326, and *PSRL*, XXV, 270–271).

once more in the hands of the Grand Prince of Moscow. In his testament, written in 1461 or 1462, Grand Prince Vasiliy II bequeathed Mozhaysk to his second son, Prince Yuriy Vasil'yevich.

IVAN III VASIL'YEVICH THE GREAT (1440–1506)

Ivan III was Grand Prince of Vladimir and Moscow from 1462 until his death in 1506. His testament was written sometime between the latter part of 1503 and June 16, 1504. The main beneficiaries of his testament were his sons, Vasiliy, Yuriy, Dmitriy, Semen, and Andrey. Ivan's first wife, Mariya Borisovna, his son Ivan (by Mariya Borisovna), and his second wife, Sofiya Paleolog, had all died prior to the writing of this testament.

To Vasiliy, his oldest surviving son, the grand prince bequeathed his father's "patrimony, the grand principalities [of Moscow and Vladimir], with which my father blessed me and which God gave me"; the city of Moscow with its customs and volosts, including Prince Vladimir's third; Radonezh; Kolomna; Kashira; Zarech'ye (the land beyond the Oka) with the cities of Teshilov, Roslavl', Venev, and Mstislavl', with the "other localities along the Ryazan' border"; Yelets; Serpukhov; Khotun'; Tarusa; Gorodets Serpukhovskiy; Princess Yevdokiya's patrimony; Mtsensk; Vorotynsk; the patrimonies of the Novosil', Odoyev, and Belev princes; Borovsk; Maloyaroslavets; Medyn'; Mozhaysk; Vyazma; Kozlov (in Smolensk); Dorogobuzh; Pereyaslavl' Zalesskiy; Vladimir; Yur'yev; Suzdal'; Rostov (both halves); [66] Yaroslavl'; Ust'-Sheksny; Beloozero; Vologda; Zaozer'ye; Kubena, Ustyug; Zavoloch'ye; Yugra; the Pechora Land; Velikaya Perm'; Kostroma; Galich; Nizhniy Novgorod with its lands of the Mordva and the Cheremisa; Murom with its lands of the Mordva and the Cheremisa; the Meshchera Land; the lands of the Mordva princes; Vyatka with the lands of the Arsk (Votyak) princes; Tver'; Novgorod the Great with its five fifths and its minor cities; Pskov with its lands and its minor cities, including Toropets and Ostrov; Prince Fedor Vasil'yevich's share of Ryazan', including Staraya Ryazan', Perevi-

---

[66] I have assumed an error in the testament of Ivan III (see below, Text 11, n. 31).

tebsk, and a share of Pereyaslavl' Ryazanskiy; and a number of volosts, villages, and other lesser holdings, including Lyshchykovo Monastery in Moscow District.

Yuriy Ivanovich, second son of the grand prince, was granted Dmitrov, Zvenigorod, Kashin (formerly an *udel* of Tver'), Ruza, Bryansk, Serpeysk, and a number of scattered volosts and settlements.

Grand Prince Ivan III bequeathed the following to his third son, Dmitriy Ivanovich Zhilka: Uglich, Ustyuzhna, Mologa (formerly an *udel* of Yaroslavl'); Khlepen'; Zubtsov and Opoki in Tver'; the half of Rzheva which had belonged to the nephew of the grand prince, Ivan Borisovich; Meshchovsk, including the half that had belonged to Prince Mikhail Mezetskiy; Opakov on the Ugra River, with a number of volosts along the river that had belonged to Lithuania; and scattered volosts and settlements.

Ivan's fourth son, Semen Ivanovich, was to receive Bezhetskiy Verkh, Kaluga, Kozel'sk, and a number of scattered volosts and settlements.

To Andrey Ivanovich, his fifth and youngest surviving son, Ivan III bequeathed Staritsa, Kholm, and the burg Novyy (all in Tver'), Vereya, Vyshegorod (in Dmitrov), Aleksin, Lyubutsk, and a number of scattered volosts and settlements.

Ivan's younger sons, Yuriy, Dmitriy, Semen, and Andrey, were granted a number of villages near Moscow and a number of courts in Moscow or its suburbs. The conditions under which they were to hold these villages and courts were clearly set forth in the testament and were of such a nature as to insure that the authority of the future grand prince, Vasiliy, would not be threatened in his "patrimony" of Moscow.

On the basis of Ivan III's testament the following should be considered acquisitions of the first type, i.e., acquisitions acquired by Moscow for the first time: Zarech'ye (the lands beyond the Oka River) including the cities of Teshilov, Roslavl', Venev, and Mstislavl' (from Lithuania by the Armistice of 1494); Yelets; Mtsensk (from Lithuania by the Armistice of 1503); Vorotynsk (with the defection of Prince Ivan Mikhaylovich to Moscow in 1490); Novosil', Odoyev, and Belev (confirmed as part of Muscovy by the Armistice of 1494); Kozlov (probably from Lithuania but method of acquisition not determined); Dorogobuzh (seized by Moscow from Lithuania in 1500); the Borisoglebsk half of Rostov (see immediately below); Yaroslavl' (ceded by its princes—perhaps for a "fitting remuneration"—to Ivan III in 1463); Yugra (the area immediately west of the Ob' River along its northern reaches, occupied by the men of Moscow in 1483–1499); the Pechora region; Velikaya Perm' (seized by Ivan's men in 1472); the lands of the Arsk (Votyak) princes in Vyatka (subjugated by Ivan's men in 1489); the former Grand Principality of Tver' (incorporated into Muscovy in 1485); Novgorod the Great, with its lands and minor cities (incorporated into Muscovy in 1478); Zavoloch'ye (in theory part of Novgorod the Great); Pskov, with its lands and minor cities (nominally independent until 1510); Prince Fedor Vasil'yevich's share of the Grand Principality of Ryazan', including the cities of Staraya Ryazan' and Perevitebsk, and part of Pereyaslavl' Ryazanskiy; Bryansk (from Lithuania by the Armistice of 1494); Serpeysk (from Lithuania by the Armistice of 1503); Meshchovsk; Kozel'sk (from Lithuania by the Armistice of 1494); and Lyubutsk (from Lithuania by the Armistice of 1494).

The cities and territories listed in the paragraph above appeared in the Testament of Ivan III for the first time as holdings of the Grand Prince of Moscow. Acquisitions of the second type, i.e., cities and territories once under the control of the Prince of Moscow, lost, and reacquired by Ivan III, were: Dmitrov, Mozhaysk, Serpukhov, Khotun', and Medyn' (all from Prince Yuriy Vasil'yevich of Dmitrov, who died childless in 1473); Uglich, Bezhetskiy Verkh, and Zvenigorod (from Prince Andrey the Elder, who died in prison in Moscow in 1494); Ruza, one half of Rzheva, and Ivan Borisovich's volosts in Volok Lamskiy (from Prince Boris Vasil'yevich and his son, Prince Ivan Borisovich); Vologda, Zaozer'ye, Kubena, Tarusa, and Gorodets Serpukhovskiy (from Prince Andrey the Younger, who died childless in 1481); Vereya, Beloozero, and Maloyaroslavets (all from Prince Mikhail Andreyevich of Vereya, who bequeathed his holdings to Grand Prince Ivan III); and the Sreten'ye half of Rostov (from Princess Mariya).

I have attempted to list all the major territorial acquisitions of Ivan III, based upon evidence of the testaments. (For brief information on most of these acquisitions, see the notes to Text 11, below.) Ivan also acquired numerous lesser holdings (including "courts") from various individuals by such diverse means as right of settlement, exchange, appropriation, and bequests from his mother and grandmother. Although not mentioned in this testament, the Seversk cities (Novgorod Seversk, Putivl', Rylsk, and others) were acquired from Lithuania during the reign of Ivan III, but at least some of these lands were in the hands of two princes, Vasiliy Shemyachich and Vasiliy Semenovich, and were not disposed of by Ivan's testaments. Interestingly enough, if Vasiliy Shemyachich was in fact a patrimonial prince—and he is called the "last of the *udel* princes"—then the grand prince should not have presumed to dispose of his holdings.[67]

Rostov

As was related above, Rostov—presumably the Sreten'ye half—was bequeathed by Vasiliy II to his wife, Princess Mariya, with the provision that, upon her death, it was to pass to Prince Yuriy Vasil'yevich. Prince Yuriy died in 1473, eleven years before the death of his mother. Rostov was not mentioned in Yuriy's testament and it appears that the Sreten'ye half of that principality escheated to the grand prince, Ivan III, for in his testament he bequeathed all of Rostov to his son Vasiliy.[68]

The Borisoglebsk half of Rostov, listed above as one of the acquisitions of Ivan III of the first type, had been acquired by Prince Konstantin Vasil'yevich, the second son of Prince Vasiliy Konstantinovich of Rostov. Prior to 1360 Prince Konstantin was allied with, or under the control of, the Grand Prince of Moscow. In 1328 Konstantin was married to Mariya, daughter of Ivan Kalita of Moscow. In 1340 Kalita was ordered by Khan Uzbek to send reinforcements to the Tartar army that was advancing against Smolensk. The grand prince sent, among

[67] See below, Text 13, n. 173.
[68] For the text of the testament of Yuriy, Prince of Dmitrov, see *DDG*, pp. 221–224. See also *PSRL*, VIII, 175, and Ekzemplyarskiy, II, 328.

others, Prince Konstantin of Rostov.[69] In 1340, following the death of Ivan Kalita and his son Semen's trip to the Horde, Semen sent a force against the city of Torzhok. Konstantin was also among the princes sent on this campaign.[70] In 1348 King Magnus of Sweden invaded the lands of Novgorod, seizing the city of Orekhovets. The people of Novgorod appealed to Grand Prince Semen for help. The latter set out for Novgorod, but was forced to turn back, receiving word that he had been summoned to the Horde. He did, however, send a force to aid Novgorod. This force was under the command of Prince Ivan (the brother of the grand prince) and Prince Konstantin of Rostov.[71]

These events indicate that until 1360 Prince Konstantin Vasil'yevich of Rostov was subservient to the will of the Grand Prince of Moscow. In 1360, however, with the death of Ivan II and the ensuing struggle between Dmitriy Ivanovich of Moscow and Dmitriy Konstantinovich of Suzdal' for the Grand Princedom of Vladimir, Prince Konstantin of Rostov began to assert his independence of Moscow. As was pointed out above, in 1360 Prince Konstantin gained the khan's patent to all of the Principality of Rostov, but was forced to flee to Ustyug in 1364, following defeat at the hands of his nephew, Prince Andrey Fedorovich, and Prince Ivan of Rzhev, the servant of Dmitriy of Moscow.

We do not know whether Prince Konstantin returned from exile during his lifetime. We do know, however, that he died of the plague in 1365 and that he was buried in the Cathedral of the Dormition in Rostov.[72]

The fate of the Borisoglebsk half of Rostov is related to two of Prince Konstantin's grandsons, Andrey and Ivan, the sons of Konstantin's fourth son, Aleksandr.[73]

Prince Andrey Aleksandrovich of Rostov was a servant of Grand Prince Vasiliy I of Moscow. In 1415 Prince Andrey was sent to rule in Pskov. He did not remain there for long, however, as the people of Pskov forced him to leave in 1417. Of his six

[69] *PSRL*, XXV, 172.   [70] *PSRL*, X, 173.
[71] *Troitskaya letopis'*, pp. 369–370.   [72] Ekzemplyarskiy, II, 50.
[73] Ekzemplyarskiy, II, 53.

sons, only one—Prince Vladimir Andreyevich—figures in this account.[74]

Prince Ivan Aleksandrovich is known only from the genealogical books, which attribute five sons to him. Concerning the three eldest nothing is known except that they were all childless. The youngest son of Prince Ivan Aleksandrovich, Aleksandr Ivanovich, probably died before his older brother, Ivan.[75] Under the year 1474 the Chronicle reports that Prince Ivan Ivanovich, the fourth son of Prince Ivan Aleksandrovich, and his cousin, Prince Vladimir Andreyevich, sold their half of Rostov—the Borisoglebsk half—to Grand Prince Ivan III.[76]

Thus, by 1474, all of Rostov had come under the direct control of the Grand Prince of Moscow. Interestingly enough, it remained the custom almost to the very end of the dynasty for Rostov to be left to the wife of the grand prince. So, in the testament of Ivan IV, dated 1572, Rostov, with its volosts, and with its *puti*, and with its villages, and with all its customs, was bequeathed to Anna, the wife of the tsar.

Any attempt to determine the essential factors in the acquisition of the Principality of Rostov by the princes of Moscow is made difficult by the paucity of evidence on this subject in the Chronicles. As the preceding account suggests, this evidence is limited almost entirely to an account of this or that action on the part of one or another of the princes of northeastern Russia. Nevertheless, some conclusions can be drawn from a summary of the most important events leading to the final absorption of Rostov by the Principality of Moscow.

In 1300, at the very beginning of Moscow's rise, Rostov must have been economically much stronger than the former principality. Why was it then that, during the fourteenth century,

[74] See *PSRL*, V, 22, and Ekzemplyarskiy, II, 56.

[75] Ekzemplyarskiy, II, 60–61.

[76] "That same winter the Rostov princes, Prince Vladimir Andreyevich and his brother [cousin] Prince Ivan Ivanovich, with all their children and nephews, sold their patrimony, a half of Rostov, with everything, to Grand Prince Ivan Vasil'yevich; now the grand prince, having purchased it of them, gave this half to his mother, Grand Princess Mariya" (*PSRL*, VIII, 180).

Rostov proved time and again to be politically weaker than her sister principality to the south? At least part of the answer to this question must lie in the fact that after the death of Prince Vasil'ko of Rostov in 1238 there was no single Prince of Rostov who was capable of seriously competing with the stronger princes of the other houses of northeastern Russia. Beginning with Prince Vasiliy Konstantinovich, who ruled early in the fourteenth century, the princes of Rostov were allies, or perhaps vassals, of one or another of the princes of Moscow, Tver', or Suzdal', who were competing for the position of Grand Prince of Vladimir, i.e., for the dominant political position among the princes of northeastern Rus'. After Konstantin Vsevolodovich of Rostov died in 1218, not one of the Rostov princes was a serious candidate for this position.

Another factor which must have seriously weakened the once powerful principality of Rostov was the series of costly military calamities which befell her during the second and third decades of the fourteenth century. In 1316 the Chronicles report that Prince Vasiliy Konstantinovich of Rostov, with Tartars, "inflicted much injury upon Rostov." Although this action on the part of the Prince of Rostov is difficult to explain, this sacking of Rostov can perhaps be related to the struggle that was taking place at that time between Prince Yuriy of Moscow and Prince Mikhail of Tver' for the position of Grand Prince of Vladimir. If this was the case, it is apparent that Prince Vasiliy of Rostov was an ally of the Prince of Moscow. How dearly Rostov was to pay for this alliance!

Rostov must have been further weakened in 1318 when it was sacked by the Tartars under the command of a "savage emissary named Kochka." This attack on Rostov may also have been related to the struggle between Moscow and Tver'.

The third attack on Rostov and the first example of the perpetration of violence on that city by Moscow is told in the "Tale of Saint Sergiy," which relates how, following his acquisition of the Grand Princedom of Moscow, Ivan Kalita sent men under the command of his voivode, Vasiliy Kochev, and "they lay great force on the city and on those living in it, and not a little of the wealth of the people of Rostov was forcibly taken away from them by the Muscovite. . . ." The Chronicle, however, gives no reason for this attack.

In about 1328 an event took place which may well have been decisive in determining the fate of Rostov. At this time the Principality of Rostov was divided between two of its princes, with Fedor receiving the Sreten'ye half and Konstantin receiving the Borisoglebsk half. This division of Rostov, at the very time that Moscow was greatly strengthening its position, must have greatly weakened the former.

During the latter part of the thirteenth and the early part of the fourteenth centuries, Rostov was greatly weakened by the loss of Beloozero and Uglich, which not only were lost by Rostov, but were acquired by Moscow, probably during the reign of Ivan Kalita. During the fourteenth century Moscow also strengthened itself at Rostov's expense by the acquisition—through purchase or by other means—of a number of holdings in Rostov.

The princes of Moscow also strengthened their position vis-à-vis Rostov by at least two marriages that are reported in the Chronicles. In 1297 Prince Yuriy of Moscow was married "in Rostov," probably to the daughter of Prince Konstantin. In 1328 Prince Konstantin Vasil'yevich of Rostov—the recipient of the Borisoglebsk half of that principality—was married to Mariya, the daughter of Grand Prince Ivan Kalita.

There is abundant evidence to show that the two princes of Rostov were subservient, from about 1328 to 1360, to the will of the Prince of Moscow who, from 1328, was also the Grand Prince of Vladimir. In 1360, however, when Konstantin Vasil'yevich of Rostov threw in his lot with Prince Dmitriy Konstantinovich of Suzdal' in the latter's competition with the young Prince of Moscow, Dmitriy, for the Grand Princedom of Vladimir, Prince Dmitriy of Moscow aided Prince Andrey of Rostov, whose patrimony—the Sreten'ye half of Rostov—was threatened by Prince Konstantin's claim to the entire Principality of Rostov. In the struggle which followed—a struggle in which the forces of the Prince of Moscow were victorious—Prince Konstantin was forced to flee. Prince Andrey of Rostov must have become even more dependent on Moscow as a result of the assistance given him by Prince Dmitriy Ivanovich.

Following the defeat of Prince Konstantin, the princes of Rostov appear to have been entirely under the control of the prince of Moscow. It was only a question of time before the princes of Rostov, the holders of both "halves" of that once mighty principality, recognized the overwhelming power of Moscow by selling their shares of Rostov to the Muscovite princes. The Sreten'ye half of Rostov was sold to Moscow sometime during the reign of Vasiliy I or during that of Vasiliy II. The Borisoglebsk half of Rostov was sold to Ivan III in 1474. There is no evidence in the Chronicles to indicate that force was employed to bring about these sales. On the contrary, considerable consideration was shown to the princes of the Sreten'ye half of Rostov by Grand Prince Vasiliy II, whose testament (1462) stipulated that these princes were to continue to "manage" their holdings following his death as they had in the past.

The decline of Rostov and its final absorption by Moscow must, then, on the basis of existing evidence, be related to the following: (1) the absence of a strong prince in Rostov during the thirteenth and fourteenth centuries, a prince who could have competed with the princes of Moscow, Tver', and Suzdal' for political supremacy in northeastern Russia; (2) the weakening of Rostov through the loss of its former holdings of Beloozero and Uglich, which were subsequently acquired by Moscow; (3) the weakening of Rostov as a result of three invasions of that principality during the second and third decades of the fourteenth century; (4) marriage alliances between the rising House of Moscow and the House of Rostov; (5) the division of Rostov in about 1328, with two of her princes each obtaining one "half" of the principality; (6) the acquisition by the princes of Moscow of a number of territorial holdings in Rostov during the fourteenth century; (7) the reliance of Andrey Fedorovich upon the Grand Prince of Moscow in the former's struggle against his uncle, Prince Konstantin; and (8) the subsequent defeat of Prince Konstantin and Prince Dmitriy Konstantinovich of Suzdal' by Grand Prince Dmitriy Ivanovich of Moscow.

Mozhaysk

It will be remembered that in his testament, written in 1461 or 1462, Grand Prince Vasiliy II granted Mozhaysk to his second son, Yuriy Vasil'yevich. Prince Yuriy died childless in 1473,[77] and his holdings must have escheated to the Grand Principality, for in 1481 Ivan III granted Mozhaysk to his brother, Andrey Vasil'yevich of Uglich.[78] Relations between the grand prince and his brother were good until 1491. In that year the Khan of the Crimea, Mengli Girey—the ally of Ivan III of Moscow—was attacked by Tartars of the Blue (Nogay) Horde. Ivan ordered his brothers, Andrey of Uglich and Boris of Volok Lamskiy, and others, to proceed to the assistance of Mengli Girey. Prince Boris followed the orders of the grand prince, but Prince Andrey failed to do so. Perhaps because of this disobedience Ivan III, in September, 1491, invited Prince Andrey to Moscow and had him arrested and placed under strict guard.[79] Prince Andrey died in confinement in Moscow in 1494.[80] Mozhaysk was once more in the hand of the Grand Prince of Moscow.

Henceforth Mozhaysk was to be kept in the senior line of the House of Moscow. Grand Prince Ivan III, in his testament dated 1503 or 1504, bequeathed Mozhaysk to his oldest son, Vasiliy Ivanovich. Vasiliy's testament has been lost, but Mozhaysk was in the hands of his son, Ivan IV, at the writing of the latter's testament in 1572, for he bequeathed that city to his oldest son, Ivan Ivanovich.

VASILIY III IVANOVICH (1479–1533)

Vasiliy, the oldest surviving son of Ivan III, was "constituted . . . autocrat in the Grand Principality of Vladimir and Moscow" in 1502. Upon the death of his father in 1506, Vasiliy became Grand Prince of All Rus', which he ruled until his death in 1533.

---

[77] See *PSRL*, VIII, 175, and Ekzemplyarskiy, II, 328.

[78] See the "Agreement of Grand Prince Ivan Vasil'yevich with Prince Andrey Vasil'yevich of Uglich" (*DDG*, pp. 252–254).

[79] *PSRL*, VIII, 223. Ivan III accused his brother of numerous other improprieties: that he had conspired (*dumal*) with his brothers "to stand as one man" against the grand prince, that he had carried on negotiations with King Casimir of Poland and Khan Sedi Akhmet, etc. (Ekzemplyarskiy, II, 149).

[80] *PSRL*, VIII, 227.

Shortly before his death Vasiliy III ordered his first testament to be burned. Thereupon he wrote another testament, but this too has been lost. A testamentary writ (*dukhovnaya zapis'*), drawn up by Vasiliy in June 1523, has been preserved. This document was concerned primarily with provisions for the construction of a monastery and several churches, in accordance with a promise made by the grand prince just before he captured Smolensk in 1514. This testamentary writ does not dispose of any significant holdings, although it does mention the acquisition of "my patrimony, the city of Smolen'sk and the Smolen'sk Land." Although they are not mentioned in the testamentary writ, Vasiliy III also acquired the Seversk cities (Novgorod Seversk, Putivl', Rylsk, and others), which had been the patrimonies of Vasiliy Shemyachich and Vasiliy Semenovich. The patrimonial principality of Volok Lamskiy was acquired in 1513 when Vasiliy's cousin, Fedor Borisovich, died childless. Prince Fedor had written a testament about 1506, willing his principality to the grand prince if Fedor should have no children.[81] Moreover, the former Grand Principality of Ryazan' was finally incorporated into Muscovy during the reign of Vasiliy III.[82]

IVAN IV VASIL'YEVICH THE TERRIBLE
(1530–1584)

Ivan Vasil'yevich was a child of three when his father died, and during his childhood Muscovy was governed by his mother and "scheming boyars." On January 16, 1547, Ivan was crowned, taking the title of Tsar. A copy of the testament that Ivan wrote (probably in 1572) has been preserved. The principal legatees were his sons, Ivan and Fedor; Princess Ul'yana, the widow of Yuriy Vasil'yevich, Ivan's brother; Anna, the fourth wife of the tsar; his prospective children; and other relatives and several persons in the service of the tsar.

The principal holdings that the tsar bequeathed to his oldest

[81] "And if my princess has no offspring, then my patrimony stands before God and before my lord, the grand prince." For the text of Fedor's testament, see *DDG*, pp. 406–409.

[82] See below, Text 13, n. 115.

51

son, Ivan, were the "Russian tsardom with which my father, Grand Prince Vasiliy, blessed me and which God gave me"; Moscow, including Prince Vladimir's third; the volosts beyond the Moskva River; the "Grand Principality" of Vladimir; the patrimonies of the Starodub princes in Starodub Ryapolovo; Kolomna; Kashira; Zarech'ye, with Teshilov, Rostovets, Roslavl', Venev, and Mstislavl'; Yelets; Serpukhov; the "city on the Solova [River]" (Kropivna?); the "Grand Principality" of Ryazan'; Mtsensk; Belev; a third of Mosal'sk; Yur'yevets (Yur'yev Volzhskiy); Belogorod (in Tver'?); Gorodets on the Volga (Radilov); Romanov on the Volga; Mozhaysk; Vyazma; Kozlov; Dorogobuzh; Belaya (Belyy); Smolensk; Pereyaslavl'; Yur'yev; Dmitrov, Borovsk; Poshekhon'ye; Vologda; Zaozer'ye; Kubena; Ustyug; Zavoloch'ye; the Yugra and Pechora regions; Velikaya Perm'; Galich; Nizhniy Novgorod; Murom; Meshchera; Koshkovo; Kadom; Temnikov; Shatsk; Kurmysh; Alatyr'; the lands of the Mordva and the Cheremisa; Arzamas; the city of Starodub Ryapolovo; Beloozero; one third of Vorotynsk; Goroden'; Mikulin; Vyatka, with the lands of the Arsk princes; the Seversk cities (Novgorod Seversk, Putivl', Mglin, Drakov, Pochap, and Karachev); the "Grand Principality" of Tver', with Klin and Kashin; Torzhok; Rzheva (both halves); the "Grand Principality" of Novgorod, with its lands and minor cities; a number of "cities" that Ivan had "founded" on the Lithuanian border; Velikiye Luki; Toropets; Rzheva Pustaya; the Karelian Land; the Lake Onega region; Kargopol'; the regions of the Onega, Dvina, Vaga, and Kokshenga rivers; Kholmogory; Pskov, with its minor cities; the "Tsardom" of Kazan', with all its lands; Sviyazhsk; Cheboksary; the "Tsardom" of Astrakhan', with all its lands; the cities in the Livonian Land, "which I took with God's help," including Yur'yev, Fellin, Narva, and others; Polotsk; Ozerishche; Usvyat; Bezhetskiy Verkh; Kaluga; the burg Malyy (Maloyaroslavets); Medyn'; Opakov on the Ugra; Bryansk; Vyshegorod on the Protva; Staritsa; Aleksin; Vereya; Dankov; and Ryazhsk.

To his second surviving son, Fedor, Tsar Ivan bequeathed Suzdal', Shuya, Kostroma, Yaroslavl', Kozel'sk, Serpeysk,

Mtsensk, Volok Lamskiy, and a large number of scattered volosts, villages, and other settlements.

The testament granted the following lifetime holdings to Princess Ul'yana, widow of Ivan's brother, Yuriy: Kremenesk (to pass to Prince Ivan at Ul'yana's death), Ustyuzhna (to pass to Prince Fedor at Ul'yana's death), the volost Kadka in Uglich, and a number of villages in Uglich and Moscow districts. Ul'yana was also granted in perpetuity two villages (Khorobrovo and Krasnoye) in Uglich. These were hers to dispose of as she saw fit.

Anna, Tsar Ivan's fourth wife, was to receive Rostov and some villages in Moscow, Yaroslavl', and Yur'yev districts.

If a son were born to Tsar Ivan and Princess Anna, the testament stipulated that he should receive Uglich, Ustyuzhna (previously granted to Ul'yana as her lifetime possession and promised to Fedor at Ul'yana's death), Maloyaroslavets and Vereya (both previously bequeathed to Prince Ivan), Kholopiy, and Kashin.

If a daughter were born to Tsar Ivan and Anna, she would receive Zubtsov, Opoki, Khlepen, Ragachev, and some villages in Moscow District.

Other relatives of Tsar Ivan's were provided for in the testament. For example, the right of the tsar's mother-in-law, Romanova (wife of Roman Yur'yevich Zakhar'in-Koshkin) and her son, Nikita Romanovich Zakhar'in-Yur'yev, to hold their patrimony (not identified) was guaranteed.

Examples of servants of the tsar who were guaranteed their holdings by this testament are Magnus, King of Livonia, who had been granted the city of Polchev in Livonia, and Mikhail Kaybulovich, son of the Khan of Astrakhan', who was to remain in possession of Zvenigorod. In all such cases the servants of the tsar were to hold their lands only as long as they continued to serve one of the tsar's sons; if they should leave to serve another, their holdings would be forfeited to Prince Ivan or Prince Fedor.

A very large number of holdings is listed in this testament as having been acquired from Yuriy Vasil'yevich, the tsar's deceased brother, from Prince Andrey Ivanovich, the tsar's uncle, from Prince Andrey's son Vladimir, from the descendants of the Starodub princes (many of whom were granted military tenures or *pomest'ya* near Moscow in 1550), and from other land-holders.

Because the testament of Ivan's father, Vasiliy III, has not been preserved, it is difficult to determine if certain territories were acquired by the father or by the son. We do know, of course, the identity of the territories willed to Vasiliy III and to Andrey of Staritsa by the testament of their father, Ivan III. The testament of Ivan the Terrible also indicates some of the territories that his younger brother, Yuriy, inherited from Vasiliy III. It is, therefore, possible to determine with reasonable assurance the identity of many of the territories that Ivan IV acquired. Many, of course, are openly identified in the testament as the tsar's acquisitions.

On the basis of evidence in his testament, the following should be considered Ivan's acquisitions of the first type: the patrimonies of the Starodub princes in Starodub Ryapolovo, including Starodub Ryapolovo city; the city on the Solova River (Kropivna?); the cities of Ryazhsk and Dankov; various "plain" patrimonies (lands in the Wild Plain associated with Kropivna, Ryazan', and Mtsensk); a third of Mosal'sk (which had belonged to Prince Vladimir Vseslav, who is not identified); Yur'yev Volzhskiy; Belogorod (probably in Tver'); Gorodets on the Volga (Radilov); Romanov on the Volga, and lands of the Nogay mirzas; Belyy (although mentioned for the first time in this testament, Belyy, or Belaya, was one of the cities that passed to Moscow from Lithuania in 1503); the patrimony of the Penkov princes in Pereyaslavl'; a number of regions and settlements in Zavoloch'ye, Velikaya Perm', and Malaya Perm' not mentioned in previous testaments; Balakhna, Vasil'sursk; Meshchera city, and Koshkovo, Kadom, Temnikov, and Shatsk cities, with the patrimonies of the Mordva princes (the Meshchera Land had been bequeathed to Vasiliy III by Ivan III); Kurmysh and Alatyr', with the patrimonies of the Mordva princes and with the Cheremisa, and with lands of the junior

54

boyars in the Wild Plain near these cities; Arzamas, with its Mordva and Cheremisa; Mikulin, and the patrimony of Prince Semen Mikulinskiy; the "plain appendages" (and the Rylsk appendages?) of the Seversk cities; Roslov (Roslavl'?); one half of Rzheva(?); cities "founded" on the Lithuanian border (Velizh, Zavoloch'ye, and others); the Khanate of Kazan', with all its lands; Sviyazhsk; Cheboksary; the Khanate of Astrakhan'; the cities in Livonia seized by Ivan IV during the Livonian War (Yur'yev, Narva, Fellin, and others, lost later to Poland); and Polotsk (lost to Bathory in 1579).

Ivan IV acquired a number of important holdings from his brother, Yuriy Vasil'yevich, who died in 1563. These included Dmitrov, Zvenigorod, Uglich, Bezhetskiy Verkh, Kaluga, Maloyaroslavets, Kremenesk, Medyn', and Bryansk (which Ivan himself had previously granted to Yuriy). The Tsar also acquired several important holdings from his cousin, Prince Vladimir Andreyevich, the son of Ivan's uncle, Prince Andrey Ivanovich.[83] These holdings were Vyzhegorod on the Protva, Staritsa, Aleksin, and Vereya.

For information on most of the holdings mentioned above see the notes to Text 13.

[83] See below, Text 13, n. 68.

CHAPTER 3

Territorial Subdivisions and Taxation in Medieval Russia

WHEN Ivan Kalita became Prince of Moscow, the principalities of northeastern Russia had already been subject to the Golden Horde of the Tartars for about eighty-five years. In theory, supremacy among these principalities was the prerogative of the Grand Principality of Vladimir, which had been the senior principality of the northeast since the days of Andrey Bogolyubskiy and Vsevolod Big Nest in the late twelfth and early thirteenth centuries. There were, however, several other principalities, sometimes also termed "grand," which on occasion asserted their supremacy over the others. These grand principalities included Tver', Ryazan', and eventually Moscow. The lesser principalities of northeastern Russia were called *udely* (patrimonial principalities). Originally the patrimonies of younger sons of the grand princes, many of these principalities had achieved varying degrees of independence in the course of the political fragmentation of Russia during and after the decline of the power of Kiev. Examples of these lesser principalities were Moscow (until its rise to the status of a grand principality in the fourteenth and fifteenth centuries), Pereyaslavl' Zalesskiy, and Mozhaysk. But the fourteenth, fifteenth, and sixteenth centuries, during which the testaments of the grand princes of Moscow were written, witnessed the reversal of this process of fragmentation and the gradual absorption of the various grand and patrimonial principalities into the Grand Principality of Moscow, which assumed the position of leadership in the northeast of Russia once held by Vladimir and succeeded in uniting all the once semi-independent principalities under its rule.

TERRITORIAL SUBDIVISIONS

The major administrative subdivision of the principality was the *uyezd,* translated here as "district." The word *uyezd* is related to *yezd,* 'traveling (about)', which may be connected with the practice of the early Russian princes called *polyud'ye.* Both terms, *polyud'ye* and *yezd,* referred to the custom of the prince and his officials of traveling about the principality to dispense justice and to collect *korm,* 'subsistence,'[1] and, in the case of *polyud'ye,* tribute in kind. The area covered in this manner came to be called an *uyezd.*[2] As the various principalities of northeastern Russia were absorbed into Muscovy, the appellation of principality was gradually discarded in favor of "district."

The term *povet* (Polish *powiat*), which occurs several times in the testament of Ivan IV, was used in western Russia in place of *uyezd.* It too has been translated "district."

The major subdivision of the *uyezd* was the *volost'* (English "volost"). If the *uyezd* was a major territorial and administrative division clearly subordinate to a city or other settlement, then the *volost'* was a rural area which was part of an *uyezd.* A *volost'* was also subordinate to some sort of settlement, usually a village (*selo*). *Volost'* is the northern or Great Russian variant of the South Slavic *vlast',* 'rule, power, authority.' In Kievan Russia *volost'* and a related word *oblast'* were often used in reference to the entire area under a prince's control, but by the fourteenth century the terms were commonly used in the more limited sense, at least in northeastern Russia.[3]

Another subdivision of the *uyezd* was the *pogost. A pogost* in Kievan Russia was a place where Russian tradesmen came

---

[1] Cf. the English term "food-rent" (see "Old English Will of Wulfwaru [984–1016]," in Dorothy Whitelock, ed., *English Historical Documents, c. 500–1042* [New York, 1955], I, 524–525).

[2] V. O. Klyuchevskiy, *Sochineniya* (Moscow, 1956–1959), VI, 134–135, and I. I. Sreznevskiy, *Materialy dlya slovarya drevne-russkogo yazyka* (Moscow, 1958), III, 1346–1347.

[3] See Sreznevskiy, I, 293, and Klyuchevskiy, VI, 134.

together for trade (*gost'ba*). The *pogost* was also often the stopping place of the prince. Later the term was applied to the settlements which grew up around such trading posts and to the areas surrounding these settlements. Occasionally *pogost* was used in the sense of *volost'*; sometimes a *pogost* was a subdivision of a *volost'*.[4]

Yet another subdivision of the *uyezd* was the *stan*. Originally a stopping place of the prince or his men, the *stan* developed into a permanent administrative center. Like the *pogost*, the *stan* was usually a subdivision of a volost, although it appears that the *stan* was sometimes used interchangeably with *volost'*, i.e., it was used to refer to the major subdivision of an *uyezd*.[5]

The principal type of urban settlement in medieval Russia was the *gorod* (Church Slavic *grad"*), which I have translated "city." Cognate with the Latin *hortus* and the English "yard" and "ward," the word originally referred to a settlement enclosed by a wall. That part of the settlement outside the wall— the unfortified area—was called the *posad*, 'suburb.' In early Russian documents the word *gorod* (or *grad"*) was sometimes used synonymously, at least in reference to Moscow, with the word *kreml'*, 'kremlin.' For example, the Chronicle relates that in 1177 Prince Gleb Rostislavich of Ryazan' burned "all Moscow, the *gorod*" and the villages."[6] A *gorod* was a comparatively large and important trading, administrative, and military center, usually the residence of a high officer of the prince, if not of the prince himself. A *gorod* was usually the center of an *uyezd* of the same name. (It should be noted that the testament of Ivan IV frequently uses *gorod* to refer to settlements that would hardly meet this definition, but this usage is understandable if one remembers that the sixteenth century was a period when many new towns were begun and many old settlements

---

[4] A church was often built at a *pogost*; hence the transition to the modern meaning, "rural graveyard," was an easy one (see Sreznevskiy, II, 1017–1018, and Klyuchevskiy, I, 128).

[5] See Alexandre Eck, *Le Moyen Age russe* (Paris, 1933), p. 568, and S. M. Solov'yev, *Istoriya Rossii s drevneyshikh vremen* (Moscow, 1959–1966), II, 36.

[6] *PSRL*, VII, 93.

newly fortified. Ivan IV, then, was using *gorod* in its original sense of a fortified settlement.) [7]

Gorodok, the diminutive of *gorod*, appears frequently in the testaments and might well be translated "small city." It would appear, however, from the location of many of these *gorodki* that their importance was primarily military. Many, if not all, of them were in frontier areas of Russia. On this assumption it seems logical to translate the term *gorodok* as "burg," "burh," or "borough," terms used in early English history to signify a fortified place or town.[8] Novyy *gorodok* (Newburg) at the confluence of the Protva and Oka rivers, mentioned in the testament of Grand Prince Ivan II, might well have been considered a frontier outpost in the mid-fourteenth century. A similar settlement was Ivan *gorodok* (Johnsburg) near the mouth of the Narva River in northwestern Russia.

The term *prigorod*, translated "minor city," was used in reference to a city in the Novgorod Land that, during the period of Novgorod's independence, was politically subordinate to the "senior city" (*starshiy gorod*), Novgorod. These cities, such as Pskov, Velikiye Luki, Torzhok, and Bezhetskiy Verkh, were centers of volosts of the Novgorod Land. Each *prigorod* was subordinate to one of the "ends" (wards) of Novgorod. Although each *prigorod* had its own popular municipal assembly (*veche*), real power belonged to the governor (*posadnik*) sent by the "end" to which the given *prigorod* was subordinate. Following the incorporation of Novgorod the Great into Muscovy during the reign of Ivan III, the *prigorods* became centers of districts (*uyezds* or *povets*).[9]

[7] Sreznevskiy, I, 555–557; V. Dal', *Tolkovyy slovar' zhivogo velikorusskogo yazyka* (Moscow, 1955), I, 380–381; Klyuchevskiy, VI, 239; and Eck, pp. 323 and 356.

[8] See the article "Borough," *Encyclopaedia Britannica* (Chicago, 1959), III, 919.

[9] The term *prigorod* was used occasionally to refer to "minor cities" in other parts of Russia. They were, however, typical of the Novgorod Land. Pskov was a *prigorod* of Novgorod until 1347, when by agreement between the two cities this relationship was altered. After 1347 Pskov was known as the "younger brother" of Novgorod (see Sreznevskiy, II, 1398–1399, and Klyuchevskiy, II, 55–56 and 73–75).

The three types of rural settlements most frequently mentioned in the testaments are *selo* (village), *sel'tso* (small village), and *derevnya* (hamlet). A *selo* was a rural settlement, larger than a *derevnya*, and usually had a church. It ordinarily varied in size from five to ten or more households. The *sel'tso* (diminutive of *selo*) was merely a small village, which is the term I have used in translating. The *derevnya* was a smaller settlement than a *selo*, usually consisting of from one to three households located at some distance from the village to which they were administratively subordinate. The *derevnya* did not have a church.[10]

Another type of rural community mentioned frequently in the testaments was the *pochinok*, translated *novale*. The *pochinok* (literally, "beginning") was a new settlement composed of people from a nearby village or even from some distant region. It usually consisted of one or two households, which enjoyed temporary relief from the payment of taxes or customs. A *pochinok* was often deserted after two or three harvests; if not, it developed into a *derevnya*.[11]

Another term which appears frequently in the testaments is *sloboda* or, less commonly, *svoboda*. The *sloboda* (the basic meaning of the word is "freedom") was a settlement or group of settlements that had been granted certain immunities or privileges. The basic characteristic of a *sloboda* was that it was freed, usually for a stipulated period, from the obligation to pay taxes or perform services for the prince. It was freed from the communal assessment of taxes to which ordinary villages were subject. *Slobodas* were of two principal types: (1) settlements whose primary function was to colonize sparsely settled or

[10] Klyuchevskiy, VI, 247–255; Dal', *Tolkovyy slovar'*, IV, 172; and Eck, pp. 275.

[11] Dal', *Tolkovyy slovar'*, III, 370 (under *pochinat'*), and Eck, p. 276.

In translating the words *selo* and *derevnya* as "village" and "hamlet," I have tried to use words which in medieval England denoted comparable rural communities. Thus E. Lipson, in discussing land tenure in England based on strip farming (the runrig or rundale system), writes: "The hamlet, with scattered homesteads covering the countryside, was in marked contrast to the 'nucleated' village with farm houses grouped together in a single street around the manor house and the church (*The Economic History of England* [London, 1956], I, 85).

disputed territories and thereby establish the eminent domain of the prince and (2) settlements whose inhabitants were engaged in the same trade or occupation (e.g., saddle makers, fishermen, post drivers). It is from the second type of *sloboda*, often located in the immediate vicinity of a city, that the modern sense of the word, "suburb," derives.[12] The diminutive forms of *sloboda* and *svoboda* are *slobodka* and *svobodka*, respectively.

TAXATION: GENERAL TERMINOLOGY

The word *potyaglo* (past tense of *potyanuti*) appears over and over in the testaments of the grand princes. The noun related to this verb, *tyaglo*, does not appear once in the testaments, although it is frequently used in other contemporary documents. The word was originally related to the concept of harvesting grain; the *tyaglo* was a tax on grain or on the harvest. Eventually the word came to signify the totality of all taxes and duties to which those who did not serve the prince were subject. These people were called *tyaglo* people (*tyaglyye lyudi*). In Klyuchevskiy's words:

He who personally served the sovereign owned land; he who did not serve personally, but paid, was subject to the *tyaglo* (*tyanul tyaglo*). The latter merely utilized another's land. The servants [of the sovereign] were landowners; the people subject to the *tyaglo* were not landowners but merely renters of another's land, private or state.[13]

The verb *potyaglo*, which occurs so often in the testaments, indicated the relationship existing between a given administrative subdivision of the prince's patrimony (city, volost, etc.) and the smaller territorial-administrative units which were subordinate to these in the discharge of the *tyaglo*. I have translated *potyaglo* as "appertained"; thus, the testament of Grand Prince Vasiliy II says, "And from among the Moscow villages I give to my son Ivan the village Ostrovskoye, and with Orininskoye, and with Kostyantinovskoye, and with Molakhovskoye, and with their hamlets, and with that which appertained [*potyaglo*] to

[12] Klyuchevskiy, VI, 247–250, and Eck, pp. 275–276.
[13] VI, 178 and 203–204.

these villages." These unnamed hamlets were subject to the *tyaglo* as were the villages, but in the discharge of their *tyaglo* the hamlets stood in a subordinate relationship to the villages. The *tyaglo* in this case was due the villages, not the prince directly. The French term which Eck uses to describe this relationship is *mouvance (mouvoir)*; though the medieval English word "to move" certainly had elements related to *mouvoir*, the relationship was most frequently expressed by "to appertain" or "to pertain." [14]

The term *poshliny* (plural of *poshlina*) has been translated as "customs." The term was used in the sense of "consuetude" (Latin *consuetudo*), i.e., any "custom, habit, social usage; usage having the force of law." *Poshlina* suggests "that which has gone before," and certainly has the connotation of tradition in the context of medieval Russian. The term *poshlina* as used in the testaments referred to any traditional revenue, any traditional impost or tribute.[15] It is frequently found in the testaments, beginning with the second testament of Dmitriy Donskoy: "And lo, I give to my son, Prince Andrey, Mozhayesk" with all its volosts, and with its *tamga*, and with its *myto*, and with its apiary, and with its villages, and with all its customs [*so vsemi poshliny*]."

The word *obrok*, translated "quitrent," occurs only three times in the testaments: in Ivan I, Ivan II, and the second testament of Dmitriy. The term *obrochniki* (quitrent tenants) also occurs in the same testaments. Certain rural inhabitants who did not cultivate land and hence were not subject to the *dan'* (princely tribute, direct tax on land) were required to pay *obrok* either in money or in kind. For instance, in the first

[14] See Eck, p. 269. The Oxford English Dictionary gives the following as one definition of the verb "to move": "to move of, by: of property: to be held by, to belong or pertain to. Obs. 'The husband that marieth an heire to haue such lands as moue by hir during his naturall life.' Cf. OF. *mouvoir (de)*" (*A New English Dictionary on Historical Principles* [Oxford, 1888–1928]).

[15] *Webster's New International Dictionary of the English Language* (2nd ed.; Springfield, Mass., 1947), and Eck, p. 101, n.

variant of Ivan Kalita's testament, it was specified that the quit-rent be in honey.[16]

DIRECT TAXES

The *dan'*, translated "tribute," was an ancient land tax due the prince. It was collected on the basis of units of cultivated land.[17] In trade and craft settlements, *slobodas*, and cities, it was levied on the basis of the number of taxable households. The *dan'* was collected by agents of the prince called *danshchiki*. It is defined as "princely tribute," as opposed to the *vykhod*, 'Tartar tribute,' which was the direct tax collected from the population for payment to the Golden Horde. Although the *vykhod* appears to have been part of the *dan'* after about mid-fourteenth century, before that time it was collected separately. It was to determine the amount of the *vykhod* that the Tartars first made a population census in 1257.[18]

The *namestnichiye dokhody*, *primetnyye den'gi*, and *kormlennyye okupy* were three direct taxes mentioned only in the testament of Ivan the Terrible. They were particular types of taxes, formerly referred to as *kormy*, 'feedings, subsistences, livings.' During the period of patrimonial principalities they consisted of payments in kind made to the prince's administrator by the inhabitants of the area which he governed. The general term was *kormleniye*, 'feeding, subsistence, living.' Later, during the Moscow period, the payments were usually made in money. The *namestnichiye dokhody*, 'lieutenant's incomes,' were payments due the prince's lieutenant.[19] The term

[16] See Klyuchevskiy, VI, 203, and Eck, p. 259.

[17] Concerning the most important of these land units, the *sokha*, see below, Text 9, n. 64.

[18] See Klyuchevskiy, VI, 201; Sreznevskiy, I, 456 and 627–628; Eck, pp. 38 and 158; and A. N. Nasonov, *Mongoly i Rus'* (*Istoriya tatarskoy politiki na Rusi*) (Moscow-Leningrad, 1940), pp. 14–23. George Vernadsky sets the date of the census of the "Grand Duchy" of Vladimir and of the Novgorod Land as 1258–1259. The census in west Russia took place even earlier, in 1245 (*The Mongols and Russia* [New Haven, 1953], p. 215).

[19] Concerning these officers, see Chapter 5.

primetnyye den'gi, translated as *contributions* by Eck,[20] has not been precisely defined, although the context in which it appears in Ivan IV's testament suggests that it too was some type of *korm*. The *kormlennyye okupy*, 'subsistence indemnities,' were payments made by the population to the prince's administrative officer after the reforms of the mid-sixteenth century enabled the people to have *kormleniye* replaced by local self-government.[21]

The term *yam*, 'post relay tax,' occurs in the three testaments of Vasiliy I and in that of Ivan IV. This tax, which financed the post system established by the Tartars, was paid either in money or in kind.[22] The term *yam* occurs once in the testament of Ivan III, in a context indicating that it referred to the post stations themselves rather than to the maintenance of the post system.

INDIRECT TAXES

The term *tamga*, which occurs in all the testaments except the first and third of Vasiliy I, has not been translated here. The word itself is Tartar, referring originally to a particular type of seal or stamp attached to the product sold. The *tamga* was a tax due from both buyer and seller; it was a tax on the product sold and on the money used to buy the product; i.e., it consisted of a certain percentage of the value of the product sold or of the money used to purchase the product. The percentage was more if a merchant was from another city or principality or from a foreign country. The *tamga* was payable on the sale and purchase of all goods except grain.[23]

The *osmnicheye*, literally "eighth," appears in the testaments of Ivan Kalita and Ivan the Fair, and, written *vosmnicheye*, in the second testament of Dimitriy Donskoy. It was a tax on the right to buy or sell, as was the *tamga*, but it was probably an

[20] Glossary of Russian terms.

[21] Klyuchevskiy, VI, 204. Concerning reforms in local self-government of the 1550's, see Klyuchevskiy, VI, 350–369.

[22] Eck, p. 111, and L. V. Cherepnin and I. A. Golubtsov, eds., *Akty sotsial'no-ekonomicheskoy istorii severo-vostochnoy Rusi, kontsa XIV-nachala XVI v.* (Moscow, 1958), II, 691.

[23] Klyuchevskiy, VI, 207–208; Sreznevskiy, III, 924; and Eck, p. 568.

older tax. The terms *osmnicheye* and *tamga* may have been used interchangeably—in some markets the tax was called *tamga* and in others *osmnicheye*.[24] Eck suggests that the *osmnicheye* was a surtax on trade, in other words, a tax added to the *tamga*.[25] This interpretation is supported by a passage from Ivan Kalita's testament that suggests that the two taxes were similar yet distinct: "And of the city revenues, I give the *osmnicheye* to my princess. But my sons shall share the *tamga* and the other city revenues . . . that which is in the district of each shall be his." The term *osmnicheye* (*vosmnicheye*) has not been translated.

The term *torg* appears only in the testaments of Ivan III and Ivan IV. This tax, more general in scope than the older *osmnicheye* and *tamga*, was a tax on the right to trade and has been translated as "tax on trading in the market place." Apparently the *torg* did not replace the *tamga*, for it is mentioned in both testaments along with the *tamga*.[26]

The term *lavka*, used in the testaments of Ivan III and Ivan IV, means "trading stand." The context suggests, however, that it was a tax on the right to maintain a trading stand. It appears to have been used in the same sense as *polavochnaya* (*polavochnoye*), a tax on trading stands.[27] Similarly, the term *gostinyye dvory*, which appears only in the testaments of Ivan III and Ivan IV, means "merchants' courts," but the context suggests that it was used in the sense of a tax on merchants' courts.

In the testament of Ivan IV the term *pod"yesnyye* villages appears. The adjective *pod"yesnyye* may be derived from *pod"yezd*, which is defined by Sreznevskiy as a type of custom tax.[28]

The term *pud* in the testament of Ivan III and the term *ves* (plural *vesy*) in the testament of Ivan IV both signify taxes on the weighing of goods, and both have been translated "tax on weighing." Similar was the *pomernoye*, which is mentioned only in the testament of Ivan III. This was a tax on the weighing of dry-measure goods (*sypuchiye tovary*). According to the "Beloozero Customs Charter" of 1551, the seller was required to pay

[24] Klyuchevskiy, VI, 207–208.   [25] Page 344.
[26] Sreznevskiy, III, 1055.   [27] Sreznevskiy, II, 1 and 1122.
[28] II, 1072.

the *pomernoye* on wheat, rye, barley, malt, oat flour, turnips, and on all grain (*zhito*), as well as on dried fish, on fish of the Osmerus family, and on *kholkhol"ki* (a variety of berry?).[29]

The term *myt* (or *myto*) appears in five of the testaments—Ivan I, Ivan II, the first and second testaments of Dmitriy, and Ivan III. The *myt* was a toll, collected for the right to pass with goods. There were two types of *myt*: the first, called the *myt sukhoy* (dry *myt*), was collected from carts; the other, called the *myt vodyanoy* (water *myt*), was collected from boats. The amount of the *myt* was based on the number of carts or boats, not on the value of the goods carried. The place where the *myt* was collected was also called *myt*.[30]

The testament of Ivan II and the first testament of Dmitriy Donskoy mention the *kostki* (or *kostka*), a tax collected from persons accompanying goods. Usually a capitation tax, it was based on the number of persons accompanying the goods (on carts or boats) and not on the value of the goods. This tax was unknown in Kievan or Novgorod Russia, having been introduced by the Tartars. It is probable that *kostka* was a corruption of *gostka*, a fee collected for the right to travel on the *gostinets*, 'the great trade road.'[31]

[29] Sreznevskiy, I, 496; II, 1724 and 1174–1175; Klyuchevskiy, VI, 207.
[30] Klyuchevskiy, VI, 206; Sreznevskiy, II, 219; and Eck, p. 344.
[31] Klyuchevskiy, VI, 206; Eck, p. 344; Nasonov, pp. 62 and 104–105.

CHAPTER 4

Classes of the Population in Medieval Russia

AT the top of the social scale among the various groups mentioned in the testaments of the grand princes of Moscow was the *knyaz'*, 'prince.' The word *knyaz'* was borrowed from one of the Germanic languages at a fairly early date. It may have come into Russian from Gothic during the third or fourth centuries, or perhaps the Varangians brought the term with them in the ninth century. It was probably the Russian form of the old Germanic word *konung* or *kuning* (Old English *cyning*, English "king").[1]

At the head of the princes, *primus inter pares*, stood the Grand Prince of Vladimir, the senior prince of northeastern Russia. This title was held, beginning with Ivan Kalita (who received it in 1328), by the grand princes of Moscow. Second in rank to the Grand Prince of Vladimir (and Moscow) stood the princes of the other major principalities of northeastern Russia, such as Tver' and Ryazan', whose princes were also sometimes called "grand prince" (*velikiy knyaz'*). The political proclivities of the chronicler sometimes determined whether a given prince was to be called "grand prince" or merely "prince." For example, the Moscow chronicler writes under the year 1326: "That same autumn, on 13 of the month of September, the tsar [khan] killed Prince Dmitriy Mikhaylovich of Tver' for Grand Prince Yuriy Danilovich [of Moscow] in the Horde, on the Kondrakla [River]." The *Tver' Chronicle*, reporting the same event, reads: "In the year 6834, on September 15, they killed, in the Horde, Grand Prince Dmitriy Mikhaylovich and Prince

[1] See V. O. Klyuchevskiy, *Sochineniya* (Moscow, 1956–1959), VI, 136.

Aleksandr Novosil'skiy on the same day . . . on the river which is called Kondrakla." [2]

There existed another category of prince. This was the *udel'nyy knyaz'*, the "patrimonial prince." He was a junior prince of one of the grand-princely families, the younger son, brother, or other relative or descendant of one of these, who had been granted, or who had inherited, an *udel*, a "princely patrimony" (or "patrimonial principality") within the grand principality of the senior member of his family. On occasion a patrimonial prince might challenge the authority of the grand prince, especially if the latter had gained his position by means not entirely in keeping with the order of seniority inherited from Kievan days. For example, when Grand Prince Vasiliy I died in 1425, his younger brother, Prince Yuriy of Zvenigorod and Galich, was in a particularly strong position to claim the grand-princely throne because, according to tradition (if not always custom), the throne of a Russian prince was to be inherited by his next younger brother, rather than by his son (the "Rota System" of Kievan times). Moreover, in this case Yuriy's claim to the Grand Principality of Vladimir and Moscow was considerably strengthened by the provision in the second testament of his father, Dmitriy Donskoy, which stipulated that "if, because of my sins, God takes away my son, Prince Vasiliy, then the patrimonial principality of Prince Vasiliy [shall pass] to my son who follows him." Although Vasiliy II was ultimately victorious in the long and terrible struggle for the Grand Princedom with his uncle, Prince Yuriy, and with Yuriy's sons, a sense of the threat to the supremacy of the grand prince inherent in the remnants of the *udel* system can be seen in Tsar Ivan the Terrible's harsh treatment of his uncle, Andrey of Staritsa, and Andrey's son, Vladimir, and in the repeated insistence in Ivan's testament that his younger son, Fedor, should in all ways subordinate himself to his older brother, Ivan.

During the Tartar period (1237–*c.* 1500), the princes of northeastern Russia represented the supreme power within their principalities, subject of course to the higher authority of the

[2] *PSRL*, XXV, 168, and XV, 415.

Grand Prince of Vladimir (or, in the case of an *udel'nyy knyaz'*, to the higher authority of the senior prince in whose territory his *udel* lay) and to the over-all supremacy of the Golden Horde. The land was the prince's.[3] Such matters as collection of tribute and custom, administration of justice, defense of his principality, granting of charters to lands and of special privileges and immunities to certain individuals and groups, and coinage of money were the prerogatives of a prince. It should be remembered, however, that the period of the first ten testaments (Ivan Kalita through Ivan III) was a time when not only the prerogatives of the princes of northeastern Russia but their very sovereignty was being successfully challenged by the grand princes of Moscow; this was the period of the formation around Moscow of the centralized Russian state.

With the breakdown of the *udel* system, a number of the lesser princes entered the service of the Grand Prince of Moscow. These were the "service princes" (*sluzhebnyye* or *sluzhilyye knyaz'ya*) mentioned in the testament of Ivan III and in that of Ivan IV. These princes, while losing their former sovereign rights, often continued to hold their patrimonies in fee of the grand prince. Even earlier, certain princes had entered the service of the Grand Prince of Moscow as his servants. These princes held much the same rank as the old boyars, although one senses that they must have stood at the head of this latter class because of their exalted genealogy. Even such a servant of the Prince of Moscow as Yuriy Patrikeyev, whose pedigree as a prince of the royal house of Lithuania was impeccable, was referred to in the first testament of Vasiliy I as one of "my boyars." Such princes were called "boyar princes" (*knyaz'ya boyarskiye*) in the testament of Ivan IV.

Immediately below the princes stood the boyars (*boyare*, singular *boyarin*).[4] This class is mentioned frequently in the

[3] Peasants referred to the lands on which they lived as *zemli velikogo knyazya, a nashego vladeniya*, 'lands of the grand prince, but of our possession' (S. G. Pushkarev, *Obzor russkoy istorii* [New York, 1953], p. 145).

[4] The origin of the word *boyarin* is not clear. It probably developed either from *boy*, 'combat,' or from *bol'*, 'larger, major.' If it developed

testaments of the grand princes. In Kievan days the boyars were the senior officers of the prince, the senior members of his retinue and his council. The prince's retinue was composed of the military class of early Russian history and came—as did the prince himself—from among the wealthy armed merchants of the great trading cities of Kievan Rus'. Similar to the prince's boyars were the *startsy gradskiye*, 'elders of the city,' the commanders of the military forces of the cities (*tysyatskiye*, 'chiliarchs,' *sotskiye*, 'commanders of a hundred,' *desyatniki*, 'commanders of ten'). At first these officers were elected by their cities; subsequently the *tysyatskiy*, at least, was appointed by the prince. The *startsy gradskiye* not only fought alongside the prince's retinue, they—at least the *tysyatskiye* and the *sotni*—also sat on the prince's council, the Council of Boyars.[5] Doubtless many of the *startsy gradskiye* came to be called boyars.

At the beginning of the eleventh century not only the principal officers of the prince but also the "notables of the different Russian regions, that is, all those who occupied an important place in the economic, social, and political life of the country" were termed boyars.[6] Boyars held important positions in city and civil administration as well as in the military organization of Kievan Russia. Frequently their voice was decisive in the councils of the princes. The boyars did not make up a caste or a closed class. It was possible for members of other classes to enter the boyar class by entering the military service of the prince.[7]

With the subjugation of Russia by the Tartars in the thirteenth century, the boyar class remained much the same in its composition. Although during the period of patrimonial principalities the typical antrustion of the Kievan prince became a landowner, he was nevertheless still primarily a military servant of the prince. Yet the power and prestige of the boyars of

---

from the latter its similarity to the English "magnate" is clear (see Klyuchevskiy, VI, 146). It is also possible that *boyarin* was of Turko-Tartar origin. If so, possible roots are *bojlu*, 'high' (Turko-Tartar), and *bajar*, 'to be rich' (Mongol) or 'man of quality' (Turkish) (Alexandre Eck, *Le Moyen Age russe* [Paris, 1933], p. 11, note).

[5] Klyuchevskiy, I, 164–165.   [6] Eck, p. 11.

[7] Eck, pp. 11 and 186.

northeastern Russia from the twelfth to the fifteenth centuries rested chiefly on the fact that they held land inhabited by peasants. Many boyars who were great landowners also served at a prince's court. This service was in theory voluntary; the boyar had the right to leave the service of his prince at any time.[8] Often a boyar served a prince other than the one in whose territory his estate was located; in spite of this he kept his estate. In the period of patrimonial principalities the boyar's two primary duties were to participate in the defense of the city and principality of the prince he served, and to pay princely tribute (*dan'*) to the prince in whose principality his estate was located.[9]

The land tenure of boyars of northeastern Russia during the period of patrimonial principalities was of two distinct types. The first was the "patrimony" (*otchina* or *votchina*), alodial property that the boyar had inherited from his father and that he could dispose of as he saw fit. The second type was a conditional form of landholding, a system of tenure under which there were two "owners": the nominal (the prince) and the actual (the boyar). The first documentary evidence of this type of land tenure is found in Ivan Kalita's testament in the passage concerning Boris Vorkov.[10]

The princes of northeastern Russia early began to disregard their boyars' right to take service with another prince. As unification of the Russian lands around Moscow progressed, this ancient practice became an anachronism. Nevertheless, some boyars continued to assert their right of freedom of movement from one prince to another. The period of the testaments was one during which a division took place in the boyar class. Some boyars supported the Grand Prince of Moscow; others supported the lesser (patrimonial) princes in their struggles to preserve their independence. After the conclusion of the civil war

[8] This right was guaranteed in numerous agreements among the princes (*a boyaram i slugam mezhi nas vol'nym volya*).

[9] B. D. Grekov, L. V. Cherepnin, and V. T. Pashuto, *Ocherki istorii SSSR: Period feodalizma IX–XV vv., Chast' vtoraya, Ob"yedineniye russkikh zemel' vokrug Moskvy i obrazovaniye russkogo tsentralizovannogo gosudarstva* (Moscow, 1953), Part 2, p. 63.

[10] See below, pp. 186–187.

between Vasiliy II and his uncle and cousins during the first half of the fifteenth century, boyars were more and more restricted in their movements. About the same time the second, conditional, type of land tenure became much more common.[11]

Although a boyar often held his rank because of birth, during the period of patrimonial principalities (and especially with the growth of the centralized state around Moscow) other elements—rich merchants, princes who had for some reason or another lost their principalities, and others—entered the boyar class. During the Moscow period the boyars, although continuing in most cases to be great landowners, also held such important administrative positions as major-domo, grand lieutenant, voivode, and chief of a *put'*.[12]

The testaments of Vasiliy II, Ivan III, and Ivan IV mention *deti boyarskiye*, literally, "boyars' children" or "boyars' sons," the plural of *syn boyarskiy*, 'boyar's son.' The term *deti boyarskiye*, which I have translated "junior boyars," began to appear in twelfth-century documents, replacing *otroki* and *detskiye*, terms used to refer to junior members of the prince's retinue in Kievan days. At first the term was used literally to mean "boyars' children." Gradually it came to be used of an entire class of service people. During the post-Kievan period, though the number of boyar families increased greatly within the numerous patrimonial principalities of northeastern Russia, the title or rank of boyar was often not conferred upon a member of such a family until he was advanced in age, or sometimes not at all. Such persons came to be known as *deti boyarskiye*. With the decline and final disappearance of the system of patrimonial principalities only some of the boyar families moved to Moscow; the great majority remained on the lands that had been part of their prince's patrimony. These were the *deti boyarskiye* of the fifteenth and sixteenth centuries; they were service people of the

[11] A case in point is that of Fedor Basenok (see below, Text 10, n. 18).

[12] Concerning the boyars, see I. I. Sreznevskiy, *Materialy dlya slovarya drevne-russkogo yazyka* (Moscow, 1958), I, 160; Klyuchevskiy, VI, 145–147; Eck, pp. 10–11, 49–50, 94–100, 108–118, and 185–203; M. N. Tikhomirov, *Srednevekovaya Moskva v XIV–XV vekakh* (Moscow, 1957), pp. 163–166; and Grekov *et al.*, pp. 63–64.

provinces. In the sixteenth century many of these came to Moscow, not as regular boyars but as servants of the grand prince's court; the former *deti boyarskiye* were now dubbed *dvoryane* (or *dvorovyye*), 'court men.' [13]

The *deti boyarskiye*, 'junior boyars,' and the *dvoryane*, 'court men,' were the two principal classes of "free servants" (*slugi vol'nyye*) of the prince which are mentioned in the testaments. Although the boyars and service princes were free servants in the general sense of the term, they were not among those specifically referred to as *slugi vol'nyye* in medieval Russia.

The great mass of the free *tyaglo* population goes all but unmentioned in the testaments of the grand princes of Moscow. The term "*tyaglo* people" (*tyaglyye lyudi*), in this or other forms, does not appear once in the testaments, although, as has been pointed out above, there are numerous references to lands or settlements which appertained (*potyaglo*) to this or that higher administrative unit. These lands and settlements were of course inhabited by *tyaglo* people. Two terms for "peasant" appear in the testaments: *siroty* (literally, "orphans") appears in the second testament of Dmitriy Donskoy; *krest'yane* (literally, "Christians," "common Christians") appears in the testament of Ivan III.

Two other special groups of the population who were *tyaglo* people are mentioned in the testaments. These were the *chislenyye lyudi* and the *ordyntsy*. The *chislenyye lyudi* (*chislyaki*), 'enrolled people,' are mentioned in almost all of the testaments (except for Semen, first Dmitriy, and the testamentary writ of Vasiliy III). In those in which the enrolled people do appear, they were "willed" to one or more of the sons of the grand prince. In the first three testaments in which they are mentioned, the grand prince commanded that his sons should "manage the enrolled people jointly and . . . as one man, care

---

[13] The term *dvoryane*, 'court men,' appears in the testaments of Ivan III and Ivan IV. With the rise of this new class (the *dvoryane*), the rank of *deti boyarskiye* declined in status and the provincial nobility came to be called "boyar court children" (*boyarskiye dvorovyye deti*) or "select court men" (*vybornyye dvoryane*). For a discussion of the *deti boyarskiye* and the *dvoryane*, see Klyuchevskiy, VI, 336 and 402–403.

for them." [14] In subsequent testaments this admonition does not appear; in the testament of Ivan III, in fact, the younger sons of the grand prince (Yuriy, Dmitriy, Semen, and Andrey) were instructed "not [to] interfere with the enrolled people . . . of my son and their older brother, Vasiliy, in any way: [they] shall not interfere in their lands, or in their waters, and they shall not do them injustice in anything."

The term *chislenyye lyudi* probably had its origin in the Tartar census (*chislo*) of 1257. The purpose of this *chislo* was to determine the amount of tribute the Tartars could demand of the Russian princes and, according to one theory, the *chislenyye lyudi* were the people enrolled in this census. There is no doubt that the *chislenyye lyudi* were under the special protection of the Russian princes. Moreover, at least late in the fourteenth century, they were landholders. In a 1389 agreement between Dmitriy Donskoy and his cousin, Prince Vladimir Andreyevich of Serpukhov and Borovsk, the two princes agreed "to take care of the *chislenyye lyudi* . . . as one man" and "not to buy their lands." [15] Prince Vladimir's testament, written about 1401 or 1402, contains a passage that directly connects the *chislenyye lyudi* with the *vykhod*, the Tartar tribute. Prince Vladimir, who held a third of Moscow, wrote, "And if God should bring about a change concerning the Horde, then the grand prince will not give *vykhod* to the Horde and neither will my children; and that *dan'* [i.e., tribute paid to a Russian prince] which is collected from the Moscow *stans*, and in the city of Moscow, and from the *chislenyye lyudi*, now my children shall take their third of the Moscow *dan'* and [a third of the *dan'*] from the *chislenyye lyudi*, and they shall share it." [16] In this same document the total amount that his sons were to contribute toward tribute to the Tartars was placed by Prince Vladimir at 320 rubles. Yet the prince then provided that the total tribute (*dan'*) that his sons were to collect was to amount to 585 rubles. This disparity seems to suggest, albeit inconclusively, that the *chislenyye lyudi* were in fact related to the calculating of that portion of tribute col-

---

[14] The quotation is from Ivan Kalita. Ivan II and second Dmitriy contain similar admonitions.

[15] *DDG*, p. 31.   [16] *DDG*, p. 16.

lected by the Russian prince (*dan'*) that was to be forwarded to the Tartars as *vykhod*. Evidence that the *chislenyye lyudi* were free, tax-paying people is to be found in a charter issued by Grand Prince Ivan III in 1504. This charter provided, in part, that on certain lands of the *chislenyye lyudi* and the *ordyntsy* "these *chislenyye lyudi* and *ordintsy* shall in all ways appertain (*tyagl' vsyakuyu tyanuti*) as of old to my son Vasiliy." [17] Admittedly this evidence is late, yet there is nothing in it which contradicts the evidence cited above from the testament of Vladimir Andreyevich.

According to another theory, the *chislenyye lyudi* were not people enrolled by the Tartar census but were a special group of the Russian population chosen to assist the Tartar census takers in carrying out the censuses and in collecting tribute due the Horde. If this interpretation is the correct one, it is quite probable that the princes of Russia would have been under a Tartar-imposed obligation to extend special protection to these people, who most certainly would have been very unpopular among the Russian population. Hence the admonition of the grand princes of the fourteenth century that their sons should "as one man care for the *chislenyye lyudi*." The omission of this admonition in the testaments of the fifteenth and sixteenth centuries can be explained by the change in the relationship between the Grand Prince of Moscow and the Horde that had taken place late in the fourteenth century: the Russian prince needed no longer to provide special protection to the *chislenyye lyudi*, because their function as census takers (if such it had been) was out of date and the Tartars were not in a position to demand that the Russian prince provide this special protection.

It seems to me that the two hypotheses concerning the nature of the *chislenyye lyudi* are not incompatible. I think they may well have been, originally, a special group of the population which assisted the Tartars in the taking of censuses and in collecting Tartar tribute. In this role they needed the special protection of the Russian princes and this protection was provided. But

[17] From the "Charter of Grand Prince Ivan Vasil'yevich to Prince Ivan Vasil'yevich Delimiting the Cities of Dmitrov and Kashin from Radonezh and the Pereyaslavl' *Stans* and Volosts" (*DDG*, p. 374).

as time passed and direct Tartar control (through military intervention) over the Russian princes became less real, the descendants of the *chislenyye lyudi* lost their special role of assistant Tartar census takers and tribute collectors. Traditionally they had been a separate, favored group of the population; by the end of the fourteenth century they were still viewed by the princes as a special group of the population, but in essence they were a free, tax-paying (*tyaglo*) people whose traditional favored status made them of special importance as sources of princely tribute (*dan'*).[18]

The term *ordyntsy* (plural of *ordynets*, from *orda* "horde") appears in the testaments of Vasiliy II and Ivan III. The word *ordynets*, freely translated, means "a Horde man." There is not unanimity among scholars as to the origin of this group or its function. Sreznevskiy, Solov'yev, and Eck generally agree that the *ordyntsy* were prisoners of the Tartars who were ransomed by the Russian princes. It is thought that the *ordyntsy* were used extensively for colonization of the princes' lands and that they may have been essentially slaves of the prince who ransomed them.[19]

Professor Vernadsky attaches a different interpretation to the term. He believes the *ordyntsy* to have been a group of the Russian population who were exempted from the direct rule of the Russian princes and were obliged to perform such duties for the Tartars as accompanying trains of Tartar envoys and fur-

[18] Concerning the *chislenyye lyudi*, see especially Eck, p. 38; S. B. Veselovskiy, *Podmoskov'ye—Pamyatnyye mesta v istorii russkoy kul'tury XIV–XIX vekov* (Moscow, 1955), p. 16; A. N. Nasonov, *Mongoly i Rus' (Istoriya tatarskoy politiki na Rusi)* (Moscow-Leningrad, 1940), p. 12; Tikhomirov, *Srednevekovaya Moskva*, p. 120; and George Vernadsky, *The Mongols and Russia* (New Haven, 1953), p. 223. Professor Vernadsky believes that the term *chislenyye lyudi* is to be derived from "chislo, number; that is men belonging to the numerical divisions" into which the Russian population under the direct control of the Tartars was divided (tens, hundreds, hordes). For a recent discussion of the *chislenyye lyudi*, the *ordyntsy*, and the *delyui* (a group not mentioned in the testaments of the grand princes), see L. V. Cherepnin, *Obrazovaniye russkogo tsentralizovannogo gosudarstva v XIV–XV vekakh* (Moscow, 1960), pp. 346–355.

[19] Sreznevskiy, II, 706; S. M. Solov'yev, *Istoriya Rossii s drevneyshikh vremen* (Moscow, 1959–1966), II, 526; and Eck, p. 387, n.

nishing wagons for Tartar envoys.[20] Some of the *ordyntsy* in the Moscow Principality may have been transferred to the jurisdiction of the Prince of Moscow by the Tartar khan during the reign of Ivan II (1353–1359). It is also possible—according to Vernadsky—that the *ordyntsy* of Moscow were a group organized "after the Mongol pattern" by Ivan II, although this origin seems less likely.[21]

M. N. Tikhomirov is in general agreement with Vernadsky as to the origin of the *ordyntsy*. He writes:

As far as the *ordintsy* are concerned, they were connected with services "as of old (*po starine*)." The name *ordinets* indicates the character of their service, which was connected with the Horde or with emissaries of the Horde. . . . Horde service in some form or other was the duty of the *tyaglo* people of the Horde Hundred (*Ordinskaya sotnya*) in Moscow. With the passage of time this service lost its significance more and more and the Horde Hundred became a regular "black hundred, or *sloboda*." [22]

The testaments mention a number of servants of the prince who stood in a position midway between that of the "free servants" and that of slaves. These people were known as "servants under the major-domo" (*slugi pod dvorskim*). The major-domo (*dvorskiy*) was the chief officer of the prince's court; he had over-all supervision of the various servants who carried out the administration of the prince's domains. According to Klyuchevskiy, the servants under the major-domo were juridically of two types: the first type, or group, were slaves of the prince; the second were personally free men who, in return for service to the prince, received lands which they held as long as they continued to serve him.[23] Tikhomirov describes the servants under the major-domo as "particular categories of dependent (*zavisimyye*) people who were, in a manner of speaking, on the border between slavery and free service." [24] The servants under

[20] *Mongols and Russia*, p. 226. Vernadsky lists these services among the duties of the "horde servitors" (*slugi ordynskiye*) of southwestern Russia but adds that "the services required of the ordyntsy in Muscovy must have been similar."

[21] Vernadsky, *Mongols and Russia*, p. 225.

[22] *Srednevekovaya Moskva*, p. 120.   [23] VI, 343–344.

[24] *Srednevekovaya Moskva*, p. 115. See also Vernadsky, *Mongols and Russia*, p. 371.

the major-domo mentioned in the testaments are listed in Chapter 5.

The testaments refer to a large number of persons who must have been essentially slaves of the prince. These were beekeepers, falconers, hunters, beaver trappers, boyars' people, people of the *puti*, palace servants, master tailors,[25] artisan slaves,[26] purchased people, purchased quitrent tenants, and slaves (*kholopi*).[27] The testament of Semen the Proud mentions persons whom the prince acquired because they had committed a penal offense.[28] Other categories of non-free people are mentioned in the testaments: "people [who belong to me on the basis of a] charter" (*lyudi gramotnyye*) and "people [who are my] full [slaves]" (*lyudi polnyye*). The terms "full charters" (*gramoty polnyye*) and "reference charters" (*gramoty dokladnyye*),[29]

---

[25] Beekeepers are mentioned in Ivan I, Ivan II, first and second Dmitriy, second and third Vasiliy I, Vasiliy II, and Ivan III. In the last they are called "*delovyye* beekeepers" (see n. 26, below). Falconers and hunters are mentioned in second Dmitriy. Beaver trappers appear in second and third Vasiliy I and in Vasiliy II. Boyars' people are referred to in Semen's testament. People of the *put'* are in second Dmitriy and third Vasiliy I. Palace servants appear in second Dmitriy, and master tailors are mentioned in Ivan III.

[26] In Semen. The term is *delovyye lyudi,* defined as *esclaves artisans* by Eck (p. 565). S. P. Obnorskiy and S. G. Barkhudarov define the adjective *delovyy (delovyi)* as "obtained through partition, division," and make particular reference to this passage from the testament of Semen (*Khrestomatiya po istorii russkogo yazyka* [Moscow, 1921], p. 363). Obnorskiy's and Barkhudarov's definition fits the example of the use of the term *delenyi lyudi* as given in Sreznevskiy, I, 789.

[27] Purchased people are mentioned in Ivan I, Semen, Ivan II, and first Dmitriy. Purchased quitrent tenants appear in Ivan I, Ivan II, and first Dmitriy. Slaves figure in first Vasiliy I ("purchased slaves"), second and third Vasiliy I, and Vasiliy II.

[28] "And concerning . . . anyone whom I have acquired because he committed a misdeed." Cf. the term "penally enslaved man" in medieval English documents (see Dorothy Whitelock, ed., *English Historical Documents, c. 500–1042* [New York, 1955], I, 544 and 549).

[29] *Lyudi gramotnyye* and *lyudi polnyye* are mentioned in Ivan II. The term *gramoty polnyye* is found in first Vasiliy I: "And to my princess [shall belong] those people whom I gave to her during my lifetime, and she has the full charters to these people." The term also occurs in Ivan III. The term *gramoty dokladnyye* appears in Ivan II.

also in the testaments, refer to persons who had sold themselves to the grand prince. Full charters or reference charters were required in cases where one person wished to sell himself to another. This voluntary enslavement required a certain set procedure: an officer of the prince—specified in the testament of Ivan III as the post relay secretary (*d'yak yamskoy*)—questioned the person concerned to determine if he were taking the step freely; then witnesses had to testify that the man was really free; finally, the prince's officer issued a document with his seal attached, certifying that the person in question had sold himself into bondage. The entire procedure was called "reference" (*doklad*) and the official document was a "reference charter" (*gramota dokladnaya*) or a "full charter" (*gramota polnaya*).[30]

The testament of Ivan III contains a reference to *zakladni* (plural of *zakladen'*).[31] The *zakladen'* was a person who commended himself (and his property) to another, usually a boyar or the prince himself. The *zakladen'* was usually given a loan in return for certain promises. He did not lose the right to leave his master, and in this his position differed from that of a slave. He was, in a sense, in a position intermediary between that of a "free servant" (*vol'nyy sluga*) and a slave.[32]

[30] Eck, p. 401.

[31] "And my son Vasiliy shall not purchase lands, or hold [lands], or hold *zakladni* in the patrimonial principalities of my children, his brothers."

[32] Klyuchevskiy, VI, 349–350, and Eck, p. 89, note.

CHAPTER 5

Princely Administration in Muscovy

THERE are numerous references throughout the testaments to various aspects of princely administration. I have attempted to bring all this information together, to expand and elucidate it by drawing upon secondary sources, and to organize it into three main categories: servants of the prince, *put'* and *prikaz*, and the holding of Moscow by thirds.

SERVANTS OF THE PRINCE

The highest officer of the prince mentioned in the testaments was doubtless the *bol'shoy namestnik,* 'grand lieutenant.' This office replaced that of the *tysyatskiy,* 'chiliarch,' which was abolished in 1373 at the death of the last Moscow *tysyatskiy,* Vasiliy Vasil'yevich Vel'yaminov.[1] The duties and prerogatives of the grand lieutenant were quite similar to those of the *tysyatskiy:* he was the chief judicial officer of the grand prince in Moscow, having authority (at least in serious cases) over the entire city population, including that of the court of the grand prince himself, of the metropolitan, and of the holdings of the various patrimonial princes. He was also concerned with determining custom duties and with the merchants' court. The position of the grand lieutenant differed from that of the *tysyatskiy*—who had frequently stood in the way of centralization of the prince's power—in that the grand lieutenant was more dependent on the grand prince than the *tysyatskiy* had been. Although the office of grand lieutenant of Moscow doubtless

---

[1] The struggle that went on during the first half of the fourteenth century for the post of Moscow *tysyatskiy* indicates that this office was particularly important. See below, Text 2, n. 16.

existed as early as the reign of Vasiliy I, it was not finally confirmed until sometime during the regency of his widow, Sofiya Vitovtovna, that is, between 1425 and 1433. The term *bol'shoy namestnik* occurs in the testaments of Ivan III and Ivan IV.

The term *namestnik,* 'lieutenant,' appears in the same testaments; but there is an earlier reference, not to the *namestnik* himself, but to his office, in the testament of Ivan II: "And [I give] to my nephew, Prince Vladimir [Andreyevich of Serpukhov-Borovsk] in his lieutenancy (*v namestnichtse*) in Moscow, a third: a third of the *tamga,* of the *myto.* . . ." Thus the lesser, *udel* princes with holdings in Moscow (thirds) exercised their authority through an officer who was also called *namestnik.* The powers and duties of such a *namestnik* must have been similar to those of the *bol'shoy namestnik.* He participated in a subordinate position in trials involving his prince's holdings—trials conducted by the *bol'shoy namestnik;* he (the *namestnik* of one of the lesser princes with holdings in Moscow) was also obliged to collect the custom due his prince in Moscow.[2]

Namestnik as used in the testaments of Ivan III and Ivan IV referred to this same officer as being in charge of one of the former thirds in Moscow (Prince Vladimir's third), only by the time of Ivan III these thirds were in the hands of the grand prince himself, so that the *namestnik* was now one of his own officers. On the other hand, the testament of Ivan III did provide that certain of the lesser princes of Muscovy should continue to maintain their *namestniks* in Moscow.

The chief officer sent by the Grand Prince of Moscow to other important cities was also called *namestnik.* For instance, about 1520 Vasiliy III sent the boyar Ivan Vasil'yevich Obraztsov-Simskiy-Khabar as *namestnik* to Pereyaslavl' Ryazanskiy.[3]

The *volosteli,* 'volost administrators,' and *slobodskiye volosteli,* '*sloboda* administrators,' also mentioned in the testaments of the grand princes, had functions analogous to those of the lieutenants

[2] M. N. Tikhomirov, *Srednevekovaya Moskva v XIV–XV vekakh* (Moscow, 1957), pp. 174–176.
[3] See below, Text 13, n. 115.

in Moscow, except that the *volosteli* administered volosts and the *slobodskiye volosteli* administered *slobodas.*[4]

Another high officer of the prince, mentioned only in the testament of Dmitriy, was the *okol'nichiy.* Among the highest officers of the prince, the *okol'nichiy* was chosen from the upper ranks of the boyars. The term itself (*okolo,* 'near') suggests that this officer was a personal aide to the prince and was always with him. The *okol'nichiy* was in charge of the prince's court during the reception of ambassadors, and he preceded the prince when the latter set out on a journey, preparing quarters and making other necessary arrangements for his master.[5]

Other free servants of the prince are mentioned in the testaments. The *putnik,* 'chief of a *put',*' was usually from the boyar class; the *konyushiy,* 'equerry,' was chief of the horse *put'*, the master of the stables. The *pechatnik* was keeper of the seal and is mentioned only in the testament of Ivan III and in the testamentary writ of Vasiliy III. The *prikazchik,* 'intendant,' was charged with the management of individual holdings (enterprises or farms) of the grand prince. This officer is mentioned only once, in the testament of Ivan III. The *pisets* was the census taker or land surveyor. I have translated the word in one or the other of these two meanings, depending on its context. The term occurs in the testaments of Vasiliy II and Ivan III; in the latter testament it is used in both senses.

[4] The term *volosteli* appears in second Dmitriy, in all three of the testaments of Vasiliy I, and in Vasiliy II (see also I. I. Sreznevskiy, *Materialy dlya slovarya drevne-russkogo yazyka* [Moscow, 1958], I, 292, and George Vernadsky, *The Mongols and Russia* [New Haven, 1953], p. 359). The term *slobodskiye volosteli* appears only in second Dmitriy.

[5] The term *okol'nichiy* (*okolnichii*) appears only once in the testaments, in first Dmitriy. During the early part of the sixteenth century the office of *okol'nichiy* appears to have disappeared, the term being used to refer to boyars of the second rank (*okol'nichiye boyare*). This change in the use of the word was a later development, however, which is not reflected in the testaments. Concerning the *okol'nichiy* of ancient and medieval Russia, see Sreznevskiy, II, 646; V. O. Klyuchevskiy, *Sochineniya* (Moscow, 1956–1959), VI, 384–385; and Vernadsky, *Mongols and Russia,* pp. 364–365. Vernadsky calls the *okol'nichiy* a "quarter-master general."

The *dvorskiy*, 'major-domo,' has already been mentioned in Chapter 4. Although this term does not appear in the testaments, a later form of it, *dvoretskiy*, appears once in the testament of Ivan III.

A considerable number of "servants under the major-domo" (*slugi pod dvorskim*) are mentioned in the testaments, and the most important are discussed briefly here.

The *posel'skiye*, '*villici*,' 'village administrators,' administered various rural districts; in some cases their range of authority extended beyond the village. Patrimonial landowners and monasteries also had their *posel'skiye*. The term appears in Semen, Ivan II, first and second Dmitriy, first and second Vasiliy I, Vasiliy II, and Ivan III.

The term *tiun* has not been translated. The primary duty of the *tiun* was to administer the prince's justice in minor cases. The *tiun* was often the assistant of a *namestnik;* boyars and high church officials also had their *tiuns*. The term appears in Semen, Ivan II, first and second Dmitriy, all three of Vasiliy I, Vasiliy II, and Ivan III.

The *dovodchiki* (*dovodshchiki*) were criminal investigators. These officers were police assistants of the prince's *namestniki, volosteli*, and *tiuny*. The term appears in all three testaments of Vasiliy I and in Vasiliy II.

The *starosty*, 'elders,' were low-ranking fiscal and administrative officers elected by the householders of a "black" (*tyaglo*) community of peasants. From the context it seems that the *starosta* was sometimes an officer of the prince. The term occurs only in Semen's testament.

The *klyuchniki*, 'somlers,' were in charge of the household supplies and menial servants of the prince's various households. The *klyuchnik* managed the various *klyuchi*, 'keys,' to the kitchen, the wine cellar, and other storerooms. Patrimonial landowners and monasteries also had *klyuchniki*. The *klyuchnik* was usually a slave.

The *kaznachey*, 'treasurer,' was in charge of the prince's *kazna*, 'treasury.' Both terms are of Tartar origin.

The *d'yaki*, 'secretaries,' were important officials of the prince because they could read and write. The second testament of

Dmitriy refers to "secretaries who have managed my income for me." The testament of Ivan III mentions a "post relay secretary" (*d'yak yamskoy*) and "palace secretaries" (*dvortsovyye d'yaki*). Ivan III specified that the "post relay secretary" was to be the officer who issued "full charters" and "reference charters"—documents required in cases where one person wished to sell himself to another.[6]

It should be noted that several of the testaments give clear evidence that some, if not all, of these servants under the major-domo were not free. Thus in the testament of Semen the following passage occurs:

And concerning my artisan slaves or anyone whom I have acquired by purchase, or anyone whom I have acquired because he committed a misdeed, as well as my *tiuns*, and *villici*, somlers, and elders, and anyone who is married to these people—to all these people I have given their freedom, [they may go] wheresoever they wish.

The only two categories of servants under the major-domo not included in this passage are the secretaries (*d'yaki*) and the treasurers (*kaznachei*) of the grand prince. Yet in the testament of Ivan II a similar provision appears in which secretaries and treasurers are included among those to whom the prince granted freedom. Similar provisions appear in the testaments of Dimitriy, Vasiliy II, and Ivan III, and yet the wording in these is different. In the latter testaments the prince merely states that his son and his other children shall not interfere with his secretaries, *tiuns*, or other servants, or with anyone married to them. On the evidence of the testaments it therefore appears that prior to the reign of Dmitriy Donskoy the servants under the major-domo were

[6] Sources consulted in determining the functions of these free servants of the prince and the "servants under the major-domo," and in determining English equivalents of their Russian designations include: Vernadsky, *Mongols and Russia;* Sreznevskiy; Tikhomirov, *Srednevekovaya Moskva;* Alexandre Eck, *Le Moyen Age russe* (Paris, 1933); V. Dal', *Tolkovyy slovar' zhivogo velikorusskogo yazyka* (Moscow, 1955); S. P. Obnorskiy and S. G. Barkhudarov, *Khrestomatiya po istorii russkogo yazyka* (Moscow, 1921); B. D. Grekov and L. V. Cherepnin, eds., *Akty sotsial'no-ekonomicheskoy istorii severo-vostochnoy Rusi, kontsa XIV-nachala XVI v.* (Moscow, 1952), I.

slaves of the grand prince but that from the second half of the fourteenth century on they may have been personally free.

PUT' AND *PRIKAZ*

Beginning with the first testament of Vasiliy I the term *puti* (the plural of *put'*) occurs frequently in all the testaments. The *puti* were departments of the prince's administration, each concerned with a specialized branch of the economic exploitation of the prince's domains. Klyuchevskiy names five *puti* that existed during the fourteenth and fifteenth centuries: the horse *put'* (*konyushiy put'*), the falconry *put'* (*sokol'nichiy put'*), the hunting *put'* (*lovchiy put'*), the table *put'* (*stol'nichiy put'*), and the drink *put'* (*chashnichiy put'*). The function of these departments is apparent. For instance, the horse *put'* was charged with managing the prince's stables and the palace lands assigned to them. All stablemen of the prince were under the horse *put'*. The drink *put'* was obliged to furnish the prince with drink; it was in charge of the wine cellars and of the servants who worked in them. Under its jurisdiction were those forests of the prince in which honey was gathered and those peasant settlements which were engaged in beekeeping (*bortnichestvo*).

Each *put'* had lands and settlements scattered throughout the prince's domains. Each was administered by an officer of the prince—usually a boyar—who was called the *putnik*, 'chief of a *put'*,' or *putnyy boyarin*, '*put'* boyar.' The *puti* were independent of the major-domo (*dvorskiy*). Besides exercising administrative power over the people of the *put'*, the *putnik* held judicial authority over them. The *putnik* was not paid from the prince's treasury, but made his profit from "feeding" (*kormleniye*), that is, by keeping a share of the income from the *put'* for himself.[7]

---

[7] The "chief of the *put'*" (*putnik*) is mentioned in Vasiliy II; the "people of the *put'*" appear in second and third Vasiliy. For a discussion of the *puti*, see Klyuchevskiy, VI, 192–193; see also, Vernadsky, p. 362.

The origin of the word *put'* in the sense of a department of economic exploitation has been the object of considerable disagreement. Basically the word meant (and means) "road, path, way." Klyuchevskiy relates the *put'* to that sense of the word that indicated anything profitable. Vernad-

Although the term *puti* occurs frequently in the testaments, in only two instances is a particular *put'* identified: the horse *put'* (*konyushiy put'*) is mentioned in the testament of Ivan II and in the second testament of Dmitriy Donskoy.

A particular office of princely administration that is mentioned in almost all of the testaments was *Vasil'tsevo vedan'ye*—Vasiliy's Department. This was the office of the boyar Vasiliy Vasil'yevich Vel'yaminov (the last *tysyatskiy* of Moscow and, probably, the "uncle Vasiliy" of the testament of Semen the Proud), which was engaged in the collection of quitrent paid in honey. The lands from which this quitrent was collected were located just west of Moscow; they doubtless were among the princes' personal lands. The testament of Ivan III refers to the tenants of these lands as slave beekeepers. Vasiliy's Department appears in the testaments of the grand princes under different names. *Vasil'tsevo vedan'ye* in the testament of Ivan Kalita, it appears in later testaments as *Vasiltsev" stan"*, 'Vasiliy's stan,' and *Vasil'tsovo sto*, 'Vasiliy's Hundred.' Vasiliy's Department must have been similar to a *put'*, although it is not so called in the testaments.[8]

The term *prikaznyye lyudi*, 'bureau people,' occurs in the testamentary writ of Vasiliy III and in the testament of Ivan IV. The term *prikaz*, 'bureau,' appeared no earlier than the sixteenth century, at least not in this sense. The *prikazy* were administrative offices that had, at least in some cases, grown out of the older *puti*. During the period of patrimonial principalities the *put'* had been a department managed by one individual (the *putnik* or *boyarin putnyy*). As a more complex administrative system developed, the chief of a *put'* became the chief official of a bureau

---

sky suggests it was the Russian equivalent of an oriental term. The use of the word *put'* in the sense of an administrative department does not seem strange when compared to the French *direction* (administrative department) or to the colloquial English "way" meaning "line of business."

[8] *Vasiltsev" stan"* in Ivan II; *Vasiltsovo sto* in second Dmitriy, in first, second, and third Vasiliy I, in Vasiliy II, and Ivan III. The *Visil'tsovyy stol"* of Ivan IV's testament is obviously an error for *Vasil'tsovo sto*. Concerning Vasiliy's Department, see M. K. Lyubavskiy, *Obrazovaniye osnovnoy gosudarstvennoy territorii velikorusskoy narodnosti* (Leningrad, 1929).

or establishment which came to be called a *prikaz*.[9] Thus the horse *put'* became known as the horse bureau (*konyushiy prikaz*), and the hunting *put'* was transformed into the hunting bureau (*lovchiy prikaz*). The table *put'* and the drink *put'* were combined in the grain (or bread) and feeding bureau (*khlebennyy i kormovoy prikaz*).

It should be pointed out that not all the *prikazy* had their origins in the *puti*. The office of the *dvorskiy* (*dvoretskiy*) or major-domo, which was not a *put'*, was transformed into the bureau of the great palace (*prikaz bol'shogo dvortsa*). Nor did the bureau of emissaries (*posol'skiy prikaz*), charged with administering a number of cities and their surrounding districts (Balakhna, Velikaya Perm', and others), derive from a *put'*.[10]

THE SYSTEM OF HOLDING MOSCOW BY THIRDS

With the death of his older brother Yuriy in 1325, Ivan Danilovich was the sole remaining son of Prince Daniil Aleksandrovich of Moscow. Ivan's four brothers had died childless, so Ivan inherited the entire "patrimony" of his father, including all of Moscow.[11] The origin of the tripartite holding of Moscow (*tretnoye vladeniye Moskvoy*), with each of the three princes being called a "prince third-man" (*knyaz'-tretnik*), dates from the testament of Ivan Kalita: "I bequeath my patrimony, Moscow, to my [three] sons."

Semen, the oldest of Kalita's three sons, bequeathed all his holdings, including his third of Moscow, to his wife, Princess Mariya. The second son, Ivan the Fair, left Moscow, including his third and the third of his deceased brother Semen, to his sons Dmitriy and Ivan. (Semen's third was disposed of even though Princess Mariya was still living.) He also confirmed the right of

---

[9] The word *prikaz* is related to the verb *prikazyvati*, 'to commit, to command, to order.' Thus the *prikazy* were "committed" or "commanded" to administer certain branches of the prince's administration.

[10] Klyuchevskiy, VI, 195–196.

[11] Yuriy was killed in the Horde in 1325; Aleksandr had died in 1308; Boris in 1320; Afanasiy in 1320 (see A. V. Ekzemplyarskiy, *Velikiye i udel'nyye knyaz'ya severnoy Rusi v" tatarskiy period", s" 1238 po 1505 g.* [St. Petersburg, 1889], II, Genealogical Table).

his nephew, Prince Vladimir Andreyevich, to hold the Moscow third of his father, Andrey, who had died in 1353. Henceforth this third was to be called "Prince Vladimir's third."

It is not known if *tret'*, 'third,' referred to a particular, geographical part of Moscow, or if it merely signified the right of each prince "third-man" to collect a third of the custom of the city. A passage in the testament of Ivan II—the first in which the term *tret'* appears—suggests that it referred only to custom: "I bequeath my patrimony, Moscow, to my sons, Prince Dmitriy and Prince Ivan. And to my nephew, Prince Vladimir, in his lieutenancy of Moscow, a third: a third of the *tamga*, of the *myto*, and a third of the city customs that have appertained to the city." But there is evidence suggesting that Prince Vladimir's third in Moscow might have actually been an area of the city. For example, in an agreement concluded by Vasiliy I and Vladimir Andreyevich in 1390, this passage appears:

And that with which your father blessed you and our father, the grand prince, conceded to you, [namely] a third of Moscow, and your patrimony, Serpukhov, and other places, [and the out]lying places, which you received in place of Lopastna, [namely] Gorodets', Borovesk.[12]

In this passage, unlike the passage cited above from the testament of Ivan II, the words "a third of Moscow" are not followed immediately by reference to particular sources of income (a third of the *tamga*, a third of the *myto*), but by geographical names. This suggests that "a third of Moscow" was also a geographical location.

The next reference to Prince Vladimir's third occurs in the second testament of Dmitriy Donskoy. The wording of the passage is such that no light is thrown on the question of the nature of the thirds.[13] A suggestive passage does occur, however, in the testament of Ivan III: "And my son Vasiliy shall maintain his grand lieutenant in Moscow as of old and as it was under me, and he shall maintain another lieutenant in Moscow in Prince

---

[12] *DDG*, p. 37.

[13] "And my brother, Prince Vladimir, shall manage his third with which his father, Prince Andrey, blessed him."

Vladimir Andreyevich's third which was given to my brothers, Yuriy and Andrey." A similar passage appears in the testament of Ivan IV.[14] These two passages support the assumption that the thirds of Moscow were indeed more than merely the right to a third of the custom of the city.

M. N. Tikhomirov suggests that Prince Vladimir's third of Moscow was the Zaneglimen'ye, or part of it, since the village Kudrino (on the spot of the former Kudrinskaya Square, now Vosstaniye Square) and the surrounding villages belonged to Prince Vladimir Andreyevich of Serpukhov.[15]

On the death of Grand Prince Semen in 1353, as has been indicated above, his third passed to his younger brother, Ivan the Fair, who then held two thirds of Moscow. Ivan the Fair bequeathed his patrimony of Moscow to his two sons, Dmitriy and Ivan. The latter died in 1364, so the two thirds of Moscow which had been held by Ivan II were reunited under his son, Dmitriy Donskoy.

In his second testament, dated 1389, Dmitriy Donskoy bequeathed his share of Moscow (two thirds) to his four sons, Vasiliy, Yuriy, Andrey, and Petr. But these two thirds were not divided equally among the four sons; Dmitriy blessed his oldest son, Vasiliy, with "the larger revenue [*starishii put'*] in the city and in the *stans* of my patrimonial principality, [namely] with one half of [my] two shares, and [I bless] my three [other] sons [with] one half, and of the city customs, one half." [16]

Dmitriy also provided that if another son should be born to the wife of the grand prince he should be granted portions of his brothers' inheritance. A son, Konstantin, was born to Dmitriy's

[14] See below, p. 327.

[15] *Srednevekovaya Moskva*, p. 200 and map opposite p. 288; see also P. V. Sytin, *Iz istorii moskovskikh ulits (ocherki)* (Moscow, 1958), p. 481. The Zaneglimen'ye was the area just west of the Neglinnaya River, which flowed from the north into the Moskva River at the southwestern corner of the Kremlin.

[16] It seems to me that the addition of the phrase "and of the city customs, one half" immediately following the disposition of the grand prince's shares is yet another indication that the thirds of Moscow were actually geographical sections of the city.

wife, and he subsequently received a portion of his father's holdings in Moscow. Probably Konstantin received a portion of the share of his oldest brother, Vasiliy I.[17]

After Dmitriy Donskoy died, the system of holding Moscow became so complex that some princes were entitled to customs from their share of the city only during certain years. This was spoken of as holding a "year" in Moscow. During the reign of Vasiliy I, the former two thirds of Dmitriy Donskoy were held as follows:

Vasiliy I	Yuriy	Andrey	Petr	Konstantin
½ of two thirds less the year of Prince Konstantin	a "year" in ½ of two thirds	a "year" in ½ of two thirds	a "year" in ½ of two thirds	a "year" in ½ of two thirds

Vasiliy I bequeathed "a third of Moscow" to his oldest son, Vasiliy II. This third must actually have been one half of two thirds less the "year" of Prince Konstantin Dmitriyevich.

Vasiliy II (1425–1462) succeeded in consolidating almost all of Moscow in his own hands. In the first place he inherited a third of Moscow less the "year" of Konstantin from his father. He also acquired the "year" of Prince Yuriy of Galich,[18] the "year" of Prince Petr of Dmitrov,[19] and the "year" of Prince Konstantin.[20]

[17] For evidence that Konstantin's "year" must have come from the *stareishiy put'* (Vasiliy's half of two thirds), see n. 33, below.

[18] Following the final defeat of Yuriy's son, Prince Dmitriy Shemyaka, by the forces of Vasiliy II in 1450, the holdings of the Prince of Galich passed to the Grand Prince of Moscow.

[19] Prince Petr died childless in 1428 and his holdings escheated to the grand prince.

[20] In accordance with a provision of the second testament of Dmitriy Donskoy, Konstantin had been granted Uglich and a "year" in one half of two thirds of Moscow. Yet Dmitriy Shemyaka and Dmitriy the Fair (cousins of Vasiliy II) held Konstantin's "year" for a time. The following passage appears in the agreement of Grand Prince Vasiliy Vasil'yevich with the princes of Galich, Dmitriy Shemyaka and Dmitriy the Fair, Yur'yevichi, dated 1434: "I [Vasiliy II] have given you as your patrimony the patrimonial principality of Prince Konstantin Dmitriyevich, [namely] Rzheva and Uglich, with his Moscow shares" (*DDG*, pp. 87–89). It is probable that among these Moscow shares was Konstantin's as yet unmentioned "year," especially in view of the fact that in previous

Grand Prince Vasiliy II also acquired the "half-year" (*pol-goda*) of his cousin, Prince Ivan Andreyevich of Mozhaysk. Ivan's father, Prince Andrey Dmitriyevich, had inherited a "year" in one half of two thirds of Moscow. Andrey died in 1432, leaving his holdings, including his "year" in Moscow, to his two sons, Ivan of Mozhaysk and Mikhail of Vereya. Prince Ivan Andreyevich fled to Lithuania in 1455, and Vasiliy II seized Mozhaysk and acquired Ivan's "half-year" in Moscow.[21]

Vasiliy II also acquired Prince Vladimir's third which Vladimir Andreyevich of Serpukhov and Borovsk had inherited from his father, Andrey Ivanovich, in 1353. Vladimir died in 1410; in his testament, dated 1401 or 1402, he bequeathed his holdings, including his third in Moscow, to his five sons:

And I commit (*prikazyvayu*) my Moscow patrimony, my third, with which my father blessed me, to my children, to my son Prince

testaments the word *zhrebii*, 'share,' was used almost interchangeably with *tret'*, 'third.'

In an agreement between Vasiliy II and Dmitriy Shemyaka dated 1441 or 1442, we find that what the grand prince had granted Shemyaka did not include—or was no longer considered as having included— Konstantin's "year" in Moscow. "And you, lord, the grand prince . . . shall hold me in brotherliness . . . and you have given me as my patrimony and as my patrimonial principality the patrimonial principal-ity of our uncle, Prince Konstantin Dmitriyevich, Rzheva and Uglich, with their volosts and villages and with all, as it used to belong to Prince Konstantin Dmitriyevich; also, in Moscow District, the villages Zaryady-liye and Sokhna, and Rameneitse, and the hamlets Ostashevskiye, except for the "year" and the Moscow customs" (*DDG*, pp. 112–117).

It appears, therefore, that as early as 1441 or 1442 the former "year" of Konstantin was in the possession of Vasiliy II. Konstantin himself had probably died either in 1433 or 1434.

[21] Concerning the bequests of Prince Andrey to his sons, see the "Agreement of Grand Prince Vasiliy Vasil'yevich with Prince Ivan Andreyevich of Mozhaysk," dated 1447 (*DDG*, pp. 146–148), and the "Agreement of Grand Prince Vasiliy Vasil'yevich with Prince Mikhail Andreyevich of Vereya and Beloozero," dated 1447 (*DDG*, pp. 126–128). Concerning Vasiliy II's seizure of Mozhaysk, see *PSRL*, VIII, 144, and XXV, 270–271, and Ekzemplyarskiy, II, 326–327. Tikhomirov, (*Sredne-vekovaya Moskva*, p. 203) states that Prince Ivan had bequeathed his Moscow "year" to Vasiliy II; I have found no evidence to substantiate this.

Ivan, to Prince Semen, to Prince Yaroslav, to Prince Andrey, and to Prince Vasiliy, [and] they shall manage (*vedayut*) it by "years." [22]

Prince Ivan Vladimirovich died in 1422, leaving a daughter; Prince Semen died in 1426, leaving no children; Prince Yaroslav died in 1426, leaving a son, Vasiliy, and two daughters, Mariya and Yelena; Prince Andrey died in 1426, leaving a daughter; and Prince Vasiliy died in 1427, leaving no children.[23] Thus the sole male representative of the House of Prince Vladimir the Brave was Prince Vasiliy Yaroslavich, the holder of the Serpukhov-Borovsk patrimonial principality and Prince Vladimir's third in Moscow (or at least a "year" in Prince Vladimir's third). The history of the unfortunate Prince Vasiliy is related below; suffice it to say that the holdings of the Prince of Serpukhov-Borovsk came directly under the jurisdiction of the Grand Prince of Moscow in 1456, when Vasiliy II ordered Vasiliy Yaroslavich seized and imprisoned in Uglich.[24]

By the end of the reign of Grand Prince Vasiliy II, the thirds of Moscow were divided as follows:

Vasiliy II	Mikhail Andreyevich of Vereya
½ of two thirds; [25]	one "half-year" in ½ of
Prince Yuriy's "year";	two thirds
Prince Petr's "year";	
the "half-year" of Ivan of Mozhaysk;	
Prince Vladimir's third	

Vasiliy held all of Moscow except for Mikhail's "half-year." The Prince of Vereya had the right to hold one half of two thirds of Moscow for six months every third year (for the "years" of the three younger sons of Dmitriy—excluding Konstantin—were "third years").

Having succeeded in concentrating almost all Moscow in his hands and certainly having experienced all the disadvantages of the system of holding Moscow by thirds, Vasiliy II nevertheless proceeded to divide the city among his five sons. To his oldest

[22] *DDG*, pp. 45–46.   [23] Ekzemplyarskiy, II, 305–311.
[24] See below, Text 9, n. 19.
[25] The *stareyshiy put'* (½ of two thirds) was whole once more, for Vasiliy II had recovered the "year" of Konstantin Dmitriyevich.

son, Prince Ivan, Vasiliy bequeathed one third of Moscow.[26] To his second son, Yuriy, he bequeathed one half of Prince Vladimir's third as well as Prince Konstantin's "year." To his son Andrey the Elder, the grand prince granted the other half of Prince Vladimir's third. Prince Yuriy and Prince Andrey the Elder were to share Prince Vladimir's third, holding it by "years." The fourth son, Boris of Volok, was given the "year" (really a "half-year") of Prince Ivan of Mozhaysk, and the youngest son, Andrey the Younger, was granted the "year" of Prince Petr Dmitriyevich:

Ivan III ½ of two thirds less the "year" of Konstantin; Prince Yuriy's "year"	Yuriy of Dmitrov ½ of Vladimir's third; Konstantin's "year"	Andrey of Uglich ½ of Vladimir's third
Boris of Volok the "half-year" of Ivan of Mozhaysk	Andrey of Vologda the "year" of Petr Dmitriyevich	Mikhail of Vereya a "half-year" in ⅓ of two thirds (from his father, Andrey of Mozhaysk)

It is interesting that, despite the complexity of this division of Moscow, the total of all the thirds and fractions thereof was still one (three thirds).[27]

Prince Yuriy of Dmitrov died childless in 1473; his holdings, including his half of Prince Vladimir's "year" and Konstantin's "year," passed to Ivan III. Prince Andrey of Uglich died in prison in Moscow in 1494; his holdings, including his half of Prince Vladimir's "year," passed to the grand prince. When

[26] The third bequeathed to Prince Ivan was really the *stareyshiy put'* ($\frac{1}{2}$ of two thirds) less the "year" of Konstantin ($\frac{1}{3}$ of $\frac{1}{2}$ of two thirds) plus the "year" of Yuriy of Galich ($\frac{1}{3}$ of $\frac{1}{2}$ of two thirds), or a total of one third.

[27] Following the death of Vasiliy II in 1462, Ivan III held $\frac{1}{2} \times \frac{2}{3}$ less $\frac{1}{3} \times \frac{1}{2} \times \frac{2}{3}$ plus $\frac{1}{3} \times \frac{1}{2} \times \frac{2}{3}$, or $\frac{1}{3}$ of Moscow; Yuriy of Dmitrov held $\frac{1}{2} \times \frac{1}{3}$ plus $\frac{1}{3} \times \frac{1}{2} \times \frac{2}{3}$, or $\frac{5}{18}$ of Moscow; Andrey of Uglich held $\frac{1}{2} \times \frac{1}{3}$, or $\frac{1}{6}$ of Moscow; Boris of Volok held $\frac{1}{2} \times \frac{1}{3} \times \frac{1}{2} \times \frac{2}{3}$, or $\frac{1}{18}$ of Moscow; Andrey of Vologda held $\frac{1}{3} \times \frac{1}{2} \times \frac{2}{3}$, or $\frac{1}{9}$ of Moscow; Mikhail of Vereya held $\frac{1}{2} \times \frac{1}{3} \times \frac{1}{2} \times \frac{2}{3}$, or $\frac{1}{18}$ of Moscow. Reduced to the common denominator of 18, the shares of the princes in Moscow were as follows: Ivan III, $\frac{6}{18}$; Yuriy of Dmitrov, $\frac{5}{18}$; Andrey of Uglich, $\frac{3}{18}$; Boris of Volok, $\frac{1}{18}$; Andrey of Vologda, $\frac{2}{18}$; Mikhail of Vereya, $\frac{1}{18}$. Total: $\frac{18}{18}$.

Prince Andrey of Vologda died childless in 1481, his holdings, including the "year" of Petr Dmitriyevich, passed to Ivan III.

In his testament, dated about 1486, Prince Mikhail Andreyevich of Vereya bequeathed his holdings, including his "half-year" in Moscow, to Ivan III. Prince Mikhail died in 1486.[28]

There remained only the share of Prince Boris of Volok: the "half-year" of Ivan of Mozhaysk. Prince Boris' testament (1477) bequeathed his holdings, including the "[half] 'year' of Prince Ivan of Mozhaysk," to his son Fedor.[29] However, as the testament of Ivan III indicates, Fedor subsequently shared his inheritance with his younger brother Ivan, Prince of Ruza, who must have been born after 1477, for he is not mentioned in his father's testament.[30] Thus, Prince Fedor was left with only one half of the "half-year" of Ivan of Mozhaysk which he had inherited from his father. Prince Ivan Borisovich in his testament (1503) bequeathed his "patrimony, Ruza and one half of Rzhova" to Ivan III.[31] Ivan confirms this bequest in his testament, noting that Ivan of Ruza had given his "half-year" to the grand prince.

Thus, at the time he wrote his testament, Grand Prince Ivan III held all of Moscow except for one half of the "half-year" of Ivan of Mozhaysk, which was still in the possession of Prince Fedor Borisovich of Volok Lamskiy. This share gave Fedor the right to hold one half of two thirds of Moscow for six months every sixth year.[32]

In his testament, Grand Prince Ivan III bequeathed to his son Vasiliy "the city of Moscow with its volosts, and with its *puti*, and with its *stans*, and with its villages . . . and with all its customs." Furthermore, he ordered that "my son Vasiliy shall maintain his grand lieutenant in Moscow as of old and as it was

[28] "And I bless my lord, Grand Prince Ivan Vasil'yevich, with my patrimony with which my father, Prince Andrey Dmitriyevich, blessed me, my share in Moscow" (*DDG*, p. 301). Similar passages occur in the other two variants of this testament (see *DDG*, pp. 306 and 308). See also, *PSRL*, VIII, 217, for the report of Mikhail's death.

[29] *DDG*, p. 250. [30] Ekzemplyarskiy, II, 362.

[31] *DDG*, pp. 351–353.

[32] Mathematically, the share of Prince Fedor amounted to $\frac{1}{2} \times \frac{1}{2} \times \frac{1}{3} \times \frac{1}{2} \times \frac{2}{3}$, or $\frac{1}{36}$ of Moscow.

Heirlooms of the grand princes. UPPER LEFT: The goblet of Yuriy Dolgorukiy (used during the mass). UPPER RIGHT: The helmet of Grand Prince Yaroslav Vsevolodovich (son of Big Nest and father of Nevskiy). BOTTOM: *Barmy* (shoulder pieces of the grand prince with holy images).

under me, and he shall maintain another lieutenant in Moscow in Prince Vladimir Andreyevich's third which was given to my brothers, Yuriy and Andrey." Nevertheless, the tradition of holding Moscow by thirds was not dead. Ivan III, later in his testament, wrote:

And I bless my son Vasiliy and my younger sons, Yuriy, Dmitriy, Semen, [and] Andrey, with Prince Konstantin Dmitriyevich's "year" in Moscow, which was given to my brother Yuriy, and with Prince Petr Dmitriyevich's "year," which was given to my brother Andrey the Younger, and with Prince Mikhail Andreyevich's "year." And my son Vasiliy and my younger sons, Yuriy and his brothers, shall keep their lieutenants in Moscow during these "years," replacing one another every five years in the "years."

Furthermore, Ivan III bequeathed the half of the "half-year" of Ivan of Mozhaysk which he had inherited from his nephew, Prince Ivan Borisovich of Ruza, to his son Vasiliy. He also provided that the brother of Ivan of Ruza, Fedor Borisovich of Volok, was to retain his share (one half of the "half-year" of Ivan of Mozhaysk) in Moscow.[33]

Tikhomirov believes that, despite these provisions of the testament of Ivan III, the system of holding Moscow by thirds had in essence come to an end by the first years of the sixteenth century.[34] In his testament, written about 1506, Prince Fedor Borisovich of Volok wrote: "And if my princess has no offspring,

[33] "And I give his [Ivan of Ruza's] 'half-year' to my son Vasiliy, and my brother's son Fedor and my son Vasiliy shall hold that 'sixth-year' each for half a year [at a time]: my son Vasiliy shall keep his lieutenant for half a year, and my brother's son Fedor shall keep his lieutenant for half a year also." It must be assumed, on the basis of this passage, that the posttestamentary allotment made to Konstantin a century earlier came from the *stareyshiy put'*, from the Moscow share of Vasiliy I. If this were not the case, that is, if Konstantin's "year" had come from the shares granted to the younger brothers of Vasiliy I, then the "year" of Ivan of Mozhaysk (the son of Andrey, the son of Dmitriy Donskoy) would have been a "fourth-year" rather than a "third-year." Yet Ivan III's testament refers to the share of Boris of Volok (one half of the "half-year" of Ivan of Mozhaysk) as a "sixth-year" rather than as an "eighth-year."

[34] *Srednevekovaya Moskva*, p. 204.

then my patrimony stands before God and before my lord, the grand prince." Fedor left no children, so all his patrimony, including his "sixth year" in Moscow, must upon his death have passed to Grand Prince Vasiliy III. The testament of Vasiliy III has not been preserved; Ivan IV bequeathed all of Moscow to his son Ivan.[35]

[35] It is interesting that Ivan IV mentioned the third of Prince Vladimir Andreyevich Donskoy, providing in his testament that the tsar's son should keep his lieutenant in this third. This is another indication that the third of Vladimir Andreyevich was a geographical area of the city of Moscow.

CHAPTER 6

Heirlooms and Princely Regalia

ASIDE from territorial bequests, the testaments of the grand princes of Moscow contain a number of items of a more personal nature that were willed to relatives of the princes, to other persons, and to religious institutions. These items, many of which became heirlooms of the family of Ivan Kalita, were of three main types: valuable objects of a purely personal nature, such as golden belts, silver dishes, and expensive items of clothing; religious objects, such as icons and crosses; and pieces of princely regalia, such as the crown and the shoulder pieces with religious images (*barmy*).

Ivan Kalita bequeathed the following personal possessions to his three sons, Semen, Ivan, and Andrey: twelve golden chains, eight golden belts (two with pearls and precious stones, one with clasps, one with a clasp on purple silk, one that was identified as "Italian," and one that was either from the Golden Horde or from Byzantium), a carnelian belt, two golden goblets with pearls, a small golden dish with pearls and precious stones, two large and two small golden bowls, two round golden cups, two golden chalices, two golden vases,[1] five silver dishes (one from Yezd in Persia), and four small dishes. These articles were divided fairly equally among the sons of the grand prince. To his daughter Fetiniya, Ivan Kalita bequeathed fourteen rings and a neckpiece that had been her mother's, a new necklace that the grand prince had caused to be made, a head band, and a neck chain. To his princess, Ul'yana, and the "younger children," Ivan left "the gold which I have acquired—that which God has given me—and the small golden box." The grand prince willed that his silver belts, not further identified, should be distributed

[1] These may not have been vases but units of gold (see below, Text 1, n. 10).

among the priests. And one hundred rubles, "which Yeska has," were to be distributed among the villages. The grand prince then specified that those silver vessels that remained were to be shared by his sons and his princess, except for a large plate "with 4 annuli," which was bequeathed to the Cathedral of the Holy Mother of God in Vladimir.

Ivan's will also provided for the disposition of a number of valuable articles of wearing apparel. To his oldest son, Semen, he left a crimson mantle and the Golden Cap, which is discussed below. To Ivan, his second son, were bequeathed the "mantle of yellow silk with pearls and the large cloak with shoulder pieces." Andrey, the youngest son, received a sable pelisse with a large pearl and precious stones and a "scarlet vestment with shoulder pieces." Kalita's two daughters, Mariya and Fedosiya, were given two mantles with breastplates and pearls which the grand prince had caused to be made. The two girls also inherited a necklace. Any remaining clothing was to be distributed among "all the priests and in Moscow."

Ivan Kalita's testament confirmed the previous gift of two herds (of horses, probably) to Semen and Ivan and provided that the sons of the grand prince and his wife should share the "other herds."

Little purpose would be served in listing all the heirlooms mentioned in the various testaments of the grand princes. It should be noted that these items are numerous throughout the testaments from Ivan Kalita to Vasiliy II (with the exception of Semen's, which is a brief document). Of special interest in these documents are an icon wrought in gold by the Moscow jeweler Paramsha, an icon of the Annunciation, golden belts made by the Moscow jewelers Makar and Shishka, a suit of golden armor from Novgorod, the great relics of the Passion of Our Lord,[2] the life-giving cross of Patriarch Philotheus, the cross of Petr the Wonder-Worker, the shoulder pieces of the grand prince with holy images (*barmy*), the carnelian box (see below), and, of course, the Golden Cap.

Beginning with Ivan III the list of such possessions alters

---

[2] See below, Text 7, n. 20.

greatly. The oldest son of the grand prince, Vasiliy, was to receive the "life-giving tree in the Tsar'grad shrine" (see below) and the cross of Petr the Wonder-Worker. Yuriy, Dmitriy, and Semen were each to receive a golden cross, and Andrey was to receive a golden icon of the Crucifixion. Then the testament specified that each of the younger sons was to receive a portion of the grand prince's treasure; each son's portion had been placed in small coffers, and "on these small coffers are my seal and that of my son . . . and the keys to these small coffers are in the possession of my son . . . and these small coffers stand in my Treasury, in the custody of my treasurer . . . and in the custody of my keeper of the seal . . . and in the custody of my secretaries." Having made these allotments to his younger sons, Ivan III then provided that all that remained should pass to his oldest son, Vasiliy.

The list of bequests of a personal nature made by Ivan IV is the shortest of all. To his oldest son, Ivan, the tsar bequeathed the cross, the great life-giving tree of Constantinople; the cross of Petr the Wonder-Worker; the Cap of Monomakh; the "entire regalia of the tsar"; all the tsar's "caps" (crowns); the staves; the tablecloth; and the *tsentur'*, which is unidentified. To his second son, Fedor, the tsar left "the golden cross and the relics of Ivan Gryaznov."

Thus, it is apparent that while the earlier testaments—of the fourteenth and fifteenth centuries—contain long lists of personal items, the testaments of Ivan III and Ivan IV contain scarcely any such items. Those listed in the last two testaments are of religious or political significance.

Among the personal possessions of the princes, three are of particular interest. These are the Golden Cap, the carnelian box, and the cross, the life-giving tree from Constantinople. The Golden Cap (*shapka zolotaya*) is mentioned in the testaments of Ivan Kalita and Ivan II, in both testaments of Dmitriy Donskoy, in the three testaments of Vasiliy I, and in the testament of Vasiliy II. In all of these the Golden Cap was willed to the oldest son of the grand prince.[3] Ivan IV blessed his son Ivan with "my Russian tsardom, with the Cap of Monomakh, and with the

[3] In the first testament of Dmitriy Donskoy the *shapka zolotaya* was

entire regalia of the tsar, which Emperor Constantine Monomachus sent from Tsar'grad to our ancestor, Tsar and Grand Prince Vladimir Monomakh." The Cap of Monomakh of the testament of Ivan IV should doubtless be equated with the Golden Cap of the earlier testaments.[4]

The carnelian box is mentioned in the testament of Ivan II, in the three testaments of Vasiliy I, and in the testament of Vasiliy II. In all of these wills the box was bequeathed to the eldest son of the grand prince.

The life-giving cross is mentioned in the testaments of Ivan III and Ivan IV. In the first it is called "the cross, the life-giving tree in the Tsar'grad shrine"; in the second, Ivan IV speaks of it as "the cross, the great life-giving tree of Tsar'grad." In both testaments this cross was willed to the oldest son of the grand prince.

Among the large number of personal possessions mentioned in the testaments, these three items are particularly interesting because of the legend, dating probably from the second half of the fifteenth century,[5] according to which Grand Prince Vladimir Monomakh of Kiev acquired these regalia from the Byzantine Emperor Constantine Monomachus. The story appears in the *Voskresenskaya Chronicle* under the year 6621 (1113):

Beginning of the reign of Vladimir Manamakh, the son of Vsevolod. On April 20 Vladimir Manamakh sat on the Grand Princedom in Kiev, and the people rejoiced. . . . And the grand prince, having

---

included among a number of items left to "my son, Prince Vasiliy, and to my princess, and to my children." The *shapka zolotaya* was not mentioned at all in Ivan III's testament even though he was married to a Byzantine princess. For excellent photographs taken by David Douglas Duncan of the Cap of Monomakh, which is preserved in the Arms Chamber of the Great Kremlin Palace, see *Life*, XLIV, No. 2 (1958), p. 43, and David Douglas Duncan, *The Kremlin* (Greenwich, Conn., n.d.), p. 44.

[4] See K. V. Bazilevich, *Vneshnyaya politika russkogo tsentralizovannogo gosudarstva (vtoraya polovina XV veka)* (Moscow, 1952), p. 87.

[5] B. D. Grekov, L. V. Cherepnin, and V. T. Pashuto, *Ocherki istorii SSSR: Period feodalizma IX–XV vv., Chast' vtoraya, Ob"yedineniye russkikh zemel' vokrug Moskvy i obrazovaniye russkogo tsentralizovannogo gosudarstva* (Moscow, 1953), Part 2, p. 378.

gathered together his army, sent his voivodes against Tsar'grad"
Thrace and conquered it sufficiently, and [they] returned in health
to their own country. Now there was at this time in Tsar'grad" a
tsar, Constantine Monomachus, and he was at war with the Persians
and with the Latins, and Tsar Constantine sent to Grand Prince
Vladimir the Metropolitan of Ephesus, Neophytus, [here follows
the names of several other emissaries] . . . and he sent with them, to
the grand prince, the cross from the life-giving tree, and he took
from his own head the tsar's [i.e., Caesar's] crown, which is called
the Cap of Monomakh, and the carnelian box—the very one from
which Augustus Caesar of Rome derived pleasure—and golden
chains, and other gifts of the tsar. And Metropolitan Neophytus and
the bishops came to Grand Prince Vladimir and they began to
beseech the grand prince in the name of the tsar: "The tsar begs of
your highness peace and love, and may the Church of God be
without disorder and may all Orthodoxy be in peace under the very
power of our empire and of your great autocracy of All Rus', and
may you be called henceforth the tsar crowned by God.". . . And
from that time Grand Prince Vladimir was called Monomakh and
Tsar of Great Rus', and he lived with Tsar Constantine henceforth
in peace and love.[6]

This story does not appear in the *Primary Chronicle*. The
Voskresenskaya Chronicle was composed during the second half
of the sixteenth century. The same story also appears in the
so-called *Nikon Chronicle*, likewise written in the second half of
the sixteenth century.[7]

Although this legend probably dates from the fifteenth century, it is interesting that the testament of Ivan IV is the first to
refer to the Cap of Monomakh by this name. Dmitriy, the
grandson of Ivan III, had been crowned grand prince (coruler
with his grandfather) in the Cathedral of the Dormition in
Moscow in February 1498. The metropolitan placed on Dmitriy's head the *shapka*, certainly the *shapka zolotaya* of the earlier
wills and the *shapka monomakhovskaya* of the testament of Ivan

[6] *PSRL*, VII, 23.
[7] *Povest' vremennykh let*, ed. V. P. Adrianova-Peretts (Moscow-
Leningrad, 1950), I, 196–202; V. O. Klyuchevskiy, *Sochineniya* (Moscow, 1956–1959), VI, 33–35; and *PSRL*, IX, v and 143–144.

IV.[8] It is surprising that this crown is not even mentioned in Ivan III's testament.

It is, of course, impossible to deny flatly that these regalia—the box, the cross, and the Golden Cap—did not come down to Ivan the Terrible from Prince Vladimir Monomakh. Yet the first two—the box and the cross—are not mentioned in the earlier testaments and it is quite possible that the Golden Cap was the work of Tartar craftsmen of the thirteenth or fourteenth centuries. Moreover, if the Golden Cap of the earlier testaments was really a crown which had been passed down from Monomakh, would not this fact in all likelihood have been indicated in the earlier testaments? Klyuchevskiy suggests that the "tale" of the Byzantine emperor sending gifts to Vladimir Monomakh should be related to the coronation of Ivan IV in 1547, when the Grand Prince of Moscow for the first time openly and officially referred to himself as tsar, i.e., Caesar. Bazilevich, stating that there is no basis for relating the acquisition of these regalia to Sofiya Paleolog (the Byzantine princess who became the wife of Ivan III), adds that "people connected them with the name of Constantine Monomachus who allegedly gave them as a gift to his grandson, Vladimir Monomakh." [9]

Although the story of the gifts from the Greek emperor, as told in the two sixteenth-century Chronicles, probably was called forth by the chroniclers' desire to strengthen the picture of the Russian tsar as the legitimate ruler of Christendom—the Orthodox autocrat who had received the regalia of his office from the Byzantine emperor—there may well have been *some* historical basis to the story. The substitution of the name of Constantine Monomachus, who died in 1054, for that of Alexius Comnenus, who was ruling in 1113, may have been merely an error—perhaps conscious—on the part of the sixteenth-century chronicler anxious to lend to an earlier story a greater aura of authenticity; for all knew that Vladimir Vsevolodovich was called Monomakh because he was, on his mother's side, the

[8] See A. N. Nasonov, L. V. Cherepnin, and A. A. Zimin, *Ocherki istorii SSSR: Period feodalizma, konets XV v.-nachalo XVII v.* (Moscow, 1955), p. 106. See also Text 12, n. 2, below.

[9] *Vneshnyaya politika*, p. 87.

grandson of Constantine IX Monomachus. Moreover, an earlier source (the *Gustinskaya Chronicle, PSRL,* II, Addenda to the *Ipat'yevskaya Chronicle,* 290) reports that Emperor Alexius Comnenus (not Constantine Monomachus) did send gifts to Vladimir.[10]

[10] See S. M. Solov'yev, *Istoriya Rossii s drevneyshikh vremen* (Moscow, 1959–1966), I, 407 and 705.

CHAPTER 7

The Changing Concept of the State as Reflected in the Testaments of the Grand Princes

THE changing concept of the state from the time of Ivan Kalita to that of Ivan the Terrible is revealed in the testaments. Three developments are of particular significance: the growth of the concept of all of Russia as the patrimony of the Grand Prince of Moscow; the gradual diminution of the authority and prestige of the patrimonial princes (younger brothers, uncles, cousins, nephews of the grand prince) and the growth of the system of conditional land tenure based on service to the grand prince; the development of the theoretical justification of the right of the grand prince to the throne of Moscow and all Russia.

To Ivan Kalita, Semen, and Ivan the Fair, Moscow (and its subordinate lands, such as Kolomna, Mozhaysk, and Zvenigorod) alone was the patrimony (*otchina* or *votchina*) of the Prince of Moscow. Although the former patrimonial principality of Pereyaslavl' had been willed to Kalita's father, Daniil of Moscow, in 1302, it was apparently not considered part of the patrimony of Moscow when the first princes wrote their testaments.[1] Dmitriy Donskoy was the first of the grand princes of Moscow to refer in his testament to the Grand Principality of Vladimir, traditionally the senior principality of northeastern Russia, as his patrimony and to bequeath it to his oldest son. Although Dmitriy's son, Vasiliy I, hesitated to consider the Grand Princedom his patrimony,[2] his successor, Vasiliy II, demonstrated that the actual seniority of Vladimir was a thing of the

[1] See the discussion of Ivan Kalita's acquisitions in Chapter 2.
[2] See the discussion of Vasiliy's acquisitions in Chapter 2.

104

past by bequeathing both "my patrimony, the Grand Princedom," and its integral parts (Vladimir, Yur'yev, Pereyaslavl', and Kostroma) to his oldest son. To the son of Vasiliy II, Ivan III, not only the grand principalities of Moscow and Vladimir, but Novgorod the Great and Tver', both of which he had seized, and Ryazan' were his patrimony. In his testamentary writ Vasiliy III referred to Smolensk and the Smolensk Land as "my patrimony." The patrimony of Tsar Ivan the Terrible was the entire "Russian tsardom."

Important in the concentration of territorial control in the hands of the oldest son of the grand prince was that provision, seen first in the testament of Ivan III, which stipulated that if one of the younger sons of the grand prince were to die without heir, then his holdings should pass to his oldest brother, the grand prince. This provision contrasted with a provision of the second testament of Dmitriy Donskoy which provided that in the event of the death of one of the younger sons of the grand prince his holdings were to be divided among his brothers.[3]

Beginning with the second testament of Dmitriy Donskoy, provisions appeared in the testaments concerning the administration of the various patrimonial principalities (*udely*) of Moscow. The first of these were directed towards establishing the amount of tribute that each patrimonial prince and the future grand princess dowager were to pay to the future grand prince. Similar provisions appeared in the testaments of Vasiliy I, Vasiliy II, and Ivan III. The testaments of Dmitriy, Vasiliy I, and Vasiliy II provided that if "God should bring about a change concerning the Horde," then all the tribute collected by the various patrimonial principalities and by the grand princess dowager should be theirs, and the future grand prince would have no claim to it. Interestingly enough, such a provision does not appear in the testament of Ivan III.

With the testament of Ivan III provisions of another type

[3] Dmitriy's second testament also provided that if the oldest son of the grand prince were to die, then his patrimony would pass to the "son who follows him." This provision appears only in second Dmitriy. None of the other testaments provided for the eventuality of the death of the oldest son.

appeared. These forbade the younger sons of the grand prince to coin money within their holdings in the Moscow Land and the Tver' Land and specified that Vasiliy, the oldest son of the grand prince, should administer the farming of the right to coin money;[4] they placed restrictions upon the younger sons' participation in trade in their Moscow holdings and they specified that the younger sons should not have the right to try cases of murder and theft within their holdings in the Moscow Land. Although the oldest son of the grand prince, Vasiliy, was enjoined not to purchase lands or to hold lands or to hold *zakladni* (bound persons) in the patrimonial principalities of his younger brothers, perhaps of greater significance was the corollary of this provision: the younger brothers of the future grand prince were not to purchase lands or hold lands or hold *zakladni* "in Moscow or in his [Vasiliy's] entire Grand Principality."

The gradual change in the relationship between the grand prince on the one hand and the lesser princes and free servants (boyars, service princes, and junior boyars) on the other, can be traced through the testaments. The only stipulation that Ivan Kalita made regarding the relationship between his oldest son and the latter's brothers was that Semen should be "the guardian—according to [the law of] God"—of his younger brothers. Most of the later testaments called upon the younger sons of the grand prince to honor and obey their mother and their oldest brother, "in the place of me, your father." The oldest son was, of course, expected to protect his younger brothers. One of the most eloquent passages in the testaments depicts the ideal relationship which should exist between the oldest son and his brothers. It is from the testament of Ivan III:

And you, my younger children, Yuriy and his brothers, hold my son Vasiliy, your older brother, in place of me, your father, and obey him in all things. And you, my son Vasiliy, hold your younger brothers—Yuriy, Dmitriy, Semen, [and] Andrey—in brotherliness and in honor, without injustice. And if any of my sons should not obey my son Vasiliy in all things, or should try to obtain the grand

---

[4] Vasiliy was to administer the *otkup*, here translated as the farming of the right to coin money. This translation is uncertain; *otkup* may have meant the ransoming of prisoners (see below, Text 11, n. 79).

principalities from him or from his children, or should leave him, or should conspire secretly or openly with anyone whomsoever to his injury, or should incite anyone against him, or should ally himself with anyone against him, now may the grace of God, and the prayers of the Most Pure Mother of God and of the Holy Wonder-Workers, and the blessing of our ancestors and of us not be upon him in this world or in the next.

A similar, if somewhat more florid, provision appears in the testament of Ivan IV.[5]

The passage in the testament of Ivan Kalita concerning the holding of the village Bogorodicheskoye by Boris Vorkov is of considerable interest. Vorkov was probably a boyar who had been especially favored by the grand prince for some service he had performed. Ivan stipulated that Vorkov was to hold his village only on condition that he continue to serve one of the sons of the grand prince. This principle is clearly enunciated in the testaments of Ivan III and Ivan IV. The latter repeated the provision a number of times and gave examples of princes who had lost their patrimonies to the grand prince.[6] The existence of the concept of treason may be inferred from the lengthy quotation from the testament of Ivan III given above and from similar passages in the testament of Ivan IV, but it should be noted that in these passages the prescribed penalty is of a religious nature ("now may the grace of God . . . and of us not be upon him in this world or in the next"). Of a much more mundane and practical nature is the passage in the testament of Ivan IV concerning the Nogay mirzas:

And I also give him [the tsar's son, Ivan] the city of Romanov on the Volga River, and my son Ivan shall maintain it in the possession of the Nagay mirzas, as it was under me. And if they should go

[5] "And you, son Fedor, should be submissive in all things to my son Ivan, your older brother." There are other passages of this nature in Ivan IV.

Of considerable interest in the quotation from Ivan III is the reference to the children of the future grand prince: ". . . or should try to obtain the grand principalities from him *or his children*" (italics supplied).

[6] A number of the princes of the House of Starodub, for instance, apparently lost their patrimonies to Ivan IV (see below, Text 10, n. 11, and Text 13, n. 78).

away anywhere, or if they should commit treason, then the city of Romanov [shall pass] to my son Ivan.

The ultimate, in the medieval Russian context, of the concept of the centralized state is found in the following passage from the testament of Ivan IV:

And the city of Ozerishche, with all its minor cities, which I founded in Polotsk and in Ozereshche District, and with Usvyat, [shall pass] to my son Fedor [the younger son of the tsar], with everything [which appertained to them], as is written in this my testament to my son Ivan, but the patrimonial principality of my son Fedor [shall be subject] to him [Ivan] also, [and] to the Grand State.

The testament of Ivan Kalita contained no passage which could be interpreted as an attempt on the part of the grand prince to set forth justification for his holding the throne of Moscow. Although the final passage of Semen's testament ("And lo, I write this to you so that the memory of our parents and of us may not die, and so that the candle may not go out") could be interpreted as the first tentative effort on the part of a Prince of Moscow to establish the right of his House to the throne, similar passages do not appear in the testaments of Ivan II, Dmitriy Donskoy, Vasiliy I, or Vasiliy II. The first prince clearly to cite the Deity as the source of his power was Ivan III, who "blessed" his son Vasiliy with "my patrimony, the grand principalities, with which my father blessed me and which God gave me." The testament of Ivan IV contains a number of similar passages.[7]

If Ivan III combined the concept of Russia as the patrimony of the grand prince with the concept of divine right, then Ivan IV added yet another dimension to the idea of divine right: he held the Russian Tsardom ("Caesardom") because, in his view,

[7] For instance, "And my son Ivan I bless with my Russian tsardom with which my father, Grand Prince Vasiliy, blessed me and which God gave me." And later, "And my son Ivan I bless with the cities that I founded, with God's will, on the Lithuanian border." The concept was not, of course, entirely new. Even Vasiliy I had written in his first testament, "And if God grants that my son, Prince Ivan, should hold the Grand Princedom. . . ."

he had inherited it from his ancestor Grand Prince Vladimir Monomakh of Kiev who had inherited it from the Byzantine emperor, Constantine IX Monomachus. Ivan IV was the first of the grand princes to refer to the Russian state, in his testament, as the Russian Tsardom. Moreover, he was the first of the Russian grand princes to identify a number of the possessions of the grand prince as "regalia of the tsar." Among these regalia were the Cap of Monomakh, the "life-giving tree," and the "carnelian box"—items that had been in the possession of the grand princes of Moscow for generations, but which had not been singled out in the testaments of previous princes as being of particular significance.[8]

Thus, a study of the testaments indicates that as early as the time of the writing of Ivan III's testament in 1503 or 1504 the state[9] was viewed as the patrimony of the Grand Prince of Moscow, who ruled it not only by right of inheritance but also because it had been granted to him by God. All others in the state held lands at the pleasure of the grand princes; even the younger brothers of the future grand prince were enjoined to obey their older brother and to refrain from any attempts to take the "grand principalities" away from him on pain of religious penalty. Ivan IV, in essence adopting this theory, elaborated it by tracing the divine right of the grand prince to the emperors of Constantinople and by strengthening the concept of the duty of all to serve the grand prince, a duty which extended equally to the second son of the tsar who, although ruling over his own patrimonial principality, was to be subject to his older brother and to the Grand State.

[8] Concerning these items, see Chapter 6.
[9] The word *gosudarstvo,* 'state,' appears first in the testament of Ivan IV.

PART TWO
Russian Texts of the Testaments

Note on the Russian Texts

THE Russian texts printed here have been reproduced, through the courtesy of the Cornell University Library, from L. V. Cherepnin and S. V. Bakhrushin, eds., *Dukhovnyye i dogovornyye gramoty velikikh i udel'nykh knyazey XIV–XVI vv.* (Moscow and Leningrad, 1950), Nos. 1, 3, 4, 8, 12, 20, 22, 61, 89, 100, and 104. The codicil to the testament of Vasiliy II appears as section b of No. 61.

The texts of the testaments, as printed in *DDG*, are taken from the originals or copies preserved in the Central State Archives of Ancient Acts in Moscow. For a discussion of the system followed by the editors of *DDG* in reproducing the texts, see "Introduction to the Texts," below, pp. 178–179.

№ 1.

[Около 1339 г.]. — Духовная грамота великого князя Ивана Даниловича Калиты.

а) Первый вариант.

Во има о(т)ца и с(ы)на и с(вѧта)го д(у)ха, се ѩзъ, грѣшныи худыи рабъ б(ож)ии Иван[ъ], пишу д(у)ш(е)вную грамоту, ида въ Ворду, никимь не нуженъ, цѣлымь своимь оумомь, въ своѥмь здоровьи. Аже б(ог)ъ что розгадаѥть о моѥмь животѣ, даю рѧдъ с(ы)н(о)мъ своимъ и кнѧгини своѥи.

Приказываю с(ы)н(о)мъ своимъ оч(и)ну свою Москву. А се ѥсмь имъ роздѣлъ оучинилъ:

Се далъ ѥсмь с(ы)ну своѥму болшему Семену: Можаѥскъ, Коломъну со всими Коломеньскими волостми, Городенку, Мѣзыню, Пѣсочну, Похране, Оусть-Мерьску, Брошевую, Гвоздну, Иван[и], [де]ревни Маковець, Лѣвичинъ, Скулневъ, Каневъ, [Гжелю, Го]рѣтову, Горки, [село Аста]фьевскоѥ, село на Сѣверьсцѣ в Похранъскомъ оуѣздѣ, село Костантиновскоѥ, село Орининьское, село Островьское, село Копотеньское, селце Микульскоѥ, село Малаховьскоѥ, село Напрудское оу города.

А при своемь животѣ далъ ѥсмь с(ы)ну своему Семену: 4 чепи золоты, 3 поѩсы золоты, 2 чаши золоты с женчуги, блюдце золото с женчугомь с каменьемь. А к тому еще далъ ѥсмь ѥму 2 чума золота болшаѩ. А исъ соудов исъ серебрьныхъ далъ ѥсмь ѥму 3 блюда серьбрьна.

А се с(ы)ну своѥму Ивану: Звенигородъ, Кремичну, Рузу, Фоминьскоѥ, Суходолъ, Великую свободу, Замошьскую свободу, Оугожь, Ростовци, Окатьева свободка, Скирминовьскоѥ, Тростна, [Нѣгуча]. А села: село Рюховьское, село Каменичьское, село Рузьскоѥ, село Бѣлжиньское, село Максимовское, село Андрѣѥвскоѥ, село Вѧземьскоѥ, село Домонтовьскоѥ, село в Замошьскои свободѣ, село Семьциньскоѥ.

А изъ золота далъ ѥсмь с(ы)ну своѥму Ивану: 4 чепи золоты, поѩсъ болшии с женчугомь с каменьемь, поѩсъ золотъ с капторгами, поѩсъ сердоничень золотомь окованъ, 2 овкача золота, 2 чашки круглыи золоты, блюдо серебрьно ѣздниньское, 2 блюдци меншии.

А се далъ ѥсмь с(ы)ну своѥму Андрѣю: Лопастну, Сѣверьску, Нару-[нижьское], Серпоховъ, Нивну, Темну, Голичичи, Щитовъ, Перемышль, Растовець, Тухачевъ. А се села: село Талежьскоѥ, село Серпоховьское, село Колбасиньскоѥ, село Нарьскоѥ, село Перемышльскоѥ, [село Битаговское], село Труфоновскоѥ, село Ѥсиновьскоѥ, [село Коломниньскоѥ], село Ногатиньское.

А изъ золота дал ѥсмь [сыну своему Андрѣю: 4 че]пи золоты, поѭсъ золотъ фрѧзьскии с женч[угомь с каменьемь], поѭсъ золотъ с крюкомь [на червчатѣ шелку, поѭсъ золотъ] ц(а)р(е)вьскии, 2 чары золот(ы), 2 чумка золота [меньшаѭ; а из блюдъ,—] блюдо серебрьно, а 2 малаѭ.

А се даю [кнѧгини своеи с ме]ньшими дѣтми: Сурожикъ, Мушк[ов]у гору, [Радонѣжское], Бѣли, Вога, Черноголовль, на Вори свободка Соф-[роновскаѭ], Вохна, Дѣиково раменье, Данилищова свободка, [Машевъ, Сел]на, Гуслица, Раменье, что было за кнѧгинею. [А села: село М]ихаиловскоѥ, село Луциньскоѥ, село у озера, [село Радонѣжс]коѥ, село Дѣигуниньскоѥ, село Тыловское, Ро[гожь, село П]ротасьевское, село Аристовьскоѥ, село Лопастеньскоѥ, [село] Михаиловскоѥ на Ѭоузѣ, 2 селѣ Коломенскии.

А из городьскихъ волостии даю кнѧгини своѥи осм[ничее]. А тамгою и иными волостми городьскими подѣл[атсѧ сынове] мои; тако же и мыты, которыи в которомъ оуѣздѣ, то тому. А оброкомь медовымь городь-скимь Василцева вѣданьѭ подѣлатсѧ с(ы)н(о)ве мои. А что моихъ борт-никовъ и оброчниковъ купленыхъ, которыи в которои росписи, то того.

А по моимъ грѣхомъ, ци имуть искати татарове которыхъ волостии, а отоимутсѧ, вамъ, с(ы)н(о)мъ моимъ, и кнѧгини моѥи подѣлити вы сѧ опѧть тыми волостми на то мѣсто.

А численыи люд(и), а тѣ вѣдають с(ы)н(о)ве мои собча, а блюд(у)ть вси с одиного. А что мои люди куплении в вел(и)комь свертцѣ, а тыми сѧ подѣлать с(ы)н(о)ве моі.

А что золото кнѧгини моѥѭ Оленино, а то ѥсмь дал дчери своѥи Фетиньи, 14 обручи и ожерелье м(а)т(е)ри ѥе, монисто новоѥ, что ѥсмь сковалъ. А чело и гривну, то есмь дал при собѣ. А что есмь придо-былъ золота, что ми дал б(ог)ъ, и коробочку золотую, а то есмь далъ кнѧгини своѥи с меншими дѣтми.

А ис портъ из моихъ с(ы)ну моѥму Семену: кожухъ черленыи женчужь-ныи, шапка золотаѭ. А Ивану, с(ы)ну моему: кожухъ желтаѭ обирь с женчу-гомь и коць великии с бармами. Андрѣю, с(ы)ну моѥму: бугаи соболии с наплечки съ великимь женчугомь с каменьемь, скорлатноѥ портище сажено з бармами. А что ѥсмь нынѣча нарѧдилъ 2 кожуха с аламы с женчугомь, а то ѥсмь дал меншимъ дѣтемъ своимъ, М(а)рьи [же] Федосьи, ожерельемъ.

А что моихъ поѭсовъ серебрьныхъ, а то роздадать по п(о)пьѭмъ. А что мое 100 руб. оу Ѥски, а то роздадать по ц(е)рквемъ. А что сѧ остало из моихъ судовъ из серебрьных, а тымъ подѣлатсѧ с(ы)н(о)ве моѥ и кнѧгини моѭ. А что сѧ останеть моихъ портъ, а то роздадать по всимъ п(о)пьѭмъ и на Москвѣ. А блюдо великоѥ серебрьноѥ о 4 колца, а то ѥсмь да[лъ] с(вѧ)тѣи Б(огороди)ци Володи-мерьскои.

А приказываю тобѣ, с(ы)ну своѥму Семену, братью твою молодшую и кнѧгиню свою с меньшими дѣтми, по б(о)зѣ ты имъ будешь печалникъ.

А что ѥсмь далъ с(ы)ну своѥму Семену стадце, а другоѥ Ивану, а иными стады моими подѣлатсѧ с(ы)н(о)ве мои и кнѧгини моѭ.

А на се послуси: о(те)ць мои д(у)ш(е)вьныи Ѥфрѣмъ, о(те)ць мои д(у)шьвныи Федосии, о(те)ць мои д(у)ш(е)вьныи, попъ Д(а)в(ы)дъ.

А грамоту п(и)салъ дьѭкъ кнѧзѧ великого Кострома.

А кто сю грамоту порушить, судить ѥму *б(о)гъ*.

На лицевой стороне грамоты привешена серебряная позолоченная печать в. кн. Ивана Даниловича Калиты.

б) Второй вариант.

Во имѧ о(т)ца и с(ы)на и с(вѧ)т(а)го д(у)ха, се ѩзъ, грѣшныи худыи рабъ б(о)жии Иванъ, пишу д(у)шевную грамоту, ида въ Ворду, никимь не нуженъ, цѣлымь своимь оумомь, въ своѥмь здоровьи. Аже б(ог)ъ что розгадаеть о моемь животѣ, даю рѧдъ с(ы)номъ своимъ и кнѧгини своѥи.

Приказываю с(ы)номъ своимъ оч(и)ну свою Москву. А се ѥсмь имъ роздѣлъ оучинилъ:

Се далъ ѥсмь с(ы)ну своему болшему Семену: Можаескъ со всими волостьми, Коломну со всими Коломеньскими вол(о)стьми, Городенку, Мѣзыню, Пѣсочну, и Середокоротну, Похрѧне, Оусть-Мерьску, Брошевую, Гвоздну, Ивани, деревни Маковець, Лѣвичинъ, Скулневъ, Каневъ, Гжелю, Горѣтову, Горки, село Астафьевьское, село на Сѣверьсцѣ в Похрѧньскомъ оуѣздѣ, село Костѧнтиновьское, село Орининьскоѥ, село Островьскоѥ, село Копотеньскоѥ, селце Микульскоѥ, село Малаховьскоѥ, село Напрудьскоѥ оу города.

А при своѥмь животѣ дал ѥсмь с(ы)ну своѥму Семену: 4 чепи золоты, 3 поѩсы золоты, 2 чаши золот(ы) с женчюги, блюдце золот(о) с женчюгомь с камен(ь)ѥмь, 2 чума золота болшаѩ. А исъ суд(о)въ исъ серебрьныхъ далъ есмь ѥму 3 блюда серьб(рь)на.

А се даю с(ы)ну своему Ивану: Звенигород, Кремичну, Рузу, Фоминьскоѥ, Суход(о)лъ, Велікую свободу, Замошьскую свободу, Оугожь, Ростовци, Охатьеву свободку, Скирминовьскоѥ, Тростну, Нѣгучю. А села: село Рюховьскоѥ, село Каменичскоѥ, село Рузьскоѥ, село Бѣлжиньскоѥ, село Максимовское, сел(о) Андрѣевьское, село Вѧземьскоѥ, село Домонтовскоѥ, село в Замошьскои свобод\ѣ), село Семциньскоѥ.

А изъ зол(о)та далъ ѥсмь с(ы)ну своѥму Ивану: 4 чепі зол(о)ты, поѩсъ зол(о)тъ болшиі с женчюгомь с каменьемь, поѩсъ золотъ с капторгами, поѩсъ сердоничѧ золотомь окованъ, 2 овкача зол(о)та, 2 чашки круглыи зол(о)ты, блюдо серебрьно ѕзднинькоѥ, 2 блюдци меншии.

А се дал ѥсмь с(ы)ну своѥму Андрѣю: Лопастну, Сѣверьску, Наруниж[ское, Серпо]ховъ, Нивну, Темну, Голичичи, Шитовъ, Перемышль, Растовець, Тухачевъ. А се села: село Талежьскоѥ, село Серпоховьскоѥ, село Колбасиньскоѥ, село Нарьскоѥ, село Перемышльскоѥ, село Битѧговьскоѥ, село Труѳ(о)новьское, село Ѩсиновьскоѥ, село Коломнинскоѥ, село Ногатиньскоѥ.

А изъ зол(о)та дал ѥсмь с(ы)ну своему Андрѣю: 4 чепи золоты, поѩсъ зол(о)тъ фрѧзьскии с женчюгомь с каменьемь, поѩсъ золотъ с крюкомь на чьрвьчатѣ шелку, поѩсъ золотъ ц(а)р(е)вьскии, 2 чары золоты, 2 чумка золота меншаѩ; а изъ блюдъ,— блюдо серебрьно, а два малаѩ.

А се даю кнѧгини своѥи с меншими дѣтми: Сурожикъ, Мушк[ов]у гору, Радонѣжьскоѥ, Бѣли, Ворѧ, Черноголовлѧ, на Вори сво(бо)дка Софроновьскаѩ, Вохна, Дѣиково раменьѥ, Данилищова свободка, Машевъ, Селна, Гуслицѧ, Раменьѥ, что было за кнѧгинею. А села: село Михаиловьское, село Луциньское, село оу озера, село Радонѣжьское, село Дѣигуниньское, село Тыловское, Рогожь, село Пѫотасьевское, село Аристовское, село Лопастеньскоѥ, село Михаиловскоѥ на Ѩоузѣ, 2 селѣ Коломеньскии.

А из городскіхъ волостии даю кнагини своюи осмничею. А тамгою и иными волостми городскими подѣлатьса с(ы)н(о)ве мои; тако же и мыты, которыи в которого оуѣздѣ, то тому. А оброкомь городскимь Василцева вѣданыа подѣлатьс(а) с(ы)н(о)ве мои. А что моих бортников и оброчников купленых, которыи в которого росписи, то тог(о).

А по моимъ грѣх(о)мъ, ци імуть искати татарове которых волостии, а отыимутьса, вамъ, с(ы)н(о)мъ моимъ, и кнагині мокеи подѣлити вы са опать тыми вол(о)стми на то мѣс(то).

А числьныи люд(и) вѣдають с(ы)н(о)ве моі собча, а блюд(у)ть вси с одиного. А что моі люд(и) купленіи въ вел(и)комъ свертцѣ, а тыми са подѣлать с(ы)н(о)ве мои.

А что зол(о)то кнагини моке Оленино, а то есмь дал дчері своеі Фетіны, 14 обруч(и) и ожерелье м(а)т(е)ри ке, моністо новое, что есмь сковал. А чело и грив(ну), то кесмь дал при собѣ. А что есмь придобыл золота, что ми дал б(ог)ъ, и коробочку золотую, а то кесмь дал кнагини своеи с меншими дѣтми.

А ис портъ изъ моихъ с(ы)ну моему Семену: кожухъ черленыи женчужныи, шапка зол(о)тага. А Ивану, с(ы)ну моему: кожухъ желтага обирь с жьнчугомь, коць вел(и)кии с б(а)рмами. Андрѣю, с(ы)ну моему: бугаи соболии с наплечки с великимь женчюгомь с каменьем, скорлатное портище с бармами. А что кесмь нын(ѣ)ча нарадил 2 кожуха с аламы с женчюгомь, а то есмь дал меншимъ дѣтемъ своимъ, М(а)рьи же Федосьи, ожерел(ь)емъ.

А что моихъ поиасовъ серебрьных, а то роздадать по п(о)пьамъ. А что мое 100 руб. оу Ески, а то роздадать по ц(е)рквамъ. А что са остало из моихъ судовъ изъ серебрьных, а тымъ подѣлатьс(а) с(ы)н(о)ве мои и кнагини моиа. А что са останеть моих портъ, а то роздадать по всимъ п(о)пымъ и на Москвѣ. А блюд(о) великое о 4 колца, а то даю с(ва)тѣи Б(огороди)ци Вол(о)димерскои.

А что есмь дал с(ы)ну своему Семену стадце, а друг(о)е Ивану, а иными стады моими подѣлатса с(ы)н(о)ве мои и кнагини моиа.

А проч(ь) Московьских селъ, даю с(ы)ну своему Семену села своиа куплена: село Аваковское въ Новѣгородѣ на Оулалѣ, другое в Володимери Борисовское.

А что есмь купилъ село Петровское, и Олексиньскою, Вседобрич(ь), и Павловьское на Масѣ, половину есмь купилъ, а пол(о)вину есмь смѣнил с мітрополитом...........¹ца на Масѣ, что есмь купилъ оу Афинѣиа, то даю с(ы)ну своему Ивану.

А что есмь купилъ село Варварьскою и Мѣловьское оу Юрьева, что есмь смѣнилъ на Матфѣищовьское село, то даю с(ы)ну своюму Андрѣю.

А что село Павловьское, бабы нашее купла, и Новое селце, что есмь купил, и Олександръ с(ва)тыи, что есмь купил на Костромѣ, то даю кнагини своеи.

А что есмь купил село в Ростовѣ Богород(и)чское, а дал есмь Бориску Воръкову, аже імѣть с(ы)ну моему которому служити, село будет за нимь, не імѣть ли служити дѣтемъ моимъ, село отоімут.

А что есмь прікупил селце на Кержачи оу Прокофьа у игумна, друг(о)е Леонтиевское, третье Шараповское, а то даю с(ва)т(о)му Олександру собѣ в поминанье.

А пріказываю тобѣ, с(ы)ну своему Семену, брат(ь)ю твою молодшую и кнаг(и)ню свою с меншими дѣтми, по б(о)зѣ ты имъ б(у)д(е)шь печалникъ.

---

¹ *Лист с текстом разорван: в этом месте может уместиться около 12 букв.*

А кто сю грамоту порушит, судить ему б(ог)ъ.

А на се послуси: о(те)ць мои д(у)шевныи Ефремъ, о(те)ць мои д(у)ш(е)вныи Федосии, о(те)ць мои д(у)ш(е)вныи, поп Дав(ы)дъ.

На обороте листа помета: Духовные, и списки з духовных, и прошнаю грамота.

На лицевой стороне грамоты след от прикрепления печати.

Основание для датировки: упоминание второй жены в. кн. Ивана Даниловича Калиты («княгини с меньшими детьми») указывает на время значительно позднее 1332 г., — *второго брака Калиты (ПСРЛ, т. XVII, стр. 30, примеч. 5б); поскольку грамота в двух вариантах написана в связи с поездкой в Орду, ее правильнее всего датировать 1339 г., когда Иван Калита с сыновьями отправился в Орду (ПСРЛ, т. X, стр. 211; т. VII, стр. 205). См. Черепнин, стр. 12—20.*

Подлинники (на пергамене) — *ЦГАДА, Гос. древлехранилище, отд. I, рубр. I, №№ 1—2. Духовная грамота ранее напечатана: Древняя Российская Вивлиофика, ч. 8, изд. 1, стр. 208—220, №№ 1—2; ч. 1, изд. 2, стр. 47—56, №№ 1—2; Мышкинское изд., т. 5, ч. 9, стр. 1—7; СГГД, ч. 1, стр. 31—35, №№ 21—22; Смирнов, стр. 53—57; Аристов, стр. 598—601; Самоквасов, стр. 179—182; Бахрушин, стр. 12—15, №№ 2—3; Фарфоровский, стр. 249—254; Влад.—Буданов, стр. 1—8; Обнорский и Бархударов, стр. 64—67; Коваленский, стр. 153—154.*

№ 3.

[1353 г. марта 18 — апреля 26.] — Духовная грамота великого князя Семена Ивановича.

Во има о(т)ца и с(ы)на и с(ва)т(а)го д(у)ха, се юзъ, худыи грешныи рабъ б(о)жии Созонтъ, при своемъ животе, целымъ своимъ оумомъ, пишу грамоту д(у)ш(е)вную. Дашю радъ своеи кнагине. Велелъ есмь у нее быти своему дяде Василью. А по б(о)зе приказываю своеи брат(ь)е, кназ(ю) Ивану и кназ(ю) Ан[др]ею, свою кнагиню, и своего [дядю?],[2] и свои боюре, положилъ есмь на б(о)зе и на вас, на своеи [братьи], [та]ко имете блюсти по нашему докончанью, како т[огды] мы це]ловали кр(е)стъ оу отна гроба.

А чимъ ма бл(а)г(о)с(ло)вилъ о(те)ць мои, кназ(ь) великии, — Коломна с волостми и съ селы и з бортью, Можаескъ с волостми и съ селы и з бортью, Заючковъ, что ма бл(а)г(о)с(ло)вила тетка мою, кнагини Анна, и Гордошевичи, а в городе на Москве жер[ебеи] мои тамги, а села на Москве в Городскомъ оуезде — сел(о) Нап[ру]дьское, сел(о) Новое на Пупавне, сел(о) Островьское, сел(о) Орининьск[ое], сел(о) Малаховьское, сел(о) Копотеньское, сел(о) на Клазме Остафьеское, сел(о) Илмовьское, сел(о) на Клазьме Хвостовьское, сел(о) Деигуниньское, сел(о) на Сулишине погостъ, а в Перьюславле купла мою сел(о) Самаровьское, сел(о) Романовьское на Кержаче, сел(о) Ортаковьское въ Юрьевьское волости, сел(о) Семеновьское Володимерьское волости, что есмь купил у Овци оу Ивана, сел(о) на Костроме Олександровьское, сел(о) в Дмитрове, что есмь купил оу Ивана у Дрюцского, и Заберегъ, что есмь купил оу Семена оу Новосильског(о), или буд(е) чего забылъ напис(а)ти своее купли и оучастка, чимъ ма бл(а)г(о)с(ло)в(и)лъ о(те)ць мои, тако же и про золото, чимъ ма бл(а)г(о)с(ло)в(и)лъ о(те)ць мои, и что буд(е) примыслилъ при своемъ животе, зол(о)та ли, женчугу ли, то все дал есмь своеи кнагине.

А ис конь изъ своихъ изъ ездовныхъ велелъ есмь дати своеи кнагини пят(ь)дес(я)тъ конь. А и стадъ из моихъ моеи кнагине стадо коломеньское, другое стадо Детино Ивашьково.

А что есмь писалъ в сю грамоту, то есмь все далъ своеи кнѧгини, ать молить б(ог)а, а д(у)шу мою поминаеть до своего живота.

А что б(у)д(е) судилъ [ког]да великомъ кнѧженьѣ и в отч(и)нѣ въ своеи на Москвѣ, или моѧ боѧре, или боѧрьскиѣ люд(и), а того вы, братья моѧ, не восчинаите.

А хто моихъ боѧръ иметь служити оу моее кнѧгини, а волости имуть вѣдати, дають кнѧгинѣ моеи прибытъка половину.

А что моихъ людии дѣловыхъ, или кого буд(е) прикупилъ, или хто ми сѧ буд(е)ть в винѣ досталъ, тако же мои тивуни, и посельскиѣ, и ключники, и старосты, или хто сѧ будеть оу тыхъ людии женилъ, всѣмъ тѣмъ люд(е)мъ далъ есмь волю, куды имъ любо. А брат(ь)ѣ моѥи, ни моеи кнѧгинѣ, тѣ люд(и) не надобны.

А сю грамоту пис(а)лъ есмь перед своими о(т)ци: перед вл(а)д(ы)кою володимерьскимъ перед Олексѣемъ, перед вл(а)д(ы)кою переѧславьскимъ Офонасеемъ, перед вл(а)д(ы)кою коломеньскимъ Офонасьемъ, перед архимандритомъ Петромъ, перед архимандритомъ перед Филимономъ, перед своимъ о(т)цемъ д(у)шевнымъ, попомъ Евсевьемъ.

А все есмь се положилъ на б(о)зѣ и на своеи братьѣ, на кнѧзи на Иванѣ и на кнѧзи на Андрѣи. А по о(т)ца нашего бл(а)г(о)с(ло)в(е)нью, что намъ приказалъ жити заодинъ, тако же и ѧзъ вамъ приказываю, своеи братьи, жити заодинъ. А лихихъ бы есте людеи не слушал(и), и хто иметь васъ сваживати, слушали бы е[сте] о(т)ца нашего, вл(а)д(ы)ки Олексѣѧ, тако же старыхъ боѧръ, хто хо[тѣ]лъ о(т)цю нашему добра и намъ.

А пишу вамъ се слово того дѣла, чтобы не перестала памѧть роди-[те]лии нашихъ и наша, и свѣча бы не оугасла.

А хто сю грамоту иметь рушити, судить ему б(ог)ъ в семь вѣцѣ и в будущемъ.

На лицевой стороне грамоты привешена серебряная позолоченная печать в. кн. Семена Ивановича и две желтовосковые печати князей Ивана и Андрея Ивановичей.

О с н о в а н и е д л я д а т и р о в к и: *грамота написана после смерти митрополита Феогноста 11 марта 1353 г. и после смерти детей великого князя Семена Ивановича, — Ивана и Семена,18 марта 1353 г.; сам великий князь Семен Иванович умер 26 апреля 1353 г. (ПСРЛ, т. VII, стр. 217; т. X, стр. 226; т. XVIII, стр. 28). См. Черепнин, стр. 25—27.*

Подлинник — ЦГАДА, Гос. древлехранилище, отд. I, рубр. I, № 3. Духовная грамота ранее напечатана: Древняя Российская Вивлиофика, ч. 8, изд. 1, стр. 226—230, № 4; ч. 1, изд. 2, стр. 61—64, № 4; Мышкинское изд., т. 5, ч. 9, стр. 10—12; СГГД, ч. 1, стр. 37—38, № 24; Карамзин, т. 4, прим. 365; Бахрушин, стр. 15—16, № 4; Фарфоровский, стр. 254—256; Дурново, стр. 38—39; Обнорский и Бархударов, стр. 68—70; Коваленский, стр. 155. Снимки: СГГД, ч. 4, табл. 2; Ивѣнов, стр. 7 и № 7; Соболевский и Пташицкий, № 2; Колесников, № 10.

№ 4.

[Около 1358 г.]. — Духовная грамота великого князя Ивана Ивановича.

а) Первый экземпляр.

Во имѧ о(т)ца [и сына] и с(вѧ)т(а)го д(у)ха, се ѧзъ, грѣшныи худыи [рабъ божии] Иванъ Ива[новичь], пишу гра[моту душе]вную, ничимъ же не нуженъ, цѣлымъ своимъ оумомъ, в своемъ здоровьѣ. [Аже чт]о б(ог)ъ розмыслить о моемъ животѣ, даю рѧдъ своимъ с(ы)номъ, кнѧз(ю) Дмитрию и кнѧз(ю) Ивану, и своему брат(а)ничу, кнѧз(ю) Володимеру, и своеи кнѧгинѣ.

Приказываю отч(и)ну свою Москву сыномъ своимъ, кназ(ю) Дмитрию
и кназ(ю) Ивану. [А братаничу] моему, кназ(ю) Володиме⌐у, на Москвѣ
в намѣстничтвѣ треть, и в тамзѣ, [в мытѣхъ и в пошлинахъ г]город-
скихъ треть, что потагло к городу. И что мед оброчныи [Василцева
стану, и что отца мое]го купленѣ бортници под вѣчныѣ варах, и кони
став[ити по станомъ и по варамъ], и конюшии путь, то имъ в[се на] трое.
А численѣ [люди вси три кнази блюдуть сопча с о]диного.

А се даю с(ы)ну своему, кназ(ю) Дмитрью: [Можаескъ со всѣми
воло]стми, и съ [селы], и з бортью, и с тамгою, и со всѣми пошлинами,
Коломну со всѣми волостми, с тамгою, и с мыт(о)мъ, и селы, и з бортью,
с оброчник(и), и с пошлинами.

А что ис тыхъ волостии за кнагинью за М(а)рьею, тѣ волости до ее живота и села, а по ее животѣ тѣ волости и села с(ы)ну моему, кназ(ю) Дмитрью:
Городна, Мѣзыни, Пѣсочна, Середокоротна, Похране, Оусть-Мерьска,
Брашевага, Гвоздна, селце Ивань, деревни Маковець, Лѣвичинъ, Скулневъ, [Каневъ, Кошира, Гжела, Горѣтовка, Горки, село] на Сѣверсцѣ,
село Малино, сел(о) Холмы, [село Костантиновское, село Ѡрининьское],
сел(о) Островьское, [село Копотеньское, село Микульское], сел(о) Мала-
ховы[ское], [село Нап]рудьское, сел(о) Илмовьское, [село] Новое, Мещерка
у Коломны.

А се даю с(ы)ну своему, кназ(ю) Ивану: Звенигород со всѣми волостми, и с мыт(о)мъ, и съ селы, и з бортью, и с оброчники, и с пошлинами, Кремична, Руза, Фоминьское, Суходолъ, Истерва, Сводъка,
свободу Замошьскую, Ростовци, Кремичну, Тростну, Нѣгучу, сел[о
Рюховьское], сел(о) Михалевьское, сел(о) Каменьское, сел(о) на Рѣпнѣ
в Боровьсцѣ, селце Мил[циньское], сел(о) Максимовьское, сел(о) в Замошьскои свободѣ, сел(о) Выславьское, [село Кузминьское, село Дѣмон-
товское], село Андрѣевьское, село Кариньское, се[ло Козловьское].

А брат(а)ничь [мои], кназ(ь) Володимеръ, вѣдаеть оуѣздъ о(т)ца своего.

А чт[о са мнѣ] достали мѣ[ста Разань]ская на сеи сторонѣ Оки,
ис тыхъ мѣстъ дал есмь кназ(ю) Володи[меру], в Лопастны мѣста, Новыи
городокъ на оусть Поротли, а инага места Р[азаньск]ага ѡтмѣньнага с(ы)-
номъ моимъ, кназ(ю) Дмитрью [и кнзю И]вану, подѣ[латса нап]олы,
безъ обиды.

[А кнагини Оульгана, по отца моего, кназа] великого, по гр[амотѣ
по душе]внои, вѣдаеть воло[сти, и осмничье, и села до своего живота,
а по ее животѣ дѣти мои, кназь Дмитрии и кназь Иванъ, и братаничь
кназь] Володимер, и мога кн(а)гини подѣлатса на четверо, безъ обиды.

А ци по грѣхомъ, имуть искати из Орды Коломны, или Лопастеньскихъ мѣстъ, или ѡтмѣньныхъ мѣстъ Разаньскихъ, а по грѣхомъ, ци
ѡт(ъ)иметса которое [мѣсто], дѣти мои, кназ(ь) Дмитрии и кназ(ь)
Иванъ, кназ(ь) Володимеръ, и кнагини [в то] мѣсто подѣлатса безъпеньными мѣсты.

А се дал есмь кнагини [своеи Оле]ксандрѣ ис Коломеньскихъ волостии:
Похране, Пѣсочну, Серед(о)ж[оротну, село Лысцевьское, да на] Москвѣ
селце Семциньское. А и Звенигород[скихъ волостии] дал есмь своеи
кнагинѣ: Оугожь, Великую свободу Юрьеву, сел(о) Кля[повьское], сел(о)
Бѣлциньское с Новымъ селцемъ.

А ис тамги ис московьское [кнагинѣ моеи] оу моего с(ы)на, у кназ(а)
оу Дмитрига, и оу кназ(а) оу Ивана из дву жер[ебьевъ треть. А по]
животѣ моее кнагини тѣ волости, и села, и треть тамги [дастса сыну]
моему, кназ(ю) Дмитрию, и кназ(ю) Ивану, в которого оуѣздѣ, то [того
и есть].

[А се] даю с(ы)ну своему, [кнзю Дмитрию: икону святыи Олександръ, чепь золо]ту врану с кр(е)сто[мъ золотымъ, чепь золоту колчату, икона золотомъ кована Па]рапшина дѣла, шапка зол(о)та, бармы, поıасъ великии зол(о)тъ [с камень]емъ с женчуги, что мıа бл(а)г(о)с(ло)вилъ о(те)ць мои, кнıаз(ь) великии, поıасъ зол(о)тъ [с крюком]ъ, сабла зол(о)та, обязь зол(о)та, и серга с женчугомъ, чечакъ зол(о)тъ с каме[ньемъ с же]нчуги, 2 овкача зол(о)та, ковшь великии зол(о)тъ гладъкии, коропка [сердони]чна зол(о)томъ кована, бадыа серебрена с наливкою серебреною......¹ с каменьемъ, опашень скорлатенъ сажень.

А се дал есмь с(ы)ну с[воему], [кнıазю] Ивану: чепь великую зол(о)ту с кр(е)ст(о)мъ, чепь зол(о)ту врану, а друга[ıа] [огнивчата] с кр(е)сты, икону бл(а)г(о)в(е)щ(е)нье, и сергу с женчугомь, поıасъ зол(о)тъ с каменьемъ [с женчуги], что ми дал бгат мои, кнıаз(ь) великии Семенъ, поıасъ зол(о)тъ сточныи, аламъ [же]нчужныи, наплечки зол(о)ты с круги с каменьемъ с женчуги, [аламъ малыи] с женчуги, что ми дала кнıагини М(а)рыıа, ковшь великии зол(о)тъ [гладъкии], овкачикъ [золотъ, чашка золота, да]стоканъ ц(а)рьгородскии золотомъ [кованъ, чечакъ] зол(о)тъ с каменьемъ с женчуги, сабла золота, обязь золота.

[А кого ми дасть богъ] зıатью, по чепи имъ по зол(о)тѣ, по поıасу по зол(о)ту.

А что за кнıагинью за [Марьею] Заıачковъ, Заберега с мѣсты, то до ее живота, а по ее животѣ [моеи кнıа]гинѣ.

А волости за кнıагинью за Оулıаною, ис тыхъ волостии [по ее жи]вотѣ дѣти мои, кнıаз(ь) Дмитрии, кнıаз(ь) Иванъ, кнıаз(ь) Володимеръ, да[дуть дчери] ее Сурожикъ, сел(о) Лучиньское.

А из моихъ суд(о)въ и серебреныхъ да[дуть блюдо серебрено] великое с колци к с(вıа)тѣи Б(огороди)ци Володимерь.

А· иными суды сер[ебреными] дѣти мои, кнıаз(ь) Дмитрии, кнıаз(ь) Иванъ, своею м(а)т(е)рью подѣлатса [на трое].

А сел(о) на Рокшь Романовьское кнıаз(ю) Дмитрию.

А сел(о) Афиньевьское [да се]лце оу Павловьского села кнıаз(ю) Ивану.

А сел(о) Павловьское дал есмь [свıатому] Олександру впрокъ, собѣ в памıать.

А что моихъ стадъ кон[евыхъ, и жереп]цевъ, и кобылиць, а то с(ы)ну моему, кнıаз(ю) Дмитрию, и с(ы)ну моему, [кнıазю Ивану], то имъ наполы.

А ис тамги ис коломеньское дал есмь чет[вертую часть] к с(вıа)тѣи Б(огороди)ци на Крутицю, собѣ в памıать. А костки московьскии [далъ есмь] на Москвѣ к с(вıа)тѣи Б(огороди)ци и к с(вıато)му Михаилу, в памıать по своемь отцѣ, [и по сво]еи брат(ь)и, и *по* собѣ, то имъ руга.

А хто буд(е)ть моихъ казначеевъ, и ти[вуновъ], и посельскихъ, или хто будеть моихъ дыıаковъ, что буд(е)ть от [мене вѣдали] прибытокъ ли которыи, или хто будеть оу тыхъ женилса, [тѣ люди не на]добни моимъ дѣтемъ, ни моеи кнıагини, дал есмь имъ [волю. Тако ıа] хто буд(е)ть моихъ люд(и)и полныхъ, купленыхъ, грамотныхъ, дал [есмь имъ свобо]ду, куды имъ любо. А дѣтемъ моимъ не надобны, [ни моеи кнıаги]ни.

А на сю грамоту послус(и): о(те)ць мои, вл(а)д(ы)ка ростово[скии Игнатии], о(т)ци мои д(у)ш(е)вныѣ, игумен Иванъ,¹ попъ Акинфъ, попъ Патрекѣи.

[А хто сю гра]моту порушить, судить ему б(ог)ъ, а моего бл(а)г(о)с(ло)в(е)ньа [не буди] ни в сии вѣкъ, ни в будущии.

---

¹ *Лист с текстом разорван: в этом месте мож тместиться около 9 букв.*
¹ *Слово Иванъ написано сверху.*

А грамоту пис(а)лъ Нестерко.

На лицевой сторонѣ грамоты привѣшена серебряная позолоченная печать в. кн. Ивана Ивановича.

б) *Второй экземпляръ.*

Во има о(т)ца и с(ы)нà и с(вА)т(а)го д(у)ха, се ıазъ, грѣшныи худыи рабъ б(о)жии Иванъ Ивановиⱬ, пишу д(у)ш(е)вную грамоту, ничимъ же не нуженъ, цѣлымъ своимъ оумомъ, во своемъ здоровьѣ. Аже что б(ог)ъ розмыслить о моемъ животѣ, даю рАдъ своим с(ы)номъ, кназ(ю) Дмит-рею и кназю Ивану, и своему брат(а)ничу, кназ(ю) Володимеру, и свои кнАгини.

Приказываю отⱬ(и)ну свою Москву с(ы)номъ своимъ, кназ(ю) Дмитрью и кназ(ю) Ивану. А брат(а)ничу моему, кназ(ю) Володимеру, на Москвѣ в намѣстничтвѣ треть, в тамзѣ, в мытѣхъ, и в пошлинах городских треть, что к городу) · потАгло. И что мед оброчныи Василцева стану, и что о(т)ца моего бортници купленыє под вѣчныѣ варахъ, и кони ста-вити по станомъ и по варАмъ, и конюшии путь, то имъ все на трое. А численыѣ люд(и) вси три кназ(и) блюдуть сопⱡа с одиного.

А се даю с(ы)ну своему, кназ(ю) Дмитрью: Можаескъ с во[лостьми] со всѣми, с тамгою, и с селы, и з бортью, и со всѣми пошлинами, Коломну со [всѣми волость]ми, и с тамгою, и с мыт(о)мъ, и съ селы, и з бортью, и со всѣми пошлинами.

[А что и с тыхъ воло]стии за кнАгинью за М(а)рьею, а тѣ волости до ее живота, а по ее жив[отѣ тѣ волости сыну моему, кназю] Дмитрью: Городна, Мѣзыни, Пѣсоⱬна, Сер(е)докоротна, Похране, Усть[-Мерьска], Брашеваıа, Гвоздна, селце Ивань, деревни Маковець, Лѣвичинъ, Скулневъ, [Кане]въ, Кошира, Гжелà, Горки, Горѣтовка, село в Похраньскомъ оуѣздѣ на Сѣ[вер-сцѣ], сел(о) Малино, сел(о) Холмы, сел(о) Костантиновьское, сел(о) Ѡри-ниньское, сел(о) Ост[ровьское], сел(о) Копотеньское, село Микульское, сел(о) Малаховьское, сел(о) Напрудьское, с[ело Илмовь]ское, сел(о) Новое. А ис тыхъ сел, котораıа буд(у)ть за кнАгинью за М(а)рь(е)ю села, т[ѣ до ее] живота, а по ее животѣ тѣ села с(ы)ну моему, кназ(ю) Дмитрью, Мещерка оу [Коломны].

А се даю с(ы)ну своему, кназ(ю) Ивану: Звенигородъ со всѣми волостми, и с мыт(о)мъ, и с селы, и з бортью, и с оброⱬники, со всѣми пошлинами, Кремичнà, Руза, Фоминьское, Сух(о)долъ, Истерва, Сводъка, свободу Замошьскую, Ростовци, Кремичну, Тростну, Нѣгучу, сел(о) Рюховьское, сел(о) Михалевьское, сел(о) Каменьское, сел(о) на Рѣпнѣ в Боровьсцѣ, селце Милциньское, сел(о) Максимовьское, сел(о) Дѣмон-говьское, сел(о) Андрѣевьское, сел(о) Кариньское, сел(о) Козловьское, сел(о) в ·Замошьскои свободѣ, сел(о) Выславьское, сел(о) Кузминьское.

А брат(а)ничь мои, кназ(ь) Володимеръ, вѣдаеть оуѣздъ о(т)ца своего.

А что сА мнѣ достали мѣста РАзаньскаıа на сеи сторонѣ Оки, ис тых мѣстъ далъ есмь кназ(ю) Володимеру, в Ломастны *[так!]* мѣста, Новыи город(о)къ на оусть Порот[ли], а инаıа мѣста РАзаньскаıа отмѣньнаıа с(ы)ну моему, кназ(ю) Дмитрию, й [кназю] Ивану, подѣлатсА наполы, безъ обиды.

А кнАгини Оулıана, по о(т)ца м[оего, кназа] великого, грамотѣ по д(у)ш(е)внои, вѣдаеть волости, и осмниⱬье, и сел(а) до св[оего живота], а по ее животѣ тѣ волости, и села, и осмниⱬье дѣтемъ моимъ, кназ(ю) Дмитрию, и кназ(ю) Ивану, и кназ(ю) Володимеру, и моеи кнАгинѣ, подѣлатсА на четверо, безъ обиды.

А ци по грѣхомъ, имуть из Орды искати Коломны, или Лопастеньскихъ мѣстъ,[1] или ѿмѣньныхъ мѣстъ Разаньскихъ, а ци по грѣхомъ отоиметса которое мѣсто, дѣти мои, кназ(ь) Дмитрии, и кназ(ь) Иванъ, и кназ(ь) Володимеръ, в то мѣсто, и кнагини подѣлатса безъпеньными мѣсты.

А се дал есмь кнаг(и)ни своеи. Олександрѣ ис Коломеньскихъ волостии: Похране, Пѣсочну, Серед(о)коротну, село Лысцевьское, сел(о) Семциньское на Москвѣ. А Звенигородскихъ волостии дал есмь кнагинѣ же своеи: Оугожь, Великую свободу Юрьеву, сел(о) Клаповьское, сел(о) Бѣлциньское с Но[вы]мъ селцемъ.

А ис тамги ис московьское кнагинѣ моеи оу моего с(ы)на, оу кназ(а) оу Дмитрыа, и оу кназ(а) оу Ивана из дву жеребьевъ треть. А по животѣ мое кнагини тѣ волости, и села, и часть тамги с(ы)номъ моимъ, кназ(ю) Дмитрью и кназ(ю) Ивану, в которого оуѣздѣ, то того и и есть.

А се дал есмь с(ы)ну своему, кназ(ю) Дмитрью: икону с(ва)тыи Олександръ, чепь золот(у) великую врану с кр(е)ст(о)мъ зол(о)тымъ, чепь зол(о)ту колчату, икона зол(о)томъ кована Парамшина дѣла, шапка зол(о)та, бармы, поисъ великии зол(о)тъ с каменьемъ с женчуги, что ма бл(а)г(о)с(ло)вил о(те)ць мои, кназь великии, поис [золотъ с] крюкомъ, облзь зол(о)та, сабла зол(о)та, и серга зол(о)та с женчугомъ, чечакъ зол(о)тъ с каменьемъ с женчуги, 2 овкача зол(о)та, ковшь великии зол(от) гладькии, [коропка золотомъ] кована сердонична, бадыа серебрена с наливкою серебреною.......[2] ца зол(о)та с каменьемъ, опашень скорлатенъ саженъ.

А се дал есмь с(ы)ну своему, [кназю] Ивану: чепь великую зол(о)ту с кр(е)ст(о)мъ, чепь зол(о)ту врану, а другую огнив.....[3] чату с кр(е)сты, икону бл(а)г(о)в(ѣ)щ(е)нье, и сергу с женчугомъ, поисъ зол(о)тъ с каменьемъ с женчуг(и), что ми дал братъ мои, кназ(ь) велик(и) Семенъ, поисъ зол(о)тъ сточныи, аламъ сженчужныи, наплечки зол(о)ты с круги с каменьемъ с женчуги, аламъ малыи с женчуги, что ми дал(а) кнагини М(а)рыа, ковшь великии зол(о)тъ гладькии, овкачикъ зол(о)тъ, чашка зол(о)та, достоканъ ц(а)рьгородскии зол(о)томъ кованъ, чечак зол(о)тъ с каменьемъ с женчуги, сабла зол(о)та, облзь зол(о)та.

А кого ми дасть б(ог)ъ затью, по чепи имъ зол(о)тѣ да по поису по зол(о)ту.

А что за кнагиню за М(а)рьею Замчковъ, Заберегъ с мѣсты, то до ее живота, а по ее живот(ѣ) моеи кнагинѣ.

А что волости за кнагинью за Оулыаною, ис тых волостии по ее животѣ дѣти мои дадуть дч(е)ри ее Сурожикъ, сел(о) Лучиньское.

А из моихъ суд(о)въ серебреныхъ дадуть к с(ва)тѣи Б(огороди)ци Володимерь блюдо великое сереброно с колци.

А иными суды серебреными дѣти мои, кназ(ь) Дмитрии и кназ(ь) Иванъ, своею м(а)т(е)рью подѣлатса на трое.

А сел(о) на Рокшѣ Романовьское кназ(ю) Дмитрью.

А кназ(ю) Ивану сел(о) Афиньевьское да селце оу Павловьского села.

А сел(о) Павловьское дал е(смь) с(ва)т(о)му Олександру впрокъ, собѣ в памать.

А что моихъ стадъ коневых, [и же ре]пцевъ и кобылицъ, а то с(ы)ну моему, кназ(ю) Дмитрью, и кназ(ю) Ивану, то им[ъ наполы].

А ис тамги ис коломеньское четвертую часть дал есмь к с(ва)тѣи

---

[1] *Слово* мѣстъ *написано сверху.*
[2] *Лист с текстом разорван: в этом* месте *может уместиться около 6 букв.*
[3] *Лист с текстом разорван: в этом* месте *может уместиться около 3 букв.*

Б(огороди)ци на Крут[ицю, со]бѣ в памать. А костки московьскии дал
есмь к с(вл)тѣи Б(огороди)ци и к с(вл)т(о)му Михаилу, [в па]мать
по своемь о(т)цѣ, и по своеи брат(ь)и, и по собѣ, то имъ руга.

А хто буд(е)ть моихъ казначѣевъ, или тивуновъ, или посельскихъ,
или хто буд(е)ть моихъ дылковъ, что от мене буд(е)ть вѣдали прибытокъ ли которыи, или оу тых хто буд(е)ть женился, тѣ люд(и) не надобни моимъ дѣтемъ, ни моеи кнагини, дал есмь имъ волю. Так же
хто буд(е)ть моихъ люд(и)и купленых, грамотных, полных, дал есмь имъ
свободу, куды имъ любо. А дѣтемъ моимъ, ни моеи кнагини не надобни.

А на сю грамоту послуси: о(те)ць мои, вл(а)д(ы)ка ростовьскии Игнатии,
о(т)ци мои д(у)ш(е)вныѣ, и[гуменъ И]ванъ, попъ Акинфъ, попъ Патрекѣи.

А хто сю грамоту порушить, суд(и)ть ему б(ог)ъ, а не буд(и) на немь
моего бл(а)г(о)с(ло)в(е)нья ни в сии вѣкъ, ни в будущии.

А грамоту пис(а)лъ Нестерко.

*На лицевой стороне грамоты привешена серебряная позолоченная
печать в. кн. Ивана Ивановича.*

*Основание для датировки: связь духовной с летописным известием 1358 г.
о том, что ордынский посол Мамат-Хожа присылал к московскому князю о «розъезде земли
Рязанскои» (ПСРЛ, т. VIII, стр. 10). См. Черепнин, стр. 27—31.*

*Подлинник — ЦГАДА, Гос. древлехранилище, отд. I, рубр. I, №№ 4—5. Духовная
грамота по двум экземплярам ранее напечатана: Древняя Российская Вивлиофика, ч. 8,
изд. 1, стр. 230—243, №№ 5—6; ч. 1, изд. 2, стр. 64—74, №№ 4—5; Мышкинское изд., т. 5,
ч. 9, стр. 12—19; СГГД, ч. 1, стр. 39—43, №№ 25—26; Карамзин, т. 4, примеч. № 386;
Аристов, стр. 707—710; Бахрушин, стр. 17—18, № 5.*

№ 8.

[Около 1375 г.]. — *Духовная грамота (первая)
великого князя Дмитрия Ивановича.*

.....[16]то......мъ[17] дѣт......[18]скую свободу, Руза, Оу.....[19]дъ, Выше-
городъ, Истерва, Дмитрьева свобода......[20] ми селы, и з бортники, и с
оброчники, и с мыт(ы). А что буд(е) прикупилъ [селъ, или] примыслилъ, или
починковъ, или которая буд(у)ть села о(т)ца моего великомъ кнаженье
купла, или моя села купленая, или брат(а) моего села, кнжи Ивановы,
тѣ села и починки с(ы)ну моему, кназ(ю) Василью, и моеи кнагини,
и моимъ дѣтемъ.

А чимъ мене бл(а)г(о)с(ло)вилъ о(те)ць мои, кназь великии, которымъ
зол(о)томъ, суды или доспѣхъ, или что язъ примыслилъ, то зол(о)то,
и шапку зол(о)тую, [и чепь, и сабли] зол(о)тыѣ, и порты саженыѣ, и суды
зол(о)тыѣ, и серебреныѣ суды, и кони, и жеребьци, и стада своя, дал
есмь своему с(ы)ну, кназ(ю) Василью, и[своеи кнаг]ини, и своим дѣтем.

А что о(те)ць мои, кназ(ь) великии, [сдалъ[1] село Павлов]ское к с(вл)-
тому Олександру, а к с(вл)тѣи Б(огороди)ци на Круцицю [четвертую
часть ис тамги ис ко]ломеньское, а костки московьскыѣ к с(вл)тѣи
Б(огороди)ци на Москвѣ [и к сватому][2] Михаило, а того не подвигнуть.

16 *Значительная часть грамоты утрачена; сохранился конец.*
17 *Лист с текстом разорван: в этом месте может уместиться около 50 букв.*
18 *Лист с текстом разорван: в этом месте может уместиться около 46 букв.*
19 *Лист с текстом разорван: в этом месте может уместиться около 35 букв.*
20 *Лист с текстом разорван: в этом месте может уместиться около 20 букв.*
1 *Лист с текстом разорван: в этом месте может уместиться около 14 букв.*
2 *Лист с текстом разорван: в этом месте может уместиться около 8 букв.*

А что моихъ [казначеевъ, или посельскихъ], и тивуновъ, и дешковъ, хто что от мене вѣдали, [тѣ всѣ сыну моему], кназ(ю) Василью, ни моеи кнагини, ни моимъ дѣтемъ не надоб[ны]. А что мо]ихъ люд(и)и купленыхъ, а тымъ дал есмь [свободу, а] с(ы)нъ мои, [кназь Василии], и моꙗ кн(аги)ни, ни мои дѣти не приимають ихъ.

А сю грамоту пис(а)лъ есмь собѣ д(у)ш(е)вную и ꙗвилъ есмь о(т)цю своему Олексѣю, митрополиту [всеꙗ] Рус(и). И о(те)ць мои Олексѣи, митрополитъ всеꙗ Рус(и), и пе[ча]ть свою при[вѣсилъ] к сеи грамотѣ.

А послус(и) на сю грамоту: Тимофѣи околничии.....[3], Иванъ Родивонович, Иванъ Федорович, Федоръ [Онд]рѣевич.

А грамоту пис(а)лъ дьꙗкъ Нестеръ.

А хто имѣть сю грамоту чимъ рушати, ...[4] д(у)ши.

На лицевой сторонѣ грамоты привѣшены двѣ серебряные позолоченые печати: в. кн. Дмитрия Ивановича и митрополита Алексея.

Основание для датировки: *грамота написана до смерти в 1378 г. митрополита Алексея, вернее всего в связи с походом Дмитрия Ивановича на Тверь в 1375 г. (ПСРЛ, т. VIII, стр. 23; т. XI, стр. 23; т. XVIII, стр. 116). См. Черепнин, стр. 58—59.*

Подлинник — ЦГАДА, Гос. древлехранилище, отд. I, рубр. I, № 6. Духовная грамота ранее напечатана: Древняя Российская Вивлиофика, ч. 8, изд. 1, стр. 259—261, № 9; ч. 1, изд. 2, стр. 86—87, № 9; Мышкинское изд., т. 5, ч. 9, стр. 27—28; СГГД, ч. 1, стр. 51, № 30; Бахрушин, стр. 19, № 6; Фарфоровский, стр. 291—292; Обнорский и Бархударов, стр. 71—72.

№ 12.

[1389 г. апреля 13 — мая 16]. — Духовная грамота (вторая) великого князя Дмитрия Ивановича.

Во имꙗ о(т)ца и с(ы)на и с(вꙗ)т(а)го д(у)ха, се ꙗзъ, грѣшныи худыи рабъ б(ож)ии Дмитрии Ивановичь, пишю грамоту д(у)ш(е)вную цѣлымъ своимъ оумомъ. Даю рꙗдъ с(ы)н(о)мъ своимъ и своеи кнагини.

Приказываю дѣти свои своеи кнагинѣ. А вы, дѣти мои, жывите заодинъ, а м(а)т(е)ри свое слушаите во всемъ.

А приказываю о(т)ч(и)ну свою Москву дѣтемъ своимъ, кнꙗзю Василью, кнꙗзю Юрью, кнꙗзю Аньдрѣю, кнꙗзю Петру. А братъ мои, кнꙗзь Володимеръ, вѣдаеть свою треть, чѣмъ его бл(а)г(о)с(ло)в(и)лъ о(те)ць его, кнꙗзь Аньдрѣи. А с(ы)на своего, кнꙗзꙗ Василью, бл(а)г(о)с(ло)в(л)ꙗю на старишии путь в городѣ и въ станѣх моего оудѣла двою жеребьевъ половина, а тремъ с(ы)н(о)мъ моим половин(а), и в пошлинах в городскихъ половин(а). А тамга из двою моихъ жеребьевъ кнꙗгинѣ моеи половин(а), а с(ы)н(о)мъ моим половин(а). А восьмничее мои два жеребьꙗ кнꙗгинѣ моеи. А на старишии путь с(ы)ну моему, кнꙗзю Василью, Василцево сто и Добратиньскаꙗ борть съ селомъ з Добрятиньскимъ. А бортъници вь станѣх в городскихъ, и конюшии путь, и соколничии, и ловчии, тѣм с(ы)н(о)ве мои подѣлатъс(а) ровно. А численых люд(и)и моих двою жеребьевъ с(ы)н(о)мъ моимъ по частем, а блюдут с одиного.

А се даю с(ы)ну своему, кнꙗзю Василью, Коломну со всѣми волостми, и с тамгою, и с мыты, и з бортью, и съ селы, и со всѣми пошлинами. А волости Коломеньские: Мещерка, Раменка, Пѣсочна, Брашева съ селцем з Гвоздною и съ Иванем, Гжелꙗ, деревни Лѣвичин, Скулневъ,

---

[3] *Лист с текстом разорван: в этом мѣстѣ можеть умѣститься около 8 букв.*
[4] *Лист с текстом разорван: в этом мѣстѣ можеть умѣститься около 8 букв.*

126

Маковець, Каневъ, Кочема, Комаревъ з берегом, Городна, Похране, Оусть-Мерьско. А из Московъских сел даю с(ы)ну своему, князю Василью: Митин починок, Малаховъское, Костантиновъское, Жырошкины деревни, Островъское, Орининьское, Копотеньское, Хвостовъское, у город(а) лугъ Велик(и)и за рѣкою. А изъ Юрьевъских сел даю с(ы)ну своему, князю Василью: своего прикупа Красное село съ Елезаровъским, съ Проватовым, да село Василевъское в Ростовѣ.

А се даю с(ы)ну своему, князю Юрью, Звенигород со всѣми волостми, и с тамгою, и с мыты, и з бортью, и съ селы, и со всѣми пошлинами. А волости Звенигородскиѣ: Скирменово з Бѣлми, Тростна, Нѣгуча, Сурожык, Замошъская слобод(а), Юрьева слобод(а), Руза город(о)къ, Ростовци, Кремична, Фоминьское, Оугожъ, Суходол с-Ыстею, съ Истервою, Вышегород, Плѣснь, Дмитриева слободка. А из Московъских сел даю с(ы)ну своему, князю Юрью: село Михалевъское, да Домантовъское, да лугъ Ходыньскии. А изъ Юрьевъских сел ему: прикупа моего село Кузмыдемъяньское, да Красного села починок за Везкою придал есмь къ Кузмыдемъяньскому, да село Бо(го)род(и)цьское в Ростовѣ.

А се даю с(ы)ну своему, князю Аньдрѣю, Можаескъ со всѣми волостми, и с тамгою, и с мыты, и з бортью, и съ селы, и со всѣми пошлинами, и с отъѣздными волостми. А волости Можаискиѣ: Исмея, Числов, Боянь, Берестовъ, Поротва, Колоча, Тушков, Вышнее, Глиньское, Пневичи съ Загорьем, Болонескъ. А Коржань да Моишин холм придал есмь к Можаиску. А се волости отъѣздныѣ: Верея, Рудь, Гордошевичи, Гремичи, Заберега, Сушов, да село Рѣпиньское, да Ивановъское Васильевич(а) въ Гремичах. А Колуга и Роща с(ы)ну же моему, князю Аньдрѣю. И что вытягал боярин мои Федоръ Аньдрѣевич на обчем рѣтѣ Товъ и Медынь оу смолнан, а то с(ы)ну же моему, князю Аньдрѣю. А из Московъских сел ему: Напрудьское село да Луциньское на Яоузѣ с мелницею, Дѣоуниньское, Хвостовъское в Перемышлѣ, да лугъ Боровъскии, а другии противу Воскр(е)с(е)ныа. А изъ Юрьевъских сел ему Олексиньское село на Пѣкшѣ.

А се даю с(ы)ну своему, князю Петру, Дмитровъ со всѣми волостми, и съ селы, и со всѣми пошлинами, и с тамгою, и с мыты, и з бортью. А се Дмитровъскиѣ волости: Вышегород, Берендѣева слобод(а), Лутосна с отъѣздъцем, Инобашъ. А из Московъских волостии князю Петру: Мушкова гора, Ижво, Раменка, слободка княжа Иванова, Вори, Корзенево, Рогожъ, Загарьѣ, Вохна, Селна, Гуслеца, Шерна городок. А из Московъских сел князю Петру: Новое село, Сулишин погост. А изъ Юрьевъских сел ему прикупа моего село Богородицьское на Богонѣ.

А се даю с(ы)ну своему, князю Ивану: Раменеице з бортники и что к нему потягло, да Звѣрковъское село съ Сохоньским починком, что отошло ото князя от Володимера. А Сохна с(ы)ну же моему, князю Ивану. А в томъ оудѣлѣ воленъ с(ы)нъ мои, кназ(ь) Иванъ, которыи брат до него будет добръ, тому дасть.

А се бл(а)г(о)с(ло)в(л)яю с(ы)на своего, князя Василья, своею о(т)ч(и)ною, вел(и)ким княженьем.

А с(ы)на своего бл(а)г(о)с(ло)в(л)яю, князя Юрья, своего дѣда куплею, Галичем, со всѣми волостми, и съ селы, и со всѣми пошлинами, и с тѣми селы, которыѣ тягли къ Костромѣ, Микульское и Борисовъское.

А с(ы)на своего, князя Аньдрѣя, бл(а)г(о)с(л)ов(л)яю куплею же дѣда своего, Бѣлымозером, со всѣми волостми, и Вольским съ Шаготью, и Милолюбъскии ѣзъ, и съ слободками, что были дѣтии моих.

А с(ы)на своего, князя Петра, бл(а)г(о)с(ло)в(л)яю куплею же своего дѣда, Оуглечим полем, и что к нему потягло, да Тошною и Самою.

А се даю своеи кнѧгинѣ из велик(о)го кнѧженьѧ оу с(ы)на оу своего, оу кнѧзѧ оу Васил(ь)ѧ, ис Переѧславлѧ Юлку, а ис Костромы Иледам с Комелою, а оу кнѧзѧ оу Юрьѧ из Галич(а) Соль, оу кнѧзѧ оу Оньдрѣѧ из Бѣлаозерѧ Вольское съ Шаготью и Милолюбьскии ѣзъ. А из Володимерских селъ кнѧгинѣ моеи Оньдрѣевьское село, а ис Переѧславъских селъ Доброе село, и что к ним потѧгло. А изъ оудѣла с(ы)на своего, кнѧжа Васильева: Каневъ, Пѣсочну, а исъ селъ Малиньское село, Лысцево. А исъ кнѧжа оудѣла изъ Юрьева: Юрьева слобод(а), Суходол с-Ыетею, с-Ыстервою, да село Оньдрѣевъское, да Каменьское. А изо кнѧжа оудѣла из Оньдрѣева: Вереѧ, да Числов, да село Луциньское на Ѧоузѣ с мелницею. А изь кнѧжа оудѣл(а) ис Петрова: Ижво да Сѧма. А что есмъ дал своеи кнѧгинѣ изъ оудѣл(а) с(ы)на своег(о), кнѧжа Васильева и изо кнѧжа изъ Юрьева, изо кнѧжа изъ Оньдрѣева, изо кнѧжа ис Петрова, волости и села, а что б(ог)ъ розмыслит о моеи кнѧгинѣ, и тѣ волости и села во чьемъ оудѣлѣ, то тому и есть.

А се даю своеи кнѧгинѣ: свои примыслъ Скирменовъскую слободку с Шепковым, Смолѧныѣ с Митлевъским починком, и з бортью, с Вышегородскими бортъник(и), Кропивну з бортн[ики] съ Кропивеньским(и)[и съ Исменьскими],[1] и зъ Гордошевъскими, и съ Рудьскими, Желѣскова слободка з бортью, съ-Ывановым селом с Хороброва, Исконьскаѧ слободка, Кузовъскаѧ слободка, и что кнѧгини мое прикупъ, и что к неи потѧнуло, то моеи кнѧгинѣ. А по котораѧ мѣста слободьскиѣ волостели судили тѣ слободы при мнѣ, и кнѧгини мое волостели судѧт по та же мѣста, какъ было при мнѣ. А что кнѧгини мое купла Лохно, то ее и есть. А на Коломнѣ мои примыслъ Самоилецевъ починокъ з деревнѧми, Савельевъскии починокъ, Микульское село, Бабышево, Ослебѧтевъское, а то кнѧгини моеи. А что ее село Рѣпеньское и прикупъ, то ее и есть. А из Московъских селъ даю своеи кнѧгинѣ: Семциньское село с Ходыньскою мелницею, да Остафьевъское село, да Илмовъское. А изъ Юрьевъских селъ даю еи: куплю свою Петровъское село, да Фроловъское, да Елохъ. А Холхол и Заѧчков, то моеи кнѧгинѣ. А что ми дала кнѧгини Федосьѧ Суду на Бѣлѣозерѣ, да Колашну, и Слободку, и что бл(а)г(о)с(ло)вила кнѧгиню мою Городком да Волочком, та мѣста вѣдает кнѧги[нѧ] Федосьѧ до своего жывота, а по ее жывотѣ то кнѧгинѣ моеи. А тѣми своими примыслы всѣми бл(а)г(о)с(ло)влѧю кнѧгиню свою, а в тѣхъ примыслѣхъ волна моѧ кнѧгини, с(ы)ну ли которому дастъ, по д(у)ши ли дастъ. А дѣти мои в то не въступаютс(ѧ).

А которыѣ деревни отоималъ был кнѧз(ь) Володимеръ от Лыткиньского села кнѧгини мое к Берендѣевѣ слобод(ѣ), а тѣ деревни потѧнутъ къ Лытькиньскому селу мое кнѧгини.

А по грѣхом, которого с(ы)на моего б(ог)ъ отъимет, и кнѧгини моѧ подѣлит того оудѣлом с(ы)н(о)въ моих. Которому что дастъ, то тому и есть, а дѣти мои в то не воли не вымутс(ѧ).

А дастъ ми б(ог)ъ с(ы)на, и кнѧгини моѧ подѣлит его, возмѧ по части у болшиѣ его братьи.

А оу которого с(ы)на моего оубудет о(т)ч(и)ны, чѣмъ есмъ его бл(а)г(о)с(ло)вилъ, и кнѧгини моѧ подѣлит с(ы)н(о)въ моихъ изъ их оудѣлов. А вы, дѣти мои, м(а)т(е)ри слушаите.

А по грѣхом, отъимет б(ог)ъ с(ы)на моего, кнѧзѧ Васильѧ, а хто будет подъ тѣм с(ы)нъ мои, ино тому с(ы)ну моему кнѧж Васильевъ оудѣл, а того оудѣлом подѣлит их моѧ кнѧгини. А вы, дѣти мои, слушѧите своее м(а)т(е)ри, что кому дастъ, то тому и есть.

---

1 *Текст стерт: в этом месте может уместиться около 15 букв.*

128

А коли дѣте*м* мои*м* вза*ти* да*н*(ь) на свои о(т)ч(и)нѣ, чѣ*мъ* ес*мъ* и*х*
бл(а)г(о)с(ло)ви*лъ*, и с(ы)*нъ* мои, кна*з*(ь) Василеи, возме*т* съ своего оудѣла
с Коломны и со всѣ*х* Коломеньски*х* волостии триста ру*б.* и соро*к*
и два ру*б.*, и кнагини мо*ıа* даст ему в то серебро с Пѣсочны
50 ру*б.* без 3-*хъ*, а с Канева дватца*т*(ь) ру*б.* и два ру*б.* А кна*з*(ь)
Юрьи возме*т* съ Звенигоро*д*(а) и со всѣ*х* съ Звенигородски*х* волостии
двѣстѣ ру*б.* и семъдес(а)*т*ь ру*б.* и два ру*б.*, и кнагини мо*ıа* даст
ему в то серебро съ Юрьевы слободы ша*т*(ь)дес(а)*т*ь ру*б.*, а съ
Суходола по*л*пата*де*с(а)*т*ь ру*б.*, *г* съ Смоланы*х* 9 ру*б.*, а съ Скирме-
новьски*ѣ* слободки 9 ру*б.* А кна*з*(ь) Оньдрѣи возме*т* с Можаиска
и со всѣ*х* волостии Можаиски*х* сто ру*б.* и семъдес(а)*т*ь ру*б.* бес тре*х*,
а с отъѣздны*х* мѣ*с*тъ семъдес(а)*т*ь ру*б.* без дву, и кнагини мо*ıа*
даст ему в то серебро дватца*т*(ь) ру*б.* и *п*о*л*трет*ьıа* ру*б.* с Вереи,
а с Числова *п*о*л*осма ру*б.*, а съ Зам*ı*чкова дватца*т*(ь) ру*б.* и два, съ
Холѣхла дес(а)*т*ь ру*б.*, съ Желѣсковы 9 ру*б.*, съ Исконьские слободки
*п*о*л*сема ру*б.*, съ Кропивны *п*о*л*сема ру*б.* А кна*з*(ь) Пе*т*ръ возме*т* съ
своего оудѣла сто ру*б.* и одинна*т*ца*т*(ь), и кнагини мо*ıа* даст ему
в то серебро съ Ижва три*т*ца*т*(ь) ру*б.* А кна*з*(ь) Ива*н* даст кна*з*ю
Василью съ Сохны *п*а*т*(ь) ру*б.*, а съ Раменеица даст кна*з*ю Пе*т*ру
*п*а*т*(ь) ру*б.* А то возму*т* в тысачю ру*б.*, а буде*т* боле или менши,
ино по тому розочту.

А перемѣни*т* б(ог)ъ Орду, дѣти мои не иму*т* давати выхода в Орду,
и которыи с(ы)*нъ* мои возме*т* да*н*(ь) на свое*м* оудѣлѣ, то тому и ес*т*.
А что ес*мъ* подава*л* свои кнагинѣ волости и села изъ оудѣловъ
дѣтии свои*х*, и свои примыс*лъ*, и слободы, и села, и Холхо*л*, и За*ıа*чко*в*,
а с тѣ*х* волостии, и съ слобо*д*, и съ се*л* что возме*т* кнагини мо*ıа*, то еи
и ес*т*. А дѣти мои в то не въступаю*т*ъс(*ı*).

А ис тѣ*хъ* волостии, и слобо*д*, и се*л*, что ес*мъ* выма*л* оу дѣтии
свои*х* изъ оудѣло*в*, а подава*л* кнагинѣ своеи, а кому буде*т* жалоба
сирота*мъ* на волостели, и тѣ*мъ* люде*м* оучини*т* исправу кнагини мо*ıа*.
А дѣти мои в то не въступаю*т*ъс(*ı*).

А что ес*мъ* да*л* с(ы)ну своему, кна*з*ю Аньдрѣю, Заберегу, за то дѣти
мои вси д*ı*ю*т* обро*к* с(*ва*)*т*(о)му Сп(а)су па*т*ьна*т*ца*т*(ь) ру*б.* на го*д*
на сп(а)с(о)въ д(е)*н*ь.

А се бл(а)г(о)с(ло)в(л)аю дѣтии свои*х*. С(ы)ну моему старишему, кна*з*ю
Василью: икона Парамшина дѣла, чепь золо*т*(а), что ми дала кнагини
Василиса, по*ıа*съ золот велик(и) с каменье*м* без ремени, по*ıа*съ золот
съ ремене*м* Мака*р*ова дѣла, бармы, шапка золо*т*(а).

А с(ы)ну моему, кна*з*ю Юрью: по*ıа*съ золот новыи с каменье*м* съ жом-
чюгом без ремени, по*ıа*съ золот Шышкина дѣла, вотола сажена.

А с(ы)ну моему, кна*з*ю Оньдрѣю: снас*т*ь золота, по*ıа*съ золот старыи
новгородскии.

А с(ы)ну моему, кна*з*ю Пе*т*ру: по*ıа*съ золот с каменье*м* пѣгии, по*ıа*съ
золот с калитою да с тузлуки, да наплечки, да ала*м*ъ.

А с(ы)ну моему, кна*з*ю Ивану: по*ıа*съ золот татаоуръ, да два ковша
золоты по двѣ гривенки.

А что с*ı* остане*т* золото, или серебро, или иное что но ес*т*ь, то все
моеи кнагинѣ.

А что с*ı* останет ста*д* мои*х*, тѣ*мъ* мо*ıа* кнагини подѣли*т*ъс(*ı*) с моими
дѣтми по часте*м*.

А хто буде*т* мои*х* казначѣе*въ*, или хто буде*т* мои*х* дь*ıа*ков прибыто*к*
мои от мене вѣда*л*, или посельски*х*, или тиоуно*въ*, или хто женил*ı*с(*ı*)
оу тѣ*х*, тѣ всѣ не надобѣ моеи кнагинѣ и мои*м* дѣте*м*.

А приказа*л* ес*мъ* свои дѣти своеи кнагинѣ. А вы, дѣти мои, слу-

шаите свое м(а)т(е)ри во все*м*, изъ ее воли не выступаите*сѧ* ни в че*м*. А которыи с(ы)нъ мои не име*т* слушати свое м(а)т(е)ри, а буде*т* не въ ее воли,
на то*м* не буде*т* моего бл(а)г(о)с(ло)в(е)нья.

А дѣти мои молодшаѧ, братьѧ кнѧжы Васильевы, чтите и слушаите
своего брата старишего, кнѧза Василья, в мое мѣсто, своего о(т)ца.
А с(ы)нъ мои, кнѧз(ь) Василии, держытъ своего брата, кнѧзѧ Юрьѧ, и свою
братью молодшюю въ братьствѣ, безъ обиды.

А хто моих бо**ѧ**ръ име*т* служыти моеи кнѧгинѣ, тѣхъ бо**ѧ**ръ, дѣти
мои, блюдите с одиного.

А хто сю грамоту мою порушит, суди*т* ему б(ог)ъ, а не буде*т*
на не*м* м(и)л(о)сти б(ож)ии, ни моего бл(а)г(о)с(лове)нья ни в сии вѣ*к*,
ни в будущии.

А писа*л* есмь сю грамоту пере*д* своими о(т)ци: пере*д* игуме[номъ] пере*д*
Сергиемъ, пере*д* игуменом пере*д* Савастьѧно*м*.

А туто были бо**ѧ**ре наши: Дмитрии Михаилович, Тимофѣи Василье-
вич, Ива*н* Родивонович, Семе*н* Васильевич, Ива*н* Федорович, Олександръ
Аньдрѣевич, Федоръ Аньдрѣевич, Федоръ Аньдрѣевич, Ива*н* Федорович,
Ива*н* Аньдрѣевич.

А писа*л* Внукъ.

*На лицевой сторонѣ грамоты привѣшена серебряная позолоченная
печать в. кн. Дмитрия Ивановича.*

*Основание для датировки: духовная грамота написана после 13 апреля
1389 г., когда уехал из Москвы митрополит Пимен, и до 16 мая 1389 г., когда у Дмитрия
Ивановича родился сын Константин (ПСРЛ, т. VIII, стр. 32). См. Черепнин, стр. 59—62.
Подлинник (на пергамене) — ЦГАДА, Гос. древлехранилище, отд. I, рубр. I, № 4.
Список первой половины XV в. — ЦГАДА, Гос. древлехранилище, отд. I, рубр. I, № 8.
Духовная грамота ранее напечатана: Древняя Российская Вивлиофика, ч. 8, изд. 1,
стр. 290—297, № 14; ч. 1, изд. 2, стр. 100—109, № 13; Мышкинское изд., т. 5, ч. 9,
стр. 37—42; СГГД, ч. 1, стр. 58—62, № 34; Ростиславич-Сагельев, стр. 142—150;
Пенинский, стр. 118—120; Смирнов, стр. 67—68; Фарфоровский, стр. 284—289;
Бахрушин, стр. 19—23, № 7.*

№ 20.

*[1406 г. сентября 16—1407 г. июня 7]. — Духовная грамота
(первая) великого князя Василия Дмитриевича.*

Во имѧ отца и с(ы)на и с(вѧ)т(а)го *[так в рукописи!]*, се ѧзъ, грѣш-   л. 1
ныи худыи рабъ божии Василеи, пишу грамоту д(у)шевную въ своемъ
смыслѣ, добръ, здоровъ. Даю рѧдъ своему с(ы)ну, кнѧзю Ивану, и своеи
кнѧгинѣ.

Бла(го)словлѧю с(ы)на своего, кнѧза Ивана, своею отчиною, трет(ь)ю
Москвы, своимъ жеребьемъ, и с пошлинами, и с путми, и з бортью,
и с Василцевым стом, и Добратинскимъ селомъ, и з бортью, и численых
людеи трет(ь), чѣм мѧ в Москвѣ бла(го)словил от(е)ць мои, как писано
в д(у)шевнои грамотѣ отца моего, великого кнѧза, да Коломною съ всѣми
волостми, и съ селы, и с бортью, и с путми, и со всѣми пошлинами.
А волости Коломенские: Похрѧне, Городна, Кочема, Каневъ, Маковець,
Лѣвичинъ, Пѣсочна, деревни Скулневъ, Брашева с-Ыванемъ и съ Гвоздною и съ селцем, Оусть-Мерска, Комаревъ, да Радоки*н* с берегом, Раменъка,
Мещерка, Крутинки, Мѣзынѧ, Гжела.

А кнѧгинѣ своеи даю ис Коломенских волостеи Брашеву да Оусть-

Мерску. А отведетъ богъ м(а)т(е)рь мою, ино по матери моие животѣ Пѣсочна моеи же кнагинѣ. А исъ селъ еи, матери моие, Малино со всѣми деревнами. А ис Коломеньскихъ же из моихъ селъ моеи кнагинѣ Оглоблино и со всѣми деревнами, и с Ольхомъ, да Колычевское и съ Змеевскимъ, да Ивановское Васил(ь)евича в Лѣвичинѣ, и с Чюхистова землею, и со всѣми прикупы, да Гжела со всѣми деревна *[так в рукописи!]*, што к неи потагло. А што села кнагининские пошлые, то ее и есть, а вѣдаетъ тѣ села пошлые кнагининские дотоле кнагини моа, доколѣ, дастъ богъ, женится с(ы)нъ мои, а потомъ ина дастъ тѣ села с(ы)на моего кнагинѣ, своеи сносѣ, которые были издавна за кнаг(и)нам(и).

А из Московскихъ селъ с(ы)ну моему, кназю Ивану: село Стровское, и с Оринискимъ, и съ Григорьевскимъ Фаоустова, и с Костантиновскимъ, и съ Жирошкинымъ, и со всѣми деревнами, и съ Малаховскимъ, да лугъ Великии противу города за рѣкою.

А кнагинѣ мои из Московскихъ селъ: село мое Починок со всѣми деревнами, да селце Хвостовское оу города и с луги, што к нему потагло.

А што мои примыслъ, а то даю кнагинѣ же своеи: Оухтюшку, куплю свою, да Фоминские села дьаконовы, да Федоровские села Свибловские на Оустюзѣ, и в Отводномъ, и на Самѣ, и в Ростовѣ, и в Бѣжицскомъ Версѣ, Максимовское съ деревнами, и в Переаславлѣ Весьское, и с Родивоновским, и со всѣми деревнами, и на Москвѣ село Буиловское и с Олексѣевьскою деревнею, да село Тимофѣевское на Маоузѣ, и в Юрьевѣ Чагино, да Савельевское, да Иворово, да Карабузино, а в Новѣгородѣ Непеицино, и всѣ села Федоровские Свибловьские, со всѣмъ, што к нимъ потагло, да што есмъ вымѣнил оу свои матери села въ Юрьевѣ, Фроловское и с Ольхомъ, да Петровское, да Б(о)г(о)р(о)д(и)цское, да Олексинское, и што к нимъ потагло, а в Новѣгородѣ в Нижнемъ Алачинские села да Мангачь.

А ис тѣхъ волостеи и съ селъ, што есмъ писал кнагинѣ своеи, хто са имет жаловати на волостелеи, или на тиоуновъ, или на посельскихъ, или на доводщиковъ, то судит кнагини моа, или кому прикажетъ, а с(ы)ну моему, кназю, в тѣ суды не вступатиса. А перемѣнит богъ татаръ, и кнагини моа емлетъ с тѣхъ волостеи и съ селъ дань себѣ, а с(ы)ну моему, кназ(ю) Ивану, так же в ту дань не вступатис(а). А коли придет дань или ѣмъ, и кнагини моа дастъ с тѣхъ волостеи и съ селъ по розочту, што са имет. А тѣ волости и се || ла кнагинѣ моеи до ее живота, а по ее животѣ, ино тѣ волости и села с(ы)ну моему, кназю Ивану. А што ее примыслъ, в томъ волна, по д(у)шѣ ли дастъ, с(ы)ну ли дастъ.

л. 2

Да к тому еи даю в опришнину два села въ Юрьевѣ, Б(о)г(о)род(и)цское да Олексинское, в тѣхъ дву селѣхъ так же волна, по д(у)шѣ ли дастъ, с(ы)ну ли дастъ.

А дастъ богъ с(ы)ну моему, кназю Ивану, кнажен(ь)е великое держати, ино кнагинѣ моеи ис Переаславла Кинела. А отведетъ богъ м(а)т(е)рь мою, ино Юлька кнагинѣ же моеи, да Доброе село, да въ Володимерѣ Ондрѣевское село. А ис Костромы еи волость Нерехта. А отведетъ богъ матерь мою, ино Иледамъ да Комела кнагинѣ моеи, а Нерехта с(ы)ну моему, кназю Ивану.

А дастъ богъ с(ы)ну моему, кназю Ивану, держати Новъгородъ Нижнии да Муромъ, ино кнагинѣ моеи из Новагорода половина пошлин новгородскихъ, да Курмышь со всѣм(и) селы, и з бортью, и с путми, и с пошлинами, и со всѣмъ, што к нему потагло, и с Алгашемъ, а из Мурома еи селце.

А с(ы)на своего, кназа Ивана, бла(го)словлаю иконою Парамшина дѣла, с чепью, чепь с каменьемъ, што ми бла(го)с(ло)вил от(е)ць мои, кназ(ь) великии. Да даю ему поѩсъ золот с каменьемъ, што мѧ бла(го)словил от(е)ць же мои, кнѧзь великии, да другии поѩсъ золотъ с каменьемъ же, што есмъ самъ сковал, да шапка золота, да бармы. А исъ судовъ ему коропка сердонична, да ковшь золотъ с лалом да съ женчюги. А опроче того, што есть казны мои и всего моего живота, то все вѣдаетъ моѩ кнѧгини, половину дастъ по д(у)шѣ по моеи, а друга половина еи.

А брата своего и с(ы)на бла(го)словлаю, кнѧза Костантина, даю ему въ оудѣл Тошню да Оустюжну, по д(у)ш(е)внои грамотѣ отца нашего, великого кнѧза.

А хто моихъ казначѣевъ, или тивуновъ, или дьѩки прибыток мои вѣдали, или посельскии, или ключники, или хто хо[ло]повъ моихъ купленыхъ, или што есмъ оу Федора оу Свибла отоимал, тѣхъ всѣх пущаю на слободу и с женами и с дѣтми, не надобны моему с(ы)ну и мои кнѧгинѣ. А кнѧгинѣ мои тѣ люди, што есмъ еи подавал при своемъ животѣ, и грамоты полные тѣх людеи оу нее.

А ты, с(ы)нъ мои, кназ(ь) Иван, держи мат(е)рь свою во чти и в матерствѣ, как богъ реклъ, а мое бла(го)словлен(ь)е на тоб(ѣ).

А о своемъ с(ы)нѣ и о свои кнѧгинѣ покладаю на бозѣ и на своемъ дадѣ, на кнази на Володимерѣ Ондрѣевич(ѣ), и на свои брат(ь)и, на кнази на Ондрѣ Дмитреевич(ѣ) и на кнази на Петрѣ Дмитреевич(ѣ), по докончанью, как сѧ имутъ печалова *[так!]*.

А оу сее грамоты были мои боѩре: кназ(ь) Юрьи Ивановичь, Костантинъ Дмитреевичь, Дмитреи Афинѣевичь, Иванъ Дмитреевичь, Во[ло]диме[ръ]...[1] Иванъ Федоровичь, Федоръ Федоровичь...

А сю грамоту писалъ....[2]

На лицевой стороне грамоты привешена серебряная позолоченая печать в. кн. Василия Дмитриевича.

Основание для датировки: грамота написана после смерти 16 сентября 1406 г. митрополита Киприана (ПСРЛ, т. II, стр. 352; т. III, стр. 103; т. IV, стр. 109; т. VI, стр. 133) и до смерти матери великого князя Василия Дмитриевича Евдокии (ПСРЛ, т. I, стр. 234; т. V, стр. 256; т. VI, стр. 134; т. VIII, стр. 81). См. Черепнин, стр. 86—89.

Подлинник — ЦГАДА, Гос. древлехранилище, отд. I, рубр. I, № 9. Духовная грамота ранее напечатана: Древняя Российская Вивлиофика, ч. 8, изд. 1, стр. 316—321, № 18; ч. 1, изд. 2, стр. 129—134, № 18; Мышкинское изд., т. 5, ч. 9, стр. 56—59; СГГД, ч. 1, стр. 72—74, № 39; Бахрушин, стр. 23—25, № 8; Фарфоровский, стр. 292—294.

№ 21.

[Около 1417 г. июля]. — Духовная грамота (вторая) великого князя Василия Дмитриевича.

Во имѧ отца и с(ы)на и свѧтаго духа, по бла(го)словленью отца нашего л. 1 Фотиѧ, митрополита киевскаго и всиѧ Руси, се ѩзъ, грѣшныи худыи рабъ божии Василеи, при своемъ здоровьѣ, пишю грамоту душевную. Даю рѧдъ своему сыну, кнѧзю Василью, и свои кнѧгинѣ.

Приказываю своего с(ы)на, кнѧза Василыѧ, свои кнѧгинѣ. А ты, с(ы)нъ

---

[1] *Лист с текстом разорван: в этом месте может уместиться около 7 букв.*
[2] *Лист с текстом разорван: в этом месте может уместиться около 8 букв.*

мои, кнѧзь Василеи, чти матерь свою и слушаи своие матери в мое мѣсто, своего отца.

А бла(го)словлѧю своего с(ы)на, кнѧзѧ Василыа, своею вотчиною, чѣмъ мѧ бла(го)словилъ от(е)ць мои, третью Москвы и с путми, своими жеребьи, и Добратинскимъ селомъ и с бортью, и Василцевымъ стомъ, и третью численыхъ людеи, и Коломною с волостьми и с путьми. А съ селъ даю с(ы)ну своему, кнѧзю Василью: на Москвѣ село Островьское, и с Оринин-скимъ, и с Костантиновскимъ, да село Малаховское, да Жирошкины деревни со всѣмъ, што к тѣмъ селомъ потѧгло, да Копотенское село, да селце оу города оу Москвы над Великимъ прудомъ, да Хвостовское селце, да лугъ Великии оу города оу Москвы за рѣкою, да Ходынскую мелницю, да дворъ в городѣ на Москвѣ Фоминскии Ивановичь(а) оу Боро-вицьскихъ воротъ, да другии дворъ, што был за Михаилом за Важемъ, да новои дворъ за городомъ оу Сватого Володимера. Да даю с(ы)ну своему, кнѧзю Васил(ь)ю, свои примыслъ въ Юрьевѣ, село Петровское, Олексинское.

А кнѧгинѣ своеи даю волости Коломенскиѣ: Пѣсочну да Брашеву и съ селцемъ и съ Гвоздною, и с-Ыванемъ, да Оусть-Мерску, да Гжелю, и с путьми, и съ селы съ своими, што в тѣхъ волостехъ ни есть. А ис Коломенскихъ селъ даю кнѧгинѣ своеи: села Малинские, што были за моею матерью, да село Ивановское и с Чюхистовымъ, да Окуловское, да Захаров-ское со всѣмъ, што к нимъ потѧгло, да село Рѣпенское, што еи дала мати моѧ. А што ее прикупъ и примыслъ, а то ее и есть. А кнѧгинѣ же своеи даю прадѣда своего примыслъ в Бѣжицьскомъ Версѣ Кистьму да села Онто-новьские, да в Ростовѣ Василевское, да свои примыслъ Троецскую сло-бодку на Волъзѣ, да Белеоутовские села на Волоцѣ и въ Юрьевѣ слободѣ, да треть тамги московские и всѣхъ пошлин в городѣ на Москвѣ, свои жеребеи. А исъ селъ из Московскихъ даю своеи кнѧгинѣ: Митинъ почи-нокъ со всѣмъ, што к нему потѧгло, да Семцинское село и съ Самсоно-вымъ лугомъ, со всѣмъ, какъ было за моею матерью, да сельце Федо-ровьское Свиблово на Ѩоузѣ и с мелницею, да Крилатьское село, што было за татаромъ, а кнѧгини моѧ дастъ с того села черницѣ Софьѣ пѧт(ь)десѧт рублевъ долгу ее. А што покупила на Москвѣ и што ее при-мыслъ, то ее и есть. А кнѧгинѣ же своеи даю отца своего примыслъ, слобод-ку на Гуси, да въ Юрьевѣ Красное село, и с Праватовъмъ, и сь Елезаров-скимъ, да свои примыслъ въ Юрьевѣ же, село Фроловское, да Елохъ, да село Богородицьское. А што ее прикупъ и примыслъ, а то ее и есть. Да свои же примыслъ даю еи на Бѣлѣозерѣ слободка, што была кнѧжа Васил(ь)ева Семеновичь(а), да на Вологдѣ Оухтюшка, да Брюховскаѧ слободка, да Федоровские села Свибловы, да свои примыслъ и прикупъ на Вологдѣ и на Тошнѣ. А што ее прикупъ и примыслъ, а то ее и есть. Да на Оустюзѣ даю еи Федоровские деревни Свибловы, да Ивановские Голо-вина, да Тутолминские, што прикупил мои поселскии Григореи Горби-шевъ, што мои примыслъ.

А с(ы)на своего, кнѧза Василыа, бла(го)словлѧю своею вотчиною, великимъ кнѧженьемъ, чѣмъ мѧ бла(го)словилъ мои от(е)ць.

А кнѧгинѣ моеи ис Костромы Иледамъ, и с Обнорою, и с Комелою, и с Волочкомъ, да Нерехта, и с варницами, и с бортники, и с бобров-ники, и со Кнѧгининьскимъ селомъ. А ис Переѩславла кнѧгинѣ же моеи Юлъка так же со всѣми людми, которого пути в неи люди ни будутъ, да Доброе село. А из Володимерѧ Ондрѣевское село. А Тошну оже вы-мѣнитъ с(ы)нъ мои, кнѧзь Василеи, оу кнѧжихъ дѣтеи оу Володимеровыхъ, по докончалнои нашеи грамотѣ съ ихъ отцемъ, ино Тошна кнѧгинѣ же моеи.

А оже ми дастъ богъ Новъгородъ Нижнии, и изъ и Новымъгородомъ Нижнимъ благ(о)словлаю с(ы)на своего, кназа Василья, со всѣмъ. А с(ы)на же своего, кназа Василья, благ(о)словлаю своимъ же примысломъ Муромомъ со всѣмъ, што к нему потагло.

А из Новагорода ‖ кнагинѣ моеи половина пошлин моихъ всѣхъ. А што л. 2 есмъ еи подавалъ села в Новѣгородѣ, или што ее примыслъ, а то ее и есть. Да Соколское село со всѣмъ еи же, да Кѣржанець со всѣмъ кнагинѣ же моеи. А из Мурома кнагинѣ же моеи Селце да Шатуръ.

А тѣ волости, и села, што есмь подавалъ своеи кнагинѣ, пославъ с(ы)нъ мои да моя кнагини, опишютъ да положатъ на них дан(ь) по людем, по силѣ, и кнагини моя дастъ с тѣхъ волостеи и съ селъ дань по розочту и ямъ, што са коли имъ иметъ. А перемѣнитъ богъ Орду, и кнагини моя емлетъ себѣ ту дань, а с(ы)ну моему, кназю Василью, не вступатиса. А волостели свои, и тиоуни, и доводщики судить кнагини моя сама. А с(ы)ну моему, кназю Василью, въ ее волости и в села не всылати ни по што. А тѣ волости и села кнагинѣ моеи до ее живота, а по ее животѣ ино с(ы)ну моему, кназю Василью, опроче Гжели, да Семциньского села, да ее прикупа. А во Гжелѣ, да в Семцинскомъ селѣ, да в своемъ примыслѣ вольна кнагини моя, кому хочетъ дати, тому дастъ. А [хто] иметъ служити оу мое кнагини бояръ, и с(ы)нъ мои, кназь Василеи, тѣхъ бояръ блюдеть.

А благ(о)словлаю с(ы)на своего, кназа Василья, страстьми болшими, да кр(е)стъ честныи животворящии патреяршь Филофѣевскии. А с(ы)на же своего бла(го)словлаю, даю ему икону Парамшина дѣла, да чепь хрестьчатую, што ма бла(го)словил от(е)ць мои, да шапку золотую, да бармы, да поясъ золотъ с каменьемъ, што ми далъ от(е)ць мои, да другии поясъ мои на чепехъ с каменьемъ, да третии поясъ ему же на синемъ ремени. А ис судовъ даю с(ы)ну моему, кназю Васил(ь)ю, коропку сердоничную, да ковшь золотъ княжь Семеновскии, да судно окованое золотомъ, што ми дала мати моя, да каменъное судно болшее, што ми от великого кназа от Витовта привезлъ кназь Семенъ, да кубокъ хрусталнои, што ми король прислалъ.

А стада кобыльи моеи кнагинѣ с моимъ с(ы)номъ наполы.

А опроче того, што ни есть оу мене, то все моеи кнагинѣ.

А холопи, которые есмь подавал своеи кнагинѣ при своемъ животѣ, тѣ еи и есть. Да дастъ моя кнагини моимъ дчеремъ из моихъ холоповъ по пати семеи, а опроче того вси холопи мои на слободу и съ женами и с дѣтми.

А приказываю своего с(ы)на, кназа Василья, и свою кнагиню, и свои дѣти своему брату и тистю, великому кназю Витовту, как ми реклъ, на бозѣ да на немъ, как са иметъ печаловати, и своеи братьѣ молодшеи, кназю Ондрѣю Дмитреевич(ю), и кназю Петру Дмитреевич(ю), и кназю Костантину Дмитреевич(ю), и кназю Семену Володимерович(ю), и кназю Яраславу Володимерович(ю), и ихъ братьѣ по ихъ докончанью, как ми рекли.

А оу сее грамоты были мои бояре: кназь Юрьи Патрекѣевич, Иванъ Дмитреевич, Михаило Ондрѣевич, Иванъ Федорович, Федоръ Иванович.

А грамоту писал мои дыякъ Тимофѣи Ачкасовъ.

А кто сю мою грамоту порушит, судит ему б(ог)ъ, а не буди на немъ моего бл(а)г(о)с(лове)нья в сии вѣкъ, ни в будущии.

Внизу подпись (на греческом языке) митрополита Фотия.

На лицевой стороне грамоты были привешены пять печатей, из которых сохранились три черновосковые печати: кн. Андрея Дмитриевича, кн. Петра Дмитриевича и кн. Константина Дмитриевича.

Основание для датировки: грамота, повидимому, написана в связи со смертью старшго сына Василия Дмитриевича — Ивана (ПСРЛ, т. VIII, стр. 88). См. Черепнин, стр. 88—90.

Подлинник —ЦГАДА, Гос. древлехранилище, отд. I, рубр. I, № 13. Список второй половины XV в. — там же, отд. I, рубр. I, № 14. Духовная грамота ранее напечатана: Древняя Российская Вивлиофика, ч. 8, изд. 1, стр. 339—345, № 20; ч. 1, изд. 2, стр. 147—152, № 20; Мышкинское изд., т. 5, ч. 9, стр. 68—71; СГГД, ч. 1, стр. 80—82, № 41; Карамзин, т. 5, примеч. №№ 226—227.

№ 22.

1423 г. марта. — Духовная грамота (третья) великого князя Василия Дмитриевича.

л. 1   Во имѧ отца и с(ы)на и сватаго д(у)ха, по бла(го)словленью отца нашего Фотѣа, митрополита киевского и всиа Руси, се аз, грѣшныи худыи раб божеи Василеи, при своемъ здоровьѣ, пишу грамоту душевную. Даю рѧд своему с(ы)ну, кнꙗзю Василью, и своеи кнꙗгинѣ.

Приказываю своего с(ы)на, кнꙗꙗ Васильꙗ, своеи кнꙗ кнꙗгинѣ *[так в рукописи!]*. А ты, сынъ мои, кнꙗзь Василеи, чти матерь и слушаи свое матери в мое мѣсто, своего отца.

А бла(го)словлꙗю своего с(ы)на, кнꙗзꙗ Василꙗ, своею вотчиною, чѣмъ мꙗ бла(го)словил от(е)ць мои, третью Москвы, и с путми, с моими жеребьи, и Добрꙗтиньским селом з бортью, и Василцевым стомъ, и третью численых людеи, и Коломною с волостми и с путми. А из сел даю с(ы)ну своему, кнꙗзю Василью: на Москвѣ село Островьское с Орининьским и с Костантиновьским, дꙗ село Малаховское, да Жирошкины деревни со всѣм, что к тѣм селом потагло, да село Копотенское, да селце оу города оу Москвы над Великим прудом, да Хвостовьское селце, да лугъ Великии за рѣкою оу города оу Москвы, да Ходынскую мелницю, да двор в городѣ Фоминьскои Ивановича оу Боровицских ворот, а другии двор, что был за Михаилом за Важемъ, да за городом новои двор оу Сватого Володимера. Да даю с(ы)ну своему, кнꙗзю Василью, свои примыслъ въ Юрьевѣ, село Петровское да Олексинское.

А кнꙗгинѣ своеи даю волости Коломеньские: Пѣсочну, да Брашеву, з селцем з Гвоздною и с-Ываном, да Оусть-Мерску, да Гжелю, и с путми и з селы з своими, что в тѣх волостех ни есть. А ис Коломеньских селъ даю своеи кнꙗгинѣ села Малиньские, что были за моею матерью, да село Ивановское с Чюхистовым, да Окуловское, да Захаровское, со всѣм, что к ним потагло, да село Рѣпинское, что еи дала мати моꙗ. А что ее прикупъ и примыслъ, а то ее и есть. А кнꙗгинѣ же своеи даю дѣда своего примыслъ в Бѣжицском Версѣ Кистму, да села Онтоновские, да Василевское в Ростовѣ, да свои примыслъ Троецскую слободку на Волзѣ, да Белевутовские села на Волоцѣ и въ Юрьевѣ слободѣ, да треть тамги московские и всѣх пошлин в городѣ на Москвѣ, свои жеребьи. А из сел из Мосъковьскихъ даю своеи кнꙗгинѣ: Митин починок со всѣм, что к нему потагло, да Семцинасое село и з Самсоновым лугом и со всѣм, как было за моею матерью, да селце Федоровское Свиблово на Ꙗоузѣ, и с мелницею, да Крилатьское село, что было за татаром, а кнꙗгини моꙗ дасть с того села Софѣѣ черницѣ долгу ее пꙗтьдесꙗт рублев.

135

А что покупила села на Москвѣ и что ее примыслъ, а то ее и есть. А княгинѣ же своеи даю примыслъ своего о(т)ца, слободку на Гуси, да въ Юрьевѣ село Красное, и с Проватовым, и сь Елизаровским, да свои примыслъ въ Юрьевѣ село Фроловское, да Елох, да село Богородицское. А что ее прикуп и примыслъ, а то ее и есть. Да на Бѣлѣозерѣ слободка, что была княжа Васильева Семеновича, да на Вологдѣ Оуктюжка, да Брюховскаа слободка, да Федоровские села Свибловы, да свои прикуп на Вологдѣ и на Тошнѣ. А что ее прикуп и примыслъ, а то ее и есть. Да на Оустюзѣ Федоровские же деревни Свибловы да Головинские деревни, мои примыслъ.

А дастъ богъ с(ы)ну моему великое княженье, ино и аз с(ы)на своего бла(го)словлаю, княза Васила.

А княгинѣ моеи ис Костромы Иледам с Комелою, и з Волочком, и с Обнорою, да Нерехта, и с варницами, и со Кнагининьским селом, и з бортники, и з бобровники. А ис Перьаславла княгинѣ моеи Юлка так же со всѣми людми, которого пути в неи люди ни будут, да Доброе село. А что ее прикупъ и примыслъ, а то ее и есть. А из Володимера Ондрѣевское село. А Тошну, оже вымѣнит с(ы)нъ мо‖и оу княжих дѣтеи оу Володимеровых, по докончалнои нашеи грамотѣ сь их отцем, и Тошна княгинѣ же моеи. *л. 2*

А с(ы)на своего, княза Васила, бла(го)с(ло)влаю своими примыслы, Новымъгородом Нижним со всѣм, да своим же примыслом бла(го)словлаю с(ы)на своего Муромом со всѣм же.

А из Новагорода княгинѣ моеи половина пошлинъ моихъ всѣх. А что есмь еи подавал село въ Новѣгородѣ или что ее примыслъ, а то еи и есть. Да Сокольское село еи же со всѣм. Да Кѣржанець со всѣм княгинѣ же моеи. А из Мурома княгинѣ моеи Селце да Шатуръ.

А тѣ волости и села, что есмь подавал своеи княгинѣ, послав с(ы)нъ мои да моа княгини, опишут да положать на них дань по людем и по силѣ, и княгини моа дасть с тѣх волостеи и з селъ дань по ро(зо)чту и ам, что са коли им имет. А перемѣнитъ богъ Орду, и княгини моа емлет ту дань собѣ, а с(ы)нъ мои, кназь Василеи, не вступаетса. А волостели свои, и тиоуни, и доводщики судит сама, а с(ы)ну моему, кназ(ю) Василью, въ ее волости, ни в села не всылаи ни по что. А тѣ волости и села княгинѣ моеи до ее живота, опроче Гжели да Семциньского села, да ее прикупа и примысла, а по ее животѣ, ино с(ы)ну моему, князю Василью. А во Гжелѣ да в Семцинском селѣ и въ своемъ примыслѣ волна княгини моа, кому то хочет дати, тому то дасть. А кто имет боаръ служити моеи княгинѣ, и с(ы)нъ мои, кназь Василеи, тѣхъ ее боаръ блюдет.

А с(ы)на своего бла(го)словлаю, княза Васила, страстми болшими, да крестъ честныи животворащии патриаршь Филофѣевьскии. А с(ы)на же своего бла(го)словлаю, даю ему икону Парамшина дѣла, да чепь хресчатую, что ма бла(го)словил от(е)ць мои, да шапку золотую, да бармы, да поас золот с каменьем, что ми дал от(е)ць мои, да другии поас мои на челех с каменьем, а третеи поасъ ему же на синем ремени. А из судов даю с(ы)ну своему, князю Василью, королку сердоничную, да ковшъ золотъ княж Семеновскои, да судно оковано золотом, [что] ми дала мати моа, да каменое судно велико, что ми от великого кназа от Витовта привезлъ кназь Семен, да кубок хрусталнои, что ми король прислал.

А стада мои кобыльи с(ы)ну моему, князю Василью, с моею княгинею наполы.

А опроче того, что ни есть оу мене, то все моеи княгинѣ.

А холопи, которые подавал есмь своеи княгинѣ при своем животѣ, тѣ еи и есть. А дастъ моа княгини дочерем моим из моихъ холопов по пати семеи, а опроче того, вси холопи мои на слободу з женами и з дѣтми.

136

А приказываю с(ы)на своего, кн҃зя Василья, и свою кн҃гиню, и свои дѣти своему брату и тьстю, великому кн҃зю Витовту, как ми реклъ, на бозѣ и на немъ, как с҃ имѣт печаловати, и свои братьѣ молодшеи, кн҃зю Ондрѣю Дмитриевич(ю), и кн҃зю Петру Дмитриевич(ю), и кн҃зю Семену Володимерович(ю), и кн҃з(ю) Ӕрославу Володимерович(ю), и их братьѣ, их док(о)нчаню, как ми ркли.

А оу сее грамоты были мои бо҃ре: кн҃з(ь) Юрьи Патрекѣевич, Иван Дмитриевич, Михаило Ондрѣевич, Ива҃ Федорович, Михаило Федорович, Федоръ Иванович.

А писал сю мою грамоту Олексѣи Стромиловъ.

Внизу грамоты подпись (на греческом языке) митрополита Фотия.

На лицевой стороне грамоты привешена желтовосковая печать в. кн. Василия Дмитриевича.

Основание для датировки: указание на списке, хранящемся в Гос. древлехранилище, отд. I, рубр. I, № 16.
Подлинник — ЦГАДА, *Гос. древлехранилище, отд. I, рубр. I, № 15.*
Список XV в. — *там же, отд. I, рубр. I, № 16. На обороте списка пометы:*
1) Список з грамоты, что поимал Олексѣи з собою в Литву, коли с митрополитом поѣхал с Фотѣем на середохрестье.
2) Список с тое грамоты, что пошла к великому кн҃зю к Витовту с Олексѣем в лѣто 30 первое, з середохрестьѧ.
Духовная грамота ранее напечатана: Древняя Российская Вивлиофика, ч. 8, изд. 1, стр. 346—353, № 21; ч. 1, изд. 2, стр. 150—158, № 21; Мышкинское изд., т. 5, ч. 9, стр. 72—75; СГГД, ч. 1, стр. 83—85, № 42; Бахрушин, стр. 25—27, № 9. Снимок: Соболевский и Пташицкий, № 3.

№ 61.

[1461 г. мая 3—1462 г. марта 27]. — Духовная грамота великого князя Василия Васильевича.

а) Основной текст.

Во им҃ с(ва)тыӕ и живоначалныѣ тро(и)ци, ѿтца и с(ы)на и с(ва)- *л. 1* т(а)го д(у)ха, и по благословленью ѿтца нашег(о) Феѡдосіа, митрополита всеіа Руси, се ӕз, многогрѣшны худы рабъ б(о)жеи Василеи, при своем животѣ, въ своем смыслѣ, пишю сію грамоту д(у)шевную. Даю рѧдъ своим дѣтем и своеи кн(а)г(и)нѣ.

Приказываю свои дѣти своеи кн(а)г(и)нѣ. А вы, мои дѣти, живите заѡдин, а м(а)т(е)ри своеѣ слушаите во всем, в мое мѣсто, своего ѿтца.

А с(ы)на своего старѣишого Ивана бл(а)гословлаю своею ѿтчиною, великим кнаженьем. А даю емȣ треть в Москвѣ и с путми, с моими жеребьи, чѣм мѧ бл(а)гословил ѿт(е)ць мои. и Добрѧтинским селом з бортью, и Василцовым стом, и числеными людми, и ѡрдинци, и Коломною с волостьми, и с путми, и с селы, и со всѣми пошлинами, Володимерем с волостьми, и с путми, и с селы, и со всѣми пошлинами, Переѕяславлем с волостьми, и с путми, и с селы, и со всѣми пошлинами, Кострома с волостьми, и с путми, и з селы, и со всѣми пошлинами, [Гал]ич с волостьми, и с путми, и з селы, и с Солью, и со всѣми пошлинами, Оустюгъ с волостьми, и с путми, и з селы, и со всѣми пошлинами. Да даю своему с(ы)ну Ивану землю Вѧтьскую. Да даю ему Суздаль с волостьми, и с путми, и з селы, и со всѣми пошлинами, да Новгород Нижнии со всѣми пошлинами, и с волостьми, и с путми, и з селы, Муромъ с волостьми, и с путми, и з селы, и со всѣми пошлинами, Юрьевом, и с Великою Солью, и со всѣми пошлинами. Да даю своемȣ

137

с(ы)ну Ивану Боровескъ со всѣми волостьми, и с путми, и з селы, и со всѣми пошлинами, как было за кн(я)зем за Васил(ь)ем, и Суходол с-Ыстьею, и с-Ыстервою, и с Красным селом, да Колугу, и с Олексиным, и с волостми, и с путми, и з селы, и со всѣми пошлинами, как было за кн(я)зем за Иваном за можаиским. А из Московских селъ даю своему с(ы)ну Ивану село Ѡстровское, и с Орининским, и с Костантиновским, и с Молаховским, и з деревнами, и что к тѣм селом потагло, да село Красное над Великим прудом оу города, и з дворы з городскими, что к нему потагло, да лугъ болшеи, оу города по рецѣ по Москвѣ.

А с(ы)на своег(о) Юрья бл(а)гословлаю третью в Москвѣ княжею Володимеровъскою, с сыном своим с Ондрѣем по половинам, а держат(и) по годом. Да Юрью же сыну придаю год в Москвѣ княжь Костантиновскои Дмитреевич(а). Да с(ы)ну же своему Юрью даю Дмитров со всѣми волостьми, и с путми, и з селы, и со всѣми пошлинами, и з Замосковъскими волостьми, и со всѣм с тѣм, как было за кн(я)зем за Петром. Да ему же даю Юлку и съ Юлотцькими бортники, и что къ Юлке потагло, да Серебожь, да Бускутово, да Рожественое, и со всѣм с тѣм, что к тѣм волостем потагло. Да даю с(ы)ну же своему Юрью Можаескъ с волостьми, и с путми, и с селы, и со всѣми пошлинами, и с Медынью, и что к Медыни потагло, да Серпоховъ, да Хотунь со всѣми пошлинами. А чѣмъ его бл(а)г(о)с(ло)в(и)ла моя м(а)ти, великая кн(я)г(и)ни Софья, его баба, и в душевнои емꙋ въ своеи написала, Семчинским селцом оу Москвы, и з дворы з городскими, и с Самсоновым лугом, да Кжелею, да и своим прикупом селцом Воробьевским, и с Семеновским, и з деревнами, да на Похрѣ селом Мачковым, и с Фаоустовским, и с Лодыгиным, и с Федоровым Левонтьева, и с Тажыным, и с рыболовлими деревнами, а ис Коломеньских сел Велина, Кривцово, Бронниче, Чевырево, Марчюково, да Рожек, да починок оу Щелина ѡзера, а изъ Юрьевъских сел Турабьевъские села всѣ, да Кучка, да Деревенка, да Шадрино, ино то его и есть. Да к тѣм селом к Турабьевъским придал есмь ему свое село Шипиловъское со всѣм. А на Костромѣ дала ему его баба село Качаловъское, да Оушаковское, да С(вя)тое село, а на Вологдѣ Масленские села, да Ѩнгосарские, да Говоровъские села, и что к ним потагло, ино то его и есть. А въсхочет мои с(ы)нъ Иван оу своего брата оу Юрья выменити[1] Коломеньские села, и с(ы)нъ мои Юрьи тѣ села ему променит, а Иван с(ы)нъ выменит оу своег(о) брата тѣ села, а его не изобидит.

А с(ы)на своего Ѡндрѣя бл(а)гословлаю, даю ему съ старешим его братом сь Юрьем треть в Москвѣ кн(я)жу Володимерову по половинам, а держат(и) по годом. Да даю ему Оуглече со всѣми волостми, и с путми, и с селы, и со всѣми пошлинами, и с Устюжною, и с Рожаловым, и с Велетовым, и с Кистьмою, и со всѣм с тѣм, как было за кн(я)з(е)мъ за Дмитреем за Шемакою. Да даю ему Бежытцки Верхъ, и с волостьми, и с путми, и с селы и со всѣми пошлинами, да Звенигород с волостми, и с путми, и з селы, и со всѣми пошлинами, а оу Москвы село Сущевъское и з дворы з городскими, что к нему потагли. А чѣм его бл(а)гословила баба ег(о) Вышелѣсом, ино то его и есть.

А с(ы)на своег(о) Бориса бл(а)гословлаю в Москвѣ годом княжым Ивановым можаиског(о), да в городе на посаде дворы шꙋколо с(вя)т(о)го Егорья, каменые ц(е)ркви, Марьиньские Федоровы. Да даю ему Ржеву с волостми, и с путми, и с селы, и з бортью, и со всѣми пошлинами. Да даю ему Волок с волостьми, и с путми, и з селы, и со

---

[1] *Слово* выменити *написано сверху.*

всѣми пошлинами, да Рузу с волостьми, и с путми, и з селы,
и с пошлинами. А что его бл(а)гословила моя мати, великая кн(а)г(и)ни
Софья, а его баба, на Волоце Белеоутовъскими селы, Съпасским селом
и з деревнями, да на Издѣтемлѣ Ѡкорокавъскими селы, ино то ему
и есть. А что ему дала М(а)рья Федорова Голтяева на Коломнѣ села
Проскурниковъские да Веденьские и з деревнями, и на Городнѣ деревня,
и на Москвѣ за Похрою Розсудовъские села, Зверевъское, и Борановъ-
ское, и иные селца, и з деревнями, и с пустошми, и в Володимере Сими-
зинские села, и Лазарьское, и Котазино, и что к тѣм селом потагло,
как было за М(а)рьею, да оу города оу Володимера Евнутьевъское село,
да на Костромѣ на Волзѣ Нижняя слобода со всѣми деревнями, да
Базѣевъское, да Мануиловское и з деревнями, да на Вологдѣ Туран-
даевъское, да Понизовное, да Кобылинские села, да Горка, да на Шомѣ
деревни, да оу Москвы село Шарапово з деревнями, да Лошаково
з деревнями, да луг на рецѣ на Москвѣ под Крутицею, да в Берендѣевѣ село Ростовцовъское з деревнями, да в Кинелѣ Суровцово, да
Тимофѣевъское, да Микульское, ино то его и есть. Да что ему дала
М(а)рья же двор свои внутри города на Москвѣ, ино то его и есть.

А с(ы)на своег(о) Андрѣя Меншог(о) бл(а)гословляю в Москвѣ годом
кн(а)ж(и)м Петровым Дмитреевич(а), да оу Москвы сел(о) Танинское
со всѣм, да Ясеневъское со всѣм, да Раменеицо со всѣм. Да даю ему
Вологду, и с Кубеною, и з Зашзерьем, со всѣм, и что к Вологдѣ,
и х Кубене, и к Зашзерью потагло, и с пошлинами, да Иледам
с Обнорою, и с Комелою, и с Волочком, да Авнегу, да Шиленгу,
да Пельшму, да Бохтюгу, да Оухтюшку, да Сяму, и Ѡтводное с Пер-
фушковъскими селы, да Тошну, да Янгосар, и со всѣм, что к тѣм
волостем потагло.

А кн(а)г(и)нѣ своеи даю Ростов ‖ и со всѣм, что к нему потагло, л. 2
и с селы своими, до еѣ живота. А кн(а)зи ростовские что вѣдали при
мнѣ,[1] при великом кн(а)зи, ини по тому и держат и при моеи кн(а)-
г(и)нѣ, а кн(а)г(и)ни моя оу них в то не въступается. А возмет б(о)гъ
мою кн(а)г(и)ню, и кн(а)г(и)ни моя дастъ Ростов моему с(ы)ну Юрью,
з шнъ держит по тому же, как держала его м(а)ти, что кн(а)зи вѣдали
свое, инѣ по тому ж держат. А что еѣ купля городок Романов княжо
Михаилово Дѣева, и княжых Лвовых детеи, и княже Давыдово
Засѣкина, и Оусть-Шокстны, что собѣ купила оу кн(а)за оу Семена и оу
кн(а)за оу Василья оу Шохонских, ино то еѣ и есть, в то ся дѣти
мои оу неѣ не въступают. А что были волости Заволские и по рецѣ по
Шокъстнѣ, кн(а)жы Ивановы можаиског(о), и села его и ѣзы, и есмь
всѣ волости, и села, и деревни тѣх сел, и ѣзы дал есмь своеи кн(а)-
г(и)нѣ, и с Петровъскими селы Костантинович(а), да Оусть-Оуглы со всѣм,
и сь езы. Да даю своеи кн(а)г(и)нѣ Нерехту с варницами и со всѣми
пошлинами. А из Московских сел даю своеи кн(а)г(и)нѣ Напрудское
оу города, и з дворы з городскими, что к нему потагло, да мелницю
Ходынскую с лугом с Ходынским, да шпосле кн(а)г(и)нина живота
Василисина, Ногатиньское моеи кн(а)г(и)ни, и з дворы, и со всѣм, что
к нему потагло, да Новинки. Да даю своеи кн(а)г(и)нѣ Ѡзерецьские
села и з деревнями, да Михалевъское и з деревнями, да Ѡлешню
и з деревнями. А что есмь оу своеѣ кн(а)г(и)ни взял село Селиванов-
ское в Медушах да дал к с(вя)тои Тро(и)цѣ, и яз в то мѣсто даю своеи
кн(а)г(и)нѣ села свои Лужские и Павшинское, да деревни Петровские
Костантянова на Истрѣ. А из оудѣла с(ы)на своег(о) Иванова, из Коломны,

---

[1] *Слова* при мнѣ *написаны сверху.*

даю свои кн(а)г(и)нѣ волостеи Городок, Брашову, и с сельцом и з Гвоздною и с-Ыванемъ, да Оусть-Мерску, да Песочну, да Малинские села. Да даю свои кн(а)г(и)нѣ село Серкизовское и с Мѣзынкою, и со всѣми селци и з деревнами, да село Высокое и з деревнами и з бортью, да село Шкинь и з деревнами, и с Федоровским селцом Степанова с(ы)на, и з Свербѣевъским, с куплею своею, да село Лысцовское и з деревнами, да Бабышово оу города оу Коломны, что еи дала моя м(а)ти, великая кн(а)г(и)ни, и з дворы з городскими, что к нему потагло, да село Чюхистово, что еи дал Михаило Федоровичь Сабуровъ, со всѣм, что к нему потагло. А в Переславле даю свои кн(а)г(и)нѣ село Рюминское з дворы з городскими,[1] да Маринину слободу, да село Доброе и з дворы з городскими, которые дворы танули к путнику. А въ Юрьеве даю свои кн(а)г(и)нѣ село Фроловское сь Елхом, да Красное село, да Курчево, да Елци, да Варварино, да Кузмѣдемьянское, да Голенищово, да Добрыньское, да Волъстиново, да Сорогошино, да Петровъские Костантинова, Матфѣищово, да Вороґово, и с-ыными селци. А в Суздалѣ даю свои кн(а)г(и)нѣ Шокшов да Давыдовское. А на Костромѣ даю еи Михаиловские села Даниловы со всѣм, что к ним потагло. А что еи дал Михаило Сабуров Колдомъские села, ино то еѣ и есть. А на Оустюзе даю свои кн(а)г(и)нѣ къ еѣ куплѣ къ Левонтьевъскому, да к Патницскому, да к Вондокурье свои села, село Мошемъское и з деревнами и с присельи, да Дымкову сторону и з деревнами и с присельи. А оу с(ы)на своег(о) оу Ондрѣя оу Болшого из оудѣла даю свои кн(а)г(и)нѣ Елду, да Кадку, да Василково з деревнами. А оу с(ы)на своег(о) оу Бориса из оудѣла даю свои кн(а)г(и)нѣ Издѣтемлю, да Июдину слободу, да Ядрово, да во Ржеве село Ондрѣевъское. А оу сына своег(о) оу Андрѣя оу Меншово даю свои кн(а)г(и)нѣ из его оудѣла Иледам с Комелою и с Обнорою. А возмет б(о)гъ мою кн(а)г(и)ню, а оу которого с(ы)на в удѣлѣ волости и села, что есмь еи подавал, ино тому то и есть, опрочѣ еѣ купель. А что еѣ купли, Романов городок, и Шокстна, и иные волости и села, в которых городѣх ни буди, в том волна моя кн(а)г(и)ни, опосле своего живота которому своему с(ы)ну въсхочет дати, ина тому дастъ.

А что моя тамга московъская, и яз даю своему с(ы)ну Ивану треть тамги и со всѣми пошлинами, а другую треть, кн(а)жу Володимерову, с(ы)ну своему Юрью да Ондрѣю Болшому по половинам, а третью треть с(ы)на с(ы)ну своему Борису да Ондрѣю Меншому по половинам. А ис тѣх изо всех трех третеи дал есмь свои кн(а)г(и)нѣ половину тамги и всѣх пошлин до еѣ живота, а по еѣ животѣ ина отдаст им ихъ жеребьи по сеи духовнои грамотѣ, как имъ написано.

Да даю свои кн(а)г(и)нѣ из Новагорода из Нижнего половину пошлин своих всѣх, как было за моею матерью, за великою кн(а)г(и)нею, да и села, которые были за моею м(а)т(е)рью, за великою кн(а)г(и)нею, и со всѣми пошлинами, и что к ним потагло, и з Соколовским селом, и с Кѣрженцом. А из Мурома даю свои кн(а)г(и)нѣ селцо Муромское да Шатуръ, и в то дѣти мои не въступаютса.

А как почнут дѣти мои жити по своим оудѣлом, и моя кн(а)г(и)ни, и мои с(ы)нъ Иван, и мои с(ы)нъ Юрьи, и мои дѣти пошлют писцев, да оудѣлы свои писци их опишут по кр(е)стному целованью, да по тому письму и обложат по сохам и по людем, да по тому окладу моя кн(а)г(и)ни и мои дѣти и в выход оучнут давати с(ы)ну моему Ивану съ своих оудѣлов. А переменит б(о)гъ Орду, и моя кн(а)г(и)ни

---

[1] *Слова* дворы з городскими *написаны сверху.*

140

и мои дѣти возмуm дань собѣ съ своих оудѣлов, а с(ы)нъ мои Иван
в то не въступаетсѧ.

А гдѣ есмь ни подаваλ своеи кн(ѧ)г(и)нѣ волости и села в удѣлеx
детеи своиx, во чьем ни буди, и тѣ волости и села данью и судоm
потануm к моеи кн(ѧ)г(и)нѣ, а дѣти мои в то не въступаютсѧ. А воло-
стелеи своиx, и поселскиx, и тиоунов, и ключников, и доводшиков
судиm моѩ кн(ѧ)г(и)ни.

А которыm есмь дѣтем своим села подаваλ во чьем оудѣле ни буди,
ино того и суд над тѣми селы, кому дано.

А кому буду даваλ своим кн(ѧ)з(е)мъ, и боѩромъ, и детем боѩрьским
свои села в жалованье, или хотѧ и в куплю кому даλ, ино тѣ мои села
моим дѣтем, во чьем оудѣле будеm, ино тому то и есть.

А по грехоm, оу которог(о) оу моег(о) с(ы)на вотчины ѿоиметсѧ,
и кн(ѧ)г(и)ни моѩ оуимеm оу своиx с(ы)н(о)въ изь их оудѣлов, да тому
вотчину исполниm, а дѣти мои из ее воли не вымутсѧ.

А с(ы)на своег(о) Ивана бл(а)гословлѧю кр(е)стъ Петров чюдотворцов, да кр(е)стъ золоm Парамшиньскои, да шапка, да бармы, да сердо-
личнаѩ коробка, да поѩз золоm болшои с каменьем.

А с(ы)на своег(о) Юрьѩ бл(а)гословлѧю икона Филафѣевъскаѩ да
кр(е)стъ золоm, что мѧ бл(а)гословила моѩ мати, великаѩ кн(ѧ)г(и)ни,
да поѩз золоm на червьчатѣ ремени.

А с(ы)на своего Андрѣѩ Болшово — кр(е)стъ золоm, кнѧж Дмитреевъ-
скои Меншег(о), ‖ с чепечкою.   л. 3

А с(ы)на своег(о) Бориса бл(а)гословлѧю кр(е)стъ золоm, что мѧ бл(а)-
гословила моѩ м(а)ти, великаѩ кн(ѧ)г(и)ни, коли есмь шоλ къ своеи
ѿчинѣ, к Великому Новугороду.

А с(ы)на своег(о) Андрѣѩ Меншого бл(а)гословлѧю икона золота на
изумрутѣ.

А приказываю свою кн(ѧ)г(и)ню, и своег(о) с(ы)на Ивана, и Юрьѩ,
и свои меншие дѣти брату своему, королю польскому и великому кн(ѧ)зю
литовъскому Казимиру, по докончалнои нашеи грамотѣ, на б(о)зе и на
нем, на моеm братѣ, как сѧ оучнеm печаловати моею кн(ѧ)г(и)нею,
и моим с(ы)номъ Иваноm, и моими детми.

А дети свои приказаλ есмь своеи кн(ѧ)г(и)нѣ. А вы, дѣти мои, слушаите своеѣ м(а)т(е)ри во всем, и из еѣ воли не выступаите ни в чем.
А которыи с(ы)нъ мои не имеm слушати своеѣ м(а)т(е)ри, а будеm не въ еѣ
воле, на том не буди моег(о) бл(а)гословленьѩ.

А вы, дѣти мои, чтите и слушаите своег(о) брата стареишог(о) Ивана
в мое мѣсто, своег(о) ѿца. А с(ы)нъ мои Иван держиm своег(о) брата
Юрьѩ и свою братью меншую въ братьствѣ, без ѡбиды.

А хто моиx боѩръ имеm служити моеи кн(ѧ)г(и)нѣ, а живуm в удѣлеx
детеи моиx, и тѣx боѩръ дѣти мои блюдуm с одинова.

А хто будеm моиx казначѣев, или хто моиx дыѩков прибытоk мои
ѿ мене вѣдали, или поселскиx, или тиоунов, или хто женилсѧ оу
тѣx, ино тѣ всѣ не надобны моеи кн(ѧ)г(и)нѣ и моиm дѣтем.

А хто сю мою грамоту переступиm, ино по е8ангильскому словеси,
хто прислушаетсѧ ѿца и м(а)т(е)ри, и заповеди их не храниm, см(е)ртью
да оумреm.

А оу духовные сидѣλ(и): ѿ(е)ць мои духовныи, архимандриm спасьскии
Трифоn, да симановскии архимандриm Афонасеи, да мои боѩре, кн(ѧ)зь
Иванъ Юрьевич, да Иван Иванович, да Василеи Иванович, да Федоръ
Васиλ(ь)евич.

А грамоту сю писаλ дыѩк мои Василеи Беда.

Внизу подпись: Смиреныи Ѳеѡд(о)сіи, архіиеп(и)с(ко)пъ всеѧ Роусіи.

На лицевой стороне грамоты следы от прикрепления двух печатей: великого князя Василия Васильевича и митрополита Феодосия.

б) Приписная грамота к духовной великого князя Василия Васильевича.

Во имѧ с(вѧ)тыѧ и живоначалныѧ тро(и)ци, ѡтца и с(ы)на и с(вѧ)т(а)го д(у)ха, и по бл(а)гословленью ѡтца нашег(о) Феѡдосіа, митрополита всеѧ Руси, се ѧз, многогрѣшныи худыи раб б(о)жеи Василеи, въ своем смысле пишу сию душевную приписную грамоту, что есмь писал болшую свою душевную грамоту, даѧ рѧд своеи кн(ѧ)г(и)нѣ и своим дѣтем. И чег(о) есмь в ту свою душевную грамоту не вписал, и ѧз в сю грамоту в приписную написал.

Даю своеи кн(ѧ)г(и)нѣ село свое Коломеньское, и з деревнѧми, и что к нему потѧгло, да село Дьѧковское, что собѣ выменила оу кн(ѧ)г(и)ни оу Василисы, со всѣм, да селцо Хвостовское оу города оу Москвы, з дворы з городскими, что к нему потѧгло, да луг княж Юрьевскои Дмитреевич(а) противу моег(о) двора, и сь Юрьевъскими лугом казначѣевым, что ѡи дал Михаило Сабуров. Да что есмь писал в болшои въ своеи грамотѣ кн(ѧ)г(и)нѣ своеи Маринину слободу, а ѡ дву станѣх, ѡ Ѡртем(ь)евъском селѣ з деревнѧми да ѡ бортницѣх и ѡ бобровникѣх с числаки, не ѡписано, и ѧз и тѣ два стану даю кн(ѧ)г(и)нѣ своеи к Маринѣнѣ слободе. Да даю своеи кн(ѧ)г(и)нѣ в Переславле Городище з деревнѧми с Волнинскими, да Бармазово з деревнѧми, да в Муроме даю еи Почап, и Заколпье, и Черсево, и что к нему потѧгло. Да на Коломне даю еи село Ѡксиньское з деревнѧми. Да что ми дала Настасьѧ Федорова Андрѣевич(а) село Мѧчково и з деревнѧми в куплю, а держати еи за собою до своег(о) живота, да что ми дала дочи еѣ Ѡрина Ѡлексѣева жена Игнатьевич(а) свои села на реце на Москвѣ в куплю же до своег(о) живота, и тѣ села Настасьины и Ѡринины ѡпосле их живота моеи кн(ѧ)г(и)нѣ. А кн(ѧ)г(и)ни моѧ по моим по купчим грамотам ѡтдастъ им цѣну за тѣ села по их д(у)ше, кому ѡни прикажут ѡпосле своег(о) живота взѧти. Да в Можаисце даю своеи кн(ѧ)г(и)нѣ село Чертановское з деревнѧми, и з дворы з городскими, да Белевици з деревнѧми, да Исмеиское село з деревнѧми, да мелницю под городом под Можаиском на Москвѣ на реце, что нарѧдил еи еѣ же поселскои Васюк. А что ми дала Анна Васил(ь)ева жена Иванович(а) села свои Муромские и в Вотском Стародубѣ с озеры и со всѣми оуходы, и ѧз то даю своеи же кн(ѧ)г(и)нѣ. Да даю своеи кн(ѧ)г(и)нѣ села Долматовские Юрьева в Хотуньском, и в Ростуновѣ, и в Перемышле, и з деревнѧми тѣх сел, и со всим, что к ним потѧгло, в тѣх селех волна, кому хочет, тому дастъ ѡпосле своег(о) живота.

А которые дѣти боѧрьские служат моеи кн(ѧ)г(и)нѣ, и слуги ее, и вси ее люди, холопи еѣ, и кому буду ѧз, кн(ѧ)зь велики, тѣм давал свои села, или моѧ кн(ѧ)г(и)ни давала свои села, или за кѣм будет их ѡтчина или купла, и в тѣх въ своих людех во всих волна моѧ кн(ѧ)г(и)ни и в тѣх селех, а дѣти мои в то не въступаютсѧ.

А что дворъ княж Ивановскои можаиског(о) на Москвѣ, и ѧз даю ег(о) с(ы)ну своему Ивану. А что дворъ княж Васил(ь)евскои Ѧрославич(а), княж Володимеровскои, за архангилом Михаилом, и ѧз даю ег(о) с(ы)ну своему Юрью. А что ему дала дворъ баба ег(о) оу с(вѧ)т(о)го Ивана Пр(е)дт(е)чи, и ѧз тот дворъ даю своеи кн(ѧ)г(и)нѣ.

А княж Дмитреевскои двор Шемякин даю своему с(ы)ну Ѡндрѣю Болшому. А что дворы оу с(вято)го Рожества, Петров, и Иванов, и Микитин Костантиновичь, да за городом которые мои дворы, ѡтчина моя и купла, примыслъ мои, и сады мои, и в тѣх дворех волна моя кн(я)г(и)ни, которым моим дѣтем которое дастъ, ино то тому и есть.

А что дала моя м(а)ти, великая кн(я)г(и)ни, Федору Басенку на Коломне село свое Ѡкуловское, да Рѣпинское, а в душевнои въ своеи ѡписала так, что в тѣх селех волен яз, еѣ с(ы)нъ, ино тѣ села ѡпосле Басенкова живота моеи же кн(я)г(и)нѣ.

А оу сеѣ грамоты оу приписные сидѣл(и): ѡт(е)ць же мои духовны архимандрит Трифон да бояре мои, кн(я)зь Иван Юрьевич да Федоръ Михаилович.

А грамоту писал дыяк мои Василеи Беда.

Внизу подпись: Смирены Ѳеѡд(о)сіи, архіиеп(и)с(ко)пъ всея Роусіи.

На лицевой стороне грамоты привешены две черновосковые печати: великого князя Василия Васильевича и митрополита Феодосия.

Основание для датировки: 3 мая 1461 г. поставлен на митрополию митрополит Феодосий (ПСРЛ, т. IV, стр. 132, 148; т. V, стр. 273; т. VI, стр. 184; т. VIII, стр. 149; т. XII, стр. 114); 27 марта 1462 г. умер Василий Темный (ПСРЛ, т. IV, стр. 148; т. V, стр. 273; т. VI, стр. 185; т. VIII, стр. 150; т. XII, стр. 151). См. Черепнин, стр. 158—161.

Подлинник — ЦГАДА, Гос. древлехранилище, отд. I, рубр. II, № 21. Список второй половины XV в. — там же № 22. Список XVI в. (первой грамоты) — Гос. ист. музей, собрание рукописей Синодальной биб-ки, кн. № 562, лл. 225—230, № 102. Духовная грамота ранее напечатана: Древняя Российская Вивлиофика, ч. 9, изд. 1, стр. 503—522, №№ 65—66; ч. 1, изд. 2, стр. 414—428, №№ 65—66; Мышкинское изд., т. 5, ч. 9, стр. 243—252, СГГД, ч. 1, стр. 202—208, №№ 86—87; Карамзин, т 5, примеч. № 372; Бахрушин, стр. 27—33, № 10.

№ 89.

[1504 г. ранее июня 16]. — Духовная грамота великого князя Ивана Васильевича.

Во имя с(вя)тыя и жывоначалныя тро(и)ца, ѡтца и с(ы)на и с(вя)- л. 1 т(а)го д(у)ха, и по бл(а)гословенію ѡтца н(а)шег(о) Симона, митрополита всеа Рѫсіи, се яз, многогрѣшны и хѫдыи раб б(о)жіи Иван, при своем животѣ, въ своем смысле, пишѫ сію грамотѫ дѫшевнѫю. Даю ряд своим с(ы)ном, с(ы)нѫ своемѫ Васил(ь)ю и меншим своим дѣтем, Юрью, Дмитрею, Семенѫ, Андрѣю.

Приказываю детеи своих менших, Юрья з брат(ь)ею, с(ы)нѫ своемѫ Васил(ь)ю, а их братѫ старѣишемѫ. А вы, дѣти мои, Юрьи, Дмитреи, Семен, Андрѣи, држыте моег(о) с(ы)на Васил(ь)я, а своег(о) брата старѣи-шаг(о), въ мое мѣсто, своег(о) ѡтца, и слѫшаите ег(о) во всем. А ты, с(ы)нъ мои Василеи, држы свою брат(ь)ю молодшѫю, Юрья з брат(ь)ею, во чти, без ѡбиды.

Бл(а)гословляю с(ы)на своег(о) старѣишаг(о) Васил(ь)я своею ѡтчиною, великими княжствы, чѣмъ мя бл(а)г(о)с(ло)вил ѡт(е)ць мои, и что ми дал б(о)гъ. А даю емѫ горѡд Москвѫ с волостьми, и с пѫтми, и з станы, и з селы, и з дворы з горѡдцкими со всѣми, и з слободами, и с тамьгою, и с пѫдом, и с помѣрным, и с торги, и с лавъками, и з дворы з гостиными, и со всѣми пошлинами, и з Добратинским селомъ, и з бортью, и с Василцовым стомъ, да числаки и ѡрдинцы.

А мои дѣти, Юрьи, Дмитреи, Семен, Андрѣи, ѹ моег(о) с(ы)на ѹ Васил(ь)ѧ, а ѹ своег(о) брата ѹ старѣишаг(о), въ числаки и въ ѡрдинцы не въстѹпаютсѧ ни во что, ни въ земли их, ни в воды не въстѹпаютсѧ, и не обидѧт их ничѣмъ.

Да емѹ ж даю селцо Семчинское, и з дворы з горѡдцкими, и з Самъсоновым лѹгомъ, да село Вориб(ь)ево, и с Володимеровским, и з Семеновским, и с Ворѡнцовским, и с Кадашовым, и з деревнами, как было при мнѣ. Да емѹ ж даю селцо Ворѡнцовское на Ѩѹзѣ, гдѣ мои дворъ, и з дворы з горѡдцкими со всѣми по ѡбе стороны Ѩѹзы, и с мелницами, как было при мнѣ, да монастыр(ь) Лыщыково и з дворы, да Ильинскѹю слобѡдкѹ, со всѣм, по томѹ, как есми выменил ѹ Андрѡнникова монастырѧ.

А с(ы)нъ мои Василеи дръжыт на Мѡсквѣ бѡлшег(о) своег(о) намѣстника по старинѣ и как было при мнѣ, а дрѹгово своег(о) намѣстника дръжыт на Мѡсквѣ на кнѧж Волѡдимерѡвскои трети Андрѣевича, что была дана братие моеи, Юрью да Андрѣю.

А что которые мои дворы взнѹтри города на Мѡсквѣ, и за городѡм на посадех, и сады мои всѣ, и пѹстые мои мѣста по посадом, то все с(ы)нѹ моемѹ Васил(ь)ю. А что которые мои дворы внѹтри города на Мѡсквѣ и за городом за моими боѧры, и за кнѧзми, и за детми боѩрскими, и за дворѧны за моими, и за дворцовыми людми, и за конюхи, и за мастеры за моими, и тѣ всѣ дворы с(ы)нѹ же моемѹ Васил(ь)ю. А ѹ кнѧг(о) бѹдѹт ѹ боѩр, и ѹ кн(а)зеи, и ѹ детеи ѹ боѩрских взнѹтри города на Мѡсквѣ и за городом на пѡсадех дворы их, ѡтчины и кѹпли, или комѹ бѹдѹ дал на Мѡсквѣ взнѹтри города и за городом по посадом на дворы грамоты свои жаловалные прѡчные, и с(ы)нъ мои Василеи въ тѣ дворы ѹ них не въстѹпаетсѧ.

Да что были къ Дмитровѹ приданы волости Мѡсковскіе: Рогѡж, Вора, Корзенево, Шерна городок, Сѡлишин и с Новым селѡм, и тѣ ѩз волости даю къ Мѡсквѣ со всѣм по старинѣ с(ы)нѹ своемѹ Васил(ь)ю. Да емѹ ж даю волости Сѹрожык, да Лѹчинское, да Радонеж с волостми, и з пѹтми, и з селы, и со всѣми пошлинами, да трет(ь) Мѹшковѹ с мытом с Липским.

Да даю емѹ горѡд Коломнѹ с волостьми, и с пѹтми, и з селы, и со всѣми пошлинами, горѡд Кошырѹ съ Зарѣч(ь)емъ, что за рекою за Ѡкою, Тѣшилѡв, и Рославль, и Венев, и Мъстиславль, и иные мѣста по Разанскои рѹбеж, и с волостьми, и с пѹтми, и з селы, и со всѣми пошлинами, и сь Елчем, и со всѣми Елечскими мѣсты, горѡд Серпохѡв, да Хотѹн(ь), и с волостми, и с пѹтми, и з селы, и со всѣми пошлинами, горѡд То,ѹсѹ з Горѡдцим, и с-Ыскан(ь)ю, и с Мышегою, и с Колѡдною, и со кнѧгининскою вотчиною Ѡвдот(ь)иною, горѡд Мченескъ с волостьми, и з селы, и со всѣми пошлинами, со всѣм, что к немѹ потагло.

Да емѹ ж даю горѡд Воротынескъ, и с Лагинском, и с Краишиным, и с-ыными мѣсты, со всѣм с тѣм, как был за Воротынскими. А что есми променил кн(а)зю Михаилѹ Мѣзетцкомѹ на ег(о) жеребеи на Мѣческъ въ Стародѹбе Ѡлексин, и ѡн дръжыт по менѡвнои грамотѣ, а сѹд и дан(ь) с(ы)на моег(о) Васил(ь)ево.

А кн(а)зи новосилские, ѡдоевские, и белевские, и з своими детми, и з своими вотчинами, и что къ их вотчинам потагло, с(ы)нѹ же моемѹ Васил(ь)ю къ нашемѹ великомѹ кнѧжствѹ.

Да с(ы)нѹ же своемѹ Васил(ь)ю даю горѡд Боровескъ с волостьми, и с пѹтми, и з селы, и со всѣми пошлинами, и з Сѹходолом,

и с-Ыстьею, и с-Ыстервою, и с Красным селом, и с Кременцом, и с Песочною з болшею, и з слободкою со Ѡсны на Шане, что садил Василеи Карамышев, горѡд Ꙗрославець с волостьми, и с пꙋтми, и з селы, и со всѣм
пошлинами, со всѣм с тѣм, как был за кн(а)зем Михаилѡмъ Андрѣеви-
чемъ, ‖ горѡд Медын(ь), и Радомль, и с Вешками по Ꙋгрꙋ, да на Шане л. 2
слобода, что Товаркѡв садил, по Ꙋгрꙋ ж, и с Песочною с меншею,
и з слободами, что садили Андрѣи Картъмазов, да Мита Загразскои,
да Ивашко Гладкои. А что Ѳилиповых детеи Полтева села и д(е)р(е)вни
на сеи сторонѣ Ꙋгры, и тѣ села и д(е)р(е)вни со всѣм, что к ним потагло,
къ Медыни с(ы)нꙋ же моемꙋ Васил(ь)ю.

Да емꙋ ж даю горѡд Можаескъ с волостьми, и с пꙋтми, и з селы,
и со всѣми пошлинами, и з Чагощъю, и с Тꙋрьевым, и с Орѣхѡвною,
и с Могилном, и с Миченками, и съ Шатѣш(ь)ю, и з Сꙋлидовым,
и з Дмитровцѡм по ѡбе стороны Ꙋгры, и с-ыными мѣсты, что к ним потагло,
горѡд Вазмꙋ, и Кизлов с волостьми, и з селы, и со всѣм пошлинами,
со всѣм с тѣм, что к Вазме и х Козлѡвꙋ и ко всѣмъ Ваземским
мѣстом потагло, как было при мнѣ.

Да с(ы)нꙋ ж своемꙋ Васил(ь)ю даю горѡд Дорогобꙋж с волостьми,
и з селы, и со всѣми пошлинами, со всѣмъ, что к немꙋ потагло,
да волости Дорогобꙋжсские Погорѣлаꙗ, Нѣгѡмле, Хотомичи, Холмъ,
Батино, Прость, селцо Заѡпье, Водоса, Некрасова, Селечна, Кремена,
Редын(ь), по рецѣ по Ꙋже ꙋстье, Косково, Рехты, Хомчичи, Вышково,
Василево, Ескино село Климова, слобѡдка вл(а)д(ы)чна въ Чертъкове,
селцо Пꙋтатино з д(е)р(е)внами, Игꙋмнова, Мъстиславець, Ѡщытѡв,
Жꙋлин, Мошкова гора, Лꙋчин городѡк, Великое поле, Лопатино, Копылеа
и Ꙋжыца, Ведрѡш(ь) и Озерища, Серковы лꙋки, со всѣм с тѣм, что
къ Дорогобꙋжꙋ и къ тѣм волостем и селом потагло, как было при
мнѣ.

Да с(ы)нꙋ ж своемꙋ Васил(ь)ю даю горѡд Переаславль с волостьми,
и с пꙋтми, и з селы, и со всѣми пошлинами, и з Солью. Да что
были къ Дмитровꙋ приданы волости Переаславльские Серебѡж, Р(о)ж(е)-
ственое, Б[ус]кꙋтово, и ꙗз тѣ волости даю къ Переꙗславлю с всѣм
по старинѣ с(ы)нꙋ своемꙋ Васил(ь)ю.

Да емꙋ ж даю горѡд Володимерь с волостьми, и с пꙋтми, и з селы,
и со всѣми пошлинами, и с Мꙋромским селцом, и з Шатꙋрѡм, и с Колꙋш-
кою, и с Вышелѣсом, и с Островом, горѡд Юрьев с волостьми, и с пꙋтми,
и з селы, и с Великою Сѡлью, и со всѣми пошлина[ми], горѡд Сꙋздал(ь)
с волостьми, и с пꙋтми, и з селы, и со всѣми пошлинами, да Солцꙋ
Малꙋю ѡбе половины, горѡд Ростов с волостьми, и с пꙋтми, и з селы,
и со всѣми пошлинами, и з Сѡлью, горѡд Ꙗрославль с волостьми,
и с пꙋтми, и з селы, и со всѣми пошлинами, и с Ꙋхрою, и с селцѡм
с Петровским, и з д(е)р(е)внами, и слободкꙋ Ѡхлабининскꙋю и с мытом,
и кнꙗж Васил(ь)евъскꙋю вотчинꙋ Щетинина Касть со всѣм, да Инопаж
и з Селцом, и сь ѣзом, что на Вѡлзе пѡд Рыбною слободою противꙋ
Инопажа и Селца. А боꙗром и дѣтемъ боꙗрским ꙗрославским с своими
вѡтчинами и с кꙋплами ѡт моег(о) с(ы)на ѡт Васил(ь)а не ѡт(ъ)ѣхати
никомꙋ никꙋдѣ. А хто ѡт(ъ)ѣдет, и земли их с(ы)нꙋ моемꙋ, а слꙋжат
емꙋ, и иꙗ з них въ их земли не въстꙋпаетса, ни ꙋ их жѡн, ни ꙋ их детеи.
Горѡд Романѡв городокъ с волостьми, и с пꙋтми, и з селы, и со всѣми
пошлинами.

Да с(ы)нꙋ же своемꙋ Васил(ь)ю даю Ꙋсть-Шокъстны по ѡбе стороны
погосты и з деревнами кнꙗж Васил(ь)евъские и кнꙗж Семеновские
Шохонских, и сь езы, и с рыбною ловлею, и со всѣми пошлинами,

145

по томѹ, как было за моею м(а)т(е)рью, за великою кнѧгинею, да волости
Заволжьские по ѡбе стороны реки Шокстны кнѧж Иванѡвские Андрѣевича, и села, и д(е)р(е)вни, что были за моею м(а)т(е)рью, за великою кнѧгинею, а волости Шохонские, Лѹковесь, Арбѹжовесь, Маткома, Веретеѧ
Бѡлшаа, городѡк Кнѧжычи, Песье село, Всесвѧтцское, Волское
и с Окишѡвским селом, и с Вонгѹемъ, Патробал, Рѹнаи, и с Шагатью,
и з слобѡдками с Кѣштомою и с Шелшедамиѡ, Бѣлое селѡ, Шыгораш
и с-ыными волостьми, и з селы, и з д(е)р(е)внами, и сь езы, и с рыбною
ловлею, и со всѣми пошлинами, со всѣм с тѣм, как было за моею
м(а)т(е)рью, за великою кнѧгинею, и с Петровскими Костантиновича селы
и з д(е)р(е)внами, и что были в Шокстнѣ ж волости бабы моеѣ, великие
кнѧгини Сѡфьи, Ѹсть-Ѹглы да Веретеика Малаѧ, и тѣ волости и сь езы,
и с рыбною лѡвлею, и со всѣми пошлинами с(ы)нѹ ж моемѹ Васил(ь)ю.

Да с(ы)нѹ же своемѹ Васил(ь)ю даю горѡд Белоѡзеро с волостьми,
и с пѹтми, и з селы, и со всѣми пошлинами, со всѣм с тѣм, как
было при мнѣ, горѡд Вологдѹ с волостьми, и с пѹтми, и з селы,
и со всѣми пошлинами, да Заѡзерье, и с Кѹбеною, и с волостьми,
и с пѹтми, и з селы, и со всѣми пошлинами, горѡд Ѹстьюг и с волос-
стьми, .и с пѹтми, и з селы, и со всѣми пошлинами, да Вычегдѹ,
и Вымь, и Ѹдорѹ, и Сысолѹ, и со всѣми их мѣсты, да въ Заволотцкои
землѣ Рости вщинѹ, Пинега, и Кѣгрола, и Чакола, Прьмьские, Мезень,
Немъюга, Пилья горы, Пинешка, Выѧ, Тоима, Кирьи горы, Емьскаа
гора на Вазе со всѣм, и Ѡнтонова перевара, Корбѡлскои ѡстров,
Шогогора, Кѣрчела, Сѹра поганаѧ, Лавела, и с-ыными мѣсты, что к тѣм

л. 3 волостем потагло, ‖ да Югрѹ и Печерѹ со всѣм, да Пермь Великѹю
со всѣм, да горѡд Костромѹ, и с Плесом, и с Нерехтою, и с-Ыледа-
мом, и с волостьми, и с пѹтми, и з селы, и со всѣми пошлинами,
горѡд Галич с волостьми, и с пѹтми, и з селы, и со всѣми пѡшли-
нами, и з Сѡлью, и с Ѹнжею, и с Чюхломою, и со всѣм, что
къ Галичю, и к Ѹнже, и къ Чюхломѣ изстарины потаглѡ, да Новгород
Нижнеи с волостьми, и с пѹтми, и з селы, и со всѣми пошлинами,
и с мордвами, и с черемисою, что к Новгородѹ потагло. А которые
села и д(е) (е)вни въ Новѣгородѣ в Нижнемъ за моими кнѧзми, и за
боѧры, и за детми за боѧрскими, за кѣм ни бѹди, и то все с(ы)нѹ же
моемѹ Васил(ь)ю.

Да емѹ ж даю горѡд Мѹром с волостьми и с пѹтми, и з селы,
и со всѣми пошлинами, и с мордвами, и с черемисою, что къ Мѹрѡмѹ
потагло, да Мещера с волостьми, и з селы, и со всѣм, что к неи
потагло, и с Кошковымъ, да кн(а)зи мордовские всѣ, и з своими
ѡтчинами, с(ы)нѹ же моемѹ Василью.

Да с(ы)нѹ же своемѹ Васил(ь)ю даю Влатцкѹю землю всю, городы,
и волости, и со всѣм, что к неи потагло, и с арскими кнѧзми, как
было при мнѣ.

А что есми пожаловал кн(а)зѧ Θеѡд(о)ра Ивановича Бѣлског(о),
дал есми емѹ въ вотчинѹ горѡд Лѹх с волостьми, да волости Вичюгѹ,
да Кинешмѹ, да Чихачев, и кнѧз(ь) Θеѡд(о)ръ и ег(о) дѣти слѹжат
с(ы)нѹ моемѹ Василью, а тѹ свою вотчинѹ држат по томѹ, как былѡ при
мнѣ. А ѡт(ъ)ѣдет кнѧз(ь) Θеѡд(о)ръ или ег(о) дѣти ѡт моего с(ы)на
ѡт Васил(ь)ѧ къ моим дѣтемъ къ меншим, или х комѹ ни бѹди,
и та ег(о) вотчина Лѹх и с тѣми волостьми с(ы)нѹ моемѹ Васил(ь)ю.

Да с(ы)на же своег(о) Васил(ь)ѧ бл(а)гословлѧю своею ѡтчиною,
великим кнѧжством Тѳерским, даю емѹ горѡд Тѳер(ь) и Городен
с волостьми, и с пѹтми, и з селы, и со всѣми пошлинами по томѹ,
по каа мѣста писал ко Тѳери писець нашъ кнѧз(ь) Θеѡд(о)ръ Алабыш,

146

горѡд Клин с волостьми, и с пѫтми, и з селы, и со всѣми пошлинами, по томѹ, по каа мѣста писал писецъ нашъ Петръ Лобан Заболотькои, ѡприч(ь) тог(о), что есми променил своим братаничем, Борисовым дѣтем Өеѡд(о)рѹ да Иванѹ, ѿ Тѵерские земли, Бѹигорѡд, да Колпь, и въ то с(ы)нъ мои Василеи не въстѹпаетсѧ. А которые кн(ѧ)зи слѹжебные в Московскои землѣ и во Тѳтрскои землѣ, и тѣ кн(ѧ)зи всѣ слѹжат с(ы)нѹ моемѹ Васил(ь)ю, а вотчины свои дръжат по томѹ, как было при мнѣ. А кто тѣх кн(ѧ)зеи слѹжебных ѿ моег(о) с(ы)на ѿ Васил(ь)ѧ ѿ(ъ)ѣдет къ моим дѣтемъ къ меньшим, или х комѹ ни бѹди, и тѣх кн(ѧ)зеи вотчины с(ы)нѹ моемѹ Васил(ь)ю.

Да с(ы)на же своег(о) Васил(ь)ѧ бл(а)гословлаю своею ѡтчиною, великимъ кнѧжен(ь)емъ Новогорѡдским, даю емѹ Великии Новгорѡд со всѣмъ, с пат(ь)ю патинами, с волостьми, и с погосты, и с пѫтми, и з селы, и со всѣми пошлинами, и з городы: Ивангорѡд, Ӏама горѡд, Копор(ь)ѧ горѡд, Ѡрѣшок горѡд, Ладога горѡд, Дѣман горѡд, Кѹрѧгорѡд, Порхѡв горѡд, Высокои горѡд, Кошкин горѡд, Рѹса горѡд. А дал есми емѹ тѣ городы всѣ с волостьми, и с погосты, и с пѫтми, и з селы, и со всѣми пошлинами, да горѡд Торжѡк с волостьми, и с пѫтми, и з селы, и со всѣми пошлинами. Да в Новогорѡдскои ж землѣ даю емѹ горѡд Холмъ, и Велилю, и Бѹецъ, и Лопастици, и с-ыными мѣсты, со всѣмъ, что к ним потагло, да горѡд Лѹки Великие с волостьми, и с погосты, и со всѣми пошлинами, да Лѹтцкие ж волости, Пѹповичи, Ваз, Чѧспла, Коротаи, Дѹбно, Комша, и с-ыными мѣсты, что к ним потагло, да Ржевѹ Пѹстѹю с волостьми, и с погосты, и со всѣми пошлинами, до Корѣлскѹю землю всю, Корѣлскои горѡд с волостьми, и с погосты, и со всѣми пошлинами, со всѣмъ с тѣмъ, что х Корѣлскои землѣ потагло, и с Лоп(ь)ю с лѣшею, и съ дикою Лопью. Да с(ы)нѹ же своемѹ Василью даю Заволотцкѹю землю всю, Ѡнѣго, и Каргополе, и все Пошнѣжье, и Двинѹ, и Варѹ, и Кокшенгѹ, и Велскои погостъ, и Колмогоры, и всю Двинскѹю и Заволотцкѹю землю.

Да с(ы)на же своег(о) Васил(ь)ѧ бл(а)гословлаю своею ѡтчиною, даю емѹ горѡд Пъскѡв, и з городы, и с волостьми, и з селы, и всю землю Пъсковскѹю.

Да с(ы)нѹ же своемѹ Васил(ь)ю даю горѡд Торопец с волостьми, и с погосты, и з селы, и со всѣми пошлинами, со всѣмъ, что к немѹ потагло, да волости Данково, Любѹта, Дѹбна, Рожна, Тѹра, Биберево, Старцева, Нежелскаа, Велижскаа, Плавѣетцкаа, Жыжетцкаа, Ѡзерскаа, Казариновскаа. Да емѹ ж даю горѡд Ѡстрее с волостми и со всѣмъ, что к немѹ потагло, а волости Березаи, Невле, Ѹсваи, Лицвцо, Веснѣболого, со всѣм с тѣм, что к Торопцѹ, и к Острею, и к тѣмъ волостем потагло, как было при мнѣ.

А что ми дал сестричич мои, кнѧз(ь) Өе(о)дѡр Васил(ь)евич рѧзанскои, свою ѡтчинѹ на Рѧзани въ городѣ и на посаде свои жеребеи, и Старѹю Рѧзан(ь), и Перевитебскъ с волостьми, и с пѫтми, и з селы, и з бортью, и с тамгою, и со всѣми пошлинами, по томѹ, как сѧ дѣлил съ своим

4 л. братомъ, со кн(ѧ)земъ с-Ываном, и ꙗз тѹ его вотчин(ѹ), || жеребеи в городѣ на Рѧзани и на посаде, и Старѹю Рѧзан(ь), и Перевитескъ с волостьми, и с пѫтми, и з селы, и з бортью, и с тамгою, и со всѣми пошлинами, со всѣм по томѹ, как было за кн(ѧ)земъ за Өеѡд(о)ром, даю с(ы)нѹ своемѹ Василью.

Да бл(а)гословлаю с(ы)на своег(о) Васил(ь)ѧ и детеи своих менших, Юрьа, Дмитреа, Семена, Андрѣа, въ Мѡсквѣ годом кнѧж Костантинѡвским Дмитреевича, что был дан братѹ моемѹ Юрью, да годомъ кнѧжым Петровским Дмитреевича, что был дан братѹ моемѹ Андрью Меншомѹ, да годомъ княж Михаилшвским Андрѣевича. А дръжыт с(ы)нъ мои Василеи и мши дѣти меншие, Юрьи з брат(ь)ею, на тѣх годѣх на Мшсквѣ своих намѣстников, переменял пять лѣт по годом.

А что был дан брату моему Борису в Мшсквѣ гшд княж Иваншвскои Андрѣевича, и тот гшд прихшдилъ брата моег(о) Борисовым дѣтем шбѣма дръжати на Мшсквѣ своег(о) намѣстника на шостои гшд, и братанич мои Иван ту полгоду дал мнѣ, и яз ту полгоду даю с(ы)ну своему Васил(ь)ю, и братанич мои Ѳе(о)дшръ съ сыном с моим с Васил(ь)емъ тшт шостои гшд дръжат по полгоду, с(ы)нъ мои Василеи дръжыт своег(о) намѣстника полгоду, а братанич мои Ѳе(о)дшръ дръжыт своег(о) намѣстника пшл же году.

Да дѣтем своим меньшим, Юрью з брат(ь)ею, даю дворы внутри города у Р(о)ж(е)ства Х(ри)с(то)ва, Петровскои, да Ивановскои, да Микитинскои Костантиновичев, да княж Александршвскои двор Шболенскшг(о), да Васил(ь)евъскои двор Сабурова, да княж Васил(ь)евъскии двор, да княж Ѳешд(о)ршвскои княж Васил(ь)евых детеи Шболенскшг(о), да княж Иваншвскои двор Стригин, да Иваншвскои двор Борисова, да дву Иванов Волшдимеровых детеи Семенова, да Иваншв Михаилова с(ы)на Семенова, да Григорьевскои дворъ Бабин, да Васил(ь)евъскои двор Тучков, да гдѣ мои портные мастеры живут, Ншздря, да Кузнецов, да ушакъ, по Новую улицу, что идет улица шт площади къ Ѳршловским воротом, а шт площади по каа мѣста кол(ь)е бито, а дѣти мои, Юрьи з брат(ь)ею, тѣ мѣста меж соба поделат поршвну.

Да с(ы)ну своему Юрью даю на Мшсквѣ селцо Сущово з дворы з горшдцкими с посадными, а по котораа мѣста дал есми ему тѣ дворы горшдные, и яз ему дал список за своею печат(ь)ю и за дьяка своег(о) пшдписью. А из Мшсковских сел даю ему село Лыткино з д(е)р(е)внами.

А с(ы)ну своему Дмитрею даю на Мшсквѣ селцо Напрудцкое з дворы з горшдцкими с посадными, а по котораа мѣста дал есми ему тѣ дворы горшдные, и яз ему дал списокъ за свою печат(ь)ю и за д(ь)яка своег(о) пшдписью. А из Мшскшвских сел даю ему Шзеретцкіе села Старое да Новое з д(е)р(е)внами.

А с(ы)ну своему Семену даю на Москвѣ селцо Луцинское, и с мелницею, и со псарнею, да слободу княж Васил(ь)евъскую Ромадановского, а по котораа мѣста дал есми ему ту слободку и селцо, и яз ему дал список за своею печат(ь)ю и за д(ь)яка своег(о) пшдписью. А из Мшсковских сел даю ему Ршзудовские села за Похрою, Зверево да Бораново, з д(е)р(е)внами, что есми выменил у братних детеи у Борисовых.

А с(ы)ну своему Андрѣю даю на Москвѣ за рекою слободу Колычевскую да монастыр(ь) Р(о)ж(е)ство пр(е)ч(и)стые на Голутвинѣ, а по котораа мѣста дал есми ему ту слободу и монастыр(ь), и яз ему дал список за своею печат(ь)ю и за д(ь)яка своег(о) пшдписью. А из Мшсковъских сел даю ему село Юсенево, да село Сарыево, да Юдино з д(е)р(е)внами.

А из тамги из московские и из всѣх пошлин с(ы)нъ мои Василеи дает дѣтем моимъ, а свои брат(ь)е молодчеи, Юрью з брат(ь)ею, на всакои гшд по сту рублев: Юрью сто рублев, Дмитрею сто рублев, Семену сто рублев, Андрѣю сто рублев.

А что есми дал дѣтемъ своим, Юрью, Дмитрею, Семену, Андрѣю, въ Мшсквѣ годы, как имъ своих намѣстников дръжати, и дворы им внутри города, и что есми им дал селца у Мшсквы, и двориш городцких, и денег из тамги, и сел въ Московских станѣх, и шни то вѣдают, как имъ в сеи

д(у)ховнои грамотѣ писано. А шприч(ь) ти‑г(о) у моег(о) с(ы)на у Васи‑
л(ь)а, а у своег(о) брата у старѣишаг(о), на Ми‑сквѣ въ дворы в гор‑дные,
и на посадех въ дворы, и в тамгу во всю, и въ пошлины во всѣ, такъ ж
и въ станы, и в волости, и в пути, и в села в Ми‑сковскіе во всѣ
не въступаютсл ни во что, а вѣдаютъ то по тому, как имъ в сеи д(у)х(о)в‑
нои грамотѣ писано.

Да бл(а)гословлꙗю с(ы)на своег(о) Юрьꙗ, даю емꙋ горшд Дмитриш
с волостми, и с путми, и з селы, и со всѣми пошлинами, шприч(ь)
Переславских волостеи, Серебожа, Р(о)ж(е)ственог(о), Бꙋскꙋтова, что есми‑
дал с(ы)нꙋ Васил(ь)ю къ Переаславлю, и шприч(ь) Замшсковских волос‑
стеи, что есми их дал с(ы)нꙋ же своемꙋ Васил(ь)ю къ Ми‑сквѣ, и в тѣ
волости с(ы)нъ мои Юрьи у моег(о) с(ы)на у Васил(ь)а, а у своег(о)
брата у старѣишаг(о), не въступаетсл ничѣмъ. А что въ Дмитришвском
ꙋѣзде, в‑Ынобаже, д(е)р(е)вни Тѣшилшвские за моим дꙗком за Шдинцом,
и тѣ д(е)р(е)вни с(ы)нꙋ же моемꙋ Юрью къ Дмитровꙋ, а с(ы)нъ мои
Василеи в тѣ д(е)р(е)вни в Тѣшиловские, в‑Ынобаже, у с(ы)на у моег(о)
у Юрьꙗ не въступаетсл и не танетъ их к Тѣши|ловꙋ ничѣмъ. Да с(ы)нꙋ же *л. 5*
своемꙋ Юрью даю къ Дмитровꙋ ис Переаславских волостеи Юлкꙋ
и з бортным станом, и в тѣ волости с(ы)нъ мои Василеи у моег(о)
с(ы)на у Юрьꙗ не въступаетсл ничѣмъ. Да емꙋ ж даю горшд Звени‑
горшд с волостьми, и с путми, и з селы, и со всѣми пошлинами,
да волость Шопьковꙋ со всѣм. Да с(ы)нꙋ же своемꙋ Юрью даю
во Тѳерскои землѣ горшд Кашин с волостьми, и с путми, и з селы,
и со всѣми пошлинами по томꙋ, по каа мѣста писал х Кашинꙋ писецъ
нашъ Василеи Карамышев. А что ми дал братанич мои, кнꙗз(ь) Иван Бори‑
сович, свою шчинꙋ горшд Рꙋзꙋ с волостьми, и с путми, и з селы,
и со всѣми пошлинами, и с тѣми волостьми, и з станы, что сл дѣлил
з братом съ своим ѳеш‑д(о)ромъ шт Волока, шприч(ь) Рюхи‑ского(о)
села з д(е)р(е)внами, что дал братанич мои Иван братꙋ своемꙋ Ѳеш‑д(о)рꙋ,
и ꙗз горшд Рꙋзꙋ с волостьми, и с путми, и з селы, и со всѣми
пошлинами, и с тѣми волостьми и з станы, что сл дѣлил з братом
съ своим съ Ѳе(о)д‑ром шт Волока, даю с(ы)нꙋ своемꙋ Юрью, со всѣмъ
с тѣм, по томꙋ, как было за моим братаничем за Иваном, шприч(ь)
Рюховского(о) села з д(е)р(е)внами. Да с(ы)нꙋ же своемꙋ Юрью даю
горшд Бранескъ с волостьми, и с погосты, и з селы, и со всѣми пошли‑
нами, со всѣмъ, что къ Бранскꙋ потагло, да волости Солшв(ь)евичи,
Прикладни, Пацꙗн, Ѳе(о)д(ш)ровскаа, Шсовикъ, Покиничи, Сꙋхар(ь),
Въсеславль, Вороница, Жерꙑн, Батогова, Хвощна. Пиꙗнова, Волконескъ.
Да емꙋ ж даю горшд Серпѣескъ с волостми и со всѣмъ, что к немꙋ
потагло, а волости Замшш(ь)е, Тꙋхачев, Дегна, Ѳоминичи, Погостище,
Ковылна, Ближевичи, Любꙗн, Снопшт(ь), Даниловичи, Шꙋа, Дѣмена,
Ꙋжеперет, Чернатици, Городечна, Мощꙑн, да Гнѣздилово, что
была вотчина кн(ꙗ)за Александра кнꙗж Иванова с(ы)на Гнѣздиловского(о)
со всѣмъ с тѣм, что къ Бранскꙋ, и къ Серпѣискꙋ, и къ тѣмъ волостемъ
потагло, как было при мнѣ.

Да бл(а)гословлꙗю с(ы)на своег(о) Дмитреꙗ, даю емꙋ горшд Ꙋглече
поле с волостьми, и с путми, и з селы, и со всѣми пошлинами, и с Ꙋстюж‑
ною, и с Рожаловым, и с Велетовым, и с Кистьмою, и со всѣм, с тѣмъ
что к Ꙋглечю и к тѣмъ волостемъ потагло, горшд Мологꙋ и з Глѣбовых
вотчиною, и съ езы на Волзѣ и на Молозе, со всѣмъ, по томꙋ, как было
при мнѣ. А что есми свел торгъ с Холшп(ь)а горшдка на Мологꙋ,
и тотъ торгъ торгꙋют на Молозе съезжаꙗсл, как было при мнѣ, а с(ы)нъ
мои Дмитреи емлетъ пошлины, как было при мнѣ, а лишних пошлин
не прибавливаетъ ничег(о), а с(ы)нъ мои Василеи и мои дѣти тог(о)

торгꙋ на свои земли не сводꙗт, ни заповеди въ своих землах не чинꙗт
к томꙋ торгꙋ ѣздити. Да емꙋ ж даю горѡд Хлепен, и с Рогачевым,
и с Нѣгомиремъ, с волостьми, и с пꙋтми, и з селы, и со всѣми
пошлинами. Да въ Тѳерскои землѣ даю емꙋ горѡд Зꙋбцов с волостьми,
и с пꙋтми, и з селы, и со всѣми пошлинами, горѡд Ѡпоки с волостьми,
и с пꙋтми, и з селы, и со всѣми пошлинами, по томꙋ, по каа мѣста
писал къ Зꙋбцовꙋ и к Опокам писец нашъ Дмитреи Пѣшков. А что ми
дал братанич мои, кнꙗз(ь) Иван Борисович, свою ѡтчинꙋ, половинꙋ Ржевы
с волостьми, и с пꙋтми, и з селы, и со всѣми пошлинами, по томꙋ,
как сꙗ дѣлил съ своим братом с Ѳе(о)дꙑромъ, и ꙗз половинꙋ Ржевы
с волостьми, и с пꙋтми, и з селы, и со всѣми пошлинами даю с(ы)нꙋ же
своемꙋ Дмитрею со всѣмъ по томꙋ, как было за моим братаничем за Иваном. Да с(ы)нꙋ же своемꙋ Дмитрею даю горѡд Мѣческъ с волостьми,
и с погосты, и з селы, и со всѣми пошлинами, со всѣмъ, что к немꙋ
потагло, как был за мѣзетцкими кнꙗзми, горѡд Ѡпакꙑв со всѣмъ,
что к немꙋ потагло, да волости Залидов, Недоходово, Лычино, Быш-
ковичи по Ꙋгрꙋ со всѣмъ с тѣмъ, что к Опаковꙋ и к тѣмъ волостемъ
потагло, как было при мнѣ.

Да бл(а)гословлꙗю с(ы)на своег(о) Семена, даю емꙋ горѡд Бѣжытцкои
Верхъ с волостми, и с пꙋтми, и з селы, и со всѣми пошлинами,
горѡд Колꙋгꙋ с волостми, и с пꙋтми, и з селы, и со всѣми пошлинами.
Да с(ы)нꙋ же своемꙋ Семенꙋ даю горѡд Козелескъ с волостми, и з селы,
а волости Козелские: Серенескъ, да Людимескъ, да Коробки, и Вырки,
на Вырке на рекѣ волости Сѣнища, да Сытичи, да Выино, и с-ыными
мѣсты, да Липици, да Възбынѡв, да Верхъ-Серена, да Лꙋган, да Мѣсти-
лово, да Кꙿцын, да Хвостовичи, да Порыски, да Боратин, да Ѡрень,
да Хостьци, да Жеремин, да Сныхово, да Ивановское Бабина село
Незнаново, и с-ыными мѣсты, со всѣм с тѣм, что к тѣм волостем и селом
потагло.

Да бл(а)гословлꙗю с(ы)на своег(о) Андрѣа, даю емꙋ горѡд Верею
с волостми, и с пꙋтми, и з селы, и со всѣми пошлинами, горѡд
Вышегорѡд с волостми, и с пꙋтми, и з селы, и со всѣми пошлинами,
горѡд Ѡлеин с волостми, и с пꙋтми, и з селы, и со всѣми пошлинами, и с Волконою, и с Конинꙑм, и з Гордѣевꙑм, и с Нюховою,
и со всѣмъ с тѣмъ, что к тѣм мѣстом потагло. Да емꙋ ж даю горѡд
Любꙋтескъ с волостми, и со всѣми пошлинами, и со всѣмъ, что к немꙋ
потагло, как было при мнѣ, и с Веприным, что за ѡдоевскими кнꙗзми.

л. 6 Да с(ы)нꙋ же своемꙋ || Андрѣю даю ꙋ Москвы Гжелю, да Раме-
неицо со всѣмъ, что к ним потагло. Да что были к Дмитровꙋ приданы
волости Московские Селна, Гꙋслица, Загарье, Вꙋхна, Кꙋнеи, и ꙗз тѣ
волости со всѣмъ даю с(ы)нꙋ своему Андрѣю, а с(ы)нъ мои Юрьи в тѣ
волости ꙋ нег(о) не въстꙋпаетсꙗ ничѣмъ. А что в Селне д(е)р(е)вни деловые
бортные Василцова ста Бекренево, Беланицино, Новое Беланицино,
Харитоновское, Деденево, Нероново, Враниково, Ꙗкимѡвское, Новое
Ꙗкимовское, да пꙋстоши Лопаково, Исачково, Грибачево, и ꙗз тѣ д(е)р(е)-
вни и пꙋстоши со всѣмъ даю с(ы)нꙋ же своемꙋ Андрѣю, а с(ы)нъ мои
Василеи ꙋ него въ то не въстꙋпаетсꙗ. Да въ Тѳерскои землѣ даю емꙋ
горѡд Старицꙋ с волостми, и с пꙋтми, и з селы, и со всѣми пошлинами
по томꙋ, по каа мѣста писал къ Старице писецъ наш Борис Кꙋтꙋзов.
Да даю емꙋ Холмꙿских вотчинꙋ, Холмъ и Новои городок, да волость
Ѡлешню, да волость Синюю, и иные волости, и пꙋти, и села, со всѣми
пошлинами по томꙋ, по каа мѣста тѣ ѡтчины, и волости, и пꙋти, и села
писал писецъ н(а)шъ Андрѣи Карамышев.

А что есми дал дѣтем своим меньшим, Юрью, Дмитрею, Семенꙋ,
Андрѣю, городов, и волостеи, и селъ, и ѡни то и вѣдаютъ по томꙋ, как

150

имъ в сеи д(ꙋ)х(о)внои грамотѣ писано, а ѡприч(ь) тог(о) ꙋ с(ы)на ꙋ моег(о) ꙋ Васил(ь)ѧ ни во что не въстꙋпаютсѧ.

А с(ы)нъ мои Юрьи з брат(ь)ею по своим ꙋдѣлом въ Московскои землѣ и въ Тфѣрскои денег дѣлати не велѧт, а денги велит дѣлати с(ы)нъ мои Василеи на Мѡсквѣ и во Тѳѣри, как было при мнѣ. А ѡткꙋп вѣдает с(ы)нъ мои Василеи, а в откꙋп ꙋ нег(о) мои дѣти, Юрьи з брат(ь)ею, не въстꙋпаютсѧ.

А что есми подавал дѣтем своим селца ꙋ Москвы з дворы з городцкими на посадех, и дѣти мои в тѣх дворех торгов не дръжат, ни жытом не велѧт торговати, ни лавок не ставѧт, ни гостеи с товаром иноземцов, и из Московскіе земли, и из своих ꙋдѣлов въ своих дворех не велѧт ставити, а ставѧтсѧ гости с товаром, иноземци, и из Московские земли, и из ихъ ꙋдѣлов, на гостиных дворех, как было при мнѣ. А дѣти мои ꙋ моег(о) с(ы)на ꙋ Васил(ь)ѧ въ тѣ дворы въ гостиные и в тѣ пошлины не въстꙋпаютсѧ. А кто ꙋчнет въ дѣтеи моих селцех и въ дворех въ горѡдных торговати сьестным товаром, и с(ы)нъ мои Василеи тѣх торгов не велит сводити, а пошлинꙋ полавочнꙋю с них берет с(ы)на моег(о) Васил(ь)евъ приказщик, как было при мнѣ.

А что есми дал дѣтем своим, Юрью з брат(ь)ею, ꙋ города ꙋ Москвы селца з дворы з горѡдцкими, и ꙋчинитсѧ въ тѣх селцех и въ дворех в городцких дꙋшегꙋбство или поличное, и то сꙋдит намѣстник болшеи с(ы)на моего Васил(ь)евъ. А что есми дал дѣтем своим, Юрью з братьею, села въ станѣх в Московских, и над тѣми селы сꙋд и дан(ь) моих детеи, а дꙋшегꙋбством и поличным тѣ села танꙋт к городу къ Москвѣ по старинѣ, ѡприч(ь) тог(о) поличног(о), что бꙋдет в тѣх селех промеж ихъ кр(е)стьѧн, то сꙋдат их приказщики, а докладывают намѣстника мѡсковског(о) болшег(о) с(ы)на моего Васил(ь)ева. А грамоты полные и докладные на Москвѣ пишет дыꙗк ꙗмьскии с(ы)на моег(о) Васил(ь)евъ, как было при мнѣ, а ѡприч(ь) тог(о) на Москвѣ грамот полных и докладных не пишет нихто. А которые есми городы и волости подавал дѣтем своим, Юрью з брат(ь)ею, в вꙋдѣлы, а танꙋли дꙋшегꙋбством къ городꙋ къ Мѡсквѣ, и тѣ городы, и ꙋѣзды, и волости тѣх городов танꙋт дꙋшегꙋбством къ городꙋ къ Мѡсквѣ по старине, а дѣти мои, Юрьи з брат(ь)ею, в то не въстꙋпаютсѧ.

А с(ы)нъ мои Василеи ꙋ моих детеи, а ꙋ своеи брат(ь)и, въ их ꙋдѣлех земел(ь) не кꙋпит, ни дръжыт, ни закладнеи не дръжыт. А мои дѣти ꙋ с(ы)на моег(о) ꙋ Васил(ь)ѧ въ Мѡсквѣ и въ всем его в великом кнѧжствѣ земел(ь) не кꙋпѧт, ни дръжат, ни закладнеи не дръжат. А что есми давал свои села боꙗром своим, и кн(ѧ)зем, и дѣтем боꙗрским, и грамоты есми им свои жаловалные подавал на тѣ села прочно им и их дѣтем, или комꙋ бꙋдꙋ въ кꙋплю дал свои грамоты, и в тѣ села с(ы)нъ мои Василеи и мои дѣти ꙋ них не въстꙋпаютсѧ.

А дѣти мои, Юрьи з брат(ь)ею, дают с(ы)нꙋ моему Васил(ь)ю съ своих ꙋдѣлѡв в выходы в ординские, и въ Крым, и в Азтарахан(ь), и в Казан(ь), и во Царевичев городок, и в-ыные цари и во царевичи, которые бꙋдꙋт ꙋ с(ы)на моег(о) ꙋ Васил(ь)ѧ въ землѣ, и в послы в татарские, которые придꙋт къ Мѡсквѣ, и ко Тѳѣри, и к Новꙋгородꙋ к Нижнемꙋ, и къ Ꙗрославлю, и к Торꙋсе, и к рѧзани къ Старои, и къ Перевитскꙋ ко кнѧж Ѳе(о)дѡровскомꙋ жеребью рѧзанског(о), и во всѣ татарские проторы, въ тысѧчю рꙋблев. С(ы)нъ мои Юрьи дает съ своег(о) ꙋдѣла со всег(о) и с Кашина восмьдесѧт рꙋблев и два рꙋблѧ без гривны. А с(ы)нъ мои Дмитреи дает съ своег(о) ꙋдѣла со всег(о), и з Зꙋпцова, и с Опок, пѧтьдесѧт рꙋблев и восмь рꙋблев с полтиною и семь денег. А с(ы)нъ мои Семен дает съ своег(о) ꙋдѣла со всег(о) шестьдесѧтъ рꙋблев и пать рꙋблев без десѧти денег. А с(ы)нъ мои Андрѣи дает съ своег(о) ꙋдѣла со всег(о), и з Старици, и з Холмъских вотчины, с Холмᲂу, и с Новог(о) городка, и с Олешни, и съ Синие, и с-ыных волостеи с Тверских, что емᲂу дано, сорᲂжк рᲂублев с полтиною и полчетверты денги. А с(ы)нъ мои Василеи дает в тᲂу ж тысачю рᲂублев с Москвы, и со всег(о) великог(о) кнжжен(ь)а Московские земли, и со Тᲂвери, и со всеᲂе Тᲂверские земли, что емᲂу дано, и с Рꙗзани съ Старые, и с Перевитска, семьсотъ рᲂублев и полᲂшсманатцата рублꙗ и пᲂшлтрет(ь)и денги. А Борисов с(ы)нъ братен(ь) ѳе(о)дᲂшръ дает с(ы)нᲂу моемᲂу Васил(ь)ю въ тᲂу же тысачю рᲂублев съ своеи ᲂштчины, и с Колпи, и з Бᲂулагорода, тритьцат(ь) рᲂублев и пᲂшлᲂшсма рублꙗ. А бᲂудет тог(о) болᲂе или менши татарскои протор, и с(ы)нъ мои Василеи, и мои дᲂети, Юрьи з брат(ь)ею, и братанич мои ѳе(о)дᲂшр, дают по розочтᲂу.

л. 7 А с(ы)нъ мои Василеи въ своем великом кнꙗжен(ь)е держꙗт ꙗмы и подводы на дорогах по тᲂемъ мᲂестом, гдᲂе были ꙗмы и подводы на дорогах при мнᲂе. А дᲂети мои, Юрьи з братьею, по своим ᲂштчинам дрꙗжꙗт ꙗмы и подводы на дорогах по тᲂемъ мᲂестом, гдᲂе были ꙗмы и подводы по дорогам при мнᲂе.

А которᲂшг(о) моег(о) с(ы)на не станет, а не ᲂустанетсꙗ ᲂу нег(о) ни с(ы)на, ни внᲂука, ино ег(о) ᲂудᲂел весь в Московскои землᲂе и въ Тᲂверскои землᲂе, что есми емᲂу ни дал, то все с(ы)нᲂу моемᲂу Васил(ь)ю, а брат(ь)а ег(о) ᲂу него въ тот ᲂудᲂел не въстᲂупаютсꙗ. А ᲂустанᲂутсꙗ ᲂу нег(о) дочери, и с(ы)нъ мои Василеи тᲂе его дочери наделив, подает замᲂуж. А что дастъ своеи кнꙗгине волостеи, и сел, и казны, и в ,то во все с(ы)нъ мои Василеи ᲂу неᲂе не въстᲂупаетсꙗ ни во что до еᲂе живота.

А с(ы)на своег(о) Васил(ь)а бл(а)гословлꙗю кр(е)стъ животворащее древо в раце цареградцкои да кр(е)стъ Петрᲂшв чюдотворцев.

А с(ы)на своег(о) Юрьа бл(а)гословлꙗю кр(е)стъ золот Борисоглᲂебъскои.

А с(ы)на своег(о) Дмитреа бл(а)гословлꙗю кр(е)стъ золот Парамшина дᲂела.

А с(ы)на своего Семена бл(а)гословлꙗю кр(е)стъ золот Михаиловъскои вл(а)д(ы)чень.

А с(ы)на своего Андрᲂеꙗ бл(а)гословлꙗю икона золота распꙗт(ь)е, дᲂелана ѳиниѳтомъ с камен(ь)емъ и з жемчюги.

А что есми дал своеи казны своим дᲂетем, Юрью, Дмитрею, Семенᲂу, Андрᲂею, и ꙗз что дал с(ы)нᲂу своемᲂу Юрью своеи казны, и то есми поклал въ ларци, а ᲂу тᲂех ларцов печати моа да с(ы)на моег(о) Юрьева, а ключи тᲂех ларцов ᲂу с(ы)на ᲂу моег(о) ᲂу Юрьа, а тᲂе ларци стоꙗт въ моеи казнᲂе, ᲂу моег(о) казначеꙗ ᲂу Дмитреа ᲂу Волᲂшдимерова, да ᲂу моег(о) печатника ᲂу Юрьа ᲂу Дмитреева с(ы)на ᲂу Грека, да ᲂу моих дьꙗкᲂшв, ᲂу Данилка ᲂу Мамырева да ᲂу Тишка ᲂу Моклокова. А что есми дал своеи казны с(ы)нᲂу своемᲂу Дмитрею, и то есми поклал в ларци, а ᲂу тᲂех ларцов печати моа да с(ы)на моег(о) Дмитреева, а ключи тᲂех ларцов ᲂу с(ы)на ᲂу моег(о) ᲂу Дмитреа, а тᲂе ларци стоꙗт въ моеи казнᲂе ᲂу моег(о) казначеꙗ ᲂу Дмитреа ᲂу Володимерова, да ᲂу моег(о) печатника ᲂу Юрьа ᲂу Дмитреева с(ы)на ᲂу Грека, да ᲂу моих дьꙗков, ᲂу Данила ᲂу Мамырева да ᲂу Тишка ᲂу Моклокова. А что есми дал своеи казны с(ы)нᲂу своемᲂу Семенᲂу, и то есми поклал в ларци, а ᲂу тᲂех ларцов печати моа да с(ы)на моег(о) Семенова, а ключи тᲂех ларцов ᲂу с(ы)на ᲂу моег(о) ᲂу Семена, а тᲂе ларци стоꙗт в моеи казнᲂе ᲂу моег(о) казначеꙗ ᲂу Дмитреа ᲂу Волᲂшдимерова да ᲂу моег(о) печатника ᲂу Юрьа ᲂу Дмитреева с(ы)на ᲂу Грека, да ᲂу моих дьꙗков, ᲂу Данилка ᲂу Мамырева да ᲂу Тишка ᲂу Моклокова. А что есми дал своеи казны с(ы)нᲂу своемᲂу Андрᲂею, и то есми поклал в ларци, а ᲂу тᲂех ларцов печати моа да с(ы)на моег(о) Андрᲂева, а ключи тᲂех ларцов ᲂу с(ы)на ᲂу моег(о) ᲂу Андрᲂеꙗ, а тᲂе ларци стоꙗт в моеи казнᲂе ȣ моег(о) казначѣа ȣ Дмитреа Волѡдимерова, да ȣ моег(о) печатника ȣ Юрьа ȣ Дмитреева с(ы)на ȣ Грека, да ȣ моих дьыков, ȣ Данилка ȣ Мамырева да ȣ Тишка ȣ Моклокова.

А ѡприч(ь) тог(о), что ни есть моеи казны ȣ моег(о) казначѣа ȣ Дмитреа ȣ Волѡдимерова, и ȣ моих дьыков, и ȣ моег(о) дьыка ȣ Семена ȣ Башенина, лалѡв, и ѩхонтов, и иног(о) камен(ь)а, и жемчюгȣ, и сажен(ь)а всаког(о), и помсов, и чепеи золотых, и сȣдов золотых, и серебраных, и каменых, и золота, и серебра, и соболеи, и шолковые рȣхлади, и иные всакие рȣхлади, что ни есть, такъ ж и в моеи казнѣ в постелнои что ни есть, икѡн, и кр(е)стовъ золотых, и золота, и серебра, и плат(ь)а, и иные рȣхлади, и что ни есть ȣ моег(о) дворетцког(о) ȣ Петра ȣ Васил(ь)ева ȣ Великог(о) и ȣ дьыковъ ȣ дворцовых моих сȣдов серебраных, и денег, и иные рȣхлади, и что ни есть ȣ моегѡ конюшег(о), и ȣ моих ѩселничих, и ȣ моих дьыков, и ȣ моих приказщиков, ȣ ког(о) ни бȣди, моих денег и иные рȣхлади всакие, такъ ж что ни есть ȣ моег(о) дворетцког(о) ȣ тверског(о), и ȣ дьыкѡв ȣ тверских, и ȣ моих приказщиков, и в Новѣгородѣ в Великомъ ȣ моег(о) дворетцког(о), и ȣ казначѣев, и ȣ дьыкѡв, и ȣ моих приказщиков, ȣ ког(о) ни бȣди, моих денег и иные рȣхлади всакие, да и на Бѣлѣѡзере и на Вологдѣ моа казна, и гдѣ ни есть моих казен, то вꙁсе с(ы)нȣ моемȣ Васил(ь)ю. А мои дѣти, Юрьи з брат(ь)ею, ȣ моег(о) с(ы)на ȣ Василья ни во что не вꙁстȣпаютса, ѡприч(ь) тог(о), что есми им дал своеи казны.

А приказываю свою дȣшȣ и детеи своих менших, Юрьа, Дмитреа, Семена, Андрѣа, с(ы)нȣ своемȣ Васил(ь)ю. А вы, дѣти мои меньшие, Юрьи з брат(ь)ею, ‖ дрꙁжыте с(ы)на моего Васил(ь)а, а своего брата л. 8 старѣишаго, въ мое мѣсто, своег(о) ѡтца, и слȣшаите ег(о) во всемъ. А ты, с(ы)нъ мои Василеи, дрꙁжи свою брат(ь)ю меньшȣю, Юрьа, Дмитреа, Семена, Андрѣа, въ братствѣ, и во чти, без ѡбиды.

А которои мои с(ы)нъ не ȣчнет с(ы)на моего Васил(ь)а слȣшати во всем, или ȣчнет пѡд нимъ под(ъ)искивати великих кнѩжствъ или пѡд его детми, или ȣчнет ѡт нег(о) ѡтстȣпати, или ȣчнет съсылатиса с кѣмъ ни бȣди таино или ѩвно на ег(о) лихо, или ȣчнȣт ког(о) на нег(о) пѡд(ъ)имати, или с кѣмъ ȣчнȣт на нег(о) ѡдиначитиса, или не бȣди на нем м(и)л(о)сти б(о)жіеи, и пр(е)ч(и)стые б(о)г(о)м(а)т(е)ри, и с(вѩ)тых чюдотворецъ м(о)л(и)твы, и рѡдител(ь) наших, и нашег(о) бл(а)г(о)с(ло)веніа и въ сіи вѣкъ и в бȣдȣщіи.

А кто бȣдеть моих казначѣев, или кто бȣдет моих дьыкѡв прибытки мои ѡт менѩ вѣдали, или тивȣни, или поселскіе, или кто женилса ȣ тѣх, тѣ всѣ не надобѣ с(ы)нȣ моемȣ Васил(ь)ю и моимъ дѣтем, Юрью з брат(ь)ею.

А кто порȣшит сию мою грамотȣ, сȣдит емȣ б(о)гъ, и не бȣди на немъ моег(о) бл(а)г(о)с(ло)веніа.

А ȣ сеѣ моеи д(ȣ)шевꙁные грамоты сидѣл ѡ(те)цъ мои д(у)хѡвнои, ѡндрѡнникѡвскои архімандрить Митрофан. А тȣто были боѩре мои: кнѩз(ь) Василеи Данилович, да кнѩз(ь) Данило Васил(ь)евич, да Ѩкѡв Захар(ь)ичь, да казначѣи мои Дмитреи Вѡлодимерович.

А сию мою д(ȣ)шевнȣю грамотȣ писал дьыкъ мои Данилко Мамыревъ.

Пометы на обороте первого листа: (почерком XVI в.). Список з д(у)ховные грамоты великог(о) кн(ѩ)за Iвана Васил(ь)евичя вꙁсеа Рȣсіи, *[почерком XVII в.]* при Симоне, митрополите всеа Рȣсіи, а в котором году д(ȣ)ховная писана, тово не написано.

*Основание для датировки: докончание в. кн. Василия Ивановича
с братьями от 16 июня 1504 г. ссылается на духовную в. кн. Ивана Васильевича (Гос. древлехранилище, отд. I, рубр. II, № 79). См. Черепнин, стр. 220—223.*

*Список начала XVI в. — ЦГАДА, Гос. древлехранилище, отд. I, рубр. I, № 34. Духов-
ная грамота ранее напечатана: Древняя Российская Вивлиофика, ч. 2, изд. 2, стр. 408—
434, № 123; Продолжение Древней Российской Вивлиофики, ч. 5, стр. 51—91; Щер-
батов, т. 4, ч. 3, № 81; СГГД, ч. 1, стр. 389—400, № 144; Бахрушин, стр. 32—43.*

№ 100.

*1523 г. июня. — Духовная запись великого князя
Василия Ивановича.*

Вꙗ имꙗ с(вѧ)тыѧ жывоначалныѧ тро(и)ца, и по бл(а)гословенію ѿца
н(а)шего Данила, митрополита всеа Рꙋсіи, пишꙋ сію запис(ь), идꙋчи на свое
дѣло х Казани.

Се ꙗз, хꙋдыи раб б(о)жіи Василеи, что есми наперед сего писал свою
д(ꙋ)х(о)внꙋю грамотꙋ, да списꙿк приписнои къ д(ꙋ)ховнои грамотѣ, а пꙉдписал тꙋ д(ꙋ)х(о)внꙋю грамотꙋ и списꙿк Варламъ, митрополит всеа Рꙋсіи,
своею рꙋкою, да и печат(ь) свою Варлам митрополит к тои д(ꙋ)х(о)внои
грамотѣ и къ сп(и)скꙋ приложил, а ꙗз к тои д(ꙋ)х(о)внои грамотѣ и къ
спискꙋ свою печат(ь) приложил, и ꙗз н(ы)нѣ свою д(ꙋ)шꙋ и свою кн(ѧ)-
г(и)ню, по тои д(ꙋ)х(о)внои грамотѣ и по тому приписному спискꙋ, приказываю ѿцꙋ своемꙋ Данилꙋ, митрополитꙋ всеа Рꙋсіи. Да и тꙋ д(ꙋ)-
х(о)внꙋю грамотꙋ и тꙉт приписнои списꙿк ем ж, ѿцꙋ своемꙋ,
приказываю.

Да коли есми з б(о)жіею волею достал своеи ѿчины, города Смоленьска
и земли Смоленьскіе, и ꙗз тогды обѣщал поставити на Мꙉсквѣ на посаде
Д(ѣ)вичь манастырь, а в нем храм во имꙗ Пр(е)ч(и)стые да Происхожде-
ніе ч(е)стнаго кр(е)ста, и иные храмы, а которые храмы в том манастырѣ
поставити, и ꙗз томꙋ велѣл написати запис(ь) діакꙋ своемꙋ Труфанꙋ
Ильинꙋ своею рꙋкою да дати печатникꙋ своемꙋ Ивану Трет(ь)ꙗкꙋ.
А дати есми обѣщал в тꙉт манастырь из своих сел дворцовых село или
два, а пашни в тѣх селех в ꙉдномъ поле тысачѧ четвертеи, а в двꙋ
полех по тому ж, да на строеніе томꙋ манастырю три тысѧчи рꙋблев
денег. И н(ы)нѣ есми тог(о) манастырѧ състроити не ꙋспѣл. И нѣчто
б(о)жьѧ волѧ надо мною състанетсꙗ, а тог(о) манастырѧ при своем жывотѣ не ꙋспѣю състроити, и ꙗз приказал казначѣм своим и приказным
своим людем на том мѣсте тꙉт манастырь състроити. А из сел из своих
из дворцовых в тот манастырь велѣл есми дати село или два, в ꙉдном
поле на тысачю четвертеи, а в двꙋ полех по тому ж. А на строеніе томꙋ
манастырю н(а)шы казначѣи дадꙋт три тысѧчи рꙋблев денег.

И сію запис(ь) ѿ(е)цъ нашъ Данил, митрополит всеа Рꙋсіи, пꙉдписал
своею рꙋкою, и печат(ь) свою к сеи записи приложил.

А мы к сеи записи свою печат(ь) приложылы.

А кто сію мою запис(ь) через мои приказ порꙋшыт, и тот сꙋдитсꙗ
сꙉ мною пред б(о)гꙉм.

А коли есми сію запис(ь) писал, и тогды был оу ѿца н(а)шего Данила,
митрополита всеа Рꙋсіи, оу сеи записи старец Васьꙗн кнꙗж Іванꙉв, да
ѿ(е)цъ мои д(ꙋ)х(о)внои Василеи, протопꙉп бл(а)говѣщеньскои.

А сію запис(ь) писал діакъ мои Меншыкъ Пꙋтꙗтинъ, лѣта 7000 трит-
цат(ь) первагꙉ, м(ѣ)с(ѧ)ца и(ю)нꙗ.

Внизу подпись: Грѣшныи и хꙋдыи инокъ Данилъ, милостию б(о)жиею митрополит всеа Рꙋсіи.

На лицевой стороне грамоты привешены две печати: в. кн. Василия Ивановича (красновосковая) и митрополита Даниила (черновосковая).

Подлинник — ЦГАДА, Гос. древлехранилище, отд. I, рубр. I, № 36. Духовная запись ранее напечатана: Древняя Российская Вивлиофика, ч. 3, изд. 2, стр. 30—32, № 129; Продолжение Древней Российской Вивлиофики, ч. 5, стр. 140—143; СГГД, ч. 1, стр. 416—417, № 150; Бахрушин, стр. 43—44.

№ 104.

[1572 г. июня—августа] — Духовная грамота царя Ивана Васильевича IV.

л. 2   Духовная царя и великаго князя Иоанна Васильевича, самодержца всероссийскаго.

Во имя отца, и сына, и святаго духа, святыя и живоначальныя троицы, и ныне, и присно, и во веки веков, аминь, и по благословению отца нашего Антония, митрополита всея России, се аз, многогрешный и худый раб божий Иоанн, пишу сие исповедание своим целым разумом. Но понеже разума нищетою содержим есмь, и от убогаго дому ума моего не могох представити трапезы, пищи ангельских словес исполнены, понеже ум убо острюпюсь, тело изнеможе, болезнует дух, струпи телесна и душевна умножишася, и не сущу врачу, исцеляющему мя, ждах, иже со мною поскорбит, и не бе, утешающих не обретох, воздаша ми

л. 2 об.   злая возблагая, и ненависть за возлюбление ‖ мое. Душею убо осквернен есмь и телом окалях. Яко же убо от Иерусалима божественных заповедей и ко ерихонским страстем пришед, и житейских ради подвиг прелстихся мира сего мимотекущею красотою; яко же к мирным гражданам привед, и багряницею светлости и златоблещанием предахся умом, и в разбойники впадох мысленныя и чувственныя, помыслом и делом; усынения благодати совлечен бых одеяния, и ранами исполумертв оставлен, но паче нежели возмнитися видящим, но аще и жив, но богу скаредными своими делы паче мертвеца смраднеиший и гнуснеиший, его же иереи видев, не внят, Левит и той возгнушася, премину мне. Понеже от Адама и до сего дни всех преминух в беззакониях согрешивших, сего ради

л. 3   всеми ненавидим есмь, ‖ Каиново убийство прешед, Ламеху уподобихся, первому убийце, Исаву последовах скверным невоздержанием, Рувиму уподобихся, осквернившему отче ложе, несытства и иным многим яростию и гневом невоздержания. И понеже быти уму зря бога и царя страстем, аз разумом растленен бых, и скотен умом и проразумеванием, понеже убо самую главу осверних желанием и мыслию неподобных дел, уста разсуждением убийства, и блуда, и всякаго злаго делания, язык срамословия, и сквернословия, и гнева, и ярости, и невоздержания всякаго неподобнаго дела, выя и перси гордости и чаяния высокоглаголиваго разума, руце осязания неподобных, и грабления несытно, и продерзания, и убийства внутрения, ея же помыслы всякими скверными и неподобными осверних, объядении и пиянства, чресла чрезъесте-

л. 3 об.   ственная блужения, и неподобнаго воздержания ‖ и опоясания на всяко дело зло, нозе течением быстрейших ко всякому делу злу, и скверно-деяниа, и убивства, и граблением несытнаго богатства, и иных неподобных глумлений. Но что убо сотворю, понеже Авраам не уведе нас, Исаак не разуме нас, и Израиль не позна нас! Но ты, господи, отец наш еси, к тебе прибегаем, и милости просим, иже не от Самарии, но от Марии девы неизреченно воплотивыйся, от пречистых тя ребр воде и крови, яко масло, возлияв, Христе, боже, язвы струп моих глаголюще душевныя и телесныя, обяжи и к небесному сочетай мя лику; яко милосерд, господи, боже мой, мир даждь нам, разве тебе иного не знаем, и имя твое разумеем; просвяти лице твое на ны и помилуй ны. Твоя бо есть держава неприкладна, и царство безначално и безконечно, и сила, и слава, и держава, ныне, и присно, и во веки веков, аминь. ||

И понеже, по писанию, не должни суть хранити имения чада родите- л. 4 лям, но родителие чадам, и яже убо вышнее имение, яко же реченно: «премудрость во исходящих поется, на краех же забралных мест проповедается, при вратех же сильных дерзающи глаголет, се предлагаю вам глас мой, сыновом человеческим, лучше бо ту куповати, паче злата и сокровища многа, честнейшии же суть камения многоценна, все честное недостойно ея есть». Глаголет господь: «мною царие царствуют и сильнии пишут правду». Сего ради и аз предлагаю учения, елико мой есть разум, от убожества моего, чадца моя, благодать и божий дар вам.

Се заповедаю вам, да любите друг друга, и бог мира да буди с вами. Аще бо сия сохраните, и вся благая достигнете; веру к богу тверду и непостыдну держите, и стоите, и научитися божественных догматов, како веровати, и како богу угодная творити, и в какове оправдании пред нелицымерным судиею стати. || То всего больше знайте: православ- л. 4 с ную христианскую веру держите крепко, за нее страждите крепко и до смерти. А сами живите в любви. А воинству, поелику возможно, навыкните. А как людей держати, и жаловати, и от них беречися, и во всем их умети к себе присвоивати, и вы б тому навыкли же. А людей бы есте, которыя вам прямо служат, жаловали и любили, их ото всех берегли, чтобы им изгони ни от кого не было, и оне прямее служат. А которыя лихи, и вы б на тех опалы клали не вскоре, по рассуждению, не яростию. А всякому делу навыкайте, и божественному, и священническому, и иноческому, и ратному, и судейскому, московскому пребыванию, и житейскому всякому обиходу, и как которыя чины ведутся здесь и в·ыных государствах, и здешнее государство с иными государствы что имеет, то бы есте сами знали. Также и во обиходе во всяких, как кто живет, и как кому пригоже быти, и в какове мере кто держится, тому б есте всему научены были. Ино вам люди не указывают, вы станите людям указывати. А чего сами не познаете, и вы сами стате *[так в рукописи!]* своими государствы владети и людьми.

А что, по множеству || беззаконий моих, божию гневу распростершуся, л. 5 изгнан есмь [1] от бояр, самоволства их ради, от своего достояния, и скитаюся [2] по странам, а може бог когда не оставит, и вам есми грехом своим беды многия нанесены, бога ради, не пренемогайте в скорбех, возвержите на господа печаль свою, и той вас препитает, по пророку глаголющу: «отец мя и мати остависта, господь же восприимет, понеже бо вся в руце господеви, яко чаша уклони от сия, в сию смиряет, а сего возносит, никто же бо приемлет честь отъ себе, но званный от бога, дает бо власть, ему же хощет, и воздвизает от земли убога и от гноища возносит нища, посадити его с князи людей, и престол славы наследует ему».

---

[1] *Примечание переписчика:* зде изгнание не значит лишение престола, но ненависть на него, в последней же духовной, учиненной въ 7090 году, яснее о сем говорит и мстить запрещает.

[2] *Примечание переписчика:* скитание свое имянует, что изволил от страха бунтов жить в городе Старице, а более в Александровой слободе.

А докудова вас бог помилует, свободит от бед, и вы ничем не разделяйтесь, и люди бы у вас заодин служили, и земля бы заодин, и казна бы у вас заодин была, ино то вам прибыльняе.

5 об.   А ты, Иван сын, ‖ береги сына Федора, а своего брата, как себя, чтоб ему ни в каком обиходе нужды не было, а всем бы был исполнен, чтобы ему на тебя не в досаду, что ему не дашь удела и казны. А ты, Федор сын, Ивана сына, своего брата старейшаго, докудова строитель, уделу и казны не прося, а в своем бы еси обиходе жил, смечаясь, как бы Ивану сыну не убыточнее, а тебя б льзе прокормити было, и оба вы есте жили заодин и во всем устроивали, как бы прибыточнее. А ты бы, сын Иван, моего сына Федора, а своего брата молодшаго, держал, и берег, и любил, и жаловал его, и добра ему хотел во всем так, как себе хочешь, и на его лихо ни с кем не ссылался, а везде бы еси был с Федором сыном, а своим братом молотшим, и в худе и в добре, один человек, занеже единородныя есть у матери своей.

И вы бы сами о себе прибежище положили, яко же рече Христос во святом евангелии: «иде же собрани аще два или три во имя мое, ту
л. 6 есмь аз посреде их». И аще ‖ Христос будет посреде вас для вашея любви, и никто может вас поколебати, вы будете друг другу стена, и забрало, и крепость. К кому ему прибегнуть и на кого уповать! Ты у него отец, и мать, и брат, и государь, и промысленник. И ты б его берег, и любил, и жаловал, как себя. А хотя буде в чем пред тобою и проступку какую учинит, и ты его понаказал и пожаловал, а до конца б его не разорял, а ссоркам бы еси отнюдь не верил, занеже Каин Авеля убил, а сам не наследовал же.

А бог благоволит вам, тебе быть на государстве, а брату твоему Федору на уделе, и ты б удела его под ними не подъискивал, а на него лиха ни с кем ни ссылался.

А где по рубежам сошлась твоя земля с его землею, и ты б его берег и накрепко бы еси смотрел правды, а напрасно бы еси не задирался, а людским бы вракам не потакал, занеже, аще кто и множество земли приобрящет и богатства, а трилакотна гроба не может избежати, и тогды то все останется, по господней притчи, — ему же угобзися нива,
6 об. иже хотяше разорити житницы ‖ и болшая создати, к нему же рече господь: «безумне, в сию нощь душу твою истяжут отъ тебе, а яже уготова, кому будет?».

А ты б любовь нелицемерную держал к брату своему, а к моему сыну Федору, яко же рече божественный апостол Павел: «любы не завидит, любы не гордится, любы не злообразуется, не вменяет злое, не радуется о неправде, радуется же о истинне, все уповает, вся терпит, любы николи же отпадает»; яко же рече той же апостол: «аще кто о ближних своих не промышляет, веры отвергся, и есть невернаго горши».

А ты, сыне мои Федор, держи сына моего Ивана в мое место, отца своего, и слушай его во всем, как мене, и покорен буди ему во всем, и добра хоти ему, как мне, родителю своему, во всем, и во всем бы
л. 7 еси Ивану сыну непрекословен был так, как мне, отцу своему, ‖ и во всем бы еси жил так, как из моего слова. А будет благоволит бог ему на государстве быти, а тебе на уделе, и ты б государства его под ним не подыскивал, и на ево лихо не ссылался ни с кем, а везде бы еси с Иваном сыном был в лихе и в добре один человек. А докуды, и по грехом, Иван сын государства не доступит, а ты удела своего,[1] и ты бы с сыном Иваном вместе был заодин, и с его бы еси изменники и с лиходеи

---

[1] *Примечание переписчика:* зде еще страх свой о лишении престола изъявляет.

никоторыми делы не ссылался. А будут тебе учнут прельщать славаю, и богатством, и честию, или учнут тебе которых городов поступать, или повольность которую учинят, мимо Ивана сына, или на государство учнут звати, и ты б отнюдь того не делал ‖ и из-Ывановой сынов- *л. 7 о* ниной воли не выходил; как Иван сын тебе велит, так бы еси был, а ни на что бы еси не прельщался. А где тебя Иван сын пошлет на свою службу или людей твоих велит тебе на свою службу послати, и ты б на его службу ходил и людей своих посылал, как коли сын мой Иван велит.

А где по рубежам Иванова сыновня земля сошлась с твоею землею, и ты б берег того наикрепко, смотрел бы еси правды, а напрасно бы еси не задирался, и людским бы еси врагам не потакал, занеже еще кто множество богатства или земли приобрящеть, а трилакатнаго гроба ‖ не может избежати, и тогда то все останется, токмо едина дела, *л. 8* что сотворихом, благо ли, или зло.

И ты б сына моего Ивана, а своего брата старейшаго, держал в мое место, отца своего, честно и грозно, и надежду бы еси держать во всем на бога да на него, и ни в чем бы еси ему не завидел, занеже единородные есте у своей матери.

И вы б сами себе прибежище положили, яко же рече Христос во святом евангелии: «иде же собрани два или три во имя мое, то есмь и аз посреде их». И аще Христос будет посреди вас для вашия любви, ино кто может вас поколебать! Он тебе стена, и забрало, и рать, и крепость. К кому тебе прибегнуть и на кого уповать! Он тебе отец, и мать, и брат старейший, и государь, и промысленик.

И ты б, Федор сын, сыну моему Ивану, а своему ‖ брату старей- *л. 8 о* шему, во всем покорен был, и добра ему хотел и во всем так, как мне и себе, и во всем воли его буди, до крови и до смерти, ни в чем ему не прикослови. А хотя будет на тебя Иванов сыновен гнев или обида в чем ни будь, и ты бы сыну моему Ивану, а своему брату старейшему, непрекословен был, и рати никакой ни вчинял, и собою ничем не боронился, а ему еси бил челом, чтоб тебя пожаловал, гнев свой сложить изволил, и жаловал тебя во всем по моему приказу. А в чем будет твоя вина, и ты б ему добил челом, как ему любо, и послушал челобитья, ино добро, а не послушал, и ты б собою не оборонялся ж, а всем бы еси печаль на радость преложа, ‖ положил *л. 9* на бога, занеже всяким неправдам местник есть бог.

А ты б, Иван сын, с братом своим молодшим, а с моим сыном Федором, жил в любви и в согласии заодин во всем, по моему приказу.

И вы б, дети мои, Иван и Федор, жили в любви и в согласии заодин, и сей мой наказ памятовали крепко. Аще бо благо учнете творити, вся вам благая будет. Аще ли злая сотворите, вся вам злая склучатся, яко же речено бысть во евангелии: «аще кто преслушает отца, смертию да умрет». Всего же болши гоните, и утвержайтеся, и разумейте от православныя веры догматех, да зде благоугодно поживши, и тамо ‖ буду- *л. 9 о* щих благ наследницы будете, яже око не виде, и ухо не слыша, и на сердце человеку не взыде, яже уготова бог любящим его. Бога любите от всего сердца, и заповедь его от всего сердца творите, елико ваша сила. Яко же речено бысть во евангелии: «Уподобися царствие небесное десяти девам, яже прияша светилники своя, изыдоша в сретение жениху, пять же бе от них мудрых и пять юродивых, яже приимши светилники своя, не взяша с собою елея, [мудрыя же] прияша елей

в сосудех, со светилники своими; коснящу же жениху, воздремаша вси, и спаша, в полунощи же вопль бысть: се жених грядет, исходите во сретение ему. Тогда воставше вся девы тыя, украсиша светилники своя,
л. 10 юродивыя же мудрым реша: ‖ дадите нам от масла вашего, яко светилницы наши угасают. Отвещаша же мудрыя: егда нам и вам не достанет, идите же паче к продающим и купите себе. Идущим же им купити, прииде жених, и готовыя внидоша с ним на браки и затворени быша двери. Последи же приидоша и протчия девы, глаголюще: господи, господи, отверзи нам. Он же отвещав, рече им: аминь, глаголю вам, [не вем вас, бдите убо], яко не весте дне и часа, в он же сын человеческии приидет». И паки глаголет: «Человек некий отходя, призва своя рабы и предаст им имение свое, овому даст пять талант, овому жь два, овому жь един, комуждо противу силы его. Имый пять талант дела в них, и сотвори другия пять талант. ‖ Такожде же иже два име, приобрете им другая два. Приемый же един, вкопа его в землю и скры сребро господина своего. По мнозе же времяни прииде господь раб тех, стезася с ними словесы. И приступл пять талант приемы, принесе другую пять талант, глаголя: господи, пять талант ми еси предал, и се другая пять при-
10 об. обретох ими. Рече же ему господь его: добрый рабе, благий и верный, в мале бысть верен, над многими тя поставлю, вниди в радость господа своего. Приступл же два талант приемый, рече: господи, два таланта ми еси предал, се другая два таланта приобретох ими». И сей тут же благодать прия. Закопавы же в землю прият наказание. Размыслите в сердце своем
л. 11 и веру имейте, ‖ яко иже глаголет, бывает, яко речет: «Глаголю вам, вся, елика аще молящеся просите, веруйте, яко приемлете, и будет вам. И егда стоите молящеся, отпущаете, и отец ваш, иже есть на небесех, отпустит вам согрешения ваша. Небо и земля преидет, словеса же моя не преидут. О дни том и о часе никто же весть, ни ангели, иже суть на небесех, ни сын, токмо отец. Блюдите, бдите, молитеся, не весте бо, когда господь дому приидет, в вечер, или в полунощь, или в петлоглашение, или утро, да пришед внезапу, обрящет вы спяща. Весте, яко царие язык господствует и велицы обладают, не тако же будет в вас, понеже
11 об. аще хощет вящий быти, ‖ да будет всем слуга; иже аще хощет в вас быти старейший, да будет всем раб, яко же сын человеческий не прииде, да послужат ему, но да послужити и дати душу свою избавление за многих». Я же вам глаголю: «Иже бо аще кто постыдится моих словес, и сын человеческий постыдится его, егда приидет во славе своей и отчей Иисус Христос. И кто бо есть строитель верный и мудрый, его же поставить господь над челядию своею, даяти во время житомерие! Блажен раб той, его же пришед господь его, обрящет тако творяща, воистину глаголю вам: над всем имением [совем поставит его. Аще же
л. 12 речет] раб той и во сердци своем, коснить господин мой медлит приити, и начнет бити рабы ‖ и рабыня, ясти же и пити и упиватися, приидет господин раба того в день, в онь же не чает, и в час, в он же не весть, опровергнет его и часть его с неверными положит. Той же раб, ведый волю господина своего, и не сотворив, биен будет много, не ведавый же сотворив, достойная мзду приимет: всякому ему же дано будет много, много взыщется от него, и ему же предаша множайша, просят от него».
И паки рече Иисус: «человек некий сотвори вечерю велию, и зва многи, и посла раб своих в год вечери рещи званным: грядите, яко же уже готово суть вся. И начаша вкупе отрицатися вси. Первый рече: село купил и имам нужду изыти и видети, молю ти ся, имей мя отреченна. И другий рече: ‖ супруг волов купих пять, и иду искусити их, молю л. 12 об. ти сь, имей мя отреченна. И другий рече: жену поях, и сего ради

не могу приити. И шед раб той, поведа господину вся сия. Тогда раз-
гневася дому владыка, рече рабу своему: изыди скоро на распутия
и стогны града, и нищия, и бедныя, и слепыя, и хромыя введи семо.
И рече раб: се есть, яко же повеле, и еще есть место. И рече господин к рабу: изыди на роспутия и халуги, убеди внити, да наполнится
дом мой. Глаголю бо вам, яко ни един мужей тех званных вкусил моея
вечери, мнози бо суть звани, мало же избранных. И паки: «Человека два
внидоста в церковь помолитися, един фарисей, а другий мытарь. Фарисей же став, ‖ сице в себе моляшеся: боже, хвалу тебе воздаю, яко   л. 13
несмь, яко же прочии человецы, хищницы, неправедницы, прелюбодее,
или яко же сей мытарь; пощуся два краты в суботу, десятину даю
всего, елика притяжу. Мытарь же издалече стоя, не хотяше ни очию
возвести на небо, но бияше в персии своя, глаголюще: боже, мило-
стив буди мне, грешнику. Глаголю вам, яко сей изыде оправдан паче
онаго, яко всяк возносяйся смириться, смирвыйся вознесется. Яко же
воздадите убо, яже кесарева кесареви, и яже божия богови. Не посла бо
бог сына своего в мир, да судит мирови, но да спасется им мир; веруя
в он не будет осужден, а не веруя уже осужден есть, яко не верова
во имя единороднаго сына божия. ‖ Се есть суд, яко свет прииде в мир,   л. 13
и возлюбиша человецы тму паче, неже свет, беша бо дела их зла.
Всяк бо делая зло, ненавидит света и не приходит ко свету, да не обли-
чатся дела его, яко лукава суть, творяй же истину, грядет ко свету,
да явятся дела его, яко о бозе делани суть. Аще кто мне служит,
и мне да последствует, иде же есмь аз, ту и слуга мой будет, и аще
кто мне служит, почтет его отец мой. И аще любите мя, заповеди моя
соблюдете, и аз умолю отца, инаго утешителя вам даст, да будет с вами
в веки дух истинныи. Аще кто любит мя, и слово мое соблюдет, и отец
мой возлюбит его, ‖ к нему приидеве и обитель у него сотвориве». Сице   л. 14
убо заповеда господь нашь Иисус Христос совершати заповеди своя,
совершавшим же и волю его сотворившим сице любовне о них молить
и благодать подает. «Отче, прииде час, прослави сына твоего, да и сын
твой прославит тя, яко же дал еси ему власть всякой плоти, да всяко,
яже дал еси ему, даст им живот вечный. Се же есть живот вечный,
да знают тебе, единаго бога, и его же посла Иисус Христа; аз просла-
вих тя на земли, и дела соверших, еже дал еси мне, сотворю; и ныне
прослави мя, отче, у тебе самаго славу, яже имех у тебе, прежде
мир не бысть; и явих имя твое человеком, их же дал еси мне от мира,
твои беша, и мне их дал еси, и слово твое ‖ сохраниша; ныне разумеша,   л. 14 о
яко вся, елика дал мне, от тебе суть; яко глаголы, их же дал еси мне,
дах им, и тии прияша и разумеша, яко от тебе изыдох, и вероваша,
яко ты мя посла, аз о сих молю, ни о всем мире молю, но о тех,
иже дал еси мне, яко твоя суть; и моя вся твоя суть, и твоя моя, и про-
славихся в них; аз дах им слово твое, и мир возненавиде их, яко не суть
от мира, яко же и аз от мира несмь; не молю, да возмеши их от мира,
но да соблюдеши их от неприязни; от мира не суть, яко же и аз несмь
от мира; спаси их во истинну твою, слово твое истинно есть; яко же
мене посла в мир, и аз послах их в мир, и за них аз свящу себе,
да и ти будут священники во истину; не о сих молю токмо, но и о ве-
рующих ‖ слове их ради в мя, да вси едино суть, яко и ты, отче,   л. 15
во мне, и аз в тебе, да и ти в нас едино будет, да и мир веру имет,
яко ты мя посла; и аз славу, ю же дал еси мне, дах им, да будут едино,
яко же и мы едино естьмы; аз в них, и ты во мне, да будут совер-
шенни во едино, и да разумеет мир, яко ты мя посла и возлюбил еси
их, яко же мене возлюбил еси. Отче, их же дал еси, хощу, дондеже

естмь аз, и тии будуть со мною, [да видят славу мою], ю же дал еси мне, яко возлюбил мя еси прежде сложения мира. Отче праведный, мир тебе не позна, аз же тя познах, и тии познаша, яко ты мя посла; и сказах им имя твое, и скажу, да любы, ею же мя еси возлюбил, в них будет,

л. 15 об. и аз в них». Видите, каково сие божие ‖ дарование, что убо сего любезнеишии, еже в бозе быти, и яко богу быти, и с богом пребывати, и божии любви в целовецех вселятися, и безконечных благ наслаждатися и наследствовати! Что убо сего злеишии, еже от бога отлучитися, и вечных благ наслаждения лишитися, и безконечных мук восприяти! И вы бы, дети моя, Иван и Федор, божиих заповедей и евангельских усердно послушали, и моего наказания и повеления так же бы есте со усердием послушали, и усердно от всея силы и крепости, елико возможно, прелестей мира сего злых отбегали, и безконечных заповедей же господних, и благих и вечных благ наслаждения наследствовати возжелети

л. 16 от всея души, и крепости, и разума, ‖ и берегучись от всякаго поползновения, и преткновения, и ветреннаго соблазна вражия.

И были есте, дети мои, Иван и Федор, в любви по сему моему наказу, заодин, неразделно, раздельны бы есте были вотчинами и казнами, а сердцем бы есте и любовию были неразделны, а никто никому ни в чем не завидел; а будет кто чем скуден, ино по любви друг друга слушал, а силою б никто ни у кого не имал, а во всяком бы еси деле были, в лихе и в добре, везде заодин, а друг бы за друга не отрекся во всяком деле не токмо что труждатися или страдати, но и кровь пролити и умерети.

И были бы есте, Иван и Федор, по моему наказу оба заедин, и во всем бы себя берегли, и жили по бозе во всяких делах. И хотя,

л. 16 об. по грехом, ‖ што и на ярость приидет в междоусобных бранях, и вы бы творили по апостолу господню: правду и равнение давайте рабом своим, послабляюще прощения, ведяще, яко и вам господь есть на небесех. Так бы и вы делали во всяких опалах и казнех, как где возможно, по разсуждению, на милость претворяли и оставливали часть душам своим, яко долготерпения ради от господа милость приимите, яко же инде речено есть: «подобает убо царю три сия вещи имети, яко богу не гневатися, и яко смертну не возноситися, и долготерпеливу быти к согрешающим». Сице аще о бозе благо поживете, и приложатся вам лета живота. Нас же, родителей своих и прародителей, не токмо что в государствующем

л. 17 граде Москве ‖ или инде где будет, но аще и в гонении и во изгнании будете, во божественных литургиях, и в панихидах, и в литиях, и в милостынях к нищим и препитаниях, елико возможно, не забывайте, понеже наших прародителей душ воспоминанием велику ползу нам и себе приобрящете зде и в будущем веце, и благостоянием святым божиим церквам, и на враги победа, и одоление, и государству строение, и своему животу покой и вечных благ наслаждение молитвою их происходит, понеже от отец благодать божия и благословение к вам пришедшее, наследником и чадом. И бог мира в троице славимый, буди с вами, молитвами пресвятыя и преблагословенныя владычицы нашея

17 об. богородицы, заступницы христианския, ‖ и милость честнаго ея образа иконы владимерския, державы Руския заступление, во всяко время, на всяком месте, буди на вас, и всех святых всея вселенныя молитва и благословение, и руских чюдотворцов, Петра, Алексея, Ионы, Ивания, Никиты, и Леонтия, Сергия, и Варлаама, и Кирила, и Похнутия, и Никиты, и всех святых руских молитвами, и благословения всего нашего роду, от великаго князя Владимера, просветившаго Рускую землю святым крещением, нареченнаго во святом крещении Василия, и до отца нашего, великаго

князя Василия Ивановича всея России, во иноцех Варлаама, и матери нашея, великия княгини Елены, и жены моей Настасии, а вашей матери,
молитва и благословение буди на вас, ныне, и присно, и во веки
веков. ‖ А что, по грехом, жон моих, Марьи да Марфы,[1] не стало, л. 18
и вы б жон моих, Марью да Марфу, а свои благодатные матери,
поминали во всем по тому, как аз уставил, и поминали бы есте их
со всеми своими родители незабвенно. А будет бог помилует, и государство свое доступите, и на нем утвердитеся, и аз благословляю вас.
Ты, сын мой Федор, держи сына моего Ивана в мое место, отца своего,
и слушай его во всем. А ты, сын мой Иван, держи сына моего Федора,
а своего брата молотшаго, без обиды, и буди ему во всем в мое
место.

Благословляю сына моего Ивана крест, животворящее древо, боль-
шей цареградской. Да сына же своего Ивана благословляю крест Петра
чудотворца, ‖ которым чудотворец благословил прародителя нашего, л. 18
великаго князя Ивана Даниловича, и весь род наш. Да сына же своего
Ивана благословляю царством Руским, шапкою мономаховскою, и всем
чином царским, что прислал прародителю нашему, царю и великому
князю Владимеру Мономаху, царь Константин Мономах из Царяграда.
Да сына же своего Ивана благословляю всеми шалками царскими
и чином царским, что аз промыслил, и посохи, и скатерть,[2] а по немецки
центурь.

Да сына же своего Ивана благословляю своим царством Руским,
чем мя благословил отец мои, князь великий Василей, и что мне бог
дал. Даю ему город Москву, с волостми, и станы, и с путми,[3]
и с селы, и з дворы с гостиными ‖ и посадскими, и с тамгою,[4] л. 19
и с мытом, и с торги, и с лавками, и с дворы гостиными, и со всеми
пошлинами, и с Добрятинским селом с бортью, и с Висильцовым
столом, и с числяки, и с сродницы.[5] Да ему ж даю село Сомчинское
с дворы городскими, и с Самсоновым лугом, да село Воробьево, и с Во-
лодимерским, и с Семеновским, и с Воронцовым, и с Кадашевым,[6]
и с деревнями, как было при мне. Да ему жь даю село Аминево,
да село Хорошово, со всем, по тому, как было при мне. Да ему жь даю
на Сетуне село Волынское с деревнями, со всем, потому жь, как было
при мне. Да ему жь даю село Воронцово, с дворы городскими, по обе
стороны реки Яузы, и с мелницами, как было при мне, да манастырь

---

[1] *Примечание переписчика:* Зде упоминает он трех жон умерших, а именно: Ана-
стасия Романовых, Мария Черкаских, Марфа Сабакиных, да живая Анна, по ней
была Марфа Нагих, итого 5. А Курпский в „Истории“ показует: прежде сея Анны
бысть 5 жен.

[2] *Примечание переписчика:* Скатерть что значит неизвестно, а видно, что между
регалиями полагалась.

[3] *Примечание переписчика:* Путь просто значит дорога, но зде разумеется доход,
от того произошло, что прежде для походов полагали дани путевые, с чего доходы
тут названы, да и денги именовали путь, как то еще на многих тиснением изо-
бражено.

[4] *Примечание переписчика:* Томга по татарски значит печать или знак, но разумеется и положенная подать, как то видно из грамот татарских и гистории, что часто
поголовные денги именуют тамгою, которые тогда положены по гривне с головы,
могущей луком владеть.

[5] *Примечание переписчика:* Вислово сто, числяне и родницы что значит, мне
неизвестно, однако ж видно, что некоторые слободы, к Москве принадлежащие, так
именованы были, равно же село и луг Самсоновской, разве по старым книгам писцовым
сыщется, понеже потом для церквей имена переменили.

[6] *Примечание переписчика:* Володимирское на Кулишках, Семеновское Воронцово
и Кодашево — все ныне внутрь Москвы.

162

9 об. Лыщиков, и с дворы. ‖ Да ему жь даю слободку Калычевскую и с лугом, что было за дядею моим, за князем Андреем Ивановичем, и за сыном его, за князем Володимером Андреевичем, да селы у Москвы, Сараевым, Едниским, Карташевым, Ясеневым, да под Москвою жь, что был есми променил князю Володимиру Андреевичу, селом Собакиным да селом Туриновым. Да сыну же моему Ивану даю Замосковские волости, что было за дядею, за князем Андреем Ивановичем, и за сыном его, за князем Володимером Андреевичем, волостью Раменейцов, волостью Загарье, волость Кунье, волость Вохна, волость Ена, волость Гуслицы, волость Гжель, и с селы подъезными, которыя в тех волостях.

А сын мой Иван держит на Москве болшаго своего наместника, по старине, как было при отце моем, при великом князе Василье

л. 20 Ивановиче всея России, и как было при мне, а другова ‖ наместника держати на трети на княжь Володимерской Андреевича Донскаго на Москве жь. Которые мои дворы на Москве, внутри города, и на посадех, и сады мои все, и пустыя места по посаду, за моими бояры, и князьми, и за детми боярскими, и за дворянами моими, и за приказными людми, и за конюхи, и за моими мастеры, и слободы стрелецкие, и ямския слободы, те все сыну моему Ивану. А у кого будут у бояр, и у князей, и у детей боярских внутри города на Москве, и за городом, и на посадах дворовых, и вотчинные, и купчие вотчинные, или у кого будут грамоты жалованныя на дворы отца, великаго князя Василья Ивановича, и сын мой Иван в те у них дворы не вступается.

А волости Московские, Рогожь, Вори, Корзенева, Шерна город, Сулешино, и с Новым селом, сыну же моему Ивану. Да ему жь волость

0 об. Сурожик, да Лучинское, да Радонежь, с волостми, ‖ и с путьми, и с селы, и со всеми пошлинами, да треть Мушкова с мытом с Лопским.

Да сына же своего Ивана благословляю своими великими княжествы, чем меня благословил отец мой, князь великий Василий Ивановичь. Да ему жь великия княжества: город Володимер с волостми, и с путьми, и с селы, со всеми пошлинами, и с Муромским селцом, и с Шатуром, и с Колужским, и с Вышелесом, и Островом, и с волостью с Крысинским, и со всем, по тому, как было при мне. Да сыну же моему Ивану даю к Володимеру в Стародубе в Ряголовим Стародубских князей вотчины, которые остались за мною у князя Михаила Воротынскаго: село Антиохово, да село Воскресенское, да село Новые Земенки, что

л. 21 было князь Федора да князь Ивана Гундоровых, да село Старые Меховицы, что было Романа Гундорова, ‖ да село Могучее, что было князь Ивана Пожарскаго Меньшова, да село Воскресенское, что было князь Никиты Тулугова, да село Серицы, да село Татарово, что было князь Петра Шарагова Ромадановскаго, да село Троицкое, да село Фалеево, что было князя Тимофея да князя Ивана Пожарских, да село Андреевское, что было князя Василья Коврова, да село Рожественское, да деревня Каменное, да три села Васильева, что было князь Ивана князь Семенова сына Пожарскаго, да деревня Ковернев, и иныя деревни, что были князь Ивана княжь Андреева сына Коврова, да село Нестеровское, что было князь Ивана Меньшова, князь Ивана сына Кривозерскаго, да село Александровское, да село Устиновское, да село Овсяниково, что было князь

1 об. Андрея Кривозерскаго съ братиею, да село Хряпово, да село ‖ Мицыно, что было князь Федора Ромодановскаго, да село Матвеевское, да село Яблонцы, что было князь Михаила Ромодановскаго, да село Татарово, да село Никольское, что было князь Афанасья Нагаева, да село Пантелеево, что было княгини Марьи княж Андреевы Стародубскаго, село Сороки, да село Кувено, что было княгини Афросиньи

княж Семеновы Стародубскаго, село Амелева, что было князь Никиты Стародубскаго, да половина села Рамадонова, что было князь Ивана Рамодановскаго, да село Дмитреевское, что было княгини Федосьи Пожарской с детми, да село Кочергино, что было князь Ивана Пожарскаго, да село Голобоково, да деревня Скореково, что было княгини Марьи княжь Борисовых Пожарскаго и сына ея, князь Михаила, да село Лучки с деревнями, что было княгини Марьи княж || Петровы Пожарскаго да княгини Федосьи княжь Семеновых дочери Мезецкаго, да село Осиново, что было князь Василья Осиповскаго, да село Палех, что было княж Дмитриевых детей Палецкаго, да село Юрьевское, да село Залесье, что были князь Никиты да князь Амы Гундоровых, да села другие всех готчины, что было Семена Образцова. л. 22

Да сыну моему Ивану даю город Коломну, и с волостми, и с путми, и с селы, и со всеми пошлинами. Да ему жь даю город Каширу, и с Заречьем, и со всеми пошлинами, и с волостми за Окою рекою, Тешилово, Ростовец, Рославль, Венев, Мстиславль, и иные места по Резанской рубеж, и с путми, и с селы, и со всеми пошлинами, и с Ельцем, и со всеми Елецкими землями. Да сыну моему Ивану даю город Серпухов с волостми, и с путми, и с селы, и со всеми пошлинами. Да ему жь даю город на Плаве || и на Солове,[1] со всеми Польскими вотчинами, и со всеми, что было к нему изстари. л. 22

Да сына ж своего Ивана благословляю, даю ему великое княжество Резанское: город Переславль Резанский, город Старая Рязань, город Ряской, город Данков, и т, еть всю,[2] со всеми пошлинами, и с волостми, и с селы, и с путми, и со всеми Полскими отхожими вотчинами, как было при мне.

Да сыну ж моему Ивану даю город Мценск с волостми, и с путми, и с селы, и со всеми пошлинами, и со всеми Польскими отхожими вотчинами, да город Белев, с волостми, и с путми, и с селы, и со всеми пошлинами. Да ему жь даю треть города Масальска княжь Володимерскую Всеславля с волостми, и с путми, и с селы, и с тамгами, и со всеми пошлинами, как было к той трети изстари. ||

А князь Михайло Воротынский ведает треть Воротынска, да город Перемышль, да город Одоев Старое, да город Новосиль, да Остров, Че ну, со всем[3] по тому, как было изстари, а Иван сын в то у него не вступается. А князи Одоевские, Оболенские, Воротынские, Трубецкие, Масальские, и их сынове своими вотчинами сыну же моему Ивану, к великому государству, и служат все сыну моему Ивану. А которой тех князей и иных детей отъедут от сына моего Ивана к сыну моему Федору, или инуды куды-нибуть, и тех вотчины сыну моему Ивану. л. 23

Да сыну моему Ивану даю город Юрьев Волской, да Белогород,[4] да Городец, с селы, и с деревнями, и с рыбными ловлями, и со всеми пошлинами, как было при мне. Да ему жь даю город Романов на реке || на Волге, а держи его, сын мой Иван, за Нагайскими мурзами по тому, как было при мне. А отъедут куды-нибуть или изведутся, и город Романов сыну моему Ивану. л. 23 об.

---

[1] *Примечание переписчика:* ныне зовется Крапивна город. Польские разумеются степные вотчины.

[2] *Примечание переписчика:* Треть разумеется по тогдашнему разделению всего государства, яко Московская, Володимерская и Рязанская.

[3] *Примечание переписчика:* Сии городы у Воротынских, Масальских, Одоевских, и Оболенских, Трубецких, взял сам царь Иван Васильевичь, а вместо оных для безопасности дал им села в разных уездах.

[4] *Примечание переписчика:* Белогород где был неизвестно, ибо нынешней Белогород на Донце тогда не был еще построен.

Да сыну жь моему Ивану даю город Можайск с волостми, и с путми, и селы, и со всеми пошлинами, и Щагощью, и с Турьевым, и с О еховкою, и с Могильным, и с Мишенками, и с Шатерою и с Сулидовым, и с Дмитровцом, по обе стороны Угры, и с иными месты, что к ним потягло, как было при мне. Да сыну жь моему Ивану даю город Вязму и Козлов с волостми, и с путми, и селы, и со всеми пошлинами, и со всем с тем, что к Вязме и Козлову и ко всем Вяземским местам потягло, как было при мне. Да сыну жь моему Ивану даю город Дорогобужь с волостми, и с путми, и с селы, и со всеми пошлинами, и со всем с тем, что к нему потягло. А волости Доргобужские: Погорелое, ||

л. 24 Негомля, Хотумичи, Холм, Бятимо, Прость, село Заопье, Водосы, Некрасово, Селечна, Кремяное, Редын по реце по Уже, Устье, Костково, Рехты, Холмичи, Вышково, Василево, Еськино, село Климово, слободка Владычня в Юртове, село Путятино с деревнями, Игумново, Мстиславец, Ощитов, Жуличь, Мошкова Гора, Лучино Городище, Великое Поле, Лопатин, Копыл, Ужида, Вед ожь, Озерище, Сверчовы Луки, и со всем с тем, что к Дорогобужу и к тем волостям и селом потягло, как было при мне. Да ему жь даю город Белою, с волостми, и с селы, и со всеми пошлинами, как было при мне.

Да сына же своего благословляю, даю ему великое княжество Смоленское, город Смоленск, с волостми, с путми, и с селы, и со всеми

л. 24 об. пошлинами, и со всем с тем, как было при мне и как писано в перемирных || грамотах с Жигимонтом Августом королем.

Да сыну же моему Ивану даю город Переславль, с волостми, и с путми, и с селы, и со всеми пошлинами, и с Солью, и с волостью Серебром же, и с Ражественным, и с Бускутовым, и с Пенковых князей вотчиною, что в Переславском уезде, да село Перевятино, да село Горы, с деревнями. Да сыну же своему Ивану даю город Юрьев Польской с волостми, и с путми, и с селы, и со всеми пошлинами. Да ему ж даю город Дмитров с волостми, и с путми, и с селы, и со всеми пошлинами. Да ему жь даю город Боровезк, с волостми, и с путми, и с селы, и со всеми пошлинами.

А что есми пожаловал царевича Муртазалея, а во крещении Михаила, Кобулина сына Ахкибекова, городом Звенигородом, по тому же, как

л. 25 был Звенигород за ца ем Симеоном || казанским, и сын мой Иван держит за ним Звенигород, по нашему жалованью, а служит царевичь Муртазалей, а во крещении Михайло, сыну моему Ивану, а отъедит куды-нибудь, и город Звенигород сыну моему Ивану.

Да сына же своего Ивана благословляю, даю ему Пешехонье, со всеми волостьми, и с путми, и с селы, и с Рыбною слободою, и с Борисоглебскою волостью, что на реке на Волге, против Романова города, и с Пешехонскимы уезды, и езы, и со езовыми деревнями, и со всеми пошлинами и доходы, по всем, по тому, как было при мне. Да сыну же моему Ивану даю город Вологду, с волостми, и с путми, и с селы, и со всеми пошлинами, как было при мне, да и Заозерьем с Кубаною, и с волостми, и с путми, и с селы, и со всеми пошлинами, и Пенко-

25 об. вых князей вотчина || в третях, Заозерским, да к Вологде село Даниловское из Костромскаго уезду, по межам. Да ему жь даю город Устег с волостми, и с путми, и с селы, и со всеми пошлинами, и Солью Вычегоцкою, да Вычегду, и Вым,[1] и Удому, и Сысолу, и со всеми их месты, да в Заволоцкой земли Ростовщину, Пенегу, Керчму, Прьмские,

---

[1] *Примечание переписчика:* Вым был тогда не малой город, где жили епископы пермские и югорские, а ныне тут монастырь небогатой.

и Мезень, Немью, Пильи горы, Пенешу, Выу, Тому, Кур-Горы, Елаская Гора на Ваге, со всем, и Онтакова перевара, и Карыалской остров, и Шалга-Гора, Корчала, Сура Паганая, Лавела, и с иными месты, что к тем местам потягло, да Югору, и по Печеру, и Великую Пермь, со всем, и с новыми городки, и с·солми, и со всеми пошлинами, как было при мне. ‖ Да сыну же моему Ивану даю город Галичь, с волостми, л. 26 и с путми, и с селы, и со всеми пошлинами, и с Кужейкою, и с Чухломою, и со всеми городки, что в Галицком уезде, и солми, и со всем, что к Галичу, и к Чюхломе, и к Уньже потягло.

Да сына же своего Ивана благословляю великим княжеством Нижегородским, даю ему Новгород Нижней с волостми, и с путми, и с селы, и со всеми пошлинами, и с мордвами, и с черемисами, да город Балахну, и с Заулусою, и с тамгою, и со всеми пошлинами, как было при мне, да город Василь на Суре, и с мордвами, и с черемисами, и со всеми пошлинами, которые села в Нижнем Новегороде и на Балахне, и за мурзами, и за князьми, и за кем ни буди, то все сыну моему Ивану. Да ему жь даю город Муром с волостми, и с путми, и со всеми пошлинами, и с мордвами, и с черемисами, ‖ и что к Мурому потягло. л. 26 Да ему жь даю город Мещеру с волостми, и с селы, и со всем тем, что к ней изстари потягло, и с Кошковым, и Кадом, и Темников, и Шацкой город, со всем, и князи мордовские со всеми же их вотчинами сыну моему Ивану. Да ему жь даю город Курмыш, да город Алатор на Алаторе, с волостми и со всеми пошлинами, и князи мордовския с их вотчинами, и с черемисами, и со всеми уезды, и угожьи, и что к тем городам потягло. А что к тем городам аз сажал детей боярских на диком поле, и те земли все сыну же моему Ивану, а вотчинникам владеть своим. Да город Арзамас с мордвами и с черемисою, со всем, по тому, как было при мне, да город Стародуб Ряполовской, да волость Мошок, ‖ село Княгинино, что было за Воротынским, в Нижегородском уезде, л. 27 да Фокино сельцо. Да ему жь даю город Белоозеро с волостми, и с путми, и с селы, и со всеми пошлинами.

Да сына жь своего Ивана благословляю, даю треть города Воротынска, с волостми, и с путми, и с селы, и со всеми пошлинами. Да ему жь даю город Городень с волостми, и с селы, и со всеми пошлинами, как было при мне. Да ему жь даю город Микулин с волостми, и с селы, и со всеми пошлинами, а со княжо Семеновскою вотчиною Микулинскаго, которая не отдана.[2]

Да сыну жь моему Ивану даю Вятскую землю, городы и волости, со всем с тем, что к ним потягло, и зъ [Ар]скими князьями, как было при мне.

Да сыну же моему Ивану даю городы Северские: Новгород Северской, город Путивль, город Рылск, и Млгинъ, и Драков, ‖ город Почап, л. 27 город Карачев, и волости и села тех городов, со всеми Северскими и Полскими угожьи и Тилскими угожеи, и со всеми пошлинами, как было при мне. А Северские городы, город Рослов, держи, сын мой Иван, со всем перемирным грамотам с Жигимонтом Августом королем.

Да сына же моего Ивана благословляю своею отчиною, великим княжеством Тверским. Да ему жь город Тверь с волостми, и с путми, и с селы, и со всеми пошлинами, со всем, по тому, как было при мне, да город Клин с волостми, и с селы, и со всеми пошлинами, как было при мне, и съ Кашиным, что было за Одоевским. А которыя князи служилыя в Московской и в Тверской земле, и те князи служат сыну

---

[2] *Примечание переписчика:* Городен и Микулин ныне села в Тверском уезде.

л. 28 моему Ивану, а вотчины свои держит, как при мне было. ‖ А кто тех князей служебных отъедет куда-нибуть, и тех князей вотчины сыну моему Ивану. Да сыну жь моему Ивану даю город Торжек с волостьми, и с путми, и селы, и со всеми пошлинами. Да ему жь даю город Ржеву Володимерову, обе половины, с волостми, и с путми, и с селы, и со всеми пошлинами.

Да сына же своего Ивана благословляю великим княжеством Новгородским, Новымгородом, со всеми пятью пятинами, и с пригородами, и со всеми пошлинами. А пригороды Новгородския: город Иван, го, од Яма, город Копорье, город Орешик, город Ладуга, городок Высокой, городок Доман, городок Куреск, городок Порхов, городок Кошкин,

л. 28 об. городок Старая Руса.[1] А дал есми Великий Новгород и с теми при- ‖ городы, и со всеми волостми, и с погосты, и с путми, и с селы, и со всеми пошлинами, что ни было при мне, к Великому Нову-городу.

Да сына же своего Ивана благословляю городы, что есми поставил, с божиею волею, на Литовском рубеже: город Велижь,[2] город Заволочье, город Себежь, город Поповичь на Невле, и волость Поповскую всю. А даю ему те городы со всем, как было при мне и как в перемирной грамоте написано с Жигимонтом Августом королем. Да сыну же Ивану в Новогородской земле город Холм, Велико, Бунца, Лапостицы, и с-ыными места, и с волостьми, и со всеми пошлинами, и со всем с тем, что им потягло. Сыну жь моему Ивану даю город Луки Великия, да город Невль,

л. 29 город Острое, с волостми, и с путми, и с селы, и со всеми ‖ пошлинами. А Луцкия волости: Березу, Невль, Усвои, Ловце, Веснеболого, и с-ыными волостьми, и с селы, и со всеми пошлинами, как было при мне. Да сыну же Ивану даю город Торопец, и волости Торопецкие, Данково, Любуту, Дубню, Рожну, Туру, Бибиреву, Ставцову, Нежельскую, Плавицкую, Жижецкую, Озерскую, Казариновскую, и со всеми пошлинами, и со всем, по тому, как было при мне, и по перемирным грамотам с Жигимонтом Августом королем. Да ему жь даю город Ржеву Пустую со всеми волостьми и погосты, по тому, как было при мне. Да сыну же моему Ивану даю Королевскую землю всю, город Корелу, с волостми, и с путми, и с селы, и с погосты, и со всеми пошлинами, и со всем с тем, что к Корелской земли потягло, и с Лопью, и с дикою Лопью. Да ему жь даю Заволоцкую землю:[3] Онего, и Каргополе, и все Поонежье, и Двину, и Вагу, и Коншегу, и Великой погост, и Холмогоры, ‖

29 об. и всю Двинскую землю, как было при мне. Да сыну же моему Ивану даю город Псков со всеми Псковскими осадами и с пригороды, город Воронежь, город Дутсов, город Выборец, город Велье, город Врев, город Володимер, город Остров, город Красной, город Вышегородок, город Кобылье городище, город Изоорск, город Олочка, город Гдов.[1] А дал есми ему город Псков и те пригороды с волостми, и засадами, и с путми, и с селы, и со всеми пошлинами, по тому жь, как было при мне.

---

[1] *Примечание переписчика:* Зде городки Высокой, Деман, Куреск, Кашкин, где были, ныне неизвестно и равно же сему и ниже горы Новгородския упомянуты, Холм Велики, Бунци, Лапостицы, о которых может быть где-либо в гисториях сыщется.

[2] *Примечание переписчика:* Велижь, Себежь, Поповичь, или Невль, уступлены к Литве при нем же по договору со Стефаном Баторием, королем полским, ниже город Острое, хотя неизвестно, но чаятелно в Литве же.

[3] *Примечание переписчика:* Заволочье во всех древних гисториях названо все, что за Ладоским озером.

[3] *Примечание переписчика:* Зде городки Высокой, Деман, Куреск, Кашкин, где были, ныне неизвестно и равно же сему и ниже горы Новгородския упомянуты, Холм Велики, Бунци, Лапостицы, о которых может быть где-либо в гисториях сыщется.

· А что есьми, с божиею волею, взял царство Казанское, и аз царством Казанским благословляю сына же своего Ивана, даю ему город Казань с Арскою стороною, и с Побережною стороною, и с Луговою стороною, и со всеми волостьми, и с селы, и с чювашею, и с черемисою, и с тарханы, и с башкирдою,[2] и с вотяки, и со всеми || их бортными землями л. 30 с Волскими и с Казанскими, и с рыбными ловлями, и со всеми угодьи, и со всеми пошлинами, а как ми бог [дал] Казанскую землю, что было изстари к Казанской земле потягло, при прежних царех. А что естми, с божею помощию, поставил город на Свиязе, на Нагорной же поставил есьми на Чебоксаре город, и яз городом Свиянским и городом Чебоксарским благословляю сына же своего Ивана, и даю ему город Свияжской, город Чебоксарской, со всею Горною стороною, и со всею чувашею, и черемисою, и с мордвами, и с их вотчинами, и с рыбными ловлями, и со всеми пошлинами, как ми бог дал Горную сторону к Свияжскому и к Чебоксарскому городу. А что есьми, с божею помощию, взял царство Астраханское, и аз царством Астраханским олагословляю сына же своего Ивана, || даю ему город Астрахань, с торги, и с тамгами, и со всеми пошлинами, л. 30 о и с езжыи, и с мочаги,[3] и со всеми Астраханскими места, и со всем по тому, как Астраханское царство прежние цари держали.

А что есми, с божиею помощию, взял городы в Ливонской земле, город Юрьев, город Вельян, город Ругодев, город Ракооор, город Алыстр, город Кереветь, город Лаюс, город Новой Городок, город Сыренец, город Тавро, город Муков, город Порхов, город Кастер Новой, город Кастер Старой, город Адежь, которои на Ругадевской стороне, город Курелов, город Рынгол, город Ранден, город Конгод, город Кавлет, город Толшебор, город Кутушен, город Сабеи, город Долговыя, двор Занганц, двор Андопеито, был || город Медвежья голова, и аз теми л. 31 городы[4] всеми, и мызами, и волостьми, и селы, и с озеры, и пристаньми морскими, и со всеми угодьи, и тамгами, и весом, и со всеми пошлинами тех городов, олагословляю сына же своего Ивана, со всем с тем, что к тем городам, и волостям, и селам, и мызам потягло. А что есьми поставил в своей отчине, в Ливонской земле, город Говью на реке на Говье, и аз тем городом Говью с волостми, и с мызами, и со всем уездом, что было в Говье, благословляю же сына своего Ивана, а держит сын мой город Говью со всем уездом к своей отчине к Юрьеву Ливонскому.

А что есми пожаловал голдовника своего, короля Арцымагнуса, в своей отчине, в Лифлянской земле, || городом Полчевым и иными л. 31 · волостми и селы, и грамоту жалованную на город Полчев, и на волости, и на селы дал есми королю Арцымагнусу, и сын мой Иван за своим голдовником, за Арцымагнусом королем, город Полчев, и волости, и селы держит по нашей жалованной грамоте, и служит король Арцымагнус сыну моему Ивану. А отъедет куды-нибудь, и город Полчев, и волости, и села, что были есми пожаловали короля Арцымагнуса, сыну моему Ивану. А что есми дал королю Арцымагнусу в заем пятнатцать тысяч пятьсот рублев денег в московское число, а в тех денгах король Арцы-

---

[2] *Примечание переписчика:* Здесь видно, что башкиры были тогда российския.

[3] *Примечание переписчика:* Мочаки видно, что учюги, слово татарское.

[4] *Примечание переписчика:* Здесь многия городы упомянуты, кои ныне неизвестны И болшая часть их же уступлены были частию к Полше, частию к Швеции, токмо Сыренец и Новой городок, помнится, остались в руском владении, и по сему видно, что сия духовная писана прежде года, когда с полским королем он мир учинил, равно сему и Полоцк со всем уступлен к Литве тогда жь, чем видится.

магнус заложил у меня в Ливонской земле городы, город Володимерец, город Ворну, город Прекат, город Смилтен, город Буртники, город Роин, и со всеми уезды, и с селами, и с мызами тех городов, и сын

л. 32 мой Иван на короле Арцымагнусе те деньги, или за денги ‖ городы, которыя въ тех денгах заложены, возмет себе, а сыну моему Федору до того дела нет.

А что, по божией воли, взял есми у брата своего Жигимонта Августа короля свою вотчину город Полоск, и аз городом Полоцком, с волостми с Полоцкими, и с селы, и с тамгами, и весы, и со всеми угодьи, и со всем Полоцким уездом, что было изстари к городу Полоцку, и аз тем городом Полоцком со всем благословляю сына своего Ивана. А что есми, с божиею помощию, поставил городы в Полоцком повете, город Сокол на реке на Дрыси, да город Копье, и аз теми городы благословляю сына же своего Ивана, со всеми волостьми, что к тем городам потянет. А что есми, за божиею помощию, взял у брата своего, Жигимонта

л. 32 об. Августа короля, город Озерище, да к Озерищу волость Усвят, и аз в Усвятской ‖ волости поставил город Усвят, и аз городом Озерищем и городом Усвятом со всеми их волостми, и уезды, и селы, и с угодьи, благословляю сына же своего Ивана, со всем с тем, как было к тем городам изстари, а держит сын мой Иван то все по перемирным грамотам с Жигимонтом Августом королем.

А что отец наш, князь великий Василей Ивановичь всея России, написал в своей душевной грамоте брату моему, князь Юрью, город Угличь и все поле, с волостми, и с путми, и с селы, и со всеми пошлинами, и с Холопьем, что торг на Мологе, да город Бежецкой Верх с волостми, и с путми, и с селы, и со всеми пошлинами, да город Калугу с волостьми, и с путми, и с селы, и со всеми пошлинами, да город Ярославец Малой с волостми, и с путми, и со всеми пошли-

л. 33 нами, и с Суходровью, да город Кременеск ‖ с волостми, и с путми, и с селы, и со всеми пошлинами, да город Медынь, Мещерск с волостми, и с путми, и с селы, и со всеми пошлинами, да Опаков[1] на Угре со всем, да волости на Угре, Товарков, Конопнарь, и иныя волости по Угре, что были даны князю Василью Шемечичу да князю Василью Стародубскому, да ему ж написал село у Москвы Озерецкое Старое, село Озерецкое Новое, с деревнями и со всеми прикупми, да село Черкизово с деревнями, что куплено у Петровых детей Яковлева Захарьина, и с прикупными селы, и с прибавочными становыми деревнями, да селцо Напрудное[2] с городскими дворы и с посадскими, а божия воля

л. 33 об. коснется, Юрья брата в живности не будет, а не останется у него ни сына, ни внука, и ту вотчину всю, его удел, ‖ отец, князь великий Василий, написал в своей душевной грамоте мне, к великому государю, и божия воля сталась, брата моего, князь Юрья, не стало в животе, а сына у него, ни внука, ни дочери не осталось, и аз ис того брата своего удела благословляю сына своего Ивана городом Бежицким Верхом с волостми, и с путми, и с селы, и со всеми пошлинами, да городом Калугою, с волостми, и с путми, и с селы, и со всеми пошлинами,

---

[1] *Примечание переписчика:* Опаков ныне село в Медынском уезде, в котором знак каменная полатка доднесь осталась. Сей был на границе Литовскаго владения во время Витолдово, но великий князь Василей Ивановичь с прочими от Литвы взял въ ... году.

[2] *Примечание переписчика:* Захарьины, как видно, писались прежде Яковля, а после стали писатся Романовы, от которых пресветлейший род Романовых счастливо воцарствующих, государей российских, происходит, и видно, что их предки знатны вотчины имели, ибо Напрудная слобода ныне внутре Москвы.

да городом Малым[1] с волостми, и с путми, и с селы, и всеми пошлинами, и с волостью Суходровью, как было преждь сего, да городом Медынью с волостьми и с путьми, и с селы, и со всеми пошлинами, да волостьми Апаковым на Угре, со всем, по тому, как было прежь сего, да волостьми жь Таварковым, и Конопкою, и иными волостьми ‖ по Угре, л. 34 что было за князем Васильем за Шемячичем и за князем Васильем Стародубским, да из сел селом Черкизовым под Москвою, оприче Черкизовские мелницы, и одиннатцать деревень, которыя к мелнице приписаны. А что есми по отце своем душевной грамоте и по брата своего, князь Юрьеву, приказу пожаловал брата своего, князь Юрьеву Васильевича, княгиню Ульяну, а свою невеску, дал есми ей на прожиток до ее живота город Кременеск с волостми, и с путми, и с селы, и со всеми пошлинами, и с ямскими, и с приметными денгами, и с кормлеными откупными денгами, и со всеми наместничьи доходы, что было доходов прежь того, да городом Устюжною Железною, посадом, и с деревнями, которыя приписаны к посаду, с ямскими, и с приметными денгами, и с кормленными окупы, да в Углицком ‖ уезде волостью Кадкою, л. 34 о с ямскими и с приметными денгами, и со всякими доходы тоя волости, да Подмосковными селы, селом Пузяевым с деревнями, селом Белом Ратом с деревнями, да деревнею Наузоловым, и иными деревнями, которыя с Наузоловым приписаны были те деревни к селу Озерецкому, да княгине же Ульяне дал есми мелницу на реке Клязме, у села Черкизова, да одиннатцать деревень, которые приписаны к той мельнице, да княгиню же Ульяну пожаловал есми на Углече дворцовыми селы, селцом Зеленцовым с деревнями, да селом Николским Ждановым с деревнями, и сын мой Иван держит за нею те городы, и волости, и села до ее живота, а после ее живота город Кременеск, и с волостью, и с волостью с Вешками, ‖ сыну моему Ивану, к великому государству, а села Черки- л. 35 зова мелница и что к ней одиннатцать деревень, сыну моему Федору, к селу Черкизову. А что был есьми благословил брата своего, князь Юрья, сверх его уделу, городом Брянским, и аз тем городом Брянским благословляю сына же своего Ивана, с волостми, и с путми, и с селы, и со всеми пошлинами, как было изстари, а село Пузяево с деревнями, да село Белой Раст с деревнями, да деревня Наузулово, и которые деревни приписаны к Наузолову, сыну моему Федору к селцу Озерецкому, Устюжна Железопольская, и волость Каргка, и села, которые въ Углицком уезде, село Николское Жданово с деревнями, сыну же моему Федору, к Угличу. А что есьми, по отца своего душевной грамоте и по брата своего, ‖ князь Юрьеву, приказу, дал есьми жене его, княгине л. 35 о Ульяне, вотчину впрок, в Углецком уезде село Хороброво с деревнями, да село Красное с деревнями, и грамоту есьми жалованную на те села и деревни, по нашей жалованной грамоте волна она отдать по душе, и продать, и променить, или буде похочет роду своему отдать, а сын мой Иван и сын мой Федор в те у ней два села не вступаются, по сей нашей жалованной грамоте.

Да сына же своего Ивана благословляю городы и волостьми, что было дяди моего, Андрея Ивановича, и сына его, князь Володимера Андреевича, городом Вышегородом на реке на Петрове,[1] с волостми, и с селы, и со всеми пошлинами, и с дворцовыми селы, да в Можай-
л. 36 ском ‖ уезде волостью Алешнею Воскресенским да волостью Петровскою, с селы, и з деревнями, и с починки, и со всеми угодьи, и с дворцо-

---

[1] *Примечание переписчика:* Городок Малой где был, неизвестно.

[1] *Примечание переписчика:* Вышегород в коем уезде было, не знаю.

выми селы, что в тех волостях, и со всеми доходы, да городом Ста-
рицею с волостми, и с путми, и с селы, и со всеми пошлинами,
с волостми, с Холмом, и с Погорелым Городищем, и с волостью
с Синею, да городом Алексиным, и с Волконою, и с волостми, и с путми,
и с селы, и со всеми пошлинами, да городом Вереею, с волостми,
и с путми, и с селы, и со всеми пошлинами. А что был дали есьми
князю Володимеру Андреевичу в мену, против ево вотчины, городов,
и волостей, и сел, городы, и волости, и села, и князь Володимер передо
мною преступил, и те городы, и волости, и села сыну моему Ивану,
а княжь Володимерова сына, князя Василья, и дочери, посмотря по настоя-
щему времяни, как будет пригоже. ‖

6 об.   А сына своего Федора благословляю крест золотой с мощьми Ива-
новской Грязнова.

Да сына же своего Федора благословляю, даю ему город Суздаль
с волостьми, и с путьми, и с селы, и со всеми пошлинами, да город Шую,
с волостми, и с путьми, и с селы, и со всеми пошлинами. Да ему жь даю
город Кострому да город Плесо[2] с волостми, и с путми, и со всеми
пошлинами. Да ему жь даю город Любим, да город Буй, да город Суди-
славль, да город Нерехту, и с Солми с Болшею и с Малою, и со всеми их
волостьми, и с путми, и с селы, и со всеми пошлинами, как было при мне.

Да сына же своего Федора благословляю, даю ему город Я,ославль
л. 37 с волостьми, и с путми, и с селы, и со всеми пошлинами. ‖ А князьям
боя,ским ярославским и детем боярским ярославцам своими вотчинами
и с купленными от сына моего Федора не отъехати к сыну моему Ивану
и никуды. А кто отъедет от сына моего Федора куды-нибудь, и земля
их сыну моему Федору. А служат у него, и он у них в земли, и у жен,
и у детей не вступается. А которые есьми вотчины поимал у князей
ярославских, и те вотчины сыну моему Федору, а сын мой Федор в том
волен, хощет те вотчины за собою держать, хощет он отдать. А у которых князей ярославских их вотчин не имал, и сын мой Федор тех вотчин
не отнимает у них, жен, и у детей их, а отъедут к сыну моему
Ивану или инуды куды-нибудь, и те вотчины сыну моему Федору.
7 об. Да сыну же моему ‖ Федору даю город Козелск и Серенеск[3] с волостми,
и с путми, и с селы, и со всеми пошлинами. Да ему жь даю город
Серпейск да Мценеск с волостьми, и с путми, и со всеми пошлинами.

Да сына же своего Федора благословляю, даю ему город Волок
Ламской с волостьми, и с путьми, и с селы, и со всеми пошлинами.
Да сыну же моему Федору даю село из Москвы, село Крылецкое
с деревнями, да село Татарово с деревнями, да село Сорочино с деревнями, Романцово с деревнями, что ,рипусканы от становых деревень,
да село Озерецкое Старое, да село Озерецкое Новое с деревнями,
и с припускными деревнями, что припусканы от остаточных деревень,
да селцо Кузяево, да селцо Белой Раст и Наузовские деревни, кото-
л. 38 рые списаны ‖ с Наузовской деревней, и те селы и деревни сыну
моему Федору, к селу Озерецкому. Да ему жь даю селцо Напрудное
с городскими с посадскими дворы, а [по] которыя места дал есьми ему
те дворы, и аз дал тому список, за своею печатью и за дьяка своего
приписью. Да сыну же моему Федору даю в Суздале село Быково,
что было князь Иваново Мстиславскаго, да волость Коряковская, со всеми
деревнями, и с починки, и с рыбными ловлями, да село Лопатниче, да

---

[2] *Примечание переписчика:* Плесо ныне село.
[3] *Примечание переписчика:* Серенеск неизвестно, разве не описано ли вместо
Серпейск.

Борисово, да полсела Гориц, да две трети села Тернеева, и с приселки, и с деревнями, и с починки, что были княжо Александровские Горбатаго, да волость Турех с деревнями и с рыбными ловлями.

А что есьми дал сыну моему Федору казны своея, и то писано в казенном списке.

А бог даст мне сына с женою ‖ моею Анною, и аз его благословляю л. 38 город Углечь, и Устюжная, Холопей, с волостми, и селы, и с двемя селы, которые даны старице Александре княжо Юрьево Васильевича, и з данью к Углечю. Да ему жь даю город Кашин, и с Задубровскою слободою и Славковым, и со всеми волостьми, и селы, и со всеми пошлинами. Да ему жь даю город Ярославец с волостми, и с селы, и со всеми пошлинами. Да ему жь даю город Верею, с волостьми, и с путьми, и с селы, и со всеми пошлинами.

А бог даст мне с женою своею с Анною дочерь, и аз ее благословляю, даю город Зубцов с волостми, и путьми, и с селы, и со всеми пошлинами. Да ей же даю Опоки, и Хлепен, и Рагачев, с волостьми, и селы, и с путми, и со всеми пошлинами. Да ей же даю Подмосковныя села, село Митрополичье, что было Михаила ‖ Тучкова, село Елде- л. 39 гино, что было Юрья Шеина, село Симоновское Васильевское Шеина, село Кленки Услюмовское, Данилово село Ивановское, Брюхово село Сулонево, Сафарынское Ивана Сафарина, село Давыдовское Дмитреевское Яковлева сына Давыдова, со всеми деревнями и с угодьи.

Да благословляю жену свою Анну, даю ей город Ростов, с волостьми, и с путми, и с селы, и со всеми пошлинами, да под Москвою село Алешня, село Болтино, село Астанково, и с приписными деревнями, что приписано от черных станов и поместных, да в Ярославле вотчина Суцких князей, село Сутки, село Щулепово, село Болонино, село Мартемьяново, село Борниское, село Новое, село Кривцово, и с деревнями, и с починки, что было княгини Аграфены Суцкой, да вь Юрьеве Польском село Городище Мстиславле, село ‖ Флолищево, село Сенмское, л. 39 село Елохово, с деревнями и со всеми угодьи, да тремя третьми Заозерских Пенковых вотчиною со всеми деревнями и угодьи.

А что есьми дал жене своей и детем своим казны своей, и то писано в казенном списке.[1]

А что отец наш, князь великий Василей Ивановичь всея России, пожаловал князя Федора Мстиславскаго, и что аз придал сыну его, князю Ивану, и сын мой Иван в ту у него вотчину и у его детей не вступается. А отъедет куда-нибудь, и та вотчина сыну Ивану.

А что есьми пожаловал князя Михаила княжь Васильева сына Львовича Глинскаго вотчиною, и сын мой Иван у княжь Михаилова сына, у князя Иванова, и у его детей не вступается у нево ничем. А буде куды-нибудь отъедет, и та вотчина сыну моему Ивану. А что есми пожаловал Раманову жену Юрьевича и ее сына Никиту волостьми и селы, ‖ и сын л. 40 мой Иван в ту вотчину, ни у них детей не вступается. А которыя у них волости и села будут в сына моего Федоров удел, и сын мой Федор по тому ж в ту вотчину не вступается по сей моей душевной грамоте. А что есьми был пожаловал князь Михаила княжь Иванова сына Воротынскаго старою его вотчиною, городом Одоевым, да городом Новасьяню, да городом на Черни, и аз ту вотчину взял на себя, а князю Михаилу дал есьми в то место вотчину, город Стародуб Ряполовской,

---

[1] *Примечание переписчика:* Здесь из всех разделов оных государей видно было, какую они от смятения опасность имеют, что хотя детем меньшим доволныя уделы определяли, но все в розни, а не сплошь, дабы им неудобно было в скорости от всего удела войска собрать и государю какое-либо воспротивление учинить.

да в Муромском уезде, в Зовском стану, волость Мошок, да в Ниже-городском уезде село Княгинино с деревнями, да на реке на Волге Фокино селище, а ведает ту вотчину князь Михайла по меновным грамо-там, по тому жь, как ведал свою вотчину, а служит он и дети ево сыну моему Ивану, а сын мой Иван в ту у него вотчину и у его детей не вступается, а отъедет куда-нибудь, и та вотчина сыну моему Ивану.

А город Озерище со всеми пригороды, которыя есьми поставил на Полоцком, и на Озегецком повете, и с Усвятом, сыну моему Федору со всем, по тому, как писано в сей моей душевной грамоте сыну моему Ивану, а удел сына моего Федоров ему жь к великому государству.

А что есьми учинил опришнину, и то на воле детей моих, Ивана и Федора, как им прибыльнее, и чинят; а образец им учинен ‖ готов.

А ныне приказываю свою душу, сына своего Федора отцу своему, бого-мольцу, Антонию, митрополиту всея России, да тебе, сыну своему Ивану.

А ты, сын мой Федор, сына моего Ивана, а своего брата старейшаго, слушай во всем и держи его в мое место, отца своего, и государства его под ним не подыскивай. А учнешь ты, сын мой Федор, под сыном под Иваном государств его подыскивать, или учнешь с кем-нибудь ссыла-тися на его лихо, тайно или явно, или учнешь на него кого подъимати, или учнешь с кем на него одиначитися, ино по евангелскому словеси, Федор сын, аще кто не чтит отца или матерь, смертью да умрет.

А кто сию мою душевную грамоту порушит, тому судит бог, и не буди на нем мое благословение.

А у сей моеи душевнои грамоты сидел...

Примечание переписчика: Сия духовная, хотя по обстоятельству дела и слогу видно, что им, государем, сочинена, однако ж действи-телною быть не могла, потому что она писана задолго до его кончины и суще видится около 7080 году, понеже...

Списку духовнои грамоты предшествует следующий заголовок, помещенный на стр. 1:

Духовная государя, царя и великаго князя Иоанна Васильевича, всея России самодержца, и прочая, и прочая, и прочая, сочинена самим около 7080-го от сотворения мира, а от рождества христова 1572 году и содержит завещание и наставление духовная, нравоучительная и поли-тическая, зело благоразумныя и мудрыя, тут же и раздел государям, царевичам, сыновьям его, царевичу Иоанну Иоанновичу и царевичу Федору Иоанновичу.

Списана с копии, которая была списана с оригинальной сей духовной человеком искусным и любопытным, как примечания показует.

А. Курбатова.

Списана въ Санктпетербурге в апреле месяце 1739.

Основание для датировки: см. статью С. Б. Веселовского: «Духовное завещание Ивана Грозного» (Изв. АН СССР, 1947, № 6, стр. 508).

Список начала XIX в. (водяной знак — 1805 г.) — ЦГАДА, портфели Малинов-ского № 3-6, дело № 79.

Духовная грамота ранее напечатана: ДАИ, т. 1, стр. 371—389, № 222.

Поправки явно испорченных мест даны в квадратных скобках, исправления географических названий см. в указателе.

PART THREE
Translations of the Testaments

Introduction to the Texts

THE testaments of the Grand Princes of Moscow are remarkably similar in nature and style. All are written in the first person and all appear to have been dictated personally by the grand prince to the secretary (*d'yak*) who penned them. The general outline of the testaments is: (1) a brief introduction in the form of an invocation; (2) a disposition of the territorial holdings and income of the prince to his widow and children in descending order of seniority, and to other persons or to ecclesiastical institutions; (3) a disposition of such personal possessions of the prince as crowns, goblets, belts, and sacred relics; (4) a disposition of the slaves and servants of the grand prince; (5) an exhortation to the prince's sons to live in peace and harmony with one another and to regard their mother or oldest brother "in the place of me, your father"; (6) a list of the attestants to the document; and (7) the curse placed upon any potential violator of the testament.

This outline is typical of the first nine testaments, beginning with Ivan Kalita and ending with Vasiliy II. The testament of Ivan III, while following the model and general style of its predecessors, differs in its more precise and detailed statement of certain aspects of princely administration in Muscovy. The testament of Ivan the Terrible is, in one respect at least, unlike any of the earlier documents. The first quarter or more of this document consists of the tsar's "confession" and of a lengthy "commandment" to his sons. His confession amounts to a long enumeration of his multifarious sins, presented in general terms, and of a number of lengthy quotations from the Bible. His commandment to his sons follows the pattern of earlier testaments but is longer. Ivan then proceeds to a disposition of his territorial and personal possessions.

Testaments of the Grand Princes

The translations are based on the texts of the testaments of the grand princes as printed in L. V. Cherepnin and S. V. Bakhrushin, eds., *Dukhovnyye i dogovornyye gramoty velikikh i udel'nykh knyazey XIV–XVI vv.* (Moscow and Leningrad, 1950), cited as *DDG*. The transliteration system is given in the accompanying table. All the texts of the testaments in *DDG* are

Russian to English Transliteration Table

Russian	English	Russian	English
а	a	т	t
б	b	у	u
в	v	оу †	u
г	g	ȣ †	u
д	d	ф	f
е	e, ye *	х	kh
ж	zh	ц	ts
з	z	ч	ch
и	i	ш	sh
й	y	щ	shch
i †	i	ъ	”
к	k	ы	y
л	l	ь	’
м	m	ѣ †	e, ye *
н	n	ю	yu
о	o	я	ya
ѡ †	o	ѥ †	ye
п	p	ꙗ †	ya
р	r	ѧ †	ya
с	s	ѱ †	ps
		ѳ †	f

* Spelled *e* after a consonant; *ye* initially and after vowels, ъ, or ь.
† Does not appear in the present Russian alphabet.

printed from originals or copies thereof preserved in the Central State Archives of Ancient Acts in Moscow. The editors of *DDG* have adhered to the following rules in reproducing the texts: (1) the texts are divided into words rather than being reproduced in a continuity of letters as in the originals; (2) marks of punctuation have been supplied in accordance with the meaning; (3) proper names and words following a full stop have been capitalized; (4) the old Russian letters ѥ, i, оу, ѣ, ꙗ, ѧ, ѡ,ѳ,ѱ, and final ъ have been preserved; (5) the old Slavic alphabetical numerals have been replaced by Arabic numerals; (6) the tittles have been removed and omitted letters restored; (7) letters written above words in the originals have been introduced into their proper places within words; (8) letters omitted in the originals have been restored in accordance with the orthography of the given text; (9) no corrections of the originals have been made; (10) corrections, glosses, and erasures of the copyists have been identified in notes; and (11) the texts have been divided into paragraphs.[1]

The translations of the testaments as given below are fairly literal, even when a freer translation would have rendered the English more readable. Russian Christian names, patronymics, epithets, and family names are rendered in their modern Russian form (transliterated). Almost all place names (except for the city and principality of Moscow) have been transliterated exactly as they appear in the text except that oblique case endings have been replaced with nominative endings.[2]

An attempt has been made to identify and locate all places mentioned in the testaments and, with a few exceptions, all persons mentioned have been identified. Any doubt as to the meaning of a given passage has been indicated in the notes.

[1] *DDG*, pp. 5–6.

[2] The reader who knows Russian will appreciate the fact that in a few instances it has not seemed advisable simply to transliterate place names. For instance, "Deacon Foma's villages" and "Fedor Sviblo's villages in Ustyug" seem to be more felicitous renderings of the original than do "Fominskiye villages d'yakonovy" and "Fedorovskiye villages Sviblovskiye in Ustyuze." Similarly, "and the [Velikiye] Luki villages" seems better than "and the Lutskiye villages."

The reader will also understand the problem of interpolating a *tverdyy znak* as the ending of a masculine place name when that place name and others in the same passage occur in a case other than nominative or accusative. This is especially true of those testaments and passages that are not at all consistent in the use of the *tverdyy znak*. As a rule I have added the *tverdyy znak* in those passages in which it seems to have been more or less regularly used by the scribe.

TEXT 1

Testament of Ivan Kalita

Commentary

IVAN DANILOVICH, called Money Bag (*Kalita*), was born in 1304, the fifth and youngest son of Prince Daniil Aleksandrovich and his wife, Mariya. Ivan was Prince of Moscow from 1325 until 1328, and Grand Prince of Vladimir and Moscow from 1328 until his death in 1341.

Ivan's testament was probably written in 1339. The mention of "my princess and the younger children" suggests a date considerably later than the prince's second marriage, to Princess Ul'yana, which took place in 1332.[1] Moreover, the reference to Ivan's trip to the Golden Horde indicates that the testament was probably written in 1339, for in that year the grand prince and his sons set out for the Horde.[2]

There are two extant variants of Ivan Kalita's testament. The originals of both, on parchment, are in the Central State Archives of Ancient Acts (TsGADA) in Moscow, in the State Repository of Ancient Documents, Section I, Heading 1, Nos. 1–2. The gilded silver seal of Grand Prince Ivan Danilovich Kalita is suspended from the face of the first variant. On the face of the second variant there is a trace of the affixture of a seal. On the reverse of the second variant the following notation appears:

---

[1] Ivan's first wife, Yelena, was the mother of Semen (b. 1317), Daniil (b. 1320, d. probably in childhood), Ivan (b. 1326), Andrey (b. 1327), Fetiniya, Mariya, Yevdokiya, and Fedosiya. Yelena died in 1331. In 1332 Ivan married Ul'yana, who subsequently gave birth to a daughter whose name is not known. For this and other biographical information on Ivan Kalita, see A. V. Ekzemplyarskiy, *Velikiye i udel'nyye knyaz'ya severnoy Rusi v" tatarskiy period", s" 1238 po 1505 g.* (St. Petersburg, 1889), I, 71–79 and 287.

[2] *PSRL*, VII, 205; see also n. 3, below.

"Testaments and copies of testaments and another document."[3]
Ivan Kalita's testament has been printed in N. I. Novikov, ed.,
Drevnyaya Rossiyskaya Vivliofika (1st ed.; St. Petersburg,
1773–1775), Part 8, Nos. 1–2; in the second edition of the
same work (Moscow, 1788–1791), Part 1, Nos. 1–2; in the
Myshkin Library edition of the same work (Myshkin,
1894), Vol. V, Part 9; in *Sobraniye gosudarstvennykh gramot i
dogovorov, khranyashchikhsya v Gosudarstvennoy kollegii
inostrannykh del* (Moscow, 1813), Part 1, Nos. 21–22; and in a
number of other collections.[4]

[3] *DDG*, pp. 9 and 11. The description of the seals attached to the two
variants of this testament as given by L. V. Cherepnin in *Russkiye
feodal'nyye arkhivy, XIV–XV vv.* (Moscow-Leningrad, 1948–1951), I,
15, is not in complete agreement with the information in *DDG* cited
above. Cherepnin writes: "Identical gilded silver seals of an octagonal
shape, made from the same stamp, were suspended from both testaments.
On the face of each is depicted Jesus Christ, standing, wearing a crown
ornamented with a cross, his right hand raised in blessing, and the Gospel
in his left hand. On the reverse is pictured John the Precursor, his right
hand raised in blessing, and a scroll in his left hand. The legend,
beginning on one side of the seals and concluding on the other, is 'Seal of
Grand Prince Ivan.' The seal on the second variant was attached, by the
cord tying it to the document, to another small lead seal (now lost). On
one side of it [the lost seal?] was a stamp [*tamga*] in the form of a plait,
and on the other side a six-cornered star composed of two triangles with
four small balls in the center. This additional lead seal, which existed
only with the second testament of the Prince of Moscow, was doubtless
of Tartar origin: representations of interlacings and of the Tartar star
are often met with on fourteenth-century coins of the Golden Horde."
Cherepnin believes that the existence of this additional Tartar seal
indicates that the second testament of Kalita was presented to the khan
for his approval in 1339 when the Moscow prince traveled to the Horde
and won a victory over Prince Aleksandr Mikhaylovich of Tver', his
competitor for the office of Grand Prince of Vladimir (*Russkiye feodal'-
nyye arkhivy*, I, 15–16).
It is of interest that the second variant—to which the seal of the Tartar
khan was affixed—contained a list of Ivan's purchases outside his proper
principality, Moscow, a list which does not occur in the first variant.
Further evidence of the successful nature of Ivan's trip to the Horde in
1339! (see n. 21, below, and Cherepnin, *Russkiye feodal'nyye arkhivy*, I,
16–17).
[4] *DDG*, p. 5.

The following translation is based on the second of the two variants of Kalita's testament (*DDG*, pp. 9–11). The second variant contains a number of passages not in the first (*DDG*, pp. 7–9). All significant items that appear in the first variant but not in the second are included in this translation and are identified in the footnotes.

THE TESTAMENT OF GRAND PRINCE IVAN I DANILOVICH

IN the name of the Father, and of the Son, and of the Holy Ghost, lo I, the sinful, poor slave of God, Ivan, on leaving for the Horde, write [this] [5] testament of my own free will, being of sound mind and body. If God should decide something concerning my life, I give [this] arrangement [*ryad"*] to my sons and to my princess.[6]

I bequeath my patrimony, Moscow, to my sons. And lo, I have arranged the [following] distribution [of it]:

Lo, to my oldest son, Semen, I have given Mozhayesk" with all its volosts, Kolomna, with all the Kolomna volosts, Gorodenka, Mezynya, Pesochna, and Seredokorotna, Pokhryane, Ust'-Mer'ska, Broshevaya, Gvozdna, Ivani, the hamlets Makovets', Levichin", Skulnev", Kanev", Gzhelya, Goretova, Gorki, the village Astaf'yev'skoye, the village on the Sever'stsa [River] in Pokhryane District,[7] the village Kostyantinov'skoye, the village Orinin'skoye, the village Ostrov'skoye, the village Kopoten'skoye, the small village Mikul'skoye, the village Malakhov'skoye, and the village Naprud'skoye near the city.[8]

And during my lifetime I have given to my son Semen: 4 golden chains, 3 golden belts, 2 golden goblets with pearls, a

---

[5] Unless otherwise indicated in the footnotes, words and phrases in brackets have been supplied by the translator.

[6] To Semen, Ivan, Andrey, and Ul'yana.

[7] Not clear. Pokhryane (mentioned immediately above in the text) is identified as a volost of Kolomna District.

[8] The village Naprud'skoye was located due north of the Kremlin on, as its name would suggest, a pond (see M. N. Tikhomirov, *Srednevekovaya Moskva v XIV–XV vekakh* [Moscow, 1957], p. 63 and map opposite p. 288).

small golden dish with pearls [and] with precious stones, [and] 2 large golden bowls. And of the silver vessels I have given to him 3 silver dishes.

And lo, I give to my son Ivan: Zvenigorod, Kremichna, Ruza, Fomin'skoye, Sukhodol'', Velikaya *svoboda*, Zamosh'skaya *svoboda*, Ugozh', Rostovtsi, Okat'yeva *svobodka*,⁹ Skirminov'skoye, Trostna, [and] Neguchya. And the villages: the village Ryukov'skoye, the village Kamenichskoye, the village Ruz'skoye, the village Belzhin'skoye, the village Maksimovskoye, the village Andreyevskoye, the village Vyazem'skoye, the village Domontovskoye, the village in Zamosh'skaya *svoboda*, [and] the village Semtsin'skoye.

And of gold I have given to my son Ivan: 4 golden chains, a large golden belt with pearls and precious stones, a golden belt with clasps, a carnelian belt bound with gold, 2 golden vases,¹⁰ 2 round golden cups, the silver dish from Yezd, [and] 2 small dishes.

And lo, I have given to my son Andrey: Lopastna, Sever'ska, Narunizhskoye, Serpokhov'', Nivna, Temna, Golichichi, Shchitov'', Peremyshl', Rastovets', [and] Tukhachev''. And lo, the villages: the village Talezh'skoye, the village Serpokhov'skoye, the village Kolbasin'skoye, the village Nar'skoye, the village Peremyshl'skoye, the village Bityagov'skoye, the village Trufonov'skoye, the village Yasinov'skoye, the village Kolomninskoye, [and] the village Nogatin'skoye.

And of gold I have given to my son Andrey: 4 golden chains, a golden Italian belt with pearls [and] precious stones, a golden belt with a clasp on purple silk, a golden belt from the Horde,¹¹ 2

⁹ A *svoboda* (or *sloboda*), 'free settlement,' was a settlement or a group of settlements which had been granted certain privileges or immunities. The diminutive form is *svobodka* (*slobodka*) (see Chapter 3).

¹⁰ *2 ovkacha zol[o]ta.* The translation of *ovkach'* as "vase" is not certain. It may have been a unit of gold (see, for example, S. P. Obnorskiy and S. G. Barkhudarov, *Khrestomatiya po istorii russkogo yazyka* [Moscow, 1921], p. 374).

¹¹ *Poyas'' zolot'' ts[a]r[e]v'skii.* The adjective *tsarev'skii* refers either to the Khan of the Tartars or to Byzantium (Tsar'grad: the city of Caesar). Alexandre Eck, in *Le Moyen Age russe* (Paris, 1933), p. 482, interprets its meaning in this document as Byzantine. Tikhomirov (*Srednevekovaya Moskva*, p. 133) prefers the alternate translation.

golden chalices, 2 small golden bowls; and of dishes: a silver dish and two small [dishes].

And lo, I give to my princess and the younger children: Surozhik", Mushkova Gora, Radonezh'skoye, Beli, Vorya, Chernogolovl', Sofronov'skaya *svobodka* on the Vorya, Vokhna, Deikovo Ramen'ye,[12] Danilishchova *svobodka*, Mashev", Selna, Guslitsya, Ramen'ye, that was the princess'. And the villages: Mikhailov'skoye village, Lutsin'skoye village, the village by the lake, Radonezh'skoye village, Deigunin'skoye village, Tylovskoye village, Rogozh', Protas'yevskoye village, Aristovskoye village, Lopasten'skoye village, Mikhailovskoye village on the Yauza, the 2 Kolomna villages.

And of the city revenues,[13] I give the *osmnicheye* to my princess. But my sons shall share the *tamga* and the other city revenues; in the same manner [they shall] also [share] the *myto*,[14] that which is in the district of each shall be his. And my sons shall share the city quitrent [in honey] [15] of Vasiliy's Department.[16] And concerning my beekeepers and purchased quitrent tenants, those who are in each [son's] list shall be his.

And if, because of my sins, the Tartars should demand certain volosts, and if they should be taken away, then you, my sons and my princess, shall again divide those volosts [that remain], in place of those [that are taken away].

And my sons shall manage the enrolled people [17] jointly and

---

[12] Not clear. Deikovo was a village (*DDG*, p. 534). Perhaps the word *ramen'ye*, 'forest along the edge of cultivated fields,' was copied by error from the following line of the testament.

[13] *A iz goro[d]skikh" volostii*. Here the word *volost'* is used to mean revenue rather than in its more usual sense of a geographic-administrative area (see A. Ye. Presnyakov, *Obrazovaniye velikorusskogo gosudarstva: Ocherki po istorii XII–XV stoletiy* [Petrograd, 1918], p. 166, n. 1).

[14] The *osmnicheye*, 'eighth,' and the *tamga* were taxes on trade; the *myto* (or *myt"*) was a toll (see Chapter 3).

[15] "In honey" occurs in the first variant but not in the second.

[16] *Vasiltsevo vedan'ye* was the administrative department of the boyar Vasiliy Vel'yaminov. It was concerned with the collection of quitrent paid in honey by tenants of the prince's lands (see Chapter 5).

[17] The *chislenyi lyud[i]*, 'enrolled people, people who have been counted in the census,' are discussed in Chapter 4.

shall, as one man, care for them. And concerning my purchased people [who are listed] in the Great Roll, now my sons shall share them also.

And concerning the gold of my princess Yelena, now I have given to my daughter Fetiniya: 14 rings and her mother's neck-piece, and a new necklace, which I [caused to be] wrought. And I myself have given [to her] a headband and a neckchain. And concerning the gold which I have acquired—that which God has given me—and the small golden box, now this I have given to my princess and the younger children.

And of my clothing [I leave] to my son Semen the crimson mantle [and] the Golden Cap.[18] And [I give] to my son Ivan the mantle of yellow silk with pearls and the large cloak with shoulder pieces.[19] And to my son Andrey [I give] the sable pelisse with a turned-down collar [and] epaulettes and with a large pearl and precious stones, [and] the scarlet vestment with shoulder pieces. And concerning the 2 mantles with breastplates [and] with pearls, which I have now caused to be made, now I have given [them] to my younger children, Mariya and Fedo-siya, with the necklace.

And concerning my silver belts, now they shall be distributed among the priests. And as for the 100 rubles which Yeska has, now they shall be distributed among the churches. And concerning those silver vessels of mine which remain, now my sons and my princess shall share them. And concerning my clothing that remains, now it shall be distributed among all the priests and in Moscow. And the large plate with 4 annuli, now it I give to the [Cathedral of the] Holy Mother of God in Vol[o]dimer'.[20]

[18] As noted in Chapter 6, the *shapka zolotaya* was probably the crown known subsequently as the Cap of Monomakh.

[19] *Barmy*, 'shoulder pieces of the grand prince, with holy images' (see I. I. Sreznevskiy, *Materialy dlya slovarya drevne-russkogo yazyka* [Moscow, 1958], I, 42).

[20] The Cathedral of the Dormition of the Most Pure Mother of God in Vladimir-on-the-Klyazma was founded by Prince Andrey Bogolyubskiy in 1158 (*PSRL*, XXV, 63 and 83–84). For a description, sketch, and photograph of this cathedral, see N. N. Voronin and M. K. Karger, *Istoriya kul'tury drevney Rusi: Domongol'skiy period, Obshchestvennyy stroy i dukhovnaya kul'tura* (Moscow-Leningrad, 1951), pp. 310–312.

And concerning the herd which I have given to my son Semen, and the second to Ivan, [now these shall be theirs], and my sons and my princess shall share the other herds.

And besides the Moscow villages, I give to my son Semen my purchased villages: the village Avakovskoye in Novgorod on the Ulala [River and] another, Borisovskoye, in Volodimer'.[21]

And concerning the village which I purchased, Petrovskoye, and Oleksin'skoye,[22] Vsedobrich['], and Pavlov'skoye on the Mas,[23] half I purchased and half I acquired by exchange from the metropolitan . . . tsya[24] on the Mas, which I bought from Afiney, now I give to my son Ivan.

And concerning the village Varvar'skoye which I purchased, and Melov'skoye near Yur'yev, which I obtained in exchange for the village Matfeishchov'skoye, now I give [them] to my son Andrey.

And concerning the village Pavlovskoye, which our grand-mother[25] purchased, and the small village Novoye, which I purchased, and [the Monastery of] Saint Aleksandr on the Kostroma [River], which I purchased, now [these] I give to my princess.

And concerning the village Bogorod[i]cheskoye in Rostov, which I bought and gave to Borisko Vor'kov, now if he serves one of my sons, then the village shall be his, [but] if he does not

[21] This paragraph and the five that follow (i.e., from "And besides the Moscow villages" to "Saint Aleksandr, for the memory of my soul") contain a list of Ivan's purchases outside the Moscow principality. These paragraphs appear in the second variant of Ivan's testament but not in the first. See also n. 3, above.

[22] The village Petrovskoye is not identified. Oleksin'skoye was a village of Zvenigorod District. This may well be one village, identical with the village Petrovskoye Aleksinskoye mentioned in the second testament of Vasiliy I.

[23] The identity of this river is obscure. It may be the Msta.

[24] The second variant is torn at this place with space for about twelve letters missing. The significance of *tsya* is not known. The passage does not occur in the first variant.

[25] Ivan Kalita's paternal grandmother was Aleksandra, wife of Grand Prince Aleksandr Nevskiy and daughter of Prince Bryachislav Izyaslavich of Polotsk. We do not know the identity of Mariya, Ivan's mother, or of her parents (Ekzemplyarskiy, II, 275).

serve my children, then the village shall be taken away [from him].[26]

And concerning the small village on the Kerzhach, which I purchased from Abbot Prokofiy, another, Leontiyevskoye, [and] a third, Sharapovskoye, now I give [them] to [the Monastery of] Saint Aleksandr, for the memory of my soul.

And I charge you, my son Semen, to be the guardian—according to [the law of] God—of your younger brothers and of my princess and the younger children.

And may God judge him who violates this testament.

And the attestants to this are my spiritual father Yefrem, my spiritual father Fedosiy, [and] my spiritual father the priest Davyd.

[And Kostroma, the secretary of the grand prince, wrote (this) document.] [27]

[26] See Chapter 7.

[27] The sentence in brackets appears in the first variant but not in the second.

TEXT 2

Testament of Semen the Proud

Commentary

SEMEN IVANOVICH, called the Proud (*Gordyy*), was the oldest son of Grand Prince Ivan Kalita and Princess Yelena. He was born in 1317. Semen was Grand Prince of Vladimir and Moscow from 1341 until his death in 1353.

Semen's testament was written sometime between March 18 and April 26, 1353. The grand prince's two young sons, Ivan and Semen, both died of the plague on March 18, 1353, and since no mention is made of them in the testament it is assumed that the document was written after this date. The testament must have been written on or before April 26, 1353, the date of the grand prince's death.[1]

The original of the testament, on parchment, is in the Central State Archives of Ancient Acts (TsGADA) in Moscow. From the face of the original are suspended the gilded silver seal of Grand Prince Semen and two yellow-wax seals, one the seal of Prince Ivan Ivanovich and the other that of Prince Andrey Ivanovich, brothers of the grand prince.[2]

The testament of Semen Ivanovich has been printed in N. I. Novikov, ed., *Drevnyaya Rossiyskaya Vivliofika*, (1st ed.; St. Petersburg, 1773–1775), Part 8, No. 4; in the second edition of the same work (Moscow, 1788–1791), Part 1, No. 4; in the Myshkin Library edition of the same work (Myshkin, 1894), Vol. V, Part 9; in *Sobraniye gosudarstvennykh gramot i dogo-*

---

[1] For the dates of Semen's life, reign, and death, see *Troitskaya letopis'* (Moscow-Leningrad, 1950), reconstructed text by M. D. Priselkov, p. 377, and *PSRL*, VII, 206 and 217. For the dating of his testament, see *PSRL*, VII, 217, and L. V. Cherepnin, *Russkiye feodal'nyye arkhivy, XIV–XV vv.* (Moscow-Leningrad, 1948–1951), I, 25.

[2] *DDG*, p. 14.

vorov, kranyashchikhsya v Gosudarstvennoy kollegii inostran-nykh del (Moscow, 1813), Part 1, No. 24; and in a number of other collections.[3]

The translation which follows is based on the text of the testament as printed in *DDG*, pp. 13–14.

THE TESTAMENT OF GRAND PRINCE SEMEN IVANOVICH

IN the name of the Father, and of the Son, and of the Holy Ghost, lo I, the poor, sinful slave of God, Sozont",[4] while living and of sound mind, write [this] testament. I give the arrangement [*ryad"*] to my princess.[5] I have commanded that my Uncle Vasiliy [6] be with her. And I charge by God my brothers, Prince Ivan and Prince Andrey, [that] I have placed my princess and my [uncle] [7] and my boyars in God's care and in your care, my [brothers], [and] you shall care for [them] according to the agreement which we made when we kissed the cross at our father's grave.[8]

[3] *DDG*, p. 14.

[4] Semen was born "in the month of September, on the seventh day, on [the day of] the memory of the holy martyr Sozont"" (*Troitskaya letopis'*, p. 355). The grand prince took monastic vows shortly before his death and probably assumed the name Sozont" at that time (see Cherepnin, *Russkiye feodal'nyye arkhivy*, I, 26).

[5] Semen's third wife, Mariya, the daughter of Prince Aleksandr Mikhaylovich of Tver' (*PSRL*, X, 218).

[6] The identity of Uncle Vasiliy has never been definitely established. Cherepnin (*Russkiye feodal'nyye arkhivy*, I, 27) believes that he was Vasiliy Vasil'yevich Vel'yaminov, the manager of "Vasiliy's Department" and the last chiliarch (*tysyatskiy*) of Moscow, who died in 1374. See also *PSRL*, XXV, 189.

[7] The original document is torn at this place, with space for about four letters missing. It is possible that the missing word is "son" (*syna*), but more probably it was "uncle" (*dyadyu*)—another reference to Vasiliy Vel'yaminov (see Cherepnin, *Russkiye feodal'nyye arkhivy*, I, 26–27).

[8] The word "brothers" (*brat'i*) is missing in the original and has been supplied by the editors of *DDG*. The Russian equivalent of "when we kissed" is defective in the original, as follows: *t . . . lovali*. The editors of *DDG* have reconstructed the phrase.

For the text of the agreement, see *DDG*, pp. 11–13.

And that with which my father, the grand prince, blessed me: Kolomna with its volosts, and with its villages, and with its apiary, Mozhayesk" with its volosts, and with its villages, and with its apiary, Zayachkov", with which my aunt, Princess Anna, blessed me, and Gordoshevichi, and in Moscow city, my share of the *tamga,* and the villages near Moscow in the city district, the village Naprud'skoye, the village Novoye on the Pupavna [River],[9] the village Ostrov'skoye, the village Orinin'skoye, the village Malakhov'skoye, the village Kopoten'skoye, the village Ostaf'yeskoye on the Klyazma, the village Ilmov'skoye, the village Khvostov'skoye on the Klyazma, the village Deigunin'skoye, the village in Sulishin *pogost,*[10] and in Per'yaslavl', the village Samarov'skoye which I purchased, the village Romanov'skoye on the Kerzhach [River], the village Ortakov'skoye in Yur'yevskaya volost, the village Semenov'skoye in Volodimer'skaya volost which I purchased from Ivan Ovtsa, the village Oleksandrov'skoye in Kostroma, the village in Dmitrov which I purchased from Ivan Dryuts'skiy, and Zabereg" which I purchased from Semen Novosil'skiy, or if I have forgotten to list any of my purchases or parcels [of land] with which my father blessed me, as well as gold with which my father blessed me, or anything which I shall acquire during my life, be it gold or pearls, now all I have given to my princess.

And I have ordered that my princess be given fifty of my riding horses. And also from among my herds, my princess [shall receive] the Kolomna herd [and] the other herd [at?] Detino Ivash'kovo.[11]

And concerning that which I have written in this document, now I have given all to my princess, [and] may she pray to God and remember my soul until her death.

And concerning that which my boyars or my boyars' people have judged when [I ruled] in the Grand Principality and in my patrimony of Moscow, now you, my brothers, shall not change this.

[9] The Kupavna River, Moscow District (*DDG*, p. 547).

[10] Sulishin *pogost* was in Moscow District. A *pogost* was essentially the same as a volost (see Chapter 3).

[11] *Drugoye stado Detino Ivash'kovo.* The meaning of this phrase is not clear. Perhaps this was the name of the herd, i.e., "Ivan's children's herd."

And those of my boyars who will serve my princess and will manage volosts, [now they] shall give one half of the income to my princess.

And concerning my artisan slaves,[12] or anyone whom I have acquired by purchase, or anyone whom I have acquired because he committed a misdeed,[13] as well as my *tiuns*,[14] and *villici*, somlers, and elders,[15] and anyone who is married to these people—to all these people I have given their freedom, [they may go] wheresoever they wish. And these people are of no concern to my brothers or to my princess.

And I have written this document in the presence of my fathers: in the presence of Bishop Aleksey of Vladimir, of Bishop Afanasiy of Pereyaslavl', of Bishop Afanasiy of Kolomna, of Archimandrite Petr, of Archimandrite Filimon, and of my spiritual father, the priest Yevseviy.

And all this I have entrusted to God and to my brothers, Prince Ivan and Prince Andrey. And according to the blessing of our father, who charged us to live as one, so I also charge you, my brothers, to live as one. And you should not heed evil persons, and if anyone incites discord between you, you should heed our father, Bishop Aleksey, as well as the old boyars who wished our father and us well.[16]

And lo, I write this to you so that the memory of our parents

[12] *Delovyye lyudi* (see above, Chapter 4, n. 26).

[13] *Ili khto mi sya bud[e]t' v vine dostal''*.

[14] The *tiun* was a servant of the grand prince whose primary duty was to administer justice (see Chapter 5).

[15] Concerning the *villici* (*posel'skiye*), somlers (*klyuchniki*), and elders (*starosty*), see Chapter 5.

[16] The mention of "evil persons" and of "the old boyars who wished our father and us well" probably is a reference to the two antagonistic groups of boyars who were active in Moscow during the reigns of Ivan Kalita and Semen the Proud. One of these groups, under the leadership of Vasiliy Vel'yaminov (Uncle Vasiliy?), supported Prince Semen in his policy of appeasing the Horde and opposing Lithuania. The other group, headed by the boyar Aleksey Petrovich Khvost, opposed this policy (see the "Agreement of Grand Prince Semen Ivanovich with Princes Ivan Ivanovich and Andrey Ivanovich," dated "about 1350–1351" [*DDG*, pp. 11–13], and Cherepnin, *Russkiye feodal'nyye arkhivy*, I, 20–27). Aleksey Petrovich Khvost was murdered 1356 (*PSRL*, VIII, 10, and *Troitskaya letopis'*, p. 375).

and of us may not die, and so that the candle may not go out.[17]

And he who violates this document, may God judge him in this life and in the next.

[17] V. O. Klyuchevskiy cites this as one of the rare occasions in which the usual coldness of the testaments warms to a degree of "fervent, pious sentiment" (*Sochineniya* [Moscow, 1956–1959], II, 51). It is also possible that a deeper meaning is hidden in this phrase. It may be that Semen, just before his death, was calling upon his brothers to keep alive the hope of eventual liberation from the Tartar yoke.

TEXT 3

Testament of Ivan II

Commentary

IVAN IVANOVICH, called the Fair (*Krasnyy*), the second surviving son of Ivan Kalita, was born in 1326. He was Grand Prince of Moscow from 1353 and Grand Prince of Vladimir and Moscow from 1354 until his death in 1359.[1]

Two testaments of Ivan II are extant. Inasmuch as they differ in only a few places, these are probably copies of one original testament that has been lost. The handwriting of both copies is identical, and the scribe who wrote both is identified as one Nesterko. L. V. Cherepnin believes that two copies of the original were made so that one might be taken to the Golden Horde to receive the seal of the khan.[2]

A reasonably certain, although rather imprecise, dating of this testament places its writing between 1356 and 1359. One of the attestants to the document was Ignatiy, Bishop of Rostov. Ignatiy became Bishop of Rostov in 1356,[3] so the document could not have been written prior to that year. It could not have been written later than 1359, the year in which Ivan died.

Cherepnin dates the testament about 1358, on the basis of the following passage:

[1] A son, Daniil, was born to Kalita in 1320, three years after the birth of Semen. Daniil apparently died in infancy, although the date of his death is not known (see A. V. Ekzemplyarskiy, *Velikiye i udel'nyye knyaz'ya severnoy Rusi v" tatarskiy period", s" 1238 po 1505 g.* [St. Petersburg, 1889], I, 79). Dates of the birth, reign, and death of Ivan II are from *PSRL*, XXV, 167, 179, and 180.

[2] L. V. Cherepnin, *Russkiye feodal'nyye arkhivy, XIV–XV vv.* (Moscow-Leningrad, 1948–1951), I, 27–31.

[3] *Troitskaya letopis'* (Moscow-Leningrad, 1950), reconstructed text by M. D. Priselkov, p. 374.

And if, because of [my] sins, the Horde should demand Kolomna, or the Lopastna localities, or the localities taken away from Ryazan', and if, because of [my] sins, any locality should be taken away, [then] my children, Prince Dmitriy and Prince Ivan, and [my nephew] Prince Vladimir, and my princess shall divide, in their stead, the uncontested places.

Cherepnin maintains that Prince Ivan II feared that the Horde, acting in accordance with its usual policy of sowing discord among the Russian princes, was preparing to support Ryazan' in an attempt by the latter to regain the lands seized by Moscow in 1353. The *Moscow Chronicle*, under the year 1358, reads in part:

That same year there came from the Horde an emissary, the tsar's [i.e., khan's] son, Mamat Khozha, to the Ryazan' Land and there did much evil [*mnogo tamo zla sotvori*]; and he sent to Grand Prince Ivan Ivanovich concerning the boundary of the Ryazan' lands. The grand prince, however, did not admit him into his patrimony, the Russian Land. And then Mamat Khozha was quickly recalled to the Horde by the tsar because he had entered into seditious activities against the tsar, and in the Horde he killed the favorite of the tsar, and himself fled to Ornach' [Urgench?] and the tsar's messengers, overtaking him, seized him and he was killed by order of the tsar.[4]

Cherepnin argues that Prince Ivan, fearing that he might be called to account by the Horde for his refusal to grant Mamat Khozha entry into the Moscow lands, wrote his testament and included in it this passage providing for a redistribution of lands should the boundary between Moscow and Ryazan' be forcibly readjusted in favor of Ryazan'. As suggested above, Ivan intended that one of the copies of the testament be sent to the Horde for the khan's approval.[5] On the other hand, this passage in the testament of Ivan II may be merely a general statement of princely policy, not related to any particular event, but stimulated by the unsettled state of the Moscow-Ryazan' border since 1353 and by the example of Ivan Kalita's testament, which con-

[4] *PSRL*, XXV, 180.
[5] Cherepnin, *Russkiye feodal'nyye arkhivy*, I, 27–30.

tains a similar proviso: "And if, because of my sins, the Tartars should demand certain volosts. . . ." [6]

Both original copies of the testament of Ivan II are in the Central State Archives of Ancient Acts (TsGADA) in Moscow, in the State Repository of Ancient Documents, Section I, Heading 1, Nos. 4–5. Gilded silver seals of Grand Prince Ivan Ivanovich are suspended from the face of both documents. [7] On the obverse of the seals is a depiction of Saint John with his right arm raised in blessing and with his left hand holding the New Testament. To the left of the picture is the word *Agios*, and to the right *Io*[ann]. On the reverse side of the seals is the inscription, "Seal of Grand Prince Ivan Ivanov[ich]." [8]

The two copies of the testament of Ivan II have been previously printed in N. I. Novikov, ed., *Drevnyaya Rossiyskaya Vivliofika* (1st ed.; St. Petersburg, 1773–1775), Part 8, Nos. 5–6; in the second edition of the same work (Moscow, 1788–1791), Part 1, Nos. 4–5; in the Myshkin Library edition of the same work (Myshkin, 1894), Vol. V, Part 9; in *Sobraniye gosudarstvennykh gramot i dogovorov, khranyashchikhsya v Gosudarstvennoy kollegii inostrannykh del* (Moscow, 1813), Part 1, Nos. 25–26; in N. M. Karamzin, *Istoriya gosudarstva rossiyskago* (St. Petersburg, 1842), Vol. IV, n. 386; and in a number of other collections. [9]

The translation which follows is based on the second copy of the testament as printed in *DDG*, pp. 17–19. All significant items which occur in the first copy (*DDG*, pp. 15–17), but not in the second, are enclosed in brackets and identified in the footnotes.

THE TESTAMENT OF GRAND PRINCE IVAN II IVANOVICH

IN the name of the Father, and of the Son, and of the Holy Ghost, lo I, the sinful, poor slave of God, Ivan Ivanovich, write [this] testament of my own free will, being of sound mind

[6] See above, p. 184.   [7] *DDG*, pp. 17 and 19.
[8] Cherepnin, *Russkiye feodal'nyye arkhivy*, I, 29, n. 84.
[9] *DDG*, p. 19.

[and] in [good] health. Should God decide something concerning my life, I give [this] arrangement [*ryad"*] to my sons, Prince Dmitriy and Prince Ivan, and to my nephew Prince Vladimir, and to my princess.[10]

I bequeath my patrimony, Moscow, to my sons, Prince Dmitriy and Prince Ivan. And to my nephew, Prince Vladimir, in his lieutenancy in Moscow, a third: [11] a third of the *tamga*, of the *myto*, and a third of the city customs that have appertained to the city. And concerning the quitrent in honey of *Vasiltsev" stan"*,[12] and concerning the purchased beekeepers of my father [who are] at the permanent breweries,[13] and the delivery of horses throughout the *stans* and at the breweries,[14] and the horse *put'*,[15] now all [I bequeath] to them [each] a third. And all three princes shall jointly [and] as one man care for the enrolled people.[16]

[10] Dmitriy Ivanovich, subsequently given the agnomen *Donskoy*, 'of the Don,' was born on October 12 of either 1350 (*PSRL*, X, 222, and *Troitskaya letopis'*, p. 371) or 1351 (*PSRL*, XXV, 178).

Ivan Ivanovich, later called Prince of Zvenigorod, was born sometime after 1350 and died in 1364 (*PSRL*, X, 230, and XXV, 181 and 182; *Troitskaya letopis'*, p. 379).

Vladimir Andreyevich, called the Brave (*Khrabryy*), Prince of Serpukhov and Borovsk, was the son of Prince Andrey Ivanovich, the younger brother of Ivan II. Prince Vladimir was born in 1353, the year of his father's death. He died in 1410 (*PSRL*, X, 226, and XXV, 240).

Aleksandra (parents not identified) (*PSRL*, XXV, 182 and 221, and Ekzemplyarskiy, I, 92).

[11] *Tret'*. The right of each of these three princes to rule a third of Moscow and to collect a third of the customs of the city goes back to the testament of Ivan Kalita, which stipulated that Moscow should pass to his three sons. For a discussion of the system of holding Moscow by thirds, see Chapter 5.

[12] Identical with *Vasiltsevo vedan'ye* (see Chapter 5). Concerning the term *stan*, see Chapter 3.

[13] *Otsa moyego bortnitsi kuplenyye pod vechnyye varyakh*. The translation of this phrase is not certain.

[14] *I koni staviti po stanom" i po varyam"*.

[15] The *put'* (pl. *puti*) was a department in the prince's administration. Each *put'* was concerned with a particular area of economic exploitation (see Chapter 5).

[16] See Chapter 4.

And lo, I give to my son, Prince Dmitriy: Mozhayesk" with all its volosts, with its *tamga*, and with its villages, and with its apiary, and with all its customs; Kolomna with all its volosts, and with its *tamga*, and with its *myto*, and with its villages, and with its apiary, [with its quitrent tenants],[17] and with all its customs.

[And concerning those volo]sts[18] that are Princess Mariya's,[19] now these volosts [and villages][20] [shall be hers] during her lifetime, but upon her death these volosts [and villages shall pass] to my son, Prince[21] Dmitriy: Gorodna, Mezyni, Pesochna, Seredokorotna, Pokhryane, Ust'-Mer'ska, Brasheva, Gvozdna, the small village Ivan', the hamlets Makovets', Levichin", Skulnev", Kanev", Koshira, Gzhelya, Gorki, Goretovka, the village in Pokhryane District on the Severtsa [River], the village Malino, the village Kholmy, the village Kostyantinov'skoye, the village Orinin'skoye, the village Ostrov'skoye, the village Kopoten'skoye, the village Mikul'skoye, the village Malakhov'skoye, the village Naprud'skoye, the village Ilmov'skoye, the village Novoye. And of those villages, the villages that are Princess Mariya's, those [shall be hers] during her lifetime, and upon her death those villages [shall pass] to my son, Prince Dmitriy, [as shall] Meshcherka, near [Kolomna].[22]

[17] The phrase in brackets appears in the first copy of the testament but not in the second (*DDG*, p. 15).

[18] The phrase in brackets appears in the first copy of the testament but not in the second (*DDG*, p. 15).

[19] Mariya was the widow of Grand Prince Semen Ivanovich.

[20] The Russian equivalent of "and villages" appears in the first copy but not in the second (*DDG*, p. 15).

[21] The translation of "these volosts [and villages shall pass] to my son, Prince" is based on the first variant of the testament (*DDG*, p. 15). The second variant is defective at this place (*DDG*, p. 17).

[22] The word "Kolomna" appears in the first copy of the testament but not in the second (*DDG*, p. 15). It is here that the two copies of this testament differ the most. The first does not contain the repetition of the condition under which Prince Dmitriy was to inherit the places listed ("And of those villages, the villages that are Princess Mariya's, those [shall be hers] during her lifetime . . ."). It should be noted that this stipulation refers to villages, whereas the earlier stipulation, which appears at least in part in both copies, refers to volosts. Cherepnin, in maintaining that the second copy of this testament is essentially identical

And lo, I give to my son, Prince Ivan: Zvenigorod" with all its volosts, and with its *myto*, and with its villages, and with its apiary, and with its quitrent tenants, with all its customs, Kremichna, Ruza, Fomin'skoye, Sukhodol", Isterva, Svod"ka, *svoboda* Zamosh'skaya, Rostovtsi, Kremichna,[23] Trostna, Negucha, the village Ryukhov'skoye, the village Mikhalev'skoye, the village Kamen'skoye, the village on the Repna [River] in Borov'sk", the small village Miltsin'skoye, the village Maksimov'-skoye, the village Demontov'skoye, the village Andreyev'skoye, the village Karin'skoye, the village Kozlov'skoye, the village in Zamosh'skaya *svoboda*, the village Vyslav'skoye, the village Kuzmin'skoye.

And my nephew, Prince Vladimir, shall manage the district of his father.[24]

And concerning the Ryazan' localities on this side of the Oka that I have acquired, from among these localities I have given the burg Novyi at the mouth of the Porotl' to Prince Vladimir, in place of Lomastna,[25] and my sons, Prince Dmitriy and Prince Ivan, shall divide equally, without injustice, the other places taken away from Ryazan'.

And Princess Ul'yana,[26] in accordance with the testament of my father, the grand prince, shall manage [her] volosts, and the *osmnich'ye*, and [her] villages during her lifetime, and upon her death those volosts, and villages, and the *osmnich'ye* shall be divided into four without injustice [and shall pass] to my children, Prince Dmitriy and Prince Ivan, and to Prince Vladimir, and to my princess.

And if, because of [my] sins, the Horde should demand Kolomna, or the Lopastna localities, or the localities taken away

---

with the first, states that this difference in the two texts can best be explained as an error on the part of the copyist (*Russkiye feodal'nyye arkhivy*, I, 28).

[23] Apparently the same as the Kremichna mentioned above.

[24] Serpukhov.

[25] Ryazan' had seized Lomastna (Lopasnya) in 1353 (*PSRL*, X, 227). See Cherepnin, *Russkiye feodal'nyye arkhivy*, I, 27–30, concerning Ivan's fear that the Horde might support Ryazan' in its attempt to regain the lands seized by Moscow in 1353.

[26] The widow of Ivan I and the stepmother of Ivan II.

from Ryazan', and if, because of [my] sins, any locality should be taken away, [then] my children, Prince Dmitriy and Prince Ivan, and Prince Vladimir, and my princess shall divide, in their stead, the uncontested places.

And lo, from among the Kolomna volosts, I have given to my princess Aleksandra: Pokhryane, Pesochna, Seredokorotna,[27] the village Lystsev'skoye, the village Semtsin'skoye on the Moskva [River]. And of the Zvenigorod volosts I have also given to my princess Ugozh', Velikaya *svoboda* Yur'yeva, the village Klyapov'skoye, the village Beltsin'skoye, with the small village Novoye.

And my princess [shall receive] a third of the two shares of the Moscow *tamga* of my son[s], Prince Dmitriy and Prince Ivan. And upon the death of my princess, those volosts, and villages, and [her] share of the *tamga*[28] [shall pass] to my sons, Prince Dmitriy and Prince Ivan, [that which is] in the district of each shall be his.

And lo, I have given to my son, Prince Dmitriy, the icon of Saint Aleksandr, the great burnished gold chain with a golden cross, the golden chain made of rings, the icon wrought in gold [which is] the work of Paramsha,[29] the Golden Cap, the shoulder pieces, the large golden belt with precious stones and pearls with which my father, the grand prince, blessed me, the [golden][30] belt with a clasp, a golden baldric, a golden sabre, a golden earring with a pearl, a golden pointed helmet with pre-

[27] The volosts Pokhryane, Pesochna, and Seredokorotna, here willed to Ivan's wife Aleksandra, were bequeathed in the same testament to Princess Mariya, the widow of Grand Prince Semen. This contradiction and another which occurs subsequently (see n. 38, below) suggest that Ivan II wrote another testament prior to this, and that one or two of the conflicting passages were copied by error from the earlier one (see Cherepnin, *Russkiye feodal'nyye arkhivy*, I, 30).

[28] The first copy of the testament reads, "and a third of the *tamga*" (*DDG*, p. 16).

[29] Paramsha was probably a jeweler attached to the court of the metropolitan. He may have been a foreigner (see M. N. Tikhomirov, *Srednevekovaya Moskva v XIV–XV vekakh* [Moscow, 1957], p. 73).

[30] The Russian equivalent of "golden" occurs in the first copy but not in the second (*DDG*, p. 16).

cious stones and pearls, 2 golden *ovkach*,[31] a large smooth golden bowl, the carnelian [box] wrought [in gold],[32] a silver drinking vessel with a silver spout . . .[33] *tsa* [34] of gold with precious stones, [and] an outer garment with sleeves made of fine cloth and embroidered with pearls and precious stones.

And lo, I have given to my son, [Prince] Ivan, a large golden chain with a cross, a burnished gold chain, and another of elongated links [35] with crosses, the icon of the Annunciation, and an earring with a pearl, the golden belt with precious stones [and] pearls which my brother, Grand Prince Semen, gave to me, a polished gold belt, a pearl breastplate, a turned-down collar with circular ornaments of precious stones and pearls, a small breastplate with pearls which Princess Mariya gave to me, a very large, smooth, golden bowl, a small golden vase,[36] a golden cup, a drinking vessel from Tsar'gorod wrought in gold, a golden pointed helmet with precious stones and pearls, a golden sabre, a golden baldric.

And whomever God gives me as sons-in-law, each [shall receive] a golden chain and a golden belt.

And concerning Zayachkov" [and] Zabereg", with their localities, which are Princess Mariya's, now [they shall be hers] during her lifetime, but upon her death [they shall pass] to my princess.

And concerning the volosts which are Princess Ul'yana's, upon her death my children, [Prince Dmitriy, Prince Ivan,

---

[31] Translation uncertain (see above, Text 1, n. 10).

[32] The Russian equivalents of "box" and "in gold" appear in the first copy but not in the second (*DDG*, p. 16).

[33] The original of the second copy is torn at this place with about six letters missing. The original of the first copy is also torn here with about nine letters missing (*DDG*, pp. 18 and 16).

[34] The meaning of the letters *tsa* is not clear.

[35] The original of the second copy reads *ogniv . . . chatu*, with about three letters missing. The word is entirely lacking in the first copy. If this word is taken to be *ogniv'chatu*, which it probably was, the meaning would be, "consisting of elongated links similar to steels" (see I. I. Sreznevskiy, *Materialy dlya slovarya drevne-russkogo yazyka* [Moscow, 1958], II, 603).

[36] *Ovkachik*, diminutive of *ovkach* (see Text 1, n. 10).

Prince Vladimir,] [37] shall give, from among those volosts, Surozhik" [and] the village Luchin'skoye to her daughter.[38]

And from among my silver vessels, the large silver plate with annuli shall be given to the [Cathedral of the] Holy Mother of God in Volodimer'.[39]

And my children, Prince Dmitriy and Prince Ivan, shall divide the other silver vessels with their mother, in three parts.

And the village Romanov'skoye on the Roksha [River shall pass] to Prince Dmitriy.

And to Prince Ivan [shall pass] the village Afin'yev'skoye and the small village near the village Pavlov'skoye.

And I have given the village Pavlov'skoye to [the Monastery of] Saint Aleksandr forever, in memory of me.

And concerning my herds of horses, both stallions and mares, now [they shall pass] to my son, Prince Dmitriy, and [to my son] [40] Prince Ivan, to them each [a half].[41]

And I have given one fourth of the Kolomna *tamga* to [the Monastery of] the Holy Mother of God in Krutitsy,[42] in memory of me. And I have given the Moscow *kostki* [43] to [the

---

[37] The words in brackets appear in the first copy but not in the second (*DDG*, p. 16).

[38] Surozhik", a volost of Zvenigorod and Moscow districts, and Luchin'skoye, a village of Moscow District, were willed to Princess Ul'yana by the testament of Ivan Kalita. This is the second apparent contradiction in the testament of Ivan the Fair (see n. 27, above). The lifetime holdings of Princess Ul'yana were, according to an earlier passage in the testament, to be divided among Princes Dmitriy, Ivan, and Vladimir, and Princess Aleksandra. Yet in this passage it is stipulated that two of Ul'yana's holdings (the volost Surozhik" and the village Luchin'skoye) were, upon her death, to pass to her daughter (name unknown).

[39] See Chapter 6.

[40] The Russian equivalent of "to my son" appears in the first copy but not in the second (*DDG*, p. 16).

[41] The Russian equivalent of "a half" appears in the first copy but not in the second (*DDG*, p. 16).

[42] Krutitsy (Steep Banks) was an area on the left bank of the Moskva River about four kilometers southeast of the Kremlin (see Tikhomirov, *Srednevekovaya Moskva*, map opposite p. 288).

[43] The *kostki* was a capitation tax on persons accompanying merchandise.

Church of] the Holy Mother of God and to [the Church of] Saint Mikhail [in Moscow],[44] in memory of my father, and of my brothers, and of myself, [and] they shall receive prestimony.

And any of my treasurers, or *tiuns*, or *villici*, or any of my secretaries, or anyone who manages my income, or anyone who marries these persons, now these people are of no concern to my children or to my princess: I have given them their freedom. Also, any of my purchased people, [people who] belong to me on the basis of a charter,[45] [and] people [who are my] complete [slaves],[46] I have given them their freedom, [and] they may go wheresoever they please. And they are of no concern to my children or to my princess.

And the attestants to this document [are] my father the Bishop of Rostov, Ignatiy, my spiritual father Abbot Ivan, the priest Akinf", [and] the priest Patrikey.

And may God judge him who violates this testament, and may my blessing not be on him in this life or in the next.

And Nesterko wrote [this] document.

---

[44] The Russian equivalent of "in Moscow" appears in the first copy but not in the second (*DDG*, p. 16).

[45] *Lyud[i] gramotnyye.*

[46] *Lyud[i] polnyye.*

TEXT 4

First (Fragmentary) Testament
of Dmitriy Donskoy

Commentary

DMITRIY, later given the agnomen *Donskoy* (of the Don) because of his participation in the battle with the Tartars on Kulikovo Plain near the Don River in 1380, was the oldest son of Grand Prince Ivan II. He was born in either 1350 or 1351.[1] A child when his father died in 1359, Dmitriy Ivanovich faced strong opposition for the position of Grand Prince of Vladimir from Prince Dmitriy Konstantinovich of Suzdal'. Prince Dmitriy of Moscow and his supporters were finally victorious in this struggle, and Dmitriy Konstantinovich "retired from the Grand Princedom in favor of Grand Prince Dmitriy Ivanovich" in 1364.[2] Dmitriy Ivanovich ruled as Grand Prince of Vladimir and Moscow until his death in 1389.[3]

Grand Prince Dmitriy wrote at least two testaments. The first, of which only the latter part is extant, has been tentatively dated 1375. Academician Cherepnin suggests this date for the testament because he believes that it was written just prior to Dmitriy's campaign against Tver' which took place in 1375.[4] An indication that the testament was written no later than 1375 is the fact that the seal affixed to it refers to Dmitriy as the grand prince, whereas the seal attached to the second testament of this prince (1389) bears the title "Grand Prince of All Rus'." Cherepnin argues that Dmitriy did not assume the title of Grand Prince of All Rus' until after his defeat of Prince Mikhail Aleksandrovich of Tver' in 1375.[5]

[1] See above, Text 3, n. 10.
[2] *PSRL*, VIII, 11–13, and XXV, 180–182.
[3] *PSRL*, XXV, 217.
[4] *PSRL*, XXV, 190.
[5] *PSRL*, XXV, 190–191, and L. V. Cherepnin, *Russkiye feodal'nyye arkhivy, XIV–XV vv.* (Moscow-Leningrad, 1948–1951), I, 58–59.

The testament was certainly written after the birth of Dmitriy's son, Vasiliy, which took place on December 30, 1371.[6] It was probably written after November 1374, when Dmitriy's son Yuriy was born,[7] because the testament makes mention of "my children." The testament was written no later than 1377, the year in which Metropolitan Aleksey died,[8] for Aleksey is mentioned in the document.

The fragmentary original of the first testament of Dmitriy Donskoy is preserved in the Central State Archives of Ancient Acts (TsGADA) in Moscow, in the State Repository of Ancient Documents, Section I, Heading 1, No. 6. From the face of the original are suspended two gilded silver seals: one of Grand Prince Dmitriy Ivanovich, the other of Metropolitan Aleksey.

The fragmentary first testament of Dmitriy Donskoy has been printed in N. I. Novikov, ed., *Drevnyaya Rossiyskaya Vivliofika* (1st ed.; St. Petersburg, 1773–1775), Part 8, No. 9; in the second edition of the same work (Moscow, 1788–1791), Part 1, No. 9; in the Myshkin Library edition of the same work (Myshkin, 1894), Vol. V, Part 9; in *Sobraniye gosudarstvennykh gramot i dogovorov, khranyashchikhsya v Gosudarstvennoy kollegii inostrannykh del* (Moscow, 1813), Part 1, No. 30; and in a number of other collections.[9]

The translation which follows is based on the text of the original as printed in *DDG*, pp. 24–25.

THE FIRST (FRAGMENTARY) TESTAMENT OF GRAND PRINCE DMITRIY DONSKOY

. . .[10] to [11] . . .[12] *m"* det [13] . . .[14] skaya *svoboda*,[15] Ruza, U . . .[16] d", Vyshegorod, Isterva, Dmitr'yeva *svoboda*, . . .[17] *mi* villages, and

[6] *PSRL*, XXV, 187.   [7] *PSRL*, XXV, 190.

[8] *PSRL*, XXV, 194.   [9] *DDG*, p. 25.

[10] "A considerable part of the document has been lost; the end has been preserved" (*DDG*, p. 24, n. 16).

[11] Italicized letters are transliterations of portions of words which cannot be translated or identified.

[12] The original is torn at this place with about fifty letters missing (*DDG*, p. 24, n. 17).   [13] Probably "to my children."

with its beekeepers, and with its quitrent tenants, and with its *myto*. And concerning the [villages] or *novalia* which I have purchased [or] [18] acquired, or any villages which were the purchases of my father in the Grand Principality, or my purchased villages, or villages of my brother, Prince Ivan,[19] [now] these villages and *novalia* [shall pass] to my son, Prince Vasiliy,[20] and to my princess,[21] and to my children.

And concerning that with which my father, the grand prince, blessed me—gold, vessels, or arms, or that which I have acquired: gold, and the Golden Cap, [and chains and sabres] [22] of gold, and clothing of fine cloth embroidered with pearls and precious stones, and golden vessels, and silver vessels, and horses, and stallions, and my herds—I have given to my son, Prince Vasiliy, and to [my princ]ess,[23] and to my children.

And concerning [the village Pavlov]skoye [24] which my father, the grand prince, [gave] [25] to [the Monastery of] Saint Alek-

---

[14] The original is torn at this place with about forty-six letters missing (*DDG*, p. 24, n. 18).

[15] Not identifiable.

[16] The original is torn at this place with about thirty-five letters missing (*DDG*, p. 24, n. 19).

[17] The original is torn at this place with about twenty letters missing (*DDG*, p. 24, n. 20).

[18] The Russian equivalent of "villages" and of "or" is not in the original but has been supplied by the editors of *DDG*.

[19] Of Zvenigorod, the younger brother of Dmitriy.

[20] Vasiliy Dmitriyevich was born in 1371. He became Grand Prince of Moscow and Vladimir upon the death of his father in 1389 and ruled until his own death in 1425 (*PSRL*, XXV, 187, 218, and 246).

[21] Yevdokiya, the daughter of Prince Dmitriy Konstantinovich of Suzdal' (*PSRL*, XXV, 215 and 236).

[22] The Russian equivalent of "and chains and sabres" has been supplied by the editors of DDG.

[23] The Russian equivalent of "my princ" has been added by the editors of *DDG*.

[24] The Russian equivalent of "the village Pavlov" is not in the original but has been supplied by the editors of *DDG*.

[25] The Russian equivalent of "gave" has been supplied by the editors of *DDG*. The place in the original document in which "the village Pavlov" and "gave" have been assumed is torn, with about fourteen letters missing (*DDG*, p. 25, n. 1).

sandr, and [the one-fourth part of the *tamga* of Ko]lomna,[26] [which he gave] to [the Monastery of] the Holy Mother of God in Krutitsy, and the Moscow *kostki,* [which he gave] to [the Church of] the Holy Mother of God in Moscow [and to the Church of Saint] [27] Mikhail, now this shall not be upset.

And concerning my [treasurers, or *villici,*] [28] and *tiuns,* and secretaries, [or] anyone who managed anything for me, [all those] shall be no concern of [my son] [29] Prince Vasiliy, or of my princess, or of my children. [And concerning] my purchased people, now to them also I have given [freedom, and] my son, [Prince Vasiliy] [30] and my princess, and my children shall not acquire them.

And I have written this testament for myself and have presented [it] to my father Aleksey, Metropolitan of [All] Rus'. And my father Aleksey, Metropolitan of All Rus', has appended his seal to this document.

And the attestants to this document [are]: the *okolnichii* [31] Timofey . . . ,[32] Ivan Rodivonovich, Ivan Fedorovich, [and] Fedor Andreyevich.

And the secretary, Nester, wrote [this] document.

And he who violates this testament in any way . . .[33] soul.

[26] The editors of *DDG* have supplied the Russian equivalent of "the one-fourth part of the *tamga* of Ko" (see also above, Text 2, for a similar passage).

[27] The original is torn at this place with about eight letters missing. The editors of *DDG* have supplied the Russian equivalent of "and to Saint" (*DDG,* p. 25, n. 2).

[28] The words "treasurers [*kaznachei*], or *villici* [*posel'skiye*]" are not in the original but have been supplied by the editors of *DDG.*

[29] The Russian equivalents of "all those" and of "my son" have been supplied by the editors of *DDG.*

[30] The Russian equivalents of "and concerning," "freedom, and," and "Prince Vasiliy" have been supplied by the editors of *DDG.*

[31] An *okol'nichii* was a high officer at the court of the prince. In rank he was just below a boyar.

[32] The text is torn at this place with about eight letters missing (*DDG,* p. 25, n. 3).

[33] The original is torn at this place with about eight letters missing (*DDG,* p. 25, n. 4).

TEXT 5

Second Testament
of Dmitriy Donskoy

Commentary

THE second testament of Grand Prince Dmitriy Donskoy was written sometime between April 13 and May 16, 1389. The mention in the testament of Dmitrov and Galich ("And lo, I give to my son, Prince Petr, Dmitrov" with all its volosts," and "my son, Prince Yuriy, I bless with my grandfather's purchase, Galich with all its volosts") indicates a date later than March 25, 1389, when, in the agreement of Grand Prince Dmitriy Ivanovich with Prince Vladimir Andreyevich of Serpukhov and Borovsk,[1] Dmitriy's possession of Dmitrov and Galich was confirmed. Furthermore, the absence of mention of Metropolitan Pimen in the testament indicates that it was written after April 13, 1389, the day on which Pimen departed from Moscow for Constantinople.[2] The passage "And if God gives me a son" suggests that the testament was written before May 16, 1389, the date of birth of Dmitriy's youngest child, Konstantin.[3] The grand prince himself died three days later, May 19, 1389.[4]

The original of this testament, on parchment, is preserved in the Central State Archives of Ancient Acts (TsGADA) in Moscow, in the State Repository of Ancient Documents, Section I, Heading 1, No. 7. A copy of the testament, dating from the first

---

[1] For text of this agreement, see *DDG*, pp. 30–32.

[2] *PSRL*, XXV, 214.

[3] *PSRL*, XXV, 215.

[4] *PSRL*, XXV, 217. For the dating of this testament, see L. V. Cherepnin, *Russkiye feodal'nyye arkhivy, XIV–XV vv.* (Moscow-Leningrad, 1948–1951), I, 59.

half of the fifteenth century, is to be found in the same place, No. 8. From the face of the original is suspended the silver gilded seal of Grand Prince Dmitriy Ivanovich.

The second testament of Dmitriy Donskoy has been printed in N. I. Novikov, ed., *Drevnyaya Rossiyskaya Vivliofika* (1st ed.; St. Petersburg, 1773–1775), Part 8, No. 14; in the second edition of the same work (Moscow, 1788–1791), Part 1, No. 13; in the Myshkin Library edition of the same work (Myshkin, 1894), Vol. V, Part 9; in *Sobraniye gosudarstvennykh gramot i dogovorov, khranyashchikhsya v Gosudarstvennoy kollegii inostrannykh del* (Moscow, 1813), Part 1, No. 34; and in a number of other collections.[5]

The translation which follows is based on the text of the testament as printed in *DDG*, pp. 33–37.

THE SECOND TESTAMENT OF GRAND PRINCE DMITRIY DONSKOY

IN the name of the Father, and of the Son, and of the Holy Ghost, lo I, the sinful poor slave of God, Dmitriy Ivanovich, write [this] testament, being of sound mind. I give [this] arrangement [*ryad"*] to my sons and to my princess.[6]

I commit my children to my princess. And you, my children, live as one and heed your mother in all things.

And I bequeath my patrimony, Moscow, to my children, to Prince Vasiliy,[7] to Prince Yuriy, to Prince Andrey, [and] to Prince Petr.[8] And my brother, Prince Vladimir,[9] shall manage his

[5] *DDG*, p. 37.

[6] Yevdokiya, the daughter of Prince Dmitriy Konstantinovich of Suzdal'.

[7] See above, Text 4, n. 20.

[8] Yuriy Dmitriyevich, later Prince of Zvenigorod and Galich, was born in 1374 and died in 1434 (*PSRL*, XXV, 190 and 251). Andrey Dmitriyevich, later Prince of Mozhaysk, was born in 1382 and died in 1432 (*PSRL*, XXV, 206 and 250). Petr Dmitriyevich, later Prince of Dmitrov, was born in 1385 and died in 1428 (*PSRL*, XXV, 212 and 247).

[9] Vladimir Andreyevich, Prince of Serpukhov and Borovsk, the first cousin of Grand Prince Dmitriy.

third with which his father, Prince Andrey, blessed him. And my son, Prince Vasiliy, I bless with the larger revenue [10] in the city [11] and in the *stans* of my patrimonial principality,[12] [namely] with one half of [my] two shares,[13] and [I bless] my three [other] sons [with] one half, and of the city customs, one half. And of my two shares of the *tamga*, my princess [shall receive] one half and my sons one half. And my princess [shall receive] my two shares of the *osmnicheye*. And in addition to the larger revenue, my son, Prince Vasiliy, [shall receive] *Vasiltsevo sto*,[14] and the Dobryatin'skoye apiary with the village Dobryatin'skoye. And the beekeepers in the city *stans*, and the horse *put'*, and the falconers, and the huntsmen: these my sons shall share equally. And of the enrolled people [15] of my two shares, my sons [shall receive] each a part and shall care for them as one man.

And lo, I give to my son, Prince Vasiliy, Kolomna with all its volosts, and with its *tamga*, and with its *myto*, and with its apiary, and with its villages, and with all its customs. And the Kolomna volosts: Meshcherka, Ramenka, Pesochna, Brasheva with the small village Gvozdna and with Ivan', Gzhelya, the hamlets Levichin, Skulnev'', Makovets', Kanev'', Kochema, Komarev'' with the shore,[16] Gorodna, Pokhryane, [and] Ust'-Mer'sko. And of

[10] *Starishii put'*, 'larger revenue.' Here the word *put'* is used to mean income from property. For the more common use of this term, see Chapter 5.

[11] That is, in Moscow.

[12] *Udel''*. An *udel*, herein translated "patrimonial principality," was the territory left to a prince by his father. See Chapter 4.

[13] Prince Dmitriy Donskoy and Prince Ivan of Zvenigorod had each inherited a third of Moscow from their father, Ivan II. Prince Ivan of Zvenigorod died in 1364 and his third passed to his brother. Hence Dmitriy here speaks of his two shares. Concerning the system of holding Moscow by thirds, see Chapter 5.

[14] "Vasiliy's Hundred," identical with *Vasiltsevo vedan'ye* (see Chapter 5).

[15] *Chislenyye lyudi* (see Chapter 4).

[16] *Z beregom*, 'with the shore.' This is probably a reference to the main Russian defense line against attack from the south. During the second half of the fourteenth century it ran along the Oka River, hence "the shore." The defense line continued to be known as "the shore" even after

209

the Moscow villages, I give to my son, Prince Vasiliy: Mitin *novale*, Malakhov"skoye, Kostyantinov"skoye, the hamlets Zhyroshkiny, Ostrov"skoye, Orinin'skoye, Kopoten'skoye, Khvostov"skoye, [and] Velikiy Meadow near the city, beyond the river.[17] And from among the Yur'yev" villages I give to my son, Prince Vasiliy, my purchase the village Krasnoye, with Yelezarov"skoye Provatovo, and the village Vasilev"skoye in Rostov.

And lo, I give to my son, Prince Yuriy, Zvenigorod with all its volosts, and with its *tamga*, and with its *myto*, and with its apiary, and with its villages, and with all its customs. And the Zvenigorod volosts: Skirmenovo and Beli, Trostna, Negucha, Surozhyk, Zamosh"skaya *sloboda*, Yur'yeva *sloboda*, the burg Ruza, Rostovtsi, Kremichna, Fomin'skoye, Ugozh", Sukhodol with Ist'ya, with Isterva, Vyshegorod, Plesn', [and] Dmitriyeva *slobodka*. And from among the Moscow villages I give to my son, Prince Yuriy, the village Mikhalev"skoye and Domantov"skoye, and Khodyn'skii Meadow. And from among the Yur'yev" villages to him [shall pass]: my purchase, the village Kuzmydem"yan'skoye, and the *novale* of the village Krasnoye beyond the Vezka [River], I have given to Kuzmydem"yan'skoye, and the village Bogorodits'skoye in Rostov.[18]

And lo, I give to my son, Prince Andrey, Mozhayesk" with all its volosts, and with its *tamga*, and with its *myto*, and with its apiary, and with its villages, and with all its customs, and with its outlying volosts. And the Mozhaisk volosts: Ismeya, Chislov, Boyan', Berestov", Porotva, Kolocha, Tushkov, Vyshneye, Glin'skoye, Pnevichi with Zagor'ye [and] Bolonesk". And I have added Korzhan' and Moishin Kholm to Mozhaisk. And lo,

---

the southern frontier of Muscovy was extended beyond the Oka. Military service at this line was termed *beregovaya sluzhba*, 'shore service' (see V. O. Klyuchevskiy, *Sochineniya* [Moscow, 1956–1959], II, 107 and 210–211, and Alexandre Eck, *Le Moyen Age russe* [Paris, 1933], p. 271).

[17] This is the first mention of Velikiy (Great) Meadow, Moscow District. The city is probably Moscow and the river the Moskva.

[18] According to the testament of Ivan Kalita, the village Bogorodicheskoye (Bogorodits'skoye) had been purchased by Ivan and given to Boris Vor"kov; it was to remain his on the condition that he continue to serve Ivan's sons.

the outlying volosts: Vereya, Rud', Gordoshevichi, Gremichi, Zaberega, Sushov, and the village Repin'skoye, and Ivanov"skoye Vasil'yevicha in Gremichi. And Koluga and Roshcha [shall pass] to my son, Prince Andrey. And Tov", and Medyn', which my boyar, Fedor Andreyevich, in our common struggle, took away from the men of Smolensk, now also [shall pass] to my son, Prince Andrey. And from among the Moscow villages [I leave] to him: the village Naprud'skoye, and Lutsin'skoye on the Yauza, with the mill, Deunin'skoye, Khvostov'skoye in Peremyshl',[19] and Borov"skii Meadow and another opposite [the Monastery of] the Resurrection. And from among the Yur'yev" villages [I give] to him the village Oleksin'skoye on the Peksha [River].

And lo, I give to my son, Prince Petr, Dmitrov" with all its volosts,[20] and with its villages, and with all its customs, and with its *tamga*, and with its *myto*, and with its apiary. And lo, the Dmitrov" volosts: Vyshegorod, Berendeyeva *sloboda*, Lutosna, with its outlying area,[21] [and] Inobash". And from among the Moscow volosts [I give] to Prince Petr: Mushkova Gora, Izhvo, Ramenka, *slobodka* Knyazha Ivanova, Vori, Korzenevo, Rogozh", Zagar'ye,[22] Vokhna, Selna, Gusletsya, and the burg Sherna. And from among the Moscow villages [I give] to Prince Petr: the village Novoye, [and] Sulishin *pogost"*. And from among the Yur'yev villages [I give] to him my purchase, the village Bogorodits'koye on the Bogon [River].

[19] Not clear. The village Khvostovskoye (Moscow District) has already been willed to Prince Vasiliy. This is the first mention in the testaments of the village Khvostovskoye in Peremyshl', which the editors of *DDG* equate with the village already bequeathed to Vasiliy (see *DDG*, p. 559).

[20] For the first time in the testaments, Dmitrov appears as a possession of the Prince of Moscow.

[21] *S ot"yezd"tsem*, 'with [its] outlying?' This translation is not certain, for the meaning of the word *ot"yezd'ts'* is not known (see I. I. Sreznevskiy, *Materialy dlya slovarya drevne-russkogo yazyka* [Moscow, 1958], II, 825).

[22] Apparently identical with the volost Zagor'ye of Dmitrov, Mozhaysk, and Moscow districts, which was left to Prince Andrey by an earlier provision of this testament (see *DDG*, pp. 539 and 552).

And lo, I give to my son, Prince Ivan: [23] Rameneitse, with its beekeepers and with that which appertained [24] to it, and the village Zverkov"skoye with the *novale* Sokhon'skiy, which has been given up by Prince Vladimir. And Sokhna also [shall pass] to my son, Prince Ivan. And in this [his] patrimonial principality, my son, Prince Ivan, is free; he may give it to whichsoever brother is kind to him.

And lo, I bless my son, Prince Vasiliy, with my patrimony, the Grand Princedom. [25]

And my son, Prince Yuriy, I bless with my grandfather's purchase, Galich [26] with all its volosts, and with its villages, and with all its customs, and with those villages which appertained to Kostroma, Mikul'skoye and Borisov"skoye.

And I bless my son, Prince Andrey, with yet [another] purchase of my grandfather, Beloozero [27] with all its volosts, and Vol'skoye with Shagot', and Milolyub"skii Weir, and with the *slobodkas* that were my children's.

And my son, Prince Petr, I bless with yet [another] purchase of my grandfather, Ugleche Plain [28] and that which appertained to it, and with Toshna and with Syama.

And lo, I give to my princess, from the Grand Principality of my son, Prince Vasiliy: Yulka in Pereyaslavl', [29] and Iledam, with

[23] The date of birth of Prince Ivan, the fifth son of Dmitriy Donskoy, is not known. His name first appears in the Chronicles under the year 1380. He died in 1393 (see A. V. Ekzemplyarskiy, *Velikiye i udel'nyye knyaz'ya severnoy Rusi v" tatarskiy period", s" 1238 po 1505 g.* [St. Petersburg, 1889], II, 290–291).

[24] *Potyaglo*, 'appertained' (see "Taxation: General Terminology," Chapter 3).

[25] This was the first instance in which one of the grand princes bequeathed the Grand Principality of Vladimir to his son.

[26] Concerning the probable purchase of Galich by Ivan Kalita, see the discussion of Kalita's acquisitions in Chapter 2. See also the discussion of Dmitriy's acquisitions in that chapter.

[27] Concerning the probable purchase by Ivan Kalita of Beloozero, see the discussion of Kalita's acquisitions in Chapter 2.

[28] Ugleche Plain (Ugleche Pole), or Uglich, was probably purchased by Ivan Kalita (see the discussion of Kalita's acquisitions in Chapter 2).

[29] Concerning the acquisition of Pereyaslavl' by Moscow, see above, Chapter 1.

Komela in Kostroma, and [from that] which belongs to Prince Yuriy in Galich, Sol',[30] and [from that which] belongs to Prince Andrey in Beloozero, Vol'skoye with Shagot', and Milolyub'skii Weir. And from among the Volodimer villages, [I give] to my princess the village On'dreyev'skoye, and from among the "Pereyaslav" villages, the village Dobroye, and that which appertained to them. And from my son's, Prince Vasiliy's, patrimonial principality [I give to my princess]: Kanev", Pesochna, and from among the villages, the village Malin'skoye, [and] Lystsevo. And from Prince Yuriy's patrimonial principality, [I give to my princess]: Yur'yeva *sloboda*, Sukhodol, with Iyet'ya, with Isterva, and with the village On'dreyev"skoye, and Kamen'skoye. And from Prince Andrey's patrimonial principality, [I give to my princess]: Vereya, and Chislov, and the village Lutsin'skoye on the Yauza, with the mill. And from Prince Petr's patrimonial principality, [I give to my princess]: Izhvo and Syama. And concerning that which I have given to my princess from the patrimonial principality of my son, Prince Vasiliy, and from Prince Yuriy's, from Prince Andrey's, from Prince Petr's, volosts and villages, now should God decide something concerning my princess, then those volosts and villages in whose patrimonial principality they are, then to him shall they belong.

And lo, I give to my princess: my acquisition Skirmenov"skaya *slobodka* with Shepkovo, Smolyanyye with the *novale* Mityayev"skiy, and with the apiary, with the Vyshegorod beekeepers,[31] Kropivna with the Kropivna beekeepers, [and with the Ismeya (beekeepers)],[32] and with the Gordoshevichi [beekeepers], and with the Rud' [beekeepers], Zheleskova *slobodka* with its apiary, with Ivan Khorobryy's village, Iskon'-skaya *slobodka*, Kuzov"skaya *slobodka*, and that which my

---

[30] That is, the Galich Salt Marshes (Sol' Galitskaya).

[31] There were at least two Vyshegorods. One, an outlying volost of Mozhaysk District, was willed to Prince Yuriy in this testament. The other, a volost of Dmitrov District, was left to Prince Petr in this testament.

[32] The text is obliterated at this place with about fifteen letters missing. The editors of *DDG* have tentatively supplied the Russian equivalent of "and with the Ismeya" (*DDG*, p. 35).

princess purchased, and that which has appertained to her, this belongs to my princess. And in those places in which *sloboda* administrators administered *slobodas* under me, the volost administrators of my princess shall administer justice in those same places, as it was under me. And concerning the purchase of my princess, Lokhno, now it is hers. And in Kolomna, my acquisition, the *novale* Samoiletsev" with its hamlets, the *novale* Savel'yev"skii, the village Mikul'skoye, Babyshevo, [and] Oslebyatev"skoye: now these belong to my princess. And concerning her village Repen'skoye and [her] purchase, now these also are hers. And from among the Moscow villages I give to my princess: the village Semtsin'skoye with Khodyn'skaya Mill, and the village Ostaf'yev"skoye, and Ilmov'skoye. And from among the Yur'yev" villages I give to her: my purchase, the village Petrov"skoye, and Frolov"skoye, and Yelokh". And Kholkhol and Zayachkov [shall pass] to my princess. And concerning that which Princess Fedosiya[33] gave me, Suda in Beloozero, and Kolashna, and Slobodka, and concerning that with which she blessed my princess, Gorodok and Volochok: Princess Fedosiya shall manage these places during her lifetime, and upon her death [they shall pass] to my princess. And I bless my princess with all these my acquisitions, and in these acquisitions my princess is free: she may give them to one of her sons or she may give them for the memory of her soul. And my children shall not interfere in this.

And those hamlets which Prince Vladimir took away from Lytkin'skoye, the village of my princess, [and added] to Berendeyeva *sloboda*, now those hamlets shall appertain to Lyt"kin'skoye, the village of my princess.

And if, because of my sins, God takes away one of my sons, then my princess shall divide his patrimonial principality among my sons. That which she gives to one is his, and my children shall not evade her will.

And if God gives me a son, then my princess shall also give a share to him, taking portions from each of his older brothers.[34]

And if the patrimony of one of my sons, with which I have

---

[33] The daughter of Ivan Kalita and the half-sister of Ivan II.

[34] A son, Konstantin, was born to Prince Dmitriy on May 16, 1389 (*PSRL*, XXV, 215).

blessed him, should be diminished, my princess shall also give a share [to him] from the patrimonial principalities of my [other] sons. And you, my children, obey your mother.

And if, because of my sins, God takes away my son, Prince Vasiliy, then the patrimonial principality of Prince Vasiliy [shall pass] to my son who follows him, and the patrimonial principality of the latter shall be divided among the others by my princess. And you, my children, obey your mother: that which she gives to one, now that is his.[35]

And when my children take tribute [*dan'*] in their patrimony, with which I blessed them, now my son, Prince Vasiliy, shall take from his patrimonial principality, from Kolomna and from all the Kolomna volosts, three hundred rubles and forty and two rubles, and my princess shall give to him towards this silver from Pesochna 50 rubles less 3, and from Kanev twenty rubles and two rubles. And Prince Yuriy shall take from Zvenigorod and from all the Zvenigorod volosts two hundred rubles and seventy rubles and two rubles, and my princess shall give to him towards this silver from Yur'yeva *sloboda* fifty rubles and from Sukhodol one half of fifty rubles, and from Smolyanyye 9 rubles, and from Skirmenov"skaya *slobodka* 9 rubles. And Prince Andrey shall take from Mozhaisk and from all the Mozhaisk volosts one hundred rubles and seventy rubles less three, and from the outlying places seventy rubles less two, and my princess shall give to him towards this silver twenty rubles and two and a half rubles from Vereya, and from Chislov fifty rubles, and from Zayachkov twenty rubles and two, from Khol"khol ten rubles, from Zheleskova 9 rubles, from Iskon'skaya *slobodka* fifty rubles, from Kropivna fifty rubles. And Prince Petr shall take from his patrimonial principality one hundred rubles and eleven, and my princess shall give to him towards this silver from Izhvo thirty rubles. And Prince Ivan shall give to Prince Vasiliy from Sokhna five rubles, and from Rameneitse he shall give Prince Petr five rubles. And now they should take a thousand rubles, but be it more or less, in any case it should be according to this reckoning.

And if God brings about a change regarding the Horde [and]

---

[35] This paragraph is of great significance in light of the struggle for the Grand Principality which ensued after the death of Vasiliy Dmitriyevich.

my children do not have to give Tartar tribute [*vykhod*] to the Horde, then the tribute [*dan'*] that each of my sons collects in his patrimonial principality shall be his. And concerning that which I have given to my princess—volosts and villages from the patrimonial principalities of my children, and my acquisitions, and *slobodas*, and villages, and Kholkhol, and Zayachkov—now that which my princess collects from these volosts, *slobodas*, and villages shall be hers. And my children shall not interfere in this.

And in those volosts, *slobodas*, and villages that I have taken away from the patrimonial principalities of my children and have given to my princess, now if any peasants should complain against the volost administrators, my princess shall decide the cases of these people. And my children shall not interfere in this.

And that which I have given to my son, Prince Andrey, Zaberega, for this my children shall all pay to [the Church? Monastery? of] the Holy Saviour [36] quitrent of fifteen rubles a year, on the Saviour's Day. [37]

And lo, I bless my children. To my oldest son, Prince Vasiliy, [I bequeath] the icon [which is] the work of Paramsha, the golden chain which Princess Vasilisa gave me, the great golden belt with precious stones without a strap, the golden belt with a strap [which is] the work of Makar, the shoulder pieces of the grand prince, [and] the Golden Cap.

And to my son, Prince Yuriy, [I bequeath] the new golden belt with precious stones [and] pearls [and] without a strap, the golden belt [which is] the work of Shishka, [and] the outer garment embroidered with pearls and precious stones.

And to my son, Prince Andrey, [I bequeath] the suit of golden armor [and] the old golden belt from Novgorod.

And to my son, Prince Petr, [I bequeath] the golden belt decorated in black [and] with precious stones, the golden belt with the moneybag and with ornaments, and [I bequeath him] the shoulder straps and a breastplate.

[36] There were a number of churches and monasteries named for the Holy Saviour. This one is not identified.

[37] There are three Saviour's Days in the Russian Orthodox calendar: August 1, 6, and 16. The meaning of this entire paragraph is obscure.

And to my son, Prince Ivan, [I bequeath] the leather belt with golden studs[38] and two golden bowls, each [weighing] two *grivenka*.[39]

And the gold or silver or other things which remain, no matter what they are, all [shall pass] to my princess.

And concerning my herds that remain, these my princess shall divide with my children, each [receiving] a share.

And any of my treasurers, or any of my secretaries who have managed my income for me, or [my] *villici*, or my *tiuns*, or anyone who has married these people, none of these are of any concern of my princess or of my children.

And I have committed my children to my princess. And you, my children, heed your mother in all things, and do not go against her will in anything. And if any of my sons does not heed his mother and goes against her will, my blessing shall not be upon him.

And my younger children, brothers of Prince Vasiliy, honor and obey your older brother, Prince Vasiliy, in the place of me, your father. And my son, Prince Vasiliy, shall hold his brother, Prince Yuriy, and his younger brothers in brotherliness and without injustice.

And those of my boyars who serve my princess, those boyars, my children, care for as one man.

And may God judge him who violates this testament, and neither God's favor nor my blessing shall be upon him in this life or in the next.

And I have written this testament in the presence of my fathers, in the presence of Abbot Sergiy[40] and Abbot Sevastian.

And present [at the writing of this testament] were our boyars Dmitriy Mikhaylovich, Timofey Vasil'yevich, Ivan Rodivonovich, Semen Vasil'yevich, Ivan Fedorovich, Aleksandr Andreyevich, Fedor Andreyevich, Fedor Andreyevich, Ivan Fedorovich, [and] Ivan Andreyevich.

And Vnuk" wrote.

---

[38] *Poyas zolot tataur.*

[39] Sreznevskiy identifies a *grivenka* merely as a weight (I, 591).

[40] Sergiy was abbot of the Trinity-Sergiy Monastery of Radonezh. He died in 1392 (*DDG*, p. 505, and *PSRL*, XXV, 219).

TEXT 6

First Testament of Vasiliy I

Commentary

VASILIY DMITRIYEVICH, the oldest son of Grand Prince Dmitriy Donskoy, was born in 1371. He became Grand Prince of Moscow and Vladimir upon the death of his father in 1389 and ruled until his own death in 1425.[1]

Vasiliy wrote three testaments, all of which are extant. His first testament, a translation of which follows, was apparently written sometime between September 16, 1406, and June 7, 1407. There is no mention in this testament of the metropolitan's blessing, which does appear in the two later testaments, so it was probably written after the death of Metropolitan Kiprian on September 16, 1406. On the other hand, it was certainly written before June 7,1407, the date of the death of Vasiliy's mother, Yevdokiya Dmitriyevna, for she is mentioned in the testament.[2]

The original of the first testament of Vasiliy I is preserved in the Central State Archives of Ancient Acts (TsGADA) in Moscow, in the State Repository of Ancient Documents, Section I, Heading 1, No. 9. The gilded silver seal of Grand Prince Vasiliy Dmitriyevich is suspended from the face of the document.

The first testament of Vasiliy I has been printed in N. I. Novikov, ed., *Drevnyaya Rossiyskaya Vivliofika* (1st ed.; St. Petersburg, 1773–1775), Part 8, No. 18; in the second edition of the same work (Moscow, 1788–1791), Part 1, No. 18; in the Myshkin Library edition of the same work (Myshkin, 1894), Vol. V, Part 9; in *Sobraniye gosudarstvennykh gramot i*

---

[1] *PSRL*, XXV, 187, 218, and 246.
[2] *PSRL*, XXV, 236 and 234; L. V. Cherepnin, *Russikiye feodal'nyye arkhivy, XIV–XV vv.* (Moscow-Leningrad, 1948–1951), I, 86.

dogovorov, khranyashchikhsya v Gosudarstvennoy kollegii inostrannykh del (Moscow, 1813), Part 1, No. 39; and in a number of other collections.[3]

The translation which follows is based on the text of the first testament of Vasiliy I as printed in *DDG*, pp. 55–57.

THE FIRST TESTAMENT OF GRAND PRINCE VASILIY I DMITRIYEVICH

IN the name of the Father, and of the Son, and of the Holy [Ghost], lo I, the sinful, poor slave of God, Vasiliy, write this testament, with a clear mind [and] in good health. I give [this] arrangement [*ryad"*] to my son, Prince Ivan, and to my princess.[4]

I bless my son, Prince Ivan, with my patrimony, with one third of Moscow, with my share, and with its customs, and with its *puti*, and with its apiary, and with *Vasiltsevo sto*, and with the village Dobryatinskoye, and with the apiary, and [with] one third of the enrolled people, with which my father blessed me in Moscow, as was written in the testament of my father, the grand prince, and [with] Kolomna with all its volosts, and with its villages, and with its apiary, and with its *puti*, and with all its customs. And the Kolomna volosts are: Pokhryane, Gorodna, Kochema, Kanev", Makovets', Levichin", Pesochna, the hamlets Skulnev", Brasheva, with Ivan', and with the small village Gvozdna, Ust'-Merska, Komarev", and Radokin, with the shore,[5] Ramen"ka, Meshcherka, Krutinki, Mezynya, [and]

---

[3] *DDG*, p. 57.

[4] Ivan Vasil'yevich, the oldest son of Grand Prince Vasiliy I, was born in 1397 and died in 1417 (*PSRL*, XXV, 227 and 243).

Sofiya Vitovtovna, whom Vasiliy married in 1391, was the daughter of Vitovt Keystut'yevich, who was living in exile among the Prussian Germans at the time of his daughter's marriage to the Grand Prince of Moscow. Vitovt became Grand Prince of Lithuania in 1392 (see *PSRL*, XXV, 219 and 220, and A. V. Ekzemplyarskiy, *Velikiye i udel'nyye knyaz'ya severnoy Rusi v" tatarskiy period", s" 1238 po 1505 g.* [St. Petersburg, 1889], I, 126–127).

[5] See above, Text 5, n. 16.

Gzhelya. And to my princess I give from among the Kolomna volosts, Brasheva and Ust'-Merska. And if God should take away my mother, then upon the death of my mother, Pesochna also [shall pass] to my princess. And of my mother's villages, Malino with all its hamlets [shall pass to my princess]. And also from among my Kolomna villages, to my princess [shall pass] Ogloblino with all its hamlets and with Ol'kh, and Kolychevskoye and Zmeyevskoye, and Ivanovskoye Vasil'-yevicha in Levichin, and with the Chyukhistova Land,[6] and with all [my] purchases, and Gzhelya with all the hamlets which appertained to it. And concerning the villages that have customarily belonged to [my] princess, now they are hers, and my princess shall manage those villages that have been customarily hers until, God willing, my son marries,[7] and then she shall give those villages which were of old in the possession of my princess to my son's princess, her daughter-in-law.

And from among the Moscow villages, [I give] to my son, Prince Ivan, the village Strovskoye,[8] with Orininskoye, and with [the village of] Grigoriy Faustov, and with Kostyantinovskoye, and with Zhiroshkino, and with all the hamlets, and with Malakhovskoye, and Velikii Meadow opposite the city beyond the river.

And to my princess [I give], from among the Moscow villages: my village Pochinok with all its hamlets, and the small village Khvostovskoye near the city, and with the meadows which appertained to it.

And concerning my acquisition[s], now I give to my princess: Uktyushka, which I purchased, and Deacon Foma's villages, and Fedor Sviblo's [9] villages in Ustyug, and in Otvodnoye,

---

[6] This is the first mention in the testaments of the Chukhistova Land (*zemlya*). It was probably an area of Kolomna District (see S. M. Solov'yev, *Istoriya Rossii s drevneyshikh vremen* [Moscow, 1959–1966], II, 777).

[7] Prince Ivan subsequently married the daughter (name unknown) of Ivan Vasil'yevich, Prince of Pronsk (see Ekzemplyarskiy, I, Genealogical Table).

[8] Probably identical with the village Ostrovskoye, Moscow District.

[9] Fedor Andreyevich Sviblo (or Svibl") was one of the leading boyars of the reign of Dmitriy Donskoy. This passage suggests that he fell into

and on the Syama, and in Rostov, and in Bezhitsskii Verkh, Maksimovskoye with its hamlets, and Ves'skoye in Pereyaslavl', with Rodivonovskoye with all its hamlets, and in Moscow the village Builovskoye with the hamlet Olekseyev'skaya and the village Timofeyevskoye on the Yauza, and in Yur'yev, Chagino and Savel'yevskoye, and Ivorovo, and Karabuzino, and in Nov"gorod, Nepeitsino, and all Fedor Sviblo's villages with all that appertained to them,[10] and that which I obtained by exchange from my mother, in Yur'yev, the villages Frolovskoye with Ol'kh,[11] and Petrovskoye, and Bogoroditsskoye, and Oleksinskoye, and that which appertained to them, and in Nizhnii Nov"gorod the villages Alachinskiye and Mangach'.

And in those volosts and villages which I have willed to my princess, if anyone should complain against the volost administrators, or against the *tiuns,* or against the *villici,* or against the criminal investigators, then [these cases] shall be judged by my princess or by him whom she commands, and my son the prince shall not interfere in these cases. And if God brings about a change concerning the Tartars, then my princess shall take the tribute [*dan'*] for herself from these volosts and villages, and my son, Prince Ivan, shall also not interfere in this tribute. And when the tribute or the post relay tax comes, then my princess shall give from these volosts and villages according to whatever reckoning there is.[12] And those volosts and villages

---

disgrace during the reign of Vasiliy I (see Solov'yev, II, 309 and 387).

[10] Apparently all places listed, beginning with "Fedor Sviblo's villages in Ustyug" and ending with "and in Nov"gorod, Nepeitsino," were acquired by Vasiliy I from Fedor Sviblo.

[11] This is the only mention in the testaments of the village Ol'kh of Yur'yev District, unless it is identical with the village Yelokh of the *sloboda* Yur'yeva, which was willed to Yevdokiya by Dmitriy Donskoy, mentioned immediately following Petrovskoye and Frolovskoye in Dmitriy's second testament.

[12] The meaning of this sentence is that should the power of the Tartars be removed and should Princess Sofiya commence to collect tribute (*dan'*) and the post relay tax (*yam*") from the holdings willed to her by this testament, she would be required to pay certain amounts to the grand prince (presumably her son Ivan), these amounts to be determined by a calculation or reckoning. In this connection, see above, Text 5, where the exact sums due the several princes from lands held by their mother

are my princess' during her lifetime, but upon her death, then those volosts and villages [shall pass] to my son, Prince Ivan. And concerning her acquisition, in this she is free: she may give [it] for remembrance of her soul, [or] she may give it to [her] son.

And in addition to this, I give her as her widow's portion two villages in Yur'yev, Bogoroditsskoye and Oleksinskoye, [and] in these two villages she is also free: she may give them for remembrance of her soul, [or] she may give them to [her] son.

And if God grants that my son, Prince Ivan, should hold the Grand Princedom, then my princess [shall receive] from Pereyaslavl', Kinela. And if God should take away my mother, then Yul"ka also [shall pass] to my princess, and the village Dobroye, and in Volodimer the village Ondreyevskoye. And to her from Kostroma [shall pass] the volost Nerekhta. And if God should take away my mother, then Iledam and Komela [shall pass] to my princess and Nerekhta [shall pass] to my son, Prince Ivan.

And if God should grant that my son hold Nov"gorod Nizhnii and Murom",[13] then my princess [shall receive] from Nov"gorod [Nizhnii] one half of the customs of Nov"gorod [Nizhnii], and Kurmysh' with all its villages, and with its apiary, and with its *puti*, and with its customs, and with all that appertained to it, and with Algash, and from Murom" to her [shall pass] a small village.

And I bless my son, Prince Ivan, with the icon [which is] the work of Paramsha, with a chain, the chain with precious stones with which my father, the grand prince, blessed me. And I give

___

within their patrimonial principalities are stipulated by Dmitriy Donskoy.

[13] Vasiliy I acquired the patent (*yarlyk*) to the Principality of Nizhniy Novgorod from the Tartar Khan Tokhtamysh in the year 1392, although there were princes in Nizhniy Novgorod after that date, princes who called themselves "grand prince." Vasiliy I obtained the patent to the Principality of Murom in 1392 or 1393 (see *PSRL*, XXV, 219; and Ekzemplyarskiy, I, 443, and II, 619). The city of Murom is on the Oka River about 280 kilometers east of Moscow. Long part of the so-called Murom-Ryazan' Principality, the city itself was a Slavic settlement among the Muroma, a people of Finno-Ugric linguistic stock.

to him the golden belt with precious stones with which my father, the grand prince, also blessed me, and the other golden belt, also with precious stones, which I myself [caused to be] forged, and the Golden Cap, and the shoulder pieces of the grand prince with holy images. And from among the vessels, to him [shall pass] the box decorated with carnelian, and the golden bowl with the yellow sapphire and with pearls. And aside from this, anything which is of my treasure or my property, now all this my princess shall manage, [and] one half she shall give in remembrance of my soul, and the other half is hers.

And my brother and son, Prince Konstantin, I bless [and] give to him as his patrimonial principality, Toshnya and Ustyuzhna, in accordance with the testament of our father, the grand prince.[14]

And any of my treasurers, or *tiuns*, or secretaries who managed my income, or *villici*, or somlers, or any of my purchased slaves, or those whom I have taken from Fedor Sviblo, all these I set free with their wives and with their children, [and] they are of no concern of my son and my princess. And to my princess [shall belong] those people whom I gave to her during my lifetime, and she has the full charters[15] to these people.

And you, my son Prince Ivan, hold your mother in respect and in the honorable state due a mother, as God has commanded, and my blessing [will be] upon you.

And concerning my son and my princess, I commit [them] to God and to my uncle, Prince Vladimir Andreyevich, and to my brothers, Prince Andrey Dmitriyevich and Prince Petr Dmitriyevich, [and] they shall care for them according to [our] agreement.[16]

[14] See above, Text 5.

[15] *Gramoty polnyye*, 'full charters,' were documents showing that persons were "full slaves" (*lyudi polnyye*) of the holder of such documents (see Chapter 4).

[16] The text is defective here. The passage reads in part: "pokladayu na boze . . . i na svoyei brat[']i, na knyazi na Ondreye Dmitreyevich[e] i na knyazi na Petre Dmitreyevich[e], po dokonchan'yu, kak sya imut" pechalova" (*DDG*, p. 57). This is probably a reference to an agreement concluded between Vasiliy I and Prince Vladimir Andreyevich about 1401 or 1402 which reads in part: "And if God should take you, the

And present at [the writing of] this testament were my boyars: Prince Yuriy Ivanovich,[17] Konstantin Dmitriyevich,[18] Dmitriy Afineyevich, Ivan Dmitriyevich,[19] Vladimir . . . ,[20] Ivan Fedorovich, Fedor Fedorovich.[21]

And this document was written by . . .[22]

---

grand prince, then I, my lord, shall have your son in your place [i.e., I shall regard your son as grand prince]. And your patrimonial principality of Moscow and Kolomna with all its volosts [here follows a list of the grand prince's lands], all this, my lord, I and my children shall defend as belonging to your princess and to your children, nor shall we treat them unjustly, [but] shall care for them and protect them." For the text of this agreement, see *DDG*, pp. 43–45.

[17] Probably the Lithuanian Prince Yuriy Patrikeyevich, grandson of Narimant (see Solov'yev, II, 388).

[18] Probably Konstantin Dmitriyevich Sheya (see Solov'yev, II, 388).

[19] Ivan Dmitriyevich Vsevolozhskiy (*DDG*, p. 495).

[20] Not identified; possibly Vladimir Danilovich Krasnyy-Snabdya (Solov'yev, II, 388). The original is torn here with about seven letters missing (*DDG*, p. 57, n. 1).

[21] Ivan and Fedor were doubtless Koshkins, sons of the boyar Fedor Andreyevich Koshka (Solov'yev, II, 387).

[22] The original is torn here with about eight letters missing (*DDG*, p. 57, n. 2).

TEXT 7

Second Testament of Vasiliy I

Commentary

THE second testament of Grand Prince Vasiliy I was probably written in the summer of 1417. L. V. Cherepnin, in maintaining that the document was written in 1417 rather than in 1421, the date proposed by Ekzemplyarskiy, cites as evidence the report given in the Chronicles of a quarrel between Vasiliy and his brother Konstantin in 1419, when the latter refused to swear allegiance to (*podpisati pod*) the grand prince's son, Vasiliy Vasil'yevich. The grand prince took Konstantin's patrimony (Uglich?) away from him and Konstantin left Moscow for Novgorod, where he was "received with honor" and given certain of the minor cities (*prigorody*) which had formerly belonged to Prince Semen Ol'gerdovich Lugven', a Lithuanian prince. In 1421, however, Konstantin returned to Moscow and made peace with his brother.[1]

Ekzemplyarskiy, in dating the testament 1421, cites this quarrel as evidence for the date he proposes. But if the fact that Konstantin's name appears among the protectors of the grand prince's son and princess in this testament is adduced to show that this testament was written after the reconciliation of the brothers, then why was Konstantin not included among the protectors of the son and princess of the grand prince in Vasiliy's third testament, which was probably written in 1423? If, as Cherepnin argues, the testament was written before the quarrel of 1419 rather than after the reconciliation of 1421, then it is

[1] See L. V. Cherepnin, *Russkiye feodal'nyye arkhivy, XIV–XV vv.* (Moscow-Leningrad, 1948–1951), I, 88–90; A. V. Ekzemplyarskiy, *Velikiye i udel'nyye knyaz'ya severnoy Rusi v" tatarskiy period", s" 1238 po 1505 g.* (St. Petersburg, 1889), II, 138–139; and *PSRL*, VIII, 90–91.

probable that it was written in the summer of 1417, shortly after the death of Vasiliy's oldest son Ivan.[2]

The original of the second testament of Grand Prince Vasiliy I is in the Central State Archives of Ancient Acts (TsGADA) in Moscow, in the State Repository of Ancient Documents, Section I, Heading 1, No. 13. Five seals were once suspended from the face of the original. Of these only three black-wax seals remain: the seals of Andrey Dmitriyevich, Petr Dmitriyevich, and Konstantin Dmitriyevich—all younger brothers of the grand prince. A copy of this testament, dating from the second half of the fifteenth century, is also preserved in the State Repository of Ancient Documents, Section I, Heading 1, No. 14.

The second testament of Vasiliy I has previously been printed in N. I. Novikov, ed., *Drevnyaya Rossiyskaya Vivliofika* (1st ed.; St. Petersburg, 1773–1775), Part 8, No. 20; in the second edition of the same work (Moscow, 1788–1791), Part 1, No. 20; in the Myshkin Library edition of the work (Myshkin, 1894), Vol. V, Part 9; in *Sobraniye gosudarstvennykh gramot i dogovorov, khranyashchikhsya v Gosudarstvennoy kollegii inostrannykh del* (Moscow, 1813), Part 1, No. 41; and in N. M. Karamzin, *Istoriya gosudarstva rossiyskago* (St. Petersburg, 1842), Vol. V, nn. 226–227.[3]

The translation which follows is based on the text of the testament as printed in *DDG*, pp. 57–60.

THE SECOND TESTAMENT OF GRAND PRINCE VASILIY I DMITRIYEVICH

IN the name of the Father, and of the Son, and of the Holy Ghost, [and] with the blessing of our father Fotiy, Metropolitan of Kiev and All Rus',[4] lo I, the sinful, poor slave of God, Vasiliy, in [good] health, write [this] testament. I give [this]

[2] See Ekzemplyarskiy, II, 138–139; Cherepnin, *Russkiye feodal'nyye arkhivy*, I, 88–90; and *PSRL*, VIII, 88.

[3] *DDG*, p. 60.

[4] Fotiy was metropolitan from 1410 until his death in 1431 (*PSRL*, XXV, 240 and 248).

arrangement [*ryad"*] to my son, Prince Vasiliy,[5] and to my princess.[6]

I commit my son, Prince Vasiliy, to my princess. And you, my son Prince Vasiliy, honor your mother, and obey your mother in the place of me, your father.

And I bless my son, Prince Vasiliy, with my patrimony with which my father blessed me, with a third of Moscow and with its *puti*, with my shares, and with the village Dobryatinskoye, and with its apiary, and with *Vasiltsevo sto*, and with a third of the enrolled people, and with Kolomna with its volosts and with its *puti*. And from among [my] villages I give to my son, Prince Vasiliy: in Moscow, the village Ostrov'skoye, and Orininskoye, and Kostyantinovskoye, and the village Malakhovskoye, and the Zhiroshkiny hamlets, with all that appertained to these villages, and the village Kopotenskoye, and the small village near the city of Moscow above Velikii Pond,[7] and the small village Khvostovskoye, and Velikii Meadow near the city of Moscow beyond the river, and Khodynskaya Mill, and the court [*dvor"*] of Foma Ivanovich in the city of Moscow by the Borovits'skiye Gates,[8] and another court which used to belong to Mikhail Vyazh, and the new court outside the city by [the Church of] Saint Vladimir.[9] And I give to my son, Prince Vasiliy, my

[5] Vasiliy Vasil'yevich, later called the Blind (*Temnyy*), was the third and, after the deaths of his older brothers Yuriy (1400) and Ivan (1417), the only surviving son of Grand Prince Vasiliy Dmitriyevich. He was born in 1415 and died in 1462 (see *PSRL*, XXV, 241 and 278, and Ekzemplyarskiy, I, Genealogical Table).

[6] Sofiya Vitovtovna.

[7] This is the first mention in the testaments of Velikii (Great) Pond, located northeast of the Kremlin. It was an enlarged portion of the Ol'khovets, a stream which flowed into the Chegora, a right tributary of the Yauza River (see M. N. Tikhomirov, *Srednevekovaya Moskva v XIV–XV vekakh* [Moscow, 1957], map facing p. 288).

[8] The Borovitskiye Gates are at the southwestern corner of the Kremlin, opposite the Neglinnaya River (see Tikhomirov, *Srednevekovaya Moskva*, "Schematic Plan of the Kremlin of the XIV–XV Centuries," p. 8).

[9] The Church of Saint Vladimir was located in or near the area known as Kulishki, just east of the Kremlin near the present Solyanka Street

acquisition in Yur'yev, the village Petrovskoye, Oleksinskoye.[10]

And to my princess I give the Kolomna volosts: Pesochna and Brasheva, with the small village Gvozdna, and with Ivan', and Ust'-Merska, and Gzhelya, and with their *puti*, and with their villages that are in those volosts. And from among the Kolomna villages I give to my princess: the villages Malinskiye which used to belong to my mother, and the village Ivanovskoye,[11] with Chyukhistovo,[12] and Okulovskoye, and Zakharovskoye, with all that appertained to them, and the village Repenskoye which my mother gave to her. And that which she has purchased or acquired, now this too is hers. And to my princess I also give the acquisition of my great-grandfather in Bezhits'skii Verkh", Kist'ma and the villages Ontonov'skiye, and in Rostov, Vasilevskoye, and my acquisition, Troyetsskaya *slobodka* on the Vol"ga, and the villages Beleutovskiye in Volok, and [that which I acquired] in Yur'yeva *sloboda*, and a third of the Moscow *tamga* and of all the customs in the city of Moscow, my shares. And from the Moscow villages I give to my princess: the Mitin" *novale*, with all that appertained to it, and the village Semtsinskoye with Samsonov Meadow, with all that used to belong to my mother, and Fedor Sviblo's small village on the Yauza, with the mill,[13] and the village Krilat'skoye which used to belong to the Tartar, and my princess shall pay from this village her debt of fifty rubles to the nun Sofiya. And concerning that which she has purchased in Moscow and that which she has acquired, now it too is hers. And to my princess I also give that which my father acquired, the *slobodka* on the Gus', and in Yur'yev, the village Krasnoye with Pravatovo Yelezarovskoye,

---

(Tikhomirov, *Srednevekovaya Moskva*, pp. 47 and 50 and map facing p. 288).

[10] Perhaps one village, Petrovskoye Oleksinskoye, identified with the Petrovskoye and Aleksinskoye of the testament of Ivan Kalita (see above, Text 1, n. 22). Vasiliy I refers to this village (or these villages) as *svoi primysl"*, 'my acquisition.'

[11] Probably identical with (the village?) Ivanovskoye Vasil'yevicha in Levichin of the first testament of Vasiliy I.

[12] Chyukhistova Land in the first testament of Vasiliy I.

[13] Concerning Sviblo, see above, text 6, n. 9.

228

and that which I acquired, also in Yur'yev, the village Frolovskoye, and Yelokh", and the village Bogorodits'skoye. And concerning her purchase and that which she has acquired, now these too are hers. And to her I also give that which I acquired in Beloozero, the *slobodka* that used to belong to Prince Vasiliy Semenovich,[14] and in Vologda, Ukhtyushka, and Bryukhovskaya *slobodka*, and Fedor Sviblo's villages, and that which I acquired, and my purchase[s] in Vologda and on the Toshna. And concerning her purchase and that which she acquired, now these are hers also. And in Ustyug, I give her Fedor Sviblo's hamlets, and Ivan Golovin's hamlets, and the Tutolminskiye hamlets, which my *villicus*, Grigoriy Gorbish-chev", purchased [and] which I have acquired.[15]

And my son, Prince Vasiliy, I bless with my patrimony, the Grand Princedom, with which my father blessed me.

And to my princess [I bequeath], from Kostroma, Iledam", and with Obnora, and with Komela, and with Volochok, and Nerekhta, and with the salt works [*varnitsy*], and with the beekeepers, and with the beaver trappers, and with the village Knyaginin'skoye. And from Pereyaslavl', to my princess [shall] also [pass] Yul"ka as well, with all its people, no matter of which *put'* in it they are,[16] and the village Dobroye. And from Volodimer' [I give her] the village Ondreyevskoye. And if my son, Prince Vasiliy, should acquire Toshna by exchange from

[14] This is the first mention in the testaments of the *slobodka* in Beloozero "that used to belong to Prince Vasiliy Semenovich." It is not further identified; it may have received its name from the infant son of Grand Prince Semen the Proud, Vasiliy, who was born in 1337 and died in 1338 (*PSRL*, XXV, 171).

[15] *Shto moi primysl"*. It may be that the term *primysl"* is used here in the sense of "appropriation," "usurpation," "conversion." On the other hand, it may mean "acquisition (by purchase)," if the meaning is that the prince's *villicus* bought the hamlets Tutolminskiye in the name of his lord.

[16] *Knyagine zhe moyei Yul"ka tak zhe so vsemi lyudmi, kotorogo puti v nei lyudi ni budut"*. In this passage the term *lyudi*, 'people,' probably refers to unfree persons who worked in the several *puti* (see I. I. Sreznevskiy, *Materialy dlya slovarya drevne-russkogo yazyka* [Moscow, 1958], II, 93).

Prince Vladimir's sons according to our agreement with their father, then Toshna also [shall pass] to my princess.[17]

And if God gives me Nov"gorod" Nizhnii, then I also bless my son, Prince Vasiliy, with Nov"gorod" Nizhnii, with all [that appertained to it].[18] And my son, Prince Vasiliy, I also bless with my acquisition Murom, with all that appertained to it.[19]

And from Nov"gorod" [Nizhnii] my princess [shall receive] one half of all my customs. And concerning the villages in Nov"gorod" [Nizhnii] which I have given to her, or that

[17] Toshna, a tributary of the Vologda River and a volost of Uglich District, was willed to Prince Petr, Vasiliy's younger brother, by the second testament of Dmitriy Donskoy, dated 1389. Toshna was mentioned in the agreement of Grand Prince Vasiliy Dmitriyevich with Vladimir Andreyevich, Prince of Serpukhov and Borovsk, dated about 1401–1402: "And if, in any manner (*kakimi dely*), Gorodets' or Kozlesk" is taken away from my brother, Prince Vladimir, or from his children, then I shall give them Toshna in place of Gorodets' " (text in *DDG*, pp. 43–45). It appears that Prince Vladimir did acquire the volost Toshna, for he wrote in his testament (also dated about 1401–1402) as follows: "And if Gorodets' is taken away from my children, then instead of it, my sons, Prince Semen and Prince Yaroslav, [shall receive] Toshna, each one half" (text in *DDG*, pp. 45–51). Toshna was granted to Prince Konstantin Dmitriyevich as his patrimonial principality by the first testament of Vasiliy I. It is probable that the sons of Prince Vladimir acquired Toshna sometime between 1406 or 1407 (the date of Vasiliy's first testament) and 1417 (the proposed date of this testament) (see Ekzemplyarskiy, II, 135).

[18] In 1417 Vasiliy I did not yet have undisputed possession of Nizhniy Novgorod. In 1412 the Nizhniy Novgorod princes had received the patent (*yarlyk*) to their principality from Zeleni-Saltan (Jalal ad-Din, son of Tokhtamysh). In 1414 Nizhniy was occupied by Yuriy, the brother of Grand Prince Vasiliy I. The local princes fled and subsequently appeared before the grand prince (1416). In 1418 Vasiliy I married his daughter Vasilisa to Aleksandr Ivanovich Bryukhatyy, the son of Ivan Vasil'yevich, one of the Suzdal'–Nizhniy Novgorod princes, and established his son-in-law as prince in Nizhniy Novgorod (see also above, Text 6, n. 13). It is quite possible that the two other claimants to the throne of Nizhniy Novgorod, Daniil and Ivan Borisovichi, who "fled from Moscow, from the grand prince," in 1418, did so as a result of the aforementioned marriage and the establishment of Bryukhatyy in Nizhniy Novgorod (*PSRL*, XXV, 243–244, and Cherepnin, *Russkiye feodal'nyye arkhivy*, I, 88–90).

[19] See above, Text 6, n. 13.

[which] she has acquired, now these too are hers. And the village Sokolskoye with all [that appertained to it shall pass] to her also, and Kerzhanets' with all [that appertained to it] also [shall pass] to my princess. And from Murom, to my princess also [shall pass] Seltse and Shatur".

And my son and my princess, having sent [persons for that purpose] shall take an inventory of those volosts and villages which I have given to my princess, and shall fix tribute [*dan'*] in them according to the number of people [and] according to their means, and my princess shall pay tribute and the post relay tax from those volosts and villages according to the reckoning which they have. And if God brings about a change concerning the Horde, then my princess shall take this tribute for herself, and my son, Prince Vasiliy, shall not interfere. And her volost administrators, and *tiuns*, and criminal investigators, my princess herself shall judge. And my son, Prince Vasiliy, shall not send [his officers] into her volosts or into her villages for any reason whatsoever. And these volosts and villages [are to belong] to my princess during her lifetime, and upon her death [they are to pass] to my son, Prince Vasiliy, except for Gzhelya and the village Semtsin'skoye, and her purchase[s]. And in Gzhelya and in the village Semtsinskoye and in that which she has acquired, my princess is free: to whomever she wishes to give [them], to him she shall give [them]. And concerning those boyars who serve my princess, now my son, Prince Vasiliy, shall protect those boyars.

And I bless my son, Prince Vasiliy, with the great [relics of the] Passion [of Our Lord] [20] and with the glorious life-giving

---

[20] *A blag[o]slovlyayu s[y]na svoyego, knyazya Vasil'ya, strast'mi bolshimi.* The *strasti bolshiye*, here translated as "the great (relics of the) Passion (of Our Lord)," were probably relics thought to have been the instruments of the Passion (*strast'*) of the Saviour, i.e., the crown of thorns, the scourge, the purple mantle, and the nails with which He was fastened to the cross. The *Voskresenskaya Chronicle* refers, under the year 6420 (from the Creation; A.D. 912), to these instruments as the *strasti Gospodni*, literally 'the Lord's Passions': "Emperor Leo [VI, the Wise,] honored the Russian emissaries [from Oleg the Wise of Kiev] with gifts, with gold, and with precious cloth, and with cloth made of gold, and appointed his men to show them the beauty of the church, and the

cross of Patriarch Philotheus.²¹ And I also bless my son: I give him the icon [which is] the work of Paramsha, and the chain decorated with crosses with which my father blessed me, and the Golden Cap, and the shoulder pieces of the grand prince with holy images, and the golden belt with precious stones which my father gave me, and my other belt of chains with precious stones, and the third belt with the blue strap [shall pass] to him also. And from among the vessels I give to my son, Prince Vasiliy, the box decorated with carnelian, and Prince Semen's golden bowl, ²²

golden chambers, and the wealth that is in them—much gold, and precious cloth, and precious stones—as well as the instruments of the Passion of the Lord, the crown [of thorns], the nails, and the purple mantle" (*PSRL*, VII, 275).

The following passage from the *Continuation of the Voskresenskaya Chronicle* may indicate the manner in which these relics came to be in the possession of the Grand Prince of Moscow: "In the year 6909 [1401] . . . concerning the instruments of the Passion of the Lord [*strasti Gospodni*]. In that same year there were acquired the instruments of the Passion of Our Lord Jesus Christ which at one time the God-fearing Bishop of Suzdal', Dionisiy, brought from Tsar'grad, having redeemed them at a very great cost, and it was through great faith and love that he acquired them, and it was with great difficulty that he brought them thence. Subsequently they were hidden for some time in the city of Suzdal', in the stone wall of the church building, [but] this spring they were found and they were brought to Moscow, and the entire clergy with their crosses and the entire city came out to meet them with reverence" (*PSRL*, VIII, 74–75).

²¹ Philotheus Kokkinos was Patriarch of Constantinople from 1354 to 1355, and from 1364 to 1376 (see Gaston Zananiri, *Histoire de l'Eglise byzantine* [Paris, 1954], p. 244). He is mentioned several times in the Chronicles. It was he who confirmed the nomination of Aleksey as metropolitan "of all the Russian Land" in 1354 (*PSRL*, XXV, 179, 194, and 195). Furthermore, in the words of Metropolitan Kiprian: "The Ecumenical Patriarch Philotheus blessed me as Metropolitan of Kiev and all the Russian Land" (*PSRL*, XXV, 192–193).

It is quite possible that the cross referred to was brought from Constantinople by either Metropolitan Aleksey or by Metropolitan Kiprian.

²² The reference is to Prince Semen Lugven' (or Lugvennyy), the son of Grand Prince Olgerd of Lithuania and therefore the first cousin of Vitovt, the father-in-law of Grand Prince Vasiliy I. Prince Semen had married Princess Mariya Dmitriyevna, the sister of Vasiliy I, in Moscow in 1394 (*PSRL*, XXV, 193 and 221).

and the vessel bound with gold which my mother gave me, and the large stone vessel which Prince Semen brought to me from Grand Prince Vitovt, and the crystal drinking glass which the king [23] sent me.

And the herd of mares [shall pass] to my princess, [and she shall share it] with my son, [and each shall receive] a half.

And apart from this, anything at all which I have, now all [shall pass] to my princess.

And the slaves that I have given to my princess during my lifetime, they are hers. And my princess shall give to each of my daughters [24] five families from among my slaves, but aside from this all my slaves shall go free, with their wives and with their children.

And I commit my son, Prince Vasiliy, and my princess, and my children to my brother and father-in-law, Grand Prince Vitovt, as [thus] he told me: [I commit them] to God and to him, [and] thus he shall care for [them]; and [I also commit them] to my younger brothers, to Prince Andrey Dmitriyevich, and to Prince Petr Dmitriyevich, and to Prince Konstantin Dmitriyevich, [25] and to Prince Semen Vladimirovich, and to Prince Yaroslav Vladimirovich, and to their brothers, [26] in accordance with their agreement, as [thus] they told me.

And present at [the writing of] this document were my

[23] Probably Jagiello, referred to as "King Yagaylo" in the Russian Chronicles. The son of Olgerd of Lithuania (and brother of Semen Lugven'), he became King of Poland in 1386, upon his marriage to Jadwiga (*PSRL*, VIII, 51).

[24] Vasiliy I had four daughters: Anna, Anastasiya, Vasilisa, and Mariya. Anna, who was married in 1411 to the future Byzantine Emperor John VIII Palaeologus (ruled 1425–1448), died in 1417, the proposed date of the writing of this testament (see Ekzemplyarskiy, I, Genealogical Table).

[25] This is the only one of the three testaments of Grand Prince Vasiliy I in which Prince Konstantin Dmitriyevich is listed among those to whom the grand prince commits his children and his princess (see Commentary to this text).

[26] Princes Semen and Yaroslav were sons of Vladimir the Brave and second cousins of Vasiliy I. Semen and Yaroslav had three brothers— Ivan, Andrey, and Vasiliy—all of whom were probably living in 1417 (see Ekzemplyarskiy, I, Genealogical Table).

boyars: Prince Yuriy Patrikeyevich,²⁷ Ivan Dmitriyevich,²⁸ Mikhaylo Andreyevich,²⁹ Ivan Fedorovich, [and] Fedor Ivanovich.³⁰

And my secretary Timofey Achkasov" wrote [this] document.

And may God judge him who violates this my testament, and may my blessing not be on him in this life or in the next.³¹

---

²⁷ See above, Text 6, n. 17.

²⁸ Ivan Dmitriyevich Vsevolozhskiy (*DDG*, p. 495).

²⁹ Perhaps the brother of Fedor Sviblo, Mikhail Andreyevich Chelyadnya (see S. M. Solov'yev, *Istoriya Rossii s drevneyshikh vremen* [Moscow, 1959–1966], II, 387).

³⁰ Probably Fedor Ivanovich Vel'yaminov, the grandson of "Uncle" Vasiliy (see above, Text 2, n. 6, and Solov'yev, II, 387).

³¹ Below appears the signature, in Greek, of Metropolitan Fotiy (*DDG*, p. 59).

TEXT 8

Third Testament of Vasiliy I

Commentary

THE third testament of Grand Prince Vasiliy I was probably
written in 1423. The original and a copy of the original of this
document are extant. On the back of the copy there appears the
following note, written in the same handwriting as that of the
original: "A copy of the document which went to Grand Prince
Vitovt with Aleksey [1] in the year 30-first [6931/1423] in Mid-
Lent week." There is another note on the same copy, written in
a different hand, which reads: "A copy of the document which
Aleksey took with him to Lithuania when he set out with
Metropolitan Fotiy in Mid-Lent week." Mid-Lent week fell
early in March in the year 1423, and therefore the testament was
probably written in February or March of that year.[2]

The original and the fifteenth-century copy of the original are
both preserved in the Central State Archives of Ancient Acts
(TsGADA) in Moscow, in the State Repository of Ancient
Documents, Section I, Heading 1, No. 15 (the original) and No.
16 (the copy). From the face of the original is suspended the
yellow-wax seal of Grand Prince Vasiliy Dmitriyevich.[3]

The third testament of Vasiliy I has been printed previously in
N. I. Novikov, ed., *Drevnyaya Rossiyskaya Vivliofika* (1st ed.;
St. Petersburg, 1773–1775), Part 8, No. 21; in the second edition
of the same work (Moscow, 1788–1791), Part 1, No. 21; in
the Myshkin Library edition of the work (Myshkin, 1894), Vol.

---

[1] Probably the secretary of the grand prince, Aleksey Stromilov, who
wrote this testament.

[2] See L. V. Cherepnin, *Russkiye feodal'nyye arkhivy, XIV–XV vv.*
(Moscow-Leningrad, 1948–1951), I, 91.

[3] *DDG*, p. 62.

V, Part 9; in *Sobraniye gosudarstvennykh gramot i dogovorov, khranyashchikhsya v Gosudarstvennoy kollegii inostrannykh del* (Moscow, 1813), Part 1, No. 42; and in other collections.[4]

The translation which follows is based on the text of the third testament of Vasiliy I as printed in *DDG*, pp. 60–62.

THE THIRD TESTAMENT OF GRAND PRINCE VASILIY I DMITRIYEVICH

IN the name of the Father, and of the Son, and of the Holy Ghost, [and] with the blessing of our father Fotiy, Metropolitan of Kiev and All Rus', lo I, the sinful, poor slave of God, Vasiliy, in [good] health, write [this] testament. I give [this] arrangement [*ryad"*] to my son, Prince Vasiliy, and to my princess.

I commit my son, Prince Vasiliy, to my princess.[5] And you, my son, Prince Vasiliy, honor your mother and obey your mother in the place of me, your father.

And I bless my son, Prince Vasiliy, with my patrimony with which my father blessed me, with a third of Moscow and with its *puti*, with my shares, and with the village Dobryatin'skoye with its apiary, and with *Vasiltsevo sto*, and with a third of the enrolled people, and with Kolomna with its volosts and with its *puti*. And from among the villages I give to my son, Prince Vasiliy: in Moscow, the village Ostrov'skoye, with Orinin'skoye, and with Kostyantinov'skoye, and the village Malakhovskoye, and the Zhiroshkiny hamlets, with all that appertained to these villages, and the village Kopotenskoye, and the small village near the city of Moscow above Velikii Pond, and the small village Khvostov'skoye, and Velikii Meadow beyond the river near the city of Moscow, and Khodynskaya Mill, and the court [*dvor"*] of Foma Ivanovich in the city by the Borovitsskiye Gates, and another court which used to belong to Mikhail Vyazh, and the new court outside the city by [the Church

[4] *DDG*, p. 62.
[5] *Svoyei knya knyagine*, 'to my prin princess'; obviously the copyist's error.

236

of] Saint Vladimir. And I give to my son, Prince Vasiliy, my acquisition in Yur'yev, the village Petrovskoye and Oleksin'skoye.

And to my princess I give the Kolomna volosts: Pesochna and Brasheva, with the small village Gvozdna, and with Ivan', and Ust'-Merska, and Gzhelya, and with their *puti* and with their villages that are in those volosts. And from among the Kolomna villages I give to my princess the villages Malin'skiye which used to belong to my mother, and the village Ivanovskoye, with Chyukhistovo, and Okulovskoye, and Zakharovskoye, with all that appertained to them, and the village Repinskoye which my mother gave to her. And that which she has purchased or acquired, now this too is hers. And to my princess I also give the acquisition of my great-grandfather in Bezhitsskii Verkh", Kistma and the villages Ontonovskiye, and Vasilevskoye in Rostov, and my acquisition, Troyetsskaya *slobodka* on the Volga, and the villages Belevutovskiye in Volok, and in Yur'yeva *sloboda*, and a third of the Moscow *tamga* and of all the customs in the city of Moscow, my shares. And from among the Moscow villages I give to my princess: the Mitin *novale*, with all that appertained to it, and the village Semtsinskoye with Samsonov Meadow, and with everything that used to belong to my mother, and Fedor Sviblo's small village on the Yauza, with the mill, and the village Krilat'skoye which used to belong to the Tartar, and my princess shall pay from this village her debt of fifty rubles to the nun Sofiya. And concerning the villages which she has purchased in Moscow and that which she has acquired, now these too are hers. And to my princess I also give that which my father acquired, the *slobodka* on the Gus', and in Yur'yev, the village Krasnoye with Provatovo Yelizarovskoye, and that which I acquired in Yur'yev, the village Frolovskoye, and Yelokh, and the village Bogoroditsskoye. And concerning her purchase and that which she has acquired, now these too are hers. And [I give to my princess] in Beloozero, the *slobodka* that used to belong to Prince Vasiliy Semenovich, and in Vologda, Ukhtyuzhka, and the Bryukhovskaya *slobodka*, and Fedor Sviblo's villages, and my purchase[s] in Vologda and on the Toshna. And concerning her purchase and that which she has acquired, now these are hers also. And [I give to her] also, in Ustyug, Fedor Sviblo's hamlets and the hamlets Golovinskiye,[6] which I have acquired.

And if God gives to my son the Grand Princedom, then I also bless my son, Prince Vasiliy, [with it].

And to my princess [I bequeath] from Kostroma, Iledam", with Komela, and with Volochok, and with Obnora, and Nerekhta, and with the salt works, and with the village Knyaginin'skoye, and with the beekeepers, and with the beaver trappers. And from Per'yaslavl' to my princess [shall] also [pass] Yulka as well, with all its people, no matter of which *put'* in it they are, and the village Dobroye. And concerning her purchase and acquisition, now these too are hers. And from Volodimer' [I give her] the village Ondreyevskoye. And if my son should acquire Toshna by exchange from Prince Vladimir's sons according to our agreement with their father, then Toshna also [shall pass] to my princess.[7]

And my son, Prince Vasiliy, I bless with my acquisitions Nov"gorod" Nizhnii with everything [that appertained to it],[8] and I also bless my son with my acquisition Murom, also with everything [that appertained to it].

And from Nov"gorod [Nizhnii] my princess [shall receive] one half of all my customs. And concerning the village in Nov"gorod" [Nizhnii] which I have given to her or that [which] she has acquired, now these too are hers. And the village Sokol'skoye also [shall pass] to her, with everything [that appertained to it]. And Kerzhanets', with all [that appertained to it shall pass] to my princess also. And from Murom, to my princess [shall pass] Seltse and Shatur".

And my son and my princess, having sent [persons for that

[6] Referred to as "Ivan Golovin's hamlets" in the second testament of Vasiliy I (see above, Text 7).

[7] See above, Text 7, n. 17.

[8] It appears that following the death (1418) of Grand Prince Vasiliy's son-in-law, Aleksandr Ivanovich Bryukhatyy, the Principality of Nizhniy Novgorod came under the uncontested rule of Moscow (see N. M. Karamzin, *Istoriya gosudarstva rossiyskago* [St. Petersburg, 1842], "Notes to Volume V," p. 109; A. V. Ekzemplyarskiy, *Velikiye i udel'nyye knyaz'ya severnoy Rusi v" tatarskiy period", s" 1238 po 1505 g.* [St. Petersburg, 1889], II, 441–442; and above, Text 6, n. 13, and Text 7, n. 18).

purpose] shall take an inventory of those volosts and villages which I have given to my princess, and shall fix tribute [*dan'*] in them according to the number of people and according to their means, and my princess shall pay tribute and the post relay tax from those volosts and villages according to the reckoning which they have. And if God brings about a change concerning the Horde, then my princess shall take this tribute for herself, and my son, Prince Vasiliy, shall not interfere. And her volost administrators, and *tiuns*, and criminal investigators, she shall judge herself, and my son, Prince Vasiliy, shall not send [his officers] into her volosts or into her villages for any reason whatsoever. And these volosts and villages [are to belong] to my princess during her lifetime, and upon her death, except for Gzhelya and the village Semtsin'skoye and her purchase[s] and acquisition[s], [they are to pass] to my son, Prince Vasiliy. And in Gzhelya and in the village Semtsin'skoye and in that which she has acquired, my princess is free: to whomever she wishes to give them, to him she shall give them. And concerning those boyars who serve my princess, now my son, Prince Vasiliy, shall protect these her boyars.

And my son, Prince Vasiliy, I bless with the great [relics of the] Passion [of Our Lord] and with the glorious life-giving cross of Patriarch Philotheus.[9] And I also bless my son: I give him the icon [which is] the work of Paramsha, and the chain decorated with crosses with which my father blessed me, and the Golden Cap, and the shoulder pieces of the grand prince with holy images, and the golden belt with precious stones which my father gave me, and my other belt of chains with precious stones, and the third belt with the blue strap [shall pass] to him also. And from among the vessels I give to my son, Prince Vasiliy, the box decorated with carnelian, and Prince Semen's golden bowl,[10] and the vessel bound with gold [which] [11] my mother gave me, and the large stone vessel which Prince Semen brought to me from Grand Prince Vitovt, and the crystal drinking glass which the king [12] sent me.

[9] See above, Text 7, nn. 20 and 21.
[10] See above, Text 7, n. 22.
[11] The word *chto*, 'which,' has been supplied by the editors of *DDG*.
[12] Probably Jagiello (see above, Text 7, n. 23).

And the herd of my mares [shall pass] to my son, Prince Vasiliy, [and he shall share it] with my princess, [and each shall receive] a half.

And apart from this, anything at all which I have, now all [shall pass] to my princess.

And the slaves that I have given to my princess during my lifetime, they are hers. And my princess shall give to each of my daughters [13] five families from among my slaves, but aside from this all my slaves shall go free, with their wives and with their children.

And I commit my son, Prince Vasiliy, and my princess, and my children to my brother and father-in-law, Grand Prince Vitovt, as [thus] he told me: [I commit them] to God and to him, [and] thus he shall care for [them]; and [I also commit them] to my younger brothers, to Prince Andrey Dmitriyevich, and to Prince Petr Dmitriyevich, and to Prince Semen Vladimirovich, and to Prince Yaroslav Vladimirovich, and to their brothers, [14] in accordance with their agreement, as [thus] they told me.

And present at [the writing of] this document were my bo-yars: Prince Yuriy Patrikeyevich, [15] Ivan Dmitriyevich, [16] Mikhaylo Andreyevich, [17] Ivan Fedorovich, [18] Mikhaylo Fedorovich, [19] [and] Fedor Ivanovich. [20]

And Aleksey Stromilov" wrote this my testament. [21]

[13] See above, Text 7, n. 24.

[14] See above, Text 7, n. 26.

[15] See above, Text 6, n. 17.

[16] Ivan Dmitriyevich Vsevolozhskiy (*DDG*, p. 495).

[17] See above, Text 7, n. 29.

[18] See above, Text 6, n. 21.

[19] Probably Mikhail Fedorovich Koshkin (see S. M. Solov'yev, *Istoriya Rossii s drevneyshikh vremen* [Moscow, 1959–1966], II, 387).

[20] See above, Text 7, n. 30.

[21] Below appears the signature, in Greek, of Metropolitan Fotiy (*DDG*, p. 62).

TEXT 9

Testament of Vasiliy II

Commentary

VASILIY, later called the Blind (*Temnyy*), was the third and, following the deaths of his older brothers Yuriy (1400) and Ivan (1417), the only surviving son of Grand Prince Vasiliy Dmitriyevich. Prince Vasiliy Vasil'yevich was born in 1415. He became Grand Prince of Moscow upon the death of his father in 1425. He was confirmed by the Tartars as Grand Prince of Vladimir in 1432, despite the efforts of his uncle, Prince Yuriy Dmitriyevich of Zvenigorod and Galich, to obtain the khan's patent to the Grand Princedom. In the ensuing struggle between Vasiliy II on the one hand and his uncle and the latter's sons on the other, Prince Yuriy and his son, Vasiliy the Cross-Eyed, held Moscow for a brief time in 1434. Vasiliy II regained his throne, however, and ruled until his death in 1462.[1]

The mention of Feodosiy, Metropolitan of All Rus', indicates that the testament of Vasiliy II was written sometime between May 3, 1461, the date of the elevation of the Archbishop of Rostov to the metropolitanate,[2] and March 27, 1462, the day on which Vasiliy died.[3]

L. V. Cherepnin suggests that this testament was written during Vasiliy's illness in March 1462, immediately following the execution of Prince Vasiliy Yaroslavich's junior boyars who had failed in their attempt to free their lord from incarceration in Uglich.[4]

[1] See *PSRL*, VIII, 98–99, and XXV, 241, 249, and 278.

[2] *PSRL*, V, 273. Feodosiy was metropolitan until 1465, when he retired to the Chudov Monastery (Monastery of the Miracle of Mikhail the Archangel) in the Kremlin (*PSRL*, VIII, 151).

[3] *PSRL*, VIII, 150.

[4] L. V. Cherepnin, *Russkiye feodal'nyye arkhivy, XIV–XV vv.* (Mos-

The original of the testament of Grand Prince Vasiliy II is preserved in the Central State Archives of Ancient Acts (TsGADA) in Moscow, Section I, Heading 2, No. 21. A copy of the document, dating from the second half of the fifteenth century, is preserved in the same place (No. 22). A sixteenth-century copy of the original is in the collection of manuscripts of the Synodical Library (Book 562, No. 102) of the State Historical Museum in Moscow.[5]

On the face of the original document there are traces of the affixture of two seals: that of Grand Prince Vasiliy Vasil'yevich and that of Metropolitan Feodosiy.[6]

A codicil to the testament of Vasiliy II (translated below as Text 10) is extant and is preserved with the original testament. The testament and its codicil have been previously printed in N. I. Novikov, ed., *Drevnyaya Rossiyskaya Vivliofika* (1st ed.; St. Petersburg, 1773–1775), Part 9, Nos. 65–66; in the second edition of the same work (Moscow, 1788–1791), Part 1, Nos. 65–66; in the Myshkin Library edition of the work (Myshkin, 1894), Vol. V, Part 9; in *Sobraniye gosudarstvennykh gramot i dogovorov, khranyashchikhsya v Gosudarstvennoy kollegii inostrannykh del* (Moscow, 1813), Part 1, Nos. 86–87; and in N. M. Karamzin, *Istoriya gosudarstva rossiyskago* (St. Petersburg, 1842), Vol. V, n. 372.[7]

The translation which follows is based on the text of the testament of Grand Prince Vasiliy II as printed in *DDG*, pp. 193–198.

THE TESTAMENT OF GRAND PRINCE VASILIY II VASIL'YEVICH

IN the name of the holy and life-giving Trinity, the Father, the Son, and the Holy Ghost, and with the blessing of our father

cow-Leningrad, 1948–1951), I, 158–159. Concerning Prince Vasiliy Yaroslavich, see n. 19, below.

[5] *DDG*, p. 199.
[6] *DDG*, p. 198.
[7] *DDG*, p. 199.

Feodosiy, Metropolitan of All Rus', lo I, the much sinning, poor slave of God, Vasiliy, while living and of sound mind, write this testament. I give [this] arrangement [*ryad"*] to my children [8] and to my princess.[9]

I commit my children to my princess. And you, my children, live as one and obey your mother in all things, in place of me, your father.

And my oldest son, Ivan,[10] I bless with my patrimony, the Grand Princedom. And I give him the third in Moscow with the *puti*, with my shares, with which my father blessed me, and with the village Dobryatinskoye with its apiary, and with *Vasiltsovo sto*, and with the enrolled people, and with the *ordyntsy*,[11] and with Kolomna with its volosts, and with its *puti*, and with its villages, and with all its customs, and with Volodimer' with its volosts, and with its *puti*, and with its villages, and with all its customs, with Pereyaslavl'[12] with its volosts, and with its *puti*, and with its villages, and with all its customs, Kostroma[13] with

[8] At the time of the writing of this testament Vasiliy II had six living children: Ivan (the oldest), Yuriy, Andrey the Elder, Boris, Andrey the Younger, and Anna (see A. V. Ekzemplyarskiy, *Velikiye i udel'nyye knyaz'ya severnoy Rusi v" tatarskiy period", s" 1238 po 1505 g.* [St. Petersburg, 1889], II, Genealogical Table).

[9] Mariya Yaroslavna, the daughter of Yaroslav Vladimirovich, Prince of Borovsk.

[10] Ivan Vasil'yevich III, called the Great (*Velikiy*), was born in 1440. He was grand prince from 1462 until his death in 1506 (*PSRL*, VIII, 108, 150, and 245).

[11] *Ordyntsy* (the plural of *ordin'ts'* or *ordyn'ts'*, from *orda*, 'the Horde'), 'Horde men.' There is disagreement as to the nature of this group of the population of Muscovy. They may have been persons taken prisoner by the Tartars and subsequently ransomed by the Russian princes. For a discussion of this term, see Chapter 4.

[12] This is the first instance in the testaments in which Vladimir and Pereyaslavl' are listed with Kolomna as part of the inheritance of the grand prince's oldest son. It is probable that at the time of the writing of the earlier testaments Pereyaslavl' and, of course, Vladimir were considered part of the Grand Principality of Vladimir and were therefore not classified with Kolomna, which had been considered part of the patrimony of the Grand Prince of Moscow since the days of Ivan Kalita.

[13] Apparently Kostroma was subordinate to the Grand Principality of Vladimir as early as 1270. The fact that Kostroma was not openly

its volosts, and with its *puti*, and with its villages, and with all its customs, [Gal]ich [14] with its volosts, and with its *puti*, and with its villages, and with Sol', and with all its customs, Ustyug" [15] with its volosts, and with its *puti*, and with its villages, and with all its customs. And I give to my son Ivan the Vyatka Land. [16] And I give to him Suzdal' [17] with its volosts, and with its *puti*, and with its villages, and with all its customs, and Novgorod Nizhnii with all its customs, and with its volosts, and with its *puti*, and with its villages, [and I give him] Murom with its volosts, and with its *puti*, and with its villages, and with all its customs, with Yur'yev, [18] and with Velikaya Sol', and with all their customs. And I give to my son Ivan, Borovesk" with all its volosts, and with its *puti*, and with its villages, and with all its customs, as it used to belong to Prince Vasiliy, [19] and Sukhodol,

---

bequeathed to the son of the grand prince in one of the earlier testaments may be explained in the same way as is the absence of Pereyaslavl' among the grants of the earlier wills (see Ekzemplyarskiy, II, 263, and n. 12, above).

[14] The letters *Gal* have been supplied by the editors of *DDG*. Galich had been willed to Prince Yuriy Dmitriyevich, the uncle of Vasiliy II, by the second testament of Dmitriy Donskoy. Vasiliy II acquired Galich from Yuriy's son, Dmitriy Shemyaka, following the defeat of the latter in a battle near Galich city in 1450 (*PSRL*, VIII, 122–123).

[15] The only previous references to Ustyug in the testaments appear in those of Vasiliy I. In all three of these testaments the grand prince willed Fedor Sviblo's hamlets ("villages" in the first testament) in Ustyug to Princess Sofiya Vitovtovna.

[16] This is the first mention in the testaments of the Vyatka Land, a vast territory to the east of Galich, along the Vyatka River and its tributaries.

[17] Here, for the first time, Suzdal' was willed to the son of the Moscow prince. The city of Suzdal' is located about two hundred kilometers northeast of Moscow (see above, Chapter 2, n. 11).

[18] This is the first time in which Yur'yev was willed to the son of the grand prince. Yur'yev was probably part of the Grand Principality of Vladimir since shortly after 1340. In that year we find the last mention of a prince of Yur'yev, Ivan Yaroslavich, who participated in a punitive expedition organized by the Tartars (with the aid of Ivan Kalita) against Smolensk. It is probable that Ivan Yaroslavich was childless and that, upon his death, Yur'yev escheated to the Grand Principality (see *PSRL*, VII, 206, and Ekzemplyarskiy, II, 260).

[19] Ivan II bequeathed "the village on the Repna in Borov'sk" " to his

with Ist'ya and with Isterva, and with the village Krasnoye, and Koluga,[20] and with Oleksin and with its volosts, and with its *puti*, and with its villages, and with all its customs, as it used to belong to Prince Ivan of Mozhaysk.[21] And from among the Moscow villages I give to my son Ivan the village Ostrovskoye, and with Orininskoye, and with Kostyantinovskoye, and with Molakhovskoye, and with their hamlets, and with that which appertained to those villages, and the village Krasnoye above

son Ivan. Prince Vladimir Andreyevich of Serpukhov received Borovsk from Dmitriy Donskoy sometime prior to 1389 (see the agreement of Grand Prince Dmitriy Ivanovich with the Prince of Serpukhov and Borovsk, Vladimir Andreyevich, dated March 25, 1389, in *DDG*, pp. 30–32).

The Vasiliy mentioned in the text was Prince Vasiliy Yaroslavich, the last Prince of Serpukhov-Borovsk and a distant cousin of Vasiliy II (their great-grandfathers were brothers). Mariya, the wife of Vasiliy II, was the sister of Vasiliy Yaroslavich. In 1456 the grand prince seized Vasiliy Yaroslavich and incarcerated him in Uglich. A number of the junior boyars (*deti boyarskiye*) of the Serpukhov-Borovsk prince plotted to secure his release in 1462. Their plot was discovered by the grand prince, who dealt with them severely (*PSRL*, XXV, 275 and 277–278). Prince Vasiliy Yaroslavich apparently was in prison in Vologda at the time of his death, "in chains," in 1483. He was buried in the Cathedral of Mikhail the Archangel in Moscow, the traditional burying place of the princes of the House of Moscow (*PSRL*, VI, 335). The holdings of the Prince of Serpukhov-Borovsk came directly into the hands of the Grand Prince of Moscow following the imprisonment of Vasiliy Yaroslavich. The cause for the seizure and imprisonment of this prince is not known; he had been a faithful ally of Vasiliy II during the latter's struggle with Yuriy of Galich and Yuriy's sons (see Ekzemplyarskiy, II, 311–315).

[20] Kaluga had been bequeathed to Prince Andrey Dmitriyevich of Mozhaysk by the second testament of Dmitriy Donskoy. Vasiliy II confirmed Kaluga as part of the patrimony of his cousin, Prince Ivan Andreyevich, the son of Andrey Dmitriyevich, in 1447 (see the agreement of Grand Prince Vasiliy Vasil'yevich with the Prince of Mozhaysk, Ivan Andreyevich, in *DDG*, pp. 146–148). In 1454 Grand Prince Vasiliy Vasil'yevich moved against Prince Ivan Andreyevich, who had acted in alliance with Dmitriy Shemyaka against the grand prince. Ivan fled to Lithuania and Vasiliy II incorporated the patrimony of Ivan—Mozhaysk and Kaluga—into the Grand Principality (see *PSRL*, VIII, 144, and "The System of Holding Moscow by Thirds" in Chapter 5, above).

[21] This is the first mention in the testaments of the city of Oleksin (Aleksin), which is located about forty kilometers east of Kaluga.

Velikii Pond near the city, and with the city courts which appertained to it, and the large meadow near the city along the river Moskva.

And my son Yuriy [22] I bless with Prince Vladimir's third in Moscow, [and he shall share it] with my son Andrey,[23] each one half, and [they] shall hold it by "years." [24] And I also give to my son Yuriy the "year" of Prince Konstantin Dmitriyevich in Moscow.[25] And to my son Yuriy I also give Dmitrov [26] with all

[22] Yuriy Vasil'yevich, Prince of Dmitrov, was born in 1442 and died in 1473. He had no children (see *PSRL*, XXV, 262 and 298, and Ekzemplyarskiy, II, Genealogical Table).

[23] Andrey Vasil'yevich the Elder, Prince of Uglich, was born in 1446 and died in 1494. He was "in prison in Moscow at the Treasury Court [*Kazennyy dvor*] of the Grand Prince [Ivan III] for two years and forty-seven days, and they buried him in the Church of Mikhail the Archangel." Prince Andrey and his sons had been seized in 1492 by the grand prince and imprisoned. Andrey's sons, Ivan and Dmitriy, who were imprisoned in Pereyaslavl', both died "in chains." Ivan died in 1522; the date of Dmitriy's death is not known (*PSRL*, VIII, 223 and 227, and Ekzemplyarskiy, II, Genealogical Table).

[24] The third of Moscow that had belonged to the House of Prince Andrey Ivanovich (the third son of Kalita) is here referred to as "Prince Vladimir's third," after Prince Vladimir Andreyevich the Brave, Prince of Serpukhov and Borovsk. This third apparently came into the hands of the Moscow line of the princely family after the incarceration of Prince Vasiliy Yaroslavich by Vasiliy II.

The system of holding Moscow by thirds had become so complex that certain princes were entitled to custom from their third only during certain years. It would appear from this document, for instance, that Princes Yuriy and Andrey were to alternate each year in their rights in the former third of Prince Vladimir.

[25] Concerning Prince Konstantin Dmitriyevich and his "year," see above, Chapter 5, nn. 20 and 33.

[26] Dmitrov was bequeathed to Prince Petr Dmitriyevich by the second testament of Dmitriy Donskoy. Prince Petr held Dmitrov until his death in 1428, at which time it escheated to the Grand Principality (*PSRL*, VIII, 94). Vasiliy II granted Dmitrov to his uncle, Yuriy of Galich, in 1432, but took it back the same year (*PSRL*, XXV, 250). In 1435 Vasiliy granted Dmitrov to his cousin, Vasiliy the Cross-Eyed, but the latter remained there for only a month before retiring to Kostroma (*PSRL*, XXV, 252). Then, in an agreement concluded about 1447, Vasiliy II granted Dmitrov to Prince Vasiliy Yaroslavich of Serpukhov and Borovsk (text of this agreement is in *DDG*, pp. 129–134; concerning

its volosts, and with its *puti*, and with its villages, and with all its customs, and with the volosts beyond the Moskva River [Zamoskov"skiye *volosti*], and with all that used to belong to Prince Petr. And to him [Yuriy] I also give Yulka and the Yulka beekeepers, and that which appertained to Yulka, and Serebozh' and Buskutovo, and Rozhestvenoye,[27] and all that appertained to these volosts. And I also give to my son Yuriy, Mozhayesk" with its volosts, and with its *puti*, and with its villages, and with all its customs, and with Medyn', and with that which appertained to Medyn', and [I give him] Serpokhov",[28] and Khotun',[29] with all their customs. And that with which my mother, Grand Princess Sofiya, his [Yuriy's] grandmother, blessed him and in her testament bequeathed to him, [namely] the small village Semchinskoye near Moscow, and her city courts, and Samsonov Meadow, and Kzhelya, and that which she purchased, the small village Vorob'yevskoye, and Semenovskoye, and with their hamlets, and on the Pokhra,[30] the village Myachkovo, and Faustovskoye, and Lodygino, and with [the village of] Leontiy Fedorov, and with Tyazhyno, and with the fishing hamlets, and from among the Kolomna villages, Velina, Krivtsovo, Bronniche, Chevyrevo, Marchyukovo, and Rozhek, and the *novale* by Lake Shchelino, and from among the Yur'yev" villages, all the villages Turab'-yev"skiye, and Kuchka, and Derevenka, and Shadrino, now these also are his. And in addition to the villages Turab'yevskiye I

Vasiliy Yaroslavich, see n. 19, above). In a subsequent agreement between Vasiliy II and Vasiliy Yaroslavich, dated 1450–1454, the latter relinquished Dmitrov to the grand prince (*DDG*, pp. 168–175).

[27] This Rozhestvenoye is identified by the editors of *DDG* (p. 552) as a village of one of the volosts "beyond the Moskva." The testament of Ivan III (1504) mentions a volost Rozhestvenoye, Pereyaslavl' District. It appears that the latter is identical with the Rozhestvenoye of this testament, which is incorrectly identified by the editors of *DDG*.

[28] Serpukhov had been part of the patrimony of Vasiliy Yaroslavich of Serpukhov and Borovsk, concerning whom, see n. 19, above.

[29] This is the first mention in the testaments of Khotun', a city on the Lopasnya River about thirty kilometers east and slightly north of Serpukhov.

[30] The Pokhra (Pakhra) River is a right tributary of the Moskva. It flows into the latter about thirty kilometers southeast of the center of Moscow.

have given to him my village Shipilov"skoye, with all [that appertained to it]. And in Kostroma his [Yuriy's] grandmother has given him the village Kachalov"skoye, and Ushakovskoye, and the village S[vya]toye, and in Vologda, the villages Maslenskiye, and the [villages] Yangosarskiye, and the villages Govorov"skiye, and that which appertained to them, now these also are his.[31] And if my son Ivan should desire to obtain by exchange the Kolomna villages from his brother Yuriy, then my son Yuriy shall give him these villages in exchange [for others], and [my] son Ivan shall obtain these villages from his brother by exchange, and he shall not cause injustice to him.[32]

And my son Andrey I bless [and] I give to him, with his older brother Yuriy, the third of Prince Vladimir in Moscow, each one half, and [they] shall hold it by "years."[33] And I give him Ugleche[34] with all its volosts, and with its *puti*, and with its vil-

---

[31] The long list of places given to Prince Yuriy Vasil'yevich by his grandmother, Grand Princess Sofiya Vitovtovna, starting with the small village Semchinskoye and ending with the villages Govorov"skiye, is, with the sole exception of the village Shipilov"skoye, a repetition of the list of places bequeathed to Prince Yuriy by the testament of Grand Princess Sofiya. For the text of this testament, dated 1451, see *DDG*, pp. 175–178.

[32] It is of interest that Sofiya in her testament confirmed the right of her son Vasiliy to acquire by exchange any "villages or other places" which she had bequeathed to her grandson, Prince Yuriy (*DDG*, pp. 175–178).

[33] See n. 24, above.

[34] Uglich, referred to as the "purchase of my grandfather," was bequeathed to Prince Petr Dmitriyevich by the second testament of Dmitriy Donskoy. The same testament provided that if another son were born to the grand prince, then "my princess shall also give a share to him, taking portions from each of his older brothers." With the birth of a son, Konstantin, to Dmitriy's princess, a complicated shuffling of holdings took place to provide the infant prince with the patrimony promised him by his father. Konstantin received Uglich, which, however, was eventually taken away from him (*PSRL*, VIII, 90). Uglich was in the hands of Vasiliy I in 1401 (or 1402), when, in an agreement with Vladimir Andreyevich the Brave, the grand prince granted Uglich to the Prince of Serpukhov and Borovsk (for text of this agreement, see *DDG*, pp. 43–45). In his testament (1401 or 1402), Prince Vladimir granted Uglich to his sons, Andrey and Vasiliy (text in *DDG*, pp. 45–51). Uglich is

lages, and with all its customs, and with Ustyuzhna, and with Rozhalovo, and with Veletovo, and with Kist'ma, and with all as it used to belong to Prince Dmitriy Shemyaka. And I give him Bezhyttski Verkh" [35] and with its volosts, and with its *puti,* and

mentioned neither in the Chronicles nor in the testaments again until 1433, although it is quite probable that it was granted to Prince Konstantin about 1421 at the time of the return of Konstantin from Novgorod and his reconciliation with his older brother, the grand prince (see *PSRL,* VIII, 98, and XXV, 245). In 1433 Uglich was in the hands of Konstantin, for in that year "his [Vasiliy II's] boyar, Ivan Dmitriyevich, fled from the grand prince to Prince Konstantin, to Uglech' and thence to Tfer'" (*PSRL,* XXV, 250). In 1434—about the time of the death of Prince Konstantin—in an agreement between Vasiliy II and Princes Dmitriy Shemyaka and Dmitriy the Fair, Uglich is mentioned as the "patrimonial principality of Prince Konstantin Dmitriyevich," which was granted to Shemyaka by the grand prince (text of this agreement in *DDG,* pp. 87–89). Shemyaka probably held Uglich until 1447, when that city was captured by partisans of Vasiliy II (*PSRL,* VIII, 120–121).

[35] Bezhetskiy Verkh, an important trading center located about 230 kilometers northwest of Moscow on the Mologa River, was one of the old cities of Novgorod the Great. Ivan Kalita seized Bezhetskiy Verkh from Novgorod in 1332 (*PSRL,* XXV, 170). Kalita apparently did not retain this town, however, because it is not mentioned in any of the testaments until the first testament of Vasiliy I (1406–1407), in which a village (Maksimovskoye) of Bezhetskiy Verkh District was willed to Princess Sofiya. Both the second and third testaments of Vasiliy Dmitriyevich make reference to the volost Kist'ma and the villages Ontonovskiye as "the acquisition of my great-grandfather [Ivan Kalita] in Bezhits'skii Verkh"." In 1397 Vasiliy I seized Bezhetskiy Verkh from Novgorod (*PSRL,* VIII, 70). In 1424, the year before his death, Vasiliy II took an oath to return Bezhetskiy Verkh to Novgorod (*PSRL,* VIII, 92). In 1433 Bezhetskiy Verkh was held by Prince Yuriy Dmitriyevich, who had received it from Vasiliy I (see the agreement of Grand Prince Vasiliy Vasil'yevich with the Prince of Galich, Yuriy Dmitriyevich, dated 1433, in *DDG,* pp. 75–80).

In 1434, following the death of Prince Yuriy Dmitriyevich, Grand Prince Vasiliy II granted Bezhetskiy Verkh to Prince Dmitriy the Fair, son of Yuriy of Galich (see *PSRL,* VIII, 99, and the agreement of Grand Prince Vasiliy Vasil'yevich with the Princes of Galich, Dmitriy Shemyaka and Dmitriy the Fair, the sons of Yuriy, dated 1434, in *DDG,* pp. 87–89). In 1435 Vasiliy entered into an agreement with Novgorod by which he relinquished Bezhetskiy Verkh (A. N. Nasonov and M. N. Tikhomirov, eds., *Novgorodskaya pervaya letopis' starshego i mladshego izvodov* [Moscow-Leningrad, 1950], p. 418).

with its villages, and with all its customs, and Zvenigorod [36] with its volosts, and with its *puti*, and with its villages, and with all its customs, and, near Moscow, the village Sushchev"skoye, and with the city courts that appertained to it. And Vysheles, with which his grandmother blessed him, now this too is his.

And I bless my son, Prince Boris,[37] with the "year" of Prince Ivan of Mozhaysk in Moscow [38] and with Mariya Fedorova's courts in the suburb [39] of the city [of Moscow] near the stone

---

In the year 1447, however, Bezhetskiy Verkh was apparently in the hands of the grand prince once more, for in that year he granted it to his cousin, Prince Ivan Andreyevich of Mozhaysk, who had deserted Shemyaka and come over to the side of the grand prince. Vasiliy II, however, soon took Bezhetskiy Verkh back from Prince Ivan (see *PSRL*, VIII, 122, and Ekzemplyarskiy, I, 177).

In an agreement concluded sometime between 1451 and 1456, Vasiliy II granted Bezhetskiy Verkh to Vasiliy Yaroslavich of Serpukhov and Borovsk (text of agreement in *DDG*, pp. 179–186). But when the grand prince seized Vasiliy Yaroslavich in 1456 and incarcerated him in Uglich, the holdings of the House of Serpukhov and Borovsk—including, presumably, Bezhetskiy Verkh—were incorporated into the Grand Principality of Moscow, i.e., Bezhetskiy Verkh ceased to be an *udel*, or patrimonial principality (see n. 19, above).

[36] Zvenigorod, part of the original patrimonial principality of Moscow, was bequeathed to Ivan the Fair by the testament of Ivan Kalita. Ivan the Fair left it to his son, Ivan the Younger. The latter died when still a child and Zvenigorod reverted to his older brother Dmitriy, who bequeathed it to his son Yuriy.

Although Yuriy willed Zvenigorod to his son, Vasiliy the Cross-Eyed, that city came back under the control of the grand prince (Vasiliy II) about 1434. Sometime between 1451 and 1456 Vasiliy II gave Zvenigorod to Prince Vasiliy Yaroslavich of Serpukhov and Borovsk. Zvenigorod must have reverted to the grand prince upon the imprisonment of Vasiliy Yaroslavich in 1456 (see *DDG*, pp. 74–75, 89–100, and 179–186; *PSRL*, VIII, 98–99; and n. 19, above).

[37] Boris, Prince of Volok, was the fourth surviving son of Vasiliy II. He was born in 1449 and died in 1494 (*PSRL*, VIII, 122 and 228).

[38] Concerning Prince Ivan Andreyevich of Mozhaysk, see n. 20, above.

[39] Mariya Fedorovna Koshkina-Goltyayeva was the second wife of Prince Yaroslav (Afanasiy) Vladimirovich of Serpukhov and Borovsk. She was the mother of both Princess Mariya (the wife of Vasiliy II) and Prince Vasiliy Yaroslavich, concerning whom, see n. 19, above.

Certain of Mariya Goltyayeva's properties were confiscated by Princes

Church of Saint Yegoriy.[40] And I give him Rzheva [41] with its volosts, and with its *puti*, and with its villages, and with its apiary, and with all its customs. And I give him Volok [42] with its

Dmitriy Shemyaka and Ivan Andreyevich of Mozhaysk in the course of their struggle with Vasiliy II (see *DDG*, pp. 140–142). In 1447 Ivan Andreyevich undertook to hand over to Vasiliy II the property of "Mariya Fedorova, the daughter of the son of Fedor," which he had seized (*DDG*, pp. 140–142 and 146–148).

The word rendered "suburb" in the passage above is *posad*. The *posad* was the area immediately adjacent to and outside the walled part of a Russian city. It was the area in which tradesmen and artisans carried on their work.

[40] The stone Church of Saint George (Yegoriy) was located in the Zaneglimen'ye, the area just west of the Kremlin beyond the Neglinnaya River (*PSRL*, VIII, 226).

[41] This is the first mention in the testaments of Rzheva (Rzhev), formerly an outlying city and volost of the Grand Principality of Tver'. It is located on the Volga, about two hundred kilometers west and slightly north of Moscow. Rzhev had come into the possession of Moscow during the reign of Vasiliy I, who in 1390 granted it to Vladimir Andreyevich of Serpukhov and Borovsk (*DDG*, p. 37). In an agreement concluded in 1401 or 1402, Vladimir Andreyevich relinquished Rzhev and Volok to Vasiliy I, in exchange for Uglich and Gorodets (*DDG*, p. 43). Following the death of Yuriy Dmitriyevich of Galich, Vasiliy II granted to Dmitriy Shemyaka "the patrimonial principality of Prince Konstantin Dmitriyevich, Rzhova and Uglich, with the Moscow shares" (*DDG*, p. 87). This indicates that Rzhev had been one of the holdings granted to Konstantin by Vasiliy I in accordance with a provision of the second testament of Dmitriy Donskoy. In 1447 Dmitriy Shemyaka relinquished his claims to "Ugleche with its volosts [and] Rzheva with its volosts" (*DDG*, p. 141).

Rzhev figures in a sworn writ (*krestotseloval'naya zapis'*) of Prince Fedor Vorotynskiy to Casimir, King of Poland and Grand Prince of Lithuania, dated February 5, 1448. In this writ Prince Fedor, speaking for his son-in-law Prince Ivan Andreyevich of Mozhaysk, promised King Casimir the city of Rzhev and the city of Medyn' if he undertook to aid the Prince of Mozhaysk in acquiring the Moscow princedom (*DDG*, p. 149).

[42] Although Volok (Volok Lamskiy, modern Volokolamsk) was mentioned in the second and third testaments of Vasiliy I ("And to my princess I also give . . . the villages Beleutovskiye in Volok"), this is the first time this city was bequeathed to a son of the Grand Prince of Moscow. Volok Lamskiy had apparently been in the possession of Ivan Kalita, for he granted it to the Kiev boyar, Rodion Nesterovich. In 1345

volosts, and with its *puti*, and with its villages, and with all its customs, and Ruza [43] with its volosts, and with its *puti*, and with its villages, and with its customs. And concerning that with which my mother, Grand Princess Sofiya, his [Boris'] grandmother, blessed him, [namely] the villages Beleutov"skiye in Volok, the village S"passkoye with its hamlets, and the villages Okorokav"skiye in Izdetemlya, now these are his. And concerning that which Mariya Fedorova Goltyayeva gave him, in Kolomna, the villages Proskurnikov"skiye and Veden'skiye with their hamlets, and the hamlet in Gorodnya, and in Moscow, the villages Rozsudov"skiye beyond the Pokhra, Zverev"skoye, and Boranov"skoye, and other small villages, with their hamlets and with their waste lands [*pustoshi*], and, in Volodimer', the villages Simizinskiye, and Lazar'skoye, and Kotyazino, and that which appertained to these villages which used to belong to

---

Grand Prince Semen Ivanovich, who had married Yevpraksiya, the daughter of Prince Fedor Svyatoslavich of Smolensk, granted Volok to that prince.

It is not known how Novgorod acquired Volok, but in 1398 Vasiliy I seized the city from the men of Novgorod (Ekzemplyarskiy, II, 354). In 1408 Grand Prince Vasiliy I gave Volok (along with Vladimir, Yur'yev Pol'skiy, and other cities) to Prince Svidrigaylo Keystut'yevich of Lithuania. This prince, however, returned to Lithuania in 1410 and his Russian holdings reverted to Moscow (Ekzemplyarskiy, II, 354, and *PSRL*, XXV, 237). Prince Boris Vasil'yevich was the first patrimonial prince (*udel'nyy knyaz'*) of Volok (Ekzemplyarskiy, II, 354).

[43] Ruza had been in the possession of the main line of the House of Moscow since the days of Ivan Kalita. It was bequeathed to Prince Yuriy of Galich by the second testament of Dmitriy Donskoy. Yuriy, in his testament, dated 1433, granted Ruza to his son Dmitriy Shemyaka (*DDG*, p. 73).

In an agreement concluded between Grand Prince Vasiliy II and Prince Vasiliy Yaroslavich of Serpukhov and Borovsk sometime between 1450 and 1454, the grand prince's possession of "that which I have taken away from my enemies, the sons of Yuriy, Prince Vasiliy [the Cross-Eyed] and Prince Dmitriy Shemyaka, [namely] Prince Yuriy's share in Moscow, with all its customs, and the entire patrimonial principality of my uncle, Prince Yuriy: his patrimony, Zvenigorod, and Ruza, and Galich" was confirmed. Vasiliy Yaroslavich undertook for himself and his sons to recognize these holdings as belonging to the grand prince and his sons (*DDG*, pp. 169 and 172).

Mariya [Goltyayeva], and the village Yevnut'yev"skoye near the city of Volodimer', and, in Kostroma, Nizhnyaya *sloboda* on the Volga, with all its hamlets, and Bazeyev"skoye, and Manuilovskoye, with their hamlets, and, in Vologda, Turanda-yev"skoye, and Ponizovnoye, and the villages Kobylinskiye, and Gorka, and the hamlets in Shoma, and near Moscow, the village Sharapovo with its hamlets, and Loshakovo with its hamlets, and the meadow on the Moskva River near Krutitsa, and, in Beren-deyeva, the village Rostovtsov"skoye with its hamlets, and, in Kinela, Surovtsovo, and Timofeyev"skoye, and Mikul'skoye, now these are his. And concerning that which Mariya [Goltyayeva] also gave him, [namely] her court in the city of Moscow, now this also is his.

And my son, Andrey the Younger,[44] I bless with Prince Petr Dmitriyevich's "year" in Moscow,[45] and [I give to him] the village Tanin'skoye near Moscow, with all [that appertained to it], and Yasenev"skoye, with all [that appertained to it], and Rameneitso, with all [that appertained to it]. And I give him Vologda,[46] and with Kubena,[47] and with Zaozer'ye,[48] and with all

---

[44] Andrey the Younger, called Prince of Vologda, was born in 1452 and died in 1481 (*PSRL*, XXV, 273 and 392).

[45] See Chapter 5.

[46] For the first time in the testaments Vologda is here granted outright to one of the sons of the Grand Prince of Moscow. Vologda, a city on the Vologda River about four hundred kilometers north and slightly east of Moscow, was part of the domains of Novgorod as early as 1265 (Ekzemplyarskiy, II, 364–369).

Vologda District was devastated by boyars of Vasiliy I in 1390 and again in 1398. It was again laid waste by the men of Moscow in 1401 and 1408. It is probable that Vologda passed back and forth between Moscow and Novgorod during the first third of the fifteenth century. Following the refusal of the younger brothers of Vasiliy the Cross-Eyed to support him in his bid for the Grand Princedom, the latter fled to Vologda "to the garrison of the grand prince" (*PSRL*, XXV, 252, under the year 1435). This would indicate that in 1435, at any rate, Vologda belonged to Moscow; otherwise it is improbable that the grand prince would have had a garrison there. Vologda was granted to Vasiliy II in 1447 by Dmitriy Shemyaka when the latter was grand prince (*PSRL*, XXV, 268, and Ekzemplyarskiy, II, 364–369).

[47] This is the first mention in the testaments of Kubena, a large area

that appertained to Vologda, and to Kubena, and to Zaozer'ye, and with their customs, and [I give him] Iledam with Obnora, and with Komela, and with Volochok, and Avnega, and Shilenga, and Pel'shma, and Bokhtyuga, and Ukhtyushka, and Syama, and Otvodnoye, with the villages Perfushkov''skiye, and Toshna, and Yangosar'', and with all that appertained to these volosts.

And to my princess I give Rostov with all that appertained to it, and with its villages [and it shall be hers] during her lifetime.[49] And the Rostov princes who managed [*vedali*] [Rostov] under me, the grand prince, now [they] shall hold [it] in the same manner under my princess, and my princess shall not interfere with them in this. And when God takes my princess, then my princess shall give Rostov to my son Yuriy, and he shall hold [it] in the same way in which his mother held it, so that the [Rostov] princes may manage that which is theirs and may hold it in the same manner [as that in which they held it under me]. And concerning her purchase, [namely] Prince Mikhail Deyev's burg, Romanov,[50] and [the holdings] of Prince Lev's children,[51] and [the village] of Prince Davyd Zasekin,[52] and Ust'-Shokstny,

---

lying northeast of Lake Kubenskoye to the north of the city of Vologda.

[48] Zaozer'ye, a part of Beloozero Principality, is mentioned here for the first time in the testaments. It is the area north of Lake Beloye.

[49] Concerning Rostov, see above, pp. 27–37 and 44–49.

[50] Prince Mikhail Deyev was a descendant of Prince Ivan Dey of Yaroslavl', who was the great-grandfather of Vasiliy Davidovich the Terrible, Prince of Yaroslavl' from 1321 to 1345. It is thought that the Deyev princes possessed a patrimonial principality not far from the city of Yaroslavl', where, at the close of the nineteenth century, their name was still preserved in the name of the village Deyevy Gorodishchi (Ekzemplyarskiy, II, 84, 89, and 98).

The burg Romanov, situated on the Volga above Yaroslavl', was built by Prince Roman Vasil'yevich, the third son of Vasiliy Davidovich the Terrible and an ancestor of Mikhail Deyev. Romanov *gorodok* may well have been the center of the patrimonial principality of Prince Roman (Ekzemplyarskiy, II, 89).

[51] Not identified.

[52] Prince Davyd Zasekin was a member of one of the lesser lines of the House of Yaroslavl'. He was the son of Ivan Zaseka, the son of Fedor, the son of Gleb, the second son of Prince Vasiliy Davidovich the Terrible of

which she purchased from Prince Semen and Prince Vasiliy Shokhonskiy,[53] now these are hers [and] my children shall not interfere with her in them. And concerning the volosts Zavolskiye [54] and the volosts along the Shok"stna River that used to belong to Prince Ivan of Mozhaysk, and his villages and weirs, now I have given all these volosts, and villages, and the hamlets of these villages, and the weirs to my princess, along with the villages of Petr Konstantinovich,[55] and Ust'-Ugly, with all [that appertained to it], and with the weirs. And I give my princess Nerekhta with its salt works, and with all its customs. And from among the Moscow villages I give to my princess Naprudskoye near the city, and with the city courts that appertained to it, and Khodyn'skaya Mill with Khodynskiy Meadow, and, after the death of Princess Vasilisa,[56] Nogatin'skoye [shall pass] to my

Yaroslavl' (Ekzemplyarskiy, II, 100). He was a distant cousin of Prince Ivan Dey, concerning whom, see n. 50, above.

[53] Princes Semen and Vasiliy Shekhonskiy were sons of Afanasiy-Andrey Ivanovich, the grandson of Prince Roman Vasil'yevich of Yaroslavl' (see n. 50, above). They were joint possessors of the Sheksna (Shekhonskoye) Principality, a petty principality that had been detached from the Principality of Yaroslavl'. The name is derived from the Sheksna River (see Ekzemplyarskiy, II, 119–120).

[54] That is, the "volosts beyond the Volga."

[55] Petr Konstantinovich Dobrynskiy was one of the three brothers—the other two were Ivan Konstantinovich and Nikita Konstantinovich—who held the office of grand lieutenant (*bol'shoy namestnik*) of Moscow during the reign of Grand Prince Vasiliy II. The Dobrynskiy brothers were not steadfast in their allegiance to Vasiliy but at times acted with his enemies. It was Nikita Konstantinovich who, with Prince Ivan Andreyevich of Mozhaysk, seized Grand Prince Vasiliy at the Trinity Monastery in 1446 (see *PSRL*, XXV, 265; *DDG*, p. 493; Cherepnin, *Russkiye feodal'nyye arkhivy*, II, 293–300; Tikhomirov, *Srednevekovaya Moskva v XIV–XV vekakh* [Moscow, 1957], pp. 174–177). Concerning the office of grand lieutenant, see "Servants of the Prince" in Chapter 5.

[56] Princess Vasilisa, the sister of Vasiliy II, was married to Prince Aleksandr Ivanovich Bryukhatyy in 1418 (see above, Text 7, n. 18). Bryukhatyy died the same year and Vasilisa was immediately married to Prince Aleksandr Danilovich Vzmeten', the son of Daniil Borisovich of Suzdal'–Nizhniy Novgorod. Prince Aleksandr is mentioned only once in the Chronicles, on the occasion of his marriage to Princess Vasilisa (see Ekzemplyarskiy, II, 441).

princess with its courts and with all that appertained to it, and Novinki. And I give to my princess the villages Ozerets'skiye with their hamlets, and Mikhalev''skoye with its hamlets, and Oleshnya with its hamlets. And concerning that which I took from my princess and gave to the [Monastery of the] Holy Trinity, the village Selivanovskoye in Medushi, now I give to my princess, in place of this, my villages Luzhskiye, and Pavshinskoye, and Petr Konstantinov's hamlets on the Istra.[57] And from the patrimonial principality of my son Ivan, from Kolomna, I give to my princess the volosts Gorodok, Brashova, and with the small village Gvozdna and with Ivan', and Ust'-Merska, and Pesochna, and the villages Malinskiye. And I give to my princess the village Serkizovskoye, with Mezynka, and with all its small villages and hamlets, and the village Vyso-koye with its hamlets and with its apiary, and the village Shkin' with its hamlets, and with the small village of Fedor, the son of Stepan,[58] and with my purchase Sverbeyev''skoye, and the village Lystsovskoye with its hamlets, and Babyshevo near the city of Kolomna which my mother, the grand princess, gave to her, and with the city courts that appertained to it, and the village Chyukhistovo, which Mikhailo Fedorovich Saburov'' gave to her,[59] with all that appertained to it. And in Pereslavl' I

[57] Concerning Petr Konstantinovich, see n. 55, above.

[58] Fedor, the son of Stepan (Fedor Stepanov *syn*), is identified merely as the owner of a patrimonial estate (*DDG*, p. 506).

[59] Chyukhistovo, a village of Kolomna District, was granted to Princess Sofiya Vitovtovna by the third testament of Vasiliy I.

Mikhail Fedorovich Saburov was a boyar in the service of Prince Dmitriy Shemyaka. He entered the service of Grand Prince Vasiliy II in the following manner: Shemyaka released Vasiliy from imprisonment in Galich in September 1447, and granted Vologda to the latter as his patrimony. In December of the same year a group of Vasiliy's sup-porters, commanded by the boyar Mikhail Pleshcheyev, entered and seized Moscow. Shemyaka and his ally, Prince Ivan Andreyevich of Mozhaysk, who were in Volok Lamskiy, hearing of the fall of Moscow to the supporters of Vasiliy, the defection of large numbers of people to the latter, and the advance of Vasiliy against them with "great forces," fled to Galich and thence to Chukhloma, where they seized Vasiliy's mother, Sofiya Vitovtovna. From Chukhloma they retreated farther, to Kargopol', taking Princess Sofiya with them. Vasiliy and his allies cap-

give to my princess the village Ryuminskoye with its city courts, and Marinina *sloboda*, and the village Dobroye, with the city courts, which courts appertained to the chief of the *put'* [*putnik*]. And in Yur'yev I give to my princess the village Frolovskoye with Yelokh, and the village Krasnoye, and Kurchevo, and Yeltsi, and Varvarino, and Kuzmedem'yanskoye, and Golenishchovo, and Dobryn'skoye, and Vol"stinovo, and Sorogoshino, and Petr Konstantinov's [villages],[60] Matfeishchovo and Vorogovo, and with the other small villages. And in Suzdal' I give to my princess Shokshov and Davydovskoye. And in Kostroma I give her Mikhail Danilov's villages, with all that appertained to them. And concerning that which Mikhail Saburov gave to her, [namely] the villages Koldom"skiye, now these are hers. And in Ustyug I give my princess, in addition to her purchase—Levont'yev"skoye, and Pyatnitsskoye, and Vondokur'ye—my villages, the village Moshem"skoye, with its hamlets, and with its small adjoining settlements [*prisel'ye*], and Dymko's Land,[61] with its hamlets and with its small adjoining settlements. And from the patrimonial principality of my son, Andrey the Elder, I give to my princess Yelda, and Kadka, and Vasilkovo, with their hamlets. And from the patrimonial principality of my son Boris, I give to my princess Izdetemlya, and Iyudina *sloboda*, and Yadrovo, and, in Rzheva, the village Ondreyev"skoye. And from the patrimonial principality of my son, Andrey the Younger, I give to my princess Iledam, with Komela, and with Obnora. And if God takes away my princess, then the volosts and villages of my sons that I have given her shall

---

tured Galich and proceeded to Yaroslavl'. From this city Vasiliy sent an emissary (Vasiliy Fedorovich Kutuzov) to Shemyaka in Kargopol', asking him to free Princess Sofiya. This Shemyaka agreed to do. "And with her [Sofiya] Prince Dmitriy sent his boyar Mikhail Fedorovich Saburov. . . . And Mikhail Saburov, with the others, having made obeisance to the grand prince, did not return to Shemyaka, but remained with the grand prince to serve him" (*PSRL*, XXV, 267–269).

[60] See n. 55, above.

[61] Dymkova *storona*, Ustyug district. It is difficult to determine the exact English equivalent of *storona*. Although the word literally means "side," it is also used in the sense of "land," "parts," "district," "locality," or even "country."

be theirs, except for her purchases. And concerning her purchases, the burg Romanov, and Shokstna, and other volosts and villages—no matter in which cities they be[62]—in these my princess is free: after her death, to whichever of her sons she wants to give, now to that one shall she give.

And concerning my Moscow *tamga*, now I give to my son Ivan a third of the *tamga*, with all the customs, and [I give] the second third—Prince Vladimir's—to my son[s], Yuriy and Andrey the Elder, each a half, and the third third I give to my son[s], Boris and Andrey the Younger, each a half. And from all these three thirds, I have given to my princess a half of the *tamga* and [a half] of all the customs, during her lifetime, and, upon her death, then [she] shall give to them [her sons] their shares in accordance with this testament, as it is [herein] allotted to them.

And I give to my princess, from Novgorod Nizhniy, a half of all my customs as my mother, the grand princess, had, and the villages which belonged to my mother, the grand princess, with all their customs, and with that which appertained to them, and with the village Sokolovskoye, and with Kerzhenets. And from Murom I give to my princess the small village Muromskoye, and Shatur", and in this my children shall not interfere.

And when my children begin to live from their patrimonial principalities, then my princess, and my son Ivan, and my son Yuriy, and my [other] children shall send census takers [*pistsy*], and their census takers shall take an inventory of their patrimonial principalities, kissing the cross,[63] and on the basis of this inventory they shall assess taxes according to plows and according to people,[64] and on the basis of this assessment my princess

---

[62] Probably the meaning here is "no matter in which *districts* they be." In the testaments the name of the principal city of a district or principality was often used to refer to the entire district or principality. For instance, from this testament: "And from the patrimonial principality of my son Boris, I give to my princess Izdetemlya . . . and, in Rzheva, the village Ondreyev"skoye."

[63] *Po kr[e]stnomu tselovan'yu.*

[64] *Po sokham i po lyudem.* A *sokha* was a type of wooden plow used in old Russia. Here, however, the word is used in the sense of a taxable unit of land. According to the *Nikon Chronicle,* "when a man plows with three horses with the help of two laborers, this is one *sokha.*" The

and my children shall also give toward Tartar tribute [*vykhod*] to my son Ivan, from their patrimonial principalities. And if God should bring about a change concerning the Horde, then my princess and my children shall take tribute [*dan'*] for themselves from their patrimonial principalities, and my son Ivan shall not interfere in this.

And wheresoever I have given to my princess volosts and villages in the patrimonial principalities of my children, no matter in whose they be, now these volosts and villages shall appertain to my princess in tribute and in the tax on the dispensing of justice [*sud*], and my children shall not interfere in this.

And my princess shall judge her volost administrators, and *villici*, and *tiuns*, and somlers, and criminal investigators.

And those of my children to whom I have given villages, no matter in whose patrimonial principality they be, now he to whom they are given shall dispense justice in these villages.

And those of my villages which I give as grants to my princes, or boyars, or junior boyars, or even if I give them as their purchase, now these my villages [shall pass] to my children, [to him] in whose patrimonial principality they are, now they are his.

And if the patrimony of one of my sons is taken away from him because of his sins, then my princess shall take away from the patrimonial principalities of her [other] sons and shall fill out his patrimony, and my children shall not escape her will.

And my son Ivan I bless with the cross of Petr the Wonder-Worker,[65] and the golden cross of Paramsha, and the Cap, and

---

amount of land that four men could work without a horse was, according to the *Novgorod Chronicle*, one *sokha*. Most likely the Moscow *sokha* of the fifteenth century was similar to the Novgorod *sokha*. The number of people to a *sokha* was probably about twenty (see George Vernadsky, *The Mongols and Russia* [New Haven, 1953], pp. 229–230).

[65] Petr, called the Wonder-Worker, was metropolitan from 1308 until 1326. He spent more time in Moscow than in Vladimir and was well disposed towards Ivan Kalita. In 1326 Petr laid the foundation of the Cathedral of the Dormition of the Holy Mother of God, the first stone church in Moscow, where he was afterwards buried. He was later canonized (see S. M. Solov'yev, *Istoriya Rossii s drevneyshikh vremen*

the shoulder pieces of the grand prince with holy images, and the box decorated with carnelian, and the large golden belt with precious stones.

And my son Yuriy I bless with the icon of Philotheus,[66] and with the golden cross with which my mother, the grand princess, blessed me, and with the golden belt on red leather.

And my son Andrey the Elder [I bless with] Prince Dmitriy the Younger's golden cross with a small chain.[67]

And my son Boris I bless with the golden cross with which my mother, the grand princess, blessed me when I went to my patrimony, Novgorod the Great.[68]

And my son Andrey the Younger I bless with the golden icon with emeralds.

And I commit my princess, and my son Ivan, and Yuriy, and my younger children to my brother Casimir, King of Poland and Grand Prince of Lithuania,[69] according to our agreement, [and I commit them] to God and to him, my brother, [and] thus he shall care for my princess, and my son Ivan, and my [other] children.

And my children I have committed to my princess. And you, my children, obey your mother in all things and do not go against her will in anything. And that son of mine who does not obey his mother but goes against her will, on him my blessing shall not be.

And you, my children, honor and obey your oldest brother, Ivan, in place of me, your father. And my son Ivan shall hold his

---

[Moscow, 1959–1966], II, 229–230). In admonishing Ivan Kalita to build this church, it is reported that Petr said: "If thou, son, obey me [and] build the Temple of the Most Pure Mother of God, and if thou give me rest in your city, then thou shalt be glorified above other princes, and thy sons and grandsons and this city will be renowned, and the holy fathers [*svyatiteli*, 'archiereis'] will live in it, and it will subject to itself all the other cities" (quoted in Solov'yev, II, 230).

[66] See above, Text 7, n. 21.

[67] Prince Dmitriy the Younger, or the Fair (1421–1441), the youngest son of Prince Yuriy Dmitriyevich of Zvenigorod and Galich.

[68] This is the first time in the testaments that Novgorod is referred to as the patrimony of the grand prince.

[69] Casimir IV (1427–1492).

brother Yuriy, and his [other] younger brothers in brotherliness, without injustice.

And those of my boyars who serve my princess or live in the patrimonial principalities of my children, now my children shall, as one, protect these boyars.

And my treasurers, or any of my secretaries who administer my income for me, or my *villici*, or my *tiuns*, or anyone who is married to them, now they are all of no concern of my princess or of my children.

And concerning him who violates this my testament, now in the words of the Gospel, he who disobeys his father and mother and does not follow their commandments shall die the death.[70]

And present at the [writing of this] testament sat my spiritual father, Archimandrite Trifon of [the Monastery of] the Saviour,[71] and Archimandrite Afanasiy of [the] Simonovo [Monastery],[72] and my boyars, Prince Ivan Yur'yevich,[73] and Ivan Ivanovich,[74] and Vasiliy Ivanovich,[75] and Fedor Vasil'yevich.[76]

And my secretary, Vasiliy Beda, wrote this document.[77]

[70] Cf. Mark 7:10.

[71] *Arkhimandrit spas'skii Trifon*. The Monastery of the Saviour, connected with the Church of the Transfiguration of the Saviour (Spasa Preobrazheniya), was located in the Kremlin. It was the court monastery of the grand princes of Moscow (Tikhomirov, *Srednevekovaya Moskva*, pp. 187–188).

[72] The Monastery of the Most Pure One in Simonovo in Moscow was founded in the latter half of the fourteenth century by Fedor, the son of Stepan, the nephew of Saint Sergiy of Radonezh, in a village called Simonovo—at that time outside Moscow (Tikhomirov, *Srednevekovaya Moskva*, p. 190).

[73] Prince Ivan Yur'yevich Patrikeyev, son of Yuriy Patrikeyevich, one of the attestants to the wills of Vasiliy I (see Solov'yev, II, 446).

[74] Perhaps Ivan Ivanovich Ryapolovskiy (see Solov'yev, II, 446).

[75] Perhaps Prince Vasiliy Ivanovich Obolenskiy (see Solov'yev, II, 446).

[76] Perhaps Prince Fedor Vasil'yevich of Tarusa (see Solov'yev, II, 447).

[77] Below appears the signature: "Humble Feodosiy, Archbishop of All Rus'."

TEXT 10

Codicil to the Testament
of Vasiliy II

Commentary

THIS codicil must have been written shortly after the writing of the testament of Vasiliy II, i.e., sometime between May 3, 1461, and March 27, 1462.[1]

The original of this document is preserved in the Central State Archives of Ancient Acts (TsGADA) in Moscow, along with the original of the testament of Vasiliy II. A copy of the codicil, dating from the second half of the fifteenth century, is preserved in the same place.[2]

From the face of the original there are suspended two black-wax seals: one of Grand Prince Vasiliy Vasil'yevich and the other of Metropolitan Feodosiy.[3]

The translation which follows is based on the text of the codicil to the testament of Grand Prince Vasiliy Vasil'yevich as printed in *DDG*, pp. 198–199.

THE CODICIL TO THE TESTAMENT OF GRAND PRINCE VASILIY II VASIL'YEVICH

IN the name of the holy and life-giving Trinity, the Father, the Son, and the Holy Ghost, and with the blessing of our father Feodosiy, Metropolitan of All Rus', lo I, the much sinning, poor

[1] See Commentary to Text 9.

[2] See *DDG*, p. 199, and Commentary to Text 9, above, for collections in which this codicil has been previously printed.

[3] *DDG*, p. 119.

slave of God, Vasiliy, being of sound mind, write this codicil to my testament [*dushevnyaya pripisnaya gramota*], having written my large testament, giving the arrangement [*ryad*] to my princess and my children. And concerning that which I did not write in my testament, now I have written in this codicil.

I give to my princess my village Kolomen'skoye with its hamlets and that which appertained to it, and the village D'yakovskoye, which I acquired by exchange from Princess Vasilisa,[4] with everything [that appertained to it], and the small village Khvostovskoye near the city of Moscow, with the city courts [*dvory*] which appertained to it, and the meadow of Prince Yuriy Dmitriyevich [5] opposite my court, and with the meadow of Yuriy's treasurer [6] which Mikhailo Saburov [7] gave to her. And although I bequeathed Marinina *sloboda* to my princess in my large testament, concerning the two *stans* and the village Ortem'yev"skoye with its hamlets, and concerning the beekeepers, and concerning the beaver trappers, and the enrolled people [*chislyaki*], nothing was written, now I also give these two *stans* to my princess [in addition] to Marinina *sloboda*. And I give to my princess, in Pereyaslavl', Gorodishche with the hamlets Volninskiye, and Barmazovo with its hamlets, and, in Murom, I give to her Pochap, and Zakolp'ye, and Chersevo, and that which appertained to it. And, in Kolomna, I give her the village Oksin'skoye with its hamlets. And that which Anastasiya Fedorova Andreyevicha [8] gave me as [my] purchase, the village Myachkovo with its hamlets, now she shall keep during her lifetime, and that which her daughter, Arina Alekseyeva, the wife of Ignat'yevich,[9] gave me as [my] purchase, her villages on the Moskva River, are also [hers] during her lifetime, and these villages of Anastasiya and Arina [shall pass] to my princess after

---

[4] The sister of Vasiliy II (see above, Text 9, n. 56).

[5] Prince Yuriy Dmitriyevich of Zvenigorod and Galich, the uncle of Vasiliy II.

[6] *I s' Yur'yev"skim lugom kaznacheyevym.*

[7] See above, Text 9, n. 59.

[8] That is, Anastasiya, the wife of Fedor Andreyevich, the owner of a patrimonial estate.

[9] That is, Arina, the wife of Aleksey Ignat'yevich, the owner of a patrimonial estate.

their death. And my princess shall, in accordance with my purchase documents, pay to them the price of these villages in memory of their souls to whomever they order shall receive [it] after their death. And, in Mozhaisk, I give my princess the village Chertanovskoye with its hamlets and with its city courts, and Belevitsi with its hamlets, and the village Ismeiskoye with its hamlets, and the mill near Mozhaisk city on the Moskva River, which her *villicus*, Vasyuk, set up for her. And that which Anna Vasil'yevna, the wife of Ivanovich,[10] gave me, [namely] her Murom villages and her villages in Votskii Starodub,[11] with the lakes and with all their advantages,[12] now this I also give to my princess. And I give to my princess Dolmat Yur'yev's villages in Khotun', and in Rostunova, and in Peremyshl', with the hamlets of these villages, and with all that appertained to them, [and] in these villages [my princess] is free: she may give them to whomever she desires after her death.

And those junior boyars who serve my princess, and her servants, and all her people, her slaves, and those to whom I, the grand prince, give my villages, or [those] to whom my princess

[10] That is, Anna, the wife of boyar Prince Vasiliy Ivanovich (Obolenskiy?), one of the attestants to the testament of Vasiliy II (see above, Text 9, n. 75, and *DDG*, pp. 439 and 487).

[11] Starodub, here called Votskii Starodub, was a small principality on the Klyazma River, about 250 kilometers east and slightly north of Moscow. In 1363 Ivan Fedorovich, Prince of Starodub, was driven from his principality by the men of young Prince Dmitriy Ivanovich of Moscow, and Andrey—the brother of Ivan—became prince in Starodub. Prince Ivan had supported or at least sympathized with Prince Dmitriy Konstantinovich of Suzdal' in the latter's attempt to obtain the patent to the Grand Principality. From this date the Starodub princes were subordinate to the grand princes of Moscow. The Principality of Starodub in the course of time broke up into a number of smaller principalities, the most important being Ryapolovo, the center of which was located about thirty kilometers northeast of Starodub. Its princes were called the Starodub-Ryapolovo princes; they were active supporters of Vasiliy II in his struggle with Dmitriy Shemyaka (see A. V. Ekzemplyarskiy, *Velikiye i udel'nyye knyaz'ya severnoy Rusi v" tatarskiy period", s" 1238 po 1505 g.* [St. Petersburg, 1889], II, 174–199).

[12] That is, fields, pastures, meadows, forests, rivers, stone quarries, etc. The Russian word used here is *ukhody*. See below, Text 13, for a like term (*ugozh'i*) in the testament of Ivan IV.

has given her villages, and those who have their patrimony or purchase: concerning these people my princess is also free in all things and [she is free] in these villages, and my children shall not interfere in this.

And concerning the court [*dvor*] of Prince Ivan of Mozhaysk in Moscow, now I give it to my son Ivan. And concerning the court of Prince Vasiliy Yaroslavich,[13] [the court] of Prince Vladimir, which is behind [the Cathedral of] Mikhail the Archangel,[14] now I give it to my son Yuriy. And concerning the court which his grandmother gave him by [the Church of] Saint Ivan the Precursor,[15] now I give that court to my princess. And I give the courts of Prince Dmitriy Shemyaka to my son Andrey the Elder. And the court of Petr, and Ivan, and Nikita, the sons of Konstantin,[16] by [the Church of] the Holy Nativity [of the Most Pure One],[17] and my courts that are outside the city, [that are] my patrimony, or purchase, [or] acquisition, and my gardens: now in these courts my princess is free, [and] to whichever of my children she gives [them], they are his.

And concerning that which my mother, the grand princess,

[13] See above, Text 9, n. 19.

[14] *Za arkhangilom Mikhailom*, 'behind [the Cathedral of] Mikhail the Archangel.' An alternate translation is "belonging to [the Cathedral of] Mikhail the Archangel." If the latter translation is adopted the reference may be to the "large court [*dvor*] of Vladimir Andreyevich on the Three Hills," located north of the Moskva River, just west of the Presnya River (see M. N. Tikhomirov, *Srednevekovaya Moskva v XIV–XV vekakh* [Moscow, 1957], map opposite p. 288). If the translation "behind [the Cathedral of] Mikhail the Archangel" is adopted, the reference could not be to the "large court of Vladimir Andreyevich," as the Cathedral of Mikhail the Archangel was in the Kremlin.

[15] The Church of Saint Ivan the Precursor was located by the Borovitskiye Gates. There had been a wooden church here, but in 1461 Vasiliy II laid the foundation of a stone church of the same name (*PSRL*, XXV, 277).

[16] See above, Text 9, n. 55.

[17] There were apparently two churches of the Nativity of the Holy Mother of God in the Kremlin. One was on the Truba, a ditch or drain in the southwestern part of the Kremlin (Tikhomirov, *Srednevekovaya Moskva*, p. 18). The other, founded by Grand Princess Yevdokiya Dmitriyevna in 1393, was in the court of the grand prince (*PSRL*, VIII, 64, and XXV, 448).

gave to Fedor Basenok,[18] in Kolomna, [namely] her village Okulovskoye, and Repinskoye, and [on the basis of the fact that] she wrote in her testament that in these villages I, her son, am free,[19] now these villages [shall], after the death of Basenok, also [pass] to my princess.

And at [the writing of] this codicil sat: my spiritual father, Archimandrite Trifon,[20] and my boyars, Prince Ivan Yur'yevich [21] and Fedor Mikhaylovich.[22]

And my secretary, Vasiliy Beda, wrote this document.[23]

[18] Fedor Vasil'yevich Basenok, boyar and voivode of Moscow, was a staunch supporter of Vasiliy II in the struggle against Dmitriy Shemyaka. In February 1446, when Vasiliy was seized at Trinity-Sergiy Monastery, blinded in Moscow, and imprisoned in Uglich, Basenok refused to swear allegiance to Shemyaka, who ordered him placed in chains. Basenok escaped and made his way to Kolomna, whence, having first plundered the Kolomna lands, he fled to Lithuania to join Prince Vasiliy Yaroslavich (Serpukhov-Borovsk), another of Vasiliy's loyal supporters. Vasiliy Yaroslavich granted Bryansk, which he had received from Casimir of Poland, to Prince Semen Ivanovich Obolenskiy and Fedor Basenok. In 1447 Basenok was among those who returned to Russia to help Grand Prince Vasiliy. Basenok and Prince Ivan Vasil'yevich Striga were in command of Grand Prince Vasiliy's garrison in Kostroma when Shemyaka launched his unsuccessful attack against that city in the spring of 1449. Basenok was one of the commanders of the detachment that the grand prince sent to Ustyug against Shemyaka in 1452. It was Fedor Basenok who defeated an invading band of Tartars commanded by the son of Khan Sedi-Akhmet in 1455. Once more accompanied by Ivan Vasil'yevich Striga, Basenok occupied and sacked the town of Staraya Rusa during Prince Vasiliy's campaign against Novgorod in 1456 (*PSRL*, XXV, 266, 268, 270, 272, and 274, and VIII, 144).

[19] "And concerning my two villages, Okulov'skoye and Repin'skoye, which I have previously given [here the document is torn with about four letters missing], now both these villages of mine [shall pass] to my son, Grand Prince Vasiliy, [and] in them he is free" (from the testament of Grand Princess Sofiya Vitovtovna in *DDG*, p. 176).

[20] See above, Text 9, n. 71.

[21] Prince Ivan Yuryevich Patrikeyev (*DDG*, p. 502).

[22] Probably Fedor Mikhaylovich Chelyadnin (see S. M. Solov'yev, *Istoriya Rossii s drevneyshikh vremen* [Moscow, 1959–1966], II, 447).

[23] Below appears the signature: "Humble Feodosiy, Archbishop of All Rus'" (*DDG*, p. 199).

TEXT 11

Testament of Ivan III

Commentary

IVAN III, later called the Great, was the oldest son of Grand Prince Vasiliy II and Grand Princess Mariya Yaroslavna. He was born in 1440 and succeeded his father as Grand Prince of Vladimir and Moscow upon the death of Vasiliy II in 1462. Ivan III ruled until his death in 1506. The chronicler, writing of the death of Ivan, refers to him as "Grand Prince Ivan Vasil'yevich of All Rus'."[1]

The testament of Ivan III was written sometime between the end of 1503 and June 16, 1504. In it the grand prince granted Ruza to his son Yuriy. Ruza had been the patrimonial principality of Prince Ivan Borisovich, the cousin of Ivan III, who died late in 1503. In his testament Ivan Borisovich granted Ruza to Ivan III.[2] Evidence that the testament of Ivan III was written prior to June 16, 1504, is contained in two agreements concluded between the sons of the grand prince, Vasiliy and Yuriy, on that date. In these agreements mention is made of the testament of "our father, the grand prince."[3]

It is possible to date the testament even more precisely. In the last week of April 1504, Prince Yuriy Ivanovich granted a charter to certain lands in Dmitrov District to the Moscow metropolitanate. This indicates that the testament of Ivan III was written prior to this date, for Dmitrov was part of the inheritance of Prince Yuriy. Thus the testament of Ivan III was written some-

---

[1] *PSRL*, VIII, 108, 150, and 245.

[2] *PSRL*, VIII, 244. For the text of the testament of Ivan Borisovich, see *DDG*, pp. 351–353.

[3] For text of these agreements, see *DDG*, pp. 366–369.

time after the death of Prince Ivan Borisovich of Ruza late in 1503 and before the last week of April 1504.[4]

The original of this testament has been lost. It was probably either destroyed in 1533 by Ivan's son, Vasiliy III, when the latter destroyed his own testament, or lost during the political struggles which occurred during the minority of Ivan IV. A copy of the testament of Ivan III, dating from the early sixteenth century, is extant and is preserved in the Central State Archives of Ancient Acts (TsGADA) in Moscow, Section I, Heading 1, No. 34.[5]

The following notation appears on the reverse of the first page of the copy of Ivan III's testament: (in script of the sixteenth century) "Copy of the testament of Grand Prince Ivan Vasil'yevich of All Rus'," (in script of the seventeenth century) "in the days of Simon, Metropolitan of All Rus', but in what year the testament was written, this is not recorded." [6]

The testament of Ivan III has been previously printed in N. I. Novikov, ed., *Drevnyaya Rossiyskaya Vivliofika*, (2nd ed.; Moscow, 1788–1791), Part 2, No. 123; in *Prodolzheniye Drevney Rossiyskoy Vivliofiki* (St. Petersburg, 1786–1801), Part 5; in *Sobraniye gosudarstvennykh gramot i dogovorov, khranyashchikhsya v Gosudarstvennoy kollegii inostrannykh del* (Moscow, 1813), Part 1, No. 144; and in other collections.[7]

The translation which follows is based on the text of the testament of Ivan III as printed in *DDG*, pp. 353–364.

THE TESTAMENT OF GRAND PRINCE IVAN III VASIL'YEVICH

IN the name of the holy and life-giving Trinity, the Father, and the Son, and the Holy Ghost, and with the blessing of our father Simon, Metropolitan of All Rus', lo I, the much sinning and poor

---

[4] See L. V. Cherepnin, *Russkiye feodal'nyye arkhivy, XIV–XV vv.* (Moscow-Leningrad, 1948–1951), I, 220–221, for the dating of this testament.

[5] Cherepnin, *Russkiye feodal'nyye arkhivy*, I, 220, and *DDG*, p. 364.

[6] *DDG*, p. 364.

[7] *DDG*, p. 364.

slave of God, Ivan, while living and of sound mind, write this testament. I give this arrangement [*ryad"*] to my sons: to my son Vasiliy,[8] and to my younger children, Yuriy, Dmitriy, Semen, [and] Andrey.[9]

I commit my younger children, Yuriy and his brothers, to my son and their older brother, Vasiliy. And you, my children—Yuriy, Dmitriy, Semen, Andrey—hold my son and your older brother, Vasiliy, in the place of me, your father, and obey him in all things. And you, my son Vasiliy, hold your younger brothers, Yuriy and his brothers, in honor, without injustice.

I bless my oldest son, Vasiliy, with my patrimony, the grand principalities, with which my father blessed me and which God gave me. And I give to him the city of Moscow with its volosts, and with its *puti*, and with its *stans*, and with its villages, and with all its city courts [*dvory*], and with its *slobodas*, and with its *tamga*, and with the tax on weighing, and with the tax on measuring dry-measure goods, and with the tax on trading in the market place, and with the tax on trading stands, and with the tax on merchants' courts, and with all its customs, and with the village Dobryatinskoye, and with its apiary, and with *Vasiltsovo*

[8] Vasiliy Ivanovich, the second son of Grand Prince Ivan, was the first son (b. 1479) of the grand prince and Sofiya Paleolog (*PSRL*, VI, 33). Vasiliy became Grand Prince of Moscow and Vladimir before the death of his father. In 1502, "on April 14 . . . Grand Prince Ivan Vasil'yevich of All Rus' favored his son Vasiliy, blessed [him] and constituted him autocrat in the Grand Principality of Vladimir and Moscow, with the blessing of Simon, Metropolitan of All Rus'" (*PSRL*, VI, 48). Upon Ivan's death in 1506, Vasiliy succeeded his father as Grand Prince of All Rus'. He died in 1533 (*PSRL*, VI, 244, and XXVI, 315).

[9] Yuriy Ivanovich, called Prince of Dmitrov, was born to Grand Prince Ivan and Grand Princess Sofiya in 1480. He died in 1536 "in confinement" (*PSRL*, XXV, 327, and VIII, 292).

Dmitriy Ivanovich Zhilka, Prince of Uglich, was born to Ivan and Sofiya in 1482. He died in 1521 (*PSRL*, VIII, 213 and 269).

Semen Ivanovich was born on March 21, 1487, and died on June 26, 1518. He was called Prince of Kaluga (*PSRL*, VIII, 217 and 263).

Andrey Ivanovich, Prince of Staritsa, was born to Ivan and Sofiya on August 5, 1490 (*PSRL*, VIII, 219). He died in 1536 (A. V. Ekzemplyarskiy, *Velikiye i udel'nyye knyaz'ya severnoy Rusi v" tatarskiy period", s" 1238 po 1505 g.* [St. Petersburg, 1889], II, Genealogical Table).

sto, and with the enrolled people, and with the *ordyntsy*.[10] And my children, Yuriy, Dmitriy, Semen, [and] Andrey, shall not interfere with the enrolled people and *ordyntsy* of my son and their older brother, Vasiliy, in any way: [they] shall not interfere in their lands, or in their waters, and they shall not do them injustice in anything.

And to him [Vasiliy] I also give the small village Semchinskoye with its city courts, and with Sam"sonov" Meadow, and the village Vorob[']yevo, and with Volodimerovskoye, and with Semenovskoye, and with Vorontsovskoye, and with Kadashovo, and with all their hamlets, as it was under me. And to him I also give the small village Vorontsovskoye on the Yauza, where my court [*dvor*] is, with all the city courts along both sides of the Yauza, and with the mills, as it was under me, and Lyshchykovo Monastery,[11] with its courts, and Il'inskaya *slobodka*, with all that I obtained by exchange from Andronnikov Monastery.[12]

[10] See Chapter 4.

[11] This is the first mention in the testaments of Lyshchykovo Monastery, which was located in Moscow District (*DDG*, p. 542).

[12] The Andronnikov (or Androniyev) Monastery of the Saviour (*Spasskiy Andronnikov Monastyr'*) was founded by Aleksey, who was metropolitan from 1353 to 1377. Its first abbot, from whom it received its name, was the monk Andronik, a disciple of Sergiy of Radonezh. The monastery was located east of the Kremlin on the southern shore of the Yauza River opposite the village Lutsinskoye (M. N. Tikhomirov, *Srednevekovaya Moskva v XIV–XV vekakh* [Moscow, 1957], pp. 188–190 and map facing p. 288).

An interesting story relates the origin of the church in this monastery: Metropolitan Aleksey, returning from a trip to Constantinople, found himself in a fierce storm at sea. During this storm he promised God that if the ship were delivered safely he would found a church in honor of the saint on whose day the ship came to shore. The storm abated and the ship came safely into harbor on August 16, the Third Day of the Saviour in the Russian Orthodox calendar; to be exact, the Day of the Translation of the Icon of the Saviour Not Made by the Hand of Man (*Pereneseniye nerukotvorennogo obraza Spasa*). Subsequently, Metropolitan Aleksey established a church in the Andronnikov Monastery and named it for the Translation of the Icon of the Saviour Not Made by the Hand of Man (*PSRL*, XI, 31–32).

And my son Vasiliy shall maintain his grand lieutenant [13] in Moscow as of old and as it was under me, and he shall maintain another lieutenant in Moscow in Prince Vladimir Andreyevich's third [14] which was given to my brothers, Yuriy and Andrey.[15]

And concerning those my courts within the city of Moscow, and outside the city in the suburbs, and all my gardens [*sady*], and my vacant places about the suburbs, now all [shall pass] to my son Vasiliy. And concerning those my courts within the city of Moscow, and outside the city, which are in the possession of my boyars, and princes, and junior boyars, and my court men, and palace people, and equerries, and my master artisans, now all these courts [shall pass] to my son Vasiliy also. And those boyars, and princes, and junior boyars who have their courts in Moscow within the city, or in the suburbs outside the city, [courts which are their] patrimony or purchase, or [concerning] those to whom I give permanent charters of grant,[16] to courts in Moscow within the city, or about the suburbs outside the city, now my son Vasiliy shall not interfere in these their courts.

And concerning those Moscow volosts which were attached to Dmitrov: Rogozh, Vorya, Korzenevo, the burg Sherna, Sulishin, with the village Novoye, now I give these volosts to Moscow with all [that appertained to them] as of old [and they shall pass] to my son Vasiliy. And I also give him the volosts Surozhyk, and Luchinskoye, and Radonezh [17] with its volosts,

This church was founded about 1367. The present stone church that stands on the site of the wooden original is of later construction (Tikhomirov, *Srednevekovaya Moskva*, p. 190).

[13] The grand lieutenant (*bol'shoy namestnik*) was the principal judicial officer of the grand prince (see Chapter 5).

[14] Concerning the Moscow thirds, see Chapter 5.

[15] Yuriy Vasil'yevich had died in 1473, leaving no children. Andrey Vasil'yevich had died in prison in 1494, and his sons had been imprisoned (see above, Text 9, n. 23).

[16] *Gramoty zhalovalnyye prochnyye.*

[17] Radonezh, located about sixty kilometers north and slightly east of Moscow, had been part of the patrimony of the princes of Serpukhov and Borovsk (Ekzemplyarskiy, II, 297 and 303). It probably came into the possession of the grand prince of Moscow at the time of the incarceration of Prince Vasiliy Yaroslavich (see above, Text 9, n. 19).

and with its *puti*, and with its villages, and with all its customs, and a third of Mushkova [Gora] with Lopskiy *myt*.[18]

And I give him the city of Kolomna with its volosts, and with its *puti*, and with its villages, and with all its customs, the city of Koshyra, with Zarech[']ye, which is beyond the Oka River, Teshilov, and Roslavl', and Venev, and M"stislavl',[19] and the other localities along the Ryazan' border with their volosts, and with their *puti*, and with their villages, and with all their customs, and with Yelech,[20] and with all the Yelech localities, [and] the city of Serpokhov, and Khotun['] with its volosts, and with its *puti*, and with its villages, and with all its customs, [and] the city of Torusa, with Gorodets,[21] and with Iskan', and with Myshega, and with Kolodna, and with Princess Avdot'ya's patrimony,[22] [and] the city of Mchenesk"[23] with its volosts, and with its villages, and with all its customs, with all that appertained to it.

[18] The word *myt* (*myto*), 'toll,' was also used to refer to the place where the *myt* was collected. Lopskiy *myt* was in Moscow District.

[19] The cities of Teshilov, Roslavl', Venev, and Mstislavl' were all confirmed as part of the Principality of Moscow by the truce concluded between Moscow and Lithuania in 1492. For the text of this truce, see *DDG*, pp. 329–332.

[20] Yelech (Yelets) was a principality located along the Bystraya Sosna River, a right tributary of the Don. Yelets city is located about 350 kilometers south of Moscow. On the east the Yelets Land bordered on the Grand Principality of Ryazan', on the west it bordered on the Verkhovskiye principalities (i.e., those of the upper Oka River region), on the north it was contiguous with the territory of the upper Don River which was claimed by both Moscow and Ryazan', and on the south it bordered on the Wild Plain (*dikoye pole*). It was semidependent on Moscow as early as 1463 (see map, below).

[21] Torusa (Tarusa) and Gorodets (Serpukhovskiy) were both among the lands of Prince Andrey the Younger, the brother of Ivan III. Upon the death of Andrey, who left no children, these two cities apparently escheated to the Grand Principality. Tarusa is located just southwest of Serpukhov; Gorodets was "near Serpukhov" (Ekzemplyarskiy, II, 373).

[22] Princess Avdot'ya (Yevdokiya) was the wife of Dmitriy Donskoy. For the holdings bequeathed to her by her husband's second testament, see above, Text 5.

[23] Mchenesk" (Mtsensk), a city on the upper Oka about 280 kilometers south and slightly west of Moscow, was formerly part of the Grand

And to him I also give the city of Vorotynesk",[24] with La-ginsk, and with Kraishino, and with other localities, with all that used to belong to the Vorotynskiy [princes]. And concerning that which I gave up to Prince Mikhail Mezetskoy in exchange for his share of Meschesk",[25] [namely] Oleksin in Starodub, now this he shall hold in accordance with the charter of exchange, but [the administration of] justice and [the collection of] tribute shall be my son Vasiliy's.

And the Novosil', Odoyev, and Belev princes,[26] with their children, and with their patrimonies, and that which appertained to their patrimonies [shall pass] also to my son Vasiliy, to our Grand Principality.

And to my son Vasiliy I also give the city of Borovesk" with its volosts, and with its *puti*, and with its villages, and with all its customs, and with Sukhodol", and with Ist'ya, and with Isterva, and with the village Krasnoye, and with Kremenets, and with Pesochna Bolshaya, and with the *slobodka* Osna on the Shana which Vasiliy Karamyshev settled, the city of Yaroslavets" with its volosts, and with its *puti*, and with its villages, and with all its customs, with all as it used to belong to Prince Mikhail Andre-

---

Principality of Lithuania. It was ceded to Moscow by the Truce of March 25, 1503, concluded between Grand Prince Aleksandr of Lithuania and Grand Prince Ivan III (S. M. Solov'yev, *Istoriya Rossii s drevneyshikh vremen* [Moscow, 1959–1966], III, 122).

[24] Vorotynsk, on the upper Oka about 175 kilometers southwest of Moscow, was one of the petty principalities near the Moscow-Lithuanian border that vacillated between the two great principalities. In 1490 Prince Ivan Mikhaylovich of Vorotynsk entered the service of the Grand Prince of Moscow (see Ekzemplyarskiy, II, 251).

[25] Meschesk" (Meshchovsk), another former Lithuanian city and principality, was located about fifty kilometers southwest of Vorotynsk. In 1493 Prince Mikhail Romanovich Mezetskoy entered the service of Ivan III (*PSRL*, VIII, 227).

[26] The Novosil', Odoyev, and Belev principalities were located along the upper reaches of the Oka; they were among the Verkhovskiye principalities. According to the Truce of 1494 between Lithuania and Moscow, Novosil', Odoyev, and Belev were confirmed as belonging to Moscow (text in *DDG*, pp. 329–332). Concerning the entry of the Odoyev and Belev princes into the service of Moscow, see Solov'yev, III, 93–95.

yevich,[27] [and] the city of Medyn['], and Radoml', and with Veshki along the Ugra, and the *sloboda* on the Shana which Tovarkov settled, also along the Ugra, and with Pesochna Menshyaya with its *slobodas* which Andrey Kart"mazov and Mitya Zagryazskoi and Ivashko Gladkoi settled. And concerning the villages and hamlets of Filipp Poltev's children on this side of the Ugra, now these villages and hamlets with all that appertained to them [shall be attached to] Medyn' [and shall pass] to my son Vasiliy also.

And I also give him the city of Mozhayesk" with its volosts, and with its *puti*, and with its villages, and with all its customs, and with Chyagoshch", and with Tur'yevo, and with Orekhovna, and with Mogilno, and with Michenki, and with Shatesh['], and with Sulidovo, and with Dmitrovets, along both sides of the Ugra, and with the other places that appertained to them, [and] the city of Vyazma,[28] and Kozlov, with their volosts, and with their villages, and with all their customs, with all that appertained to Vyazma, and to Kozlov, and to all the Vyazma localities, as it was under me.

And to my son Vasiliy I also give the city of Dorogobuzh [29] with its volosts, and with its villages, and with all its customs, with all that appertained to it, and the Dorogobuzh volosts [are]: Pogorelaya, Negomle, Khotomichi, Kholm", Byatino,

[27] Yaroslavets (Maloyaroslavets, west of Serpukhov) was presented to Prince Mikhail Andreyevich of Vereya at the time of his marriage to Yelena, daughter of Prince Yaroslav Vladimirovich of Serpukhov-Maloyaroslavets, which took place no later than 1448. In 1484 Mikhail Andreyevich and Grand Prince Ivan III concluded an agreement in which Mikhail was forced to promise that he would bequeath his patrimony—Maloyaroslavets—to the grand prince; Mikhail's son Vasiliy had defected to Lithuania in 1484 (see Ekzemplyarskiy, II, 307–333). In his testament dated "about 1486," Prince Mikhail Andreyevich did bequeath Yaroslavets to Grand Prince Ivan III (*DDG*, p. 301).

[28] Vyazma was in effect ceded to Moscow by the Truce of 1494 between Moscow and Lithuania (*DDG*, p. 330).

[29] Dorogobuzh, on the Dnieper east of Smolensk, was seized from Lithuania by Russian forces under the boyar Yuriy Zakhar'yevich in the spring of 1500. It was near Dorogobuzh that the battle on the Vedrosha Brook took place on July 14, 1500; this was an important victory for the Muscovites (*PSRL*, VIII, 239–240).

Prost', the small village Zaop'ye, Vodosa, Nekrasova, Selechna, Kremena, Redyn['], along the mouth of the Uzha, Koskovo, Rekhty, Khomchichi, Vyshkovo, Vasilevo, the village of Yeska Klimov, the *slobodka* of the bishop in Chert"kovo, the small village Putyatino with its hamlets, Igumnova, M"stislavets", Oshchytov, Zhulin, Moshkova Gora, the burg Luchin, Velikoye Pole, Lopatino, Kopylea and Uzhytsa, Vedrosh['], and Ozerishcha, [and] Serkovy Luki, with all that appertained to Dorogobuzh and to these volosts and villages, as it was under me.

And to my son Vasiliy I also give the city of Pereaslavl' with its volosts, and with its *puti*, and with its villages, and with all its customs, and with Sol'. And concerning the Pereaslavl' volosts that were attached to Dmitrov, [namely] Serebozh, R[o]zh[e]stvenoye, [and] B[us]kutovo, now I give these volosts to Pereyaslavl', with everything [that appertained to them] as of old, [and I give them] to my son Vasiliy.[30]

And to him I also give the city of Volodimer' with its volosts, and with its *puti*, and with its villages, and with all its customs, and with the small village Muromskoye, and with Shatur, and with Kolushka, and with Vysheles, and with Ostrov, [and I also give him] the city of Yur'yev with its volosts, and with its *puti*, and with its villages, and with Velikaya Sol', and with all its customs, [and] the city of Suzdal['] with its volosts, and with its *puti*, and with its villages, and with all its customs, and Soltsa Malaya both halves, [and] the city of Rostov [31] with its volosts, and with its *puti*, and with its villages, and with all its customs,

[30] Or, perhaps: "now I give these volosts in addition to Pereyaslavl', with everything [that appertained to them] as of old, to my son Vasiliy." The original reads: "i yaz te volosti dayu k" Pereyaslavlyu s vsem po starine s[y]nu svoyemu Vasil[']yu" (*DDG*, p. 355).

[31] It is possible that the editors of *DDG* have not punctuated this passage correctly and that a comma should follow Soltsa Malaya, rather than "both halves." In such a case, the translation would read ". . . both halves [of] the city of Rostov." It is more probable, however, that the scribe made an error and wrote "both halves" before the "city of Rostov" instead of after it. If this is the case, then the translation would read, quite understandably: ". . . and Soltsa Malaya, [and] the city of Rostov, both halves."

and with Sol', [and] the city of Yaroslavl' [32] with its volosts, and with its *puti*, and with its villages, and with all its customs, and with Ukhra, and with the village Petrovskoye, and with its hamlets, and the *slobodka* Okhlyabininskaya, and with the *myto*, and Prince Vasiliy Shchetinin's patrimony, Kast', with everything [that appertained to it], and Inopazh and Seltso, and with the weir which is on the Volga near Rybnaya *sloboda* opposite Inopazh and Seltso. And the Yaroslavl' boyars and junior boyars, with their patrimonies and with their purchases, shall not leave [the service of] my son Vasiliy to go to anyone, anywhere. And concerning those who leave, their lands [shall pass] to my son, but he shall not interfere in the lands of them that serve him, nor [shall he interfere in the lands] of their wives, or of their children. The city of Romanov burg with its volosts, and with its *puti*, and with its villages, and with all its customs [shall also pass to my son Vasiliy].

And to my son Vasiliy I also give Ust'-Shok"stny, along both sides [of the Sheksna River, and] the *pogosts*,[33] and with the hamlets of Prince Vasiliy and Prince Semen Shokhonskiy,[34] and with the weirs, and with the fishing places, and with all the customs, as it was when my mother, the grand princess,[35] owned it, and Prince Ivan Andreyevich's volosts Zavolzh"skiye [36] along

[32] "That same year [6971/1463] the Yaroslavl' princes ceded their patrimony to Grand Prince Ivan Vasil'yevich, through the efforts of Aleksey Poluyekhtovich, the secretary of the grand prince" (*Ustyuzhskiy letopisnyy svod* [*Arkhangelogorodskiy letopisets*], text prepared by K. N. Serbina [Moscow-Leningrad, 1950], p. 85). Ekzemplyarskiy, citing the *Novgorod Fourth Chronicle*, suggests that the Yaroslavl' princes ceded their patrimony to the grand prince for a "fitting remuneration" (II, 95). L. V. Cherepnin questions the validity of the notion that the Yaroslavl' princes ceded their patrimony to Ivan III in 1463, pointing out that Yaroslavl' does not begin to figure in agreements among the princes before 1473 (*Obrazovaniye russkogo tsentralizovannogo gosudarstva v XIV–XV vekakh* [Moscow, 1960], pp. 825–826).

[33] Concerning the term *pogost*, sometimes used in the sense of "volost," see Chapter 3.

[34] Concerning the Shokhonskiy (Shekhonskiy) princes, see above, Text 9, n. 53.

[35] Mariya Yaroslavna.

[36] See above, Text 9, n. 20.

both sides of the Shokstna River, and the villages and hamlets
that belonged to my mother, the grand princess, and the volosts
Shokhonskiye, Lukoves['], Arbuzhoves['], Matkoma, Vereteya
Bolshaa, the burg Knyazhychi, Pes[']ye village, Vsesvyattskoye,
Volskoye, with the village Okishovskoye, and with Vonguy,
Patrobal, Runai, and with Shagat', and with the *slobodkas* Keshtoma and Shelshedam, the village Beloye, Shygorash, with the
other volosts, and with the villages, and with the hamlets, and
with the weirs, and with the fishing places, and with all the
customs, with all that used to belong to my mother, the grand
princess, and with the villages and hamlets of Petr Konstantinovich,[37] and also the volosts of my grandmother, Grand Princess Sofiya, in Shokstna, Ust'-Ugly and Vereteika Malaya, now
these volosts with their weirs, and with their fishing places, and
with all their customs [shall pass] to my son Vasiliy also.

And to my son Vasiliy I also give the city of Beloozero[38] with
its volosts, and with its *puti*, and with its villages, and with all its
customs, with all as it was under me, [and] the city of Vologda
with its volosts, and with its *puti*, and with its villages, and with
all its customs, and Zaozer'ye, and with Kubena[39] with its volosts, and with its *puti*, and with its villages, and with all its
customs, [and] the city of Ust'yug with its volosts, and with its
puti, and with its villages, and with all its customs, and Vychegda, and Vym', and Udora, and Sysola, and with all their
localities, and in the Zavolottskaya Land, Rostovshchina, Pinega,

[37] Petr Konstantinovich Dobrynskiy. See above, Text 9, n. 55.

[38] Beloozero was willed to Prince Andrey Dmitriyevich of Mozhaysk by
the second testament of Dmitriy Donskoy. Upon the death of Prince
Andrey his patrimony was divided into two parts: his oldest son, Ivan,
received Mozhaysk; his second son, Mikhail, received Vereya and Beloozero; and some of the Beloozero volosts passed to Grand Prince Ivan
III. Upon the death of Prince Mikhail his entire patrimony passed into
the hands of Ivan III in accordance with the provisions of an agreement
concluded between the two princes on December 12, 1483 (see
Ekzemplyarskiy, II, 173 and 333). For the text of the December 12, 1483,
agreement, see *DDG*, pp. 293–295.

[39] Vologda, Zaozer'ye, and Kubena were bequeathed to Prince Andrey
the Younger by the testament of his father Vasiliy II (see above, Text 9,
nn. 46–48).

and Kegrola, and Chyakola, Pr'm"skiye, Mezen['], Nem"yuga, Pil[']i Gory, Pineshka, Vyya, Toima, Kir'i Gory, Yem"skaa Gora on the Vaga, with everything [that appertained to them], and Ontonova Brewery, Korbolskoi Island, Shogogora, Kerchela, Sura Poganaa, Lavela, with the other localities that appertained to these volosts, and Yugra and Pechera, with everything, and Perm' Velikaya,[40] with everything, and the city of Kostroma, and with Ples, and with Nerekhta, and with Iledam, and with its volosts, and with its *puti*, and with its villages, and with all its customs, [and] the city of Galich with its volosts, and with its *puti*, and with its villages, and with all its customs, and with Sol', and with Unzha, and with Chyukhloma, and with everything that from of old appertained to Galich, and to Unzha, and to Chyukhloma, and [I give my son Vasiliy] Novgorod Nizhnei with its volosts, and with its *puti*, and with its villages, and with all its customs, and with the Mordva, and with the Cheremisa,[41] which appertained to Novgorod. And those villages and hamlets in Novgorod Nizhnei which are in the possession of my princes, and boyars, and junior boyars—to whomsoever they belong—now all these [shall pass] to my son Vasiliy also.

And I also give to him the city of Murom with its volosts, and

[40] The area formerly known as Velikaya Perm' included the basins of the Kama, Kolva, and Vichera rivers, north of the present city of Perm'. Its center was Cherdyn', at the confluence of the Kolva and Vichera.

Velikaya Perm' had been a volost of Novgorod the Great. In 1472 Grand Prince Ivan III sent Prince Fedor Davydovich Pestryy "as voivode to Velikaya Perm'." That same year "there came news from Perm' that the voivode, Prince Fedor Davydovich Pestryy, had taken the Velikaya Perm' Land and had delivered it into the hands of the grand prince, and the army was intact, and [this news arrived] on the 26th day of June" (*Ustyuzhskiy letopisnyy svod*, p. 90).

[41] The Mordva and Cheremisa were peoples of Finno-Ugric stock whose descendants, known respectively as Mordvins (Mordvinians, Mordovians, and Marii), still inhabit the area south (Mordvins) and northeast (Marii) of Gor'kiy (see James S. Gregory and D. W. Shave, *The USSR, A Geographical Survey* [New York, 1946; first published in London, 1944], p. 166; see also the section "Ethnic Groups," p. 724 of the article "Russia" in *Encyclopaedia Britannica* [Chicago, 1959], XIX, 682–746).

with its *puti,* and with its villages, and with all its customs, and with the Mordva, and with the Cheremisa, which appertained to Murom, and the Meshchera [42] with their volosts, and with their villages, and with all that appertained to them, and with Kosh-kovo, and all the Mordva princes,[43] with their patrimonies, [shall pass] also to my son Vasiliy.

And to my son Vasiliy I also give all the Vyatka Land, its cities, and its volosts, and with everything that appertained to it, and with the Arsk princes,[44] as it was under me.

And concerning that which I granted to Prince Fedor Ivano-vich Belskiy,[45] that which I gave to him as his patrimony, the city

[42] The Meshchera were a Finno-Ugric tribe. Their descendants (Mesh-cheryaks, or Meshchers) have either been Russified or have amalgamated with Bashkirs. Some of the Mordvins called themselves Meshchers. Their name is preserved in the city of Meshchovsk, Kaluga district (see *Encyclopaedia Britannica,* XV, 287). The Meshchera inhabited the area adjacent to the northeast border of the Principality of Ryazan'. The principal city of the Meshchera area was Gorodets Meshcherskiy (Kasi-mov) on the Oka River.

[43] The Mordva princes had served the princes of Suzdal'–Nizhniy Novgorod in their struggle against Moscow. For example, in 1410 the Mordva princes participated in a campaign with the princes of Suz-dal'–Nizhniy Novgorod against Prince Petr Dmitriyevich (*PSRL,* XV, 485).

[44] The Arsk (Votyak) princes were brought to Moscow in 1489, following the subjugation of Khlinov (Vyatka) by the forces of Ivan III. The grand prince favored them, however, and permitted them to return to their land, which was, of course, then subject to him (see Ekzemplyarskiy, II, 243). The town of Arsk on the Kazanka River northeast of Kazan' still exists. The descendants of the Votyaks (a Finnish people now called Udmurts) are concentrated in the Udmurt Autonomous Soviet Socialist Republic which is located between the Vyatka and Kama rivers northeast of Kazan'.

[45] In 1482 Prince Fedor Ivanovich Bel'skiy left the service of Casimir of Lithuania and fled to Moscow, having been implicated in an unsuccessful plot to "take away from the grand prince land along the Berezynya." Fedor was received by Ivan III, who granted him Demon (Deman in Novgorod?) and the Novgorod volost of Moreva. In 1493 Bel'skiy was involved in a plot to murder Ivan III and was exiled to Galich, although he was apparently later reinstated in Ivan's favor. In 1498 he was married in Moscow to the daughter of Anna (the sister of Ivan III and Princess of Ryazan'). Bel'skiy was dispatched to Kazan' in 1499 to command an

of Lukh with its volosts, and the Vichyuga volosts, and Kineshma, and Chikhachev, now if Prince Fedor and his children serve my son Vasiliy, then they shall hold their patrimony as it was under me. And if Prince Fedor or his children should leave [the service of] my son Vasiliy [and should go over] to my younger children, or to anyone whomsoever, then this his patrimony, Lukh with these volosts, [shall pass] to my son Vasiliy.

And my son Vasiliy I also bless with my patrimony, the Grand Principality of Tfer': [46] I give him the city of Tfer['], and Goroden with its volosts, and with its *puti*, and with its villages, and with all the customs in the localities which our land surveyor, Prince Fedor Alabysh, assigned to Tfer', [and] the city of Klin with its volosts, and with its *puti*, and with its villages, and with all its customs, in those places which our land surveyor, Petr Loban Zabolottskoi, assigned [to Klin], except for that which I have given in exchange to my nephews—Boris' children, Fedor and Ivan—from the Tfer' Land, [namely] Buigorod and Kolp', [47] and in this my son Vasiliy shall not interfere. And concerning the service princes in the Moscow Land and in the Tfer' Land, now these princes shall all serve my son Vasiliy, and they shall hold their patrimonies as they did under me. And concerning those service princes who leave [the service of] my son Vasiliy [and go over] to my younger sons, or to anyone whomsoever, now the patrimonies of these princes [shall pass] to my son Vasiliy.

And my son Vasiliy I also bless with my patrimony, the Grand Principality of Novgorod: [48] I give him Novgorod the

---

army to support the "tsar" of Kazan' (Ivan's appointee) against an attack by Agalak, a prince of the Shibanskaya (Tyumen') Horde (see Ekzemplyarskiy, I, 252, 270, and 274).

[46] Concerning the manner in which the Grand Principality of Tver' came into the possession of Ivan III in 1485, see Solov'yev, III, 43–45; Ekzemplyarskiy, II, 512–515; and *PSRL*, VIII, 216–217.

[47] In 1407 Fedor and Ivan, the sons of Boris Vasil'yevich, Prince of Volok Lamskiy, petitioned their uncle, Ivan III, to grant them villages in Tver' that would be nearer their patrimonial principality in exchange for the Moscow villages that Mariya Goltyayeva had given to their father. Ivan III granted their request and gave them the volosts Buygorod and Kolp'. For the text of this grant, see *DDG*, pp. 341–344.

[48] Concerning the manner in which Novgorod the Great finally came

Great, with everything [that appertained to it], with its five fifths,[49] with its volosts, and with its *pogosts*, and with its *puti*, and with its villages, and with all its customs, and with the cities of Ivangorod, Yam city, Kopor[']ye city, Oreshok city, Ladoga city, Deman city, Kur"gorod, Porkhov city, Vysokoi city, Koshkin city, [and] Rusa city. And I have given him all these cities with their volosts, and with their *pogosts*, and with their *puti*, and with their villages, and with all their customs, and [I have given him] the city of Torzhok[50] with its volosts, and with its *puti*, and with its villages, and with all its customs. And, also in the Novgorod Land, I give him the city of Kholm", and Velilya, and Buyets", and Lopastitsi, and with other localities, with everything that appertained to them, and the city of Luki Velikiye with its volosts, and with its *pogosts*, and with all its customs, and the [Velikiye] Luki volosts [are] Pupovichi, Vyaz, Chyaspla, Korotai, Dubno, [and] Komsha, and with the other localities which appertained to them, and Rzheva Pustaya

---

into the possession of Ivan III, see Solov'yev, III, 9–36, and *PSRL*, VIII, 166–199.

[49] The territory of Novgorod the Great (except for the Novgorod lands in the far north and northeast) was divided into five areas called *pyatiny*, 'fifths.' They were the following: (1) the Vodskaya *pyatina* was the area stretching north of the city of Novgorod to Lake Ladoga, a narrow strip along the western shore of Lake Ladoga, and a small area north of the lake; (2) the Obonezhskaya *pyatina* extended northeast from the city of Novgorod, around both sides of Lake Onega, and reached the White Sea north of Lake Vyg; (3) the Shelonskaya *pyatina* was the area west of the city of Novgorod, extending almost to Pskov and including Ivangorod in the northwest; (4) the Derevskaya *pyatina* was the area southeast of the city of Novgorod, with its eastern boundary the Msta River and extending almost to Torzhok in the southeast and including Kholm in the southwest; and (5) the Bezhetskaya *pyatina* was east of the city of Novgorod, with its western boundary the Msta River, reaching almost to Ustyuzhnya and Bezhetskiy Verkh in the east, and bordering on the Obonezhskaya *pyatina* in the north. These boundaries are those of 1462.

[50] Torzhok, also called Novyy Torg (New Market), was an old trading town on the Tvertsa River, sixty kilometers northeast of Tver'. It was for long a "minor city" (*prigorod*) of Novgorod the Great. Although occupied by the forces of Vasiliy I in 1393, Torzhok was not finally incorporated into Muscovy until 1478 (*PSRL*, XXV, 220, 311, and 319).

with its volosts, and with its *pogosts,* and with all its customs, and [I give him] all the Korelskaya Land, Korelskoi city with its volosts, and with its *pogosts,* and with all its customs, with all that appertained to the Korelskaya Land, and with the Forest Lop['], and with the Wild Lop'.[51] And to my son Vasiliy I also give all the Zavolottskaya Land, Onego, and Kargopole, and all Poonezh'ye, and the Dvina, and the Vaga, and the Kokshenga,[52] and the *pogost"* Velskoi, and Kolmogory, and all the Dvinskaya and Zavolottskaya lands.

And my son Vasiliy I also bless with my patrimony: I give him the city of P"skov, and with its cities, and with its volosts, and with its villages, and all the P"skov Land.[53]

And to my son I also give the city of Toropets" with its volosts, and with its *pogosts,* and with its villages, and with all its customs, with all that appertained to it, and the [Toropets] volosts are Dankovo, Lyubuta, Dubna, Rozhna, Tura, Biberevo, Startseva, Nezhelskaa, Velizhskaa, Plaveyettskaa, Zhyzhettskaa, Ozerskaa, [and] Kazarinovskaa. And I also give him the city of Ostreye with its volosts, and with all that appertained to it, and the volosts Berezai, Nevle, Usvai, Lovtso, Vesnebologo, with everything that appertained to Toropets", and to Ostreye, and to these volosts, as it was under me.

And that which my sister's son, Prince Fedor Vasil'yevich of Ryazan', gave me, his patrimony, his share in the city of Ryazan', and in the suburb [*posad*], and Staraya Ryazan['], and Perevitebsk", with their volosts, and with their *puti,* and with their villages, and with their apiaries, and with their *tamga,* and with all their customs, as he shared them with his brother, Prince Ivan, now this his patrimony, his share in the city of Ryazan' and in the suburb, and Staraya Ryazan['], and Perevitesk", with

[51] The Forest Lop' (*Lop' leshaya*) and the Wild Lop' (*Dikaya Lop'*) were Finnish tribes.

[52] Ivan III was referring to the Northern Dvina River. The Vaga is a left tributary of the Northern Dvina. The Kokshenga is a right tributary of the Vaga.

[53] Pskov was nominally independent of Moscow until 1510 (see *PSRL,* VIII, 251). Concerning the incorporation of Pskov into the Russian state, see N. N. Maslennikova, *Prisoyedineniye Pskova k russkomu tsentralizovannomu gosudarstvy* (Leningrad, 1955).

their volosts, and with their *puti*, and with their villages, and with their apiaries, and with their *tamga*, and with all their customs, with all as it used to be in the possession of Prince Fedor, I give to my son Vasiliy.[54]

And I bless my son Vasiliy and my younger sons, Yuriy, Dmitriy, Semen, [and] Andrey, with Prince Konstantin Dmitri-yevich's "year" in Moscow, which was given to my brother Yuriy, and with Prince Petr Dmitriyevich's "year," which was given to my brother Andrey the Younger, and with Prince Mikhail Andreyevich's "year." And my son Vasiliy and my younger sons, Yuriy and his brothers, shall keep their lieutenants [*namestniki*] in Moscow during these "years," replacing one another every five years in the "years."

And concerning that which was given to my brother Boris, [namely] Prince Ivan Andreyevich's "year" in Moscow, now that "year" passed to the sons of my brother Boris, each of them

---

[54] Anna Vasil'yevna, the sister of Ivan III, married Grand Prince Vasiliy Ivanovich of Ryazan' in 1464. Two sons and one daughter were born of this marriage: Ivan Vasil'yevich (1467–1500), Grand Prince of Ryazan' from 1483 to 1500; Fedor Vasil'yevich *Tretnoy* (1483–1503); and a daughter (name unknown) who was married to Prince Fedor Ivanovich Bel'skiy (concerning whom, see n. 45, above). By an agreement concluded between Grand Prince Ivan Vasil'yevich of Ryazan' and his younger brother in 1496, Prince Fedor agreed that upon his death, if he had no children, his patrimony would pass to his older brother. It is not known under what circumstances he gave his patrimony to his uncle, Ivan III, rather than to his nephew Ivan Ivanovich, the son of the Grand Prince of Ryazan' (Ekzemplyarskiy, II, 600–605).

The "city of Ryazan'," as used here, obviously refers to the main city of the principality, Pereyaslavl' Ryazan'skiy (modern Ryazan'). The time at which this city became the principal city of the grand principal-ity is not known; it may have superseded Staraya Ryazan' as early as the thirteenth century, following the Tartar invasion (Ekzemplyarskiy, II, 567–568).

Staraya Ryazan' was located on the Oka River, opposite the modern town of Spassk Ryazanskiy and near the point where the Pronya River joins the Oka. It was the original center of the Grand Principality of Ryazan' and is first mentioned in the Chronicles under the year 1096 (*PSRL*, XXV, 16).

Perevitebsk (Perevitesk, Perevitsk) was located on the Oka River, about midway between Pereyaslavl' Ryazanskiy and Staraya Ryazan'.

keeping his lieutenant in Moscow every sixth year; and my brother's son Ivan gave his "half-year" to me, and I give his "half-year" to my son Vasiliy, and my brother's son Fedor and my son Vasiliy shall hold that "sixth year" each for half a year [at a time]: my son Vasiliy shall keep his lieutenant for half a year, and my brother's son Fedor shall keep his lieutenant for a half a year also.[55]

And to my younger sons, Yuriy and his brothers, I give within the city [of Moscow], the courts of Petr, and Ivan, and Nikita, the sons of Konstantin,[56] near the [Church of the] Nativity of Christ, and the court of Prince Aleksandr Obolenskiy, and the court of Vasiliy Saburov, and the court of Prince Vasiliy, and [the court] of the children of Prince Fedor Vasil'yevich Obolenskiy, and the court of Prince Ivan Striga, and the court of Ivan Borisov, and [the court] of the two children of Ivan Vladimirovich Semenov, and [the court] of Ivan the son of Mikhail Semenov, and the court of Grigoriy Baba, and the court of Vasiliy Tuchkov, and where my master tailors Nozdrya and Kuznetsov and Ushak" live along Novaya Street, which street goes from the square [57] to the Frolovskiye Gates: now from the square along those places where a picket fence has been erected,[58] now my children, Yuriy and his brothers, shall divide these places equally among themselves.

And to my son Yuriy I give, in Moscow, the small village Sushchovo, with its courts in the city and in the suburb, and to those places in which I have given him these city courts, now [to these places] I have given him a deed with my seal and with the signature of my secretary. And from among the Moscow villages I give him the village Lytkino with its hamlets.

And to my son Dmitriy I give, in Moscow, the small village Naprudtskoye, with its courts in the city and in the suburb, and to those places in which I have given him these city courts, now [to these places] I have given him a deed with my seal and with

[55] For a discussion of the holding of Moscow by thirds and "years," see Chapter 5.

[56] Concerning the brothers Dobrynskiy, see above, Text 9, n. 55.

[57] Not identified. Perhaps Red Square.

[58] *Po kaa mesta kol'ye bito.*

the signature of my secretary. And from among the Moscow villages I give him the [two] villages Ozerettskiye, Staroye and Novoye, with their hamlets.

And to my son Semen I give, in Moscow, the small village Lutsinskoye, with the mill and with the kennel, and the *slobodka* of Prince Vasiliy Romodanovskiy, and to those places which I have given him, the *slobodka* and the small village, now I have given him a deed with my seal and with the signature of my secretary. And from among the Moscow villages I give to him the villages Ruzsudovskiye beyond the Pokhra, Zverevo and Boranovo, with their hamlets, which I acquired by exchange from the children of my brother Boris.[59]

And to my son Andrey I give, in Moscow, beyond the river, the *slobodka* Kolychevskaya and the Monastery of the Nativity of the Most Pure One in Golutvino, and to those places that I have given him, the *slobodka* and the monastery, I have given him a deed with my seal and with the signature of my secretary. And from among the Moscow villages I give him the village Yasenevo, and the village Saryyevo, and Yudino, with their hamlets.

And from the Moscow *tamga* and from all the customs, my son Vasiliy shall give to my children, his younger brothers, Yuriy and his brothers, each one hundred rubles every year: to Yuriy one hundred rubles, to Dmitriy one hundred rubles, to Semen one hundred rubles, [and] to Andrey one hundred rubles.

And concerning that which I have given to my children, Yuriy, Dmitriy, Semen, [and] Andrey, [namely] "years" in Moscow during which they keep their lieutenants [there], and [concerning] the courts [that I have given to] them within the city, and concerning the small villages that I have given them near Moscow, and the city courts, and the money from the *tamga*, and the villages in the Moscow *stans*, now they shall administer them, as is written in this testament. And aside from this, [my younger sons] shall in no way interfere at all in the Moscow city courts, or in the courts in the suburb, or in all the *tamga*, or in all the customs, as well as in the *stans*, or in the volosts, or in the *puti*, or in all the Moscow villages of my son

[59] Concerning this exchange, see n. 47, above.

and their older brother Vasiliy, but they shall administer that which has been assigned to them in this testament.

And I bless my son Yuriy [and] give him the city of Dmitrov with its volosts, and with its *puti*, and with its villages, and with all its customs, except for the Pereaslav volosts—Serebozh, R[o]zh[e]stvenoye, Buskutovo—which I have given to my son Vasiliy [and have caused to appertain] to Pereaslavl', and except for the volosts beyond the Moskva, which I have also given to my son Vasiliy, to Moscow, now in these the volosts of my son and his older brother Vasiliy, my son Yuriy shall not interfere in any way. And concerning the hamlets Teshilovskiye in Dmitrov District, in Inobazh, which are in the possession of my secretary Odinets, now these hamlets also [shall pass] to my son Yuriy, [and I have caused them to appertain] to Dmitrov, and my son Vasiliy shall not interfere in these the hamlets Teshilovskiye, in Inobazh, that belong to my son Yuriy, and [Vasiliy] shall not cause them to appertain to Teshilov in any way.[60] And to my son Yuriy I also give [and cause to appertain] to Dmitrov, from among the Pereaslav volosts, Yulka with its apiarian *stan*, and in these volosts that belong to my son Yuriy, my son Vasiliy shall interfere in no way. And to him [Yuriy] I also give the city of Zvenigorod with its volosts, and with its *puti*, and with its villages, and with all its customs, and the volost Shop"kova, with all [that appertained to it]. And to my son Yuriy I also give, in the Tfer' Land, the city of Kashin with its volosts, and with its *puti*, and with its villages, and with all its customs, on the basis of those localities that were assigned to Kashin by our land surveyor, Vasiliy Karamyshev.[61] And concerning that which my brother's son, Prince Ivan Borisovich, gave me, [namely] his

[60] *I ne tyanet ikh k Teshilovu nichem.* That is, the future grand prince, Vasiliy, shall not require the hamlets Teshilovskiye to pay dues or to perform the other duties included in the term *tyaglo* to Teshilov, the volost to which they formerly appertained.

[61] Kashin was the most important of the patrimonial principalities of the Grand Principality of Tver'. The city of Kashin was located in the northeastern part of Tver', about 175 kilometers due north of Moscow. Kashin, along with Tver', was incorporated into the Grand Principality of Moscow in 1485 (Ekzemplyarskiy, II, 523 and 536).

patrimony, the city of Ruza with its volosts,[62] and with its *puti*, and with its villages, and with all its customs, and with those volosts and with the *stans* of Volok [Lamskiy] which he obtained as his share from his brother Fedor, except for the village Ryukhovskoye with its hamlets, which my brother's son Ivan gave to his brother Fedor,[63] now I give the city of Ruza with its volosts, and with its *puti*, and with its villages, and with all its customs, and with those volosts and with the *stans* of Volok [Lamskiy] which he obtained as his share from his brother Fedor, [these I give] to my son Yuriy, with everything as it used to be in the possession of my brother's son Ivan, except for the village Ryukhovskoye, with its hamlets. And to my son Yuriy I also give the city of Bryanesk" [64] with its volosts. and with its *pogosts*, and with its villages, and with all its customs, with all that appertained to Bryanesk", and the [Bryanesk"] volosts [are] Solov[']yevichi, Prikladni, Patsyn, Fe[o]d[o]-rovskaa, Osovik", Pokinichi, Sukhar['], V"seslavl', Voronitsa, Zheryn, Batogova, Khvoshchna, Piyanova, [and] Volkonesk". And to him I also give the city of Serpeyesk" [65] with its volosts

---

[62] See the testament of Ivan Borisovich, Prince of Ruza (*DDG*, pp. 351–353).

[63] *DDG*, pp. 351–353. Although the testament of Prince Boris of Volok Lamskiy provided that the patrimony of this prince should pass to his son Fedor, it is apparent that the latter subsequently shared it with his younger brother Ivan (see "The System of Holding Moscow by Thirds" in Chapter 5).

[64] Bryanesk" (Bryansk) was confirmed as part of the Grand Principality of Lithuania by the Armistice of 1494 (see *DDG*, pp. 329–332). Bryansk passed to Moscow by the Armistice of 1503 (Solov'yev, III, 122).

[65] Serpeyesk" (Serpeysk) was a city of the upper Oka River principalities, located just west of Meshchovsk. It was occupied in the name of Ivan III by Prince Semen Fedorovich Vorotynskiy and his nephew, Prince Ivan Mikhaylovich, in 1493. These two princes had left the service of Lithuania and entered that of Moscow. The next year (1494) Serpeysk was confirmed as part of Lithuania by an armistice concluded between Lithuania and Moscow. By the Armistice of 1503, however, Serpeysk passed formally to Moscow (Ekzemplyarskiy, II, 603, and Solov'yev, III, 122).

and with all that appertained to it, and the [Serpeyesk"] volosts [are] Zamosh[']ye, Tukhachev, Degna, Fominichi, Pogostishche, Kovylna, Blizhevichi, Lyubun, Snopot['], Danilovichi, Shuya, Demena, Uzheperet, Chernyatitsi, Gorodechna, Moshchyn, and Gnezdilovo, which was the patrimony of Prince Aleksandr, the son of Ivan Gnezdilovskiy, [and] with everything that appertained to Bryanesk", and to Serpeisk", and to these volosts, as it was under me.

And I bless my son Dmitriy [and] give him the city of Ugleche Pole with its volosts, and with its *puti*, and with its villages, and with all its customs, and with Ustyuzhna, and with Rozhalovo, and with Veletovo, and with Kist'ma, and with all that appertained to Ugleche and to these volosts, [and] the city of Mologa, with the patrimony of the Glebovs, and with the weirs on the Volga and on the Mologa, with everything as it was under me. And concerning the market which I moved from the burg Kholopiy to Mologa, now this market shall carry on trade at Mologa [with traders] gathering [there],[66] as it was under me, and my son Dmitriy shall take the customs, as it was under me, and he shall not add any additional customs at all, and my son Vasiliy and my children shall not bring this trade to their lands, neither shall they prohibit, through fines, trade in their lands from going to this market.[67]And to him I also give the city of Khlepen, with Rogachovo, and Negomir' with its volosts, and with its *puti*, and with its villages, and with all its customs. And in the Tfer' Land I give him the city of Zubtsov with its volosts, and with its *puti*, and with its villages, and with all its customs, [and] the city of Opoki with its volosts, and with its *puti*, and with its villages, and with all its customs, on the basis of those

[66] *I tot torg" torguyut na Moloze s"yezzhayasya.*

[67] *Ni zapovedi v" svoikh zemlyakh ne chinyat k tomu torgu yezditi.* The town of Mologa, formerly located at the confluence of the Mologa and Volga rivers (the area is now inundated by the Rybinsk Reservoir), had been the center of one of the patrimonial principalities of the Grand Principality of Yaroslavl', which Ivan III acquired—probably by purchase—in 1463 (see above, n. 32). According to Ekzemplyarskiy (II, 102), Kholopiy Monastery, at the mouth of the Mologa, took its name from the burg Kholopiy that had stood at this spot and had been famed for its market.

localities which my land surveyor, Dmitriy Peshkov, assigned to Zubtsov and Opoki. And concerning that which my brother's son, Prince Ivan Borisovich, gave me, [namely] his patrimony, half of Rzheva with its volosts, and with its *puti*, and with its villages, and with all its customs, which he obtained as his share from his brother Fedor, now I [this] half of Rzheva with its volosts, and with its *puti*, and with its villages, and with all its customs, also give to my son Dmitriy, with everything as it used to belong to my brother's son Ivan.[68] And to my son Dmitriy I also give the city of Meschesk" [69] with its volosts, and with its *pogosts*, and with its villages, and with all its customs, with everything that appertained to it, as used to belong to the Meschesk" princes, [and] the city of Opakov,[70] with everything that appertained to it, and the volosts Zalidov, Nedokhodovo, Lychino, Byshkovichi along the Ugra, with everything that appertained to Opakov and to these volosts, as it was under me.

And I bless my son Semen [and] give him the city of Bezhyttskoi Verkh" with its volosts, and with its *puti*, and with its villages, and with all its customs, [and] the city of Koluga with its volosts, and with its *puti*, and with its villages, and with all its customs. And I also give to my son Semen the city of Kozelesk" [71] with its volosts, and with its villages, and the Kozelesk" volosts [are] Serenesk", and Lyudimesk", and Korobki,

[68] See "The System of Holding Moscow by Thirds" in Chapter 5, and nn. 62 and 63.

[69] Meschesk" (Meshchovsk), one of the upper Oka principalities, was located west and slightly south of Kaluga. The Moscow-Lithuanian Armistice of 1494 provided that those Meschesk" princes who were serving Lithuania at the time would remain, with their principalities, as part of Lithuania; those who were serving Moscow would remain as part of Moscow (*DDG*, pp. 329–332). Meschesk" is not listed among those cities recognized as belonging to Moscow by the Armistice of 1503. This omission would indicate that the principality had been considered part of Moscow since 1494 (see Solov'yev, III, 122).

[70] Opakov was located on the Ugra River about 180 kilometers southwest of Moscow. It was confirmed as belonging to Moscow by the Armistice of 1503 (Solov'yev, III, 122 and 366).

[71] Kozelesk" (Kozel'sk), one of the upper Oka principalities located southwest of Kaluga, was confirmed as part of the Grand Principality of Moscow by the Armistice of 1494 (*DDG*, pp. 329–332).

and Vyrki on the Vyrka River, the volosts Senishcha, and Syti-chi, and Vyino, and with other localities, and Lipitsi, and V"zbynov, and Verkh"-Serena, and Lugan, and Mestilovo, and K"tsyn, and Khvostovichi, and Poryski, and Boryatin, and Oren', and Khost'tsi, and Zheremin, and Snykhovo, and Ivan Baba's village Neznanovo, and with the other localities, with everything that appertained to these volosts and villages.

And I bless my son Andrey [and] give him the city of Vereya [72] with its volosts, and with its *puti*, and with its villages, and with all its customs, [and] the city of Vyshegorod with its volosts, and with its *puti*, and with its villages, and with all its customs, [and] the city of Olein [73] with its volosts, and with its *puti*, and with its villages, and with all it customs, and with Volkona, and with Konino, and with Gordeyevo, and with Nyukhova, and with everything that appertained to these places. And to him I also give the city of Lyubutesk" [74] with its volosts, and with all its customs, and with all that appertained to it, as it was under me, and with Veprino, which is in the possession of the Odoyev princes.[75] And to my son Andrey I also give, near Moscow, Gzhelya and Rameneitso, with everything that appertained to them. And concerning the Moscow volosts which were annexed to Dmitrov, [namely] Selna, Guslitsa, Zagar'ye, Vokhna, [and] Kunei, now I give these volosts with everything [that appertained to them] to my son Andrey, and my son Yuriy shall not interfere in these his volosts in any way. And

[72] Vereya, a city and "outlying volost" of Mozhaysk, was left to Prince Andrey Dmitriyevich by the second testament of Dmitriy Donskoy. In 1485 upon the death of Prince Andrey's son Mikhail, Vereya passed into the hands of Ivan III (see "The System of Holding Moscow by Thirds" in Chapter 5).

[73] Apparently a distorted form of Oleksin (Aleksin).

[74] Lyubutesk" (Lyubutsk), located just up the Oka (south) from Aleksin, was confirmed as part of the Grand Principality of Lithuania by the Armistice of 1494 (*DDG*, p. 330). It was formally ceded to Moscow by the Armistice of 1503 (see Solov'yev, III, 122).

[75] Concerning the Odoyev (Odoyevskiy) princes, some of whom served Moscow, others Lithuania, see Ekzemplyarskiy, II, 251–252.

Odoyev city, the center of the upper Oka River principality of the same name, is located on the Upa River about sixty-five kilometers west and slightly south of Tula.

concerning, in Selna, the hamlets of slave beekeepers[76] of *Vasil-tsovo sto,* [namely] Bekrenevo, Belyanitsino, Novoye Belyani-tsino, Kharitonovskoye, Dedenevo, Neronovo, Vranikovo, Yakimovskoye, Novoye Yakimovskoye, and the waste lands of Lopakovo, Isachkovo, [and] Gribachevo, now I these hamlets and waste lands, with everything [that appertained to them] also give to my son Andrey, and my son Vasiliy shall not interfere with him in this. And in the Tfer' Land I give to him the city of Staritsa[77] with its volosts, and with its *puti,* and with its villages, and with all its customs, on the basis of those places that were assigned to Staritsa by our land surveyor, Boris Kutuzov. And I give to him the patrimony of the Kholm" [princes], Kholm" and the burg Novoi, and the volost Oleshnya, and the volost Sinyaya,[78] and the other volosts, and the *puti,* and the villages, with all their customs, on the basis of the places assigned to these patrimonies, and volosts, and *puti,* and villages, by our land surveyor, Andrey Karamyshev.

[76] *A chto v Selne d[e]r[e]vni delovyye bortnyye.* An alternate transla-tion is: "And concerning, in Selna, the apiarian hamlets that are my share. . . ."

[77] The city of Staritsa is located on the Volga, about sixty-five kilome-ters southwest of Tver' (Kalinin). Although Staritsa was doubtless one of the patrimonial principalities of the Grand Principality of Tver', there is not, according to Ekzemplyarskiy, a single mention of a prince of Staritsa during the entire period of Tartar domination in Russia. Evi-dence of the existence of such princes during this period is to be found in the coins of Staritsa (Ekzemplyarskiy, II, 559).

[78] Kholm, the center of a patrimonial principality of the Grand Princi-pality of Tver', was probably located about fifty kilometers southeast of Staritsa. There is some uncertainty as to the location of this old city because, in the latter part of the nineteenth century, there were eight settlements within the former boundaries of Tver' bearing the name Kholm. Moreover, there was a village in the same area with the name Krasnyy Kholm; it is this which was probably the old city of Kholm (see Ekzemplyarskiy, II, 538–539). At the fall of Tver' to the forces of Grand Prince Ivan III in September 1485, Prince Mikhail of Kholm, his brothers, his son, and Bishop Vassian of Tver' "opened" the city to the men of Moscow (*PSRL,* VIII, 216).

The burg Novyy (Novoi *gorodok*) was located about twelve kilome-ters northwest of Kholm. The volosts Oleshnya (Aleshnya) and Sinyaya were both located in Kholm District.

And concerning the cities, and volosts, and villages that I have given to my younger children—to Yuriy, Dmitriy, Semen, [and] Andrey—now these they shall rule as is written to them in this testament, but otherwise they are not to interfere with my son Vasiliy in anything whatsoever.

And my son Yuriy and his brothers shall not order money coined in their patrimonial principalities in the Moscow Land or in the Tfer' [Land], but my son Vasiliy shall order money coined in Moscow and in Tfer', as it was under me. And my son Vasiliy shall administer the *otkup*,[79] and my children, Yuriy and his brothers, shall not interfere with him in the *otkup*.

And concerning the small villages that I have given to my children near Moscow, with their city courts in the suburb, now my children shall not maintain trading places in these courts, nor shall they permit grain to be traded, nor shall they set up trading stands, nor shall they permit merchants with goods, [be they] foreigners, or merchants from the Moscow lands, or merchants from their patrimonial principalities, to set up [business], but merchants with goods, [be they] foreigners, or from the Moscow Land, or from their patrimonial principalities, shall set up [business] in the merchant courts, as it was under me. And my children shall not interfere with my son Vasiliy in these merchant courts and in these customs. And whoever trades in foodstuffs in the small villages and city courts of my [younger] children, now my son Vasiliy shall not order these trading places removed, but the intendant of my son Vasiliy shall collect the tax on trading stands from them, as it was under me.

And concerning the small villages and city courts that I have given to my children near Moscow city, to Yuriy and his brothers, now if murder or theft is committed in these small villages or

[79] *A otkup vedayet s[y]n" moi Vasilei.* The word *otkup* meant both farming (letting out to farm) and the ransoming of prisoners (see I. I. Sreznevskiy, *Materialy dlya slovarya drevne-russkago yazyka* [Moscow, 1958], II, 792, and V. Dal', *Tolkovyy slovar' zhivogo velikorusskogo yazyka* [Moscow, 1955], II, 732). Solov'yev interpreted the use of *otkup* in this passage of the testament of Ivan III in the sense of farming, suggesting that the reference was to the farming of the right to coin money. Under Ivan III one Ivan Fryazin obtained this right (III, 143 and 369).

in the city courts, the grand lieutenant of my son Vasiliy shall judge these [cases]. And concerning the villages in the Moscow *stans* which I have given to my children, Yuriy and his brothers, now in these villages [the dispensing of] justice and [the collecting of] tribute shall be by my children, but in [cases of] murder and theft these villages shall be under the jurisdiction of the city of Moscow as of old, except for [cases of] theft which occur in these villages among their peasants, now they shall be judged by their intendants,[80] and they shall report to the grand lieutenant of Moscow of my son Vasiliy. And, in Moscow, the post relay secretary of my son Vasiliy shall write full charters and reference charters [81] as it was under me, and, except for him, no one shall write full charters or reference charters in Moscow. And concerning the cities and volosts which I have given to my children, to Yuriy and his brothers, as their patrimonial principalities, now if they were under the jurisdiction of Moscow in [cases of] murder, these cities and the districts and volosts of these cities shall be under the jurisdiction of the city of Moscow in [cases of] murder, as of old, and my children, Yuriy and his brothers, shall not interfere in this.

And my son Vasiliy shall not purchase lands, or hold [lands], or hold *zakladni*[82] in the patrimonial principalities of my children, his brothers. And my children shall not purchase lands, or hold [lands], or hold *zakladni* of my son Vasiliy in Moscow or in his entire Grand Principality. And concerning my villages which I have given to my boyars, and to my princes, and to my junior boyars, and concerning the charters of grant to these villages which I have given them, [now these villages] shall be permanently theirs and their children's, or [they shall belong] to anyone to whom I give my charters of purchase,[83] and my son Vasiliy and my children shall not interfere with them in these villages.

[80] That is, they shall be tried by the intendants (*prikazchiki*) of Yuriy and his brothers.

[81] Concerning full charters (*gramoty polnyye*) and reference charters (*gramoty dokladnyye*), see Chapter 4.

[82] A *zakladen'* (pl. *zakladni*) was a person who commended himself and his land to a prince.

[83] *Ili komu budu v" kuplyu dal svoi gramoty.*

And my children, Yuriy and his brothers, shall give to my son Vasiliy, from their patrimonial principalities, as Tartar tribute [*vykhod*] to the Hordes, [namely] to Krym,[84] and to Aztarakhan['],[85] and to Kazan['], and to Tsarevichev burg,[86] and to the other tsars and tsars' sons, who are in the land of my son Vasiliy, and to the Tartar envoys who come to Moscow, and [to the Tartar envoys who come] to Tfer', and to Novgorod Nizhniy, and to Yaroslavl', and to Torusa, and to Ryazan' Staraya, and to Perevitsk, [namely] the share of Prince Fedor of Ryazan',[87] and for all the expenses of the Tartars, one thousand rubles. My son Yuriy shall give from his whole patrimonial principality and from Kashin eighty rubles and two rubles less a *grivna*. And my son Dmitriy shall give from his whole patrimonial principality, and from Zuptsov, and from Opoki, fifty rubles and eight rubles with a *poltina* and seven *denga*. And my son Semen shall give from his whole patrimonial principality sixty rubles and five rubles less ten *denga*. And my son Andrey shall give from his whole patrimonial principality and from Staritsa, and from the Kholm" patrimonies, from Kholm", and from the burg Novyy, and from Oleshnya, and from Sinyaya, and from the other Tver' volosts that were given to him, forty rubles with a *poltina* and three and one-half *denga*. And my son Vasiliy shall also give towards this one thousand rubles, from Moscow, and from the whole Grand Princedom of the Moscow Land, and from Tfer', and from the whole Tfer' Land that was given him, and from Ryazan' Staraya, and from Perevitsk, seven hundred rubles and seventeen-and-one-half rubles and two and one-half *denga*. And Fedor, the son of [my] brother Boris, shall also give to my son Vasiliy towards this one thousand rubles, from his patrimony, and from Kolp', and from Buygorod, thirty rubles and seven and

---

[84] The Khanate of the Crimea.   [85] The Khanate of Astrakhan'.

[86] Tsarevichev burg (*gorodok*), 'the burg of the son of the [Tartar] tsar,' was Kasimov, formerly called Gorodok Meshcherskiy, 'the burg of the Meshchera.' It was the center of the holdings of the sons of the Tartar Khan Mengly-Girey, who were in the service of the grand princes of Moscow (see K. V. Basilevich, *Vneshnyaya politika russkogo tsentralizovannogo gosudarstva* [*vtoraya polovina XV veka*] [Moscow, 1952], p. 190).

[87] See n. 54, above.

one-half rubles. And be the Tartar expenses more or less than this, my son Vasiliy and my children, Yuriy and his brothers, and my brother's son Fedor, shall give according to [this] reckoning.[88]

And my son Vasiliy shall maintain, in his Grand Princedom, post stations and post carts with horses on the roads at those places where there were post stations and post carts with horses on the roads under me. And my children, Yuriy and his brothers, shall maintain post stations and post carts with horses on the roads throughout their patrimonies, at those places where there were post stations and post carts with horses along the roads under me.

And if any one of my sons should pass away and not leave a son or a grandson, then his entire patrimonial principality in the Moscow Land and in the Tfer' Land that I have given him, now all [shall pass] to my son Vasiliy, and his brothers shall not interfere with him in this his patrimonial principality. And if he should leave daughters, then my son Vasiliy, having made allocations to these his daughters, shall give them in marriage. And concerning that which he gives his princess—volosts, and villages, and treasure—now my son Vasiliy shall not interfere with her in all this in any way during her lifetime.

And my son Vasiliy I bless with the cross, the life-giving tree in the Tsar'grad shrine,[89] and [also] the Cross of Petr the Wonder-Worker.[90]

---

[88] A *grivna* at this time was one tenth of a ruble—"Grivna, da grivna, an" i dvadtsat' kopeyek!" (see Dal', *Tolkovyy slovar'*, I, 394, and *Slovar' russkogo yazyka* [Moscow, 1957], I, 466). A *poltina* equalled one half of a ruble, or five *grivna*; a *denga* equalled one two-hundredth part of a ruble. Yuriy was to contribute 81.9 rubles, Dmitriy 58.535 rubles, Semen 64.95 rubles, Andrey 40.5175 rubles, Vasiliy 717.5125 rubles, and Fedor 37.5 rubles. On the basis of the values assumed for the *poltina* (.5 rubles), the *grivna* (.1 rubles), and the *denga* (.005 rubles), the contributions that the sons and nephew of Ivan III were to make towards the one thousand rubles to be paid to the Tartars totalled 1000.915 rubles.

[89] *Kr[e]st" zhivotvoryashcheye drevo v ratse tsaregradtskoi.* The word "shrine" is employed here in the sense of a case, box, or receptacle, especially for sacred relics.

[90] See above, Text 9, n. 65.

And my son Yuriy I bless [with] the golden cross of Boris and Gleb.[91]

And my son Dmitriy I bless [with] the golden cross, the work of Paramsha.

And my son Semen I bless [with] the golden cross of Bishop Mikhail.

And my son Andrey I bless [with] the golden icon—the Crucifixion—done in enamel with precious stones and pearls.

And concerning the treasure that I have given to my children, to Yuriy, Dmitriy, Semen, [and] Andrey, and [first of all] concerning my treasure that I have given to my son Yuriy, now this I have placed in small coffers, and on these small coffers are my seal and that of my son Yuriy, and the keys to these small coffers are in the possession of my son Yuriy, and these small coffers stand in my Treasury, in the custody of my treasurer Dmitriy Volodimerov, and in the custody of my keeper of the seal Yuriy, the son of Dmitriy the Greek, and in the custody of my secretaries Danilko Mamyrev and Tishko Moklokov.[92] And concerning my treasure that I have given to my son Dmitriy, now this I have placed in small coffers, and on these small coffers are my seal and that of my son Dmitriy, and the keys to these small coffers are in the possession of my son Dmitriy, and these small coffers stand in my Treasury in the custody of my treasurer Dmitriy Volodimerov, and in the custody of my keeper of the seal Yuriy, the son of Dmitriy the Greek, and in the custody of my secretaries Danil Mamyrev and Tishko Moklokov. And concerning my treasure that I have given to my son Semen, now this I have placed in small coffers, and on these small coffers are

---

[91] That is, the cross of the martyrs Boris and Gleb, princes murdered in 1015 by order of their brother, Svyatopolk the Accursed (*PSRL*, V, 125–131).

[92] In Russian medieval documents the first, or Christian, names of persons of lower social status appear more often than not in the diminutive or pejorative forms. This is also true of the names of servants of the grand prince, as in the text under discussion. Thus, Mamyrev's name was Daniil (Daniel) and Moklokov's was Tikhon. See *DDG*, p. 499; Solov'yev, IV, 14; and V. K. Chicagov, *Iz istorii russkikh imen, otchestv i familiy* (Moscow, 1959), for a general exposition of the development of Russian names.

my seal and that of my son Semen, and the keys to these small coffers are in the possession of my son Semen, and these small coffers stand in my Treasury in the custody of my treasurer Dmitriy Volodimerov, and in the custody of my keeper of the seal Yuriy, the son of Dmitriy the Greek, and in the custody of my secretaries Danilko Mamyrev and Tishko Moklokov. And concerning my treasure that I have given to my son Andrey, now this I have placed in small coffers, and on these small coffers are my seal and that of my son Andrey, and the keys to these small coffers are in the possession of my son Andrey, and these small coffers stand in my Treasury in the custody of my treasurer Dmitriy Volodimerov, and in the custody of my keeper of the seal Yuriy, the son of Dmitriy the Greek, and in the custody of my secretaries Danilko Mamyrev and Tishko Moklokov.

And aside from this, any of my treasure that is in the custody of my treasurer Dmitriy Volodimerov, and of my secretaries, and of my secretary Semen Bashenin—rubies, and sapphires, and other precious stones, and pearls, and any articles of dress decorated with precious stones, and belts, and golden chains, and golden vessels, and silver ones, and stone ones, and gold, and silver, and sables, and silk goods, and divers other belongings, whatever there is—as well as whatever there is in my private treasure [93]—icons, and golden crosses, and gold, and silver, and clothing, and other belongings—and whatever is in the custody of my major-domo Petr Vasil[']yev Velikiy, and of my palace secretaries—silver vessels, and money, and other belongings—and whatever is in the custody of my equerry, and of my grooms, and of my secretaries, and of my intendants, and of anyone at all—my money and divers other belongings—as well as anything that is in the custody of my major-domo in Tver', and of my Tver' secretaries, and of my [Tver'] intendants, and in Novgorod the Great, [anything] that is in the custody of my major-domo, and of my treasurers, and of my secretaries, and of my intendants, and of anyone at all—my money and divers other belongings—and in Beloozero and in Vologda my treasure and my treasures, wherever they be, now all [shall pass] to my son Vasiliy. And my children, Yuriy and his brothers, shall not inter-

[93] "I v moyei kazne v postelnoi." Literally, "in my bed treasury."

fere with my son Vasiliy in anything, except in that of my treasure that I have given to them.

And I commit my soul and my younger children—Yuriy, Dmitriy, Semen, [and] Andrey—to my son Vasiliy. And you, my younger children, Yuriy and his brothers, hold my son Vasiliy, your older brother, in place of me, your father, and obey him in all things. And you, my son Vasiliy, hold your younger brothers—Yuriy, Dmitriy, Semen, [and] Andrey—in brotherliness and in honor, without injustice.

And if any of my sons should not obey my son Vasiliy in all things, or should try to obtain the grand principalities from him or from his children, or should leave him, or should conspire secretly or openly with anyone whomsoever to his injury, or should incite anyone against him, or should ally himself with anyone against him, now may the grace of God, and the prayers of the Most Pure Mother of God and of the Holy Wonder-Workers, and the blessing of our ancestors and of us not be upon him in this world or in the next.

And concerning my treasurers, or any of my secretaries who have managed my income for me, or my *tiuns*, or my *villici*, or anyone married to them, none of these are of any concern of my son Vasiliy or of my children, Yuriy and his brothers.

And may God judge him who violates this my testament, and may my blessing not be upon him.

And at [the signing of] this my testament sat my spiritual father, Archimandrite Mitrofan of the Andronnikov [Monastery].[94] And here were my boyars: Prince Vasiliy Danilovich, and Prince Danilo Vasil'yevich, and Yakov Zakhar'ich,[95] and my treasurer Dmitriy Volodimerov.

And my secretary Danilko Mamyrev" wrote this my testament.

[94] See n. 12, above.

[95] Prince Vasiliy was probably Vasiliy Danilovich Kholmskoy, son-in-law of Ivan III and voivode of Moscow after Ivan Yur'yevich Patrikeyev fell from favor (Solov'yev, III, 154). Prince Danilo was probably Daniil Vasil'yevich Shchenya-Patrikeyev (Solov'yev, III, 154). Yakov Zakhar'ich was probably Yakov Zakhar'yevich Koshkin-Zakhar'in, boyar, voivode of Kolomna, and son of the boyar Zakhar Ivanovich Koshkin (Solov'yev, III, 154 and 771).

TEXT 12

Testamentary Writ of Vasiliy III

Commentary

VASILIY IVANOVICH, the oldest son of Grand Prince Ivan III and Sofiya Paleolog, was born in 1479.[1] Vasiliy became Grand Prince of Vladimir and Moscow prior to the death of his father. In 1502 "on April 14 . . . Grand Prince Ivan Vasil'-yevich of All Rus' favored his son Vasiliy, blessed [him], and constituted him autocrat in the Grand Principality of Vladimir and Moscow, with the blessing of Simon, Metropolitan of All Rus'."[2] Vasiliy Ivanovich, known as Vasiliy III, became Grand Prince of All Rus' in 1506, upon the death of his father Ivan III. He died in 1533.[3] Shortly before his death Grand Prince Vasiliy ordered that his testament be burned. He then wrote another testament, but this too has been lost.[4]

[1] *PSRL*, VI, 33.

[2] *PSRL*, VI, 48. Ivan III married Mariya Borisovna (daughter of Grand Prince Boris Aleksandrovich of Tver') in 1452. A son, Ivan Ivanovich, called the Young (*Molodoy*), was born of this marriage in 1458 (*PSRL*, XXV, 275). Grand Princess Mariya Borisovna died in 1467; Ivan Ivanovich the Young died in 1490.

In 1498 Grand Prince Ivan III brought about the coronation of his grandson Dmitriy Ivanovich (son of Ivan Ivanovich the Young), blessing him in the presence of the metropolitan with the grand principalities of Moscow, Vladimir, and Novgorod. Subsequently, as a result of alleged seditious activity by a number of boyars who supported young Dmitriy against Sofiya (whom Ivan married in 1473) and her son Vasiliy, Grand Prince Ivan disgraced Dmitriy and his mother and placed them under guard. Three days later, Vasiliy (the son of Ivan and Sofiya) was "constituted autocrat of All Rus' in the Grand Princedom of Vladimir and Moscow" (see Solov'yev, *Istoriya Rossii s drevneyshikh vremen* [Moscow, 1959–1966], III, 54–64).

[3] *PSRL*, VI, 244 and 274.

[4] For a detailed account of the events leading up to the death of Vasiliy III, see *PSRL*, VI, 267–275, and Solov'yev, III, 287–293.

The original of Vasiliy's testamentary writ [*dukhovnaya zapis'*], written in June 1523, is preserved in the Central State Archives of Ancient Acts (TsGADA) in Moscow, in the State Repository of Ancient Documents, Section I, Heading 1, No. 36. Two seals are suspended from the face of the original: the red-wax seal of Grand Prince Vasiliy Ivanovich and the black-wax seal of Metropolitan Daniil.[5]

The testamentary writ of Vasiliy III has been previously printed in N. I. Novikov, ed., *Drevnyaya Rossiysakaya Vivliofika* (2nd ed.; Moscow, 1788–1791), Part 3, No. 129; in *Prodolzheniye Drevney Rossiyskoy Vivliofiki* (St. Petersburg, 1786–1801), Part 5; and in *Sobraniye gosudarstvennykh gramot i dogovorov, khranyashchikhsya v Gosudarstvennoy kollegii inostrannykh del* (Moscow, 1813), Part 1, No. 150.[6]

The translation which follows is based on the text of the testamentary writ as printed in *DDG*, p. 415.

THE TESTAMENTARY WRIT OF GRAND PRINCE VASILIY III IVANOVICH

IN the name of the holy, life-giving Trinity, and with the blessing of our father Daniil, Metropolitan of All Rus', [I] write this writ, leaving on my business for Kazan'.[7]

Lo I, the poor slave of God, Vasiliy, having prior to this written my testament and a codicil to my testament, and Varlaam, Metropolitan of All Rus',[8] having signed that testament

---

[5] *DDG*, p. 415. Daniil, Abbot of the Iosif of Volokolamsk Monastery of the Dormition, became metropolitan on February 27, 1523 (*PSRL*, VI, 264). In 1539 he was removed from this position by Prince Ivan Vasil'yevich Shuyskiy and his associates (*PSRL*, VIII, 295).

[6] *DDG*, p. 415.

[7] Vasiliy III undertook a campaign against Khan Saip-Girey of Kazan' in 1523. Although the Chronicle does not give the date of the departure of the grand prince from Moscow, it does report that he reached Nizhniy Novgorod on August 23 (*PSRL*, VI, 264).

[8] Varlaam, Archimandrite of the Simonovo Monastery, became metropolitan in 1511, after the death of Metropolitan Simon (*PSRL*, VI, 252). In December 1522 he resigned—probably because of his unwilling-

and codicil with his own hand, and Metropolitan Varlaam having affixed his seal to that testament and to the codicil, and I having affixed my seal to that testament and to the codicil, now I, in accordance with that testament and that codicil, commit my soul and my princess [9] to my father Daniil, Metropolitan of All Rus'. And that testament and that codicil I also commit to him, my father.

And when, by God's will, I acquired my patrimony, the city of Smolen'sk and the Smolen'sk Land,[10] now I then promised to found, in the suburb of Moscow, the Monastery of the Virgin, and in it the Temple of the Most Pure One and of the Invention of the Holy Cross,[11] and other temples, and concerning those temples that were to be founded in that monastery, now I have ordered my secretary Trufan Il'in to write, with his own hand, a writ and give it to my keeper of the seal Ivan Tret[']yakov. And I promised to give to this monastery, from my palace villages, a village or two, and of cultivated land in these villages, a thousand quarters in one field,[12] or the same in two fields, and, toward the building of this monastery, three thousand rubles of money. And now I have not succeeded in building this monastery. And if, by the will of God, something happens to me and I do not succeed in building this monastery during my lifetime, then I have ordered my treasurers and my bureau people [13] to build this monastery on this spot. And from among my palace villages, I have

---

ness to approve Vasiliy's divorce from Grand Princess Solomonida—and retired to the Simonovo Monastery. He was later exiled to the Kamennyy (Spasokamennyy) Monastery in Vologda (*PSRL*, VI, 264).

[9] The first wife of Vasiliy III, Solomonida Yur'yevna Saburova, whom the grand prince divorced in 1525 (Solov'yev, III, 286 and 780).

[10] An account of the capture of Smolensk by Vasiliy III in 1514 is in *PSRL*, VI, 254–257. Smolensk had been part of the Grand Principality of Lithuania since its seizure by Vitovt in 1404 (*PSRL*, V, 253).

[11] The festival of the Invention (or Discovery) of the Holy Cross is celebrated on August 1 (O.S.) in the Greek Orthodox Church. It is also called the First Saviour's Day. Grand Prince Vasiliy III and his men entered Smolensk on August 1, 1514 (*PSRL*, VI, 255).

[12] A quarter (*chetvert'*) was equal to one half of a dessiatine, or 1.35 acres.

[13] *Prikaznyye lyudi*. See "*Put*' and *Prikaz*" in Chapter 5.

ordered that this monastery be given a village or two, a thousand quarters in one field, or the same in two fields. And for the building of this monastery, our treasurers shall give three thousand rubles of money.

And our father Daniil, Metropolitan of All Rus', has signed this writ with his own hand and has affixed his seal to this writ.

And we have affixed our seal to this writ.

And he who violates this writ against my order, now he shall be judged with me before God.

And when I wrote this writ, then there were in the presence of our father Daniil, Metropolitan of All Rus', at [the writing of] this writ, Elder Vassian, Prince Ivan's [son],[14] and my spiritual father Vasiliy, Archpriest of the [Cathedral of the] Annunciation.[15]

---

[14] Elder Vassian was the former Prince Vasiliy Ivanovich Patrikeyev the Cross-Eyed. The Patrikeyevs were one of the leading princely families in Moscow. Descendants of Gedimin of Lithuania, they were related by marriage to the House of Moscow: Prince Yuriy Patrikeyev, an attestant to the second and third testaments of Grand Prince Vasiliy I, was married to Mariya, the daughter of Vasiliy I. The Patrikeyevs fell into disfavor when they opposed Sofiya Paleolog and her party, who wished to see Vasiliy Ivanovich, Sofiya's son, succeed to the throne instead of Dmitriy Ivanovich, the grandson of Ivan III. Early in 1499 Ivan Yur'yevich Patrikeyev, voivode of Moscow, and his oldest son, Vasiliy Ivanovich, were forced to enter monasteries. The father retired to the Trinity-Sergiy Monastery, his son to the Kirill of Beloozero Monastery.

During the reign of Vasiliy III, Vassian returned to Moscow to the Simonovo Monastery. He was highly respected by the grand prince for his intelligence and erudition; but he opposed Vasiliy's divorce from Solomonida, which took place in 1525 with the approval of Metropolitan Daniil.

Vassian is also remembered for his stand on one of the most pressing questions of the day: Should monasteries be permitted to own large landed properties? On this question Vassian, a pupil of Nil Sorskiy, opposed Iosif of Volokolamsk, the great proponent of the right of the church to own such properties. Bravely refusing to recant before a Church Council that was considering his case and that of Maxim the Greek, Vassian was sentenced to incarceration in the Iosif of Volokolamsk Monastery (see Solov'yev, III, 62–63, 285–287, and 327–334).

[15] The foundation of the Cathedral of the Annunciation (*Blagoveshchenskiy sobor*) was laid by Ivan III in his court in the Kremlin on May

And my secretary Menshyk" Putyatin" [16] wrote this writ in the year 7000 thirty the first [17] in the month of June.[18]

6, 1484. It was on the site of a church founded by Grand Prince Vasiliy Dmitriyevich (*PSRL*, XXV, 330).

[16] Menshyk Putyatin was apparently one of the most trusted servants of Vasiliy III. Late in 1533 when the grand prince was ill at Volok Lamskiy, he secretly dispatched both his secretary Menshoy (Menshyk) Putyatin and his attendant (*stryapchiy*) Yakov Mansurov to Moscow, to fetch his and his father's testaments. When the testaments were brought to him, Vasiliy ordered his own burned (*PSRL*, VI, 268).

[17] 7031/1523.

[18] The following signature appears on the original: "The sinful and poor monk Danil", by the grace of God, Metropolitan of All Rus'."

TEXT 13

Testament of Ivan IV the Terrible

Commentary

IVAN IV, called the Terrible, or the Dread (*Groznyy*), was born on August 25, 1530, the oldest son of Grand Prince Vasiliy III and Yelena Glinskaya, the niece of Prince Mikhail L'vovich Glinskiy, who had deserted Lithuania and entered the service of the Grand Prince of Moscow in 1507. Ivan was only three when his father died; he was not yet eight when his mother died, perhaps by poison, on April 3, 1538. Ivan's boyhood, an unhappy time during which the heir to the throne of Muscovy was mistreated by scheming boyars, ended on January 16, 1547, when he was crowned, taking the title of tsar. According to contemporary reports Ivan IV died in a state of mental and emotional anguish on March 18, 1584.[1]

In an excellent article on the historical significance of the testament of Ivan IV, Academician S. B. Veselovskiy has analyzed the circumstances leading up to the writing of this document.[2] This, the only surviving testament of Ivan the Terrible, was not his first. He had written one in 1553 at the time of his illness, when it appeared that a number of boyars would refuse to swear allegiance to Dmitriy, his infant son. The following year (1554), after the accidental death by drowning of Tsarevitch Dmitriy, Ivan wrote another testament in favor of his new-born heir, Ivan Ivanovich. Neither of these early testaments has been preserved.

Veselovskiy demonstrates that the one surviving testament of

[1] See S. M. Solov'yev, *Istoriya Rossii s drevneyshikh vremen* (Moscow, 1959–1966), III, *passim*.

[2] S. B. Veselovskiy, "Dukhovnoye zaveshchaniye Ivana Groznogo kak istoricheskiy istochnik," *Izvestiya Akademii Nauk SSSR: Seriya istorii i filosofii*, IV, No. 6 (1947), 505–520.

Ivan IV was written in Novgorod sometime between the beginning of June 1572 and August 6, 1572. In the first place, it must have been written after the tsar's marriage to Anna Koltovskaya in early May 1572, for Ivan writes in the testament: "And if God should give a son to me and my wife Anna." Secondly, the testament certainly was written after the elevation of Antoniy, Bishop of Polotsk, to the office of metropolitan in mid-May 1572, for it was written "with the blessing of our father Antoniy, Metropolitan of All Russia." Ivan was also concerned during May with preparations for the defense of Moscow against the expected invasion by the Crimean Tartars under Khan Devlet-Girey and most likely did not undertake to write a testament before his departure for Novgorod about May 20 with his bride and a large entourage. The tsar arrived in Novgorod on June 1, 1572; on July 31 word came that Devlet was marching against Moscow; on August 6 runners arrived in Novgorod with news of the rout of the Tartars near Moscow. Veselovskiy maintains that Ivan's "doleful testament" (*skorbnoye zaveshchaniye*) was written sometime between the tsar's arrival in Novgorod on June 1 and August 6 when the good news of the Tartars' defeat arrived. It was set down at a time "when the tsar, under the reliable guard of several thousand streltsy, with the tsarina and the tsarevitches, was living in Novgorod in apprehension of the imminent bloody struggle between his voivodes and the Tartars." Veselovskiy does not believe the testament could have been written between August 6 and August 17 when Ivan set out on his return to Moscow.

But the question remains whether the testament could not have been written after Ivan's return to the capital. Shortly after he arrived in Moscow Ivan dissolved the Oprichnina. In view of this, Veselovskiy concludes that the testament must have been written before Ivan's return to Moscow, for in his testament Ivan speaks of the Oprichnina as an institution which is still functioning.

Ivan wrote another testament in 1582, but it is no longer in existence.[3]

[3] Veselovskiy, pp. 506–508.

The original of the one surviving testament, that of 1572, has also been lost. On the first page of the extant copy of the 1572 testament appears the following heading:

The testament of the Sovereign, Tsar and Grand Prince Ivan Vasil'yevich, Autocrat of All Russia, etc., etc., etc., was composed by him about the year 7080 from the Creation of the World and from the birth of Christ 1572, and contains his will and spiritual commandments, moral and political, extremely judicious and wise, and here also are made allotments to the sovereigns, the tsarevitches, his sons, Tsarevitch Ivan Ivanovich and Tsarevitch Fedor Ivanovich. Copied from a copy which was copied from the original by a man artful and curious, as the notes indicate.
A. Kurbatov.
Copied in St. Petersburg in the month of April, 1739.[4]

The surviving copy of the testament bears a watermark of 1805.[5] Hence it appears that it is the *third* in a descending line of copies, as follows:

1. the original, written in Novgorod in the summer of 1572—now lost.
2. copy 1, date unknown, made by a man "artful and curious"—now lost.
3. copy 2, made in St. Petersburg in April 1739 by one A. Kurbatov—now lost.
4. copy 3 (extant), made early in the nineteenth century by a "barely literate copyist" (Veselovskiy's expression) and preserved in the Central State Archives of Ancient Acts in Moscow, Malinovskiy's Portfolio, Nos. 3–6, Item 79.[6]

The text of the testament of Ivan IV has previously been printed in *Dopolneniya k" Aktam" istoricheskim", sobrannyye i izdannyye Arkheograficheskoyu Komissiyeyu* (St. Petersburg, 1846), Vol. I, No. 222, and, in part, in N. M. Karamzin, *Istoriya gosudarstva rossiyskago* (St. Petersburg, 1842), Book 3, notes to Vol. IX, Chap. 7.

The translation which follows is based on the text of the

[4] *DDG*, p. 444.
[5] *DDG*, p. 444.
[6] *DDG*, p. 444.

nineteenth-century copy of the testament of Ivan IV as printed in *DDG*, pp. 426–444.

THE TESTAMENT OF GRAND PRINCE AND TSAR IVAN IV VASIL'YEVICH

THE testament of Tsar and Grand Prince Ioann Vasil'yevich, Autocrat of All Russia.

In the name of the Father, and of the Son, and of the Holy Ghost, and of the holy and life-giving Trinity, now and always and in the ages to come, amen, and with the blessing of our father Antoniy, Metropolitan of All Russia,[7] lo I, the much sinning and poor slave of God, Ivan, write this confession, being of sound mind. But inasmuch as I am guided by a poverty of reason and from the miserable house of my mind I could not offer a table spread with the food of angelic words, [and] inasmuch as [my] mind has become covered with sores, [my] body has become weak, [my] spirit is afflicted, [my] spiritual and bodily wounds have increased, and there is no physician to heal me, I waited for someone to pity me, but there was no one, I found no comforters, they have repaid me with evil for my kindness and with hatred for my love.[8] For I am defiled of soul

[7] Metropolitan Filipp had been removed from office and imprisoned in the Tver' Otroch Monastery in 1568. In 1569, having refused to give his blessing to Ivan's campaign against Novgorod, Filipp—who was later canonized—was strangled by one of the leading *oprichniks*, Grigoriy Luk'yanovich Skuratov-Bel'skiy (Malyuta-Skuratov) (Solov'yev, III, 557).

The successor of the murdered Filipp was Kirill, Archimandrite of the Trinity-Sergiy Monastery, who was metropolitan from 1568 to 1572. Antoniy, Bishop of Polotsk, was named metropolitan in May 1572. Both Kirill and Antoniy were merely "silent witnesses of that which was taking place about them; they did not even protest against the marriages of the tsar which violated the canon statutes of the church" (F. A. Brokhaus and I. A. Efron, eds., *Entsiklopedicheskiy slovar'*, [St. Petersburg, 1898], XXXVII, 466).

[8] Cf. Psalm lxix.20; also cf. Romans xii.17, I Thessalonians v.15, and Proverbs xiii.21. When biblical quotations from Ivan's testament can be positively identified, the wording of the King James Version (A.V.) has

and corrupt of body. Indeed, having passed from the Jerusalem of God's commandments to the passions of Jericho, I was tempted by the transient beauty of this world for the sake of earthly pursuits and, led among people of this world, I in my mind gave myself over to the brilliance of the purple and the glitter of gold, and I fell among thieves of the mind and the senses, in thought and in deed; I was stripped of the raiment of shelter of grace and was left half dead of wounds, but more than seeing can show, still alive but, because of my sordid actions, worse to God than a stinking and abominable corpse which the priest sees but does not heed, and even the Levite, with aversion, passed me by. Indeed, from Adam to this day I have surpassed all sinners in unlawfulness, [and] because of this I am hated by all: having surpassed the murder done by Cain I was like unto Lamech, the first murdered, I was like unto Esau in my profane lack of restraint, I was like unto Reuben who defiled his father's bed, and [I was like unto] many others in insatiability and in the wrath and indignation of my lack of restraint. And although the mind should contemplate God and be aware of the tsar's passions, I was most corrupt of reason and bestial in mind and thought; for my very head I had defiled in my wish and desire for improper deeds, [and I had defiled] my mouth with discourse on murder, and on fornication, and on all evil doings; [and I had defiled] my tongue with improper speech, and vile language, and wrath, and indignation, and intemperance in all kinds of improper deeds; [and I had defiled] my neck [9] and breast with pride and the expectations of pompous-sounding reason; [and I had defiled] my hands with the touch of improper things, and insatiable rapine, and presumption, and inner murder; [and] I also had defiled [my head] with all sorts of detestable and improper thoughts, with gluttony and drunkenness; [and I had defiled] my loins with excessive fornication, and with improper restraint, and by surrounding everything with evil; [and I had defiled] my feet with a most rapid striving after all

---

been used. Such quotations have been compared with the pertinent versions of the Church Slavic Version (C.S.V.), the American Standard Revised Version (A.R.V.), and the Revised Standard Version (R.S.V.).

[9] Cf. Deuteronomy xxxi.27.

things evil, and with foul doings, and with murder, and with an insatiable plundering of [others'] wealth, and with other improper amusements. But what then shall I do, for Abraham will not know us, Isaac will not be cognizant of us, and Israel will not recognize us. But Thou, O Lord, art our Father; to Thee we flee and beg mercy, [to Thee] who art not from Samaria, but of the Virgin Mary ineffably incarnate; [10] from Thy most pure side water and blood flowed like oil; [11] O Christ God, bind up the telling sores of my spiritual and bodily wounds and unite me with the Heavenly Chorus; and as One compassionate, O Lord my God, give us peace, for we know none but Thee, and Thy name we know; shine Thy face on us and have mercy on us. For Thine is the unexampled dominion, and the kingdom without beginning and without end, and the power, and the glory, and the dominion now, and everlasting, and in the ages to come, amen.

And inasmuch as, according to the Scriptures, children need not preserve possessions for their parents, but parents for their children, and that which is the highest possession is, as was said: "Wisdom [which] crieth aloud in the street, She crieth at the head of the noisy streets, at the gates of the mighty she crieth aloud, Unto you, O men, I call, and my voice is to the sons of men, for the gaining of it is better than the gaining of silver, and the profit thereof than fine gold, she is more precious than rubies, and none of the things thou canst desire are to be compared to her." [12] The Lord saith: "By me kings reign and princes decree justice." [13] Because of this, now I offer advice to you, my

[10] The word *Samarii* is perhaps an error on the part of one of the copyists. The text in Karamzin reads *semeni*, 'seed,' instead of *Samarii*, 'Samaria.' The translation "who art not from the seed, but of the Virgin Mary ineffably incarnate" would appear to make more sense. On the other hand, Ivan is perhaps continuing his paraphrase of the Parable of the Good Samaritan, in which case his intention may have been to use the word "Samaria."

[11] Cf. John xxix.34.

[12] It appears that the tsar, probably quoting from memory, has combined portions of Proverbs i.20–21, viii.1–4, and iii.14–15, in that order.

[13] Proverbs viii.15.

children, to the extent that I, in my miserable state, have the wisdom, the grace, and God's gift.[14]

Lo, I command you, love one another, and may the God of Peace be with you. For if you keep this, then you will acquire all goodness; keep a firm and fearless faith in God, and stand [firm] and learn the dogmas of God—how to believe, and how to do that which is pleasing to God, and [learn] in what manner you should justify yourself before the impartial Judge. Know this more than all else: hold firmly to the Orthodox Christian faith, suffer for it manfully, even unto death. And you yourselves live in love. And accustom yourselves to [the art of] war as much as possible. And how to rule over people, and how to favor them, and how to protect yourselves from them, and how to be able to make them yours in all things—to this you should also become accustomed. And those people who serve you in a straightforward manner you should favor and love, you should protect them from all, so that they be not persecuted by anyone, and they will serve in an [even] more straightforward manner. And upon those that are evil you should place your disfavor, not hurriedly but after consideration, not in wrath. And accustom yourselves to all affairs: God's, the priest's, the monk's, the soldier's, the judge's; [and accustom yourselves] to the way of life in Moscow, and to all the customs of daily life, and how the various ranks [of government] are dealt with here and in other states, and [the relations] which this state has with other states—this you yourselves should know. Also, in all everyday relationships: how one man lives, and what befits him, and what is the measure of his behavior—all this you should learn. And people will not direct you but you will direct people. And that which you yourselves do not know,[15] you will rule by yourselves your states and people.

And if, because of the multitude of my sins which caused God's wrath to spread, I were exiled [16] by the boyars—because

[14] "God's gift" is "grace" (*blagodat'*).

[15] *A chego sami ne poznayete, i vy sami state.* An obviously deficient sentence, as indicated by the editors of *DDG*, p. 427.

[16] Copyist's note: "Here exile does not signify deprivation of the throne but hatred of him, [and] in his last testament, done in 7090 [1582], he speaks more clearly of this and forbids revenge."

of my wilfulness—from my possessions, and I wander [17] about my lands, and may God never leave [me], and I have caused you much misfortune through my sinning, [but] for the sake of God do not languish in your sufferings, place your sorrow upon the Lord and He will sustain you,[18] for as the prophet saith: "My father and my mother have forsaken me, but the Lord will take me up, for all is in the hand of the Lord, as the cup passes from one, humbles another, and exalts another. For no one shall receive honor of himself but he who is called of God, for [He] gives power to whom He desires, and He raiseth up the poor out of the dust, He lifteth up the needy from the dunghill to make them sit with the princes of His people and inherit the throne of glory."[19]

And as long as God has mercy on you [and] frees you from evils, be divided by nothing; and the people should serve you as one man, and the land should [serve you] as one man, and your treasure should belong to you as to one man, for this will be of profit to you.

And you, son Ivan,[20] protect [my] son Fedor,[21] your brother, as yourself, so that he should be wanting in no necessity, and so

[17] Copyist's note: "His wandering signifies that he preferred, because of fear of revolts, to live in the city of Staritsa or, even more, in the Aleksandrova *sloboda*."

[18] "Cast thy burden upon the Lord, and he shall sustain thee" (Psalm lv.22).

[19] For the first part of the quotation, see Psalm xxvii.10; for the latter part, beginning with "He raiseth up," see I Samuel ii.8; see also Psalm cxiii.7–8.

[20] Dmitriy, the first son born to Ivan IV and Anastasiya (1552), died in 1553. Anastasiya was the daughter of the boyar Roman Yur'yevich Zakhar'in-Koshkin. Ivan, the second son of Ivan and Anastasiya, was born in 1554. As a young man he took part in his father's rule but played no important political role. He was killed by his father in a fit of anger on November 19, 1581, at Aleksandrova *sloboda* (Solov'yev, pp. 473, 530, 557–560, 575, 584, 627, 667, and 703–704, and *Entsiklopedicheskiy slovar'*, XXVI, 699–700).

[21] Fedor, the youngest son of Ivan IV and Anastasiya Romanova, was born in 1557 and ruled as tsar from 1584 to 1598. He was indolent and absent-minded, and his reign was dominated by his brother-in-law, Boris Godunov. His death in 1598 marked the end of the House of Ryurik in the Muscovite line.

that all should be done that he should not complain of you that you did not give him a patrimonial principality and of the treasure. And you, son Fedor, not asking for a patrimonial principality or of the treasure of [my] son Ivan, your older brother, as long as he is the steward [*stroitel'*], should live within your wealth, considering in what manner [my] son Ivan should not suffer loss, and [how] it would be possible [for him] to maintain you, and both of you should live as one and should arrange all things in a manner most profitable. And you, son Ivan, should hold, and protect, and love my son Fedor, your younger brother, and should favor him and wish him well in all things, as you wish for yourself, and should conspire with no one to his harm; and you should be with [my] son Fedor, your younger brother, for better and for worse, everywhere [as] one man, for you are the only ones born of your mother.

And you within yourselves should build a refuge, for as Christ said in the Holy Gospel: "For where two or three are gathered together in my name, there am I in the midst of them." [22] And if Christ is in the midst of you because of your love, then no one can shake you; you will be a wall one to the other, and a defense, and a fortress. To whom is he [Fedor] to flee, and in whom is he to place his hopes? You are his father, and his mother, and his brother, and his sovereign, and his guardian. And you should protect him, and love him, and favor him as yourself. And even if he should commit an offense against you in some way, then you should punish him and forgive him, but should not bring him to final ruin; and you should in no way trust to petty quarrels, for Cain killed Abel and yet he did not come into an inheritance.

And God will show good will toward you and you are to be over the state, and your brother Fedor is to be over his patrimonial principality, and you should not covet his patrimonial principality, neither should you conspire with anyone to his injury.

And where along the borders your land joins with his land, this you should protect, and you should strictly observe justice and should not begin to quarrel without reason, and you should not indulge in worldly bickering; for even if one acquires much

[22] Matthew xviii.20.

land and wealth he will not avoid the three-cubit-long grave, and then that is all that will remain. [For] according to the Lord's parable, the grain field of him who wanted to pull down his barns and build larger ones had brought forth plentifully, and God said to him: "Thou fool, this night thy soul shall be required of thee: then whose shall those things be, which thou hast provided?" [23]

And you should have sincere love for your brother and my son Fedor, for as the divine Apostle Paul said: "Love envieth not, love vaunteth not itself, love doth not behave itself unseemly, thinketh no evil, rejoiceth not in iniquity, but rejoiceth in the truth, hopeth all things, endureth all things, love never faileth"; [24] and, as the same apostle said: "But if any provide not for his own, [and specially for those of his own house,] he hath denied the faith, and is worse than an infidel." [25]

And you, O my son Fedor, hold my son Ivan in the place of me, your father, and obey him in all things, as me, and be subject to him in all things, and wish him well as [you do] me, your parent, in all things, and in all things you should be not contradictory to [my] son Ivan as [you are not] to me, your father, and in all things you should live by my word. And God will favor him [Ivan] and he will be over the state, and [God will favor] you and you will be over your patrimonial principality; and you should not covet the state of him and should not conspire with anyone to his harm, and you should everywhere be with [my] son Ivan, for better or for worse, [as] one man. And until such time as [my] son Ivan, because of [my] sins, attains the state, and you your patrimonial principality,[26] you should be together as one with [my] son Ivan, and you should not negotiate in any matters with traitors and evildoers. And if they should tempt you with glory and wealth and honor, or should release any cities to you, or offer you freedom to do as you please, without the knowledge of [my] son Ivan, or call you to reign

[23] Luke xii.16–20.   [24] I Corinthians xiii.4–8, in part.
[25] I Timothy v.8. Note that the phrase in brackets that Ivan omits is defective in the C.S.V.
[26] Copyist's note: "Here he evinces once more his terror of being deprived of the throne."

over the state, you should in no way do this, and you should not remove yourself from the will of [my] son Ivan; as [my] son Ivan commands you, thus you should be, and you should not be tempted by anything. And where [my] son Ivan sends you on his service or orders you to send your people on his service, [there] you should go on his service and send your people, just as my son Ivan commands.

And where along the borders the land of [my] son Ivan joins your land, you should strictly defend this, [and you] should observe justice and should not without reason begin to quarrel, and you should not indulge in worldly bickering, for even if one acquires much wealth or land he will not avoid the three-cubit-long grave, and then all that remains is only one thing: that which we have done, be it good or evil.

And you should hold my son Ivan, your older brother, in place of me, your father, in honor and in awe, and in all things you should place your hope in God and in him, and you should not envy him in anything, for you are both born of the same mother.

And you should build a refuge unto yourselves, [for] as Christ said in the Holy Gospel: "For where two or three are gathered together in my name, there am I in the midst of them." [27] And if Christ is in the midst of you because of your love, then who can shake you? He will be your wall, and your defense, and your army, and your fortress. To whom should you [Fedor] flee, and in whom should you place your hopes? He is to you father, and mother, and older brother, and sovereign, and guardian.

And you, son Fedor, should be submissive in all things to my son Ivan, your older brother, and should wish him well in all things, as [you do] me and yourself, and follow his will in all things, [even] unto blood[shed] and death, [and] do not contradict him in anything. And even though the anger and disfavor of [my] son Ivan be upon you in something, you should not be contradictory to my son Ivan, your older brother, and you should not make any kind of war [against him], and you should

[27] Matthew xviii. 20.

314

in no way defend yourself, but you should petition him that he forgive you, that he be pleased to remove his anger [from you], and that he favor you in all things in accordance with my command. And no matter in what your guilt is, you should petition him, [and] if it pleases him and he heeds your petition, then it is good, but if he does not heed, even then you should not defend yourself but, in all things changing sorrow into happiness, you should place everything on God, for God is the avenger of all injustices.[28]

And you, son Ivan, should live with your younger brother, my son Fedor, in love and agreement, as one man in all things, according to my commandment.

And you, my children, Ivan and Fedor, should live in love and agreement, as one man, and should firmly remember this my instruction. For if you do good, all good will be yours. If you do evil, all evil will come to you, for as it was said in the Gospel: "If one disobeys his father, he shall die the death." [29] Most of all, pursue, strengthen yourselves in and understand the dogmas of the Orthodox faith, and having lived here in a manner pleasing [to the Lord], then there [in the next world] you will be the inheritors of future blessings which "eye hath not seen, nor ear heard, neither have entered into the heart of man, the things which God hath prepared for them that love him." Love God with all your heart and do his commandments with all your heart, to the extent that you have the strength.[30] For as it was said in the Gospel: "[Then] shall the kingdom of heaven be likened unto ten virgins, which took their lamps, and went forth to meet the bridegroom. And five of them were wise, and five were foolish. They that were foolish took their lamps, and took no oil with them: [But the wise] took oil in their vessels with their lamps. While the bridegroom tarried, they all slumbered and

[28] Cf. I Thessalonians iv.6: "That no man go beyond and defraud his brother in any matter: because that the Lord is the avenger of all such."

[29] Mark vii.10. Cf. Matthew xv.4, Exodus xii.21, Leviticus xx.9, and Deuteronomy v.16.

[30] The passage beginning "eye hath not seen" is from I Corinthians ii.9. For the sentence beginning "Love God," cf. Deuteronomy vi.5, Matthew xxii.37, and Luke x.27.

slept. And at midnight there was a cry made, Behold, the bridegroom cometh; Go ye out to meet him. Then all those virgins arose, and trimmed their lamps. And the foolish said unto the wise, Give us of your oil; for our lamps are gone out. But the wise answered, saying, Not so; lest there be not enough for us and you: but go ye rather to them that sell, and buy for yourselves. And while they went to buy, the bridegroom came; and they that were ready went in with him to the marriage: and the door was shut. Afterward came also the other virgins, saying, Lord, Lord, open to us. But he answered and said, Verily I say unto you [I know you not. Watch therefore], for ye know neither the day nor the hour wherein the Son of man cometh." [31] And then [Jesus] says: "A certain man, departing, called his own servants, and delivered unto them his goods. And unto one he gave five talents, to another two, and to another one; to each man according to his several ability; [and straightway took his journey]. Then he that had received the five talents [went and] traded with the same, and made other five talents. And likewise he that had received two, he also gained other two. But he that had received one [went and] digged in the earth, and hid his lord's money. After a long time the lord of those servants cometh, and reckoneth with them. And so he that had received five talents came and brought other five talents, saying, Lord, thou deliveredst unto me five talents: behold, I have gained beside them five talents more. His lord said unto him, Well done, thou good and faithful servant: thou hast been faithful over a few things, I will make thee ruler over many things: enter thou into the joy of thy lord. He also that had received two talents came and said, Lord, thou deliveredst unto me two talents: behold, I have gained two other talents beside them." [32] And this one then and there received grace. He that had digged in the earth received punishment. Ponder in your heart and have faith, as He

[31] The Parable of the Ten Virgins is in Matthew xxv.1–13. A.R.V. and R.S.V. do not have the last phrase, "in which the Son of man cometh," although it appears in A.V. and C.S.V. For comparable passages in A.R.V. and R.S.V., see Matthew xxiv.39, 42, 44.

[32] The Parable of the Talents is found in Matthew xxv.14–30. Ivan quotes through xxv.23.

spake several times, saying: "[Therefore] I say unto you, What things soever ye desire, when ye pray, believe that ye receive them, and ye shall have them. And when ye stand praying, forgive, [if ye have aught against any:] that your Father also which is in heaven may forgive you your trespasses.[33] Heaven and earth shall pass away: but my words shall not pass away. But of that day and that hour knoweth no man, no not the angels which are in heaven, neither the Son, but the Father only.[34] Take ye heed, watch and pray: for ye know not when the master of the house cometh, at even, or at midnight, or at the cockcrowing, or in the morning: Lest coming suddenly he find you sleeping.[35] Ye know that the princes of the Gentiles exercise dominion over them, and they that are great exercise authority upon them. But it shall not be so among you: but whosoever will be great among you, let him be your servant; and whosoever will be chief among you, let him be your servant: even as the Son of man came not to be ministered unto, but to minister, and to give his life a ransom for many." [36] And I say unto you: "For whosoever shall be ashamed of my words, then the Son of man also shall be ashamed of him, when Jesus Christ cometh in his and in the Father's glory.[37] And who then is that faithful and wise steward, whom his lord shall make ruler over his household, to give them their portion of meat in due season? Blessed is that servant, whom his lord when he cometh shall find so doing. Of a truth I say unto you, that [he will make him ruler] over all that he hath. [But and if] that servant [say] in his heart, My lord delayeth his coming [and] tarries; [38] and shall begin to beat the menservants and the maidens, and to eat and drink, and to be drunken; the lord of that servant will come in a day when he looketh not for him, and at an hour when he is not aware, and will cut him in sunder,[39] and will appoint him his portion with

[33] Mark xi.24–25.   [34] Mark xiii.31–32.

[35] Mark xiii.33, 35–36. Ivan has combined portions of these.

[36] Matthew xx.25–28.   [37] Cf. Mark viii.38 and Luke ix.26.

[38] Ivan adds a second word (*medlit*) to the original word for "delayeth" (*kosnit'*) (see Luke xii.45 [C.S.V.]).

[39] Or, "severely scourge him," as in C.S.V. (*i rasteshet' yego*). Ivan has "overthrow him" (*oprovergnet yego*).

the unbelievers. And that servant, which knew his lord's will, [and prepared not himself], neither did [according to his will], shall be beaten with many stripes; but he that knew not, and did commit things worthy of recompense, shall receive.[40] For unto whomsoever much is given, of him shall be much required: and to whom men have committed much, of him they will ask the more." [41]

And again Jesus said: "A certain man made a great supper, and bade many: and sent his servant at supper time to say to them that were bidden, Come; for all things are now ready. And they all with one consent began to make excuse. The first said unto him, I have bought a piece of ground, and I must needs go and see it: I pray thee have me excused. And another said, I have bought five yoke of oxen, and I go to prove them: I pray thee have me excused. And another said, I have married a wife, and therefore I cannot come. And so that servant came, and shewed his lord these things. Then the master of the house being angry said to his servant, Go out quickly into the streets and lanes of the city, and bring in hither the poor, and the needy, and the blind, and the halt. And the servant said, lo, [Lord,] it is done as thou hast commanded, and yet there is room. And the lord said unto the servant, Go out into the highways and hedges, and compel them to come in, that my house may be filled. For I say unto you, That none of those men which were bidden has tasted of my supper, for many are called, but few are chosen." [42] And

---

[40] Obviously an error on the part of either Ivan or the copyist. The passage should read: "and did commit things worthy of stripes, shall be beaten with few stripes" (Luke xii.48 [A.V.]); or "shall be beaten little" (C.S.V.).

[41] For the passage beginning "who then is that," see Luke xii.42–48. Cf. Matthew xxiv.45–51.

[42] The Parable of the Great Supper (Luke xiv.16–24). A.V. has "the poor, and the maimed, and the halt, and the blind"; R.S.V. has "the poor and maimed and blind and lame." Ivan has quoted accurately from C.S.V.

Ivan is in error in writing "has tasted of my supper." Both A.V. and C.S.V. have "shall taste of my supper."

A.V. and R.S.V. do not have "for many are called, but few are chosen." These words do appear at this place in C.S.V.; they also appear in Matthew xx.14 in all three versions, following a similar parable.

then: "Two men went up into the temple to pray; the one a Pharisee, and the other a publican. The Pharisee stood and prayed thus with himself, God, I thank thee, that I am not as other men are, extortioners, unjust, adulterers, or even as this publican. I fast twice in the week, I give tithes of all that I possess. And the publican, standing afar off, would not lift up so much as his eyes unto heaven, but smote upon his breast, saying, God be merciful to me a sinner. I tell you, this man went out justified rather than the other: for every one that exalteth himself shall be abased; and he that humbleth himself shall be exalted.[43] Likewise: Render therefore unto Caesar the things which are Caesar's; and unto God the things that are God's.[44] For God sent not His Son into the world to condemn the world; but that the world through him might be saved. He that believeth on him is not condemned, but he that believeth not is condemned already, because he hath not believed in the name of the only begotten Son of God. And this is the condemnation, that light is come into the world, and men loved darkness rather than light, because their deeds were evil. For every one that doeth evil hateth the light, neither cometh to the light, lest his deeds should be reproved, that they are evil. But he that doeth truth cometh to the light, that his deeds may be made manifest, that they are wrought in God. If any man serve me, let him follow me; and where I am, there shall also my servant be: if any man serve me, him will my Father honour.[45] And if ye love me, keep my commandments. And I will pray the Father, [and] he shall give you another Comforter, that he may abide with you for ever; even the Spirit of truth.[46] If a man love me, he will keep my words: and my Father will love him, and we will come unto him, and make our abode with him." [47] For thus commanded our

---

[43] The Parable of the Pharisee and the Publican (Luke xviii.10–14). A.V., R.S.V., and C.S.V. all have "went down to his house"; Ivan has "went out" (*izyde*).

[44] Matthew xx.21; Mark xii.17; Luke xx.25.

[45] The words beginning "For God sent not" is from John iii.17–21. The words "that they are evil" do not occur here in A.V. or R.S.V., but they do appear in C.S.V. at this place.

The passage beginning "If any man serve me" is from John xii.26.

[46] John xiv.15–17.   [47] John xiv.23.

Lord Jesus Christ to do his commandments; for those who do them and do his will, he will in love pray for them and give [them] grace. "Father, the hour is come; glorify thy Son, that thy Son also may glorify thee: as thou hast given him power over all flesh, that he should give eternal life to as many as thou hast given him. And this is life eternal, that they might know thee the only [true] God, and Jesus Christ whom thou hast sent. I have glorified thee on the earth: I have finished the work which thou gavest me to do. And now, O Father, glorify thou me with thine own self with the glory which I had with thee before the world was. I have manifested thy name unto the men which thou gavest me out of the world: thine they were, and thou gavest them me; and they have kept thy word. Now they have known that all things whotsoever thou hast given me are of thee. For I have given unto them the words which thou gavest me; and they have received them, and have known [surely] that I came out from thee, and they have believed that thou didst send me. I pray for them: I pray not for all the world, but for them which thou hast given me; for they are thine. And all mine are thine, and thine are mine; and I am glorified in them.[48] I have given them thy word; and the world hath hated them, because they are not of the world, even as I am not of the world. I pray not that thou shouldest take them from the world, but that thou shouldest keep them from the evil. They are not of the world, even as I am not of the world. Save them through thy truth: [49] thy word is truth. As thou hast sent me into the world, even so have I also sent them into the world. And for their sakes I sanctify myself, that they also might be sanctified through the truth. Neither pray I for these alone, but for them also which shall believe on me through their word; that they all may be one; as thou, Father, art in me, and I in thee, that they also may be one in us: that the world may believe that thou hast sent me. And the glory which thou gavest me I have given them; that

---

[48] John xvii.1–10.

[49] "Save" (*spasi*) should read "sanctify." Probably an error on the part of either the copyist or the editors of *DDG*.

they may be one, even as we are one: I in them, and thou in me, that they may be made perfect in one; and that the world may know that thou hast sent me, and hast loved them, as thou hast loved me. Father, I will that they also, whom thou hast given me, be with me where I am; that they also may be with me, [that they may behold my glory,] which thou hast given me: for thou lovedst me before the foundation of the world. O righteous Father, the world hath not known thee: but I have known thee, and these have known that thou hast sent me. And I have declared unto them thy name, and will declare it: that the love wherewith thou hast loved me may be in them, and I in them." [50] You see, of such nature is God's gift; for what is more pleasant than to be in God [and] to be like unto God, and to live with God, and to dwell in the kisses of God's love, and to delight in and inherit eternal bliss! For what is more evil than to be separated from God, and to be deprived of the delights of eternal bliss, and to receive endless torments! And you, my children, Ivan and Fedor, should zealously obey the commandments of God and of the Gospel, and you should also obey my instructions and commands with zeal, and you should zealously flee, to the extent that this is possible, from all the power and bondage of the evil allurements of this world, and [you should obey] the immortal commandments of the Lord, and [you should] wish to inherit delight in eternal bliss with all your soul, and with all your strength, and with all your mind, and you should guard yourselves against all backsliding, and stumbling, and windy temptation by the Enemy.

And you, my children, Ivan and Fedor, in love should be as one man, indivisible, in accordance with this my instruction, [and] you should be divided in your patrimonies and in your treasures, but in your hearts and your love you should be indivisible, and neither should envy the other in anything, and if one should be lacking in something, then you should listen one to the other in love, but one should not take [anything] from the other

[50] The passage beginning "I have given them thy word" is from John xvii.14–26.

by force, but in all matters, in evil and in good, you should ever be as one man, and one should not deny the other in any matter, not only in laboring and struggling, but even in spilling blood and dying.

And you, Ivan and Fedor, should be, in accordance with my instruction, both as one man, and should guard one another in all things, and should live by God in all matters. And even if, because of your sins, something should lead you to the wrath of internecine wars, you should even then act as the apostle of the Lord: justice and equality give to your servants, tempering these with forgiveness, knowing that even your Lord is in heaven. Likewise, you should act in all cases of disgrace and punishments, where possible, according to reason, [and you should] change them into mercy and [should] reserve a part [of it] to your souls, for you will receive mercy from the Lord because of your long suffering, for as was said elsewhere: "For it is fitting for a king to understand these three things: how not to provoke God to wrath, and how not to exalt himself over mortals, and [how] to be long-suffering towards sinners." [51] Thus, if you live in the goodness of God, then [long] years of life will be given you. Do not forget us—your parents and grandparents—not only in the capital city of Moscow or in other places wherever you may be, but even if you should be persecuted or in exile, [do not forget us] in divine services, and in funeral services, and in prayers for the dead, and in giving alms and food to the poor, to the extent that it is possible; for in remembering the souls of our ancestors you shall obtain great benefit for us and for yourselves here and in the future life, and [you shall obtain] the welfare of the holy, divine churches, and victory over your enemies, and overcoming, and the ordering of the state, and rest during your life and the enjoyment of eternal bliss that comes from their prayers, for the grace of God and [His] blessing has come to you, heirs and children, from [your] fathers. And may the God of Peace, glorified in the Trinity, be with you, [and may] the prayers of our most holy and most blessed Lady, the Mother of God, the intercessor for Christians, and may the grace of her

[51] This quotation is not identified.

holy image, the icon of Vladimir,[52] the intercession for the Russian state at all times and at all places, be with you; and may the
prayers and blessings of all the saints of the whole universe, and
of the Russian wonder-workers Petr, Aleksiy, Iona, Ioann, Nikita, Leontiy, Sergiy, and Varlaam, and Kirill, and Pokhnutiy,
and Nikita,[53] and of all the Russian saints in their prayers [be
with you], and [may] the blessings of our entire family—from
Grand Prince Vladimir who enlightened the Russian land with

[52] Concerning this icon, see N. N. Voronin and M. K. Karker, *Istoriya
kul'tury drevney Rusi: Domongol'skiy period, Obshchestvenny stroy i
dukhovnaya kul'tura* (Moscow-Leningrad, 1951), pp. 354–357.

[53] Concerning Metropolitan Petr, see above, Text 9, n. 65.

Saint Aleksiy, metropolitan from 1353 to 1377, was a strong supporter
of the princes of Moscow and did much to raise the prestige of the
Russian church (see *PSRL*, XXV, 179 and 194–196, and Solov'yev, II,
567–570; see also above, Commentary to Text 4 and Text 11, n. 12).

Saint Iona was appointed metropolitan in 1431 by a council of the
Russian hierarchy, but his appointment was not confirmed by Constantinople. In 1448 another Russian council confirmed his position. A great
partisan of Grand Prince Vasiliy II, Iona addressed the grand prince as
"grand sovereign, the Russian tsar" (*velikiy gospodar', tsar' russkiy*) (see
Russkiy biograficheskiy slovar' [St. Petersburg, 1896–1918], Vol. Ibak-
Klyucharev, pp. 313–314).

Probably Ioann, Metropolitan of Kiev, a Greek who became metropolitan no later than 1077. He died in either 1088 or 1089 (see *Russkiy
biograficheskiy slovar'*, Vol. Ibak-Klyucharev).

Saint Nikita, Bishop of Novgorod from 1096 to 1108, and Nikita
Stolpnik (the Stylite) of Pereyaslavl' Zalesskiy (twelfth century) (*Russkiy biograficheskiy slovar'*, Vol. Na-Ni, p. 288).

Probably Saint Leontiy, Bishop of Rostov in the eleventh century
(*Russkiy biograficheskiy slovar'*, Vol. La-Lya, p. 221).

Concerning Saint Sergiy, founder and abbot (fourteenth century) of
the Trinity Monastery of Radonezh, see Solov'yev, II, 596–597.

The reference may possibly be to Metropolitan Varlaam, concerning
whom, see above Text 12, n. 8.

Either Saint Kirill, the twelfth-century Bishop of Turov, or Kirill
Belozerskiy (*c.* 1337–1427), who founded the Kirill of Beloozero Monastery (see *Russkiy biograficheskiy slovar'*, Vol. Ibak-Klyucharev, pp.
655–657; concerning Kirill of Beloozero, see also Solov'yev, II, 597–598).

Probably Pafnutiy Borovskiy, founder and first abbot of the Borovsk
(Pafnutiyev) Monastery near Kaluga (fifteenth century) (*Russkiy biograficheskiy slovar'*, Vol. Pa-Pe, p. 408, and Solov'yev, II, 741).

holy baptism [and who was] called Vasiliy in holy baptism,[54] even to our father, Grand Prince Vasiliy Ivanovich of All Russia, [called] as a monk Varlaam,[55] and to our mother, Grand Princess Yelena, and to my wife Anastasiya, your mother:[56] may [their] prayers and blessing be with you now, and forever, and in the ages to come. And because of my sins, my wives Mariya and Marfa[57] passed away, and you should remember my wives, Mariya and Marfa and your gracious mother, in your prayers, in all things, as I have ordered, and you should remember them in your prayers along with all your ancestors, without forgetfulness. And if God is gracious and you attain your state and establish yourself over it, then I bless you. You, my son Fedor, hold my son Ivan in the place of me, your father, and obey him

[54] Saint Vladimir was baptized in 988, receiving the Christian name of Vasiliy in honor of the Byzantine emperor Basil II (see *Povest' vremennykh let*, ed. V. P. Adrianova-Peretts, text prepared by D. S. Likhachev, trans. D. S. Likhachev and B. A. Romanov [Moscow-Leningrad, 1950], I, 75–83, and George Vernadsky, *Kievan Russia* [New Haven, 1948], pp. 60–70).

[55] "Grand Prince Vasiliy Ivanovich of All Rus', as a monk called Varlaam, died in the year 7042, on 3 of the month of December" (*PSRL*, VI, 274).

[56] On February 3, 1547, Ivan married Anastasiya, daughter of the boyar Roman Yur'yevich Zakhar'in-Koshkin. She was the mother of Dmitriy (who died in infancy), Ivan, and Fedor. She died in 1560, perhaps from poison, as Ivan claimed (see Solov'yev, III, 433 and 702).

[57] Copyist's note: "Here he mentions three of his deceased wives, namely: Anastasiya of the Romanovs, Mariya of the Cherkaskiys, Marfa of the Sabakins, and the living Anna, after her was Marfa of the Nagoys, all told, 5. A[ndrey] Kurpskiy in [his] *Istoriya* points out: before this Anna there were 5 wives."

After unsuccessful efforts to arrange a marriage with the sister of Sigismund Augustus of Poland, in 1561 Ivan married Mariya, the daughter of a Circassian prince named Temryuk. Mariya died in 1569 (see Solov'yev, III, 572–573 and 702). In 1571 Ivan married Marfa Sobakina, daughter of a merchant of Novgorod, but she died less than a month after the wedding. She too was probably poisoned (Solov'yev, III, 702). In 1572, in violation of church rules, Ivan married Anna Koltovskaya; three years later she was sent to a monastery (Solov'yev, III, 702–703). Ivan married Mariya Fedorovna Nagaya in 1580. She became the mother of his youngest son, Dmitriy (Solov'yev, III, 703).

in all things. And you, my son Ivan, hold my son Fedor, your younger brother, without injury, and be in my place towards him in all things.

I bless my son Ivan [with] the cross, the great life-giving tree of Tsar'grad.[58] And my son Ivan I also bless [with] the cross of Petr the Wonder-Worker with which the Wonder-Worker blessed our ancestor Grand Prince Ivan Danilovich and our entire family.[59] And my son Ivan I also bless with the Russian tsardom, with the Cap of Monomakh, and with the entire regalia of the tsar, which Emperor Constantine Monomachus sent from Tsar'grad to our ancestor, Tsar and Grand Prince Vladimir Monomakh.[60] And my son Ivan I also bless with all the tsar's caps [crowns], and with the regalia of the tsar which I have acquired, and the staves, and the tablecloth,[61] and, in German, the *tsentur'*.[62]

And my son Ivan I also bless with my Russian tsardom with which my father, Grand Prince Vasiliy, blessed me and which God gave me. I give him the city of Moscow with its volosts, and *stans*, and with its *puti*,[63] and with its villages, and with its merchants' courts and courts in the suburbs, and with its *tamga*,[64] and with its *myto*, and with its taxes on trading in the market place, and with its tax on trading stands, and with its tax on merchants' courts, and with all its customs, and with the village

[58] Probably the relic bequeathed to Vasiliy III by Ivan III (see Chapter 6 and Text 11, n. 89).

[59] See above, Text 9, n. 65.

[60] Concerning this legend, see Chapter 6.

[61] Copyist's note: "The meaning of *skatert'* is not known, but apparently it was among the regalia."

[62] *Zentur*, or ceinture?

[63] Copyist's note: "*Put'* simply means road [*doroga*], but here it is to be understood as income, from the fact that for campaigns 'road tributes' [*dani putevyye*] were formerly levied, from which incomes are here named, and monies were also called *put'*, as is still stamped on many."

[64] Copyist's note: "*Tomga* in Tartar means a seal or sign, but it is also understood as a levied tax [*podat'*], as is apparent from Tartar charters and from history, as poll monies are often called *tamga*, which in such case are levied at the rate of one *grivna* from each person who owns a *luk*" of land [i.e., two *obzha*, or 18.144 acres]."

Dobryatinskoye with its apiary, and with *Visil'tsovyy stol*",[65] and with the enrolled people, and with their relatives.[66] And to him I also give the village Somchinskoye with the city courts, and with Samsonov Meadow, and the village Vorob'yevo, and with Volodimerskoye, and with Semenovskoye, and with Vorontsovo, and with Kadashevo,[67] and with their hamlets, as it was under me. And to him I also give the village Aminevo, and the village Khoroshovo, with everything as it was under me. And to him I also give, on the Setun' [River], the village Volynskoye, with its hamlets [and] with everything, also as it was under me. And to him I also give the village Vorontsovo, with its city courts along both sides of the Yauza River, and with the mills, as it was under me, and Lyshchikovo Monastery with its courts. And to him I also give the *slobodka* Kalychevskaya with the meadow, which used to belong to my uncle, Prince Andrey Ivanovich, and to his son, Prince Vladimir Andreyevich,[68] and the villages near Moscow: Sarayevo, Yedninskoye, Kartashevo, Yasenevo, and—also near Moscow—the village Sobakino and the village Turinovo, which Prince Vladimir Andreyevich obtained from me in exchange. And to my son Ivan I also give the volosts beyond the Moskva which used to belong to my uncle, Prince Andrey Ivanovich, and to his son, Prince Vladimir An-

---

[65] An error for *sto*, 'hundred.' The reference is to Vasiliy's Hundred.

[66] Copyist's note: "The meaning of Vislovo Hundred, enrolled people [*chislyane*, as compared to *chislyaki* in the text of the testament], and *rodnitsy* [*srodnitsy* in the text] is unknown to me, although it is apparent that certain *slobodas* belonging to Moscow were thus named, as well as the village and meadow Samsonovskoy, but they must be searched out in the old cadastres, for they were subsequently renamed for churches."

[67] Copyist's note: "Volodimirskoye in Kulishki, Semenovskoye Vorontsovo, and Kodashevo are now all within Moscow."

[68] Prince Vladimir Andreyevich was imprisoned with his father in 1537 during the rule of Yelena. After the fall of Vasiliy Shuyskiy from power, Vladimir was released and in 1541 was given his father's patrimonial principality of Staritsa (see Solov'yev, III, 424). Concerning Prince Vladimir's claim to the throne, his refusal to kiss the cross to Ivan's infant son Dmitriy at the time of the tsar's illness in 1553, his loss of his patrimonial principality (Staritsa and Vereya, in exchange for which he received Dmitrov and Zvenigorod), and his mysterious death in 1569, see Solov'yev, III, 524–528 and 557–558.

dreyevich: the volost Rameneytsov, the volost Zagar'ye, the volost Kun'ye, the volost Vokhna, the volost Yena,[69] the volost Guslitsy, the volost Gzhel', and with the *pod"yesnyye* villages [70] that are in those volosts.

And my son Ivan shall maintain his grand lieutenant [71] in Moscow as of old, as it was under my father, Grand Prince Vasiliy Ivanovich of All Russia, and as it was under me, and he shall maintain another lieutenant in the third of Prince Vladimir Andreyevich Donskoy, also in Moscow.[72] And concerning my courts in Moscow within the city and in the suburbs, and [concerning] all my gardens and the waste lands about the suburbs [which are] in the possession of my boyars, or princes, or in the possession of my junior boyars, or in the possession of my court men, or bureau people,[73] or equerries, or in the possession of my master artisans, and [concerning] the *slobodas* of the *streltsy*,[74] and [concerning] the *slobodas* of the post relay men, now all these [shall pass] to my son Ivan. And those boyars, and princes, and junior boyars who have their courts within the city of Moscow, or outside the city, or in the suburbs—be they patrimonial or purchased patrimonial—or anyone who has charters of grant to courts of my father, Grand Prince Vasiliy

[69] The volost Yena has not been identified. It is probably an error for the volost Selna, willed to Prince Andrey Ivanovich by the testament of Ivan III.

[70] Not clear. The word *pod"yesnyy* may be related to *pod"yezd"*, a type of custom tax (see I. I. Sreznevskiy, *Materialy dlya slovarya drevne-russkogo yazyka* [Moscow, 1958], II, 1072).

[71] See Chapter 5.

[72] It is interesting that Ivan IV applies the epithet *Donskoy* to Prince Vladimir Andreyevich. This epithet has subsequently been reserved for Grand Prince Dmitriy Ivanovich.

[73] See Chapter 5.

[74] The *streltsy* (shooters, arquebusiers) were the standing troops of Muscovy. They were paid in money and were quartered in special *slobodas*. Figures are available for the number of *streltsy* in Moscow during the reigns of Fedor and Boris Godunov, that is, twenty to thirty years following the writing of this testament: under Fedor there were 7000 *streltsy* in Moscow; under Boris 10,000. For this and other information on the *streltsy*, see Solov'yev, IV, 379.

Ivanovich, now my son Ivan shall not interfere in these their courts.[75]

And the Moscow volosts Rogozh', Vori, Korzeneva, Sherna city, Suleshino, and the village Novoye, also [shall pass] to my son Ivan. And to him also [I give] the volost Surozhik, and Luchinskoye, and Radonezh' with their volosts, and with their *puti*, and with their villages, and with all their customs, and one third of Mushkova [Gora], with the Lopskiy *myt*.[76]

And my son Ivan I also bless with my grand principalities with which my father, Grand Prince Vasiliy Ivanovich, blessed me. And to him [shall pass] the [following] grand principalities: the city of Volodimer with its volosts, and with its *puti*, and with its villages, with all its customs, and with the small village Muromskoye, and with Shatur, and with Koluzhskoye,[77] and with Vysheles, and with Ostrov, and with the volost Krysinskoye, and with everything as it was under me. And to my son Ivan I also give, in addition to Volodimer, the patrimonies of the Starodub princes[78] in Starodub Ryapolovo, which came to me from Prince Mikhail Vorotynskiy,[79] [namely] the

---

[75] For a similar passage in the testament of Ivan III, see above, p. 271.

[76] See above, Text 11, n. 18.

[77] Or Kolushka (*DDG*, p. 539.) Kolushka was a volost of Vladimir District, bequeathed to Prince Vasiliy III by Ivan III. Koluzhskoye (or Kolushskoye) was a village, perhaps the center of the volost Kolushka (*DDG*, p. 539).

[78] See above, Text 10, n. 11. The patrimonies of the descendants of the House of Starodub—the princes Gundorov, Pozharskiy, Tulupov, Romadanovskiy, Kovrov, Krivoyezerskiy, Nagayev, Starodubskiy, and Paletskiy—were taken away from them, probably by Ivan IV. Solov'yev, IV, 12–13, cites the testament of Ivan IV as the source of this information. Concerning the princely families descended from the Starodub princes, see A. V. Ekzemplyarskiy, *Velikiye i udel'nyye knyaz'ya sever-noy Rusi v" tatarskiy period", s" 1238 po 1505 g.* (St. Petersburg, 1889), II, 188–189.

[79] Mikhail Ivanovich Vorotynskiy was the descendant of an old princely family of Chernigov (Prince Mikhail Vsevolodovich, thirteenth century). He participated in the campaign against Kazan' in 1551 and was made a boyar in 1552. For some unknown reason, he was relieved of his holdings by Ivan IV in 1561 and exiled to Beloozero. He was pardoned in 1565 and in 1572 commanded the Muscovite troops which defeated the

village Antiokhovo, and the village Voskresenskoye, and the village Novyye Zemenki, which used to belong to Prince Fedor and Prince Ivan Gundorov,[80] and the village Staryye Mekhovitsy, which used to belong to Roman Gundorov, and the village Mogucheye, which used to belong to Prince Ivan Pozharskiy the Younger,[81] and the village Voskresenskoye,[82] which used to belong to Prince Nikita Tulupov,[83] and the village Seritsy and the village Tatarovo, which used to belong to Prince Petr Sharapov Romadanovskiy,[84] and the village Troitsskoye and the village Faleyevo, which used to belong to Prince Timofey and Prince Ivan Pozharskiy,[85] and the village Andreyevskoye, which used to belong to Prince Vasiliy Kovrov,[86] and the village Rozhestvenskoye, and the hamlet Kamennoye, and the three villages Vasil'yevo, which used to belong to Prince Ivan, the son of Prince Semen Pozharskiy,[87] and the hamlet Kovernev, and the

---

invading Tartars. Accused by his servant of wizardry and of planning to murder the tsar, Vorotynskiy was seized in 1577 and died as the result of torture (see *Entsiklopedicheskiy slovar'*, XIII, 230–231). The holdings of which Vorotynskiy was deprived were his patrimony: the city of Odoyev and others. In return he was granted Starodub Ryapolovo, the volost Moshok in Murom, and lesser places (see Solov'yev, IV, 12).

[80] See n. 78, above.   [81] See n. 78, above.

[82] *DDG*, p. 531, lists only one village Voskresenskoye of Starodub Ryapolovo District, yet two are mentioned in this testament.

[83] See n. 78, above. Prince Nikita Tulupov participated in Ivan's campaign in Estonia and in the capture of the city of Payda in the autumn of 1572 and in early 1573 (see Karamzin, IX, 128, and "Notes to Volume IX," n. 412, cols. 92–93).

[84] See n. 78, above. Prince Petr Borisovich Romodanovskiy-Sharap was taken prisoner with his father after the defeat of the Russians by the Lithuanians in the battle on the Orsha River, September 8, 1514 (Karamzin, VII, 42–43, and "Notes to Volume VII," n. 125, col. 23).

[85] See n. 78, above. Ivan and Timofey Pozharskiy were granted military tenures (*pomest'ya*) near Moscow by order of the tsar in October 1550 (see A. A. Zimin, ed., *Tysyachnaya kniga 1550 g. i dvorovaya tetrad' 50-kh godov XVI v.* [Moscow-Leningrad, 1950], p. 63).

[86] See n. 78, above. Prince Vasiliy Ivanovich Kovrov was granted a military tenure near Moscow in 1550 (*Tysyachnaya kniga*, p. 63).

[87] See n. 78, above. Prince Semen Borisovich Pozharskiy was listed as a military tenant (*pomeshchik*) in the "Court Book of the Fifties of the XVI Century" (see *Tysyachnaya kniga*, p. 123).

other hamlets which used to belong to Prince Ivan, the son of Prince Andrey Kovrov,[88] and the village Nesterovskoye, which used to belong to Prince Ivan the Younger, the son of Prince Ivan Krivozerskiy,[89] and the village Aleksandrovskoye, and the village Ustinovskoye, and the village Ovsyanikovo, which used to belong to Prince Andrey Krivozerskiy and his brothers,[90] and the village Khryapovo and the village Mitsyno, which used to belong to Prince Fedor Romodanovskiy,[91] and the village Matveyevskoye, and the village Yablontsy, which used to belong to Prince Mikhail Romodanovskiy,[92] and the village Tatarovo, and the village Nikol'skoye,[93] which used to belong to Prince Afanasiy Nagayev,[94] and the village Panteleyevo, which used to belong to Princess Mariya, [the wife] of Prince Andrey Starodubskiy,[95] the village Soroki and the village Kuveno, which used to belong to Princess Yevfrosin'ya, [the wife] of Prince Semen Starodubskiy,[96] the village Ameleva, which used to belong to Prince Nikita Starodubskiy,[97] and one half of the village Ramadonovo,[98] which used

[88] See n. 78, above. Prince Ivan Andreyevich Kovrov was granted a military tenure near Moscow in 1550 (*Tysyachnaya kniga*, p. 63).

[89] Concerning the Krivozerskiy (Krivoyezerskiy) princes, see n. 78, above.

[90] See n. 78, above.

[91] See n. 78, above. Prince Fedor Borisovich Romodanovskiy was granted a military tenure near Moscow in 1550 (*Tysyachnaya kniga*, p. 58).

[92] See n. 78, above.

[93] A village called Tatarovo, Starodub Ryapolovo District, was listed above as having formerly belonged to Prince Petr Sharapov Romodanovskiy. This is presumably another village of the same name located in the same district. The village Nikol'skoye was in Starodub Ryapolovo District.

[94] See n. 78, above.

[95] See n. 78, above. Prince Andrey Ivanovich Starodubskiy was listed in the "Court Book" as being in Moscow "with the tsarina" (*u tsaritsy*) (*Tysyachnaya kniga*, p. 125).

[96] See n. 78, above. Prince Semen Ivanovich Starodubskiy was listed in the "Court Book" as having died (*Tysyachnaya kniga*, p. 125).

[97] See n. 78, above. Prince Nikita (Mikita) Mikhaylovich Starodubskiy was listed in the "Court Book" as being in Moscow (*Tysyachnaya kniga*, p. 125).

to belong to Prince Ivan Ramodanovskiy,[99] and the village Dmitreyevskoye, which used to belong to Princess Fedosiya Pozharskaya and her children,[100] and the village Kochergino, which used to belong to Prince Ivan Pozharskiy,[101] and the village Golobokovo and the hamlet Skorekovo, which used to belong to Princess Mariya, [the wife] of Prince Boris Pozharskiy, and to her son, Prince Mikhail,[102] and the village Luchki with its hamlets, which used to belong to Princess Mariya, [the wife] of Prince Petr Pozharskiy,[103] and to Princess Fedosiya, the daughter of Prince Semen Mezetskiy,[104] and the village Osipovo, which used to belong to Prince Vasiliy Osipov-

---

[98] The village Ramadonovo (Romodanovo) was in Starodub Ryapolovo District (*DDG*, p. 553). It was from this village that the Romodanovskiy princes took their name.

[99] See n. 78, above. Prince Ivan Borisovich Romodanovskiy was among those who were granted military tenures near Moscow in 1550 (*Tysyachnaya kniga*, p. 63).

[100] See n. 78, above.

[101] See n. 78, above. Two princes named Ivan Pozharskiy (Ivan the Elder Ivanovich and Ivan the Younger Ivanovich) are listed in the "Court Book" as Yaroslavl' military tenants (*Tysyachnaya kniga*, p. 123). Two princes named Ivan Pozharskiy (Ivan Ivanovich Tret'yakov, Prince of Starodub, and Ivan the Black Vasil'yevich) were among those who received military tenures near Moscow in 1550 (*Tysyachnaya kniga*, p. 63). Prince Ivan Ivanovich Tret'yakov Pozharskiy is listed in the "Court Book" as a Yaroslavl' military tenant who "has passed his military tenure to Mikhail [Pozharskiy], he serves" (*Tysyachnaya kniga*, p. 123).

[102] See n. 78, above. Prince Mikhail Borisovich Pozharskiy is listed in the "Court Book" as a Yaroslavl' military tenant (*Tysyachnaya kniga*, p. 123).

[103] See n. 78, above. The reference is either to Prince Petr Borisovich Pozharskiy or Prince Petr Vasil'yevich Pozharskiy. Prince Petr Borisovich of Starodub received a military tenure near Moscow in 1550. (*Tysyachnaya kniga*, p. 63). Petr Vasil'yevich Pozharskiy, Prince of Starodub, also received a military tenure near Moscow in 1550. He is listed as a Yaroslavl' military tenant in the "Court Book" (*Tysyachnaya kniga*, pp. 63 and 123).

[104] Prince Semen Mikhaylovich Mezetskiy is listed as a Starodub military tenant in the "Court Book." The same source reports that he had died (*Tysyachnaya kniga*, p. 123).

skiy, and the village Palekh,[105] which used to belong to the children of Prince Dmitriy Paletskiy,[106] and the village Yur'yevskoye and the village Zales'ye, which used to belong to Prince Nikita and Prince Ama Gundorov,[107] and all the other villages which were of the patrimony that used to belong to Semen Obraztsov.[108]

And to my son Ivan I give the city of Kolomna with its volosts, and with its *puti*, and with its villages, and with all its customs. And to him I also give the city of Kashira, with Zarech'ye, and with all its customs, and with the volosts beyond the Oka River: Teshilovo, Rostovets, Roslavl', Venev, Mstislavl', and other localities along the Rezan border, with their *puti*, and with their villages, and with all their customs, and with Yelets

[105] The village Palekh, from which the Paletskiy princes took their name, was in Starodub Ryapolovo District (*DDG*, p. 549).

[106] See n. 78, above. Prince Dmitriy Fedorovich Paletskiy is listed among those who received military tenures near Moscow in 1550 (*Tysyachnaya kniga*, p. 54). He was listed as a boyar in the "Court Book" (*Tysyachnaya kniga*, p. 111). Prince Dmitriy Paletskiy was the commander of a detachment of Russians that defeated the Tartars near Ryazan' in August 1533. Though one of the first to kiss the cross to young Dmitriy during Ivan's illness in 1553, Paletskiy informed the tsar's cousin, Prince Vladimir of Staritsa (whom many boyars supported in preference to Dmitriy), that he would not oppose Vladimir's elevation to the throne if Vladimir and his mother, Yevfrosin'ya, would promise a patrimonial principality to Paletskiy's son-in-law Yuriy, the incompetent younger brother of Tsar Ivan. Paletskiy even promised to serve Vladimir if he became tsar (Solov'yev, III, 274 and 528). Apparently still in the good graces of the tsar, in 1555 Paletskiy was named voivode and lieutenant of the tsar (*namestnik*) in Novgorod, and later in the year commanded a Russian campaign against the Swedes (Solov'yev, IV, 37–39).

Two Paletskiy princes (unidentified) were killed in the battle between the Russians and the Lithuanians on the Ula River in 1564 (Solov'yev, III, 579).

[107] see n. 78, above. Prince Nikita (Mikita) Grigor'yevich Gundorov is listed in the "Court Book" as a Yaroslavl' military tenant (*Tysyachnaya kniga*, p. 123). Prince Ama Gundorov is not identified.

[108] The junior boyar Semen Romanovich Obraztsov was among those granted military tenures near Moscow in 1550. He was listed in the "Court Book" as a junior boyar of the court (*dvorovyy syn boyarskiy*) from Mozhaysk (*Tysyachnaya kniga*, pp. 76 and 184).

and all the Yelets lands. And to my son Ivan I give the city of Serpukhov with its volosts, and with its *puti*, and with its villages, and with all its customs.[109] And I also give to him the city on the Plava [River] and on the Solova [River],[110] with all the "plain" patrimonies,[111] and with all that has belonged to it from of old.

And my son Ivan I also bless [and] give to him the Grand Principality of Rezan: the city of Pereslavl' Rezanskiy, the city of Staraya Ryazan', the city Ryaskoy, the city of Dankov,[112] and the entire third[113] with all its customs, and with its volosts, and

[109] For similar passages in the testament of Ivan III, see above, p. 272.

[110] Copyist's note: "Now called the city of Krapivna. *Pol'skiye* means steppe patrimonies."

[111] *So vsemi Polskimi votchinami*, 'with all the plain patrimonies.' The "plain" cities were located in part of the area formerly known as the Wild Plain (*dikoye pole*). The area of the plain cities stretched southwest from Yelets and included the areas around Kursk and Belgorod. It reached the Polish-Russian border in the southwest and also included an area southeast of Yelets which encompassed the city of Kursk. Concerning the word *pol'skiy* (or *pol'skoy*), see Sreznevskiy, II, 1150, and V. Dal', *Tolkovyy slovar' zhivogo velikorusskogo yazyka* (Moscow, 1955), III, 258.

Krapivna, about thirty-five kilometers southwest of Tula, was in the latter half of the sixteenth century on or near the northern boundary of the plain region. In 1574 Krapivna was one of a number of cities (Ryazhsk, Donkov, and others) concerned with guarding the southern boundaries of Russia (see Solov'yev, IV, 26–27).

[112] This is the first mention in the testaments of the city of Ryaskoy (Ryazhsk), which was located about ninety kilometers south and slightly west of Staraya Ryazan'. Dankov, also mentioned here for the first time in the testaments, was located on the upper Don River about eighty kilometers southwest of Ryazhsk. Ivan IV founded (or fortified) Ryazhsk and Dankov about 1571 (see Karamzin, IX, 276).

[113] Copyist's note: "Third (*tret'*) meant a division at that time of the entire state, such as the Moscow [third], the Volodimer' [third], and the Ryazan' [third]." It appears that Ryazan' was divided into thirds at an early date. Prince Vasiliy Ivanovich (1448–1483) and Prince Fedor Vasil'yevich (1483–1503), both of Ryazan', bore the epithet *Tretnoy*, 'Third.' Tsar Ivan's reference to "the entire third" probably refers to that which his grandfather, Ivan III, received from Prince Fedor Vasil'yevich of Ryazan' (see Ekzemplyarskiy, II, 601, n. 1926; see also above, Text 11, n. 54).

with its villages, and with its *puti,* and with all its outlying
"plain" patrimonies,[114] as it was under me.[115]

[114] *I so vsemi Polskimi otkhozhimi votchinami* (see n. 111, above). The
word *otkhozhiy* is here translated "outlying." It is probable that such
outlying lands were not subject to the taille (*tyaglo*). Certainly land
tenures on the periphery of the Muscovite state (e.g., in the Wild Plain)
enjoyed a privileged position in carrying out their duties to the grand
prince. Their principal duty was to act as defensive outposts of the state
(see Sreznevskiy, II, 822, and Dal', *Tolkovyy slovar'*, II, 764 [under
otkhazhivat']).

[115] Ryazan' was under the *de facto* control of the Grand Prince of
Moscow as early as 1503–1504 when Ivan III wrote his testament (see
above, Text 11, n. 54). Ivan Ivanovich, the last prince of Ryazan', was
only four when, following the death of his father in 1500, he came under
the protection of his paternal grandmother, Anna Vasil'yevna, favorite
sister of Grand Prince Ivan III of Moscow. Upon the death in 1503 of the
young prince's uncle, Fedor Vasil'yevich (Anna had died in 1501), Ivan
III could easily have incorporated the Principality of Ryazan' into the
Muscovite state. For some reason he did not do this, and Ryazan'
retained its semblance of independence for about seventeen years longer.

By the time Ivan was about twenty, two competing parties had arisen
at the court of Ryazan'. One faction desired to end Moscow's control
over Ryazan', and it particularly aspired to remove Princess Agrippina
Vasil'yevna, the young prince's mother, from her controlling position in
the principality. The second faction favored continuing the Moscow
orientation. Sometime between 1516 and 1520 Prince Ivan, perhaps encouraged by the anti-Moscow party and certainly aided by the Tartars
of the Crimea, succeeded in seizing power from his mother. Learning of
this, Grand Prince Vasiliy III induced Ivan to come to Moscow, where
he was seized and placed under guard. Vasiliy III then dispatched his
lieutenants (*namestniki*) to the principal cities of Ryazan'; the Moscow
boyar and voivode Ivan Vasil'yevich Obraztsov-Simskiy-Khabar was sent
as lieutenant to Pereyaslavl' Ryazanskiy.

In July 1521, in the confusion of Mahmet-Girey's campaign against
Moscow, Prince Ivan escaped, setting out by a circuitous route for
Pereyaslavl'. Perhaps he hoped to reestablish himself in Ryazan' with the
assistance of Khan Mahmet-Girey. When his escape became known in
Pereyaslavl', Khabar (Moscow lieutenant in Pereyaslavl') forced the
inhabitants to swear to oppose the prince if he attempted to regain his
principality assisted by the khan. Mahmet attacked Pereyaslavl' Ryazan'skiy but was repulsed. In the meantime, Grand Prince Vasiliy III
learned of Prince Ivan's intention to go to Pereyaslavl' to contact his

And to my son Ivan I also give the city of Mtsensk with its volosts, and with its *puti,* and with its villages, and with all its customs, and with all its outlying "plain" patrimonies, and the city of Belev [116] with its volosts, and with its *puti,* and with its villages, and with all its customs. And I also give to him the third of the city of Masal'sk,[117] which belonged to Prince Vladimir Vseslav, with its volosts, and with its *puti,* and with its villages, and with its *tamga,*[118] and with all its customs, as belonged to this third of old.

And Prince Mikhail Vorotynskiy shall rule one third of Vorotynsk, and the city of Peremyshl', and the city of Odoyev Staroye, and the city of Novosil', and Ostrov, Cherna, with everything [119] as it was of old, and [my] son Ivan shall not interfere in this, [which is] his. And the Odoyevskiy, Obolenskiy, Vorotynskiy, Trubetskoy, [and] Masal'skiy princes and their sons also [shall be subject], with their patrimonies, to my son Ivan and to the Grand State,[120] and they shall all serve my

---

supporters in the hope of reestablishing his power. Now, however, Ivan apparently realized the hopelessness of his cause and fled to Lithuania, where he was given the town of Stoklishki in Kovno District. Thus ended the independent existence of the once powerful Grand Principality of Ryazan' (see Ekzemplyarskiy, II, 605–608).

[116] Belev, the center of a principality of the same name, was located on the upper Oka River about ninety kilometers south of Kaluga (see above, Text 11, n. 26).

[117] Masal'sk (Mosalesk, modern Mosal'sk) was part of the Grand Principality of Lithuania during most of the fifteenth century. It was ceded to Moscow by the Armistice of March 25, 1503, concluded between Grand Prince Ivan III and Grand Prince Aleksandr of Lithuania (see Solov'yev, III, 122 and 366). Mosal'sk is located about eighty kilometers west of Kaluga.

[118] The word appears in the plural in the testament (*s tamgami*).

[119] Copyist's note: "These cities of the Vorotynskiys, Masal'skiys, Odoyevskiys, and Obolenskiys, [and] Trubetskoys, Tsar Ivan Vasil'yevich took himself, and in place of them gave them for [their] security villages in various districts."

[120] *Velikomu gosudarstvu.* This is perhaps a carry-over from the older expression *velikoye knyazhestvo,* 'grand principality.' Cf. also, *gospodin velikiy Novgorod,* 'Lord Great Novgorod.'

son Ivan.[121] And should any of these princes or their children leave [the service of] my son Ivan and [enter the service of] my son Fedor, or [go] anywhere else, then these patrimonies [shall pass] to my son Ivan.

And to my son Ivan I give the city of Yur'yev Volskoy, and Belogorod,[122] and Gorodets, with their villages, and with their hamlets, and with their fishing places, and with all their customs, as it was under me. And I also give him the city of Romanov on the Volga River, and my son Ivan shall maintain it in the possession of the Nagay mirzas, as it was under me.[123] And if they should go away anywhere, or if they should commit treason, then the city of Romanov [shall pass] to my son Ivan.

And to my son Ivan I also give the city of Mozhaysk with its volosts, and with its *puti*, and villages, and with all its customs, and with Shchagoshch', and with Tur'yevo, and with Orekhovka, and with Mogil'noye, and with Mishenki, and with Shater', and with Sulidovo, and with Dmitrovets, along both sides of the Ugra, and with the other localities that appertained

[121] In ancillary ukases to the Code of Ivan IV (1550) the Yaroslavl', Starodub, Rostov, Suzdal', Tver', Obolensk, Beloozero, Vorotynsk, Mosal'sk, Trubchevsk (Trubetsk), Odoyev, and other service princes were forbidden to sell or exchange their patrimonies. This measure certainly accelerated the transfer of many of these lands to the tsar (Solov'yev, IV, 13).

[122] Copyist's note: "It is not known where Belogorod was, for the present Belogorod on the Donets was not yet then built." The reference may be to Belgorod in Tver'. Belgorod on the Donets was not built until the reign of Ivan's son, Fedor (Solov'yev, II, 276, and IV, 289).

[123] Bashkiria, an ill-defined area lying generally to the east of Kazan' and including part of the middle Ural region, had been largely controlled by the Nogay Horde (to the south) for more than a century. Following the subjugation of Kazan' and Astrakhan' (1552–1556) and the gradual, generally peaceful absorption of Bashkiria by Muscovy, the Nogay Horde was restricted to the general area between the middle and lower Volga and the Yaik (Ural) rivers. Although technically a part of the Russian state, the Nogay Horde retained its own traditional self-government. Apparently some of the Nogay mirzas, or princes, were in possession of Romanov on the Volga (see A. N. Nasonov, L. V. Cherepnin, and A. A. Zimin, *Ocherki istorii SSSR: Period feodalizma, konets XV v.-nachalo XVII v.* [Moscow, 1955], pp. 674–682).

to them, as it was under me. And to my son Ivan I also give the city of Vyazma and Kozlov with their volosts, and with their *puti*, and villages, and with all their customs, and with everything that appertained to Vyazma and Kozlov and to all the Vyazma localities, as it was under me. And to my son Ivan I also give the city of Dorogobuzh' with its volosts, and with its *puti*, and with its villages, and with all its customs, and with everything that appertained to it. And the Dorogobuzh volosts [are] Pogoreloye, Negomlya, Khotumichi, Kholm, Byatimo, Prost', the village Zaop'ye, Vodosy, Nekrasovo, Selechna, Kremya-noye, Redyn, along the Uzha River, Ust'ye, Kostkovo, Rekhty, Kholmichi, Vyshkovo, Vasilevo, Yes'kino, the village Klimovo, the *slobodka* Vladychnya in Yurtova, the village Putyatino with its hamlets, Igumnovo, Mstislavets, Oshchitov, Zhulich', Moshkova Gora, Luchino Gorodishche, Velikoye Pole, Lopatin, Kopyl, Uzhida, Vedrozh', Ozerishche, Sverchovy Luki, and with everything that appertained to Dorogobuzh and to these volosts and villages, as it was under me. And to him I also give the city of Belaya with its volosts, and with its villages, and with all its customs, as it was under me.

And my son I also bless [and] give him the Grand Principality of Smolensk: the city of Smolensk with its volosts, with its *puti*, and with its villages, and with all its customs, and with everything as it was under me, and in accordance with that which was written in the armistice agreements with King Sigismund Augustus.[124]

And to my son Ivan I also give the city of Pereslavl' with its volosts, and with its *puti*, and with its villages, and with all its customs, and with Sol', and also with the volost Serebro, and with Razhestvennoye, and with Buskutovo, and with the patrimony of the Penkov princes [125] which is in Pereslavl' District,

[124] Sigismund Augustus was King of Poland from 1548 to 1572. Concerning the incorporation of Smolensk into the Moscow state, see above, Text 12, n. 10.

[125] The Penkov princes traced their line from Daniil Penko, son of Prince Aleksandr Fedorovich Bryukhatyy (1420–1472), Prince of Yaroslavl'. Daniil was a Moscow boyar. It was during the reign of Aleksandr Fedorovich that Ivan III acquired Yaroslavl' (see above, Text

and the village Perevyatino, and the village Gory, with their hamlets. And to my son Ivan I also give the city of Yur'yev Pol'skoy with its volosts, and with its *puti*, and with its villages, and with all its customs. And to him I also give the city of Dmitrov with its volosts, and with its *puti*, and with its villages, and with all its customs. And I also give him the city of Borovezk with its volosts, and with its *puti*, and with its villages, and with all its customs.

And concerning that which I granted to Tsarevitch Murtazaley, in baptism Mikhail Kobulin, the son of Akhkibek, [namely] the city of Zvenigorod, in the same manner as Zvenigorod used to belong to Tsar Simeon of Kazan',[126] now my son Ivan shall maintain Zvenigorod in his [Mikhail Kobulin's] possession according to our grant, and Tsarevitch Murtazaley, in baptism Mikhaylo, shall serve my son Ivan, and if he should go away anywhere, then the city of Zvenigorod [shall pass] to my son Ivan.

And I also bless my son Ivan [and] give him Peshekhon'ye with all its volosts, and with its *puti*, and with its villages, and with the *sloboda* Rybnaya, and with the volost Borisoglebskaya [127] which is on the Volga River opposite the city of Romanov,[128] and with the Peshekhon'ye districts, and with the

11, n. 32, and Ekzemplyarskiy, II, 95–96 and 99). The only Penkov listed in the "Court Book" is Ivan Vasil'yevich Pen'kov, Prince of Yaroslavl', junior boyar and boyar (*Tysyachnaya kniga*, p. 120).

[126] Tsarevitch Murtazaley (Mikhail Kabulin or Mikhail Kaybulovich) was appointed in 1572 to the position of head of the Council of Boyars of the Land (the Zemshchina, that part of Muscovy outside Ivan's preserve, the Oprichnina) (see Nasonov, Cherepnin, and Zimin, pp. 313 and 917). Ivan IV had previously granted Zvenigorod to Semen Bekbulatovich, the "tsarevitch" of Kasimov and "tsar" of Kazan'. Semen subsequently succeeded Mikhail Kabulin as head of the Council of Boyars of the Land (see Ekzemplyarskiy, II, 286, and Nasonov, Cherepnin, and Zimin, pp. 313 and 922).

[127] *DDG*, p. 529, identifies Borisoglebskaya as a volost of Poshekhon'ye District. However, there was apparently more than one Poshekhon'ye District, as the following text of the testament indicates.

[128] In the testament of Vasiliy II, Romanov was identified as a burg (*gorodok*) (see above, Text 9, n. 50). In the testament of Ivan III it is spoken of as the "city of Romanov burg."

weirs, and the hamlets at the weirs, and with all the customs and income, with everything as it was under me. And to my son Ivan I also give the city of Vologda with its volosts, and with its *puti*, and with its villages, and with all its customs, as it was under me, and with Zaozer'ye, with Kubana, and with their volosts, and with their *puti*, and with their villages, and with all their customs, and the patrimony in thirds of the Penkov princes, [with?] Zaozerskoye [129] and the village Danilovskoye, which [appertains] to Vologda from Kostroma District, following the boundaries.[130]

And to him I also give the city of Usteg with its volosts, and with its *puti*, and with its villages, and with all its customs, and with Sol' Vychegotskaya, and Vychegda, and Vym',[131] and Udoma, and Sysola, and with all their localities, and in the Zavoloch'ye Land, Rostovshchina, Pinega, Kerchma, the Pr'm' [volosts], and Mezen', Nem'ya, Pil'i Gory, Penesha, Vyy, Toma, Kur-Gory, Yelaskaya Gora on the Vaga, with everything, and Ontakova Brewery, and Karyalskoy Island, Shalga-Gora, Korchala, Sura Paganaya, Lavela, and with the other localities that appertained to these localities, and Yugora, and Pechora,[132] and Velikaya Perm', with everything [that appertained to them], and with the new burgs, and with the salt marshes, and with all the customs, as it was under me. And to my son Ivan I also give the city of Galich' with its volosts, and with its *puti*, and with its villages, and with all its customs, and with Kuzheyka, and with Chukhloma, and with all the burgs that are in Galich District, and with the salt marshes, and with every-

---

[129] *I Penkovykh knyazey votchina v tretyakh, Zaozerskim.* Not clear. Concerning the Penkov princes, see n. 125, above.

[130] *Da k Vologde selo Danilovskoye iz Kostromskago uyezda, po mezham.* Perhaps: "and, in addition to Vologda, the village Danilovskoye, from Kostroma District, following the boundaries."

[131] Copyist's note: "Vym was then a not small city, where the Perm and Yugora bishops lived, and now there is a poor monastery there." The town is now called Ust' Vym' and is at the confluence of the Vym' and Vychegda rivers.

[132] The original reads *po Pecheru*. The meaning may be "the area along the Pechora."

thing that appertained to Galich, and to Chyukhloma, and to Un'zha.

And I also bless my son Ivan with the Grand Principality of Nizhniy Novgorod: I give him Novgorod Nizhney with its volosts, and with its *puti,* and with its villages, and with all its customs, and with the Mordva, and with the Cheremisa, and the city of Balakhna, with Zaulusa, and with its *tamga,* and with all its customs, as it was under me, and the city of Vasil' on the Sura, with the Mordva and the Cheremisa, and with all its customs, [and] concerning those villages that are in Nizhniy Novgorod and in Balakhna, or in the possession of mirzas, or princes, or of anyone at all, now they all [shall pass] to my son Ivan. And I also give him the city of Murom with its volosts, and with its *puti,* and with all its customs, and with the Mordva and the Cheremisa, and with [everything] that appertained to Murom. And I also give him the city of Meshchera [133] with its volosts, and with its villages, and with everything that appertained to it from of old, and with Koshkovo, and Kadom, and Temnikov, and Shatskoy city, with everything, and the Mordva princes, with all their patrimonies, [shall pass] to my son Ivan. And I also give to him the city of Kurmysh, and the city of Alator on the Alator [River] with their volosts, and with all their customs, and the Mordva princes with their patrimonies, and with the Cheremisa, and with all their districts and appendages [*ugozh'i*], and [with everything] that appertained to these cities. And concerning the junior boyars that I have settled in the Wild Plain near these cities, now these lands [of these junior boyars shall] all [pass] to my son Ivan, but these patrimonial estate owners shall hold their own [estates]. And [I also give to my son Ivan] the city of Arzamas, with the Mordva and with the Cheremisa, [and] with everything as it was under me, and the city of Starodub Ryapolovskoy,[134] and the volost Moshok, the village Knyaginino in Nizhniy Novgorod District which used to belong to [Prince Mikhail] Vorotynskiy, and the small

[133] Kasimov? See above, Text 11, nn. 42 and 86. The editors of Solov'yev identify Meshchera as a city and volost and do not equate it with Kasimov (see III, 794 and 798).

[134] See above, Text 10, n. 11.

village Fokino. And I also give him the city of Beloozero with its volosts, and with its *puti*, and with its villages, and with all its customs.

And my son Ivan I also bless [and] give him a third of the city of Vorotynsk with its volosts, and with its *puti*, and with its villages, and with all its customs. And I also give him the city of Goroden' with its volosts, and with its villages, and with all its customs, as it was under me. And I also give him the city of Mikulin with its volosts, and with its villages, and with all its customs, and with the patrimony of Prince Semen Mikulin-skiy,[135] which has not been given away.[136]

And to my son Ivan I also give the Vyatka Land, its cities and volosts, with everything that appertained to them, and with the [Ar]sk princes, as it was under me.

And to my son Ivan I also give the Seversk cities: Novgorod Severskoy, the city of Putivl', the city of Rylsk, and Mlgin'', and Drakov, the city of Pochap, the city of Karachev, and the volosts and villages of these cities, with all the Seversk and "plain" [*polskiye*] appendages [*ugozh'i*], and with the *tilskiye*[137] appendages, and with all their customs, as it was under me.

And hold, my son Ivan, the Seversk cities [and] the city of Roslov, according to all the armistice agreements with King Sigismund Augustus.

And my son Ivan I also bless with my patrimony the Grand Principality of Tver'. And [I] also [give] him the city of Tver' with its volosts, and with its *puti*, and with its villages, and

---

[135] Prince Semen Ivanovich Mikulinskiy was one of the outstanding military leaders of Ivan IV's reign. He participated in Ivan's campaign against Kazan' in 1552, and in the spring of that year was sent as Ivan's lieutenant from Sviyazhsk to Kazan' (see Solov'yev, III, 446, 449, 460–462, 465, 472, and 478). In 1550 Prince Semen was granted a military tenure near Moscow (*Tysyachnaya kniga*, 54). The Mikulinskiy princes were descended from Prince Saint Mikhail Yaroslavich of Tver' (1272–1318) (see Solov'yev, I, 339, Table 2, bb).

[136] Copyist's note: "Goroden and Mikulin are now villages in Tver' District."

[137] The word *tilskiye* is a copyist's error; undoubtedly it should read *Rylskiye*.

with all its customs, with everything as it was under me, and the city of Klin with its volosts, and with its villages, and with all its customs, as it was under me, and with Kashin, which used to be in the possession of Odoyevskiy.[138] And concerning the service princes in the Moscow and Tver' lands, now these princes shall serve my son Ivan, and they shall hold their patrimonies as it was under me. And if any of these service princes go away any-where, then the patrimonies of these princes [shall pass] to my son Ivan. And to my son Ivan I also give the city of Torzhek with its volosts, and with its *puti*, and with its villages, and with all its customs. And to him I also give the city of Rzheva Volodimerova—both halves—with its volosts, and with its *puti*, and with its villages, and with all its customs.[139]

And my son Ivan I also bless with the Grand Principality of Novgorod, with Novgorod, with all its five fifths, and with its minor cities, and with all its customs. And the minor cities of Novgorod [are]: the city of Ivan, the city of Yama, the city of Kopor'ye, the city of Oreshik, the city of Laduga, Vysokoy burg, Doman burg, Kuresk burg, Porkhov burg, Koshkin burg, [and] the burg Staraya Rusa.[140] And I have given [to my son Ivan] Novgorod the Great, with these minor cities and with all its volosts, and with its *pogosts*, and with its *puti*, and with its villages, and with all its customs, and [with everything that appertained] to Novgorod the Great under me.

[138] Odoyevskiy's identity is not established; however, see Text 11, n. 75, above.

[139] Concerning Rzheva (here called Rzheva Volodimerova), see above, Text 9, n. 41.

[140] Copyist's note: "Here the burgs Vysokoy, Deman, Kuresk, Kashkin, where they were is not now known, as well as the below-mentioned mountains [cities?] of Novgorod—Kholm[,] Veliki, Buntsi, Lapostitsy —concerning which something may perhaps be searched out some-where in the histories." The preceding is a fairly literal translation; its difficulties compare with those of Ivan's testament.

This passage is similar to a passage in the testament of Ivan III (see above, p. 280). It is of interest that a number of settlements called "city" (*gorod*) in the earlier testaments are referred to in this document as "burg" (*gorodok*).

And my son Ivan I also bless with the cities that I founded, with God's will, on the Lithuanian border: the city of Velizh',[141] the city of Zavoloch'ye, the city of Sebezh', the city of Popovich' on the Nevl', and all the volost Popovskaya. And I give him these cities with everything as it was under me and as it is in the armistice agreement signed with King Sigismund Augustus. And also to my son Ivan, in the Novgorod Land [I give] the city of Kholm, Veliko, Buntsa, Lapostitsy, and with other localities, and with their volosts, and with all their customs, and with everything that appertained to them. And to my son Ivan I also give the city of Luki Velikiya, and the city of Nevl', the city of Ostroye, with their volosts, and with their *puti,* and with their villages, and with all their customs. And the [Velikiye] Luki volosts [are]: Bereza, Nevl', Usvoi, Lovtse, Vesnebologo, and with the other volosts, and with the villages, and with all the customs, as it was under me. And to my son Ivan I also give the city of Toropets and the Toropets volosts: Dankovo, Lyubuta, Dubnya, Rozhna, Tura, Bibireva, Stavtsova, Nezhel'skaya, Plavitskaya, Zhizhetskaya, Ozerskaya, Kazarinovskaya, and with all their customs, and with everything as it was under me, and in accordance with the armistice agreements with King Sigismund Augustus. And to him I also give the city of Rzheva Pustaya with all its volosts and *pogosts,* as it was under me. And to my son Ivan I also give all the Korolevskaya Land, the city of Korela with its volosts, and with its *puti,* and with its villages, and with its *pogosts,* and with all its customs, and with everything that appertained to the Korelevskaya Land, and with the [Forest] Lop', and with the Wild Lop'. And to him I also give the Zavolotskaya Land: [142] [the Lake] Onego [region], and Kargopole, and all of Poonezh'ye, and the Dvina, and the Vaga, and the Konshega, and the *pogost* Velikoy, and Kholmogory, and all

---

[141] Copyist's note: "Velizh', Sebezh', Popovich', or Nevl' were ceded to Lithuania during his reign, in accordance with a treaty with Stefan Bathory, the Polish king; the city of Ostroye [mentioned below], although unknown, is felt to be also in Lithuania."

[142] Copyist's note: "All that is beyond Lake Ladoga was called Zavoloch'ye in all the ancient histories."

343

the Dvina Land, as it was under me. And to my son Ivan I also give the city of Pskov with all the Pskov *osadas*,[143] and with its minor cities: the city of Voronezh', the city of Dutsov, the city of Vyborets, the city of Vel'ye, the city of Vrev, the city of Volodimer, the city of Ostrov, the city Krasnoy, the city of Vyshegorodok, the city of Kobyl'ye *gorodishche*, the city of Izborsk, the city of Opochka, [and] the city of Gdov.[144] And I have given to him the city of Pskov and these minor cities with their volosts and *zasadas*,[145] and with their *puti*, and with their villages, and with all their customs, just as it was under me.

And concerning the Tsardom of Kazan', which I took with God's will,[146] now I also bless my son Ivan with the Tsardom of Kazan', [and] I give him the city of Kazan', with the Arsk Land, and with the land along the [higher, right] bank [of the Volga], and with the land along the [lower, left] bank [of the Volga],[147] and with all its volosts, and with its villages, and with the Chuvash,[148] and with the Cheremisa, and with the holders of

[143] Alexandre Eck defines *osada* as "a subdivision of a canton [volost]" (*Le Moyen Age russe* [Paris, 1933], pp. 108 and 567). Dal' defines *osada* as "a settlement abroad [*na chuzhbine*], a colony, from which the Little Russian *osadchiy:* the founder of a new settlement, the chief of settlers" (*Tolkovyy slovar'*, II, 693).

[144] Copyist's note: "The minor cities of Pskov, except for Opochka and Gdov, are all villages, and the majority of them are in the possession of military tenants." Gdov is about 110 kilometers north of Pskov.

[145] The word *zasada*, as well as *osada*, is defined by Eck as "a subdivision of a canton [volost]" (pp. 108 and 569).

[146] Concerning Ivan's incorporation of the Khanate of Kazan' into the Russian state, see Solov'yev, III, 455–480.

[147] The Arskaya *storona*, 'Arsk Land,' was the area between the city of Kazan' and Arsk, a town on the Kazanka River northeast of Kazan'. It was the side (*storona*) of the Volga and of Kazan' towards Arsk.

The rivers of European Russia which flow south have a higher right bank (*bereg*) and a lower left bank (*lug*). Thus Ivan bequeaths his son the *poberezhnaya storona*, 'the land along the [higher, right] bank,' of the Volga, and the *lugovaya storona*, 'the meadow side,' which was the land along the lower, left bank. Both terms referred here to parts of the region around the city of Kazan'.

[148] The Chuvash are a Finno-Tartar people inhabiting the area between Nizhniy Novgorod (Gor'kiy) and Kazan'. During the sixteenth century they occupied the same general area.

immunity lands,[149] and with the Bashkirs,[150] and with the Vo-
tyaks,[151] and with all their Volga and Kazan' beekeeping lands,
and with their fishing places, and with all their appendages, and
with all their customs, and as God [has given] me the Kazan'
Land, [I give my son Ivan all] that appertained to the Kazan'
Land from of old, during the days of the former tsars [khans].
And concerning the city which, with God's will, I built on the
Sviyaga [River, and] the city which I built in the Nagornaya
[Land] [152] on the Cheboksara [River], now I also bless my son
Ivan with the city Sviyanskoy, and with the city Cheboksarskoy, and I give him the city Sviyazhskoy, the city Cheboksarskoy, with all the Gornaya Land, and with all the Chuvash, and
the Cheremisa, and the Mordva, and with their patrimonies, and
with their fishing places, and with all their customs, as God gave
me the Gornaya Land, [which appertained] to [the city]
Sviyazhskoy and to the city Cheboksarskoy. And concerning
the Tsardom of Astrakhan' which I took with God's help,[153]
now I also bless my son Ivan with the Tsardom of Astrakhan',
[and] I give him the city of Astrakhan', with its taxes on trading
in the market place, and with its *tamgas,* and with all its customs,
and with its weirs, and with its salt lakes [*mochagi*],[154] and with

---

[149] "And with the *tarkhans.*" A *tarkhan* was a patrimonial landholder
(*votchinnik*) who was freed of the obligation to pay taxes. He was
sometimes granted other privileges as well (see Dal', *Tolkovyy slovar'*,
IV, 391).

[150] Copyist's note: "Here it is apparent that the Bashkirs were then
Russian." The copyist uses the word *rossiyskiya* in the sense of a subject
of the Russian state. The Bashkirs, of course, are not ethnic Russian;
actually they are a Turkic people living to the east of Kazan'.

[151] See above, Text 11, n. 44.

[152] The Nagornaya, or Gornaya, *storona,* 'the upper land or side (of
the Volga),' was a region of the Khanate of Kazan' (see above, Text 9, n.
61, and n. 147, this text.

[153] Concerning the subjugation of the Khanate of Astrakhan' in 1556,
see Solov'yev, III, 483–487.

[154] Copyist's note: "*Mochaki,* it is apparent, are *uchyugi,* a Tartar
word." The word *mochag* signified, in the area of Astrakhan', a salt lake
or a "sea bay with little water, with silt, overgrown with reeds." The
word *uchug,* which the copyist erroneously equates with *mochag,* is a
Tartar word meaning much the same as the Russian *yez* (weir), except

all the Astrakhan' localities, and with everything as it was when the former tsars held the Tsardom of Astrakhan'.

And concerning the cities in the Livonian Land which I took with God's help: the city of Yur'yev, the city of Vel'yan, the city of Rugodev, the city of Rakobor, the city of Alystr, the city of Kerevet', the city of Layus, the city Novyy Gorodok, the city of Syrenets, the city of Tavrs, the city of Mukov, the city of Porkhov, the city of Kaster Novoy, the city of Kaster Staroy, the city of Adezh' which is in the Rugadev Land, the city of Kurelov, the city of Ryngol, the city of Randen, the city of Kongod, the city of Kavlet, the city of Tolshebor, the city of Kutushen, the city of Sabei, the city of Dolgovyya, Zangants Court, Andopeito Court, there was the city of Medvezh'ya Golova; now I also bless my son Ivan with all these cities [155] with their farmsteads [*myzy*], and volosts, and villages, and with their lakes, and maritime wharves, and with all their appendages, and their *tamgas*, and their tax on weighing [*ves"*],[156] and with all the customs of these cities, with everything that appertained to these cities, and volosts, and villages, and farmsteads. And concerning the city of Gov'ya that I founded on the Gov'ya River in my patrimony, the Livonian Land, now I also bless my son Ivan with this city of Gov'ya with its volosts, and with its farmsteads, and with the entire district that is in the Gov'ya [region], and my son Ivan shall hold the city of Gov'ya with its

---

that an *uchug* was a larger device for catching fish than was a *yez* (see Dal', *Tolkovyy slovar'*, II, 353, and IV, 529).

[155] Copyist's note: "Here many cities are mentioned that are now unknown. And the majority of these were ceded, some to Poland and some to Sweden; only Syrenets and Novoy Gorodok, it is remembered, remained in Russian possession, and it is therefore apparent that this testament was written prior to the year in which he [Ivan IV] made peace with the Polish king; in the same manner Polotsk with everything was then also ceded to Lithuania, by which this is seen [*chem viditsya*]." The reference in the copyist's note is to the peace concluded between Ivan IV and Stefan Bathory (negotiated by the papal envoy Possevinus in 1582) in which Russia lost all her acquisitions in Livonia. Bathory had seized Polotsk in 1579 (see Solov'yev, III, 653–654 and 665–673).

[156] See Chapter 3.

entire district in addition to his patrimony,[157] Yur'yev in Livonia.

And that which I have granted to my vassal,[158] King [and] Arch[duke] Magnus,[159] in my patrimony the Liflyandskaya Land,[160] [namely] the city of Polchev and other volosts and villages, and I have given to King [and] Arch[duke] Magnus a charter of grant to the city of Polchev and to its volosts and villages, and my son Ivan shall maintain the city of Polchev and its volosts and villages in the possession of his vassal, King [and] Arch[duke] Magnus, in accordance with our charter of grant, and King [and] Arch[duke] Magnus shall serve my son Ivan. And if [Magnus] goes away anywhere, then the city of Polchev and its volosts and villages which I granted to King [and] Arch[duke] Magnus [shall pass] to my son Ivan. And concerning the fifteen thousand five hundred rubles in Moscow money which I lent to King [and] Arch[duke] Magnus, and for which money King [and] Arch[duke] Magnus pledged to me the [following] cities in the Livonian Land: the city of Volodimerets, the city of Vorna, the city of Prekat, the city of Smilten, the city of Burtniki, the city of Roin, and with all the districts, and with the villages, and with the farmsteads of these cities, now my son Ivan shall take unto himself this money from King [and] Arch[duke] Magnus, or the cities which are the pledge for this

[157] Or perhaps "attached to," or "as part of his patrimony." The text reads: *so vsem uyezdom k svoyey otchine.*

[158] *Goldovnik,* 'vassal.' Cf. Polish *holdownik,* from *hold,* 'homage,' from German *Huld.*

[159] In 1560 Frederick III, King of Denmark, purchased the bishopric of Oesel (modern Saaremaa, an island off the coast of Estonia) for his younger brother, Magnus. Magnus journeyed to Moscow in 1570, where he was named King of Livonia by Tsar Ivan IV, and later married Mariya, the daughter of Ivan's cousin, Vladimir Andreyevich of Staritsa. Magnus once betrayed Ivan but was forgiven; again he betrayed the tsar and entered the service of Stefan Bathory of Poland. The only king of Livonia, he died in 1583 in Piltene, Estonia. For this and other information on Magnus, as well as for a detailed account of Ivan's Livonian war, see Karamzin, IX, Chaps. 1–5. Ivan refers to Magnus as *korol' Artsymagnus.*

[160] *V Liflyandskoy zemle.* Liflyandiya was another name for Livonia.

money, and my son Fedor shall have no concern in this matter.

And concerning my patrimony the city of Polosk, which by the will of God I took from my brother, King Sigismund Augustus,[161] now I, with the city of Polotsk, with the Polotsk volosts, and with the villages, and with the *tamgas,* and taxes on weighing [*vesy*], and with all the appendages, and with the entire Polotsk District which belonged to the city of Polotsk from of old, now I with this city of Polotsk, with everything, bless my son Ivan. And concerning the cities which I founded with God's help in the Polotsk District: the city of Sokol on the Drys' River,[162] and the city of Kop'ye,[163] now I bless my son Ivan with these cities, with all the volosts that will appertain [*potyanet*] to those cities. And concerning that which with God's help I took from my brother, King Sigismund Augustus, [namely] the city of Ozerishche and, in addition to Ozerishche, the volost Usvyat—now I in the volost Usvyat founded the city of Usvyat [164]—now I also bless my son Ivan with the city of

[161] The old Russian city of Polotsk on the Western Dvina had been part of Lithuania since 1307, when the Lithuanians purchased it from the German knights. It was captured by Ivan IV in 1563, and the Russians held it until 1579, when it was taken by Stefan Bathory (see Karamzin, IV, 100, and Solov'yev, III, 575–576 and 753–654).

[162] "That same year [1566], in December, in Polotsk District [there was founded] the city of Sokol on the Drys' River . . . thirty versts from Polotsk, seventy versts from Sibezh" (from the *Aleksandr Nevskiy Chronicle,* as quoted in Karamzin, "Notes to Volume IX," col. 47). The Drissa (Dris') River, a right tributary of the Western Dvina, flows from east to west, and at the point at which it is closest to Polotsk is about twenty-two versts from that city.

[163] "In the month of August [1567] there was founded in Polotsk District, beyond the [Western] Dvina, towards the Wilno border, on Lake Susha on an island, a city; and the Sovereign commanded that this city be called Kopiye, [and it is] seventy versts from Polotsk" (from the *Aleksandr Nevskiy Chronicle,* as quoted in Karamzin, "Notes to Volume IX," col. 47).

[164] Usvyat was a volost and city of Ozerishche District (*DDG,* p. 559). Once more Ivan speaks of "founding a city" (*Az . . . postavil gorod Usvyat*). He probably fortified or built a (new) wall around Usvyat, for a settlement of that name had existed since at least the early eleventh century: "And from there he [Grand Prince Yaroslav the Wise] summoned Bryachislav [Izyaslavich, Prince of Polotsk,] and, having given

Ozerishche and with the city of Usvyat with all their volosts, and districts, and villages, and with their appendages, with everything that those cities had from of old, and my son Ivan shall hold all this in accordance with the armistice agreements with King Sigismund Augustus.

And concerning that which our father, Grand Prince Vasiliy Ivanovich of All Russia, assigned in his testament [165] to my brother, Prince Yuriy,[166] [namely] Uglich' and all the Plain [167] with its volosts, and with its *puti*, and with its villages, and with all its customs, and with Kholopiy which is a market on the Mologa,[168] and the city of Bezhetskoy Verkh with its volosts, and with its *puti*, and with its villages, and with all its customs, and the city of Kaluga with its volosts, and with its *puti*, and with its villages, and with all its customs, and the city of Yaroslavets Maloy [169] with its volosts, and with its *puti*, and with all its customs, and with Sukhodrov', and the city of Kremenesk [170] with its volosts, and with its *puti*, and with its villages, and with all its customs, and the city of Medyn', [and] Meshchersk [171] with its volosts, and with its *puti*, and with its villages, and with all its customs, and Opakov [172] on the Ugra, with everything, and

him the two cities of V"svyach' [Usvyat] and Vidbesk" [Vitebsk], said to him, 'Be with me as one.' But Bryachislav fought against Prince Yaroslav for all the days of his life" (*PSRL*, V, 134, under the year 1021).

[165] Not extant. See above, Commentary to Text 12.

[166] Yuriy Vasil'yevich, Prince of Uglich, was born to Vasiliy III and Yelena Glinskaya on October 30, 1531 (*PSRL*, VIII, 280–281). He died on November 24, 1563 (Karamzin, "Notes to Volume IX," col. 18).

[167] See above, Text 9, n. 34.   [168] See above, Text 11, n. 67.

[169] Called Yaroslavets in the testament of Ivan III (see above, Text 11, n. 27.

[170] Kremenesk is mentioned here for the first time in the testaments. Although not positively identified, it should probably be equated with the modern town of Kremenskoye, located on the Luzha River approximately thirty-five kilometers west and slightly north of Maloyaroslavets.

[171] Meshchovsk (see above, Text 11, nn. 25, 42, and 69).

[172] Copyist's note: "Opakov is now a village in Medyn' District, in which a stone marker remains to this day. It was on the border of Lithuanian territory during the time of Vitovt, but Grand Prince Vasiliy Ivanovich and others took it from Lithuania in the year . . ." (see above, Text 11, n. 70).

the volosts on the Ugra, [namely] Tovarkov, Konopnar', and the other volosts along the Ugra that were given to Prince Vasiliy Shemechich and to Prince Vasiliy Starodubskiy; [173] and [concerning that which our father, Grand Prince Vasiliy Ivanovich] also assigned to him [Prince Yuriy, namely] the village Ozeretskoye Staroye near Moscow, the village Ozeretskoye Novoye, with their hamlets and with all their purchases, and the village Cherkizovo with its hamlets, which was purchased from the children of Petr Yakovlev Zakhar'in, with the purchased villages, and with the additional hamlets in the *stans* and the small village Naprudnoye, [174] with the city courts, and with the courts in the suburb; now [according to the testament of my father] if, depending on God's will, [my] brother Yuriy should not live, and if he should not leave a son, or a grandson, then all of this patrimony—his patrimonial principality—[my] father, Grand Prince Vasiliy, assigned to me, the Grand Sovereign, in his testament; and God's will was fulfilled—my brother, Prince Yuriy, passed away, and neither a son of his, nor a grandson, nor a daughter remained—and I from this the patrimonial principality of my brother Yuriy bless my son Ivan with the city of Bezhitskiy Verkh with its volosts, and with its *puti*, and with its

[173] Prince Vasiliy Ivanovich Shemyachich, the "last of the *udel* princes," was known as the Prince of (Novgorod) Seversk. He was the grandson of Dmitriy Shemyaka and the youngest son of Ivan Dmitriyevich Shemyaka, who deserted to Lithuania in 1453. Ivan Dmitriyevich received Novgorod Seversk and Rylsk from King Sigismund (?), and Vasiliy inherited these as his patrimony. In 1500 Vasiliy entered the service of Ivan III of Moscow. He spent most of the remainder of his life fighting the Lithuanians and the Tartars. For repulsing an invasion of the latter he was granted the city of Putivl' in 1518. He died in a Moscow prison in 1529, having been accused of negotiating with the Lithuanians (*Russkiy biograficheskiy slovar'*, Vol. Sh-Shyu, pp. 86–89). Concerning the enmity between Vasiliy Semenovich, Prince of Starodub, and Vasiliy Ivanovich Shemyachich, see Solov'yev, III, 280–282.

[174] Copyist's note: "The Zakhar'ins, as is apparent, formerly were written [i.e., were called] Yakovlya and subsequently came to be called the Romanovs, from whom the most radiant family of the Romanovs, who are most happily reigning—the Russian sovereigns—take their origin, and it is apparent that their ancestors possessed noble patrimonies, for the *sloboda* Naprudnaya is now inside Moscow."

villages, and with all its customs, and [I bless him] with the city
of Kaluga with its volosts, and with its *puti*, and with its villages,
and with all its customs, and [I bless him] with Malyy city [175]
with its volosts, and with its *puti*, and with its villages, and with
all its customs, and with the volost Sukhodrov', as it was before
this, and [I bless him] with the city of Medyn' with its volosts,
and with its *puti*, and with its villages, and with all its customs,
and with the volosts Apakov on the Ugra, with everything as it
was before this, and with the volosts Tovarkov also, and with
Konopka, and with the other volosts along the Ugra which used
to be in the possession of Prince Vasiliy Shemyachich and Prince
Vasiliy Starodubskiy, and from among the villages [I bless him]
with the village Cherkizovo near Moscow, except for the Cherkizovo Mill and the eleven hamlets which were annexed to the
mill. And concerning that which, in accordance with the testament of my father and the command of my brother, Prince
Yuriy, I granted to my brother Prince Yuriy Vasil'yevich's
wife, Princess Ul'yana [176]—my sister-in-law—[now] I have
given her for her support during her lifetime the city of Kremenesk with its volosts, and with its *puti*, and with its villages, and
with all its customs, and with its post relay taxes, and with its
contributions [*primetniye dengi*], and with its subsistence indemnities [*kormlennyye okupy*], and with all its lieutenant's
incomes [*namestnich'i dokhody*], [with all] that was income
prior to this time, and [concerning that which I granted
Ul'yana, namely] the city of Ustyuzhna Zheleznaya with its
suburb, and with the hamlets that were annexed to the suburb,
with the post relay taxes, and with the contributions, and with
the subsistence indemnities, and in Uglich District the volost
Kadka, with its post relay moneys and with its contributions,
and with all the incomes of that volost, and the villages near
Moscow: the village Puzyayevo with its hamlets, the village
Belyy Rat with its hamlets, and the hamlet Nauzolovo with the

---

[175] Copyist's note: "The burg Maloy, where it was is unknown."
"Malyy city" was Yaroslavets Malyy, or modern Maloyaroslavets
(*DDG*, p. 543).

[176] Karamzin asserts that Ul'yana (in orders, Aleksandra) was drowned
in the Sheksna River at the behest of Ivan IV in 1569! (see IX, 84).

other hamlets, which hamlets were, with Nauzolovo, annexed to the village Ozeretskoye, and to Princess Ul'yana I have also given the mill on the Klyazma River near the village Cherkizovo, and the eleven hamlets that were annexed to this mill, and I have granted to Princess Ul'yana, in Uglech, court villages, [namely] the small village Zelentsovo with its hamlets, and the village Nikolskoye Zhdanovo with its hamlets, and my son Ivan shall maintain these cities, and volosts, and villages in her possession during her lifetime, but after her death, the city of Kremenesk with its volosts, and with the volost Veshki [shall pass] to my son Ivan, to the Grand State, and the mill of Cherkizovo village and the eleven hamlets [annexed] to it [shall pass] to my son Fedor, to the village Cherkizovo. And concerning that with which I blessed my brother Prince Yuriy, in addition to his patrimonial principality, [namely] the city of Bryansk, now I also bless my son Ivan with the city of Bryansk with its volosts, and with its *puti*, and with its villages, and with all its customs, as it was of old, but the village Puzyayevo with its hamlets, and the village Beloy Rast with its hamlets, and the hamlet Nauzulovo, and those hamlets that were annexed to Nauzolovo, [I give] to my son Fedor, in addition to the small village Ozeretskoye, [and] Ustyuzhna Zhelezopol'skaya, and the volost Kargka, and the villages that are in Uglich District, [and] the village Nikolskoye Zhdanovo with its hamlets also [shall pass] to my son Fedor, in addition to Uglich.[177] And concerning the patrimony which, in accordance with the testament of my father and in accordance with the command of my brother, Prince Yuriy, I have given to his wife, Princess Ul'yana, in perpetuity, in Ugleche District, the village Khorobrovo with its hamlets, and the village Krasnoye with its hamlets, now I have [given to Ul'yana] a charter of grant to these villages and hamlets, [and] in accordance with our charter of grant, she is free to give [them] for [remembrance of] her soul, or sell [them], or exchange [them], or she may want to give them to her family, and

[177] *K Uglichu*. The meaning may be "[and shall be] annexed to Uglich."

my son Ivan and my son Fedor in these her two villages shall not interfere, in accordance with this our charter of grant.

And I also bless my son Ivan with the cities and volosts that used to belong to my uncle, Andrey Ivanovich, and to his son, Prince Vladimir Andreyevich, [namely] the city of Vyshegorod on the Petrova River [178] with its volosts, and with its villages, and with all its customs, and with its court villages, and in Mozhaysk District the volost Aleshnya Voskresenskoy and the volost Petrovskaya with their villages, and with their hamlets, and with their *novalia*, and with all their appendages, and with the court villages that are in those volosts, and with all their income, and the city of Staritsa with its volosts, and with its *puti*, and with its villages, and with all its customs, with the volosts Kholm, and with Pogoreloye Gorodishche, and with the volost Sinyaya, and the city of Aleksin, with Volkona, and with its volosts, and with its *puti*, and with its villages, and with all its customs, and the city of Vereya with its volosts, and with its *puti*, and with its villages, and with all its customs. And concerning the cities, and volosts, and villages that I gave to Prince Vladimir Andreyevich in exchange, in recompense for his patrimony of cities, volosts, and villages, now Prince Vladimir having committed a crime against me,[179] these cities, and volosts, and villages [shall pass] to my son Ivan, and Prince Vladimir's son, Prince Vasiliy, and [Prince Vladimir's] daughter [180] [shall be given allotments] as will be fitting, taking into consideration the present time.[181]

---

[178] Copyist's note: "I do not know in what district Vyshegorod was." The reference here is probably to Vyshegorod on the Protva, just west of Borovsk, and not to Vyshegorod in Dmitrov. A certain amount of confusion on the part of the copyist is understandable, however, as Vyshegorod in Dmitrov was part of the inheritance of Prince Andrey Ivanovich (see above, Text 5, n. 31, and Text 11).

[179] See n. 68, above.

[180] Almost nothing is known about the son (or sons) of Prince Vladimir (see Solov'yev, III, 734, n. 90). Prince Vladimir's daughter is not identified further.

[181] *A knyazh' Volodimerova syna, knyazya Vasil'ya, i docheri, posmotrya po nastoyashchemu vremyani, kak budet prigozhe.*

353

And my son Fedor I bless with the golden cross and the relics of Ivan Gryaznov.[182]

And my son Fedor I also bless [and] give him the city of Suzdal' with its volosts, and with its *puti*, and with its villages, and with all its customs, and [I give him] the city of Shuya with its volosts, and with its *puti*, and with its villages, and with all its customs. And I also give him the city of Kostroma and the city of Pleso [183] with their volosts, and with their *puti*, and with all their customs. And I also give him the city of Lyubim,[184] and the city of Buy, and the city of Sudislavl', and the city of Nerekhta, with Sol' Bolshaya and [Sol'] Malaya with all their volosts, and with their *puti*, and with their villages, and with all their customs, as it was under me.

And my son Fedor I also bless [and] give him the city of Yaroslavl' with its volosts, and with its *puti*, and with its villages, and with all its customs. And the Yaroslavl' princes-boyars and the Yaroslavl' junior boyars shall not leave [the service of] my son Fedor [and] go to my son Ivan or anywhere [else], with their patrimonies and purchases. And he who leaves my son Fedor [and goes] anywhere whatsoever, now his land [shall be forfeited] to my son Fedor. And he [Fedor] shall not interfere in the lands of them that serve him, nor in those of their wives or children. And concerning those patrimonies which I took away from the Yaroslavl' princes, now these patrimonies [shall pass] to my son Fedor, and in these my son Fedor is free: if he wants to keep these patrimonies in his possession [he may do so], if he wants to give them away [he may do so]. And whosoever of the Yaroslavl' princes have patrimonies, now my son Fedor shall not

---

[182] Ivan Gryaznov is not positively identified. Karamzin mentions an Ivan Gryaznoy as being voivode in Toropets in 1576 ("Notes to Volume IX," col. 103).

[183] Copyist's note: "Pleso is now a village."

[184] The Russians captured the fortress of Fellin (Vil'yandi) in 1560, taking prisoner the Master of the Teutonic Order, Furstenberg. He was taken to Moscow and was well treated by Ivan, who granted him the "small town" of Lyubim in Kostroma, where he lived out his days (see Karamzin, IX, 15–16).

Lyubim is located approximately sixty-five kilometers north and slightly west of Kostroma.

take these patrimonies away from them, from their wives, or from their children, but if they should leave [the service of my son Fedor and go] to my son Ivan, or anywhere whatsoever, then these patrimonies [shall pass] to my son Fedor. And to my son Fedor I also give the city of Kozelsk and Serenesk [185] with their volosts, and with their *puti*, and with their villages, and with all their customs. And also to him I give the city of Serpeysk and Mtsenesk with their volosts, and with their *puti*, and with all their customs.

And I also bless my son Fedor [and] give him the city of Volok Lamskoy with its volosts, and with its *puti*, and with its villages, and with all its customs. And also to my son Fedor I give the village from Moscow [District, namely] the village Kryletskoye with its hamlets, and the village Tatarovo with its hamlets, and the village Sorochino with its hamlets, Romantsovo with the hamlets that have been annexed [to it] from among the hamlets of the [city] *stan*, and the village Ozeretskoye Staroye, and the village Ozeretskoye Novoye, with their hamlets and with the annexed hamlets which have been annexed [to the Ozeretskoye villages] from among the remaining hamlets, and the small village Kuzyayevo, and the small village Beloy Rast, and the hamlets Nauzovo which are listed with the hamlet Nauzovo, now these villages and hamlets [shall pass] to my son Fedor, [and have been annexed] to the village Ozeretskoye. [186] And also to him I give the small village Naprudnoye with its courts in the suburb of the city, and to the places in which [are located] those courts that I have given him I have given [him] a deed, with my seal and with the signature of my secretary. And also to my son Fedor I give, in Suzdal', the village Bykovo which used to belong to Prince Ivan Mstislavskiy, [187] and the volost

---

[185] Copyist's note: "Serenesk is not known unless, perhaps, it was written in place of Serpeysk." Serenesk (Serensk, Sheren'sk) was doubtless the center of the volost of the same name which was in Kozel'sk District.

[186] Or, perhaps, "[in addition to] the village Ozeretskoye."

[187] Prince Ivan Fedorovich Mstislavskiy was one of Ivan's most trusted military commanders, participating in the campaigns to subjugate the peoples of the Kama Region in the mid-1550's and commanding an army

Koryakovskaya with all its hamlets, and with its *novalia*, and with its fishing places, and the village Lopatniche, and Borisovo, and half of the village Goritsy, and two thirds of the village Terneyevo, and with the small adjoining settlements, and with the hamlets, and with the *novalia*, that used to belong to Prince Aleksandr Gorbatyy,[188] and the volost Turekh with its hamlets, and with its fishing places.

And concerning that which I have given to my son Fedor from my treasure, now this has been recorded in the Treasury Roll.

And if God should give a son to me and my wife Anna,[189] I bless him with the city of Uglech', and Ustyuzhnaya, Kholopey, with their volosts, and villages, and with the two villages which were given to Prince Yuriy Vasil'yevich's [widow], the nun

---

sent in 1555 to intercept a Tartar invasion. Mstislavskiy was one of the first to swear allegiance to Ivan's son, Dmitriy, during the tsar's illness in 1553. Mstislavskiy was named one of the ruling boyars of the Land (that part of Muscovy outside the Oprichnina). In 1571 he made the following confession: "I, Prince Ivan Mstislavskiy, have failed to keep faith in God, God's holy churches, and all Orthodox Christianity and have betrayed my Sovereign, his children, and his lands, all Orthodox Christendom, and all the Russian land; I and my comrades brought [into Russia] the godless Crimean Tsar Devlet-Gerai." But upon the intercession of Metropolitan Kirill and other church worthies, Ivan pardoned Mstislavskiy, receiving pledges of his future faithfulness from three other boyars (see Solov'yev, III, 478–479, 490, 526–528, 532, 552, 555, and 564–567). Prince Ivan Mstislavskiy was among the boyars who were granted military tenures near Moscow in 1550 (*Tysyachnaya kniga*, p. 54).

[188] Aleksandr Borisovich Gorbatyy-Suzdal'skiy (Shuyskiy), prince and voivode, was an active participant in Ivan's campaign against Kazan'. In October 1552, following the fall of Kazan' to the Russians, Prince Aleksandr was named lieutenant (*namestnik*) in that city. In 1565 he and his son, Petr, were both executed, having been accused of being in league with Andrey Kurbskiy and of having plotted "all kinds of evil things" against the tsar and his wife and children (see Solov'yev, III, 449, 468, 473, 553, and 766). Prince Aleksandr Borisovich Gorbatyy was among those boyars who were granted military tenures near Moscow in 1550 (*Tysyachnaya kniga*, p. 54).

[189] See n. 57, above. A son, Dmitriy, was born to Ivan and Mariya Nagaya in 1583. Immediately after his father's death, Dmitriy was exiled to his patrimonial city of Uglich, where he was reportedly killed in 1591 (Karamzin, IX, 251, and Solov'yev, III, 678 and 703).

Aleksandra, and with the tribute [*dan'*] which is due Uglech'. And to him I also give the city of Kashin, with the *sloboda* Zadubrovskaya and Slavkovo, and with all its volosts, and villages, and with all its customs. And to him I also give the city of Yaroslavets with its volosts, and with its villages, and with all its customs. And I also give him the city of Vereya with its volosts, and with its *puti*, and with its villages, and with all its customs.

And if God should give a daughter to me and my wife Anna, now I bless her [and] give her the city of Zubtsov with its volosts, and *puti*, and with its villages, and with all its customs. And I also give her Opoki, and Khlepen, and Ragachev with their volosts, and villages, and with their *puti*, and with all their customs. And I also give her the [following] villages near Moscow: the village Mitropolich'ye which used to belong to Mikhail Tuchkov,[190] the village Yeldegino which used to belong to Yuriy Shein, Vasiliy Shein's[191] village Simonovskoye, the village Klenki, Uslyumovskoye, the village Danilovo Ivanovskoye, Bryukhov's village Suponevo, Ivan Safarin's [village] Safarynskoye, the village Davydovskoye of Dmitriy, Yakov's son, Davydov, with all their hamlets and with their appendages.

And I bless my wife Anna [and] give her the city of Rostov with its volosts, and with its *puti*, and with its villages, and with

---

[190] Mikhail Vasil'yevich Tuchkov was an *okol'nichiy* of Vasiliy III and Ivan IV. In her letters to Prince Kurbskiy, Ivan IV accused Tuchkov (Kurbskiy's maternal grandfather) of having misappropriated or mismanaged some of the possessions of Yelena, Ivan's mother, and of having made treasonable utterances during Ivan's minority (Solov'yev, III, 264, 289, 291, 300–301, 428, 429, 549, and 782).

[191] Yuriy, Vasiliy, and Ivan Shein, sons of the boyar Dmitriy Vasil'yevich Shein and grandsons of Vasiliy Mikhaylovich Morozov-Sheya, were boyars at the beginning of Ivan IV's reign. Yuriy Dmitriyevich Shein served as voivode in Velikiye Luki from 1534 to 1536, in Mtsensk in 1537, and later in Vladimir. In 1541 he was made a boyar. He died in 1546. Vasiliy Dmitriyevich Shein served as voivode in the Dvina Land in 1532. In 1544 he was made a boyar and became deputy to the lieutenant (*namestnik*) in Novgorod. In 1547 he served in the southern Ukraine. In 1550, when the tsar was absent on the campaign against Kazan', Vasiliy and others remained in Moscow "to manage [*vedat'*]" the capital. He died in 1550. The Sheins were one of the few "old" families to survive Ivan IV (see *Russkiy biograficheskiy slovar'*, Vol. Shebanov-Shyutts, pp. 41, 59–60, and 39).

all its customs, and, near Moscow, the village Aleshnya, the village Boltino, the village Astankovo, and with the annexed hamlets that were annexed [to these villages] from the black *stans* [192] and from the military tenure [lands], [193] and, in Yaroslavl', [I give Anna] the patrimony of the Sutskiy princes: the village Sutki, the village Shchulepovo, the village Bolonino, the village Martem'yanovo, the village Borniskoye, the village Novoye, the village Krivtsovo, and with their hamlets, and with their *novalia*, that used to belong to Princess Agrafena Sutskaya, and, in Yur'yev Pol'skiy, the village Gorodishche Mstislavle, the village Flolishchevo, the village Senmskoye, [and] the village Yelokhovo with their hamlets, and with all their appendages, and with two thirds of the patrimony of the Zaozerskiy-Penkov [princes] [194] with all their hamlets and appendages.

And that which I have given to my wife and to my children from my treasure, now this is recorded in the Treasury Roll. [195]

And concerning that which our father, Grand Prince Vasiliy Ivanovich of All Russia, granted to Prince Fedor Mstislavskiy, and concerning that which I gave in addition to this to his son, Prince Ivan, now my son Ivan shall not interfere in this his patrimony nor in his children's. But if he should go away anywhere, then this patrimony [shall pass] to my son Ivan.

And concerning the patrimony which I granted to Prince Mikhail, the son of Prince Vasiliy L'vovich Glinskiy, [196] now my

[192] *Ot chernykh stanov.* The reference is to hamlets that had formerly been free and had been obliged merely to pay the *tyaglo* to the prince but that had subsequently been annexed to the villages named.

[193] *I pomestnykh.* That is, hamlets that had formerly been held in military tenure by one of the prince's servants but that had subsequently been annexed to the villages named.

[194] See above, Text 13, nn. 125 and 129.

[195] Copyist's note: "Here it is apparent that they, among all branches of rulers, have fear of revolts, that, although they apportioned rather large patrimonial principalities to their younger children, they [were] all scattered and not contiguous, so that it would be inconvenient for them to gather troops rapidly from their entire patrimonial principality and bring about any opposition to the sovereign."

[196] Prince Mikhail Vasil'yevich Glinskiy, brother of Ivan's mother, served as adviser to his nephew during the latter's minority. In 1547, at the time of the great fires in Moscow, Prince Mikhail escaped death at

son Ivan shall not interfere in any way with Prince Mikhail's son, Prince Ivan, nor with his children. But if he should go away anywhere, then this patrimony [shall pass] to my son Ivan. And concerning the volosts and villages that I have granted to Rama-nova, the wife of Yur'yevich,[197] and to her son Nikita,[198] now my son Ivan shall not interfere in this patrimony nor in [that of] their children. And those of their volosts and villages that are in the patrimonial principality of my son Fedor, now my son Fedor likewise shall not interfere in this patrimony, in accordance with this my testament. And concerning that which I granted to Prince Mikhail, the son of Prince Ivan Vorotynskiy, [namely] his old patrimony the city of Odoyev, and the city of Novas'iya, and the city on the Chern', now I took this patrimony to myself, and in place of it I have given to Prince Mikhail a patrimony, the city of Starodub Ryapolovskoy, and in Murom District in the *stan* Zovskiy, the volost Moshok, and in Nizhniy Novgorod District the village Knyaginino with its hamlets, and on the Volga River the large village [*selishche*] Fokino, and Prince Mikhail shall manage this patrimony according to the charters of exchange in the same manner in which he ruled his [former] patrimony, and he and his children shall serve my son Ivan, and my son Ivan shall not interfere in this his patrimony or [in that] of his children, but if he should go away anywhere, then that patrimony [shall pass] to my son Ivan.[199]

the hands of a mob inspired by some of the boyars against the Glinskiys only because he was not in Moscow at the time. Prince Mikhail Va-sil'yevich served in the campaign against Kazan' in 1552; later, he partici-pated in the Livonian war as a commander (see Solov'yev, III, 430, 434, 463, 472, 501, and 526).

Prince Vasiliy L'vovich Glinskiy was the father of Ivan's mother, Yelena, and of Prince Mikhail Vasil'yevich Glinskiy. He was the brother of Prince Mikhail L'vovich Glinskiy (Solov'yev, III, 45, 160, 287, and 765).

[197] That is, to the wife of Roman Yur'yevich Zakhar'in-Koshkin, an *okol'nichiy* and the father of Anastasiya, Ivan's first wife.

[198] Boyar and voivode Nikita Romanovich Zakhar'in-Yur'yev, Ivan's brother-in-law, the son of Roman Yur'yevich (mentioned above).

[199] This paragraph appears to conflict with that concerning Prince Mikhail's continued holding of a third of Vorotynsk, the city of Pere-myshl', etc., which appeared earlier in the testament (see above, p. 335).

And the city of Ozerishche, with all its minor cities, which I founded in Polotsk and in Ozereshche District, and with Usvyat, [shall pass] to my son Fedor, with everything [which appertained to them], as is written in this my testament to my son Ivan, but the patrimonial principality of my son Fedor [shall be subject] to him [Ivan] also, [and] to the Grand State.[200]

And concerning the Oprichnina which I have established, now it is within the power [*volya*] of my children, Ivan and Fedor, [to do with it as they see fit]; in the manner in which it is most advantageous to them, so they should do, but the pattern has been made ready for them.

And now I commit my soul and my son Fedor to my father and intercessor Antoniy, Metropolitan of All Russia, and to you, my son Ivan.

And you, my son Fedor, obey my son Ivan, your older brother, in all things, and hold him in the place of me, your father, and do not covet the State of him. And if you, my son Fedor, should covet the states of Ivan, or if you should conspire with anyone to his harm, secretly or openly, or if you should raise up anyone against him, or should ally yourself with anyone against him, then, by the words of the Gospel, son Fedor, he who does not honor his father or mother shall die the death.[201]

And may God judge him who violates this my testament, and may my blessing not be on him.

And at [the writing of] this my testament sat . . .[202]

[200] Although the wording of this paragraph is obscure, it means that Fedor is to receive a patrimonial principality, but he is not to consider it his *udel* in the traditional sense. In the final analysis it is to be subject to Ivan's will and is to be part of the "Grand State."

[201] See Mark vii.10. Cf. also Matthew xv.4; Exodus xx.12 and xxi.17; Leviticus xx.9; and Deuteronomy v.16.

[202] Copyist's note: "Although by the circumstances of things and by the style of writing it appears that this testament was composed by him, the Sovereign, it could not, however, actually have been, because it was written long before his death and really appears [to have been written] about the year 7080 [1572], for. . . ." Here the extant text of the testament of Ivan IV breaks off.

Appendix and Bibliography

APPENDIX

Territories Bequeathed
in the Testaments*

1. TESTAMENT OF IVAN KALITA

To Semen:

Cities	Kolomna, Moscow (one third), Mozhaysk
Volosts	Broshevaya, Goretova, Gorodenka, Gzhelya, Kanev", Mezynya, Pesochna, Pokhyrane, Seredokorotna, Ust'-Mer'ska
Villages	Astaf'yev'skoye, Avakovskoye (Novgorod), Borisov-skoye (Vladimir), Gorki, Gvozdna, Ivani, Kopoten'-skoy, Kostyantinov'skoye, Malakhov'skoye, Mikul'-skoye, Naprud'skoye, Orinin'skoye, Ostrov'skoye, village on the Sever'stsa River in Pokhryane district
Hamlets	Levichin", Makovets', Skulnev"
Other	One third of quitrent of Vasiliy's Department

To Ivan:

Cities	Moscow (one third), Ruza, Zvenigorod
Slobodas	Okat'yeva *svobodka*, Velikaya *svoboda*
Volosts	Fomin'skoye, Kremichna, Neguchya, Rostovtsi, Skirmi-nov'skoye, Sukhodol", Trostna, Ugozh', Zamosh'skaya *svoboda*
Villages	Andreyevskoye, Belzhin'skoye, Domontovskoye, Ka-menichskoye, Maksimovskoye, Oleksin'skoye, Pavlov'-skoye on the Mas, Petrovskoye, Ruz'skoye, Ryukhov'-skoye, Semtsin'skoye, . . . tsya on the Mas, Vsedob-rich('), Vyazem'skoye, village in Zamosh'skaya *svoboda*

* The district was usually bequeathed along with the city, although often the grand princes would enumerate subdivisions of the districts. The modern spelling of cities and principalities is used in this Appendix; volosts, villages, and other smaller holdings are spelled as they appear in the testaments.

Appendix

To Andrey:

Cities	Moscow (one third), Peremyshl', Serpukhov, Shchitov" *gorodok* (burg)
Volosts	Golichichi, Lopastna, Narunizhskoye, Nivna, Sever'ska, Temna, Tukhachev"
Villages	Bityagov'skoye, Kolbasin'skoye, Kolomninskoye, Melov'skoye, Nar'skoye, Nogatin'skoye, Peremyshl'skoye, Serpokhov'skoye, Talezh'skoye, Trufonov'skoye, Varvar'skoye, Yasinov'skoye
Hamlet	Rastovets'

To Ul'yana and "the younger children":

Slobodas	Danilishchova *svobodka*, Sofronov'skaya *svobodka*
Volosts	Beli, Chernogolovl', Guslitsa, Mashev", Mushkova Gora, Selna, Surozhik", Vokhna, Vorya
Villages	Deikovo (Ramen'ye?), Deygunin'skoye, Lutsin'skoye, Mikhailov'skoye, Mikhailovskoye on the Yauza, Novoye, Pavlovskoye, Protas'yevskoye, Radonezh'skoye, Ramen'ye, Rogozh', two Kolomna villages, Tylovskoye, village by the lake, Aristovskoye, Lopasten'skoye
Other	Monastery of St. Aleksandr, the *osmnicheye* of Moscow (to Ul'yana)

To Boris Vorkov:

Village	Bogorod(i)cheskoye in Rostov (conditionally confirmed)

To the Monastery of St. Aleksandr:

Villages	Leontiyevskoye, Sharapovskoye, small village on the Kerzhach

2. TESTAMENT OF SEMEN THE PROUD

To Mariya, wife of the Grand Prince:

Cities	Kolomna, Moscow ("my share of the *tamga*"), Mozhaysk
Volosts	Gordoshevichi, Zabereg, Zayachkov
Villages	Deigunin'skoye, Ilmov'skoye, Khvostov'skoye, Kopoten'skoye, Malakhov'skoye, Naprud'skoye, Novoye on the Kupavna, Oleksandrov'skoye, Orinin'skoye, Orta-

| Villages (*cont.*) | kov'skoye, Ostaf'yeskoye, Ostrov'skoye, Romanov'-skoye, Samarov'skoye, Semenov'skoye, village in Dmitrov purchased from Ivan Dryuts'skiy, village in Sulishin *pogost* |

3. TESTAMENT OF IVAN II

To Dmitriy:

Cities	Kashira, Kolomna, Moscow (one third), Mozhaysk
Volosts *	Brasheva, Goretovka, Gorodna, Gzhelya, Kanev", Meshcherka, Mezyni, Pesochna, Pokhryane, Seredokorotna, Ust-Mer'ska
Villages *	Gorki, Gvozdna, Ilmov'skoye, Ivan', Kholmy, Kopoten'skoye, Kostyantinov'skoye, Malakhov'skoye, Malino, Mikul'skoye, Naprud'skoye, Novoye, Orinin'-skoye, Ostrov'skoye, Romanov'skoye on the Roksha, the village in Pokhryane district on the Severstsa
Hamlets	Levichin", Makovets', Shulnev"
Other	One fourth of Princess Ul'yana's volosts, villages, and the *osmnicheye* (upon her death); one third of the quitrent of Vasiliy's Department; "other places taken away from Ryazan' "

To Ivan:

Cities	Moscow (one third), Ruza, Zvenigorod
Volosts	Fomin'skoye, Isterva, Kremichna, Negucha, Rostovtsi, Sukhodol", Trostna, Zamosh'skaya *svoboda*
Villages	Afin'yev'skoye, Andreyev'skoye, Demontov'skoye, Kamen'skoye, Karin'skoye, Kozlov'skoye, Kuzmin'-skoye, Maksimov'skoye, Mikhalev'skoye, Miltsin'skoye, Ryukhov'skoye, Vyslav'skoye, the small village near the village Pavlov'skoye, the village in Zamosh'skaya *svoboda*, the village on the Repna in Borovsk
Other	Svod"ka; one fourth of Princess Ul'yana's volosts, villages, and the *osmnicheye* (upon her death); "other places taken away from Ryazan' "

To Vladimir Andreyevich, nephew of the Grand Prince:

Cities	Moscow (one third, confirmed), Novyy burg (*gorodok*) (in place of Lopasnya), Serpukhov (confirmed)

* Some of these were lifetime holdings of Princess Mariya, wife of the deceased Semen. Upon her death they were to pass to Dmitriy.

Other   One fourth of Princess Ul'yana's volosts, villages, and
           the *osmnicheye* (upon her death); one third of Vasiliy's
           Department

To Aleksandra, wife of the Grand Prince:

City   One third of two shares of the Moscow *tamga* of
           Dmitriy and Ivan (to pass to the latter upon the death
           of Aleksandra)
Volosts   Pesochna, Pokhryane, Seredokorotna, Ugozh', Velikaya
           svoboda Yur'yeva, Zayachkov and Zabereg (upon the
           death of Grand Princess Mariya)
Villages   Beltsin'skoye, Klyapov'skoye, Lystsev'skoye, Novoye
           (small village), Semtsin'skoye
Other   One fourth of Princess Ul'yana's volosts, villages, and
           the *osmnicheye* (upon her death)

To Ul'yana, widow of Ivan Kalita:

           Confirmed in the holding of her volosts, villages, and
           the *osmnicheye* during her lifetime

To Mariya, widow of Semen:

           Confirmed in the holding of Zayachkov and Zabereg,
           both to pass to Princess Aleksandra upon the death of
           Mariya

To an unidentified daughter of Princess Ul'yana:

Volost   Surozhik (upon death of Ul'yana)
Village   Luchin'skoye (upon death of Ul'yana)

To the Monastery of the Holy Mother of God in Krutitsy:

           One fourth of the Kolomna *tamga*

To the Monastery of St. Aleksandr:

Village   Pavlov'skoye

4. FIRST (FRAGMENTARY) TESTAMENT OF DMITRIY DONSKOY

To unidentified person or persons, probably Prince Vasiliy:

City   Ruza
Slobodas   . . . skaya *svoboda*, Dmitr'yeva *svoboda*
Volosts   Isterva, Vyshegorod

To the Church of the Holy Mother of God in Moscow and to the Church of St. Mikhail:

The Moscow *kostki* (confirmed)

To the Monastery of the Holy Mother of God in Krutitsy:

One fourth of the Kolomna *tamga*

To the Monastery of St. Aleksandr:

Village   Pavlovskoye

5. SECOND TESTAMENT OF DMITRIY DONSKOY

To Vasiliy:

	The Grand Princedom
Cities	Kolomna, Moscow (one half of two thirds)
Volosts	Brasheva, Gorodna, Gzhelya, Kanev", Kochema, Komarev" (with the shore), Meshcherka, Pesochna, Pokhryane, Ramenka, Ust-Mer'sko
Villages	Dobryatin'skoye, Gvozdna, Ivan', Khvostov"skoye, Kopoten'skoye, Kostyantinov"skoye, Krasnoye, Malakhov"skoye, Mitin *novale*, Orinin'skoye, Ostrov"skoye, Vasilev'skoye, Yelezarov"skoye Provatovo
Hamlets	Levichin', Makovets', Skulnev", Zhyroshkiny
Other	Dobryatin'skoye apiary, *Vasiltsevo sto* (Vasiliy's Department), Velikiy Meadow

To Yuriy:

Cities	Galich, Moscow (a "year" in one half of two thirds), Ruza (burg, listed among volosts), Zvenigorod
Slobodas	Dmitriyeva *sloboda* (listed among volosts), Yur'yeva *sloboda* (listed among volosts)
Volosts	Beli, Fomin'skoye, Isterva, Ist'ya, Kremichna, Negucha, Plesn', Rostovtsi, Skirmenovo, Sukhodol, Surozhyk, Trostna, Ugozh", Vyshegorod, Zamosh"skaya *sloboda*
Villages	Bogorodits'skoye, Borisov"skoye, Domantov"skoye, Kuzmydem"yan'skoye (with the *novale* of the village Krasnoye beyond the Vezka), Mikhalev"skoye, Mikul'skoye
Other	Khodyn'skii Meadow

Appendix

To Andrey:

Cities — Beloozero, Kaluga, Medyn', Moscow (a "year" in one half of two thirds), Mozhaysk, Vereya (an "outlying volost")

Volosts — Berestov", Bolonesk", Boyan', Chislov, Glin'skoye, Gordoshevichi, Gremichi, Ismeya, Kolocha, Korzhan', Moishin Kholm, Pnevichi, Porotva, Roshcha, Rud', Shagot', Sushov, Tov", Tushkov, Vyshneye, Zaberega, Zagor'ye

Villages — Deunin'skoye, Ivanov"skoye Vasil'yevicha in Gremichi, Khvostov'skoye (in Peremyshl'), Lutsin'skoye, Naprud'skoye, Oleksin'skoye (on the Peksha), Repin'skoye, Vol'skoye

Other — Borovskii Meadow; the meadow opposite the Monastery of the Resurrection; Milolyub"skii Weir; "the *slobodkas* that were my children's [in Beloozero?]"

To Petr:

Cities — Dmitrov, Moscow (a "year" in one half of two thirds), Uglich

Volosts — Berendeyeva *sloboda*, Gusletsya, Inobash", Izhvo, Korzenevo, Lutosna, Mushkova Gora, Ramenka, Rogozh", Selna, Sherna (burg), *slobodka* Knyazha Ivanova, Syama, Toshna, Vokhna, Vori, Vyshegorod, Zagar'ye

Villages — Bogorodits'skoye (on the Bogon), Novoye

Other — Sulishin *pogost*

To Ivan:

Volosts — Rameneitse, Sokhna

Village — Zverkov"skoye

Other — *Novale* Sokhon'skiy

To Vladimir Andreyevich, cousin of the Grand Prince:

City — Moscow (one third—"Prince Vladimir's third") (confirmed)

To Yevdokiya, wife of the Grand Prince: *

Cities — Moscow (one half of the Moscow *tamga* and two shares of the Moscow *osmnicheye*), Vereya (from Andrey's *udel*)

* A large number of these holdings were willed to Princess Yevdokiya as lifetime holdings only; they were from the *udels* of her four oldest sons.

Slobodas   Iskon'skaya *slobodka*, Kuzov"skaya *slobodka*, Skirmenov"skaya *slobodka*, Yur'yeva *sloboda*, Zheleskova
slobodka

Volosts   Chislov, Iledam, Isterva, Iyet'ya (Ist'ya), Izhvo, Kanev",
Kholkhol, Komela, Kropivna, Lokhno (her purchase,
confirmed), Pesochna, Smolyanyye, Shagot', Sukhodol,
Syama, Zayachkov

Villages   Babyshevo, Dobroye, Frolov"skoye, Ilmov'skoye, Ivan
Khorobryy's village, Kamen'skoye, Lutsin'skoye, Lys-
tsevo, Malin'skoye, Mikul'skoye, On'dreyev'skoye (in
Vladimir), On'dreyev"skoye (probably in Zvenigorod),
Oslebyatev"skoye, Ostaf'yev"skoye, Petrov"skoye,
Repen'skoye, Semtsin'skoye (with Khodyn'skaya Mill),
Shepkovo, Vol'skoye, Yelokh", Yulka

Hamlets   Hamlets which Prince Vladimir took away from Yevdokiya's village Lytkin'skoye

Other   Gordoshevichi beekeepers; Gorodok, Kolashna, Slobodka, Suda (River region), and Volochok (all to
Yevdokiya upon the death of Princess Fedosiya); Ismeya
beekeepers (interpolated in the text); Kropivna beekeepers; Milolyub'skii Weir; *novale* Mityayev"skiy; *novale*
Samoiletsev"; *novale* Savel'yev"skii; Rud' beekeepers;
Sol' Galitskaya (Galich Salt Marsh); "that which my
princess purchased and that which has appertained to
her"; Vyshegorod beekeepers

6. FIRST TESTAMENT OF VASILIY I

To Ivan:

Cities   Kolomna, Moscow (one third of Moscow [probably
one half of two thirds less the "year" of Prince Kon-
stantin])

Volosts   Brasheva, Gorodna, Gzhelya, Kanev", Kochema, Komarev", Krutinki, Malakhovskoye, Meshcherka, Mezynya, Nerekhta (if mother of the grand prince should
die), Pesochna, Pokhryane, Radokin with the shore,
Ramenka, Ust'-Merska

Villages   Dobryatinskoye, Gvozdna, Ivani, Kostyantinovskoye,
Orininskoye, Strovskoye (Ostrovskoye), village of
Grigoriy Faustov

Hamlets   Levichin", Makovets, Skulnev", Zhiroshkino[y]

Other   *Vasiltsevo sto*, Velikii Meadow

Appendix

To Sofiya, wife of the Grand Prince: *

Cities	Kurmysh' with all its villages (if Ivan should hold Nizhniy Novgorod and Murom), Nizhniy Novgorod—one half of the customs (if Ivan should hold Nizhniy Novgorod and Murom)
Volosts	Algash (if Ivan should hold Nizhniy Novgorod and Murom), Brasheva, Gzhelya, Iledam (if mother of grand prince dies), Kinela (if Ivan receives the Grand Princedom), Komela (if mother of grand prince dies), Nerekhta, Pesochna (if mother of grand prince dies), Ukhtyushka, Ust'-Merska, Yul''ka (if mother of grand prince dies)
Villages	Alachinskiye villages, Bogoroditsskoye (as widow's portion), Builovskoye, Chagino, Deacon Foma's villages, Dobroye (if mother of grand prince dies), Fedor Sviblo's villages, Frolovskoye, Ivanovskoye Vasil'-yevicha in Levichin, Ivorovo, Karabuzino, Khvostovskoye, Kolychevskoye, Maksimovskoye, Malino (belongs to mother of grand prince), Mangach', Nepeitsino, Ogloblino, Oleksinskoye (as widow's portion), Ol'kh, Ondreyevskoye (if the mother of the grand prince dies), Petrovskoye, Pochinok, Rodivonovskoye, Savel'yevskoye, small village from Murom" (if Ivan should hold Nizhniy Novgorod and Murom), Timofeyevskoye on the Yauza, Ves'skoye, Zmeyevskoye
Hamlets	Olekseyev'skaya, Ol'kh
Other	Chyukhistova Land

To Konstantin, brother of the Grand Prince:

City	Ustyuzhna
Volost	Toshnya

7. SECOND TESTAMENT OF VASILIY I

To Vasiliy Vasil'yevich:

	The Grand Princedom
Cities	Kolomna, Moscow (one half of two thirds less "year" of Konstantin), Murom, Nizhniy Novgorod (if God gives it to Vasiliy I)

* Lifetime holdings except Bogoroditsskoye and Oleksinskoye.

Villages	Dobryatinskoye, Khvostovskoye, Kopotenskoye, Kostyantinovskoye, Malakhovskoye, Orininskoye, Ostrov'skoye, Petrovskoye Oleksinskoye [perhaps two villages], small village near the city of Moscow above Velikii Pond
Hamlets	Zhiroshkiny hamlets
Other	Court of Foma Ivanovich, court which used to belong to Mikhail Vyazh, Khodynskaya Mill, new court outside the city by [the Church of St. Vladimir], *Vasiltsevo sto*, Velikii Meadow

To Sofiya, wife of the Grand Prince:

Cities	Moscow (one third of the *tamga* and "of all the customs in the city of Moscow, my shares"), Nizhniy Novgorod (one half of all customs)
Slobodas	Bryukhovskaya *slobodka*, *slobodka* (in Beloozero) that used to belong to Prince Vasiliy Semenovich, *slobodka* on the Gus', Troyetsskaya *slobodka*
Volosts	Brasheva, Gzhelya, Iledam, Kist'ma, Komela, Nerekhta, Obnora, Pesochna, Shatur", Toshna (if Vasiliy Vasil'yevich should acquire it from Prince Vladimir's sons), Ukhtyushka, Ust'-Merska, Volochok, Yul"ka
Villages	Beleutovskiye villages, Bogorodits'skoye, Chyukhistovo, Dobroye, Fedor Sviblo's small village on the Yauza with the mill, Fedor Sviblo's villages in Vologda, Frolovskoye, Gvozdna, Ivan', Ivanovskoye, Knyaginin'skoye, Krasnoye, Krilat'skoye, Malinskiye villages, Okulovskoye, Ondreyevskoye, Ontonov'skiye villages, Pravatovo Yelezarovskoye, Repenskoye (gift of Yevdokiya, confirmed), Semtsinskoye, Sofiya's villages in Nizhniy Novgorod, Sokolskoye, Vasilevskoye, Yelokh", Zakharovskoye
Hamlets	Fedor Sviblo's hamlets in Ustyug, Ivan Golovin's hamlets in Ustyug, Tutolminskiye hamlets in Ustyug
Other	"Her purchase and that which she acquired," Mitin" *novale*, Samsonov Meadow, Seltse, "that which I acquired and my purchase[s] in Vologda and on the Toshna," ["that which I acquired"] in Yur'yeva *sloboda*

Appendix

8. THIRD TESTAMENT OF VASILIY I

To Vasiliy Vasil'yevich:

	The Grand Princedom ("if God gives to my son the Grand Princedom")
Cities	Kolomna, Moscow (one half of two thirds less "year" of Konstantin), Murom, Nizhniy Novgorod
Villages	Dobryatin'skoye, Khvostov'skoye, Kopotenskoye, Kostyantinov'skoye, Malakhovskoye, Oleksin'skoye, Orinin'skoye, Ostrov'skoye, Petrovskoye, the small village near the city of Moscow above Velikii Pond
Hamlets	Zhiroshkiny
Other	Court of Foma Ivanovich, court which used to belong to Mikhail Vyazh, Khodynskaya Mill, new court outside the city by the Church of St. Vladimir, *Vasiltsevo sto*, Velikii Meadow

To Sofiya, wife of the Grand Prince: *

Cities	Moscow (one third of the *tamga* and "of all the customs in the city of Moscow, my shares"), Nizhniy Novgorod (one half of all the customs)
Slobodas	Bryukhovskaya *slobodka*, *slobodka* on the Gus', *slobodka* that used to belong to Prince Vasiliy Semenovich, Troyetsskaya *slobodka*
Volosts	Brasheva, Gzhelya, Iledam", Kistma, Komela, Nerekhta, Obnora, Pesochna, Shatur", Toshna (if Vasiliy Vasil'yevich should acquire it from Prince Vladimir's sons), Ust'-Merska, Volochok, Yulka
Villages	Belevutovskiye villages in Volok and in Yur'yeva *sloboda*, Bogoroditsskoye, Chyukhistovo, Dobroye, Fedor Sviblo's small village on the Yauza with the mill, Fedor Sviblo's villages in Vologda, Frolovskoye, Gvozdna, Ivan', Ivanovskoye, Kerzhanets', Knyaginin'skoye, Krasnoye, Krilat'skoye, Malin'skiye villages, Okulovskoye, Ondreyevskoye, Ontonovskiye villages, Provatovo Yelizarovskoye, Repinskoye, Semtsinskoye, Sokol'skoye, Vasilevskoye, villages which she has purchased in Moscow and that which she has acquired, Yelokh, Zakharovskoye

* Lifetime holdings except for the volost Gzhelya, the village Semtsin'-skoye, and her acquisitions.

| Hamlets | Fedor Sviblo's hamlets in Ustyug, the hamlets Golovinskiye |
| Other | "Everything that used to belong to my mother," "her purchase and that which she has acquired," Mitin *novale,* purchase(s) of the grand prince in Vologda and on the Toshna, Samsonov Meadow |

9. TESTAMENT OF VASILIY II

To Ivan:

	The Grand Princedom
Cities (principalities, lands, districts)	Aleksin, Borovsk, Galich, Kaluga, Kolomna, Kostroma, Moscow ("my shares," i.e., one half of two thirds less the "year" of Prince Konstantin), Murom, Nizhniy Novgorod, Pereyaslavl', Suzdal', Ustyug, Vladimir, Vyatka, Yur'yev
Volosts	Isterva, Ist'ya, Sukhodol
Villages	Dobryatinskoye, Kostyantinovskoye, Krasnoye above Velikii Pond, Krasnoye (in Borovsk), Molakhovskoye, Orininskoye, Ostrovskoye
Hamlets	Hamlets of the villages Kostyantinovskoye, Molakhovskoye, Orininskoye, and Ostrovskoye
Other	Dobryatinskoye apiary, Large meadow near the city along the river Moskva, Sol' Galitskaya (Galich Salt Marsh), *Vasiltsovo sto,* Velikaya Sol' (Great Salt Marsh)

To Yuriy:

Cities (principalities, lands, districts)	Dmitrov, Khotun', Medyn', Moscow (Prince Vladimir's third, alternating "years" with Prince Andrey the Elder), Mozhaysk, Serpukhov
Volosts	Buskutovo, Kzhelya (Gzhelya),* Serebozh', Zamoskov"skiye volosts (with all that used to belong to Prince Petr)
Villages *	Bronniche, Chevyrevo, Derevenka, Faustovskoye, Govor"ovskiye villages, Kachalov"skoye, Krivtsovo,

* Gzhelya, and all the villages except Rozhestvenoye, the Shipilov"-skiye villages, and Yulka, were willed to Yuriy by his grandmother, Grand Princess Sofiya, as were the fishing hamlets, the *novale* by Lake Shchelino, Samsonov Meadow, and Sofiya's courts in the city.

	Kuchka, Lodygino, Marchyukovo, **Maslenskiye** villages, Myachkovo, Rozhek, Rozhestvenoye, Semchinskoye, Semenovskoye, Shadrino, Shipilov"skoye, Svyatoye, Turab'yev'skiye villages, Tyazhino, Ushakovskoye, Velina, village of Leontiy Fedorov, Vorob'yevskoye, Yangosarskiye villages, Yulka
Hamlets *	Fishing hamlets on the Pokhra
Other	*Novale* by Lake Shchelino,* Samsonov Meadow,* Princess Sofiya's city courts,* the Yulka beekeepers

To Andrey the Elder:

Cities (principalities, lands, districts)	Bezhetskiy Verkh, Moscow (Prince Valdimir's third, alternating "years" with Prince Yuriy), Uglich, Ustyuzhna, Zvenigorod
Volosts	Kist'ma, Rozhalovo, Vysheles (which his grandmother gave him)
Village	Sushchev"skoye
Other	(Moscow) city courts that appertained to the village Sushchev"skoye, Veletovo (unidentified)

To Boris:

Cities (principalities, lands, districts)	Moscow (the "year" of Prince Ivan of Mozhaysk), Ruza, Rzheva, Volok Lamskiy
Sloboda	Nizhnyaya *sloboda* on the Volga †
Villages †	Bazeyev"skoye, Beleutov"skiye villages in Volok, Boranov"skoye, Gorka, Kobylinskiye villages, Kotya-

* Gzhelya, and all the villages except Rozhestvenoye, the Shipilov"-skiye villages, and Yulka, were willed to Yuriy by his grandmother, Grand Princess Sofiya, as were the fishing hamlets, the *novale* by Lake Shchelino, Samsonov Meadow, and Sofiya's courts in the city.

† Nizhnyaya *sloboda*, all villages named (except the Beleutov"skiye villages, the Okorokav"skiye villages, and S"passkoye), the hamlets listed, Mariya Goltyayeva's court in the city of Moscow, and the meadow on the Moskva River near Krutitsy, were left to Prince Boris by his maternal grandmother, Princess Mariya Fedorovna Koshkina-Goltyayeva. The Beleutov"skiye villages, the Okorokav"skiye villages, and S"passkoye were given Boris by his paternal grandmother, Princess Sofiya.

zino, Lazar'skoye, Loshakovo, Manuilovskoye, Mikul'-skoye, Okorokav"skiye villages in Izdetemlya, Ponizov-noye, Proskurnikov"skiye villages, Rostovtsov"skoye in Berendeyeva, Rozsudov"skiye villages, Sharapovo, Simizinskiye villages, S"passkoye, Surovtsovo, Timo-feyev"skoye, Turandayev"skoye, Veden'skiye villages, Yevnut'yev"skoye, Zverev"skoye

Hamlets *   Hamlet in Gorodnya, hamlets in Shoma

Other *   Mariya Goltyayeva's court in the city of Moscow, Mariya Goltyayeva's courts in the suburb of Moscow, the meadow on the Moskva River near Krutitsy

To Andrey the Younger:

Cities (princi-palities, lands, districts)   Kubena, Moscow (Prince Petr Dmitriyevich's "year"), Vologda, Zaozer'ye

Volosts   Avnega, Bokhtyuga, Iledam, Komela, Obnora, Pel'shma, Shilenga, Syama, Toshna, Ukhtyushka, Volochok, Yangosar"

Villages   Otvodnoye, Perfushkov"skiye villages, Rameneitso, Tanin'skoye, Yasenev"skoye

To Mariya, wife of the Grand Prince: †

Cities (princi-palities, lands, districts)   Moscow (one half of the *tamga* and of all the customs), Nizhniy Novgorod (one half of all the customs), Romanov burg (her purchase), Rostov (the Sreten'ye half)

* Nizhnyaya *sloboda*, all villages named (except the Beleutov"skiye villages, the Okorokav"skiye villages, and S"passkoye), the hamlets listed, Mariya Goltyayeva's court in the city of Moscow, and the meadow on the Moskva River near Krutitsy, were left to Prince Boris by his maternal grandmother, Princess Mariya Fedorovna Koshkina-Goltyayeva. The Beleutov"skiye villages, the Okorokav"skiye villages, and S"passkoye were given Boris by his paternal grandmother, Princess Sofiya.

† Many of these holdings are from the *udels* of Mariya's sons. Upon her death they were to revert to the son in whose territory they were. Exceptions were Romanov burg and Shokstna (Ust'-Shokstny) and her other purchases: these were hers to dispose of as she saw fit. Rostov was to pass to Yuriy.

Appendix

Slobodas	Iyudina *sloboda*, Marinina *sloboda*
Volosts	Brashovo, Gorodok, Iledam, Izdetemlya, Komela, Mezynka, Nerekhta, Obnora, Pesochna, Shatur, Ust'-Merska, Ust'-Shokstny (her purchase), Ust'-Ugly, Yadrovo
Villages	Babyshevo (given Mariya by Sofiya), Chyukhistovo (given Mariya by Mikhail Fedorovich Saburov), Davydovskoye, Dobroye, Dobryn'skoye, Frolovskoye, Golenishchovo, Gvozdna, Ivan', Kadka, Kerzhanets, Koldom"skiye villages (which Mikhail Saburov gave her), Krasnoye, Kurchevo, Kuzmedem'yanskoye, Levont'yev"skoye, Luzhskiye villages, Lystsovskoye, Malinskiye villages, Matfeishchovo, Mikhail Danilov's villages, Mikhalev"skoye, Moshem"skoye, Muromskoye, Naprudskoye, Nogatin'skoye (upon the death of Princess Vasilisa), Oleshnya, Ondreyev"skoye, Ozerets'skiye villages, Pavshinskoye, Pyatnitsskoye, Ryuminskoye, Serkizovskoye, Shkin', Shokshov, small village of Fedor the son of Stepan, Sokolovskoye, Sorogoshino, Sverbeyev"skoye, Varvarino, Vasilkovo, village of Prince Davyd Zasekin, villages of Petr Dobrynskiy, villages of Prince Ivan of Mozhaysk, Vol"stinovo, Vorogovo, Vysokoye, Yelda, Yelokh
Hamlets	Novinki, Petr Konstantinov's hamlets on the Istra
Other	City courts of the *putnik* in Pereyaslavl', city courts that appertained to Babyshevo and Naprudskoye and Ryuminskoye, Dymko's Land, holdings of Prince Lev's children, Khodyn'skaya Mill, Khodynskiy Meadow, Nerekhta Salt Works, Vondokur'ye, Vysokoye apiary, Yeltsi

10. CODICIL TO THE TESTAMENT OF VASILIY II

To Ivan:

Court of Prince Ivan of Mozhaysk in Moscow

To Yuriy:

Court of Prince Vasiliy Yaroslavich (the court of Prince Vladimir)

To Andrey the Elder:

Courts of Prince Dmitriy Shemyaka

376

To Mariya, wife of the Grand Prince:

Volost	Pochap
Villages	Belevitsi, Chertanovskoye, Dolmat Yur'yev's villages, D'yakovskoye, Ismeiskoye, Khvostovskoye, Kolomen's-koye, Murom villages and villages in Votskiy Starodub (given the grand prince by Anna Vasil'yeva, the wife of Ivanovich), Myachkovo (purchased by the grand prince from Anastasiya Fedorova Andreyevicha and to be held by her until her death), Oksin'skoye, Okulovskoye (upon the death of Fedor Basenok), Ortem'yev''skoye, Repinskoye (upon the death of Fedor Basenok), villages on the Moskva River (sold to grand prince by Arina Alekseyeva, the wife of Ignat'yevich, who will hold them until her death)
Hamlets	Kolomen'skoye hamlets, Volninskiye hamlets
Other	Barmozovo, Chersevo, city courts which appertained to Chertanovskoye, city courts which appertained to Khvostovskoye, court by the Church of St. Ivan the Precursor which his grandmother gave Yuriy, courts of Petr and Ivan and Nikita Dobrynskiy and "my courts outside the city and my gardens" (which Mariya is free to dispose of as she sees fit), Gorodishche, meadow of Prince Yuriy Dmitriyevich, meadow of Yuriy's treasurer (which Mikhail Saburov gave her), mill near Mozhaysk on the Moskva River, two *stans* and the beekeepers and the beaver trappers and the enrolled people of Marinina *sloboda*, Zakolp'ye

II. TESTAMENT OF IVAN III

To Vasiliy:

	The Grand Principalities
Cities (princi-palities, lands, districts)	Beloozero, Borovsk, Buyets, Chukhloma, Deman, Doro-gobuzh, Dvina Land, Galich, Gorodets Serpukhovskiy, Ivangorod, Karelian Land, Kargopol'ye, Kashira, Kholm (in Novgorod), Kholmogory, Khotun', Kineshma (if Prince Fedor Ivanovich Bel'skiy or his children should leave the service of Moscow), Klin, Kokshenga, Kolomna, Kopor'ye, Korela (Korelskoy city), Koshkin, Koshkovo, Kostroma, Kozlov, Kremenets, Kubena,

Kurgorod, Ladoga, lands of the Arsk princes and of the Cheremisa and of the Meshchera, and of the Mordva and Mordva princes, and of princes and boyars in Nizhniy Novgorod, Lukh (if Prince Fedor Ivanovich Bel'skiy or his children should leave the service of Moscow), Medyn', Mogilno, Moscow (all, except that the younger brothers of Vasiliy were to share with their older brother Prince Konstantin's "year," Prince Petr Dmitriyevich's "year," and Prince Mikhail Andreyevich's "year," and Prince Fedor Borisovich of Volok was to retain one half of the "half-year" of Ivan of Mozhaysk), Mozhaysk, Mstislavl', Mtsensk, Murom, Nizhniy Novgorod, Novgorod the Great, Onega region, Oreshok, Ostreye, Pechora region, Perevitebsk, Pereyaslavl', Perm' Velikaya, Pleso, Porkhov, Pskov, Radoml', Radonezh, Romanov burg, Roslavl', Rostov (both halves), Ryazan' (the share of Prince Fedor Vasil'yevich), Rzheva Pustaya, Serpukhov, Sherna burg (listed among volosts), Staraya Rusa, Staraya Ryazan', Suzdal', Sysola region, Tarusa, Teshilov, Toropets, Torzhok, Tver', Udora region, Ustyug, Vaga region, Velikiye Luki, Venev, Vladimir, Vologda, Vorotynsk, Vyatka Land, Vyazma, Vychegda region, Vym region, Vysokoy, Yam, Yaroslavets (Maloyaroslavets), Yaroslavl', Yelets, Yugra region, Yur'yev, Zaozer'ye, Zarech'ye, Zavoloch'ye, Zhulin (listed among volosts)

Slobodas — Il'inskaya *slobodka, slobodas* of Pesochna Menshyaya which Andrey Kart"mazov and Mitya Zagryazskoi and Ivashko Gladkoi settled, *sloboda* on the Shana which Tovarkov settled, *slobodka* Keshtoma, *slobodka* of the bishop in Chert"kovo, *slobodka* Okhlyabininskaya, *slobodka* Osna on the Shana, *slobodka* Shelshedam, *slobodka* Shygorash

Volosts — Arbuzhoves('), Berezai, Biberevo, B(us)kutovo, Byatino, Chikhachev (if Prince Fedor Ivanovich Bel'skiy or his children should leave the service of Moscow), Chyagoshch", Chyakola, Chyaspla, Dankovo, Dubna (Toropets district), Dubno (Velikiye Luki district), Igumnova, Iledam, Inopazh, Iskan', Isterva, Ist'ya, Kazarinovskaa, Kegrola, Kerchela, Kholm" (Dorogobuzh district), Khomchichi, Khotomichi, Kir'i Gory,

Volosts (*Cont.*)	Knyazhichi burg, Kolodna, Kolushka, Komsha, Kopylea, Korotai, Korzenevo, Koskovo, Kremena, Lavela, Lopastitsi, Lopatino, Lovtso, Luchin burg, Luchinskoye, Lukoves('), Lyubuta, Matkoma, Mezen('), Michenki, Moshkova Gora, M''stislavets'', Mushkova Gora (one third), Myshega, Negomle, Nekrasova, Nem''yuga, Nerekhta (volost and city), Nevle, Nezhelskaa, Orekhovna, Oshchytov, Ozerishcha, Ozerskaa, Patrobal, Pesochna Bol'shaya, Pesochna Menshyaya, Pil'i Gory, Pinega, Pineshka, Plaveyettskaa, Pogorelaya, Pr'm''skiye (Perm') volosts, Prost', Pupovichi, Redyn('), Rekhty, Rogozh, Rostovshchina, R(o)zh(e)stvenoye, Rozhna, Selechna, Seltso, Serebozh, Serkovy Luki, Shatesh('), Shatur, Shogogora, Shokhonskiye volosts, Startseva, Sukhodol, Sulidovo, Sura Poganaa, Surozhyk, Toima, Tura, Tur'yevo, Ukhra, Unzha, Ust'-Shok''stny, Usvai, Uzhytsa, Vasilevo, Vedrosh('), Velikoye Pole, Velilya, Velizhskaa, Vereteya Bolshaa, Veshki, Vesnebologo, Vichyuga (if Prince Fedor Ivanovich Bel'skiy or his children should leave the service of Moscow), Vodosa, volosts of Grand Princess Sofiya in Shokstna, Ust'-Ugly, and Vereteika Malaya, Vorya, Vyaz, Vysheles, Vyshkovo, Vyya, Yem''skaa Gora, Zaop'ye, Zavolzh''skiye volosts of Prince Ivan Andreyevich, Zhulin (volost and city), Zhyzhettskaa
Villages	Aleksin in Starodub, Beloye, Dobryatinskoye, Goroden, Kadashovo, Kraishino, Krasnoye, Muromskoye, Novoye, Okishovskoye, Ostrov, Pes(')ye, Petrovskoye, Putyatino, Runai, Semchinskoye, Semenovskoye, Shagat', village of Yeska Klimov, villages and hamlets of Filip Poltev's children, villages and hamlets of Petr Konstantinovich Dobrynskiy, Volodimerovskoye, Volskoye, Vonguy, Vorob'yevo, Vorontsovskoye, Vorontsovskoye on the Yauza, Vsesvyattskoye, Zaop'ye (small village and volost)
Hamlets	Hamlets of Prince Vasiliy and Prince Semen Shokhonskiy
Other	All that the grand prince obtained by exchange from the Andronnikov Monastery, city courts along both sides of the Yauza, courts of the grand prince in the city and in the suburbs, Dmitrovets *gorodishche*,

Dobryatinskoye apiary, the Forest Lop('), Kast' (the patrimony of Prince Vasiliy Shchetinin), Korbolskoi Island, Laginsk, Lopskiy *myt*, Lyshchykovo Monastery, mills along the Yauza, Ontonova Brewery, other localities along the Ryazan' border, patrimonies of the Novosil', Odoyev, and Belev princes, patrimonies of the Yaroslavl' boyars (if they leave the service of Moscow), *pogost* Velskoi, Princess Yevdokiya's patrimony, Samsonov" Meadow, Sheksna *pogosts*, Sol' (Galitskaya), Sol' (Pereyaslavskaya), Sol' (Rostovskaya), Soltsa Malaya, Sulishin (*pogost*, listed among volosts), Velikaya Sol', weir on the Volga near Rybnaya *sloboda*, Wild Lop'

To Yuriy:

Cities (principalities, lands, districts)	Bryansk, Dmitrov, Kashin (in Tver'), Moscow (a share of Prince Konstantin's "year," of Prince Petr Dmitriyevich's "year," and of Prince Mikhail Andreyevich's "year," and 100 rubles a year from the *tamga*), Ruza, Serpeysk, Zvenigorod
Volosts	Batogova, Blizhevichi, Chernyatitsi, Danilovichi, Degna, Demena, Fe(o)d(o)rovskaa, Fominichi, Gnezdilovo, Gorodechna, Khvoshchna, Kovylna, Lyubun, Moshchyn, Osovik", Patsyn, Piyanova, Pogostishche, Pokinichi, Prikladni, Shop"kova, Shuya, Snopot('), Solov(')-yevichi, Sukhar('), Tukhachev, Uzheperet, Volkonesk", Voronitsa, V"seslavl", Yulka, Zamosh(')ye, Zheryn
Villages	Lytkino, Sushchovo
Hamlets	Teshilovskiye hamlets
Other	Apiarian *stan* in Yulka volost, courts (of Petr, Ivan, and Nikita Dobrynskiy, of Prince Aleksandr Obolenskiy, of Vasiliy Saburov, of Prince Vasiliy, of the children of Prince Fedor Vasil'yevich Obolenskiy, of Prince Ivan Striga, of Ivan Borisov, of the two children of Ivan Vladimirovich Semenov, of Ivan Mikhaylovich Semenov, of Grigoriy Baba, of Vasiliy Tuchkov, and "where my master tailors live"—to be shared by Yuriy and his younger brothers), volosts and *stans* of Volok Lamskiy obtained by the grand prince from Prince Ivan Borisovich

To Dmitriy:

Cities (principalities, lands, districts)	Khlepen, Meshchovsk, Mologa, Moscow (a share of Prince Konstantin's "year," of Prince Petr Dmitriyevich's "year," and of Prince Mikhail Andreyevich's "year," and 100 rubles a year from the *tamga*), Opakov, Opoki (in Tver'), Rzheva (the half obtained from Prince Ivan Borisovich), Uglich, Ustyuzhna, Zubtsov (in Tver')
Volosts	Byshkovichi, Kist'ma, Lychino, Nedokhodovo, Negomir', Rozhalovo, Zalidov
Villages	Naprudtskoye, Novoye Ozerettskoye, Staroye Ozerettskoye
Other	Courts of the village Naprudtskoye in the city and in the suburb, courts shared with Yuriy and his younger brothers (see above, under Yuriy), patrimony of the Glebovs, Rogachevo (not identified), weirs on the Volga and on the Mologa

To Semen:

Cities (principalities, lands, districts)	Bezhetskiy Verkh, Kaluga, Kozel'sk, Moscow (a share of Prince Konstantin's "year," of Prince Petr Dmitriyevich's "year," and of Prince Mikhail Andreyevich's "year," and 100 rubles a year from the *tamga*)
Sloboda	*Slobodka* of Prince Vasiliy Romodanovskiy
Volosts	Boryatin, Khost'tsi, Khvostovichi, Korobki, K"tsyn, Lipitsi, Lugan, Lyudimesk", Mestilovo, Oren', Poryski, Senishcha, Serenesk", Snykhovo, Sytichi, Verkh"-Serena, Vyino, Vyrki, V"zbynov, Zheremin
Villages	Boranovo, Lutsinskoye, Neznanovo (Ivan Baba's village), Ruzsudovskiye villages, Zverevo
Other	Courts shared with his brothers Yuriy, Dmitriy, and Andrey (see above, under Yuriy)

To Andrey:

Cities (principalities, lands, districts)	Aleksin, Kholm (patrimony of Kholm princes), Lyubutsk, Moscow (a share of Prince Konstantin's "year," of Prince Petr Dmitriyevich's "year," and of Prince Mikhail Andreyevich's "year," and 100 rubles a year from the *tamga*), the burg Novyy (Novoi, in the Tver'

	Land), Staritsa (in the Tver' Land), Vereya, Vyshegorod
Sloboda	*Slobodka* Kolychevskaya
Volosts	Gordeyevo, Guslitsa, Gzhelya, Konino, Kunei, Nyukhova, Oleshnya (patrimony of the Kholm princes), Rameneitso, Selna, Sinyaya (patrimony of the Kholm princes), Veprino (in possession of the Odoyev princes), Vokhna, Volkona, Zagar'ye
Villages	Saryyevo, Yasenevo, Yudino
Hamlets	Hamlets of the slave(?) beekeepers of *Vasiltsovo sto* in Selna volost, namely, Bekrenevo, Belyanitsino, Dedenevo, Kharitonovskoye, Neronovo, Novoye Belyanitsino, Novoye Yakimovskoye, Vranikovo, Yakimovskoye
Other	Courts shared with his brothers Yuriy, Dmitriy, and Semen (see above, under Yuriy), Monastery of the Most Pure One in Golutvino, and the waste lands Gribachevo, Isachkovo, and Lopakovo

To Fedor Borisovich, nephew of the Grand Prince:

Cities (principalities, lands, districts)	Buygorod, Moscow (one half of a "sixth year"), Rzheva (one half, confirmed indirectly)
Volost	Kolp' (confirmed)
Village	Ryukhovskoye (confirmed)

12. TESTAMENTARY WRIT OF VASILIY III

Toward building, in the suburb of Moscow, the Monastery of the Virgin and in it the Temple of the Most Pure One and of the Invention of the Holy Cross, and other temples:

A village or two from among the palace villages and a thousand quarters of land, and 3,000 rubles

13. TESTAMENT OF IVAN IV THE TERRIBLE

To Ivan:

The Grand Principalities (listed below)
The Russian Tsardom

Cities (principalities, lands, districts)

Adezh' (Neimil), Alator (Alatyr'), Aleksin, Alystr (Alyst), Arzamas, Astrakhan' (Khanate and city, with the weirs and salt lakes), Balakhna, Belev, Belgorod, Beloozero, Belyy, Bezhetskiy Verkh, Borovsk, Bryansk, Cheboksary, Chukhloma, city on the Plava, city on the Solova (Krapivna?), Dankov, Dmitrov, Dolgovyya (Dolgaya), Doman burg, Dorogobuzh, Drakov, Dutsov, Dvina Land, Galich, Gdov, Goroden', Gorodets (Radilov), Gov'ya, Ivan, Izborsk, Kadom, Kaluga, Karachev, Kargopol'ye, Kashin, Kashira, Kaster Novoy, Kaster Staroy, Kavlet, Kazan' (Khanate and city, with lands along both banks of the Volga), Kerevet' (Kerepet'), Kholm (in Novgorod), Kholmogory, Klin, Kobyl'ye *gorodishche*, Kolomna, Kongod, Konshega (Kokshenga) region, Kopor'ye, Kop'ye, Korela city, Korolevskaya (Karelian) Land, Koshkin burg, Koshkovo, Kozlov, Krasnoy, Kubena, Kurelov (Kurslov), Kuresk burg, Kurmysh, Kutushen, Laduga (Ladoga), Layus, Malyy city (Maloyaroslavets), Medvezh'ya Golova, Medyn', Meshchera (volost?), Mglin, Mikulin (with the patrimony of Prince Semen Mikulinskiy), Mosal'sk (the third which belonged to Prince Vladimir Vseslav), Moscow (all), Mozhaysk, Mstislavl', Mtsensk, Mukov, Murom, Nevl', Nizhniy Novgorod (Grand Principality and city), Novgorod (Grand Principality and city), Novgorod Seversk, Novyy Gorodok, (Lake) Onega region, Opochka, Oreshik (Oreshek), Ostrov (in Pskov), Ostroye (Ostrov), Ozerishche (also willed to Fedor), Pechora region, Pereyaslavl' (Zalesskiy), Pereyaslavl' Ryazanskiy, Pochap, Polotsk, Poonezh'ye (region of the Onega River), Popovich' on the Nevl', Porkhov burg, Poshekhon'ye, Pskov, Putivl', Radonezh, Rakobor (Rakvere), Randen, Romanov on the Volga (which Ivan should maintain in the possession of the Nogay mirzas as long as they remained loyal), Roslavl', Rugodev (Narva), Ryazan' (Grand Principality), Ryazhsk, Rylsk, Ryngol (Ringen), Rzheva (both halves), Rzheva Pustaya (burg in Novgorod), Sabei, Sebezh, Serpukhov, Shatskoy (Shatsk), Smolensk (Grand Principality and city), Sokol, Staraya Rusa (burg), Staraya Ryazan', Staritsa, Starodub Ryapolovo, Sviyazhsk, Syrenets, Sysola, Tavrs (Tarvas), Temnikov, Teshilovo, Tolshebor, Toropets, Torzhok, Tver' (Grand Principality and city), Udoma, Ustyug, Usvyat (also willed to Fedor), Vaga region, Vasil' on the Sura (Vasil'sursk), Velikaya Perm' with the new burgs and salt marshes, Velikiye Luki, *pogost* Velikoy Velizh, Vel'yan, Vel'ye, Venev, Vereya, Vladimir, Volodimer (in Pskov), Vologda, Voronezh' (Voronoch'), Vorotynsk (one third), Vrev, Vyatka Land, Vyazma, Vyborets, Vychegda region, Vym region, Vyshegorod on the Protva, Vyshegorodok, Vysokoy burg, Yama, Yelets, Yugra region, Yur'yev (in Livonia), Yur'yev (Pol'skiy), Yur'yev Volzhskiy, Zaozer'ye, Zarech'ye, Zavoloch'ye (northwest of Velikiye Luki), Zavolotskaya Land (Zavoloch'ye)

Slobodas

Sloboda Rybnaya, *slobodas* of the *streltsy* and post relay men, *slobodka* Kalychevskaya with the meadow, *slobodka* Vladychnya in Yurtova

Volosts

Aleshnya Voskresenskoy, Bereza (Berezai), Bibireva, Borisoglebskaya, Buntsa (Buytse), Buskutovo, Byatino, Dankovo, Dubnya, Guslitsy, Gzhel', Igumnovo, Kazarinovskaya, Kerchma (Kegrola), Kholm (in Dorogobuzh), Kholm (in Staritsa), Kholmichi, Khotumichi, Konopka, Kopyl, Korchala, Kremyanoye, Krysinskoye, Kun'ye, Kur-Gory (Kir'i Gory), Kuzheyka (Unzha?), Lapostitsy, Lavela, Lopatin, Lovtse, Luchino Gorodishche, Lyubuta, Mezen', Mishenki, Moshkova Gora (in Dorogobuzh), Mogil'noye, Mstislavets, Mushkova (Gora) (one third), Nekrasovo, Nem'ya (Nem'yuga), Nevl', Nezhel'skaya, Orekhovka, Oserishche, Oshchitov, Ozerskaya, Penesha (Pineshka?), Petrovskaya, Pil'i Gory, Pinega, Plavitskaya, Pogoreloye, Pogoreloye Gorodishche, Popovskaya (Pupovichi?), Pr'm (Perm') volosts, Prost', Rameneytsov, Razhestvennoye, Redyn, Rekhty, Rostovets, Rostovshchina, Rozhna, Selechna, Serebro, Shalga-Gora, Shater' (Shatesh'), Shatur, Shchagoshch' (Chagoshch'), Sherna city, Sinyaya, Stavtsova (Startseva), Sukhodrov', Suleshino, Sulidovo, Sura Poganaya, Surozhik, Sverchovy Luki, Toma, Tovarkov, Tura, Tur'yevo, Ust'ye, Usvoi, Uzhida, Vasilevo, Vedrozh', Veliko (Velilya), Velikoye Pole, Vesnebologo, Vodosy, Vokhna, Volkona, volosts Apakov (Opakov) on the Ugra, other volosts along the Ugra which used to be in the possession of Prince Vasiliy Shemyachich and Prince Vasiliy Starodubskiy, volosts beyond the Moskva which belonged to Prince Andrey of Staritsa and his son Prince Vladimir, Vysheles, Vyshkovo, Vyy, Yelaskaya Gora (Yemskaya Gora), Yena (Selna?), Yes'kino, Zagar'ye, Zaulusa, Zhizhetskaya, Zhulich'

Villages   Aleksandrovskoye, Ameleva, Aminevo, Andreyevskoye, Antiokhovo, Cherkizovo, Danilovskoye, Dmitreyevskoye, Dobryatinskoye, Faleyevo, Fokino, Golobokovo, Gory, Kadashevo, Kartashevo, Khoroshovo, Khryapovo, Klimovo (village of Yeska Klimov), Knyaginino, Kochergino, Koluzhskoye, Kuveno, Luchinskoye, Luchki, Matveyevskoye, Mitsyno, Mogucheye, Muromskoye, Nesterovskoye, Nikol'skoye, Novoye, Novyye Zemenki, Osipovo, Ostrov, Ovsyanikovo, Palekh, Panteleyevo, Perevyatino, the *pod"yesnyye* villages of the volosts beyond the Moskva, Putyatino, Ramadonovo (one half), Rozhestvenskoye, Sarayevo, Semenovskoye, Seritsy, Sobakino, Somchinskoye, Soroki, Staryye Mekhovitsy, Tatarovo (two villages), Troitskoye, Turinovo, Ustinovskoye, Vasil'yevo (three villages), the villages which were the patrimony of Semen Obraztsov, Volodimerskoye, Volynskoye, Vorob'yevo, Vorontsovo, Voskresenskoye, Yablontsy, Yasenevo, Yedninskoye, Yur'yevskoye, Zales'ye, Zaop'ye

Hamlets   Kamennoye, Kovernev and other hamlets which belonged to Prince Ivan Andreyevich Kovrov, Nauzolovo, Skorekovo

Other   Andopeito Court, Arsk land (Kazan'), cities and volosts and villages of Prince Vladimir Andreyevich, city courts of Somchinskoye, city courts of Vorontsovo, Dmitrovets *gorodishche*, Dobryatinskoye apiary, (Forest) Lop', Karyalskoy (Korbolskoy) Island, lands (of Chuvash, Cheremisa, Bashkirs, Votyaks, Mordva), lands in Nizhniy Novgorod in possession of mirzas or princes, lands of junior boyars in the Wild Plain, lands of the Arsk princes, fishing places, beekeeping lands, Lopskiy *myt*, Lyshchikovo Monastery (with its courts), the Mordva and Cheremisa in Nizhniy Novgorod and Murom, Moscow courts (of boyars and princes), Ontakova (Ontonova) Brewery, other localities along the Ryazan' border, the patrimonies of the service princes in Moscow and Tver' (if they should leave the service of the Grand Prince), patrimonies of the Penkov princes in Pereyaslavl', patrimonies of the Starodub princes in Starodub Ryapolovo (listed above), "plain" patrimonies, Samsonov Meadow, Seversk and "plain" and Rylsk (?) appendages, Sol' (Pereyaslavskaya), Sol' Vychegotskaya, Vasiliy's Department, weirs and hamlets at the weirs in Poshekhon'ye, Wild Lop', Zangants Court, Zaozerskoye

To Fedor: *

Cities (principalities, lands, districts)	Buy(gorod), Kostroma, Kozel'sk, Lyubim, Mtsensk, Nerekhta, Ozerishche, Pleso, Serenesk, Serpeysk, Shuya, Sudislavl', Suzdal', Uglich (?), Ustyuzhna Zhelezopol'skaya, Usvyat, Volok Lamskiy, Yaroslavl'
Volosts	Kargka, Koryakovskaya (with its hamlets, *novalia*, and fisheries), Turekh (with its hamlets and fishing places)
Villages	Beloy Rast (Belyy Rat), Borisovo, Bykovo, Goritsy (one half), Kryletskoye, Kuzyayevo, Lopatniche, Naprudnoye, Nikolskoye Zhdanovo, Ozeretskoye Novoye, Ozeretskoye Staroye (both with hamlets), Puzyayevo, Romantsovo, Sorochino, Tatarovo, Terneyevo (two thirds), villages in Uglich
Hamlets	Nauzovo (Nauzulovo) (with hamlets annexed)
Other	Courts of Naprudnoye in the city and in the suburb, minor cities founded in Polotsk and in Ozerishche districts, patrimonies and purchases of princes-boyars and junior boyars of Yaroslavl' (if they should leave the service of Fedor), patrimonies (already) taken away from Yaroslavl' princes, small adjoining settlements and hamlets and *novalia* that used to belong to Prince Aleksandr Gorbatyy, Sol' Bolshaya, Sol' Malaya

* "The patrimonial principality of my son Fedor [shall be subject] to him [Ivan] also, [and] to the Grand State."

To unborn son of the Tsar:

Cities (princi- palities, lands, districts)	Kashin, Kholopey (Kholopiy), Uglich, Ustyuzhnaya, Vereya, Yaroslavets (Maloyaroslavets)
Sloboda	Zadubrovskaya
Volost	Slavkovo
Other	The *dan'* which is due Uglich, two villages given to Yuriy's widow

To Anna, wife of the Tsar:

City (princi- palities, lands, districts)	Rostov (all)
Villages	Aleshnya, Astankovo, Bolonino, Boltino, Borniskoye (Borinskoye), Flolishchevo, Gorodishche Mstislavle, Krivtsovo, Martem'yanovo, Novoye, Senmskoye (Sem- skoye), Shchulepovo, Sutki (the patrimony of the Sut- skiy princes), Yelokhovo
Hamlets	Hamlets and appendages of Gorodishche Mstislavle and of Flolishchevo and of Senmskoye and of Yelokhovo, hamlets annexed to Aleshnya and Boltino and Astan- kovo from the black *stans* and from the military tenure lands, hamlets and *novalia* that used to belong to Prin- cess Agrafena Sutskaya
Other	Two thirds of the patrimony of the Zaozerskiy-Penkov princes with all their hamlets and appendages

To unborn daughter of the Tsar:

Cities (princi- palities, lands, districts)	Khlepen, Opoki, Ragachev (Rogachev), Zubtsov
Villages (with their hamlets)	Danilovo Ivanovskoye, Davydovskoye, Klenki, Mitro- polich'ye, Safarynskoye, Simonovskoye, Suponevo, Uslyumovskoye, Yeldegino

Appendix

To Ul'yana, widow of the Tsar's brother, Yuriy: *

Cities (principalities, lands, districts)	Kremensk, Ustyuzhna Zheleznaya
Volosts	Kadka, Veshki
Villages	Belyy Rat, Khorobrovo, Krasnoye, Nikolskoye Zhdanovo, Puzyayevo, Zelentsovo
Hamlets	Eleven hamlets annexed to the mill at Cherkizovo, Nauzolov, other hamlets
Other	Mill on the Klyazma near the village Cherkizovo

To Prince Vladimir's son, Prince Vasiliy, and to his daughter:

Testament provided that they should be given allotments "taking into consideration the present time."

To King and Archduke Magnus:

Confirmed in his holding of the city of Polchev "and other volosts and villages." It was noted that Magnus held the cities of Burtniki, Prekat, Roin, Smilten, Volodimerets, and Vorna, but that he had offered them as security to the tsar for a loan of 15,500 rubles (Moscow money). If this loan was not repaid, Ivan, the son of the tsar, should take these cities and their lands. Ivan was to receive Polchev, also, if Magnus should cease to serve him.

Prince Mikhail Vorotynskiy:

Confirmed in his holding of Cherna (Chern'), Novosil', Odoyev Staroye, Ostrov, Peremyshl', and one third of Vorotynsk. Later in the testament, however, the tsar states that he had taken Chern', Novas'iya (Novosil'), and Odoyev away from Prince Mikhail and had given him in exchange the city of Starodub Ryapolovo, the volost Moshok, the villages Knyaginino (with hamlets)

* Lifetime holdings only except for the villages Khorobrovo and Krasnoye, which were hers to dispose of as she saw fit. Upon her death Kremensk and the volost Veshki were to pass to Ivan; Ustyuzhna and other holdings, to Fedor.

and Fokino, and the *stan* Zovskiy, with the warning that if he or his children should cease to serve, then his patrimony would pass to Ivan.

Tsarevitch Murtazaley (Mikhail Kobulin, son of Akhibek):

Confirmed in his holding of Zvenigorod

Following were confirmed in holdings granted them or their fathers by the Tsar or his father:

Mosal'skiy, Obolenskiy, Odoyevskiy, Trubetskoy, and Vorotynskiy princes; Prince Fedor Mstislavskiy and his son Ivan; Prince Mikhail Vasil'yevich Glinskiy and his son Ivan; Ramanova (Romanova), the wife of Yur'-yevich, and her son Nikita

Bibliography

SOURCES

Akty sotsial'no-ekonomicheskoy istorii severo-vostochnoy Rusi, kontsa XIV-nachala XVI v. 2 vols. Vol. I: ed. B. D. Grekov and L. V. Cherepnin (Moscow, 1952). Vol. II: ed. L. V. Cherepnin and I. A. Golubtsov (Moscow, 1958).

Dukhovnyye i dogovornyye gramoty velikikh i udel'nykh knyazey XIV–XVI vv. Ed. L. V. Cherepnin and S. V. Bakhrushin. Moscow-Leningrad, 1950.

Novgorodskaya pervaya letopis' starshego i mladshego izvodov. Ed. A. N. Nasonov and M. N. Tikhomirov. Moscow-Leningrad, 1950.

Polnoye sobraniye russkikh letopisey [PSRL]. 30 vols. to date:

Vol. I. *Lavrent'yevskaya letopis' i Suzdal'skaya letopis' po akademicheskomu spisku.* Moscow, 1962. A reprint of the 1926 Leningrad edition.

Vol. II. *Ipat'yevskaya letopis'.* Moscow, 1962. A reprint of the 1908 St. Petersburg edition.

Vol. V. *Pskovskaya II letopis'.* St. Petersburg, 1851.

Vols. V and VI. *Sofiyskaya I i II letopisi.* St. Petersburg, 1851 and 1853.

Vol. VII. *Voskresenskaya letopis'.* St. Petersburg, 1856.

Vol. VIII. *Prodolzheniye k Voskresenskoy letopisi.* St. Petersburg, 1859.

Vols. IX and X. *Patriarshaya ili Nikonovskaya letopis'.* Moscow, 1965. A reprint of the 1862 St. Petersburg edition of Vol. IX and of the 1885 St. Petersburg edition of Vol. X.

Vol. XV. *Tverskaya letopis'.* St. Petersburg, 1863.

Vol. XXV. *Moskovskiy letopisnyy svod.* Moscow-Leningrad, 1950.

Vol. XXVI. *Vologodsko-Permskaya letopis'.* Moscow-Leningrad, 1959.

Povest' vremennykh let. Ed. V. P. Adrianova-Peretts, text prepared by D. S. Likhachev, trans. D. S. Likhachev and B. A. Romanov. 2 vols. Moscow-Leningrad, 1950.

Bibliography

Troitskaya letopis'. Reconstructed text by M. D. Priselkov. Moscow-Leningrad, 1950.

Tysyachnaya kniga 1550 g. i dvorovaya tetrad' 50-kh godov XVI v. Ed. A. A. Zimin. Moscow-Leningrad, 1950.

Ustyuzhskiy letopisnyy svod (Arkhangelogorodskiy letopisets). Text prepared by K. N. Serbina. Moscow-Leningrad, 1950.

SECONDARY MATERIALS

Bakhrushin, S. V., A. A. Novosel'skiy, A. A. Zimin, and N. V. Ustyugov. *Istoriya Moskvy*. 6 vols. Vol. I: Moscow, 1952.

Bazilevich, K. V. *Vneshnaya politika russkogo tsentralizovannogo gosudarstva (vtoraya polovina XV veka)*. Moscow, 1952.

Bibliya, ili knigi svyashchennago pisaniya vetkhago i novago zaveta. City and date of publication not legible; published during the reign of Emperor Alexander I. A Church Slavic version of the Bible.

Bibliya, ili knigi svyashchennogo pisaniya vetkhogo i novogo zaveta. Moscow: Publishing House of the Moscow Patriarchate, 1956.

Buslayev, F. I. *Istoricheskaya grammatika russkogo yazyka*. Moscow, 1959. A new edition based on the Moscow 5th edition of 1881.

Cherepnin, L. V. *Obrazovaniye russkogo tsentralizovannogo gosudarstva v XIV–XV vekakh*. Moscow, 1960.

——. *Russkiye feodal'nyye arkhivy, XIV–XV vv.* 2 vols. Moscow-Leningrad, 1948–1951.

Chichagov, V. K. *Iz istorii russkikh imen, otchestv i familiy*. Moscow, 1959.

Chicherin, B. *Opyty po istorii russkago prava: Dukhovnyya i dogovornyya gramoty velikikh" i udel'nykh" knyazey*. Moscow, 1858.

Dal', Vladimir. *Tolkovyy slovar' zhivogo velikorusskogo yazyka*. Moscow, 1955. Reproduced from the St. Petersburg 2nd edition of 1880–1882.

Duncan, David Douglas. *The Kremlin*. Greenwich, Conn., n.d.

Eck, Alexandre. *Le Moyen Age russe*. Paris, 1933.

Ekzemplyarskiy, A. V. *Velikiye i udel'nyye knyaz'ya severnoy Rusi v" tatarskiy period", s" 1238 po 1505 g.* 2 vols. St. Petersburg, 1889.

Encyclopaedia Britannica. Chicago-London-Toronto, 1959.

Entsiklopedicheskiy slovar'. Ed. F. A. Brokhaus and I. A. Efron. St. Petersburg, 1898.

Gregory, James S., and D. W. Shave. *The USSR: A Geographical Survey.* New York, 1946; first published by George G. Harrap and Co., Ltd., London, in 1944.

Grekov, B. D., L. V. Cherepnin, and V. T. Pashuto. *Ocherki istorii SSSR: Period feodalizma IX–XV v.v., Chast' vtoraya, Ob"yedineniye russkikh zemel' vokrug Moskvy i obrazovaniye russkogo tsentralizovannogo gosudarstva.* Moscow, 1953.

Hastings, James, ed. *Dictionary of the Bible.* New York: 1909.

Holy Bible (American Standard Revised Version). New York: Thomas Nelson and Sons, 1901.

The Holy Bible (King James Version). Philadelphia: National Bible Press, n.d.

Holy Bible (Revised Standard Version). New York: Thomas Nelson and Sons, 1952.

Karamzin, N. M. *Istoriya gosudarstva rossiyskago.* 5th ed. 12 vols. St. Petersburg, 1842.

Klyuchevskiy, V. O. *Sochineniya.* 8 vols. Edition issued under the general direction of M. N. Tikhomirov. Moscow, 1956–1959.

Lebedev, V. I., M. N. Tikhomirov, and V. Ye. Syroyechkovskiy. *Khrestomatiya po istorii SSSR.* Moscow, 1951.

Life, XLIV, No. 2 (1958), 43, 46, 54.

Lipson, E. *The Economic History of England.* Vol. I: London, 1956.

Lyubavskiy, M. K. *Obrazovaniye osnovnoy gosudarstvennoy territorii velikorusskoy narodnosti.* Leningrad, 1929.

Maslennikova, N. N. *Prisoyedineniye Pskova k russkomu tsentralizovannomu gosudarstvu.* Leningrad, 1955.

Nasonov, A. N. *Mongoly i Rus' (Istoriya tatarskoy politiki na Rusi).* Moscow-Leningrad, 1940.

Nasonov, A. N., L. V. Cherepnin, and A. A. Zimin. *Ocherki istorii SSSR: Period feodalizma, konets XV v.-nachalo XVII v. Ukrepleniye russkogo tsentralizovannogo gosudarstva (konets XV–XVI vv.) Krest'yanskaya voyna i bor'ba russkogo naroda protiv inostrannoy interventsii v nachale XVII v.* Moscow, 1955.

Nechkina, M. V., B. A. Rybakov, A. A. Novosel'skiy, A. V. Fadeyev, L. V. Cherepnin, and V. I. Lebedev. *Istoriya SSSR.* Vol. I: Moscow, 1956. This is the first volume of a two-volume work released as a university text by the Ministry of Higher Education of the USSR.

A New English Dictionary on Historical Principles. Ed. James A. H. Murray, *et al.* Oxford, 1888–1928.

Bibliography

Novyy zavet" gospoda nashego Iisusa Khrista. St. Petersburg, 1912.

Obnorskiy, S. P., and S. G. Barkhudarov. *Khrestomatiya po istorii russkogo yazyka*. Moscow, 1921.

Presnyakov, A. Ye. *Obrazovaniye velikorusskogo gosudarstva: Ocherki po istorii XII–XV stoletiy*. Petrograd, 1918.

Pushkarev, S. G. *Obzor russkoy istorii*. New York, 1953.

Russkiy biograficheskiy slovar'. 25 vols. to date. St. Petersburg, 1896–1918.

Slovar' russkogo yazyka. Edited by a board under the chairmanship of S. G. Barkhudarov (Vol. I) and A. P. Yevgen'yeva (Vols. II–IV). Moscow, 1957–1961.

Solov'yev, S. M. *Istoriya Rossii s drevneyshikh vremen*. 15 vols. Moscow, 1959–1966. A new edition of the *Istoriya*, published under the editorship of L. V. Cherepnin. I have translated *kniga* as "Volume" when referring to this work.

Sreznevskiy, I. I. *Materialy dlya slovarya drevne-russkogo yazyka*. 3 vols. Moscow, 1958. A reprint of the St. Petersburg edition of 1893–1902.

Svyashchennyya knigi vetkhago i novago zaveta. Vienna, 1889.

Sytin, P. V. *Iz istorii moskovskikh ulits (ocherki)*. 3rd ed. rev. and enlarged. Moscow, 1958.

Tatishchev, V. N. *Istoriya Rossiyskaya*. 7 vols, 6 vols. to date. Moscow-Leningrad, 1962–1966.

Tikhomirov, M. N. *Drevnyaya Moskva*. Moscow, 1947.

——. "Osnovaniye Moskvy i Yuriy Dolgorukiy," *Izvestiya Akademii Nauk SSSR: Seriya istorii i filosofii*, V, No. 2 (1948), 143–148.

——. *Srednevekovaya Moskva v XIV–XV vekakh*. Moscow, 1957.

Vernadsky, George. *Kievan Russia*. New Haven, Conn., 1948.

——. *The Mongols and Russia*. New Haven, Conn., 1953.

Veselovskiy, S. B. "Dukhovnoye zaveshchaniye Ivana Groznogo kak istoricheskiy istochnik," *Izvestiya Akademii Nauk SSSR: Seriya istorii i filosofii*, IV, No. 6 (1947), 505–520.

——. *Podmoskov'ye—Pamyatnyye mesta v istorii russkoy kul'tury XIV–XIX vekov*. Moscow, 1955.

Voronin, N. N., and M. K. Karger. *Istoriya kul'tury drevney Rusi: Domongol'skiy period. Obshchestvennyy stroy i dukhovnaya kul'tura*. Moscow-Leningrad, 1951.

Webster's New International Dictionary of the English Language. 2nd ed. Springfield, Mass., 1947.

Whitelock, Dorothy. *English Historical Documents, c. 500–1042*. New York: 1955. The first volume in a series of English historical documents published under the general editorship of David C. Douglas.

Zabelin, Ivan. *Domashniy byt" russkago naroda v XVI i XVII st.: Domashniy byt" russkikh" tsarey v XVI i XVII st.* Moscow, 1862.

Zananiri, Gaston. *Histoire de l'Eglise byzantine.* Paris, 1954.

Glossary and Indexes

Glossary of Russian Terms

barmy, shoulder pieces of the grand prince, 97, 98, 185

bereg, shore, 344; defense line south of Moscow, 209

beregovaya sluzhba, shore service, service on the defense line south of Moscow, 210

bol'shoy namestnik, grand lieutenant, 80–81, 255, 271

bortnichestvo, beekeeping, 85

boyare (sg. *boyarin*), boyars, 69–70

boyarin putnyy, see *putnyy boyarin*

boyarskiye dvorovyye deti, boyar court children, 73

chashnichiy put', drink *put',* 85; see also *put'*

chetvert', quarter (of land), one half of a dessiatine, 301

chislenyye lyudi (chislyaki, chislyane), enrolled people, 73–76, 184, 209, 263, 326

chislo, census, 94

chislyaki, chislyane, see *chislenyye lyudi*

dan', princely tribute, 62, 63, 71, 74–76, 215, 216, 221, 231, 239, 259, 357, 387

dani putevyye, road tributes, 325

danshchik, collector of *dan',* 63

delenyi lyudi, people acquired through partition (?), 78

delovyye lyudi, artisan slaves (?), 78, 191

delyui, 76

denga, one two-hundredth of a ruble, 294, 295

derevnya, hamlet, 60

desyatnik, commander of ten, 70

deti boyarskiye (sg. *syn boyarskiy*), junior boyars, 72–73

detskiye, junior members of the prince's retinue in Kievan Russia, 72

dikoye pole, wild plain, 272; *see also* Wild Plain *in* Index of Place Names

doklad, reference, 79

dokladnaya gramota, see *gramoty dokladnyye*

dovodchik, criminal investigator, 83

dukhovnaya zapis', testamentary writ, 51, 300

dushevnaya pripisnaya gramota, codicil, 263

dvor, court, 25, 227, 236, 263, 265, 269, 270

dvoretskiy, major-domo, 83, 87; see also *dvorskiy*

dvorovyy syn boyarskiy, junior boyar of the court, 332

dvorovyye, court men, see *dvoryane*

dvorskiy, major-domo, 77, 83, 85, 87

dvortsovyye d'yaki, palace secretaries, 84; see also *d'yak*

dvoryane (dvorovyye), court men, 73

d'yak, secretary, 83, 84, 177

d'yak yamskoy, post relay secretary, 79, 84

goldovnik, vassal, 347

gorod, city, 4, 5, 12, 58, 59, 342

gorodishche, large city, ruins of a city, 344

gorodok, burg, 3, 4, 59, 342, 365

gost'ba, trade, 58

gostinets, great trade road, 66

gostinyye dvory, tax on merchants' courts, 65

gostka, see *kostki*

gosudarstvo, state, 109

grad, city, 4, 5, 12, 58; see also *gorod*

gramota dokladnaya, see *gramoty dokladnyye*

Glossary of Russian Terms

gramota polnaya, see *gramoty polnyye*

gramoty dokladnyye, reference charters, 78–79, 293

gramoty polnyye, full charters, 78–79, 223, 293

gramoty zhaloval'nyye prochnyye, permanent charters of grant, 271

grivenka, a weight, 217

grivna, one tenth of a ruble (c. 1500), 294, 295, 325

kazennyy dvor, treasury court, 246

kazna, treasure, treasury, 83

kaznachey, treasurer, 83, 84, 206

khlebennyy i kormovoy prikaz, grain (or bread) and feeding bureau, 87; see also *prikaz*

kholopi, slaves, 78

klyuchi, keys, domestic departments, 83

klyuchniki, somlers, 83, 191

knyaz' (pl. *knyaz'ya*), prince, 67; *knyaz'ya boyarskiye*, boyar princes, 69; *sluzhebnyye* (*sluzhilyye*) *knyaz'ya*, service princes, 69; *udel'nyy knyaz'*, patrimonial prince, 44, 68, 69, 81, 252; *velikiy knyaz'*, grand prince, "grand duke," 67

knyaz'-tretnik, prince third-man, 87

konyushiy, equerry, 82

konyushiy prikaz, horse bureau, 87

konyushiy put', horse *put'*, 85, 86

korm (pl. *kormy*), subsistence, (pl.) feedings, livings, 57, 63, 64

kormleniye, feeding, subsistence, living, 63, 64, 85

kormlennyye okupy, subsistence indemnities, 63, 64, 351

kostki (*kostka*), tax on persons accompanying goods, 66, 201, 206, 367

kreml', kremlin, 58

krestnoye tselovan'ye, kissing the cross, taking an oath, 258

krestotseloval'naya zapis', sworn writ, 40, 251

krest'yane, peasants (literally Christians, common Christians), 73

lavka, trading stand, tax on trading stands, 65; see also *polavochnaya*

lovchiy prikaz, hunting bureau, 87

lovchiy put', hunting *put'*, 85; see also *put'*

lug, meadow, lower side or bank of a river, 344

lugovaya storona, the meadow side, the lower (left) bank (of the Volga), 344

luk, measure of land (6.72 dessiatines), 325

lyudi gramotnyye, people who are slaves (or indentured) on the basis of a charter (*gramota*), 78, 202

lyudi polnyye, full slaves, people who are slaves on the basis of a *gramota polnaya*, 78, 202, 223; see also *gramoty polnyye*

mochag (*mochak*), salt lake, 345

myt (*myto*), toll, 12, 62, 66, 81, 88, 184, 196–198, 205, 209–211, 272, 276, 325; *myt sukhoy*, dry *myt*, 66; *myt vodyanoy*, water *myt*, 66

myzy, farmsteads, 346

namestnichiye dokhody, lieutenants' incomes, 63, 351

namestnik, lieutenant, 81, 83, 283, 332, 334, 356, 357

oblast', district, 87; see also *uyezd*

obrochniki, quitrent tenants, 62

obrok, quitrent, 62

obzha, measure of land (one half of a *luk*, or 3.36 dessiatines), 325

okol'nichiy, high officer of the prince, 82, 206, 357, 359

okol'nichiye boyare, boyars of the second rank, 82

Oprichnina, 305, 338, 356, 360

orda, horde, 76, 243

Ordinskaya sotnya, Horde Hundred, 77

ordyntsy (*ordintsy*), 73, 75, 76–77, 243, 270

osada, subdivision of a volost, 344

osadchiy, founder of a new settlement (Ukr.), 344

osmnicheye (*vosmnicheye*), 12, 64–65, 184, 198, 209, 364–366, 368

otchina (*votchina*), patrimony, 71, 104

otkhozhiy, outlying, 334

otkup, ransoming of prisoners, farming (of the right to coin money, etc.), 106, 292

otroki, junior members of the

otroki (cont.)
   prince's retinue in Kievan Russia, 72
ovkach, vase (?), unit of gold (?), 183, 200

pechatnik, keeper of the seal, 82
pisets, scribe, census taker, land surveyor, 82, 258
poberezhnaya storona, the shore side, the higher (right) bank (of the Volga), 344
pochinok, novale, 19, 60
podat', tax, 325
pod"yesnyye villages, 65, 327, 385; see also *pod"yezd*
pod"yezd, a custom tax, 65, 327
pogost, 20, 57–58, 190, 276, 281, 282, 287, 289, 342, 343
polavochnaya (polavochnoye), tax on trading stands, 65; see also *lavka*
polgoda, half-year, 91
polnaya gramota, see *gramoty polnyye*
pol'skiye (sg. *pol'skiy*), plain (adj.), 333, 341; *see also* Wild Plain *in* Index of Place Names
poltina, one half of a ruble, 294, 295
polyud'ye, 57
pomernoye, tax on weighing dry-measure goods, 65, 66
pomeshchik, military tenant, 329
pomest'ya (sg. *pomest'ye*), military tenures, 54
pomest'ye system, military tenure system, xiv
posad, suburb, 4, 58, 251, 282
posadnik, governor, 59
posel'skiye, villici, village administrators, 83, 191, 206
poshliny (sg. *poshlina*), customs, 62
posol'skiy prikaz, bureau of emissaries, 87
potyaglo, appertained, 33 (*potyagnusha*), 61, 73, 212, 348 (*potyanet*)
povet (Polish *powiat*), district, 57, 59
prigorod, minor city, 27, 59, 225, 281
prikaz, bureau, 86, 87
prikaz bol'shogo dvortsa, bureau of the great palace, 87
prikazchik, intendant, 82, 293
prikaznyye lyudi, bureau people, 86, 301

primetnyye den'gi, contributions, 63, 64, 351
primysl, acquisition, appropriation, 21, 229
prisel'ye (priselka), small adjoining settlement, 257
pud, tax on weighing, 65
pustoshi, waste lands, 252
put' (pl. *puti*), 46, 78, 82, 85–87, 94, 196, 209, 219, 222, 227–229, 236–238, 243–245, 247–252, 269, 272–283, 285–291, 325, 328, 332–344, 349–355, 357
putnik, chief of a *put',* 72, 82, 85, 86, 257
putnyy boyarin, put' boyar, 85
pyatiny (sg. *pyatina*), fifths (of Novgorod), 281

ryad, arrangement, disposition, 182, 189, 196, 208, 219, 227, 236, 243, 263, 269

sad, garden, 271
selishche, large village, 359
selo, village, 57, 60
sel'tso, small village, 59, 60
shapka monomakhovskaya, Cap of Monomakh, 101; see also *shapka zolotaya*
shapka zolotaya, golden cap, Cap of Monomakh, 99–101, 185
siroty (sg. *sirota*), peasants, (lit.) orphans, 73
sloboda (svoboda), 60–61, 63, 77, 82, 183, 214, 216, 269, 274, 326, 327, 384
slobodka (svobodka), 12, 61, 183, 212, 285, 368
slobodskiye volosteli, sloboda administrators, 81, 82
slugi ordynskiye, Horde servitors, 77
slugi pod dvorskim, servants under the major-domo, 77, 78, 83
slugi vol'nyye (sg. *sluga vol'naya*), free servants, 73, 79
sluzhebnyye knyaz'ya, sluzhilyye knyaz'ya, see *knyaz', sluzhebnyye (sluzhilyye) knyaz'ya*
sokha, wooden plow, taxable unit of land, 63, 258, 259
sokol'nichiy put', falconry *put',* 85
sotskiye (sg. *sotskiy*), commanders of one hundred, 70
stan, 58, 74, 75, 89, 94, 196, 209, 263,

stan (cont.)
  269, 285, 287, 293, 325, 350, 377, 380; apiarian *stan*, 286; black *stan*, 358, 387; city *stan*, 355
stareyshiy put' (*starishii put'*), senior *put'*, larger revenue (Vasiliy Dmitriyevich's half of two thirds in Moscow), 89, 90, 92, 93, 95
starosty (sg. *starosta*), elders, 83, 191
starshiy gorod, senior city, 59
startsy gradskiye, elders of the city (in Kievan Russia), 70
stol'nichiy put', table *put'*, 85
storona, side, region, district, country, land, 33, 257
strel'tsy, 327, 384
sud, tax on the dispensing of justice, 259
svoboda, see *sloboda*
svobodka, see *slobodka*
strasti bol'shiye, strasti Gospodni, relics of the Passion of the Lord, 231, 232
syn boyarskiy, see *deti boyarskiye*

tamga, 12, 23, 62, 64, 65, 81, 88, 184, 190, 196, 197, 199, 201, 206, 209–211, 228, 237, 258, 269, 282, 283, 285, 325, 335, 340, 345, 346, 348, 364, 366–368, 371, 372, 375, 380, 381; stamp, 181
tarkhan, holder of immunity lands, 345
tiun, 83, 84, 191, 202, 206, 217, 221, 223, 231, 239, 252, 261, 298
torg, tax on trading in the market place, 65
tret', third, 88, 91, 196, 333
tretnoye vladeniye Moskvoy, tripartite holding of Moscow, 87
tsentur', 99, 325
tyaglo, 61–62, 334, 358
tyaglo people (*tyaglyye lyudi*), 61, 73, 76, 83
tysyatskiy, chiliarch, 4, 70, 80, 86, 189

uchug (*uchyug*), large weir, 345, 346
udel, patrimonial principality, 7–9, 20, 42, 56, 68–69, 105, 209, 250, 360, 368, 375

udel'nyy knyaz', udel prince, see *knyaz', udel'nyy knyaz'*
ugozh'i, appendages, 264, 340, 341
ukhody, advantages, 264
ulus, "province" of a Tartar horde, 14
uyezd, district, 57–59

varnitsy, salt works, 229
Vasiltsev" stan", Vasiltsevo sto, see *Vasiltsevo vedan'ye*
Vasiltsevo vedan'ye (*Vasiltsev" stan", Vasiltsevo sto*), Vasiliy's Department, 86, 184, 196, 209, 219, 227, 236, 243, 269, 291, 326, 367, 369, 371–373, 382
veche, city assembly, 27, 59
velikiy knyaz', see *knyaz', velikiy knyaz'*
veliko-knyazheskiy udel, grand-princely patrimonial principality, 38; see also *udel*
ves, tax on weighing, 65, 346, 348
vlast', rule, power, authority, see *volost'*
vol'nyy sluga, see *slugi vol'nyye*
volost', 32, 57, 58, 184
volosteli, volost administrators, 81–83
vosmnicheye, see *osmnicheye*
votchina, see *otchina*
votchinnik, patrimonial landholder, 345
vybornyye dvoryane, select court men, 73
vykhod, Tartar tribute, 63, 74, 75, 216, 259, 294

yam, post relay tax, 64, 221
yarlyk, patent, 222, 230
yez, weir, 345, 346
yezd, traveling about, 57

zakladni (sg. *zakladen'*), 79, 106, 293
zasada, subdivision of a volost, 344
Zemshchina, the Land, that part of Muscovy outside Ivan IV's preserve (the Oprichnina), 338
zhrebii, share, 91; see also *tret'*

Index of Personal Names*

Abdullah (Abdul, Abdulla), Khan of the Golden Horde, 35

Abel (bib.), 312

Abraham (bib.), 309

Achkasov, Timofey, secretary of Vasiliy I, 234

Adam (bib.), 308

Aepa, Polovetsian khan, 4

Afanasiy, Archimandrite of the Simonovo Monastery, 261

Afanasiy, Bishop of Kolomna, 191

Afanasiy, Bishop of Pereyaslavl', 191

Afanasiy Danilovich, Pr., son of Daniil Aleksandrovich of Moscow, 87

Afanasiy-Andrey Ivanovich, Pr. of Yaroslavl', 255

Afiney, owner of a patrimonial estate, 13, 186

Agalak, Pr. of the Shibanskaya (Tyumen') Horde, 280

Agrippina Vasil'yevna, Gr. Princess of Ryazan', wife of Ivan Vasil'yevich, 334

Akhibek, Tartar khan, 338, 389

Akinf, priest, 202

Alabysh, Fedor, Pr., land surveyor of Ivan III, 280

Aleksandr Andreyevich, boyar of Dmitriy Donskoy, 217

Aleksandr Borisovich, Pr., see Gorbatyy-Suzdal'skiy (Shuyskiy), Aleksandr Borisovich

Aleksandr Danilovich, Pr., son of Daniil Aleksandrovich of Moscow, 87

Aleksandr Danilovich Vzmeten', Pr., son of Daniil Borisovich of Suzdal'-Nizhniy Novgorod, 255

Aleksandr Fedorovich, Pr. of Yaroslavl', see Bryukhatyy, Aleksandr Fedorovich

Aleksandr Ivanovich, Pr. of Rostov, son of Ivan Aleksandrovich, 46

Aleksandr Ivanovich Bryukhatyy, Pr., see Bryukhatyy, Aleksandr Ivanovich

Aleksandr Kazimirovich, Gr. Pr. of Lithuania, King of Poland, 273, 335

Aleksandr Konstantinovich, Pr. of Rostov, son of Konstantin Vasil'yevich, 45

Aleksandr Konstantinovich, Pr. of Uglich, son of Konstantin Borisovich, 30–32

Aleksandr Mikhaylovich, Gr. Pr. of Tver' and Vladimir, son of Gr. Pr. Mikhail Yaroslavich, 16, 181, 189

Aleksandr Yaroslavich Nevskiy, Saint, Pr. of Novgorod and Pskov, Gr. Pr. of Vladimir, 8, 9, 29, 186

Aleksandra, nun, see Ul'yana, Princess, wife of Yuriy Vasil'yevich of Uglich

Aleksandra, Gr. Princess, wife of Aleksandr Nevskiy, 186

Aleksandra, Gr. Princess, wife of Ivan II, 17, 196, 199, 201, 366

Aleksey (Aleksiy), Saint, Bishop of Vladimir, Metropolitan, 191, 204, 206, 232, 270, 323

Aleksey Ignat'yevich, owner of a patrimonial estate, 263

Alexius Comnenus, Byzantine emperor, 102, 103

Anastasiya, wife of Fedor Andreyevich, owner of a patrimonial estate, 263, 377

Anastasiya Romanovna, Tsarina, first wife of Ivan IV, daughter of the *okol'nichiy* Roman Yur'yevich Zakhar'in-Koshkin, 311, 324, 359

Anastasiya Vasil'yevna, daughter of Vasiliy I, 233

Andrey Aleksandrovich, Gr. Pr. of

* Abbreviations: Pr.—prince; Gr. Pr.—grand prince.

Index of Personal Names

Index of Personal Names

Dolmat Yur'yev, *see* Yur'yev, Dolmat

Donskoy, Dmitriy, *see* Dmitriy Ivanovich Donskoy

Donskoy, Vladimir Andreyevich, *see* Vladimir Andreyevich the Brave

Dryuts'skiy, Ivan, owner of a patrimonial estate, 190, 365

Eck, Alexandre, 62, 64, 65, 76, 183, 344

Ekzemplyarskiy, A. V., 31, 34, 37, 225, 276, 288, 291

Esau (bib.), 308

Faustov, Grigoriy, owner of a patrimonial estate, 369

Fedor, grandfather of Mariya Fedorovna Koshkina–Goltyayeva, *see* Koshka, Fedor Andreyevich

Fedor, son of Stepan, owner of a patrimonial estate, 256

Fedor Andreyevich, boyar of Dmitriy Donskoy, 19, 206, 211, 217

Fedor Andreyevich, *okol'nichiy* of Dmitriy Donskoy, 217

Fedor Andreyevich, owner of a patrimonial estate, 263

Fedor Borisovich, Pr. of Volok Lamskiy, son of Boris Vasil'yevich, 51, 94–96, 280, 284, 287, 289, 294, 295, 378, 382

Fedor Fedorovich, *see* Koshkin, Fedor Fedorovich

Fedor Glebovich, a lesser prince of Yaroslavl', 254

Fedor Ivanovich, Tsarevich, son of Ivan IV and Anastasiya Romanovna, 51–53, 68, 99, 107, 108, 306, 311–315, 321, 322, 324, 325, 327, 336, 348, 352–356, 359, 360, 383, 384, 386, 388

Fedor L'vovich, Pr. of Vorotynsk, 40, 251

Fedor Stefanovich, founder of the Simonovo Monastery, later Archbishop of Rostov, 261

Fedor Sviblo, *see* Sviblo, Fedor Andreyevich

Fedor Svyatoslavich, Pr. of Smolensk, son of Svyatoslav Glebovich, 252

Fedor Vasil'yevich, Pr. of Rostov, son of Vasiliy Konstantinovich, 31–34, 48

Fedor Vasil'yevich, Pr. of Tarusa, 261

Fedor Vasil'yevich *Tretnoy*, Pr. of Ryazan', son of Vasiliy Ivanovich, 41, 43, 282, 283, 294, 333, 334, 378

Fedorov, Leontiy, owner of a village, 247, 374

Fedosiy, spiritual father of Ivan Kalita, 187

Fedosiya, Princess, daughter of Ivan Kalita, 20, 98, 180, 185, 214, 369

Fedosiya Semenovna, Princess, daughter of Pr. Semen Mikhaylovich Mezetskiy, 331

Feodosiy, Archbishop of Rostov, Metropolitan, 241, 243, 261, 262, 266

Fetiniya, Princess, daughter of Ivan Kalita, 97, 180, 185

Filimon, Archimandrite, 191

Filipp, Saint, Metropolitan, 307

Finnish tribes, 282

Foma Ivanovich, owner of a court (*dvor*) in Moscow, 227, 236, 371, 372

Forest Lop', a Finnish tribe, 282, 343, 380, 385

Fotiy, Metropolitan, 226, 234–236, 240

Frederick III, King of Denmark, 347

Fryazin, Ivan, 292

Furstenberg, Master of the Teutonic Order, 354

Gedimin, Gr. Pr. of Lithuania, 302

Gentiles, 317

German knights, 348

Gladkoy, Ivashko (Ivan), 274, 378

Gleb Rostislavich, Pr. of Ryazan', son of Rostislav Yaroslavich, 6, 58

Gleb Vasil'kovich, Pr. of Beloozero and Rostov, son of Vasil'ko Konstantinovich, 30, 33

Gleb Vasil'yevich, one of the lesser princes of Yaroslavl', 254

Gleb Vladimirovich, Saint, Prince of Murom, son of Gr. Pr. Vladimir Svyatoslavich, 33, 296

Glebov, family, 288, 381

Glinskaya, Yelena, Gr. Princess, second wife of Vasiliy III, 304, 324, 326, 349, 357, 359

Glinskiy, family, 359

Glinskiy, Ivan Mikhaylovich, Pr., 359, 389

Glinskiy, Mikhail L'vovich, Pr., 304, 359

Index of Personal Names

Ivan Ivanovich the Young (*Molodoy*), Gr. Pr. of Tver', son of Ivan III and Mariya Borisovna, 41, 299

Ivan Kalita, *see* Ivan I Danilovich Kalita

Ivan Mikhaylovich, *see* Vorotynskiy, Ivan Mikhaylovich

Ivan Rodivonovich, *okol'nichiy* of Dmitriy Donskoy, 206, 217

Ivan Semenovich, Pr., son of Semen the Proud, 188

Ivan the Precursor, *see* John the Precursor

Ivan Vasil'yevich, Gr. Pr. of Ryazan', son of Gr. Pr. Vasiliy Ivanovich of Ryazan', 282, 283

Ivan Vasil'yevich, Pr., 75

Ivan Vasil'yevich, Pr., son of Vasiliy I, 21, 22, 108, 219–223, 226, 227, 241, 369, 370

Ivan Vasil'yevich, Pr. of Pronsk, 220

Ivan Vasil'yevich, Pr. of Suzdal'–Nizhniy Novgorod, 230

Ivan III Vasil'yevich the Great, Gr. Pr. of Vladimir and Moscow, xiv, xv, 24–26, 41–44, 46, 50, 54, 59, 61, 65, 69, 75, 93, 94, 98–102, 105, 108, 243–246, 248, 256, 258–260, 265, 267–269, 272–274, 276–283, 287, 288, 290–292, 295, 298, 299, 302, 325, 327, 328, 333–335, 337, 350, 376, 377

Ivan IV Vasil'yevich the Terrible, Tsar, xv, 46, 49–55, 58, 59, 63–65, 68, 96, 99, 102, 104, 105, 109, 177, 268, 304–307, 311, 324, 326, 327, 329, 332, 333, 335, 341, 344, 346, 347, 351, 354–357, 359, 360, 382

Ivan Vladimirovich, Pr. of Serpukhov, son of Vladimir Andreyevich the Brave, 92, 233

Ivan Yaroslavich, Pr. of Yur'yev, 244

Ivan Yur'yevich, Pr., *see* Patrikeyev, Ivan Yur'yevich

Jadwiga, Queen of Poland, wife of King Jagiello, 233

Jagiello, Gr. Pr. of Lithuania, King of Poland, 233, 239

Jalal ad-Din, *see* Zeleni–Saltan

Jesus, 33, 181, 232, 306, 309, 312, 314, 316–318, 320

John VIII Palaeologus, Byzantine emperor, 233

John the Precursor (the Baptist), 181, 195

Kalita, House of, *see* Moscow princes

Karamyshev, Andrey, land surveyor of Ivan III, 291

Karamyshev, Vasiliy, land surveyor of Ivan III, 273, 286

Karamzin, N. M., 14, 351, 354

Kartmazov, Andrey, elder of a *sloboda*, 274, 378

Kazanchiy, Tartar emissary, 31

Khabar, *see* Obraztsov–Simskiy–Khabar, Ivan Vasil'yevich

khans, 53, 67, 77, 181, 183

Kholm princes, 291, 381, 382

Kholmskoy, Vasiliy Danilovich, Pr., son-in-law of Ivan III, voivode of Moscow, 298

Khvost, Aleksey Petrovich, boyar of Ivan Kalita and Semen the Proud, *tysyatskiy* of Moscow, 191

Kiev princes, 27, 70

Kiprian, Metropolitan, 218, 232

Kirill, Archimandrite of the Trinity-Sergiy Monastery, Metropolitan, 307, 356

Kirill, Saint, Bishop of Turov, 323

Kirill Belozerskiy, founder of the Kirill of Beloozero Monastery, 323

Klyuchevskiy, V. O., xv, 77, 85, 102, 192

Kobulin, Mikhail, son of Akhibek, 53, 338, 389

Kochev, Vasiliy, voivode of Ivan Kalita, 33, 34, 47

Kochka, Tartar emissary, 32, 34, 47

Koltovskaya, Anna, Tsarina, wife of Ivan IV, 46, 51, 53, 305, 324, 356–358, 387

Konstantin Borisovich, Pr. of Rostov, son of Boris Vasil'kovich, 30, 32, 48

Konstantin Dmitriyevich, *see* Sheya, Konstantin Dmitriyevich

Konstantin Dmitriyevich, Pr., son of Dmitriy Donskoy, 19–23, 89–91, 95, 207, 214, 223, 225, 226, 230, 233, 248, 249, 251, 369, 370

Konstantin Romanovich, Pr. of Ryazan', 8, 10

Index of Personal Names

Mariya Dmitriyevna (*cont.*)
Dmitriy Donskoy, 232

Mariya Fedorovna Koshkina–Goltyayeva, Princess, wife of Pr. Yaroslav Vladimirovich of Serpukhov–Borovsk, daughter of the boyar Fedor Fedorovich Goltyay–Koshkin, mother-in-law of Vasiliy II, 25, 250–253, 280, 374, 375

Mariya Fedorovna Nagaya, *see* Nagaya, Mariya Fedorovna

Mariya Ivanovna, Princess, wife of Konstantin Vasil'yevich of Rostov, daughter of Ivan Kalita, 44, 48, 98, 180, 185

Mariya Vasil'yevna, Princess, wife of Pr. Yuriy Patrikeyev, daughter of Vasiliy I, 302

Mariya Vladimirovna, Princess, wife of King Magnus of Livonia, daughter of Pr. Vladimir Andreyevich of Staritsa, 347

Mariya Yaroslavna, Gr. Princess, wife of Vasiliy II, daughter of Pr. Yaroslav Vladimirovich of Serpukhov–Borovsk, 24–26, 43, 44, 46, 92, 243, 245, 250, 267, 276, 375–377

Mary, mother of Jesus, 6, 107, 309, 322

Masal'skiy (Mosal'skiy) princes, 335, 336, 389

Maxim the Greek, 302

Mengli Girey, Khan of the Crimea, 50, 294

Meshchera (Meshchers, Meshcheryaks), people, 279, 294

Meshchovsk (Meschesk, Mezetskiy) princes, 289

Mezetskiy, Mikhail, Pr., *see* Mikhail Romanovich

Mezetskiy, Semen Mikhaylovich, Pr., Starodub military tenant, 331

Mikhail, Bishop, 296

Mikhail, Pr. of Kholm, 291

Mikhail Aleksandrovich, Gr. Pr. of Tver' and Mikulin, son of Aleksandr Mikhaylovich, 36, 203

Mikhail Andreyevich, Pr. of Vereya and Beloozero, son of Andrey Dmitriyevich of Mozhaysk, 39, 40, 43, 91–94, 273, 274, 277, 290

Mikhail Deyev, a prince of Yaroslavl', 254

Mikhail Glebovich, Pr. of Beloozero, son of Gleb Vasil'kovich, 30, 32

Mikhail Fedorovich Saburov, *see* Saburov, Mikhail Fedorovich

Mikhail Kaybulovich, *see* Kobulin, Mikhail

Mikhail Kobulin, *see* Kobulin, Mikhail

Mikhail Romanovich, Pr. of Meshchovsk (Mezetskiy), 42, 273

Mikhail Vsevolodovich, Pr. of Chernigov and Novgorod, son of Vsevolod Svyatoslavich, Gr. Pr. of Kiev, 328

Mikhail Yaroslavich, Saint, Gr. Pr. of Tver', 8–10, 31, 47, 341

Mikhail Yaroslavich the Brave (*Khorobit*), Pr. of Moscow, son of Gr. Pr. Yaroslav Vsevolodovich, 7

Mikhail (Mikhalko) Yur'yevich, Gr. Pr. of Suzdal', son of Yuriy Dolgorukiy, 5, 6

Mikhaylo Andreyevich, *see* Chelyadnya, Mikhail Andreyevich

Mikhaylo Fedorovich, *see* Koshkin, Mikhail Fedorovich

Mikulinskiy, Semen Ivanovich, Pr., 55, 341, 383

Mikulinskiy princes, 341

Minyay, boyar of Ivan Kalita, emissary, 33

Misail, Bishop of Smolensk, 40

Mitrofan, Archimandrite of the Andronnikov Monastery, 298

Moklokov, Tishko (Tikhon), secretary of Ivan III, 296, 297

Mordva (Mordvins, Mordovians, Mordvinians, Marii), people, 41, 52, 55, 278, 279, 340, 345, 378, 385

Mordva princes, 279, 340

Morozov-Sheya, Vasiliy Mikhaylovich, 357

Mosal'sk, Mosal'skiy princes, *see* Masal'skiy princes

Moscow, men of, *see* Muscovites

Moscow princes, House of Moscow, xiii, xv, 8, 10, 12, 16, 19, 21, 26, 29, 34–37, 46–50, 75, 77, 81, 211, 232, 243, 246, 252, 261, 264, 294, 302, 304, 311, 334, 386

Mstislav Mstislavich the Daring (*Udaloy*), Pr. of Toropets, Novgorod and Galich, 28, 29

Index of Personal Names

Petr Aleksandrovich (*cont.*)
Suzdal'skiy (Shuyskiy), 356
Petr Dmitriyevich, Pr. of Dmitrov, son of Dmitriy Donskoy, 19, 20, 89, 90, 207, 208, 211–213, 215, 216, 223, 226, 230, 233, 240, 246–248, 279, 368, 373
Petr Konstantinovich, *see* Dobrynskiy, Petr Konstantinovich
Petr the Wonder-Worker, Saint, Metropolitan, 98, 99, 259, 260, 295, 323, 325
Philotheus Kokkinos, Patriarch of Constantinople, 98, 232, 239, 260
Pimen, Metropolitan, 207
Pleshcheyev, Mikhail Andreyevich, boyar of Vasiliy II, 256
Pokhnutiy, *see* Pafnutiy Borovskiy
Poltev, Filipp, owner of a patrimonial estate, 274
Poluyekhtovich (Poluyekhtov), Aleksey, secretary of Ivan III, 276
Possevinus (Antoniy Possevin), papal envoy, 346
Pozharskaya, Fedosiya, Princess, 331
Pozharskiy, Boris, Pr., 331
Pozharskiy, Ivan Ivanovich the Elder, Yaroslavl' military tenant, 331
Pozharskiy, Ivan Ivanovich the Younger, Yaroslavl' military tenant, 329, 331
Pozharskiy, Ivan Ivanovich Tret'yakov, Pr. of Starodub, military tenant, 331
Pozharskiy, Ivan Semenovich, Pr., 329
Pozharskiy, Ivan Vasil'yevich, the Black, military tenant, 331
Pozharskiy, Mikhail Borisovich, Pr., Yaroslavl' military tenant, 331
Pozharskiy, Petr Borisovich, Pr. of Starodub, military tenant, 331
Pozharskiy, Petr Vasil'yevich, Pr. of Starodub, Yaroslavl' military tenant, 331
Pozharskiy, Semen Borisovich, Pr., military tenant, 329
Pozharskiy, Timofey, Pr., 329
Pozharskiy princes, 328
Prokofiy, Abbot, 187
Prussian Germans, 219
Putyatin, Menshyk (Menshoy), secretary of Vasiliy III, 303

Ramadanovskiy, Ramodanovskiy, *see* Romodanovskiy

Ramanova, *see* Romanova
Reuben (bib.), 308
Rodion Nesterovich, boyar of Ivan Kalita, 251
Romadanovskiy, *see* Romodanovskiy
Roman Vasil'yevich, Pr. of Yaroslavl', 254, 255
Roman Vladimirovich, Pr. of Uglich, son of Vladimir Konstantinovich, 30
Romanov, family, 324, 350
Romanova, wife of the *okol'nichiy* Roman Yur'yevich Zakhar'in-Koshkin, mother of Tsarina Anastasiya Romanovna, 53, 359, 389
Romodanovskiy, Fedor Borisovich, Pr., military tenant, 330
Romodanovskiy, Ivan Borisovich, Pr., military tenant, 331
Romodanovskiy, Mikhail, Pr., 330
Romodanovskiy, Vasiliy Vasil'yevich, Pr., 285, 381
Romodanovskiy-Sharap, Petr Borisovich (Petr Sharapov Romodanovskiy), Pr., 329
Rostov, men of, 29
Rostov princes, House of Rostov, 25, 29, 30, 32, 37, 47–49, 254, 336
Rus', princes of, *see* Russian princes
Russian princes, 8, 16, 35, 57, 74–76, 194, 243, 350
Russians, 30, 39, 57, 75, 76, 231, 274, 329, 332, 348, 354
Ryapolovskiy, Ivan Ivanovich, Pr., boyar of Vasiliy II, 261
Ryazan' princes, 67
Ryurik, Varangian Pr. of Rus', 27; house of, 311
Rzhev princes, 35

Sabanchey, Tartar emissary, 31
Saburov, Mikhail Fedorovich, boyar of Vasiliy II, 256, 257, 263, 376, 377
Saburov, Vasiliy, 284, 380
Saburova, Solomonida Yur'yevna, *see* Solomonida Yur'yevna Saburova
Safarin, Ivan, owner of a village, 357
Saip-Girey, Khan of Kazan', 300
Sedi-Akhmet (Sedi-Ahmed), Khan of the Blue (Nogay) Horde, 40, 50, 266
Semen Bekbulatovich, Khan of Kasimov, "Tsar" of Kazan', 338
Semen Ivanovich, Pr. of Kaluga, son of Ivan III, 41, 42, 74, 95, 99, 106,

Index of Place Names *

* Abbreviations: d.—district; Pr.—prince; vil.—village; vol.—volost.

Index of Place Names

Index of Place Names

Estonia, 329, 347

Faleyevo, vil., Starodub Ryapolovo d., 329, 385
Falkenau, city, *see* Mukov
Faustovskoye, vil., Moscow d., 247, 373
Faustov, Grigoriy, vil. of, Moscow d., 220, 369
Fedor, the son of Stepan, small vil. of, 256, 376
Fellin, city, *see* Vel'yan
Feodorovskaa (Fedorovskaya), vol., Bryansk d., 287, 380
Filipp Poltev's children, vils. and hamlets of, 274, 379
Flolishchevo, vil., Yur'yev d., 358, 387
Fokino, vil., Nizhniy Novgorod d., 341, 359, 385, 389
Foma, Deacon, vils. of, *see* Deacon Foma's vils.
Fominichi, vol., Serpeysk d., 288, 380
Fomin'skoye, vol., Zvenigorod and Ruza ds., 183, 198, 210, 363, 365, 367
Frolovskiye (Frolo-Lavrskiye) Gates, in the Kremlin, 284
Frolovskoye, vil., Yur'yev d., 214, 221, 229, 237, 257, 369, 370, 371, 372, 376

Galich, city, 26, 207, 212, 244, 256, 257, 278, 279, 339, 340, 367, 373, 377, 383
Galich, d., 14, 19, 21, 24, 26, 41, 52, 213, 244, 252, 339
Gauya (Gauja), city and river, *see* Gov'ya, city and d., *and* Gov'ya, river
Gdov, minor city of Pskov, 344, 383
Glebovs, patrimony of the, 288, 381
Glin'skoye, vol., Mozhaysk d., 210, 368
Gnezdilovo, vol., Serpeysk d., 288, 380
Golden Gates, Vladimir city, 6
Golden Horde (the Horde), 9, 10, 14, 15, 18, 31, 34–36, 45, 56, 63, 67, 74, 75, 77, 97, 105, 180–183, 191, 193, 194, 198, 215, 216, 231, 239, 259
Golenishchovo, vil., Yur'yev d., 257, 376
Golichichi, vol., Borovsk d., 183, 364
Golobokovo, vil., Starodub Ryapolovo d., 331, 385

Golovinskiye, hamlets, Ustyug, 229, 238, 371, 373
Gomel', city, 40
Gordeyevo, vol., Aleksin d., 290, 382
Gordoshevichi, vol., Mozhaysk d., 190, 211, 212, 364, 368, 369
Goretova (Goretovka), vol., Kolomna d., 182, 197, 363, 365
Goritsy, vil., Suzdal' d., 356, 386
Gorka, vil., Vologda d., 253, 374
Gorki, vil., Kolomna d., 182, 197, 363, 365
Gor'kiy, city, *see* Nizhniy Novgorod, city
Gornaya Land (*storona*), *see* Nagornaya Land
Gorodechna, vol., Serpeysk d., 288, 380
Goroden (Goroden', Gorodets, Gorodnya), vil. (later city?) on the Volga, Tver', 52, 280, 341, 379, 383
Gorodenka (Gorodna, Gorodnya, Gorodok), vol., Kolomna d., 182, 197, 209, 219, 252, 256, 363, 365, 367, 369, 375, 376
Gorodets, 251; *perhaps identical with* Goroden, *q.v.*
Gorodets, vol., Serpukhov d., 230
Gorodets (Serpukhovskiy), city, 41, 43, 88, 272, 377
Gorodets Meshcherskiy, city, *see* Kasimov
Gorodets on the Volga, city, *see* Radilov
Gorodishche, Pereyaslavl' d., 263, 377
Gorodishche Mstislavle, vil., *see* Mstislavle Gorodishche
Gorodna, vol., *see* Gorodenka
Gorodnya, vol., *see* Gorodenka
Gorodok, in Beloozero, 214, 369
Gorodok, vol., *see* Gorodenka
Gorodok Meshcherskiy, city, *see* Kasimov
Gory, vil., Pereyaslavl' d., 338, 385
Govorovskiye, vils., Vologda d., 248, 373
Gov'ya, city, d., 346, 383
Gov'ya, river, 346
Great Posad, *see* Kitaygorod
Gremichi, vol., 211, 368
Gribachevo, waste land, Moscow d., 291, 382

Index of Place Names

Marinina, *sloboda*, Pereyaslavl' d., 257, 263, 376, 377
Martem'yanovo, vil., Moscow d., 358, 387
Mas (Masa), river, 13, 186, 363
Masal'sk, city, *see* Mosal'sk
Mashev, vol., Moscow d., 184, 364
Maslenskiye, vil., Vologda d., 248, 374
Matfeishchovskoye (Matfeyshchovo), Yur'yev d., 186, 257, 376
Matkoma, vol., Poshekhon'ye, 277, 379
Matveyevskoye, vil., Starodub Ryapolovo d., 330, 385
meadow on the Moskva River near Krutitsy, Moscow d., 253, 374, 375
Medushi, 256
Medvezh'ya Golova (Odenpe, Otepyaa), city, Livonia, 346, 383
Medyn', city and d., 19, 21, 24–26, 40, 41, 52, 55, 211, 247, 251, 274, 349, 351, 368, 373, 378, 383
Melov'skoye, vil., Yur'yev d., 186, 364
Meschesk, city and principality, *see* Meshchovsk
Meshchera, city and vol., land, 41, 52, 54, 279, 340, 383
Meshchera, lands of the, 279, 378
Meshcherka, vol., Kolomna d., 197, 209, 219, 365, 367, 369
Meshchersk, city and principality, *see* Meshchovsk
Meshchovsk (Meschesk, Meshchersk), city and principality, Kaluga d., 42, 43, 273, 279, 287, 289, 349, 381
Mestilovo, vol., Kozel'sk d., 290, 381
Mezen', river and region, 278, 339, 379, 384
Mezynya (Mezyni, Mezynka), vol., Kolomna d., 183, 197, 219, 256, 363, 365, 369, 376
Mglin, city, 52, 341, 383
Michenki (Mishenki), vol., Mozhaysk d., 274, 336, 379, 384
Mikhail Danilov's vils., *see* Danilov, Mikhail, vils. of
Mikhail Deyev, Pr., burg of, *see* Romanov, burg
Mikhailovskoye, vil., 184, 364
Mikhailovskoye, vil. on the Yauza, Moscow d., 184, 364
Mikhalevskoye, vil., Moscow d., 198, 210, 256, 365, 367, 376

Mikulin, city, 52, 55, 341, 383
Mikulinskiy, Pr. Semen, patrimony of, 55, 341, 383
Mikul'skoye, small vil., Kolomna d., 182, 197, 214, 363, 365
Mikul'skoye, vil., Kostroma d., 212, 367, 369
Mikul'skoye, vil., Pereyaslavl' d., 253, 375
Milolyubskiy Weir, Beloozero d., 212, 213, 368, 369
Miltsin'skoye, small vil., 198, 365
Mishenki, vol., *see* Michenki
Mitin (Mityayevskiy), *novale*, vil., Moscow d., 210, 228, 237, 367, 371, 373; *see also* Mityayevskiy
Mitropolich'ye, vil., 357, 387
Mitsyno, vil., Starodub Ryapolovo d., 330, 385
Mityayevskiy, *novale*, 213, 369; *perhaps identical with* Mitin, *q.v.*
Mlgin", city, *see* Mglin
Mogilno (Mogil'noye), city and vol., Mozhaysk d., 274, 336, 378, 384
Mogucheye, vol., Starodub Ryapolovo d., 329, 385
Moishin Kholm, vol., Mozhaysk d., 210, 368
Molakhovskoye, vil., *see* Malakhovskoye
Mologa, city and former *udel* of Yaroslavl', 42, 288, 381
Mologa, river, 249, 288, 349, 381
Monasteries: Andronnikov (Androniyev) Monastery of the Saviour, Moscow d., 270, 298, 379; Borovsk (Pafnutiyev) Monastery, near Kaluga, 323; Chudov Monastery, in the Kremlin, 241; Holy Mother of God in Krutitsy, Monastery of the, 17, 201, 206, 366, 367; Holy Saviour, Monastery of the, 216; Holy Trinity Monastery, *see* Monasteries, Trinity-Sergiy Monastery; Iosif of Volokolamsk Monastery of the Dormition, 300, 302; Kamenny (Spasokamenny) Monastery, Vologda d., 301; Kholopiy Monastery, 288; Kirill of Beloozero Monastery, 302, 323; Lyshchikov Monastery, Moscow d., 42, 270, 326, 380, 386; Miracle of Mikhail the Archangel, Monastery of the, *see* Monasteries, Chudov Monastery; Nativity of

428

Index of Place Names

Rauna, city, *see* Rovnoy

Razhestvennoye, vol., *see* Rozhestvenoye, vol.

Red Square, 284

Redyn', vol., Dorogobuzh d., 275, 337, 379, 384

Rekhty, vol., Dorogobuzh d., 275, 337, 379, 384

Repen'skoye (Repin'skoye), vil., Kolomna d., 211, 214, 228, 237, 266, 368, 369, 371, 372, 377

Repna River, vil. on the, Borovsk d., 198, 244, 365

Ringen, city, *see* Ryngol

Rodivonovskoye, vil., Pereyaslavl' d., 221, 370

Rogachev, city, Vyazma d., 53, 288, 357, 381, 387

Rogachovo, city, *see* Rogachev

Rogozh, vol., Moscow d., 211, 271, 328, 367, 379

Roin, city, Livonia, 347, 388

Roksha, river, 201, 365

Romanov, burg on the Volga above Yaroslavl', 254, 258, 276, 375, 378

Romanov, city on the Volga, 52, 54, 107, 108, 254, 336, 338, 383

Romanovskoye, vil. on the Kerzhach, 190, 365

Romanovskoye, vil. on the Roksha, 201, 365

Romantsovo, vil., Moscow d., 355, 386

Rome, 101

Romodanovo, vil., Starodub Ryapolovo d., 330, 331, 385

Romodanovskiy, Pr. Vasiliy, *slobodka* of, 285, 381

Ronneburg, city, *see* Rovnoy

Roshcha, vil. and vol., Tarusa d., 211, 368

Roslavl', city southeast of Smolensk, 41, 42, 55, 271, 332, 341, 378, 383

Roslov, city, *see* Roslavl'

Rostov (the Great), city, 5–7, 27–35, 39, 45, 48, 275, 357, 378, 387

Rostov, principality, d., 11–13, 15, 19, 26–38, 41, 44–48, 53, 186, 210, 221, 228, 237, 254, 364, 375; Borisoglebsk half of, 33, 34, 43–46, 48, 49; Sreten'ye half of, 25, 26, 33–37, 43, 44, 48, 49, 375

Rostov-Suzdal', Rostov-Suzdal'-Vladimir, land, 27

Rostovets, vol., Kashira d., 47, 52, 332, 384

Rostovshchina, vol., Zavoloch'ye, 339, 379, 384

Rostovtsi, vol., Zvenigorod d., 183, 198, 210, 363, 365, 367

Rostovtsovskoye, vil., Dmitrov d., 253, 375

Rostunova *slobodka*, Serpukhov d., 264

Rotozh (Rogozh), vil., 184, 364

Rovnoy (Rauna, Ronneburg, Vorna), city, Livonia, 347, 388

Rozhalovo, vol., Uglich d., 249, 288, 374, 381

Rozhek, vil., Kolomna d., 247, 374

Rozhestvenoye, vil. of the vols. beyond the Moskva, 247, 373, 374

Rozhestvenoye, vol., Pereyaslavl' d., 247, 275, 286, 337, 379, 384

Rozhestvenskoye, vil., Starodub Ryapolovo d., 329, 385

Rozhna, vol., Toropets d., 282, 343, 379, 384

Rozsudovskiye, vils., Moscow d., 252, 285, 375, 381

Rud', vol., Mozhaysk d., 211, 213, 368, 369

Rudino, vil., Yaroslavl' d., 40

Rugodev (Rugadev, Rugodiv), city, *see* Narva, city and land

Runai, vol., Shokhonskiy d., 277, 379

Russian state, 69, 109, 282, 323, 336, 344, 345

Russian Tsardom, 52, 99, 105, 108, 109, 325, 382

Ruza, city, 183, 198, 204, 210, 252, 287, 363, 365–367, 374, 380

Ruza, *udel* of Moscow, d., 12, 17, 19, 21, 24, 26, 42, 43, 94, 252, 267

Ruz'skoye, vil. on the Ruza, 183, 363

Ruzsudovskiye, vils., *see* Rozsudovskiye

Ryapolovo, principality, 264; *see also* Starodub Ryapolovo, principality

Ryaskoy, city, *see* Ryazhsk

Ryazan' (Pereyaslavl' Ryazanskiy), city, 6, 7, 8, 42, 43, 81, 282, 283, 332–334, 383

Ryazan', grand principality, land, 8, 12, 17, 18, 41, 51, 52, 54, 56, 67, 105, 194, 198, 199, 272, 279, 283, 332–335 365, 380, 383, 386; Prince Fedor

Index of Place Names

Topical Index

acquisition, appropriation (of lands), 229

administration (in Testament of Ivan III), 105–106

Arms Chamber of the Great Kremlin Palace, 100

bureau, 86–87

burg, 59

Cap of Monomakh (the Golden Cap), 98–103

carnelian box, 98–103

city, 58–59

classes of the population, 67–79; boyars, 69–72; court men, 73; enrolled people, 73–76; Horde men (*ordyntsy*), 76–77; junior boyars, 72–73; peasants, 73; princes, *see* princes; servants under the major-domo, 77–78; slaves, non-free people, 78–79, 84, 106; *streltsy*, 327; *tyaglo* people, 73

coining of money, 106

Council of Boyars, 70

Council of Boyars of the Land, 338

cross from Constantinople (life-giving cross of Patriarch Philotheus), 98–103

district, 57

divine right, 108–109

ends of Novgorod, 59

feeding (feedings, livings), 63–64, 85

fifths of Novgorod, 281

Grand State, 109, 352, 360, 386

Great Roll, 185

hamlet, 60

heirlooms of the princes, 97–103

Icon of the Virgin of Vladimir, 323

justice, dispensing of, 106, 190, 216, 221, 231, 238–239, 259, 292–293

Land, the (Zemshchina), 338, 356

manumission, 191, 202, 206, 217, 223, 233, 240, 261, 264–265, 298

minor cities, 59

Mozhaysk, absorption of, by Moscow, 37–41, 49–50

names, 4; pejoratives, 296

novale, 60

officers of the prince, 70; *see also* servants of the prince

oprichnik, 307

Oprichnina, 305, 338, 356, 360

otkup, 292

parables of Jesus: Faithful and Unfaithful Servants, 317–318; Good Samaritan, 317–318; Great Supper, 318; Pharisee and the Publican, 319; Rich Fool, 313; Talents, 316; Ten Virgins, 315–316

patrimonial principalities, 56

patrimony, concept of, 15, 19, 71, 104–105, 108–109, 215, 349–350, 353–355, 358–360

pogost, 57–58

prikaz, see bureau

Prince Vladimir's third, 88–89, 96; *see also* Moscow, thirds of, *in* Index of Place Names

princes: boyar, 69; grand, 67–69; patrimonial (*udel'nyy*), 68–69; service, 69

put', 85–87